Polaris

NORTHERN LIGHTS SERIES
COPUBLISHED WITH THE ARCTIC INSTITUTE OF NORTH AMERICA
ISSN 1701-0004 (PRINT) ISSN 1925-2943 (ONLINE)

This series takes up the geographical region of the North (circumpolar regions within the zone of discontinuous permafrost) and publishes works from all areas of northern scholarship, including natural sciences, social sciences, earth sciences, and the humanities.

No. 1 · **Nunavik: Inuit-Controlled Education in Arctic Quebec** Ann Vick-Westgate · Copublished with the Katutjiniq Regional Development Council

No. 2 · **Many Faces of Gender: Roles and Relationships through Time in Northern Indigenous Communities** Edited by Lisa Frink, Rita S. Shepard, and Gregory A. Reinhardt · Copublished with University Press of Colorado

No. 3 · **New Owners in their Own Land: Minerals and Inuit Land Claims** Robert McPherson

No. 4 · **War North of 80: The Last German Arctic Weather Station of World War II** Wilhelm Dege, translated and edited by William Barr · Copublished with University Press of Colorado

No. 5 · **Writing Geographical Exploration: Thomas James and the Northwest Passage 1631-33** Wayne K.D. Davies

No. 6 · **As Long as This Land Shall Last: A History of Treaty 8 and Treaty 11, 1870–1939** René Fumoleau

No. 7 · **Breaking Ice: Renewable Resource and Ocean Management in the Canadian North** Edited by Fikret Berkes, Rob Huebert, Helen Fast, Micheline Manseau, and Alan Diduck

No. 8 · **Alliance and Conflict: The World System of the Inupiaq Eskimos** Ernest S. Burch · Copublished with the University of Nebraska Press

No. 9 · **Tanana and Chandalar: The Alaska Field Journals of Robert A. McKennan** Edited by Craig Mishler and William E. Simeone · Copublished with University of Alaska Press

No. 10 · **Resurrecting Dr. Moss: The Life and Letters of a Royal Navy Surgeon, Edward Lawton Moss, MD, RN, 1837–1880** Paul C. Appleton, edited by William Barr

No. 11 · **Lands that Hold One Spellbound: A Story of East Greenland** Spencer Apollonio

No. 12 · **Biocultural Diversity and Indigenous Ways of Knowing: Human Ecology in the Arctic** Karim-Aly S. Kassam

No. 13 · **Arctic Scientist, Gulag Survivor: The Biography of Mikhail Mikhailovich Ermolaev, 1905–1991** A.M. Ermolaev and V.D. Dibner, translated and edited by William Barr

No. 14 · **The Reindeer Botanist: Alf Erling Porsild, 1901–1977** Wendy Dathan

No. 15 · **The Fast-Changing Arctic: Rethinking Arctic Security for a Warmer World** Edited by Barry Scott Zellen

No. 16 · **Shipwreck at Cape Flora: The Expeditions of Benjamin Leigh Smith, England's Forgotten Arctic Explorer** P.J. Capelotti

No. 17 · **A Historical and Legal Study of Sovereignty in the Canadian North: Terrestrial Sovereignty, 1870–1939** Gordon W. Smith, edited by P. Whitney Lackenbauer

No. 18 · **Baffin Island: Field Research and High Arctic Adventure, 1961–1967** Jack D. Ives

No. 19 · ***Polaris*: The Chief Scientist's Recollections of the American North Pole Expedition, 1871–73** Emil Bessels, translated and edited by William Barr

The Chief Scientist's Recollections of the American North Pole Expedition, 1871–73

Emil Bessels

Translated from the German:
Die Amerikanische Nordpol-Expedition
(Leipzig: Verlag von Wilhelm Engelmann, 1879)

BY WILLIAM BARR

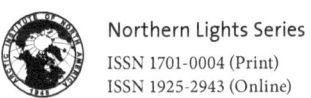

Northern Lights Series
ISSN 1701-0004 (Print)
ISSN 1925-2943 (Online)

UNIVERSITY OF CALGARY
Press

© 2016 William Barr

University of Calgary Press
2500 University Drive NW
Calgary, Alberta
Canada T2N 1N4
press.ucalgary.ca

This book is available as an ebook which is licensed under a Creative Commons license. The publisher should be contacted for any commercial use which falls outside the terms of that license.

LIBRARY AND ARCHIVES CANADA CATALOGUING IN PUBLICATION

Bessels, Emil, 1847-1888
[Die amerikanische Nordpol-Expedition. English]
    Polaris : the chief scientist's recollections of the American North Pole expedition, 1871-73 / Emil Bessels ; translated from the German: Die amerikanische Nordpol-Expedition (Leipzig: Verlag von Wilhelm Engelmann, 1879), by William Barr.

(Northern lights series ; no. 19)
Includes bibliographical references and index.
Issued in print and electronic formats.
ISBN 978-1-55238-875-4 (paperback).—ISBN 978-1-55238-876-1 (open access pdf).—
ISBN 978-1-55238-877-8 (pdf).—ISBN 978-1-55238-878-5 (epub).—ISBN 978-1-55238-879-2 (mobi)

    1. Polaris (Ship). 2. Arctic regions—Discovery and exploration—American. 3. Bessels, Emil, 1847-1888—Travel—Arctic regions. 4. Hall, Charles Francis, 1821-1871. I. Barr, William, 1940-, editor, translator II. Arctic Institute of North America, issuing body III. Title. IV. Title: Die amerikanische Nordpol-Expedition. English V. Series: Northern lights series ; no. 19

G670.1871.B4713 2016   919.804   C2016-907071-9

                                                  C2016-907072-7

The University of Calgary Press acknowledges the support of the Government of Alberta through the Alberta Media Fund for our publications. We acknowledge the financial support of the Government of Canada through the Canada Book Fund for our publishing activities. We acknowledge the financial support of the Canada Council for the Arts for our publishing program.

      Canada Council   Conseil des Arts
                                                for the Arts   du Canada

This book has been published with the help of a grant from the Federation for the Humanities and Social Sciences, through the Awards to Scholarly Publications Program, using funds provided by the Social Sciences and Humanities Research Council of Canada.

 An electronic version of this book is freely available, thanks to the support of libraries working with Knowledge Unlatched. KU is a collaborative initiative designed to make high quality books Open Access for the public good. The Open Access ISBN for this book is 978-1-55238-876-1. More information about the initative and links to the Open Access version can be found at www.knowledgeunlatched.org.

Cover Image: Top - Colour box image #2395643. Bottom - Fig. 26. Separation of the party.
Copyediting by Peter Enman
Cover design, page design, and typesetting by Melina Cusano

MAPS

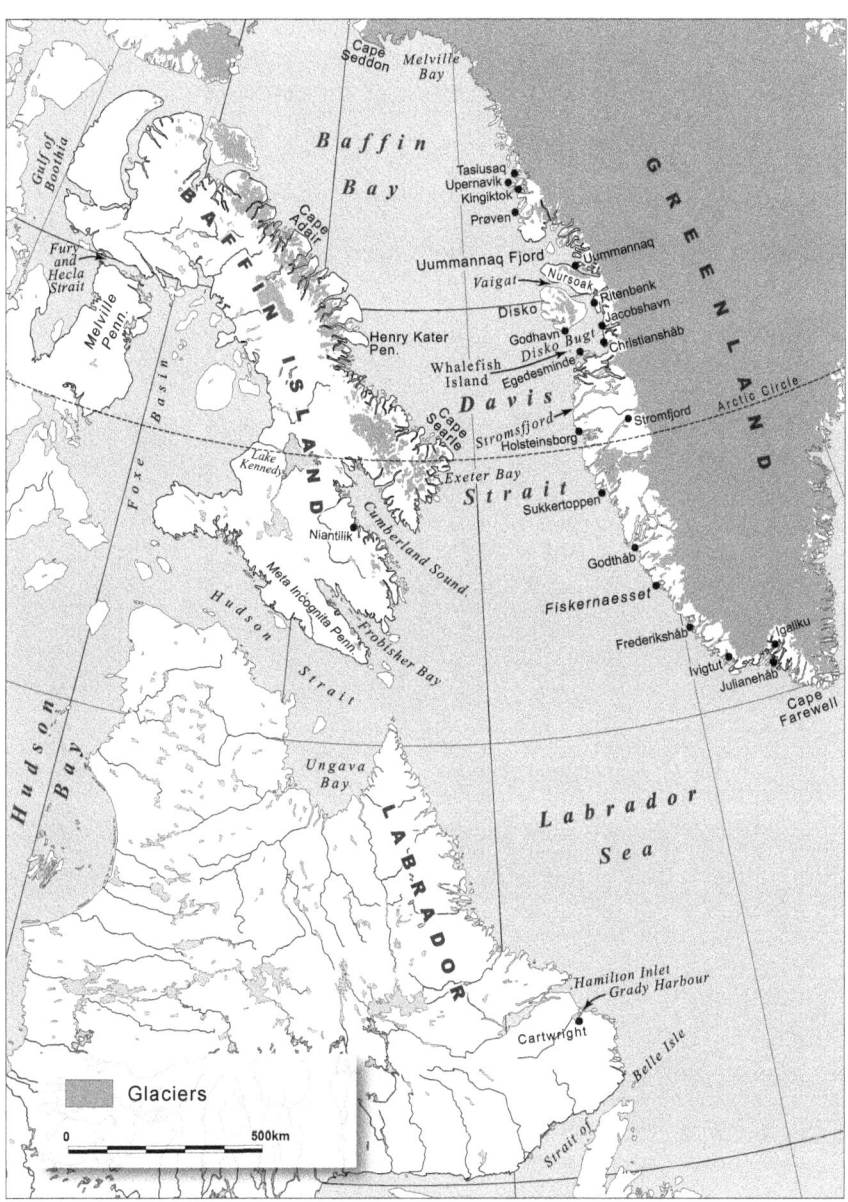

Map 1. West Greenland and the full extent of the ice-floe drift.

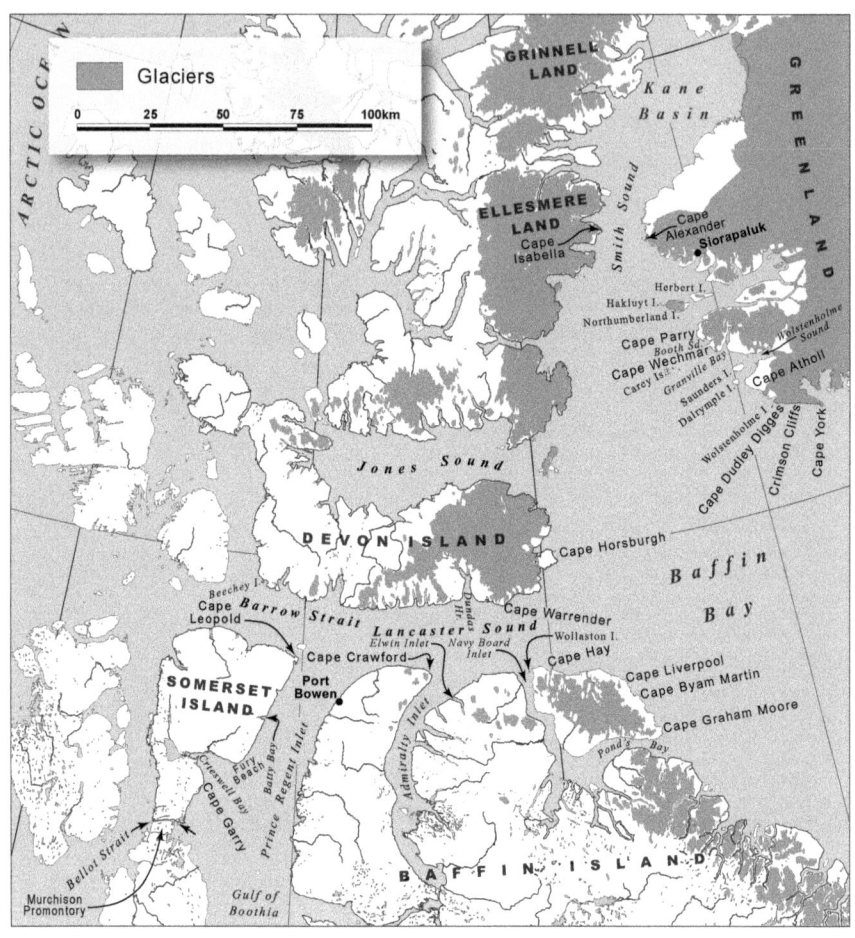

MAP 2. Northwest Greenland and the area of the *Arctic*'s whaling cruise.

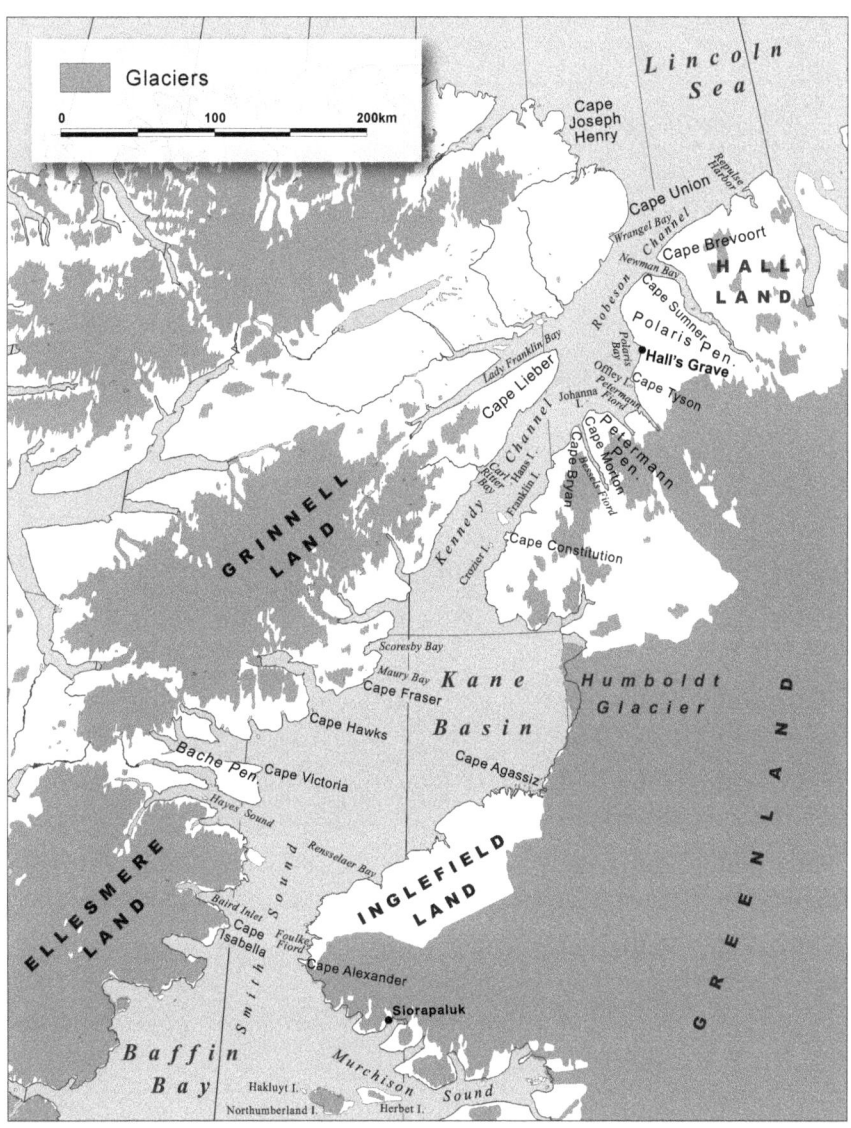

MAP 3. Nares Strait and the area of the expedition's first winter quarters.

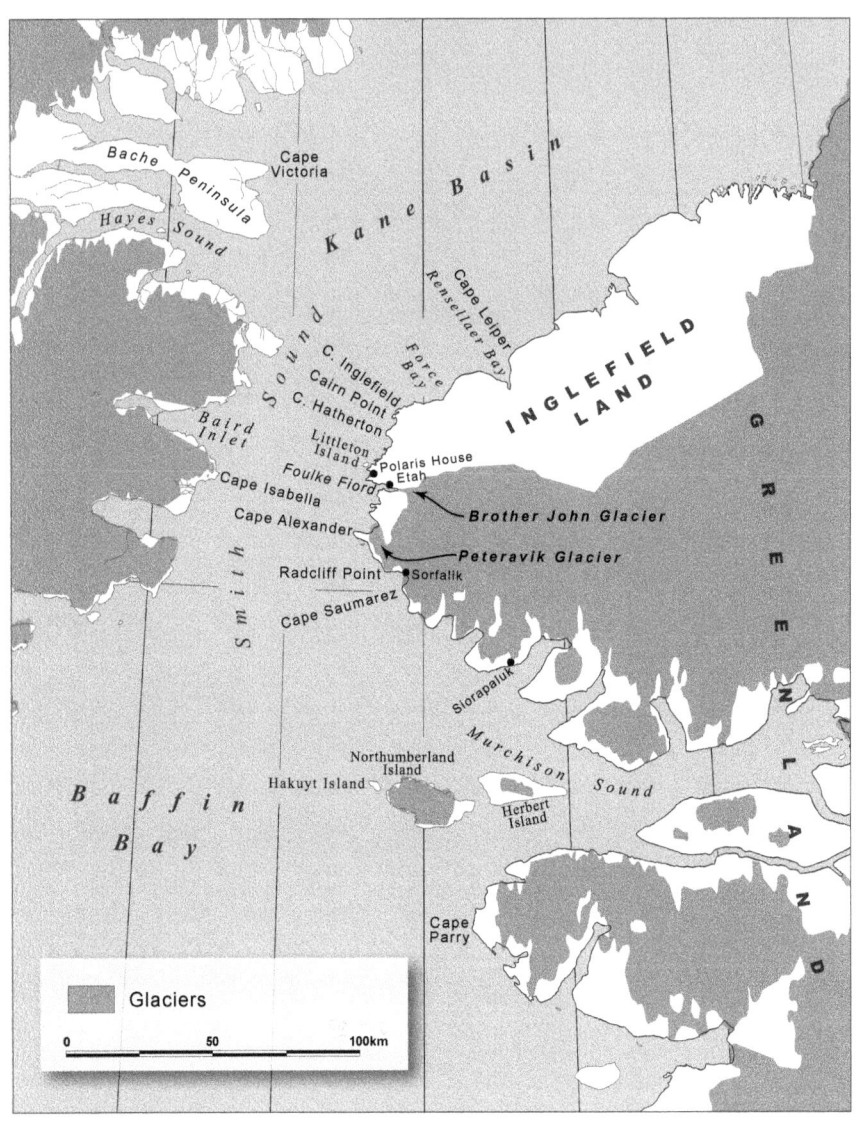

Map 4. Area of the second wintering, and of the retreat by boat.

Contents

List of Figures	xi
Expedition Members	xiii
Acknowledgments	xv
Foreword	xvii

The American North Pole Expedition by Emil Bessels

Dedication		1
Preface		3
1	Origin of the expedition and its outfitting	9
2	From New York to Newfoundland	27
3	From Newfoundland to Greenland	47
4	From Holsteinsborg to the northernmost settlement on Earth	81
5	Historical review	111
6	Into unknown territory	131
7	The first days in Polaris Bay	153
8	The first sledge journey	175
9	Hall's sledge trip	197
10	In the realm of darkness	219
11	The New Year	241
12	Through darkness to the light	257
13	The southern sledge trip	273

14	Early summer	291
15	The boat voyage north	303
16	The summer	315
17	Southward	331
18	On terra firma	347
19	An ethnographic sketch	363
20	Further progress	385
21	The start of the ice floe drift	415
22	Between hopelessness and optimism	431
23	Spring on the floe	441
24	The seals	455
25	Salvation	463
26	The boat voyage in arctic waters	469
27	Whaling	495
28	The search	521
29	Homeward bound	531

Epilogue: Motive for Murder	537
Appendix 1 Scientific appendix (outline)	543
Appendix 2 Hall's Instructions	545
Appendix 3 The Board of Inquiry	549
Appendix 4 Biographical sketches	555
Notes	565
Bibliography	609
Index	615

LIST OF FIGURES

Fig. 1. Arrangement of the chronometers.
Fig. 2. Fiskernæsset.
Fig. 3. Lichtenfels.
Fig. 4. Holseinsborg.
Fig. 5. Inuit lamps.
Fig. 6. Inuit cooking pot.
Fig. 7. Godhavn.
Fig. 8. Upernavik.
Fig. 9. Tasiusaq.
Fig. 10. Beset.
Fig. 11. The observatory.
Fig. 12. *Polaris* in winter quarters.
Fig. 13. A muskox hunt.
Fig. 14. The tide-gauge.
Fig. 15. The thermometer screen.
Fig. 16. Reading the tide-gauge.
Fig. 17. The pendulum apparatus in the observatory.
Fig. 18. At the magnetometer.
Fig. 19. Ptarmigan.
Fig. 20. Petermann Fiord.
Fig. 21. A bear hunt.
Fig. 22. Difficult sledging along the ice-foot.

Fig. 23. About to fire.
Fig. 24. Hall's grave.
Fig. 25. The refuge hut.
Fig. 26. Separation of the party.
Fig. 27. Polaris House.
Fig. 28. Snow-houses and Polaris House.
Fig. 29. Arctic foxes.
Fig. 30. The abandoned wreck of *Polaris*.
Fig. 31. Inuit gloves: figs. 1 and 2 from Etah, the rest from the North American Arctic.
Fig. 32. Inuit boots and shoes from various locations.
Fig. 33. Inuit at home.
Fig. 34. 1. Inuit stool. 2. Old Inuit sledge (after Ross). 3. Modern Inuit sledge.
Fig. 35. Inuit weapons from Smith Sound.
Fig. 36. Inuit weapons from Smith Sound and elsewhere.
Fig. 37. Ivory carving of human torso.
Fig. 38. Inuit song.
Fig. 39. A walrus hunt.
Fig. 40. Measuring glacier flow on Brother John Glacier.
Fig. 41. Netting dovekies.
Fig. 42. The boats setting off.
Fig. 43. A narwhal hunt.
Fig. 44. In a tight spot.
Fig. 45. A campsite near Cape York.
Fig. 46. Ivittuut: from a photograph.

EXPEDITION MEMBERS

Charles Francis Hall (Commander) – American
Emil Bessels (Chief scientist/Surgeon) – German*
Sidney O. Budington (Sailing master) – American*
George Tyson (Assistant navigator) – American #
Hubbard C. Chester (First Mate) – American*
William Morton (Second Mate) – American*
Emil Schumann (Chief Engineer) – German*
Alvin Odell (Assistant Engineer) – American*
Frederick Meyer (Meteorologist) – German #
Richard W.D. Bryan (Astronomer/Chaplain) – American*
Nathaniel Coffin (Carpenter) – American*
John W.C. (Robert) Krüger (Seaman) – German #
Friedrich Jamka (Seaman) – German #
William Nindemann (Seaman) – German #
Friedrich Anthing (Seaman) – German #
Gustav Lindquist (Seaman) – Swedish #
Peter Johnson (Seaman) – Danish #
Noah Hayes (Seaman) – American*
Hermann Siemens (Seaman) – German*
Heinrich Hobby (Seaman) – German*
Joseph Mauch (Seaman) – German*
John Booth (Fireman) – English*

Walter Campbell (Fireman) – American*
William Jackson (Cook) – American*
John Herron (Steward) – English*
Ebierbing (Joe, Ipiirviq) (Hunter, Dog driver) – Inuk #
Tookoolito (Hannah, Taqulittuq) (Seamstress) – Inuk #
Punny (Sylvia, Pannik) – Inuk #
Hans Hendrik (Suersaq) (Hunter, Dog driver) – Inuk #
Merkut Hendrik (Wife and mother) – Inuk #
Augustina (Josephine) Hendrik – Inuk #
Tobias Hendrik – Inuk #
Sussi Hendrik – Inuk #
Charlie Polaris Hendrik – Inuk #

\# Member of ice-drift party
* Member of party remaining with ship

Acknowledgments

I wish to thank Dr. Maria Pia Casarini-Wadhams. Director of the Istituto Geografico Polare Silvio Zavatti, Fermo, Italy, for supplying translations of Bessels's two brief quotations from Dante's *Inferno*, and Dr. James Hume of the Department of Greek and Roman Studies, University of Calgary, for his translation of Bessels's brief quotation from Homer's *Odyssey*. I am also extremely grateful to Dr. Ludger Müller-Wille, Retired Professor, Department of Geography, McGill University, for directing me to several German biographical sources with entries on Emil Bessels, and also to the two anonymous reviewers for their very useful suggestions for improvements and additions. And finally I am indebted to Mr. Robin Poitras, Department of Geography, University of Calgary, for producing the excellent maps.

Foreword

On 10 May 1873 every major newspaper in the United States, and indeed around the world, carried a startling telegram, which raised more questions than it answered. The coverage in the *New York Times* reads as follows:

Bay Roberts, via St. John's, N.F.,

May 9, 1873

The steamer *Walrus* arrived from the seal fishery at the port of St. John's, this morning, bringing news that the steamer *Tigress* had come into Roberts Bay, eighteen miles from here, having on board nineteen survivors of Hall's Arctic Expedition. The following are the names of those rescued: H.C. Tyson, assistant navigator; Frederick Meyer, meteorologist; John Heron, steward; W.C. Kruger, seaman; Fred. Jamka, seaman; Wm. Nindemann, seaman; Fred. Anring, seaman; Gustavs C. Linquist, seaman; William Jackson, cook; Esquimaux Joe, interpreter; Hannah and child, Esquimaux; Hans Christian, of Cane's (sic) expedition; Hans Christian's wife and four children, the youngest only eight months old.

    This party, which had been landed from the *Polaris*, were driven from her by a gale, which burst her moorings on the 15th of October, 1872, in latitude 72° 35′.

When they last saw the Polaris she was under steam and canvas, making for a harbor on the east side of Northumberland Island.

She had no more boats left of the six which she brought with her from the port of New York. Two were lost in a northern expedition, two were landed on the ice with Capt. Tyson's party, one was burnt as firewood to make water for the crew, and the other is on board the *Tigress.*

The *Polaris* was in command of Capt. Budington, who had thirteen of a crew along with him, and a plentiful stock of provisions.

Her bow was somewhat damaged, and it is the opinion of the survivors they will be unable to get clear until July, and even then, if the ship is unseaworthy, they should have to make new boats to effect an escape.

On the 8th of October 1871, in latitude 81°38', longitude 71°44', Capt. Hall died of apoplexy, and was buried on shore, where they erected a wooden cross to mark his grave.

He had recently returned from a northern sledge expedition, in which he had attained the latitude of 82°16'. He seemed in his usual health, and had called the crew into the cabin to encourage them with hopes of the future rewards, when he was suddenly struck down and expired, to the great grief of those around, to whom he had endeared himself by his kindness and devotion.

In September 1871 the *Polaris* entered winter quarters, and left Aug. 12, 1872. The ice was very heavy and set in a southern direction. She was forced south, and so continued drifting till Capt. Tyson and party were driven from her.

The sledge party crossed Kane's Polar Sea, which they pronounced to be a strait about fifteen miles wide. There was an appearance of open water to the north.

The rescued party suffered very much during their dreary drift from hunger and cold. For the last two months they ate raw seal and polar bear as they could get it.

When met by the *Tigress* they showed evident signs of their great sufferings, but during the nine days that they have been on board they have improved vastly, and are now in fair health.

> The party is in charge of the United States consul, and will arrive in St. John's on Monday next.

The events of the expedition were so unlikely, and also so complex, that it is not surprising that this account, derived by a reporter only at second-hand from the survivors of an almost incredible drift on an ice floe, from Smith Sound almost to the Strait of Belle Isle, should have become somewhat garbled.

The editor of the *New York Times* quickly realized this and on the following day (11 May) published a follow-up note:

> The news which appeared in *The Times* yesterday of the death of Captain Hall, the probable loss of the *Polaris*, and the breaking up of the American Polar expedition, add another to the long list of Arctic failures. The story of the little band rescued by the *Tigress* is a strange one, and needs further explanation before its statements can be fully understood. We have, however, the consolation of knowing that whatever may be the fate of Capt. Buddington and his thirteen men, who were last seen on board the leaky and drifting *Polaris*, eighteen people at least are alive.

But even at this stage, before the full details emerged, it was clear that this expedition, quite lavishly equipped and dispatched, with great fanfare and at considerable government expense, had not only not reached its goal, the North Pole, but had somehow disintegrated and that its leader had unexpectedly died.

Charles Francis Hall was one of the most unlikely Arctic explorers. An engraver and newspaper publisher by trade, resident in Cincinnati, Ohio, in the late 1850s he became fascinated by the fate of the missing Franklin expedition in the Arctic, and decided to mount his own expedition to search for survivors and/or records of the expedition. Through sheer persistence and the cooperation of whaling captains he managed to achieve his objective twice, once in 1860–62 (to the Frobisher Bay area) and again in 1864–69, to the Repulse Bay/King William Island area. Thereafter, however, he changed his focus and decided to make an attempt at reaching the North Pole. Through an impressive display of chutzpah he managed to persuade the Senate and the House of Representatives to provide an allocation of $50,000, and on 20 July 1870 received from President Ulysses S. Grant his appointment "to command the expedition toward the North Pole, to be organized and sent out pursuant to an act of Congress approved July 12, 1870."[1]

The expedition's ship, *Polaris*, sailed from New London on 3 July 1871 and, having encountered unusually favourable ice conditions in Nares Strait (between northwest Greenland and Ellesmere Island), attained the record high latitude of 82°11'N in the Lincoln Sea on 30 August. But thereafter *Polaris* became beset in the ice and drifted south and was forced to go into winter quarters on the Greenland shore of Hall Basin on 10 September. By 10 November Hall was dead, having died in his bunk on board ship under somewhat suspicious circumstances. During the last two weeks of his life he was tended by the expedition's medical officer and chief scientist, Dr. Emil Bessels. Bessels's version of the events leading up to Hall's death and of the dramatic events which followed are published here in English for the first time.

Following the return south of both parties of survivors an official Board of Inquiry was held, and the transcript of its hearings was published almost immediately in the *Annual report of the Secretary of the Navy on the operations of the Department for the year 1873*.[2] Until now there has been only one first-hand English account of the *Polaris* expedition, namely that of the assistant navigator, George Tyson.[3] The official narrative, almost contemporaneous, was compiled by Rear-Admiral C.H. Davis, USN[4] and relies quite heavily on Tyson's account, and on the report of the Board of Inquiry. While these two latter sources reveal much as to the tensions and interpersonal frictions and even enmities on board *Polaris*, Davis's account sugar-coats the expedition, and provides little or no information as to these discordant themes. Emil Bessels's book, published in German in 1879, also relies quite heavily on Tyson's account, but it too is largely silent as to the schisms and enmities which plagued the expedition even from the start, and tells us nothing at all about the Board of Inquiry.

A few examples of these interpersonal frictions will suffice. Thus, as Blake notes in her introduction to Tyson's journal, right at the start of the expedition problems had already risen:

> While in Washington previous to sailing, a want of mutual respect was known to exist between Captain Hall and Dr. Bessel (sic) and so far was Dr. Bessels' discourtesy carried, on several occasions, that Captain Hall would have been quite justified in refusing to take him in his company, and calling for a volunteer in his place.[5]

By the time *Polaris* had reached St. John's the situation had clearly deteriorated further:

> While lying in this pleasant port, a point of discussion arose as to the authority of the commander over the Scientific Corps. Strong feeling was mutually exhibited, which extended to the officers, and even to the crew, among whom was developed an unmistakable feeling of special affinity on the score of national affiliation. At this point it really appeared as if the foreign element [the majority of the crew were German] were far more in sympathy with each other, as fellow countrymen, than they were with furthering the hopes of Captain Hall, and the main object of the expedition. However, matters were smoothed over; the Scientific Corps were left free to follow their own course, and the threatened disruption of the party avoided.[6]

Concerning this same situation at St. John's, Tyson himself had written, "I see there is not perfect harmony between Captain Hall and the Scientific Corps, nor with some others either. I am afraid things will not work well. It is not my business, but I am sorry for Hall; he is fearfully embarrassed."[7]

Even as early as this in the voyage Hall had occasion to reprimand Sidney Budington, the sailing master, for covertly helping himself to various food items. At the Board of Inquiry, challenged with this, Budington admitted his misdemeanour as follows: "Captain Hall had a very slight difference with me about some of my—well it was a very careless trick in me, and he gave me a reprimand on leaving St. John's."[8]

Bessels may or may not have been aware of this disagreement; certainly there is no mention of it in his book. But even when he was directly involved in a serious difference of opinion, also early in the expedition, he does not report it. Thus when Frederick Meyer, the meteorologist, was asked by Hall to be his secretary, especially to keep the expedition journal, he refused, arguing that it would interfere with his weather observations. When Hall insisted, Meyer threatened to leave the ship at Disko. Bessels backed him up, also threatening to leave, and with the further threat that all eight German members of the crew would also defect. Hall backed down. When the supply ship *Congress* reached Disko, her captain, H.K. Davenport, on learning of this mutinous behaviour, threatened to take Meyer back to Washington in irons. Hall, however, declined to take advantage of this offer, determined at all costs to avoid the total disruption of his expedition which this would almost certainly have caused.[9] He was fully aware of the anomalous and inconvenient situation in which he found himself: while Meyer was on loan from the Army, Hall was not a naval officer, and Bessels, of course, was a civilian, as were most of the crew. Nevertheless Davenport managed to extract from Meyer a signed statement that he would obey Hall's orders. But even after that Hall backed down, countermanding his earlier order that Meyers should act as his secretary.

Later, while Hall was on shore, making a preliminary sledge trip, suspecting Budington of helping himself to the supply of alcohol Bessels had brought for preserving specimens, Bessels set a trap for him and caught him red-handed.[10] Even though this incident presents Bessels in a positive light, as being the aggrieved party, there is no mention of it in his book.

These are only a few samples of the numerous schisms and enmities which developed on board *Polaris*. As to why he makes no mention of them, in situations (as in the penultimate situation just mentioned) where he does not appear in a very positive light, one can understand why he would not want to publicize it. But in the final case mentioned, where he appears in a positive light, one can only assume that it was due to his desire to present the entire expedition to his German readers (who would not have been exposed to the less glamorous details revealed in the American press) in the best possible light.

On the other hand there is considerable detail in Bessels's book which does not appear elsewhere. For example, he provides much more information than in the other accounts on the various Greenland settlements *Polaris* visited on her way north. His is the only published firsthand account of the second wintering of part of the ship's complement on shore at Polaris House, near Littleton Island, and of that party's attempt at travelling south by boat until picked up by the Scottish whaler *Ravenscraig*. The same applies with regard to the cruise of the whaler *Arctic*, after Bessels and his companions transferred to that ship. It will probably come as a surprise to many readers that *Arctic* visited Fury Beach on the east coast of Somerset Island; here Bessels provides details of the remains of the depot left there by Parry in 1825 and of Somerset House where John Ross and his crew wintered in 1832–33. Indeed, *Arctic* penetrated even farther south into the Gulf of Boothia, and it appears that it was not at all an unusual occurrence for British whaling vessels.

But where Bessels's account differs so conspicuously (and so valuably) from the other published accounts is in the scientific details and descriptions inserted into the narrative, including such topics as birds, mammals, insects, flora, geology, hydrography (tidal observations, currents and ice conditions); magnetism and aurora; glaciology and meteorology (including air temperature, wind, barometric pressure, humidity, precipitation, cloud cover and solar radiation). And this is in addition to the Scientific Appendix, totalling 120 pages, the major headings of which will be found in Appendix 2. The information interspersed through the text on flora, fauna and geology is particularly valuable in that Volume 2 of the official *Scientific Results*,[11] which would have covered these topics, was never published. It should also be noted that Bessels devotes an entire chapter (Chapter 19) to the Inuit. While the information and attitudes are obviously dated, this chapter does provide a useful indication of the knowledge about the Inuit in Europe at the time.

While Loomis consulted Bessels's book in preparing his excellent biography of Charles Francis Hall,[12] none of the various recent studies of the expedition, namely those of Parry (2001), Henderson (2001) and Nickerson (2002), gives any indication that they had consulted it, or even knew that it existed.

Even although he was a member of an American expedition, Emil Bessels's participation in Hall's expedition represented an effective step in Germany's contribution to polar science and exploration. That contribution was closely linked to the ideas and aspirations of geographer and cartographer August Petermann.[13] He first proposed the idea of a preliminary arctic expedition at a meeting of the Versammlung deutscher Geographen und Hydrographen (Assembly of German Geographers and Hydrographers) in Frankfurt on 23 July 1865.[14] To demonstrate that he was serious, on 30 July he offered a prize of 1000 to 2000 thaler to any German mariner who would undertake a "reconnaissance voyage" to the region between Svalbard and Novaya Zemlya (and if possible to 80°N) to investigate currents and water temperatures. The challenge was accepted by Korvettenkapitän Reinhold Werner of the Prussian Navy, who even refused the prize offered. He chartered the British iron steamer *Queen of the Isles* (200 tons, 40 hp). Since Werner was unable to negotiate leave from the navy, Captain Hegemann took command of the vessel in his stead. With an English crew the ship reached Hamburg on 30 August 1865 and sailed again next day, now with a mixed German and English crew. Unfortunately the ship suffered an engine breakdown, which brought it to a halt off Otterndorf in the Elbe estuary, just west of Cuxhaven, that same afternoon. There were even rumours of sabotage by English members of the crew. The ship was towed back to Hamburg; since repairs would take more than a week it was decided to abandon the voyage.

Although Petermann stubbornly continued to lobby for a German arctic expedition, the Austro-Prussian War of 1866 not surprisingly diverted attention away from such enterprises. But in 1868 conditions were much more favourable and things fell into place in the shape of the First German North Pole Expedition. Once it was advertised, financial contributions flooded in, including 5000 thaler from König Wilhelm. Leader of the expedition was Karl Koldewey, who purchased the expedition's vessel in Bergen: *Grönland*—a ketch built only the previous year. At a length of 25.8 m, beam 6.00 m, it had a draft of 3.00 m. Koldewey's instructions were to try to reach the east coast of Greenland at about 75°N and then to follow it north as far as possible, possibly even as far as the North Pole. If unsuccessful there he was to head east to Svalbard and to try to find the elusive "Gillis Land" (in fact Kvitøya, located just east of Nordaustlandet).[15]

Koldewey's instructions reflected two ideas to which Petermann clung obsessively: firstly, the widely held concept of an "open polar sea" surrounded by an annular belt of pack ice and, secondly, that Greenland extended right across the Arctic to Ostrov Vrangelya (Wrangel Island), just off the arctic coast of Chukotka.

Grönland put to sea from Bergen on 24 May 1868 and headed north past Jan Mayen. Blocked by ice at about 75°N, Koldewey ran south, probing the ice edge, and although the Greenland coast was sighted on 16 June at about 73°30'N he was unable to reach it and the ship was beset for some time. Following instructions, Koldewey headed east to and past Sørkapp on Spitsbergen, hoping to reach "Gillis Land." Blocked again by ice, he headed north along the west coast of Spitsbergen and, after calling at Bellsund for water and ballast, continued north until again blocked by ice at about 80°30'N. Hoping that ice conditions off the east coast of Greenland might have improved, he headed back there but was again thwarted by ice. Returning to the north coast of Spitsbergen, Koldewey ran south through Hinlopenstretet and there managed to make some original discoveries; place names such as Wilhelmøya and Augustabukta still commemorate that minor success. Finally, pushing north from Verlegenhuken, the northern tip of Spitsbergen, *Grönland* reached a latitude of 81°04'N, the highest latitude ever known to have been attained by a sailing vessel. By 29 September the expedition was back at Bergen. The scientific results, with an emphasis on currents and water temperatures, were published the following year.[16]

Public reaction to Koldewey's voyage was very positive, and a subscription campaign to fund a follow-up expedition was very successful. Despite Koldewey's failure to reach the east coast of Greenland, the stated aims for this second expedition were to attempt to reach that coast again, to establish a wintering base, to explore inland and, if possible, to again push north toward the North Pole. This would be the Second German North Pole Expedition.[17] The fact that Fram Strait (between Greenland and Svalbard) and Denmark Strait (between Iceland and Greenland), i.e., precisely the same waters Petermann considered to be the optimal route for attempting to reach the North Pole, represent precisely the main route by which multi-year ice is exported from the Arctic Ocean in a constant stream, carried by the East Greenland Current, clearly had not yet registered with Petermann. The outcome of his plan would be a terrifying ordeal for half the personnel of the expedition.

One ship, *Germania*, was built especially for the expedition in the Tecklenborg yards in Geestemünde, now a suburb of Bremerhaven. Only slightly larger than *Grönland*, it possessed the advantage of a steam engine. A second vessel, *Hansa*, was to act as a supply vessel. Koldewey himself commanded *Germania* as well as being expedition leader, while Captain Paul Hegemann, a whaling captain from Oldenburg, was in command of *Hansa*. The two ships put to sea from Bremerhaven on 15 June 1869, the intention being that they would stay in company. They encountered the first ice on 15 July, and on the 20th at about 74°13'N they became separated due to the misreading of a signal hoist

Hansa became beset in the ice and was carried south by the ice-drift.[18] It was crushed and sank on 22 October at 70°52'N; 21°W. Prior to this a house had been built on the ice and substantial amounts of provisions and equipment (including all the boats) had been salvaged. The shipwrecked party drifted steadily south throughout the winter. Finally, after a drift of some 1200 n. miles (2222 km) they took to the boats on 7 May 1870 and finally reached the Moravian mission station at Frederiksdal (now Narsarmijit), just west of Cape Farewell, on 13 June.

Meanwhile, on 5 August *Germania* dropped anchor in a bay, Germaniahavn, on the southeast coast of Sabine Ø (one of the Pendulum Øer). Unlike the situation with the previous expedition on board *Grönland*, there were three scientists on board *Germania*: Carl Nicolai Jensen Börgen (magnetologist), Ralph Copeland (astronomer) and Adolf Pansch (surgeon and zoologist). Also on board, as surveyor and mountaineer, was Oberleutnant Julius Payer of the Austrian army, who had just spent four summers surveying the mountains of the Ortler and Adamello-Presenella mountains of the Eastern Alps. All of them now began their studies of the island's environment. On the 10th the ship got underway again, pushing north, but was totally blocked by ice at 75°31'N, the highest latitude she would reach. Returning to Germaniahavn, shore parties were landed to continue their surveys of Sabine Ø while the ship cruised around the nearby islands. By 13 September

Germania was back at Germaniahavn, and went into winter quarters. But first, in the fall several relatively short man-hauled sledge trips were made around Clavering Ø and to Fligely Fjord. In the spring the major sledge trip of the expedition was mounted, northward to Dovebugt and what is now Danmarkshavn, from where a further penetration was made northward into the interior of Germania Land, reaching 77°N. Once back at Germaniahavn a further sledge trip was made to Ardencaple Fjord. *Germania* got underway again on 1 August, heading south along the coast. On 8 August a party climbed a mountain above Cape Franklin, and from there spotted the entrance to the spectacular Kejser Franz Joseph Fjord, and it was explored by ship over the following week. From the ship's farthest point Payer climbed Payer Tinde. Thereafter *Germania* started for home, reaching Bremerhaven on 11 September.

A particularly interesting discovery made by the expedition was the common occurrence of old Inuit dwellings, tent rings and food caches, including those at the site where Douglas Clavering had encountered a small group of Inuit during his visit to this coast in HMS *Griper* in 1823.[19] No Inuit were ever seen on this coast thereafter.

Simultaneously with the first season of the expedition on board *Germania* and *Hansa*, Bessels was also in the Arctic for the first time.[20] With Petermann acting as intermediary, he headed north on board shipowner Albert Rosenthal's vessel *Albert* (Captain Hashagen). *Albert* reached Svalbard and pushed north beyond it, reaching 80°14'N, before being blocked by ice. As with so many other expeditions, the elusive "Gillis Land" was one of the objectives, but the ship was unable to reach it due to ice. *Albert* next tried to reach the coast of Novaya Zemlya, but without success. Among Bessels's achievements was correcting the coordinates of the island of Hopen and confirming the penetration of the relatively warm waters of the Gulf Stream (or more correctly, its continuation, the North Atlantic Drift) far north into the Barents Sea.[21]

It was on the basis of this arctic voyage that, on Petermann's recommendation, Bessels was assigned to the position of chief scientist and medical officer on Hall's expedition, Thus his contribution as an arctic scientist represented a legitimate step in the history of German polar exploration.

To Captain Albert Hastings Markham, R.N.[1]

MY DEAR MARKHAM

While on our retreat from the far North, after the cruise described in the following pages, you were the first one deeply interested in the geography of the Polar regions whom I had the good fortune to meet.[2] Since then you have taken an active part in Arctic exploration as commanding officer of that gallant little band of sailors who, after struggling against obstacles unsurpassed in the record of exploration, attained a higher latitude than had ever before been reached.[3]

Upon this success let me offer my most hearty congratulations. As an expression of friendship and high esteem, in remembrance of bygone times and pleasant days spent in common scientific pursuits, and as a reminder of rough sports in chasing the whale, the polar bear and the walrus, as well as of quieter ramblings in two hemispheres, permit me to inscribe to you this volume. Accept it as a token of gratitude from the shipwrecked waif with whom you kindly shared your berth and cabin in the good old ship "Arctic," which later met the same fate as our own "Polaris."

Very sincerely yours,

Emil Bessels.

Preface

The expedition, the history and results of which are dealt with in the present book, owes its origins to the generosity of the United States of America. Its admirable aim was to reach the North Pole via the northern continuation of Smith Sound, the strait which American drive and American perseverance had revealed and had already made the scene of glorious discoveries.

So as not to interrupt the flow of the narrative which I have selected for this work, I have included the physical-geographical results of the expedition in a scientific appendix, and have dealt with them there in some detail. It was originally my intention to present the natural history results there also, but I have not done so, since I do not want to anticipate the Government, which has the right of first publication.[1]

Of the not inconsiderable funds that Congress had approved for the production of illustrations for the official scientific account of the voyage, only a small part was used for this purpose. By far the major portion, under the previous naval administration, ended up in other hands, and as a result completion of the natural history and ethnological volumes was delayed in a distressing fashion. For this reason I consider it my duty to limit the extent of the scientific appendix. But at the same time I could not refrain from including all the worthwhile data either as notes or as inclusions in the narrative in popular form.

I completed the text of the book in the summer of 1874, shortly after my return from the expedition; but some parts were later substantially rewritten and some remarks were inserted into the ethnological chapter. All the expedition documents plus the archives of the Navy Department were made available for my unrestricted use. I must acknowledge this fact all the more gratefully, since the greater part of my journal entries, that I had saved from the shipwreck and that were contained in my trunk along with other papers, went missing during the railway journey through Scotland.[2]

The first four chapters are based on a series of letters, whose content is rendered almost word-for-word. The relevant sections have probably gained in completeness as a result, but their origin is unmistakable, as is indicated by their somewhat casual style, as well as by various unnecessary details. These aspects now appear more conspicuous to me than two years ago, when the writing of the book began.

In order to provide the most faithful and vivid description possible of the ice journey, I used the brief journal entries published in the annual report of the Naval Ministry, supplemented by an oral account by the Inuk Joseph.[3]

The reason that I did not immediately publish this account lay solely in the fact that my sense of justice would not allow me to forestall the publication of the official account of the voyage.[4] I also took pains not to appear to compete with its editor, who was not familiar with the arctic regions from personal experience, thereby appearing to woo the favour of the public.

The appearance of the official account of the voyage, which has been edited by Rear-Admiral Davis, was delayed until last summer.[5] Although the book claims to be an account of the voyage and bears that title, one can scarcely describe its content as anything more than just a meagre itinerary. Many of the illustrations published in it also occur in my book. But I must note that it was not I who borrowed them from the editor of the "account of the voyage," but rather the latter who acquired them from me.

It is scarcely necessary to discuss the "Narrative" in more detail. But I can state with pleasure that I am the anonymous reviewer who discussed it in the *Nation*. In the meantime I have only been strengthened in the view that I expressed there on this so-called "narrative." I now consider it an even more insignificant make-work than I did then. If this vast tome can make any claim at all to being a narrative, I would today describe it as the most vacuous and worthless of all narratives.

Before the "narrative" appeared, the British expedition that had followed the same route as *Polaris*, under the command of Sir George Nares, returned. Since I had anticipated that the conclusions of the scientific appendices would be modified by the discoveries of the British, it seemed advisable to me not to hurry with publication, but to wait for the appearance of the British results. Moreover, I nurtured the hope that Congress would approve the necessary funds to complete the illustrations of the two missing volumes of the official narrative, and hence that it would have been possible for me to include the remaining scientific results in the appendix.

Thus far this hope has not been fulfilled. By contrast, Sir George Nares was so kind as to support me in the most obliging fashion, and to send me in manuscript many of the still unpublished observations which he and his officers had made. I used them to the best of my abilities in compiling the appendix, which, in general, may be considered an extract from the first scientific volume of the narrative.[6]

The latter contains many gross errors, which unfortunately were not discovered until after this book of about 1000 quarto pages was published. A young man who had relieved me of part of the burden of the mechanical tasks of compiling it abused my trust in an irresponsible fashion, in that in adding up long rows of figures he attained the totals by impermissible means, and also used similar dishonest procedures on other occasions.

Although these objectionable errors involve almost exclusively the meteorological results in that volume, I still subjected the entire contents of the volume to a thorough revision, the results of which are presented in the appendix to this work. I handled the tidal observations particularly carefully, since they provide the first proof of the insularity of Greenland and show clearly that the tide wave reaches Polaris Bay from the north. In the meantime not only has this fact been confirmed by Sir George Nares, but the latter also determined by direct observations that this northern wave meets the one from the south at the same spot that I had identified on theoretical grounds.

For the compilation of the map, which I submitted for printing in the summer of 1877, I used the most recent British surveys as well as all the older sources in order to supplement our own measurements, the elements of which, almost without exception, were lost during the shipwreck. While I took pains to straighten out the confusion in nomenclature produced by earlier explorers and to include the original names, I have retained almost all those which Sir George Nares and his officers used. The conflicts between the British and American surveys were thus resolved.

The most significant deviation in my nomenclature from the British consists of the fact that I did not use Nares's term "Paleocrystic Sea."[7] This was for two reasons. In the first place it was to respect the honour of the flag under which specific discoveries are made; secondly, fairness demands that the sole minor priority to which the discoverer himself can lay claim should be protected. The part of the central Arctic Basin which Sir George Nares labels the "Paleocrystic Sea" was discovered under the flag of the United States and was named the "Lincoln Sea" by the Americans. Hence priority is due to this latter name.

Only the future will decide whether the ice conditions in this marine area are always as unfavourable as the British encountered. Markham's push for the North Pole from Cape Joseph Henry across the shattered ice of the Lincoln Sea will always remain memorable in the history of discovery voyages. But we could only conditionally agree with the statement of the brave British officers that the North Pole is not accessible from Smith Sound. There is scarcely any doubt that the Pole was unattainable when the British made their attempt to reach it. At the same time this circumstance does not allow us to render a generally applicable verdict, since we know that the ice cover of the polar seas is subject to significant fluctuations.

I am far from advocating the route via Smith Sound; at the moment the marine area east of Svalbard, as well as Bering Strait, promise much better results that would be more valuable to geographers. But it seems to me advisable to point out here the variable nature of the ice, and I should like to emphasize this aspect in particular.

When Cook reached his highest southerly latitude on 30 January 1774, not only was he of the view that it was impossible to get any closer to the South Pole, but he expressed this view with total conviction.[8] Almost half a century passed before other explorers dared to penetrate beyond the latitude he had reached. But finally the step was taken. It was made by British whalers[9] who made their richest haul in precisely the region of which Cook had said that it would never provide the slightest profit for mankind.

Exactly the same thing happened with the Kara Sea, the "inaccessible ice cellar,"[10] in which Russian and Scandinavian fishermen now ply their trade every year.

If the latest reports are correct, descendants of the old Norsemen are now even close to accomplishing the deed which the most eminent civilized nations of Europe have striven in vain to achieve for three centuries. *Vega*, which last summer was fitted out by a generous Swede as an arctic expedition ship, had already passed the mouth of the Lena this fall, as we are reliably informed.[11] Now vague reports are reaching us of a vessel lying alone in icy fetters near that Siberian cape[12] where the first rays of the gloomy dawn break on the coasts of both worlds. If these reports are indeed true, that vessel is *Vega*, and we may expect important contributions toward the solution of the polar question.

The author.

CHAPTER 1

Origin of the expedition and its outfitting

> *America's part in exploration of the Far North. Hall, the originator of the expedition. The Congress of the United States. A bill. Selection of the ship, its refitting in Washington and voyage to New York. The* Polaris *instruments. Provisions. The arctic trefoil. Extraordinary session of the Geographical Society in New York.*

When, about 25 years ago, the population of Britain raised its voice and impetuously demanded a glimpse of the final act in the Franklin drama,[1] and when Great Britain was obliged to outfit a squadron to search for its sons, this exhortation penetrated far beyond the borders of Old England and found a sympathetic echo in the hearts of American kinsmen.

Given the prominent position that the United States occupied as a sea power, it was perhaps the duty of the government to render help to the martyrs of a maritime enterprise. But at that time the slave question was beginning to assume quite a serious tone; in the south, American freebooters were fighting to help Cuba to throw off Spanish domination; and if the government took no decisive steps to satisfy public opinion, at least it had no lack of excuses.

Hence all the greater is the gratitude due to the man who made a nation's business his own and stretched out a helping hand to search for the missing seafarers. The latter had set out to solve a problem, whose origin was rooted in the dreams of wealth which had once made the two greatest sea powers in Europe greedy for the treasure of the fabulous kingdom of Cathay. Now, after more than three centuries, the latter had been discovered; thousands were working amidst feverish excitement to bring them to light. But they were not found where people expected but in the country which the gold-hungry conquistadores had long possessed without suspecting its significance. The mass migration to the West had reached its high point but had not yet passed it; the wave of settlers rolled endlessly on across the prairies and through forests toward the Pacific coast; more American sails than ever before swarmed around the notorious Cape Horn. Anybody owning ships loaded them with goods and manpower, since the profits promised on the shores of California were large and certain.

Two vessels, originally intended for this purpose, found another use, however. Their owner, Henry Grinnell, a benevolent merchant from New York, quietly outfitted them for a polar voyage and placed them at the disposal of the US Navy, in order to dispatch them to the scene of the Northwest Passage, in order to investigate the loss of the missing Britons and to bring the survivors back home.

After more than a year, *Advance* and *Rescue* returned to New York but without having penetrated the secret which surrounded the fate of the polar travellers.[2] The problem had advanced closer to a solution, certainly, but only far enough to arouse in the families of the explorers even more anxious doubts than before. The winter quarters of the expedition had been discovered and graves had been found;[3] partially contradictory articles had been recovered; but nobody could say where the seafarers had gone after leaving their wintering harbour.[4]

Barely 18 months had passed since the return of the ships when one of them, the larger and stronger *Advance*, put to sea again, largely fitted out by Henry Grinnell again and partly with the same crew as previously, but under a different commander. The command had been entrusted to Elisha Kent Kane, the doctor on the first Grinnell Expedition, and he chose the Smith Land[5] area as his base of operations.[6]

After a double wintering beyond the 78th parallel, during which he had every opportunity to taste to the full the terrors of the polar regions, he returned to America in early October 1855, bleeding from all the wounds which the crown of thorns of the explorer can inflict. Part of the crew had died from the privations of the voyage; the vessel herself had been abandoned after all the available wood had been torn from it in order to combat the cold of the second winter. Since no traces of the missing Englishmen were found, the main object of the enterprise must be considered as a failure, but important geographical discoveries had been made which richly compensated for the loss of human life and of the ship.

To complete these discoveries, in 1860 Isaac Hayes, who had shared in the pains and joys of the Second Grinnell Expedition as doctor, left the United States.[7] For the ship and its outfitting he was indebted to the keen interest which learned societies and warm personal friends invested in an enterprise, toward the realization of which he had worked for a full five years. Although in many aspects fate was more favourable to him than to his predecessor, despite all his efforts he was unable to reach a higher latitude in his little schooner than Kane. After the vessel had suffered assorted serious damage, Hayes found himself obliged, due to unfavourable ice conditions, to establish winter quarters close to the entrance to Smith Land, and to wait for the arrival of spring to traverse the stretch of icy wastes that lay between him and his goal. Without being able to claim any more significant results than a partial confirmation of Kane's discoveries, he returned to Boston in October of the following year.

Thus I have sketched, in brief outline, the part which America had played in the exploration of the Far North up until 1861. Later we will repeatedly find occasion to examine these last two voyages in greater detail, and to linger longer over the brilliant sidelights they throw on the history of arctic voyages of discovery.

While there was a lapse of only five years between Kane's and Hayes's expeditions, it would now be a full decade before America again took up the polar question. The reason for this is to be sought in political circumstances on the one hand, but largely in the natural indifference with which one views all enterprises whose success will not be either pecuniary or religious, in a relatively young country where material interests dominate and naturally must dominate.

In the meantime a number of expeditions had set out from Sweden, Germany and England that were likely to shake even America out of its indifference. Toward the end of the 1860s the polar question was repeatedly brought up for discussion at the Geographical Society; repeatedly ardent speeches were made, but after a short time their effect was negated by the commonest everyday interests. No rich private individuals could be won over to this costly undertaking; even less could Congress, thrown together from the most heterogeneous elements, and the majority of whose members always viewed science as the Cinderella of the great republic, become enthusiastic for a North Pole expedition in which, according to the experts, in the most favourable situation human lives and ships would be lost, and at most a few ice-covered islands might be gained.

And yet an expedition was to be outfitted from government funds. Admittedly every permissible and impermissible means had to be brought into play in order to place a bill before Congress and to defend it successfully; every lever had to be set in motion which either certain hands were unwilling to grasp or were unable to touch without becoming soiled. But the scheme worked; the enterprise came about; America's star-spangled flag was to fly at high latitudes again.

The initial impulse for the expedition came solely from Francis C. Hall;[8] he is also largely to be thanked for its realization. Two sojourns in the Hudson Bay area and its vicinity, which lasted for over seven years, had made him an experienced traveller, and even although he lacked the general and scientific education which is necessary to crown a voyage of exploration with complete success, he was possessed of a rare, indomitable energy, and had accustomed himself so completely to the less-than-enviable conditions of an arctic campaign that (one can say without exaggeration) they seemed to him the normal conditions of life. Hunger and cold, deprivations of all kinds, had become the norm for him; his powerful, muscular form could boldly defy hardships with impunity. Such qualities weighed heavily in the choice of a participant in a voyage of exploration.

During the winter of 1869 he travelled to the capital. For a long time his ideas and pleas went unheard. Malevolent policies threatened to strangle his plans in the bud when, unexpectedly, helping hands were extended to him.[9] On 8 March 1870 the delegate for the State of Ohio[10] brought a bill before the House of Representatives which would authorize the President of the United States[11] to fit out a North Pole expedition and appoint Hall as its leader. A similar bill was presented to the Senate by the Senator for the same state[12] on the 25th of March; the Senate passed it to the Committee on Foreign Affairs[13] to report on it. On 19 April the bill was returned in a modified form; Hall's name had been left off and it was now so worded that command of the expedition was to be entrusted to "one or several persons," unidentified.[14] In this altered form the bill passed both the House and Senate on 11 July[15] and was signed by the President next day. Its text reads as follows:

> Sec. 9. *Be it enacted*, That the President of the United States be authorized to organize and send out one or more expeditions toward the North Pole, and to appoint such person or persons as he may deem most fitted to the command thereof; to detail any officer of the public service to take part in the same, and to use any public vessel that may be suitable for the purpose; the scientific operations of the expedition to be prescribed in accordance with the advice of the National Academy of Sciences; and that the sum of fifty thousand dollars,[16] or such part thereof as may be necessary, be hereby appropriated, out of any moneys in the Treasury not otherwise appropriated, to be expended under the direction of the President.[17]

Once the enterprise had been assured to this extent, others, who until now had silently observed the course of events, tried to usurp the command, and important voices were raised against Hall and his abilities. But he succeeded in eliminating his antagonists from the field, and with the help of influential Congress members and Senators to maintain the position for which he had fought so hard. On 20 July his commission was completed and signed by the President and he received orders to report for duty to the Secretary of the Navy.[18]

The next step was the procurement of a ship. If the sum approved by Congress, which in fact was quite modest, was to suffice, the ship had to be selected from the available vessels in the Navy, but at that time these were far from numerous. After a long search Hall decided on *Periwinkle*, a small vessel of 387 tons burden,[19] which the government had bought during the Civil War in order to maintain contact between various points on the Delaware River when the river was heavily ice-covered.[20]

In terms of strength and ability the ship scarcely left anything to be desired, but before she could be used for a polar expedition, it seemed advisable to undertake various major changes in her construction and interior arrangements. Toward the end of the year the vessel was docked in the Navy Yard at Washington in order to be totally refitted.[21] For the impending new guise a new name was also called for instead of *Periwinkle*, whereby, depending on mood or preference, one can imply either a gastropod or a flower. Mr. Grinnell, the zealous promoter of arctic exploration, preferred *Polaris*, and since no objections were raised to this new name, this was the one selected, corresponding appropriately to the ship's mission.

On 15 April 1871, I reached New York from Bremen on board the Norddeutsche Lloyd steamer *Rhein* after a fast, pleasant crossing;[22] two days later I arrived in Washington and Hall took me to the shipyards where the ship was lying in dock, immediately next to a proud frigate. The masts were not yet stepped, heavy ice-sheathing was being put in place, and the vessel looked very unprepossessing; three weeks later she left the dock. Since the responsibility for the scientific equipment for the expedition was almost exclusively mine,[23] I had enough to do in the meantime, and the time passed faster than was pleasant, given the circumstances. We were waiting impatiently for a crate of instruments from England that finally arrived in mid-May.

I must mention with gratitude the help that was extended to us from every side in the most liberal fashion, and note with pleasure the warm interest that Professors Henry,[24] Baird,[25] the head of the Smithsonian Institution, Admiral Sands,[26] then director of the Naval Observatory, Commodores Ammen[27] and Wyman,[28] and Messrs Hilgard[29] and Schott[30] of the Coast Guard, took in the enterprise.

Although the carpenters and other craftsmen worked with every diligence at the rigging and the ship's interior arrangements, early June was approaching before *Polaris* was approximately completed. On the morning of June 10th orders came from the Navy Department to put to sea, and shortly after noon the vessel weighed anchor to proceed to New York,[31] her next destination, where the rest of the provisions were to be loaded and where we intended completing our inventory and provisioning. In a flat calm she quickly ran down the Potomac under steam; when night fell the ship anchored with her fires banked, in 15 fathoms of water in a gentle bend of the river. At 4.00 next morning she continued her voyage, but it took her until the morning of the 14th to reach New York, since for two days the vessel had to battle foul winds and heavy seas. In order to save time, and to be able to complete various preparations, I opted to make the journey to New York by train. When I arrived there on the 17th, it looked so uninviting on board ship that it seemed advisable to find lodgings in town; the wheel-house had been carried away and had to be refitted; the inner woodwork had received a second coat of paint; every usable space was filled with bales, casks and boxes; everywhere craftsmen or seamen were busy. Everything was in that stage of confused disorder that such an occasion produces. Despite this, inquisitive visitors were constantly crowding in from all sides to view the little North Pole traveller, which was rapidly approaching completion under the management of a superb shipbuilder.

Scarcely a plank had been transferred from the old *Periwinkle* to *Polaris*;[32] the lines of the ship's hull were now completely different and her rig had been changed to that of a schooner. The gently and pleasingly curving exterior of the hull now concealed a skeleton whose massive tween-deck beams and knees, angle irons and bands might have served to build a full-rigged ship. Over the actual hull planking stretched a solid oak ice-skin, firmly fastened to the hull while, in addition, thick armour plates covered the bow. The saloon, the engine room and four small cabins were located in a superstructure on deck; a narrow, covered passageway led along both port and starboard sides. Only the saloon door opened aft into the open air; the doors to the other compartments gave onto the longitudinal passages, which could be closed by doors. Aft of the saloon lay the wheelhouse, and aft of it the small structure into which the twin-bladed propeller could be housed; it could be quickly raised by a simple mechanism. A sentry box–like cubby-hole located forward of the mainmast formed the galley; somewhat farther forward rose the main hatch that led down to the crew's quarters, which contained 12 bunks. From here one gained access forward to two small store rooms and to the lower chain locker; aft of it lay the lower engine room, with coal bunkers to starboard and port; then came the main provisions stores and the powder magazine.

The saloon, which served as the general assembly point, was lit by a large skylight and was delicately, almost elegantly furnished, but unfortunately was of rather small dimensions. In the middle stood a table that occupied most of the space; to starboard and port lay four bunks on each side, hidden by grey damask curtains. Directly forward of the table the little compartment was traversed by the stout shape of the mast; a tolerably good harmonium, donated by some friendly soul, was squeezed between two cupboards which housed the library, while another cupboard, barely 9 square feet in area, later converted into a "study room," separated the double row of bunks on the port side. Various armchairs and folding chairs competed with the chronometer cases to reduce the space in which one could move to a minimum. Photographs of the President of the Republic and the Secretary of the Navy, and steel engravings of various senators, served as decoration; several chromo-lithographed pictures whose gaudy mixture of colours was a pleasant titillation for the optical nerves of my comrades, formed an extremely dubious ornamentation on the walls and the covering of the skylight. From the latter hung the clock, which monitored the progress of the year with pedantic conscientiousness by means of a complicated system of dials and proclaimed months, days, hours, minutes and seconds in a monotonous "tick-tock."

The ship's inventory was of masterly completeness; in terms of spare parts it included a mast, various topmasts, a rudder, a screw and an assortment of sails. The four large whaleboats were of superb construction; a small jolly-boat was exclusively available for scientific work. In addition we had on board a collapsible boat about 20 feet long; it weighed not more than about 250 lbs. and in case of necessity could carry 15 men. Oak frames, equipped with hinges, formed a skeleton, and the covering consisted of waterproof canvas. It took barely 15 minutes to assemble it and make it seaworthy, but despite this it turned out not to be practical. The sledges were to be made en route, as required; selected planks, cut from Norwegian spruce, were intended for making the runners; in addition we possessed two assembled sledges that had been used by the First Grinnell Expedition. Particular care was paid to the selection of the weapons; the rifles were mainly breech-loaders of the latest design (Remingtons, Sharps, Springfields), as were most of

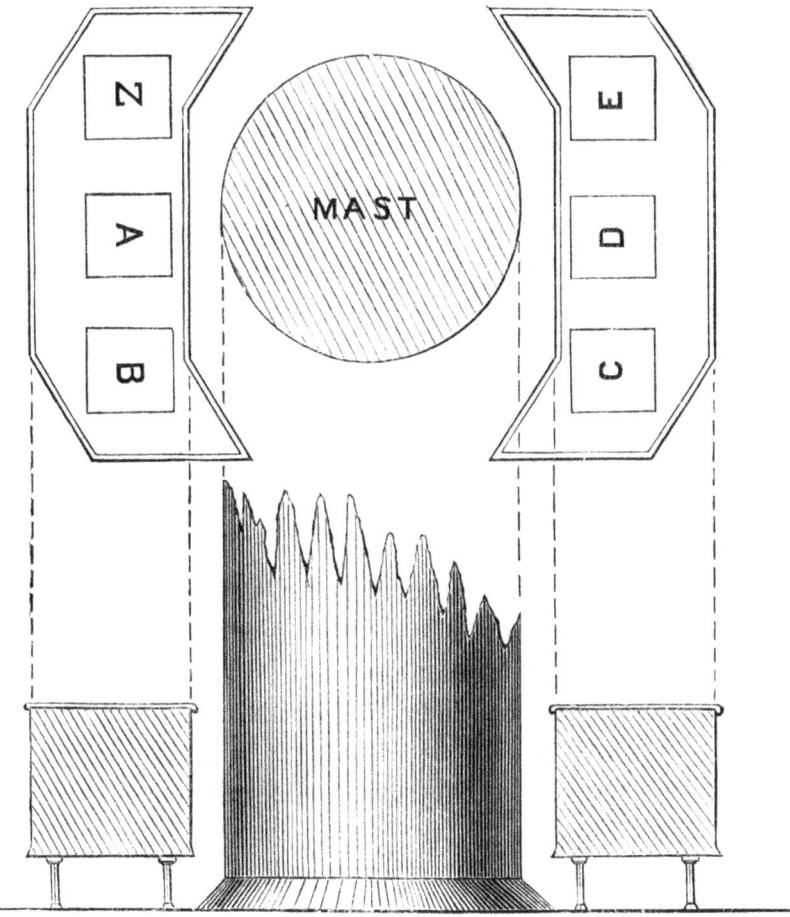

Fig. 1. Arrangement of the chronometers.

the shotguns and the long-barrelled pistols (Remingtons), which could be sighted-in for considerable ranges and whose rifling ensured great accuracy for the trajectory of the bullet. The ship's inventory included complete equipment for whaling, since there was a small apparatus attached to the engine whose overrated function was allegedly heating the boiler with blubber. Given the circumstance that it might have daily consumed the blubber of a medium-sized whale in order to give the ship a speed of 6 knots, it was totally inappropriate and was never used.

We could consider ourselves fortunate that we had available not only a significant number of box chronometers but also instruments whose regular functioning exceeded the boldest anticipations. They had all been made by Negus of New York; three kept standard time, the other three star time. In addition we possessed four pocket chronometers produced by various English makers, but their reliability never attained a superlative calibre. Apart from the care with which the six Negus chronometers had been made, we were indebted for their regular functioning in part to the special way in which they were set up, which may be seen from the preceding diagram.

The two boxes in which the clocks were housed (Z, A, B, C, D & E) consisted of strong walnut wood; they were insulated from the mast and rested on four low, wooden legs. Partly to dampen possible shocks the ship might experience due to impacts with the ice, partly in order to ensure an even temperature, the latter were provided with horsehair cushions covered with doubled billiard cloth. The containers were opened only when the clocks were compared and wound; this occurred daily at a specific time and we deviated from it by more than a minute only in exceptional situations. In order to demonstrate what superb service these poor conductors performed it should suffice to note that even in the coldest part of the winter the temperature inside the boxes was subject to only insignificant fluctuations. The other astronomical instruments, which we owed in part to the generosity of the Navy Department and to the friendliness of the Director of the Coast Guard, were as follows:

> 1 portable passage instrument by Würdemann.
> 6 sextants, mostly readable to 10", by Gambey, Stackpole,
>   Pistor & Martins and Wurdemann.
> 1 Repeating Circle by Pistor & Martins.
> 3 pocket sextants.
> 5 artificial horizons; 4 with mercury; one made of glass
>   ' with a level.
> 1 Casella travelling theodolite (also a universal
>   instrument).
> 1 pendulum apparatus (property of Dr. Isaac Hayes).
>   For hydrographic work we had at our disposal:

2 ship's compasses.
1 azimuth compass.
2 alcohol compasses.
8 boat's compasses.
2 patent logs.
1 Massey sounding instrument.
2 Brook's instruments, along with 50 30-lb weights with holes drilled through them.
4 Miller-Casella deep-sea thermometers.
1 metal thermometer (Six).
6400 fathoms of assorted lines,
6 sensitive hydrometers, giving reliable readings to the third decimal place.

To determine the elements of earth magnetism we had:

1 unifilar magnetometer for determining the absolute declination and the horizontal intensity and for taking variation observations.
1 needle inclinometer, with Lloyd's needles.
6 prismatic compasses; 2 of these being by Casella with divisions on an aluminum ring.

We were abundantly provided with meteorological instruments, of which the following may be listed here:

3 marine barometers by Adie (reading to within 0.005").
3 standard barometers, made by Green & Fortin (reading to within 0.002").
6 aneroids of various sizes, by Casella, Beck and Green.
3 Robinson anemometers.
2 Casella pocket anemometers.
20 standard thermometers (10 of them mercury thermometers) by Casella.
1 standard thermometer (mercury) by Green.
1 metal thermometer, by Casella, for determining very low temperatures.
2 maximum thermometers.

3 minimum thermometers.
4 psychrometers (one of them an alcohol psychrometer) by Casella and Green.
1 Regnault instrument for determining the melting point.
2 rain gauges.
3 blackened thermometers, sealed in evacuated glass containers, by Casella.
2 standard blackened thermometers.
1 silver spherical concave mirror, 21.67" in diameter, with thermometer, for determining the reradiated energy from the earth's surface.
1 polarizing apparatus, consisting of two Nicol's prisms.
2 spectroscopes, one a Browning hand spectroscope, the other by Desaga of Heidelberg after Bunsen's design.
1 electrometer with dry piles.
2 miles of rubber-covered telegraph wire.
2 ozonometers.

In addition we had available a plane-table with chain and a standard steel yard in a case; cameras; a microscope; a trawl net with accessories; a reagent box; glasses and also copper containers for preserving plants and animals in alcohol; geological tools; and many other items, to list which would take too long.[33]

Our physical needs were taken care of just as well, on the assumption that we were engaged on a three-year expedition. The provisions list was as long as a medium-sized volume; in its pages, in small writing, the products of the animal and vegetable kingdoms were recorded, arranged in groups, according to a system newly developed by the commissariat officer, which one could only describe as more ingenious than Linné's botanical system.

The class of mammals was represented by: 10,000 lbs. of pemmican, made from the best beef; 4500 lbs. of the rear extremities of the common pig; 600 lbs. of veal; 800 lbs. of lamb; 5300 lbs. of beef; 49 casks of pork; and by other minor items such as roast venison and hares, concentrated soups, hygienically preserved in cans, and 1000 lbs. of butter. The main representatives of the avifauna were geese, ducks, chickens, turkeys, pheasants and snipe, while salmon, mackerel, cod, sardines, sole, herring and anchovies worthily represented the fish; several hundred turtles in the form of soup, and numerous lobsters and shrimp and legions of oysters and soft Venus mussels completed the zodiac.

The fruits of Ceres had been partly mutilated at the hands of the miller and appeared in the form of 45 barrels of wheat flour, 14 barrels of milled corn, maize and oats, supplemented by impressive amounts of split peas; Lima beans, broken beans, white beans and lentils completed the array of *leguminosae*. We received, as "Java coffee," 1500 lbs. of slim beans whose telltale smell indicated a Brazilian origin; the ten cases of tea were delightfully adorned on the outside with brightly coloured paper and covered with cabalistic Chinese characters. However, their contents had made eventful Ulyssean journeys through the teapots of various American hotels and had then been re-dried and treated with a tannin solution. Later, when necessity forced us to use syrup which contained some iron, instead of sugar, the tea drinkers saw the contents of their cups change into a blue-black liquid, which in sufficient concentration could have served as ink. As our poverty increased, and we had to search for tobacco with a magnifying glass in the seams of our tobacco pouches, we contentedly smoked the abused tea leaves, which burned better than they tasted, although the government had paid top market price for them. Before we made the discovery that the tea could be used for tobacco, the crew never uttered the supplier's name without cursing at the same time. But when our pipes were drawing and were comfortingly warming our cold noses, this hatred turned to love and we were full of praise for the gentleman, whose speculative spirit had provided us with this pleasure. But if his coffee was bad and his tea scarcely drinkable, as compensation he had provided us with superb pineapples, peaches, plums and other canned fruits which were not to be despised. The 5000 lbs. of dried potatoes tasted like the fresh item, while the cabbage and asparagus were superb.

So as not to arouse the suspicion that I have written a cook book, let me say simply that the list of stores was much more extensive than these lines would indicate; for apart from the spices of India, we also had 2 centners[34] of fresh onions, various casks of salt and several cheeses like medium-sized millstones. Also many other items, known to all and sundry as solid and liquid states of aggregation, also known as the secrets of kitchen and storeroom; but for others, such as the ship's crew, they were totally worthless.

Since apart from the flag of the US Navy *Polaris* also flew the water-coloured pennant of the Temperance Society, whose brotherhood is widely distributed in the United States, just as the Freemasons are in Europe, and which dispatches watchful missions to every point of the compass, less innocent drinks than milk and herb tea had to be brought aboard surreptitiously. Because of its name, wine was banned; those few cases of Rothspohn that might delight one's palate, and also alcohol, were disguised as medicine containers; a massive array of bottles, filled with liquid that had been distilled from sugar and corn from the fields of Kentucky according to the rules of the distiller's art, suffered a similar fate.

Before the cabins had been made habitable, the Eskimo family whose fate was closely linked with that of the expedition and its originator arrived.[35] When Hall returned from his first trip he brought two natives with him, Tookoolito and her spouse, who showed to advantage amongst their countrymen and had acquired a certain veneer of civilization during a trip to England on board a whaler. As long as Hall remained in the United States, Joseph and his wife Hannah were his inseparable friends; they loved him like a father and later accompanied him on his second voyage to the Hudson Bay area. On a sledge trip to King William Island, in which they both also participated, Hannah, whose only child had died,[36] saw a small girl, of whom she grew passionately fond. Like Americans, many Eskimos consider a large family to be an unwelcome addition to a marriage; girls in particular are not very welcome. And thus it happened that Hall traded a sledge and several old knives for little Pannik and made a gift of her to Hannah. The little girl, now a dainty little creature, eight years old, with the warm complexion of a dark brunette, displayed strikingly little sign of Eskimo features.[37]

When she was baptized her original name had been replaced with Sylvia, but her mother paid little heed to this new appellation and generally called the little tomboy Pannik.

If Hannah did not know her own age, it was not because she was trying to conceal it; the date of her birth was obscured in the total darkness of a polar night, and if we had wanted to celebrate her birthday, in order to hit the right date the celebrations would have had to last a full leap year.

Although the teeth of time can gnaw for quite a long time at an Eskimo's fat face without leaving visible traces, there were certain wrinkles around Hannah's mouth and eyes which, combined with other clues in the area of the brow and the side of the neck, under normal circumstances would have indicated that she was in her early thirties. In any case she was in her relatively senior years; but she had made good use of her time. She had mastered the secrets of writing and was on more comfortable terms with the spelling of the English language than many free citizens of the United States. She had not only assumed the modern fashions of the female world but had also acquired tolerably good manners and possessed that tact which is more or less peculiar to the feminine nature. One of the most eminent anthropologists in Germany, to whom I sent her bust, considered her "quite presentable" and was of the view that she could "enter any drawing-room without her facial features arousing any notice." Her cheekbones were moderately developed; her eyes somewhat slit-like; her nose showed well in profile, with the tip somewhat turned down; her mouth was small, with its outlines curving gently. Mentally she was far superior to her spouse and spoke English quite fluently, whereas he could express himself only with difficulty; like the Japanese and the inhabitants of the Celestial Kingdom he regularly used an L instead of an R. He was an Eskimo from head to foot, a superb hunter and an enviable shot, but he liked the small pleasures of civilization and placed great value on fine clothes, alcoholic beverages and strong tobacco. Joseph possessed one of those physiognomies that respond to the burden of the years only indifferently; he might have passed for a 20-year-old rather than an older man but, he assured us, he had a greater number of years behind him than Hannah, whom he had known from childhood. The latter was formally married to him according to European custom. According to the custom of his people, to whom polygamy is not forbidden, he possessed two wives. The first of his life's companions languished beyond the Arctic Circle in the cold shadow of pinnacled icebergs; his second love languished in the protection of an enormous crinoline at his side. Who was the more beautiful of the two remained a secret, toward the clarification of which Joseph was reluctant to contribute. Any mention of the first inclination of his easily influenced Eskimo soul immediately produced some discomfort. He had an eye for female beauty, and whenever the conversation swung to women he would praise the kindness of the Queen of England, whom he knew from first-hand experience; when visitors came on board he always stayed beside the prettiest ladies.

The arctic trio had their modest accommodations in a small cabin near Hall's. Apart from the latter and myself, nobody on board was so fortunate as to have at his disposal, as undisputed owner, living accommodations that ensured privacy. Hall's cabin was small; mine was of much more limited extent and apart from its function as living and sleeping quarters (which were not to be underestimated) might have served as a model for lectures on experimental physics, in order to demonstrate the thesis (worthy of observance) that two bodies cannot occupy the same space at the same time. In wet weather I was reminded regularly of this truth in the most unequivocal fashion, since before I could put on my sea boots I always had to open the door in order to provide some space in the communal passageway for my legs. My cabin, which had originally been intended as a pantry, still retained the character of a pantry more or less, even after I took possession of it. Along the long wall opposite the door stood a low chest of drawers exactly 6 feet long and 18 inches wide. A bed stood upon a pedestal and could be closed with a hinged lid, so that this article of furniture could be used as a cupboard, bed or table, as occasion demanded. The shelves were covered with green baize and had been converted into book shelves on which sat a modest library. A narrow closet served as a wardrobe; it was barely large enough to accommodate a single person. The free floor space was 7 feet long and 1½ feet wide, providing an area of exactly 10½ square feet; it was reduced to less than half this area by a washstand and a miniature writing desk. If one adds to this a folding chair, which had to be built specially in order to fit the dimensions of the cabin, it is easy to see that its occupant could make only such movements as could be made around his own long axis. Curtains and other minor items helped to make this corner the cosiest little spot aboard ship, where one could work undisturbed.

While preparations on board were approaching completion, the Geographical Society in New York organized an extraordinary meeting, whose main purpose was to present the crew of *Polaris* to the curious public.[38] The event was held in the great hall of the Cooper Institute[39] on a warm June evening. The polar travellers sat, their faces sweating, atop the podium while the curious crowd thronged into the auditorium. Whenever one of the speakers had finished, loud clapping and cheering followed, while the brilliant attire of the ladies provided a somewhat theatrical tone to the celebration.

The most solemn event of the session came when, in conclusion, old Henry Grinnell unfolded the small Union flag which had flown over the ice fields of the South Pole during Wilkes's expedition,[40] which had accompanied De Haven,[41] which Hayes[42] had carried with him, and which now was again to be carried to a region where day and night cease to alternate in regular sequence.

CHAPTER 2

From New York to Newfoundland

Departure from New York. Down the East River to New London. Meteorological observations. Church services on land and at sea. A prayer for the North Pole. Departure from New London. The Gulf and Polar streams. Sailing abilities of Polaris. *Storm petrels and whales. We sight the coast of Newfoundland. The entrance to St. John's. Harbour and town. The dogs. The time signal. A physical-geographical sketch. The people and their occupations.*

Finally we were to take our leave of New York. The 29th of June had arrived and with it the long-awaited final instructions from the Navy Department, the lack of which, for the past two days, had been the only obstacle preventing our sailing. No matter how keenly each person was looking forward to the expedition, this delay was not unpleasant for anyone; when an absence of several years is involved, necessitating being cut off from all civilization, one is not particularly angry at fate which provides one with a short breathing space. Many items that one had cast aside during the rush of the past few days as totally worthless now seemed like indispensable requirements and had to be bought. And there were so many stores that one finally had to wander through that these last hours were certainly not leisurely.

As the last boat, laden with friends and good wishes, rowed ashore from our anchorage, it was almost 7.00 p.m. The anchor had already been weighed; as the ship's bell rang for 7 o'clock the ship got underway.

Crowds of people had assembled on shore; a loud cheer that seemed reluctant to end rang out from a sea of waving handkerchiefs.

Our course lay through the Sound, a wide arm of the sea which here is as narrow as a river and is known as the East River; it separates the Metropolis of the New World from its sister-city of Brooklyn. Long, uninterrupted rows of quays and wharves stretch along the shore; steamers and sailing ships of every type and size lay at anchor, flying the flags of every nation. A lively traffic plied the river itself: ships entering and departing, ferries crossing from shore to shore, tugs with their engines panting loudly, pilot boats and fishing craft. Astern of us the scene was bounded by the fortifications on Governor's Island and the heights of Staten Island farther back. Opposite, the forest of masts and the endless masses of houses of New York and Brooklyn stood out in sharp outline from the unusually clear evening air. Ahead of us lay the gradually widening channel with its lively, exciting panorama, and with its ships gliding along, with which we exchanged signals of greeting.

To starboard Brooklyn ended here, whereas on the other side the rows of houses of New York bordered the shore for some distance farther. Blackwell's Island,[1] dividing the river into two arms, lay here, with its magnificent buildings, the Charity Hospital,[2] the prison[3] and the mental institution.[4] Then one passed two more islands, from which large buildings glistened at us in the last glow of the evening sun: reformatories for children, hospitals and poor-houses where sick and indigent immigrants can find free care.

The shores had now retreated and had assumed a more rural character; the channel became wide and its surface rougher, hinting at the swell on the sea that was now so close. Here and there rows of white-capped wave crests appeared and amongst them funnel-shaped eddies and racing currents, the shoals which have been given the popular names of the Frying Pan and Hell Gate.[5] While we glided along slowly and safely, guided by the alert pilot between the rocks and eddies, beneath us, under the surface of the sea, hundreds of men were at work, undermining this reef in every direction. Galleries and passages already ran out from shore into the heart of this rock mass, and when the enormous project is complete, a charge of explosives, larger than any ever used before, will blow up the reef and create a safe channel.

Around noon on the 30th we dropped anchor in New London's spacious harbour, opposite the town of that name. Just as in England there is a River Thames here too, with the houses of this new London rising on its western shores, but there are only few of them, and its population does not exceed 10,000. But the harbour is one of the best in the United States, about 3 miles long, sheltered by hills all around, and defended at its entrance by Fort Trumbell (*sic*),[6] a superbly arranged fortification with 80 pieces of artillery. Opposite New London, on the other side of the river, lies Groton, a small town to which some historic significance attaches due to Fort Griswold, where the well-known encounter between British and American troops occurred in 1781.[7]

We were ferried ashore after lunch, but New London had nothing of interest to offer. Hall had the good fortune to acquire the services of a second engineer here without any difficulty; he was to take the place of his predecessor, who had deserted in New York.[8] The cook had also deserted and was now replaced by a black.[9] The expedition received an addition in the person of George Tyson, an experienced whaler who had spent many years in the arctic seas and was seen by Hall as a good acquisition.[10] Initially he was appointed to the position of Hall's private secretary, but in the official communication which was sent to the [Navy] Department at the time he was listed as sledge master and navigator;[11] later he received the appointment of assistant navigator.

In order to be able to start the meteorological observations the instruments were now set in order. Apart from a thermometer, intended to record the air temperature, the screen on deck contained a psychrometer, a mercury barometer and an aneroid, while the anemometer was fastened to the deckhouse on the port side amidships to avoid the area of most violent movements. Observations every three hours of air temperature, barometric pressure, atmospheric humidity, wind speed and direction and cloud cover now began. At the same interval the temperature of the sea water was measured, and its specific gravity was determined initially twice per day, using a sensitive hydrometer.

The following day was a Sunday. Early in the morning the seamen were sent to church under the mate's supervision; the clergyman wove the expedition into his sermon and he is said to have said many edifying things about it. As a teetotaller, ex officio—and what clergyman could not present himself as such to the public here—he seemed to feel deep satisfaction at the Temperance Association's rules, which allegedly prevailed on board.

Poor, God-pleasing man! If only you'd known how abstinence was actually observed there, you would have been thundering from the height of your pulpit and would have been cursing Hell, Purgatory and the Devil, instead of expressing your thoughts in honey-sweet words. You would not have come down, followed by your pious flock, to give the blessing on that sinful ship, would not have made the ladies and girls languish in the heat on the unshaded deck in order to exalt your afternoon service with their singing.[12]

The service on board lasted over an hour, while the sermon was spiced with expectorations that disclosed the most loving sentiments. He referred to the North Pole and icebergs, the joys and dangers we would be facing, the fascination of the aurora-bright nights and also the terror of the blizzards with their blood-freezing impact. Once the sermon was over Hall gave a speech; then the full tones of the harmonium wafted through the open saloon doors. A well-trained baritone sang "Glory, Glory, Hallelujah," and numerous silver-clear voices piously joined in. Slowly the last notes died away, the congregation dispersed and the pretty ladies of the town, in flowing summer dresses, began flitting, joking and laughing through the various compartments of the ship. Many were honoured with a brochure containing delightful prayers, composed for the occasion by the pious Brother Newman, pastor to the Senate. There were hundreds of copies of this brochure on board, but it never reached the book trade; hence I may be permitted here to quote one of the prayers which it contained, and which, one cannot deny, possesses a certain cultural-historical interest.

Just as one has embraced various views on our planetary system at different times, so one has adopted various ideas as to individual parts of it, from the time of the Alexandrian mystics who espoused a domed disc-shaped earth, to the ingenious Symmes,[13] who would have had vast, cylindrical abysses yawning at the poles of our planet. Just as eternal sunshine plays around the mountain peaks of the moon, the venerable Brother Newman[14] appears to believe that the North Pole of the earth is warm enough to ensure a home there for science and the fine arts.

But I don't want to anticipate the content of his prayer, which teaches us that the earth is hung upon a great nothing, instead I shall let him speak for himself:

Prayer for the North Pole

Great God of the universe, our hearts are filled with gratitude and joy in recognition of the wonderful goodness which thou wouldst have us share. We have seen thy wonders in the depths of the sea and amidst the eternal icebergs and now we are seeing that place, which has so long escaped the gaze of man, and the glory of thy might. Thanks be to thee, who spreadest the North over this vacuum, who hangest the earth on a nothing, and who hast dammed up the waters, until day and night will one day cease. We thank thee for the glimpse which thou hast allowed our gaze; we thank thee for the feeling which now swells our hearts.

Honour to thee, O God, who art enthroned on high, peace on earth.

We praise thee; we honour thee; we pray to thee; we thank thee for thy great magnificence, O Lord our God, our heavenly king! God, almighty Father! Praise him, works of his hands! Praise him, ye sun, moon and stars! Praise him, ye heavens, and ye waters, which are spread out above the heavens. Praise him, the God of Earth, ye dragons and ye deeps, ye fire and hail, snow and steam, and ye storms, which obey his words! Praise him, ye cold and frost, ye snow and ice, ye day and night, ye summer and winter, ye seas and waves. Praise him, rulers and peoples of the earth. All that has breath, praise the Lord!

In thy name, O God, we devote this part of our globe to *freedom, education and religion; may future generations bring to maturity the fruit of our discovery*. Protect the nation which has sent us forth; protect the President of this great republic; protect all inhabitants of our favoured country, whose banner we unfolded in this distant region.

And now may God our Father guide and lead our steps back to those, who will greet us joyfully and to the land which we love. May no evil afflict us; may no sins soil the purity of our souls and may nothing deflect us from the path of virtue. Hear us, O God! Lead us not into temptation, and deliver us from evil, for thine is the kingdom, thine is the power, and thine is the glory, for all time. Amen!

As we shall see later, we managed to set up an observatory nearer to the Pole than any other expedition, in which, apart from other tasks, temperature observations and pendulum experiments were carried out. But unfortunately the cosmogonic views that the worthy vicar sent with us on our way do not completely agree with them.

The residents of New London were still in deep sleep when we left port on the morning of 3 July. Grey clouds covered the sky; one of those fine, drizzling rains made everything appear in a dismal light; and a high sea was running. Everyone not writing letters of farewell stood in his oilskins on deck and stared toward land. At 5.20 a.m. we stopped off Rave Rock in order to drop the pilot.[15] A dear friend who had accompanied us from Washington to here took charge of our mail; a last handshake, a "bon voyage," then he too climbed down into the pilot cutter. The men climbed into the shrouds, at a command three cheers rang out, then the screw began churning in the green flood; we were underway. Toward evening the rain ceased, a fresh wind swelled the sails and shortly before midnight we passed the South Shoal lightship.[16]

July 4th, the great national holiday of the Americans, was spent in quiet celebration. Battling a foul wind, we made only slow progress as we headed eastward; at noon we were at 41°10′N; 68°24′W. We had scarcely measured the sun's noon altitude when a thick fog descended; we were approaching the banks of Newfoundland and hence could scarcely expect fair weather. Not until around noon on the 5th did it begin to clear somewhat; an astronomical observation placed us at 40°58′N, since our course had been somewhat south of east. We did not succeed in determining the longitude either in the morning or the afternoon.

With the barometer dropping, at 6 o'clock the wind swung into the southwest. We were alternately travelling through the warm water of the Gulf Stream and the cold water of the Polar Current,[17] which here interlock in a comb-like fashion. Apart from their colour, their temperature and their different specific gravities, the two currents were distinguishable by means of the meteorological instruments in the screen. Whenever we were in the Polar Current the temperature dropped, the humidity of the air decreased, and the mercury column in the barometer climbed, while the reverse occurred whenever we passed through the waters of the Gulf Stream. The alternation was so noticeable that it could be detected by the relative feelings of cold and warmth, without the help of instruments. In one tongue of the Polar Current we measured a temperature of +4.3°C at a depth of 60 fathoms, whereas the surface temperature was +5.2° and the air temperature 15.4°.[18] By noon we were at 41°40'N; 62°51'W, with a heavy swell from the southwest; then we sighted two sails, a steamer and a small fishing vessel.

At 7 o'clock our position was determined to be 42°24'N, 59°45'W. Toward evening the light southerly wind, which until now had not exceeded 2 miles per hour, assumed a more definite character and began to blow more strongly; and hence the engine was stopped. All available canvas was set, since we wanted to investigate the ship's sailing abilities. The result was what anyone must have anticipated who had examined the ship's lines and rigging carefully. After various fruitless manoeuvres, which evoked long faces, the shrugging of shoulders, and gentle curses, the engine again began chugging in its rhythmic fashion and we made 6 knots instead of one. The result was depressing, but now there was no help for it; without power the sails appeared almost useless. If the coal ran out during the expedition we could whistle patiently for a fair wind and, under favourable circumstances, proceed at one n. mile per hour.

Numerous storm petrels were following our wake next morning; the sky was dark and the seas high.[19] Divided into flights of 8 to 10, the dusky throng at times hurried with a trippling gait over the wave crests, their wings outspread, and at times circled among the waves with swallow-like flight. "Wiehb, wiehb, nawah!" rang out their screaming calls; one protracted call followed another; but the gale held off. The clouds massed threateningly and then, with violent thunder and lightning, a severe storm broke. Once the rain had ceased a dense fog fell; it stubbornly covered the sea throughout the 9th and robbed us of any distant view. Being unable to make any determination of position we had to proceed cautiously, since we were in tricky waters. A sounding made at 4.00 p.m. gave a depth of 40 fathoms.

The 10th was almost as bad as the two preceding days; the dense fog was accompanied by a light drizzling rain; at 10.00 a.m. we got no bottom with 70 fathoms of line. Around noon, when it was clearing somewhat at times, we sighted land to the west, but it was impossible to identify it. We learned from a fishing vessel with which we closed to within hailing distance that it was Morton's Bay. At times we heard whales blowing, and then the animals, which our mates called bottlenoses, came close alongside so that we could examine them quite closely.[20] There were three of them; the largest may have measured about 20 feet. From their external appearance a zoologist would classify them as dolphins. The snout appeared blunt and not at all bottle-shaped; the dorsal fin, which extends along about the last third of the length of the body, is small; the colour is brownish-black. The tail was never clearly visible. When they dived, which occurred every three minutes, the back arched quite significantly; when they surfaced they showed their porpoise-like heads to just behind the eye. After less than 15 minutes they disappeared.

When the fog lifted on the morning of the 11th we sighted the coast ahead of us: a steep rock massif, apparently little dissected, which seen from a distance could evoke neither a picturesque nor a comforting impression. Not a tree adorned the dark heights, around which fluttered fantastically shaped rags of fog; not a house interrupted the monotony of the landscape, which appeared to our eyes as untouched by civilization as it had once done to its first discoverers.

Setting first a northerly, then a westerly course, we soon found numerous fishing vessels swarming around us; their blackened sails, tended by ragged forms, gave the picture a very peculiar touch and, combined with the lowering, grey clouds, spread a breath of melancholy, fully in accord with the mood of the dark, cliffed background. Around 10 o'clock the pilot came aboard to bring our ship into the harbour.[21] It was not until we were opposite the harbour that we were able to spot the entrance; a fiord-like defile with almost vertical walls, barely 900 feet wide at its widest point. This narrow strait is about half a mile long and ships have to feel their way cautiously down the middle of it to the actual harbour, which only becomes visible after one has almost passed the narrows, which are aligned roughly east–west.[22] On the right the steeply dropping sandstone rocks of Signal Hill rise in three vaguely demarcated terraces to a height of over 500 feet; to the left lie sheer, gullied faces whose highest point carries a lighthouse[23] and rises about 100 feet above the opposite side with its tower.[24] Along the second third of the length of the narrows, the hills flanking them approach so close to each other that the distance between them is not more than 100 paces; involuntarily one feels tempted to hurl a stone at the shores which, on the west, elongated by perspective, appear almost close enough to touch. On both sides a rock lies in front of the cliffs: Chain Rock to the north and Pancake Rock to the south. In wartime they are connected by a chain, thus making the entrance to the harbour impassable.[25] Given the present state of the ordnance such precautionary measures are scarcely necessary, especially since two batteries sit atop the cliffs where they can barely be reached by projectiles from below, whereas every shot fired from their cannon must be fatal to any hostile ship.

As one reaches the point where the narrows widen like a boot, the capital of the island appears, clinging to the hill-face and clambering up it from the water; its most prominent building is the cathedral. We dropped anchor opposite it shortly before noon and waited for the cannon shot that daily announces the time when the sun crosses the meridian, to give ships' captains an opportunity to adjust their chronometers. Surrounded by assorted small boats whose scantily clad occupants constantly begged for food, until the shot was fired we were able to absorb a good view of the harbour, which now appeared more favourable than we had first anticipated, since the gloomy clouds had dispersed in the meantime and the sun was shining brightly and warmly.

The basin, about 1¼ miles long and 1200 feet wide, is surrounded on all sides by mountains or hills which reach their greatest height near the entrance; along the waterfront, with few interruptions stretch wooden wharves and scaffoldings covered with spruce branches on which cod are dried;[26] the smell of the latter fills the air and, especially when the pressure is low, is more noticeable than one might really wish. On the west shore the town rises in a pyramid from a base about a mile long; it is only the more scattered houses farther up that prevent it from appearing boring to the observer. It is altogether difficult to understand what caused the original settlers to found a town here, unless it is the easterly location of the place, which lies closer to Europe than any other point on the island, or indeed in North America. To the southwest, at the back of the bay, a few mills appear on the slopes, their clattering wheels set in motion by a small stream that flows down the slopes on its way to the sea, forming cheerful waterfalls and rapids, around which the sun produces pale-coloured rainbows. Apart from some storehouses and the inevitable drying stages the shore opposite the town offers little reminiscent of civilization. The hills have more pleasing outlines than on the opposite side, while behind the chain lying closest to the shore rises a second, running parallel to it, and whose five-peaked crest reaches an average height of 700 feet.

In the course of the afternoon the consul came aboard to offer us his services; later, in a walk into town we took advantage of them in order to exchange American money for Newfoundland currency. In so doing we had full opportunity to admire the business acumen of this honest fellow, whose name is Molloy,[27] and in whose eyes American bills were of very little value vis-à-vis Newfoundland dollars, or at least of much lower value than that offered by the other merchants in St. John's who did not enjoy the advantage of being consul. This, however, was not a motive for us to value them less highly. These merchants were all prepared to be pleasant to us in every conceivable fashion, but at the same time without being motivated by interests other than those by which respectable people are impelled to do anything that they are not obliged to do.

The time required to stroll through the town, whose population according to the latest census (1869) is 22,553, is directly related to the available sights; these are limited to many wooden houses, a few stone and brick buildings, the cathedral[28] and the Governor's residence. Earlier the latter lived aboard a warship which lay in the harbour under his command; only later was a wooden building erected for him in the garrison. Here during the three or four summer months when he was in residence, he found meagre accommodations. Once the temporary sojourn of the highest authority had become more permanent, Sir Thomas Cochrane[29] had a new house built of sandstone during the 1820s. This is still the Governor's residence,[30] located in a park; it is neither comfortable nor tasteful, and cost an amount for which one could have built a small palace anywhere else. Most of the building stone had to be brought from a distance since there was no suitable material in the vicinity of the capital, while the interior fittings were ordered from England.

It would appear that in laying out the town no consistent plan was followed, or if regularity was intended it was foiled by the topography of the site. Many of the streets are narrow; few are attractive, and all the cross-streets which run up to the upper town with endless bends and twists are steeper than is desirable for people who do not count mountain climbing among the pleasures of life. The remarkable cathedral rises from the narrow, fairly level crest of the hill, overlooking the town; in its construction various building styles were abused in the most despicable fashion. Somewhat to the southwest of it lie the remains of the dismantled Fort Townshend, while to the north-northeast, little more than half an English mile away, rises Fort William. About 100 feet lower than the cathedral and lying opposite it, one can see another church whose tower carries a permanent light; when this is lined up with the light on the customs house, it shows a captain the way to a safe anchorage at night.

The canine species is abundantly represented but, in St. John's at least, fine, purebred animals are as rare as handsome people; even amongst the female population few handsome individuals caught our eye, in sharp contrast to England.

The true Newfoundland dog occurs only rarely; only with difficulty did Hall succeed in acquiring a perfect adult specimen, which cost $60 on the spot. Two pups, from a litter of five barely four weeks old, were sold to us for a quarter of that price. Most of the dogs of the Newfoundland type were of rather weakly build, with wide, but short heads, only slightly thickened snouts and narrow chests; their necks appeared less powerfully developed than in good, purebred animals, their silky coats were denser and less curly; their legs seemed short and weak; their feet too small and their webs poorly developed, while their tails were too large and in the majority of cases too cylindrical. If the ancestors of the Newfoundland are truly the large poodle and the French mastiff, the degeneration of the present generation should perhaps be seen as a throwback to the latter, although the shortness of the limbs would tend more to suggest the poodle. Obviously crosses with every possible mongrel are far from rare; short, outward-turned front legs seemed to indicate fairly incontrovertibly some "turnspit" blood, while long heads with wide skulls, delicate, elegant limbs and feathered tails indicated some mixture with a setter.

To conclude from an ordinance that Governor Edwards[31] released in 1780, the species either no longer seemed pure then, or the beauty of the animals was not in proportion to the disturbances that they caused.

It reads:

> Since it has come to my notice that the number of dogs kept by merchants, ferrymen and others in this city has become very considerable, so that the animals cause the inhabitants great annoyance and even inflict damage on them, I hereby issue an ordinance, by the power of which those same merchants, ferrymen or other persons who, after 31 August should be found to be keeping more than one dog will pay a penalty of 25 shillings for every second or further dog that should be found in their possession, and I hereby empower anyone to kill all dogs that are owned by merchants, ferrymen or other persons, beyond one dog per owner.

How much time the residents of St. John's were given to get rid of their dogs is not clear from *The history of Newfoundland from the earliest times to the year 1860*, by the Rev. Charles Pedley,[32] from which I have extracted this announcement.

Leaving the rather uninteresting city behind us, we made our way to Signal Hill, whose summit we reached shortly before twilight fell. To the west, beyond dark blue rows of hills, the first glow of sunset was gleaming, its light reflected by Quidi Vidi Pond.[33] On the other side, reaching to the distant horizon, stretched the sea, which foamed around the cliffs at the foot of the hill, its roar carrying clearly to the summit, borne on the uprushing air currents. Across the grey shadows that lay on its agitated surface, long rows of fishing boats glided toward the entrance of the harbour, in order to bring their catches to safety before nightfall. To the north a thin mist rose, hiding the farthest headlands of this steep coast, and to the south the lighthouse on Cape Spear[34] flashed. Although not magnificent, the view was certainly worthwhile, and we contentedly started back on our return trip to the ship, where we found a telegram from New York, the reply to a dispatch that we had sent only in the late afternoon.

Next morning we made the obligatory visit to the Governor, Colonel Hill,[35] then returned on board in order to listen for the cannon shot in order to check the chronometers. The signal rang out; standing on deck we noted the time by a pocket chronometer. But when, shortly after this, we compared it with the actual ship's chronometers in the saloon, we discovered a suspicious difference as compared to yesterday; however, this lost much of its alarming character when it turned out to be the same in the case of all the chronometers. In my opinion the shot must have been fired too early; but in order to entirely reassure myself I equipped myself with a pocket chronometer, which had first been carefully compared with several of the ship's chronometers, and set off to take the gunner to task. After I had taken several wrong turns on streets with the most appalling gradients, a weather-tanned man, whose walk and manners betrayed that he was a seaman, put me on the right track. The building that he pointed out to me was a small three-windowed house, adorned with a massive sign that bore the awe-inspiring inscription "Nautical Academy." I reproached myself bitterly that I had accused this institution of such a black crime, and, in order to assuage my conscience, rang the doorbell. An old gentleman who was hard-of-hearing and whose name must unfortunately be withheld from the present and future generations due to the loss of my journals, opened the door and showed me into a ground-floor room. It was with some difficulty that I managed to make myself understood to the Colony of Newfoundland's worthy teacher of navigation and chronometer adjuster, who urged me to shout as loudly as possible. Once I had won his confidence he led me through a courtyard to a hut which revealed a similarity to certain small buildings on whose doors a number is usually painted which, when it follows a 5, gives the latter the value of half a hundred.[36] He cautiously thrust a large key into the lock, which yielded noisily, and once we had entered he showed me his passage instrument;

it was bound with string at various points and showed the signs of age even more clearly than its owner.

This was where the sun's transit of the meridian was observed on clear days, and on this observation in turn the time of the noon gun depended. Once the sun had crossed the instrument's first hair the old gentleman lit a slow match, and before it had crossed the second one he hurried to the cannon to fire the shot. Naturally this sometimes took more and sometimes less time, and for precisely this reason one might be advised to be suspicious of the signal when the sky was not completely overcast; in the latter case the gentleman provided himself with a clock and fired the gun at the right moment. In reply to my question as to why the arrangements were not better, lack of money was identified as the cause; but given the importance of this service this could be remedied at very little cost. For only a few pounds sterling, a galvanic connection could be arranged between the gun and the passage instrument and gentle pressure of a finger would close the circuit, make a platinum wire start to glow and thus provide a usable signal which, if given a little before the correct time, would, for normal purposes, adequately compensate for the time difference which results from the propagation of the noise. I satisfied myself with bringing this to the attention of my friendly guide and once we had returned to the "Academy" asked to have my chronometer compared, so that I could take the exact local time back on board with me. But my intention was complicated more than I had expected by mutual suspicion. I wanted to make the comparison myself, but he stubbornly refused me access to his chronometers, which were located in the adjacent bedroom and which he would not bring into the other room, to avoid disturbing their running. I probably must have tried to persuade him in a louder voice than was really necessary since, as a result of the noise, which to the uninitiated must have sounded like a violent dispute, a flaxen-haired young lady appeared, the daughter of the house. She gazed at her papa with fearful looks and at me with suspicious looks. Once I had informed her of my wishes, she offered to collaborate with me in checking the chronometer; she said that she had experience at this since she sometimes had to compare the clocks when her father was prevented from doing so. Each carrying out our allotted roles, she in front of the chronometers in the bedroom, I in the other room, the task was achieved to my fullest satisfaction; at a given signal we compared the chronometers three times. With the prospect of soon seeing the young lady on board in order to show her the arctic chronometers, as she called ours, I started on the return journey.

We had to linger at St. John's for eight full days, in part because repairs to the boiler were required, in part in order to take on coal and water. Shortly before our arrival the army had left St. John's. Life in the city offered little entertainment; hence as often as the weather permitted we made excursions into the surrounding area in order to pass the time. We had the good fortune to meet an English mining engineer, a former German student, who in the most obliging fashion undertook the role of Cicerone and gave us much valuable information. Unfortunately the means of transport were of rather a restricted nature; unless one wanted to use carts in order to drive around the old, beaten trails, there was no option but to use riding horses, since no railways exist. But the only acceptable animals are in the possession of a few private individuals and generally are not available to strangers. Even the brown Rosinante[37] which carried me on a ride to the nearby Mental Home[38] had to be treated with caution, since for her age she was extremely mean and her training must have been very deficient. She understood only two gaits, completely ignored both knee and bit, and in addition kicked so brutally that it seemed advisable to walk in future.

The interior of the island is practically unknown. It has been crossed only once, in 1822, by a Scot by the name of Cormack, who travelled with a single companion from Trinity Bay to St. George's Bay. But Cormack's little publication[39] is so meagre that one can scarcely extract any positive information from it; the geological survey that has been underway since 1840 generally sticks near the coast due to its limited funds. Despite this, it has produced important information on the disposition of the island, which is easily understandable when one is aware of its geological nature. Almost every formation from coal to the Lower Laurentian is represented; the latter forms the main mountain chains and either breaks through the younger deposits along the lines of anticlines in order to reach the surface or is exposed by faults which are all more or less parallel to each other, striking generally north-northeast to south-southwest. It is the alignment of these strike lines that has a controlling influence on the configuration of the coast and of the interior, as far as the latter is known. A glance at the map reveals clearly that all the major coastal indentations form an angle with the meridian which deviates little from the alignment in question and which rarely reaches approximately 45°, e.g., in Fortune Bay. Even the direction of the line of separation from the American continent, which we see represented by the narrow Strait of Belle Isle, deviates little from this angle. None of Newfoundland's peninsulas extend from east to west; nor do the major areas of the numerous lakes run in this direction. Despite these water bodies, which occupy about a third of the surface area of the entire island, it scarcely possesses a single navigable river; the Humber, Exploits and Terra Nova, as well as the other major streams, are passable only by ordinary boats.

The flora very much resembles that of Vancouver Island, although it is much tamer and the tree-growth less luxuriant, since the warm waters of the Pacific Ocean are absent here and the insolation is significantly reduced due to the frequent fogs. However, the latitude of both islands is approximately the same and the humidity of the air is clearly evident by the numerous fallen trees that are all quite young. The terrain is broken by forest, swamp and barren areas. The majority of the forests consist of conifers, along with birch, aspen and alder. Spruce and birch attain the greatest heights, while the other timber is generally low, at times even of dwarf dimensions, for example the juniper, which has an almost level crown that gives the impression that it has been trimmed with shears. Generally the forests extend along the mountain slopes if they receive sufficient moisture; they commonly follow the course of a stream or frame the shores of small water bodies. More extensive than the forest is the swampland whose vast covers of *Sphagnum* and *Hypnum* absorb and hold the bulk of the moisture from the surrounding area, especially where they fill the valleys. The rain water which flows down the mountain slopes accumulates in them, as does the overflow from the lakes; perhaps they are in part responsible for the fact that the rivers are not navigable to any great extent. The "barrens" or sterile areas are devoid of all vegetation. Sometimes they consist of widespread erratic material, sometimes of bedrock, on which blueberries and other low, berry-bearing plants grow abundantly, alternating with lichen-covered areas, whose bright colours are somewhat too turbulent to make a pleasant effect.

Although the most northerly tip of the island lies at the latitude of London and the most southerly farther south than Nantes, the climate is raw and unpleasant, although it is less cold and less prone to extremes than that of the neighbouring part of continental America. The cold arctic current that flows south along the west side of Davis Strait and bears the name of the Labrador Current, once it has been joined by the cold waters of Hudson Strait, flows along the east and southeast coasts of the island; in late fall and spring it often carries significant quantities of ice, and as a result the temperatures, already low, are depressed even more. The impact of this current is especially noticeable in the months of February and March, and at times even in April, since at this time the prevailing winds are northeasterlies, whereas at other times they fluctuate between southwest and northwest. As a result the cold current surges with its full force against the coast, cooling the surrounding area and, at the same time, the air flowing over it from the North Atlantic Ocean. The weather is extremely changeable and cold days are far from rare in summer. It is then that the fogs, which have become proverbial for Newfoundland, are the most frequent on the south and southwest coasts and along the coasts of the Avalon Peninsula, but they do not extend into the interior.

Continuous meteorological observations thus far are taken only at St. John's. The mean annual temperature for that station over the period 1857–64 inclusive was 5.1°C, and the highest mean annual temperature, based on the observations in 1863 was 6.7°C, whereas the lowest during this period (1864) was 2.8°. The maximum temperature (31.7°) was observed in July 1857 and the lowest –25.6° in February 1863. During my stay in St. John's we recorded a maximum of 22.3° with a northwest wind on 16 July and a minimum of 9.3° with a gentle northeasterly on 13 July. The mean annual amount of atmospheric precipitation during the above-mentioned period was 59.94 English inches; the maximum, in 1860, was 82.4 inches and the minimum, in 1857, 42 inches.

Since the productivity of agriculture in any area depends exclusively on its climatic conditions, one may conclude *a priori* how much one may expect of Newfoundland in this regard.

Wheat ripens only exceptionally, and until now its cultivation could be attempted at only a few favoured localities; by contrast, oats and barley mature without difficulty, as do peas and beans. The yield of potatoes is generally good, and cabbage heads as well as white and yellow turnips reach a considerable size. According to the statistical data computed two years before our visit, the arable acreage was then 41,715 acres.[40] Recently various proposals have been made for upgrading agriculture; the government was petitioned to allot quite large areas of land to the capitalists living in Newfoundland, who would then immediately make it their duty to encourage immigration. Obviously little would be achieved by such an arrangement, since the capitalists would immediately exploit agriculture just as they now do the fishermen and the miners. The area of cultivated land would probably increase, but not the well-being of the bulk of the population, since as soon as the capitalist has ensured a sufficiently large fortune, he bids farewell to the inhospitable shores of Newfoundland and heads for more favoured areas in order to conclude his life in comfort. As long as the United States continues to give away land under the present conditions the wave of migration from Great Britain will continue to head for the great West, where the freedom-seeking Irishman and the thrifty Scot can find a new home which will appeal to them more than Newfoundland even if the land there is transferred to them under equally favourable conditions.

According to the last published census, the population in 1869 was 146,536,[41] almost without exception living in the coastal strip; there are scarcely any settlements in the interior. The bulk of the male population earns its living from the sea, in part from cod fishing, in part from seal hunting, which, however, is pursued only in certain months of the year. Mining is a more subordinate branch of the economy.[42] Iron and lead have been worked at scattered locations, but after a short period the workings were abandoned again, although the lead mines were very productive. Copper mining produces the greatest profit, especially the Tilt Cove mine, which has been in continuous operation since 1865 and during the past five years has produced more than 22,000 tonnes of ore; however, it is not processed metallurgically on site but is exported as raw material to England since the necessary coal is not available on the island.[43] Not incorrectly, the latest report of the Geological Survey draws attention to the need to make experimental borings for coal, but as long as the government does not take the matter in hand itself it will simply remain a well-intentioned proposal, since the workers lack the funds to acquire the tools and the capitalist can get a return on his money much more safely and, for the moment, much more advantageously by investment in seal hunting or fishing.

CHAPTER 3

From Newfoundland to Greenland

Departure from St. John's. Aurora borealis. The first icebergs. Green water. The Greenlanders' house. In sight of the coast. Gulf Stream and driftwood. The first Eskimos. The entrance to Fiskernæsset. The administration of the colony. An excursion. A ball. The settlement. A Greenland scholar; his sphere of activity and his spouse. A trip to Lichtenfels. German missionaries. The Greenland raven. Statistical data. Return on board and departure from Fiskernæsset. The arctic petrel. Meeting with the Swedish expedition. Meteors. The Danes of the colony. Horticulture. The natives. Remarks on their customs. Departure of the Swedes. An unfortunate kayak trip.

On the 18th the various repairs to the boiler were completed, the coal was loaded and our supplies of wood and fresh meat replenished; but we still had not managed to find a ship's carpenter. Next day, when all our efforts were still fruitless, and since our stay had become seriously protracted, we weighed anchor at 3.30 p.m. The honest consul, in the hopes of drinking one more stirrup cup with us, insisted on accompanying us; it was not until we dismissed the pilot that we were able to dispense with the pleasant company of this conscientious official, whose noble selflessness later became proverbial.

Under sail and steam our vessel glided rapidly over the mirror-smooth sea before a gentle southerly breeze; around 9 o'clock we passed the

47

lighthouse on Baccalieu Island[1] about 15 n. miles off; its blinking light flashed at us at short intervals through the gathering darkness.

The lighthouse, which is visible for 28 miles, had barely disappeared from sight when reddish-yellow clouds rose in the northern sky, expanding rapidly to become a glowing aurora borealis. Above a dark sector of a circle, which included about one-sixth of the sky's circumference, there rose an arc of light, about 20° of arc in height, which for some time maintained its position, apparently motionless. Then violent undulations extended from east to west throughout its entire extent, following quickly upon one another; its upper edge, which until now had been sharply demarcated, became jagged, sending out numerous rays, some of which shot up halfway to the zenith and often even beyond it. Around 10 o'clock the arc split lengthwise, the upper half seeming to sway upward freely and soon afterward assuming the appearance of a sinuous belt which waved to and fro, as if moved by the wind. Its main mass was an intense carmine-red, shading at individual spots to a whitish yellow; its edges were of a faint sea-green colour. Near it the movements appeared to be strongest, sometimes top to bottom, sometimes running approximately in a horizontal direction. Suddenly the belt broke into a number of cones of light, their points facing downward. In the relatively narrow dark interstices separating them, a pale yellow mist billowed, but of a much lower light intensity than the main body of the belt. Without visibly changing its shape these cones made bobbing motions; they became narrower and narrower, their colour faded and by 10.15 there was nothing left of the entire formation but a small, faintly glowing cloud, strikingly reminiscent in shape of the patch of fog that under normal conditions a sharp eye can detect near the star in Orion's Belt.

In the meantime the lower arc of light, which still rested on the dark segment, had scarcely changed perceptibly. Now rays began to shoot restlessly upward from its upper edge; it expanded in vertical extent and attained about four times the width of a rainbow. Its colour became almost pure white, with a greenish play only in isolated spots. A dark bank of cloud which almost seemed to touch its western end began to push eastward, and almost simultaneously the arc split into two pieces of unequal size. The eastern part was only a third of the extent of the other; it became paler and by 10.30 had completely disappeared, while glowing rays constantly rose from the surviving piece of the arc. Until 11 o'clock they shot up uninterruptedly, sometimes individually, sometimes joined in bundles. The piece of the arc swayed upward, and all of a sudden the entire northwest quadrant of the sky was covered with a waving mass of light, through which the subdued shimmer of the stars penetrated. Ten minutes later the phenomenon had disappeared.

Early on the morning of the 20th, around 4.00 a.m., we passed several icebergs, one of which towered about 80 feet above the water surface. At noon the ship's position was 49°33'N; 52°16'W. The sea was beginning to run high, and over the course of the afternoon fog descended but it soon dispersed again. Around midnight it rolled in again; this was accompanied by a gentle drizzle, and next day the cloud cover was so thick that it was impossible to determine the ship's position astronomically. According to our patent log which had been streamed constantly, the distance we had covered toward the northeast during the past 24 hours was 120¼ miles.

We appeared to leave the cold Labrador Current between 6.00 and 7.00 p.m., since the water temperature, which had not risen above 6° since we had left Newfoundland, rose to 12.3°, while the air temperature was 13.5°. As it began to grow dark, a flock of small land birds flew over toward the coast to the west, but too high for an accurate observation.

According to a number of sun's altitudes that were shot under fairly favourable conditions, at noon on the 22nd *Polaris* was at 53°19'N; 53°10'W. At 9 o'clock that morning the deep, dark-green colour of the water had changed, giving way to a dirty light green; around 1 o'clock this colour became much more distinct than it had been during the morning, but the temperature remained the same as on the previous day. Water hauled up on deck in a bucket turned out to be totally clear and transparent; even when it was poured into a glass cylinder and examined with the light shining through it, one could not detect any cloudiness or pollution. Once one of the glasses had stood quietly on deck for some time one could notice that its contents near the bottom broke the light more strongly than higher up. On more careful examination one could detect with the naked eye small flickering bodies which, under the magnifying glass, revealed themselves to be shining needles and under the microscope as siliceous diatoms (*Melosia arctica*). When it was towed behind the ship for only a short time the pelagic net brought up vast numbers; even on board, in the glass cylinders in which we kept them, they quickly increased in numbers. A number of water samples, taken from different depths with the greatest possible care, and examined in cylinders, revealed that at a depth of 12 feet the organisms were present in equal abundance as at the surface. At the same time we collected innumerable small crustaceans (copepods) whose food appeared to consist exclusively of these diatoms since their intestinal canals were completely filled with them.

The facts I have reported here are certainly not new; Scoresby[2] has already drawn attention to the fact that certain species of organisms give the arctic seas at various places an artificial coloration, and many other polar travellers have confirmed the accuracy of his observation. In our case it is interesting that we discovered the organisms at such a low latitude, so far south of the Arctic Circle, and that we succeeded in approximately determining their vertical distribution. Until 7.00 p.m. the ship was running through this coloured water, and since we were travelling about 6 miles per hour, the organisms thus covered a zone whose extent, measured from north to south, was about 60 miles.

Although we streamed the pelagic net throughout the following day and checked it hourly, we found no more of these diatoms; by contrast the first specimens of the so-called whale-lice appeared, pteropods to which the zoologists refer as *Limacina arctica*.[3] They were hauled up around 11.00 a.m., and at noon the ship was at 54°38'N, 52°10'W by dead reckoning. The latitude indicated here is probably too low due to the strong northward-setting current, and hence in this case the area of distribution of the animals did not extend so far south.

On the 24th it was again impossible to get an astronomical fix due to the overcast sky, just as on the previous day; but on the 25th we got several good observations which strengthened our suspicions. They revealed the ship's position to be 58°21'N; 52°14'W, so that the current had set us north quite substantially. Next day, the 26th, we were at 60°39'N; 52°55'W; we had thus drawn closer to the Greenland coast by about 93 n. miles.

Anyone who has leafed through the account of the Second Grinnell Expedition[4] may recall that at Fiskernæsset,[5] a small Danish mission settlement in South Greenland, Kane found an intelligent Eskimo whom he persuaded to accompany him. Hans[6] (that was the name of the young man, then about 17 years old) parted with a heavy heart from his darling, his mother and his place of birth and joined the expedition, to which he rendered very impressive service. When the ship did not get free during the second summer and hard times were in the offing for the polar travellers, despicably forgetting his distant flame, Hans conceived the not uncommon idea of falling in love with the most beautiful girl from a neighbouring band, so as to be able to endure better the harshness of life. The deed followed the decision and his love was answered, since, as Kane tells us, apart from his physical attributes he was the most prominent man in the country and was also rich. One day he left the ship, supposedly to buy sealskins in one of the more southerly settlements. Week after week passed and month after month, but Hans did not return. He was under the spell of Schangu's little daughter, and was last seen by one of Kane's people racing along on a dog sledge with his beloved. Shortly afterward, in view of the advanced season, Kane had to start on his return journey, and since Hans did not reappear in time he was left behind.

Five years later Hayes set out on his polar voyage. As a member of Kane's expedition he had known Hans, and when his vessel reached the vicinity of Cape York he hugged the coast since he expected to spot natives and gather news of Hans. He was not deceived in his postulations, since it was not long before a group of people appeared and tried to attract the ship's attention. Hayes had a boat lowered and rowed ashore with Sonntag,[7] the expedition's astronomer. The first person he met was none other than Hans, who immediately recognized him and Sonntag and addressed them by name. His sojourn of almost six years among the savages of this desolate coast had sufficed to bring him down to the level of those dirty people.[8] He was accompanied by his wife, who carried the hopeful offspring of their marriage in her hood on her back, his mother-in-law, an old Eskimo woman with a wrinkled face, and his brother-in-law, a cheerful lad of about 12. They were all dressed in the native dress of the country, and their skins were far from clean and were not in good condition.

Hans led his visitors over rough rocks and massive snowdrifts up a steep slope to his sealskin tent, which he had pitched on an almost inaccessible spot about 200 feet above the sea; it was barely large enough to accommodate the little family. But it was his lookout at the same time. Year after year he had watched out for the longed-for ship, but summer after summer had passed without a vessel being sighted; he was seized by a wild longing for his more southerly home, his relatives and the friends of his youth. Now the hour of deliverance might have arrived, had he faithlessly abandoned his wife and child to follow Hayes; but the latter took pity on Mrs. Merkut and their offspring and loaded the family plus their tent and household goods in his boat. The mother-in-law and son-in-law pleaded to be taken along too, but given the smallness of the boat, it could not possibly handle this load, and these two were left behind with their tribe. Once on board, the seamen immediately set to work by means of soap and comb to make this worthy family ready for red shirts and other luxury items of the civilized world. At first the procedure of washing and combing gave them great pleasure; but the dirt had accumulated over the years and the process of cleaning demanded so much effort and time that the wife began to shout and complain loudly about their fate. She wanted her husband to tell her whether this was a religious custom of the whites; one could clearly read from her expression that she imagined herself a victim of a refined Christian torture. In a matter of a few hours the task was completed and the family paraded gravely around the deck, delighted at their new finery. Hans's better half was short and fat. Due to her light skin colour the blush on her cheeks was clearly visible; her baby, about 10 months old, seemed to have as great a natural inclination to cold as ducklings to water, since almost daily he crawled out of his parents' tent, which had been pitched on deck, and despite the low temperatures, crawled around naked.

When Hayes returned home a year later he put Hans and his family ashore at the Danish colony of Upernavik. Since we hoped to find him at Fiskernæsset, his place of birth, on the evening of the 26th we set an easterly course. We intended to hire him as dog-driver for the expedition and to let Mrs. Merkut enjoy the delights of grass-widowhood for a few years. Next morning around 4.00 a.m. we came within sight of land. Similar in shape and formation to the Scandinavian massif between Gilleskaal and Melfjord, the coast rises steeply here; the dark rock masses rise sheer, almost vertical, out of the sea, but they are not wooded like the Scandinavian coast, and the lack of trees makes the boldly curving forms appear harsh and of imposing wildness. The sun gleamed as a brighter patch through the masses of cloud that hung over the rock faces, concealing them. The brows of the rock formations lay in deep blue-purple shadows; outside on the sea scattered lights sparkled on the short waves and produced a play of mixed cold and warm tones on the scattered ice floes, a play which till now no palette has tried to capture.

Slowly our ship steamed northward along the coast. A massive spruce trunk about 30 feet long came drifting along, betraying the existence of a current coming from the south; on its barkless surface both traces of an axe and those of the pack ice could be clearly distinguished.[9] We lowered a boat and took it in tow, in order to cut off a piece for our driftwood collection at an appropriate moment. Some parts of it were covered by inch-wide barnacles, an indicator that it had been adrift in the sea for a long time. The green slime which adhered between the clumps of seaweed that had colonized its surface in a scattered pattern, provided a varicoloured sample card of diatoms, small crustaceans and annelid larvae. While the boat was lowered we measured the water temperature: 7.2°, while the air temperature was only 5.5°; combined with the presence of the drifting log, this set the existence of the Gulf Stream beyond any doubt.

It may have been about 8 o'clock when the fog bank which had been hovering around the summits of the cliffs dispersed. Numerous rounded summits, about 2000 feet high and packed close together, appeared; they extended quite far inland and only in places were they lightly covered with snow. The sun's noon altitude gave a latitude of 63.5°N; hence we were a little more than two miles north of Fiskernæsset. Turning back, we immediately headed south, toward the coast, to find the entrance to the harbour. Having approached to within about a mile of the coast, on a rise we spotted numerous figures who were waving their arms animatedly. We had only just fired a cannon shot when they suddenly disappeared. We let our steam whistle blow, but they did not return. Having decided to run in without a pilot, we swung in sharply toward a slot that cut the cliffs and that appeared to us to be the harbour entrance.[10] We had barely covered a few ship's lengths when two natives in kayaks swung around a projecting cape; they handled them with enviable skill, playfully dipping the delicate double-paddles first on the right side, then the left. Since there was quite a high sea running, we lowered a boat once they had approached close enough, in order to fetch them both on board more easily. But they did not succeed in extricating themselves immediately from their skin boats, and hence two stalwart seamen hoisted first one, then the other kayak into the boat, which was then hoisted on deck along with its crew and with the Eskimos still secured firmly in their kayaks.

I have never heard Danish or English abused in a more inhuman fashion than by these two converted heathens from the north, in their skin clothing, with their wide, dirty faces, whose basic colour one could at best only guess at. Joseph and his wife Hannah tried to talk to them, but due to their dialect they had difficulty, although this may sound strange. Hannah's reply was very enlightening when I raised the matter with her. "They cut their words too short," she said, and with her fingers imitated the movements of scissor blades. But the two men knew what we needed. Striking his chest with his fist, the elder of them said: "Me Umiak soak bring havn," and pointed in the direction in which Fiskernæsset lay. And we trusted him and let him pilot the ship into the harbour. In the meantime the other man pulled out a goat's horn which he used as a snuff box. He let me have it in return for some trifle; on trying the contents I found them to be snuff heavily mixed with a white powder. Later I was told that many of the natives, for reasons of economy, mix their tobacco with cryolite,[11] which irritates the mucous membranes of the nose more severely than prepared tobacco.

At its entrance the shores of Fiskefjord swing round from their east–west alignment toward the south, and here three islands project from the sea; they have been named the "Three Brothers" by the resident Danes. Fiskernæsset lies on the most northerly tip of the largest of them. Maintaining an almost northerly course, we had the steep cliffs of the mainland to starboard, and to port the gullied gneiss cliffs of the largest of the Three Brothers. After we had proceeded a little more than two miles along this strait, in view of a high cape our pilot had us swing sharply to the northwest; we maintained this direction for about a quarter mile and then spotted the buildings of the colony.

Fig. 2. Fiskernæsset.

It was 3 o'clock when we dropped anchor; the settlement lay barely 50 paces from us. Like figures from a fairy-tale, strangely-clad figures thronged down to the shore, gesticulating animatedly and gazing at us inquisitively. The women must have become bored; they attempted to conjure up the amusing side of life by lying on the sun-warmed rocks, their bottoms up, stretching their legs in the air, and singing a song without words. Some of our German seamen, who were rowing a cable out, provided the missing words; the echo sent back a confused "bridal wreath" from the mountains, while beheaded cod-fish, spread out near the singers to dry, exhaled that unmistakable odour that we had so richly enjoyed during our sojourn in Newfoundland.

A boat rowed toward us from the headland, and a few moments later the colony's administrator stood on deck, en route to the saloon. After we had exchanged the usual civilities, our first question was as to the whereabouts of Hans, for whose sake we had called here. At the moment he was not living in Fiskernæsset; Mr. Schönheyter did not know where he was but he suggested that it would not be difficult to locate him, since his brother was still living in the settlement.

Hall and I accompanied the obliging official ashore and to his home. Although he was badly asthmatic, the Greenland climate seemed to suit him; when he lay stretched out he was of impressive height and hence very good-natured. But he had not been very fortunate in the choice of his name, which did not match his appearance at all well.[12] Herr Schönheyter did not have a loving wife to sweeten his life, but mindful of the well-devised saying, he was not ill-disposed toward the other accessories. Draped in a blue ribbon, a guitar hung on the wall; on a small side-table stood various bottles filled with strong liquor. In a sparkling red wine, which even those envious of him had to declare as superb, he bade us "Willekumm," and amidst cheerful conversation the bottle made many rounds. But I could not stay long; I had ordered a seaman to accompany me on an excursion and the time for that had now come; leaving the two men to their liquid devotions, I took my leave.

We climbed a steep slope to a narrow, rocky slab which led to an undulating plateau about 200 feet high and covered in many places with dwarf willows and blueberry bushes; the numerous pools of water were surrounded by *Eriophorum*[13] which, when seen from a distance, was not dissimilar to the seed-bearing flower-heads of our common dandelion. The yellow blossoms of the arctic poppy that waved above their dark clumps of leaves on stems almost a foot high glowed from a distance; here and there a blue harebell bloomed, while in shady cracks in the rocks delicate ferns grew. A thick cover of purple saxifrage and numerous *Draba* flowers[14] covered the dry peat cover, from which erratic blocks of varying size and assorted materials projected. Lichens had colonized these boulders.

We were constantly followed by a pack of natives. If we dug a plant up we could be sure that next moment a dozen dirty hands would be stretched toward us, holding out a clump of grass or some other worthless object. If we broke off geological hand specimens from the various types of gneiss in which there were often excrescences of garnets up to an inch across, the natives, young and old, would come dragging any old rocks. In one case an elderly matron brought us a granite boulder which weighed 30 lbs. and drew my attention to a large feldspar crystal which lay embedded in it. Probably grandmother considered it very valuable since she wanted my hammer in return for it; she appeared to have a great liking for the latter's brightly polished steel.

From a point about 900 feet high a fine view of the other two "brothers" and of the fiord opened before us; but a projecting cape prevented us from seeing far into the latter.

Once I had sketched the landscape we started back to the ship, heavily laden. It was almost 11 o'clock when we got down, but it was far from dark. The notes of a fiddle carried to us from the colony's warehouse; the beauties of Fiskernæsset had assembled there in their holiday attire, to amuse themselves dancing with our sailors. Reddishly burning blubber lamps, which smoked and sputtered badly, illuminated the room, in which the couples wove to and fro. The old Greenlandic fiddler sat on an upturned barrel, attempting to compensate for the lack of clarity in his playing with comical facial distortions. The feet of our sailors seemed impossibly clumsy as compared to the extremely delicate little feet of the ladies, whose movements revealed an amazing grace. Dancing seemed to rivet all their senses; every movement was accompanied by an expressive play of the features, while in their dark eyes there glowed a passion which one would never have suspected in these inhabitants of the north.

Although in her homeland Mrs. Hannah had disdained to wear the becoming native dress, she was whirling around with the bosun in a green dress, puffed out by a crinoline and adorned with a fiery red sash, and a hat on which there were enough feathers to fill a pillow. Joseph stood in a corner with his arms folded; his stay in America had made him too materialistic and serious for him to find pleasure in the enjoyment that was thrilling the others.

The female dancers wore short fur jackets that reached to their hips and concealed the movements of their limbs somewhat excessively. Some had the hair side of this garment outside; others had covered the hair side with brightly coloured calico; a dark trim of dog fur clung around the neck and sleeve openings. The lower garments, also made from sealskin, were not more than a foot in length, not unlike swimming trunks, and gave way downward to boots which reached halfway up the thigh.

It would appear that great care had been spent on the footwear, which was made from white, red or yellow sealskin and was embroidered at the upper part of the legs with delicate mosaics of leather. The majority of the native women wore their hair combed tightly up on top of the head, and with the upstanding clump of hair wound around with coloured ribbons. Some wore brightly coloured kerchiefs wound round their heads, after the fashion of Andalusian peasant women. Here and there some imitation jewellery glittered in their hair.

The men's dress differed little from that of the women. In their case the jacket was of a somewhat different cut; the watertight footwear was less artistic and revealed the natural colour of the leather; and the pants stretched to below the knee, where they were tucked into the legs of the boots and were fastened securely to them.

No matter how picturesque and unique the scene was, and it certainly provided sufficient material for observation, we could not linger long. My collections of the afternoon had to be put in order, the plants pressed and the hand specimens packed, since on the following day we wanted to make a boat trip to Lichtenfels,[15] a neighbouring German colony,[16] and to visit Fiskernæsset itself.

The clear night sky promised fine weather, but in the morning it was raining. It was 8 o'clock but the Eskimo pilot whom I had ordered for 7 was nowhere to be seen. I rowed ashore and went to see Mr. Schönheyter, who had promised to send the man to me; there I learned that the latter had refused to accompany me because of the rain. Since there were prospects of the weather improving, and since it was still early I took a stroll through the little colony, which consisted of eight wooden houses and about the same number of huts. The only two-storeyed building is the administrator's house, which, since it stands on a rise near the flagpole, is visible from a great distance. Since there is no wood in Greenland which might be used as building lumber, apart from tree trunks which happen to drift ashore, all the boards, beams and planks required for house construction are imported from Denmark. Generally the lumber is entirely cut to length there so that once it has reached its destination it can be assembled with minimum effort. Only the foundations of the houses consist of stone; the walls consist of beams about 6 inches thick, which are covered with boards outside and in; as a result the cold is countered tolerably well. The roof and the rest of the exterior are usually tarred, while the window frames are a show of various gaudy colours.

The majority of the Greenlanders live in low huts built of rocks and turf, whose flat, slightly sloping roofs consist of driftwood over which turf sods have been spread. Depending on whether these buildings are occupied by one or several families, they vary in length between 10 and 30 feet; they are rarely more than 12 to 15 feet wide, and scarcely over 8 feet in height. A typical Greenlander's hut is built as close to the beach as possible and possesses a tunnel leading to the door; this tunnel is so low that one has to crawl on all fours to get through it to reach the interior. To right and left of the door are windows which sometimes consist of glass, sometimes of marine mammal intestines; in the latter case the daylight can only penetrate in subdued fashion. The interior of the hut is lined with skins, generally old boat coverings or the material of worn-out tents. A raised plank bed extends along one wall and serves as marriage bed, nursery, kitchen and workshop. The smell which prevails in such a dwelling is far from inviting; the ventilation is inadequate since the only exchange of air occurs by way of the tunnel entrance. The effluvium from inhabitants, skins, lamps and kitchen refuse is so strong that a European nose takes quite some time to get accustomed to this atmosphere.

Cleanliness is a quality that the Eskimo does not include among the virtues, and his personal use of water is limited just to what is needed for drinking. The lack of sensitivity of his organ of smell may be realized most clearly from the heaps of refuse of every kind that lie around his hut in immediate proximity. Although the distance between the sea and his dwelling is very small, he cannot resolve to carry the remains of his meals to the water. Convenience wins and he throws bones, shells, fish, skins which are unusable, and anything else that for the moment is no longer of any value to him, in front of his hut. As a result a luxuriant vegetation develops whose fresh green is visible for long distances. It takes only a short time to find traces of almost all the usable vertebrates of the Greenland fauna in these kitchen middens. In many cases it would not even be difficult to determine at what season the deposit was formed; in places the remains of birds predominate, in places those of fish, or else there are strata which consist almost exclusively of mussel shells. Several well-preserved dog skulls were added to our collection as important objects as well as a number of crushed seal marrow bones.

We made our way to the home of the catechist, which was in somewhat better condition than the other huts. It possessed glass windows and a small stove, while brightly painted picture screens, which were very cheerful to look at, adorned the walls. Where everything proceeds at such a leisurely pace as in Greenland, there is no urgent business to perform, yet despite that I was surprised to still find the family deep in sleep. I wanted to withdraw quietly but the people on the sleeping platform began to stir; there were movements under the skins. Two feet appeared, then two legs and then the rest of the catechist's wife, wearing little more than her birthday suit. Once she had torn her spouse from his dreams by a gentle poke in the ribs, she jumped up to make me coffee. When I thanked her, she turned her attention to her nursing baby, who soon afterward was imbibing his morning drink with greedy suckings. There were two chairs in the room; I was obliged to take a seat on one of them while the catechist sat on the other. He told me about his community in broken Danish, but it was far from easy to understand him since he spoke rapidly and used many expressions which, if they were not Greenlandic, certainly did not belong to the Germanic group of languages. He had received his education at the high school in Godthåb[17] and was one of the country's scribes; he could write and possessed a champagne bottle full of ink which hung on the wall near the window,

Anybody who wants to hold the position of catechist in Greenland must have attended the seminary in Godthåb or, if he is from North Greenland, the one at Jakobshavn,[18] where instruction is given in the Greenlandic and Danish languages and in theology. During this period the students receive an annual allowance of 25 Reichsthaler and the local natives provide their board and lodgings. If they assume office on completion of their years of study, they are obliged to instruct the children who are hungry for knowledge and to call the faithful to church service every Sunday. They are allowed to perform baptisms but their authority does not extend to joining loving hearts in the bonds of matrimony. Only the missionary may do this. As Mr. Schönheyter told us, the annual stipend of a priest is 70 Reichsthaler, a small sum even by Greenland standards.

Whether these well-intentioned efforts of the authorities can achieve anything remains to be seen. In any case the Eskimo would feel happier with his traditional beliefs than under the influence of any other religion, which can never be appropriate to him with his limited range of ideas. The graft of European culture, transplanted to Greenland's soil, will never bear the fruit which is expected of it; the effect of heredity is too powerful and despite the most careful training can be eliminated only very slowly. The Eskimo will always have to adapt to Greenlandic conditions; but if indeed the European element ever starts to become dominant through constant mixing with Whites, the coming generations will have to look around for other places to live, since only people who are at the cultural level of the Eskimo are capable of surviving for a prolonged period in a country like Greenland. Since needs grow with increasing civilization, with prolonged civilization the Eskimo will, of necessity, have to abandon hunting, on which he relies for his livelihood. But he cannot apply himself to cultivating the land, and hence missionary work and civilization produce a disadvantageous rather than a favourable effect. Yet the zeal of the missionaries has to be recognized, as long as it flows from true conviction. But in a country with the physical properties of Greenland, where even agriculture, that powerful lever of human culture, is impossible, all their efforts will be expended in vain.

The catechist's blonde wife, of mixed ancestry, understood barely a word of Danish; apart from her hair she could be distinguished from full-blooded Greenlandic women only by her light skin colour and her blue eyes, although she also had in common with them a total lack of cleanliness. Once she had adequately carried out her maternal duties to the little girl, who seemed to me to bear more of a resemblance to the father than to her, she did her toilet. If I had accepted the coffee which she offered to make for me, I would probably have robbed her momentarily of her wash basin, since the cup had to serve that function; as a sponge she used the hem of her shirt, which she had slipped on in the interim and was somewhat dark in colour.

The rain was now pouring down; on the way to the ship I found a native who stated that he was prepared to accompany me. While we rowed out to the ship he told me the reason why Christian, whom the administrator had lined up for me, had declined to come with me to Lichtenfels. Like most Greenlanders, the poor man owned only a single suit and when it was soaked its owner was confined to his own fireside. With two seamen volunteers and the first engineer[19] we set off on our trip; our course lay about southwest and led through a channel flanked on the left by the largest and on the right by the smallest of the "Three Brothers." At some points the rocky gneiss cliffs approach each other to less than half a n. mile and here and there are seamed by quartz veins, recognizable from a distance by their white colour. The tide was rising; the seaweed, rooted firmly to the almost vertical rocks, still projected about a foot above the water. Above this came a strip, on average about 2 feet wide, devoid of all vegetation, while above that again the crustose lichens began above a fairly sharply demarcated line. As we continued on our journey this bare strip occurred everywhere, more or less distinctly; its upper edge probably marks the maximum height of the high spring tide. We had brought a trawl along, in order to dredge the sea bed, but it was still raining too heavily to be able to make use of it. Rowing against wind and current, about 45 minutes after we had left the ship we spotted the little tower at Lichtenfels, and shortly afterward we clambered ashore.

One of the missionaries,[20] who was already aware of the expedition's arrival at Fiskernæsset, hurried toward us and in very broken English invited us into the house to wait out the rain and to take a little refreshment. Great was his delight when I started to speak German after introducing myself since, during his 14-year sojourn in West Greenland, fate had brought countrymen to see him only three times. In the mission house we met Mrs. Starik, our host's spouse, as well as another missionary, Mr. Uellner,[21] along with his spouse. While we were chatting with the pious Moravian brothers, the ladies made arrangements to take care of our physical well-being. Plates clattered in the adjacent room; a native serving girl carried several covered dishes past us; on the bosom of the

Fig. 3. Lichtenfels.

massive enamelled stove nestled various bottles whose shape, in conjunction with their location, indicated Rothspohn[22] to any non-Eskimo. Without being too concerned as to whether we were about to consume lunch or supper, I escorted the younger of our hostesses, who had been assigned to me, to the table. Since I had neither expected such an impressive reception nor had suspected what lay before me, apart from the outfit I was wearing I had brought no other garments with me; for better or for worse I therefore had to take my seat in a short jacket and sea boots.

The menu was entirely Greenlandic: fowl soup, salmon, roast reindeer and young eider duck; the small beds of the kitchen garden had provided assorted seasonal vegetables and the goats had supplied excellent butter. When it stopped raining we got up, since our time was limited and I had expressed to Mr. Starik a desire to see the mission station. First of all we were shown the communal dwelling of the two childless couples; then we proceeded to the small unadorned prayer hall, which offered little worthy of note. In general we found the natives less well clothed than in Fiskernæsset; the huts were generally in poor condition, and some even in miserable condition; just as there, those creations were abundantly represented with which the noble handicrafts of Neu-Ruppin flood the market,[23] delighting the spirit and the eyes of the masses. A madonna, taken from Van Dyck's group of repentant sinners,[24] seemed to enjoy particular favour; here it was suddenly equipped with a halo, and appeared in a fullness reminiscent of Rubens; in some cases it had a jaundiced complexion and sometimes the face was flooded with a purplish-red.

Whereas at Fiskernæsset we had encountered an alpine flora of delightful luxuriance, the vegetation on the neighbouring heights seemed rather wretched, although the soil here was no worse. The latitude of both sites is almost the same; indeed Lichtenfels even lies farther south than the other colony, but at the same time it is closer to the sea. As a result the fog can obtain easier access, and just as in Newfoundland this exerts an influence by clearly making the lower insolation an important factor and by delaying growth. A few ravens sat on the nearby rocks; we were able to kill three specimens for our collection with very little effort.

The Greenland raven, which our ornithologists consider a separate variety,[25] is not at all shy, and unlike its other cousins is a coastal species in the fullest sense of the word. Although large amounts of animal refuse lie scattered around the huts, it prefers to search for its food along the shore; it catches fish, hunts for crabs and mussels, and if it has difficulty in opening the latter with its bill, it drops them from the tops of the cliffs in order to shatter the shells. It nests on the cliffs near the shore and, I was informed, lays its eggs in mid-April. Our obliging host offered to show me some nests in the vicinity, but due to the lack of time I had to decline, since I was planning to extract information from the church records.

Unfortunately the documents provided information only on the population of the German brethren, which was 221 at the end of 1870, namely 64 married couples, 1 widower, 37 widows, 9 males over 18 years of age, 20 between 12 and 18, and 16 under 12; 40 females over 18, 14 between 12 and 18, and 20 under 12. They are distributed among the colonies as follows: Lichtenfels 142, Tornait, 38, Kangersuk, 14 and Fiskernæsset 27 members. We compiled a more-or-less complete census for the 10 preceding years but I will leave it out as being too voluminous. In 1860 the population was 315; at that time 123 people lived at Lichtenfels, and the rest at the six other colonies. Hence we were able to establish a decrease of 94 people; the church records provide no definite information as to whether this was caused exclusively by mortality, or by some people leaving the brethren.

Having taken leave of our friendly hosts we re-embarked to row back to the ship. The dredge produced a rich haul of invertebrates, algae and seaweed; my shotgun produced a number of black guillemots for the table.

We found the entire female population of Fiskernaesset assembled on board, in the saloon; the table had been removed and the ladies were squatting on the floor, huddled close together in the most varied positions. Once I had safely pushed my way through to the chronometers in order to wind them, a noisy crowd pressed around me; numerous hands stretched toward me to grasp the large, brass clock keys which were the object of great admiration. The catechist's blonde wife even asked me to give her one of them, so that she could fasten it to the string of pearls she wore around her neck. Instead I just sprayed some perfume, since the smell of skins and people was more penetrating than was pleasant even to fairly insensitive olfactory nerves. I had scarcely poured a few drops on the handkerchief of one of those present when every woman wanted to be perfumed; those who did not possess a handkerchief would pull out the hem of their shirt between their jacket and their pants and, once it had been sprayed, rub it energetically around their nose.[26] Hans's brother sat to one side, busy since early morning at ineffectually composing a letter to the latter in the Greenlandic language. After many unsuccessful attempts, to the detriment of our supply of paper, he had written half a page. Hall urged him to hurry since he intended putting to sea with the next high tide.

When the order was given to weigh anchor at 3.00 a.m. on 29 July, the seamen had great difficulty in turning the capstan; the anchor chain appeared to be wedged between the rocks on the sea bed and would not budge, even when the engine was brought in to help. It was not until half an hour later, after several vain attempts, that we were ready to sail. Our old pilot guided us out to sea; after we had paid him and dismissed him, we set a course to the north.

Around 6 o'clock we had to stop involuntarily since the grating on one of the boilers was broken; repairs took two hours. Thereafter we followed the coast, some 15–18 n. miles off; unfortunately it was hidden from us due to fog. At noon on the 30th we were at 65°16'N; 53°47'W and about an hour later passed Sukkertoppen, a boldly curving peak about 3000 feet high; it towers above the other points on the coast and is recognizable from a great distance and serves as a landmark for seafarers. A violent southwest gale, which at times increased to hurricane force, obliged us to reef all our sails and made the Newfoundland dogs pitiably seasick. The ship rolled and pitched in the most unpleasant fashion; one of the pigs, whose pen had broken loose, was almost washed overboard along with it.

For the first time during the voyage we spotted fulmar petrels.[27] They circled the vessel with slight, barely perceptible wing-strokes, sometimes swinging high in the air, sometimes diving to the surface of the water in a sudden turn; they would then settle on the water after making various circles with rapid wing-beats. This bird, called a mallemuck by the seamen, is about the size of a raven. The colour of the plumage is extremely variable, ranging from white to dark grey-brown. Younger individuals are generally darker-coloured than the adults, but there exists a variety that in the mature stage is a very dark gull-blue with the exception of a light patch on the wings.[28] Only rarely does one see solitary birds; generally they appear in quite large flocks. They follow ships for short distances and examine everything that is thrown overboard with inquisitive looks. Their movements in the water are strange and clumsy; with their heads nodding constantly and deliberately they paddle alternately, as if pacing, first with the right foot then the left, often cackling, engaged in mutual conversation. When they have bustled about sufficiently, they lay their heads close to their bodies, sticking them under the mantle feathers up to their eyes, and sleep for a while as they let themselves drift in a carefree manner on the smooth sea. In West Greenland they never nest south of Godhavn;[29] there they nest in large numbers on high cliffs and fulfill their maternal duties so faithfully and devotedly that one has to forcibly push them aside to reach the large, white egg. Both it and the birds itself are quite tasty during the nesting period. At other seasons the birds taste unpleasantly oily, even when one skins them carefully and removes all the fat. A peculiar penetrating smell clings to their plumage and is very difficult or impossible to remove. At least all our efforts at dealing with a pillow that we had had stuffed in the eastern Arctic Ocean[30] were totally in vain.

Once the storm had died down, we threw out hooks baited with bacon and caught a number of these birds to fill out our collection. Once on deck they are completely helpless; they looked extremely unhappy and puked up their foul-smelling stomach contents; in so doing some of them fouled their plumage so badly that we were glad to let them go again. They are trusting and harmless and generally peck boldly at the bait; but at times they seem to be suspicious, examining the bait from all sides, pecking at it cautiously and letting it go again until the treacherous hook lodges securely in their bills.

During the night we crossed the Arctic Circle, then headed closer in toward the severely dissected coast, and around 10.00 a.m. on the morning of the 31st we sighted the entrance to Holsteinsborg[31] harbour. After we had fired a number of shots a pilot came aboard, and we then proceeded between the off-lying skerries to the anchorage, which we reached around 11.

There was no sign of the transport ship; on the other hand we had the pleasure of meeting the Swedish expedition that had left Scandinavia in the late spring in order to fetch the meteoric iron that Nordenskiöld[32] had found the previous year and, in addition, to carry out hydrographical and other investigations. The head of the expedition, Baron Fr. von Otter,[33] a naval captain, was in command of the gunboat *Ingegerd*, while Captain von Krusenstjerna commanded the brig *Gladan*. *Ingegerd* had been damaged and lay on the beach, heeling heavily to port, in order to be careened; Holsteinsborg harbour, with its considerable tidal range, offers a superb opportunity for this.[34] In order to make the expedition as productive as possible, various scientists had been sent with it, some of whom had earned their laurels on the earlier Swedish voyages to Svalbard. On board the brig, Professor Thore Fries[35] was employed as botanist and Dr. Gustav Nauckhoff as geologist; Dr. Carl Nyström and Joshua Lindahl[36] were housed on board *Ingegerd*. While Hall went to see the colony's administrator, I rowed over to *Gladan* and then, since that vessel was totally deserted, to the brig, where I found Captain von Otter and Professor Fries; later the rest of the gentlemen appeared and we shared our experiences. Several years previously common interests had taken us to Svalbard, and now they were concentrated on Greenland. The news that von Otter brought us concerning ice conditions in the north of Davis Strait was highly encouraging and justified our boldest hopes; as they cruised to and fro both ships had invariably encountered open water. The fairly numerous deep-sea soundings made mainly by the gentlemen on board *Gladan* seemed to be of particular value, as too did the simultaneous temperature determinations taken at various depths, which definitely argued against any warmer subsurface current.[37] Unfortunately these investigations have not yet been worked up, or at least not published; since our return I have seen no publication coming from the Arctic Ocean that made these measurements an object of study.

The meteorites have fared better; one of them, weighing 21,000 kg, may be considered the largest known thus far. The occurrence of meteoric iron in Greenland is certainly nothing new; it was first established in 1818 by Ross's expedition, which purchased knives made from this material from the natives near Cape York (75°55'N). Later Rink[38] and others found several pieces, the largest of which weighed 21 lb. When Nordenskiöld spent some time in northern Greenland in the summer of 1870, he charged the natives to look for masses of iron that might be lying around; their investigations were crowned with the most brilliant results. In late August a Greenlander informed him that he had found several of the rocks that he was seeking, and Nordenskiöld immediately travelled with two boats to Ovifak, located on the island of Disko (69°19' 5"N; 54°1'W), to have the site shown to him. When they landed the men moored the boat to a large boulder which, to Nordenskiöld's great joy, turned out to be a meteorite. Over a short period of time no fewer than five fairly large pieces and a number of smaller pieces were found; their total weight was over 15,325 kg.

The occurrence of this mineral in such large masses is, in itself, of quite great interest. That interest is heightened by the geological conditions of the surrounding area, which quite incontrovertibly suggest that this meteor-fall occurred during an earlier geological epoch, probably the Miocene, when Greenland's climate was warmer than now and when a luxuriant growth of trees covered the heights on which, at best, the dwarf arctic willow now grows.

The finds were made particularly on basalts, in which small pieces of iron lay embedded; these too turned out to be meteoric iron. Using explosives, Nauckhoff obtained from the rocks masses similar to those we had seen on board *Gladan* and which were of impressive size. Moreover, some of the meteorites discovered by Nordenskiöld turned out to be covered with a basalt crust in various places; this was adhering firmly to the mineral and, as was determined later, its chemical composition turned out to be identical to the outcropping and underlying rock.[39] The largest of the meteorites, which unfortunately is starting to crumble despite all precautionary measures, is now located in the Rijksmuseum in Copenhagen, while one of the smaller ones is housed in the British Museum's collection.

Together, over the course of the afternoon, we visited the colony, the most beautiful we saw in Greenland, and perhaps the most beautiful in the whole country.

Facing mountains rising to 2000 feet and more, the colony rises in the entrance of a delightful valley, at one of the outermost points on the coast. If one could imagine the roaring sea to be Lake Tannick or Loch Shin,[40] and forget for a moment that one is beyond the Arctic Circle, one could be in a Scottish hamlet in the full abundance of its idyllic charms. Freshly stacked piles of peat, warmed by the sun, spread that unique earthy smell which, without being pleasant, titillates the senses; blue columns of smoke curl up above moss-covered hut roofs; a homely church rises among scattered houses which betray a comfortable well-being, and cheerful goats graze on the green slopes.

Fig. 4. Holsteinsborg.

Isolated from the din of the world, a few Europeans live here who are rooted with every fibre of their mind and soul in their dear homeland, from whence news trickles only sparingly to them. Once per year the ships of the Royal Greenland Trading Department call here, bringing letters, coal, provisions and trade goods.[41] Perhaps a whaler which has been damaged, or which wants to take on water, may call; perhaps an exploration ship, in order to acquire the indispensable products of the Greenland market or to buy sledge dogs. The most trivial incident, if sufficient to bring some variety in their existence, will live on for years in the traditions of these people, in whose hearts, along with the joy of living, there gnaws an unquenched longing. If, having served their period of service, they finally return to where the golden wheat waves, with onset of winter or the sight of the first snow they are seized by a wild longing for the loneliness of the north and for the uplifting air of the mountains, which they breathe as the free residents of magnificent nature. Leaving civilization behind, with its pleasures and ailments, after a short period many of them return to their self-chosen place of exile until death finally smooths over the split in their hearts and they can find a resting place in the narrow strip of ground which, itself frozen at no great depth, separates the mighty glaciers, behind which the sun rises from the ice-covered sea.

Mr. Elberg received us with benevolent sincerity.[42] This honest Danish administrator had lived in Greenland for years, first as an assistant, then as a higher official. According to the custom of the country he wore sealskin pants and boots of the same material, cut according to Eskimo style, whereas the rest of his clothing was European. He guided us to his home, where we made the acquaintance of his family, and then to the little kitchen garden which he showed us, displaying justified pride. It had certainly not been a small task to build up this little garden on naked rock; every handful of earth had to be painfully hauled in; in general the dark loam was almost 2 feet deep. Carefully tended cabbage, white turnips, lettuce, rhubarb and sorrel grew here; a cucumber was blooming in a hot frame but the fruit it had produced were only small. If one can succeed in sheltering the plants from the cold winds many of them grow with encouraging luxuriance despite the relatively low air temperatures. At these latitudes the summer days are long; for some time the sun does not drop below the horizon, and if fog does not blanket the landscape, vegetative conditions here are much more favourable than in the Alps for example, at places with similar mean summer temperatures. The first attempts at growing grain, made by Egede,[43] were repeated at Rink's instructions, but they were a failure, both at Godthåb and at Julianehåb[44] located farther south. Here and there some barley is planted, but it develops only meagrely and barely manages to form ears. Strawberries are said to flourish as well under glass as in Denmark, but on the other hand the growing of potatoes encounters serious difficulties. The plants never reach the blooming stage; the tubers are generally small and watery and one scarcely finds more than four of them on the roots of a single plant.

Here we encountered a larger number among the natives who displayed pure Eskimo features than at Fiskernæsset, and we succeeded in taking some photographs of them. At first nobody wanted to sit; but when Mr. Elberg placed himself in the middle and when I promised the men tobacco and the women glass beads, the shyness gradually disappeared. But it was not easy to make the people keep still during the brief exposure time. The difficulty increased when I made preparations to photograph the interior of a hut with the family busy with its domestic activities, since only a meagre light penetrated, and it acted only very slowly on the sensitive plate. I had scarcely specified good poses for everyone when an arm would move here, or a head would shake there; hence after several unsuccessful attempts I dismissed the family and satisfied myself with a photo of the empty hut. In contrast to Fiskernæsset most of the huts here have plank roofs; in many of them one encounters Schwarzwald clocks which, in combination with the tiled stoves, contrasting with the Greenland lamps, give the rooms a very strange appearance.

Despite Christianity and civilization, the Eskimo cannot persuade himself to part with his lamp; but as long as he owns it he will remain an Eskimo with every beat of his pulse, since where a lamp exists cleanliness is impossible. According to old traditional custom this utensil is carved from soapstone,[45] which plays a significant role among the peoples of North America and is to be found in various districts in Greenland. The following illustrations show two of these lamps; they consist more or less of hollow troughs, the straight edges of which usually bulge in slightly, while the concave sides generally drop vertically and are somewhat higher than the opposite sides.

The fuel used is blubber, which is either beaten on a rock in order to break the fat cells, or else the housewife, to whom alone care of the lamp falls, takes care of this operation with her teeth, spitting the well-chewed mass into the tray. The wick, consisting of peat, moss or arctic willow catkins, is spread along the straight edge of the tray; it is then lit at one end and skilfully guided by the keeper of the fire along the full extent of the rim by means of a small wooden or bone stick. But the lamp requires careful handling. If the rapidly charring wick projects too far up into the flame, too much heat escapes from the latter; it burns

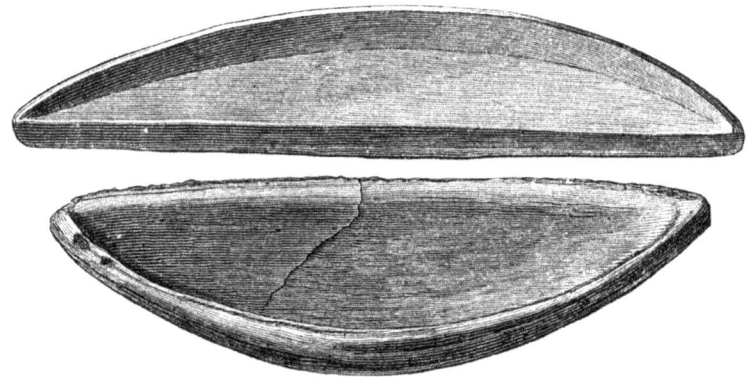

Fig. 5. Inuit lamps.

feebly, with a deep-red colour, and its outer edge is no longer hot enough to burn up the carbon and the latter spreads throughout the hut as sooty clouds. If I am not seriously mistaken, a high percentage of fatalities during the spring is due to the use of this lamp, since many Greenlanders succumb to lung ailments, which probably are primarily caused by the penetration of foreign bodies into the air passages, and which then develop further due to the extremes of temperature until they finally manifest themselves by causing death.

Where two or more families occupy one hut, there will be several lamps, since a lamp is the sole property of the head wife. It either rests on a low, wooden tripod or on some flat stones which are gently inclined to produce a sloping surface, whereby the oil pressure on the wick is enhanced. In general this device, which has barely experienced any modification for millennia, is well designed, since as the stone warms up it transmits some of its heat to the blubber; as a result the latter melts and hence constantly feeds more oil to the wick. The cooking vessel hangs above the lamp by four sealskin thongs, only a short distance above it. Like the lamp, it is carved from soapstone, since the making of clay dishes is alien to the Greenlanders and was unknown to them until the arrival of Whites. Unfired pots would be totally useless for their purposes but there is no fuel for firing them; pottery shards which have been found in southern Greenland and which are considered to be quite old were certainly not produced by the natives but probably by the old Norse colonists. The cooking vessel is rectangular with a somewhat curved bottom, as is shown in the following illustration; its walls are about ¼ of an inch thick and are very uniformly heated over the lamp, thereby preventing the shattering of the vessel.

In some of the huts the women were engaged in sewing. The leather almost without exception is sewn with animal sinew; the needle is usually three-sided and the seamstress handles it quickly and in a somewhat peculiar fashion: instead of sewing from right to left she holds the needle point toward her so that the wrist forms almost a right angle with the lower arm. While the needle is held between thumb and middle finger the index finger rests on its blunt end and exerts a gentle pressure on it. Apart from European models a small rectangular piece of sealskin is generally used as a thimble; it is equipped with a loop which is looped over the finger near the root of the nail while the flat little cap covers the tip of the finger. This represents the original form, the same in Greenland as one encounters in North America and on the islands of the Parry Archipelago and also on the Aleutians. The old style of needle, made from bone or fishbone, which was still in general use in Cranz's[46] time, has disappeared completely and has been replaced by the steel needle; the latter is kept in a delicately carved bone cylinder.

Several families had given up staying in their huts in favour of a cone- or pyramid-shaped tent. Depending on whether it was occupied by a larger or smaller number of natives, its diameter varied between 3 and 4 paces; the height of the apex was about 6 feet. The framework consisted of wooden poles with their lower ends rammed into the ground, and tied at the top with a leather thong or cord. The framework was covered with tanned, waterproof sealskin secured at the bottom with stones placed on it; where the skins did not lie snugly on the ground chunks of turf had been pushed under them to prevent draughts. The entrance hole was covered by a skin curtain, the upper part of which was cut away and fitted with translucent animal membranes in order to allow daylight to enter. Seal or dog skins, generally still hair-covered, were used to line the interior. Dry moss was piled up to form a bed, over which fur blankets were spread. Almost everywhere we went and found

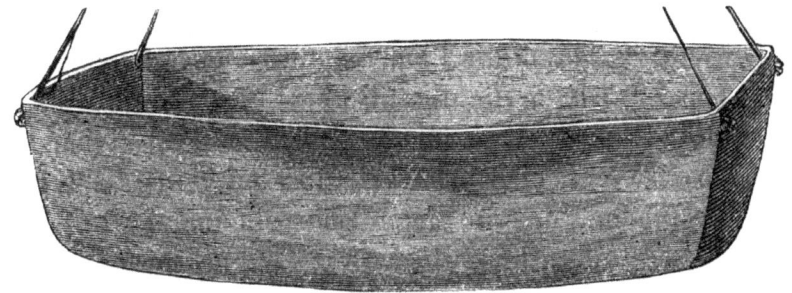

Fig. 6. Inuit cooking pot.

natives, they were cooking birds: over the lamp in the tents or huts, or over an open fire in the open, the latter being fed with small pieces of peat, or the skins or bones of eider ducks.

Toward evening we set off in one of *Gladan*'s boats between the skerries which lie off the entrance to the harbour and worked with the trawl-net for some time. Our haul was surprisingly abundant; the number of individuals was enormous, but the number of species relatively small. Nearby the natives were amusing themselves by killing black guillemots and gulls with the bird-spear; they had achieved an enviable degree of skill and only rarely did their prey escape. They often hit their target at a range of over 30 feet; they would then immediately shoot toward it as quick as an arrow in their small skin boats to retrieve the spear and the game before the current carried them away.

In order to be able to hurl the weapon with greater force and accuracy they use a throwing stick, in which the spear is placed. The spear itself consists of a wooden shaft about 6 feet long, fitted with an iron tip. In addition, midway down it possesses three pieces of bone set at equal intervals in a circle, each of which resembles a slightly curved harpoon point, equipped with several barbs. They make a fairly sharp angle with the shaft; if one imagines the spear standing upright, their arrow-shaped points face upward and their object is to wound the prey, in the event that the iron tip misses. Although the resistance encountered by the spear in its flight is increased by these protruding barbs, the weapon offers the great advantage that it won't miss its target so easily as if it possessed only the main tip. Usually the birds are not at all wary; the hunter can approach quite close to them and since the same thrust is effective at shorter distances, the probability of a hit is enhanced and completely counteracts the apparent disadvantage of the greater resistance which the weapon encounters in its flight.

Equally ingenious is the construction of the small skin boats whose shape ensures maximum speed, attained with minimum expenditure of energy. If one were to attempt to build a vessel according to the laws of mechanics, such as to produce minimum friction, one could scarcely choose any shape other than that of the kayak,[47] which can be thought of as the ideal of its type. With an average length of about 15 feet, at its widest point, located at the centre, a kayak measures barely 14 inches, while the height is not much more than half the maximum width. In shape it forms a double wedge, not unlike that of a shuttle; the bottom is absolutely flat and the deck, which has a circular hole in the centre to accommodate the paddler, is slightly convex. Bow and stern are sharp, like the breast-bone of a fast-flying bird; they curve upward from the water surface regularly and quite rapidly so that the boat is almost symmetrical not only laterally but also almost as between bow and stern sections. Not only is it elegant in shape, it is also surprisingly light, rarely heavier than 50–60 lbs., and can be carried by a single person without difficulty over rugged ice or mountainous terrain.

While it probably took quite a long time before the most appropriate design was achieved, the small weight of the craft must have been dictated from the beginning by the unique conditions under which the Eskimo lives. He uses very little wood or, in the event that a current were ever to land an adequate amount of it in his hands, he would lack the tools to craft a boat from it. Thus his only choice would be between a raft or else an almost equally primitive craft, one hollowed from a trunk of driftwood, which, given sufficient expenditure of time, could be produced with the crudest of tools, or with the help of fire. Hence nothing could be more obvious than that he should make a framework out of bones and pieces of wood and fit it with a leather skin; the result is the traditional design of the two types of boat that are used by the Eskimo.

Although their way of life and the highly dissected nature of the coast have developed the seamanship of the Greenland women to a high degree, and although the clothing of the women is fully suited to the kayak, it is used exclusively by the men. If there is a heavy sea running, or if the Eskimo is making a long trip, he pulls on a second skin jacket over his normal one; the former, like the skin of the kayak, consists of waterproof sealskin. The lower hem of the garment is provided with a draw-cord, and once the paddler has taken his seat in his boat, he ties the jacket securely over the projecting rim of the round opening; as a result the craft is almost hermetically sealed. Thus, from the hips down, he is ensconced in the kayak while from there up he is covered by the snugly fitting garment; high waves can break over him without wetting more than just his face and hands. The water runs down from the jacket onto the narrow decking but the interior of the boat remains completely dry. Thus equipped, he can kill seals and is not afraid of doing battle with a whale or a walrus. Dipping his elegant double-paddle alternately left and right, he shoots agilely over the wave crests, ready at any instant to hurl his spear or harpoon, which always lie ready at his side. The inflated stomach of a seal or of some other sea mammal lies secured behind him on the deck; it is hurled with the harpoon at the prey and prevents it from diving. A line cut from raw walrus hide lies coiled in front of him on a small, raised frame; it is secured to the harpoon head and runs out quickly when the weapon is thrown.

While we were busy hauling in the trawl one of the natives harpooned a shark near us (*Selachus maximus* Gunn.[48]), and he let us have it in exchange for a few cigars. Apart from a few half-decomposed leaves of *Laminaria*, the animal's stomach contained the remains of various amphipods; clearly the shark had been hungry and had forfeited its life when he snapped at an eider-duck's head which hung over the edge of the kayak, in the water. The fish measured barely 4 feet and was probably a young specimen since adults commonly reach a length of 15–18 feet. Their livers are used for oil extraction and form a not-insignificant item of trade. According to Rink, the Greenlanders catch the sharks mainly by two different methods. If the ice near the coast is solid they chop holes of varying sizes in it and hang seal intestines in the water to attract the predator. They congregate around the bait and are landed without any trouble using a dull iron hook, which is driven into their heads. Occasionally torches are used, making the bait redundant; the fish readily follows the light of the torch and is killed as soon as it surfaces. The other means of catching them is by using the well-known shark hooks. Baited with meat, they are hung at a depth of 4 to 6 feet. Less commonly, as in Uummannaqfjord, for example, cod hooks are used; just as in fishing for cod they are lowered to the bottom. While one can leave the big hook untended on the bottom, one has to keep a careful eye on the line, since the shark often swims away with the hook.

Hall had intended buying reindeer skins for our winter clothing here but unfortunately he was disappointed in this. Hunting had been extremely poor for the past few years and the natives had kept the few skins they had acquired; hence there was not a single skin in the government warehouse. The few dog skins that Mr. Elberg could have let us have were in poor condition and totally useless for our purpose. Altogether, apart from a bear pelt there was nothing for sale that would have repaid the effort of bringing it aboard.[49]

Like the first day of our stay, the following days were also used for excursions in the vicinity of the colony, during which we found sufficient opportunity to enrich our collections. On 2 August the Swedish expedition left the harbour. Hall and I accompanied the two ships for a short distance and returned in one of our whaleboats, after we had handed our mail over to the gentlemen.

It was almost a fatal day for one of our seamen. The natives took every opportunity to give displays of their skill in kayak handling. They commonly rolled over in the water so that the bottom of the boat was turned upward and the paddler was forced to stay under water until he succeeded in changing the craft's equilibrium by a quick movement in order to bring it back to the correct position. Several of the Greenlanders possessed such considerable skill that, secured in their kayaks, they could turn four or five of these lateral somersaults without staying on the surface longer than was necessary to catch a breath. Usually a single paddle stroke was sufficient to overturn the craft and a second one quickly brought it right way up again. William,[50] a model of foolhardiness and self-confidence, thought he could do the same. He climbed into a kayak that lay off to one side on the beach, paddled silently out into deeper water and involuntarily overturned the kayak. It was more difficult to right it again; in his panic to save himself he lost the paddle and barely escaped the danger of drowning. When the natives spotted the capsized kayak and paddled out to it to right it, the poor man had already swallowed so much water that he was half-unconscious and incapable of moving.[51] Brought back aboard, he recovered after some time, but it was several days before he was completely recovered.

CHAPTER 4

From Holsteinsborg to the northernmost settlement on Earth

Departure from Holsteinsborg. Sole. Greenland's political boundaries. A belt of pack ice and beluga. A gyrfalcon out at sea. More driftwood. A change in the coastal panorama. At anchor off Godhavn. An umiak. Coal. Godhavn. Topography and geology. A musical evening's entertainment. Boat trip to Jakobshavn. Trip to the high plateau. Arrival of the transport ship and the inspector. Unloading the cargo. The Greenlanders' church service. Eskimo dogs. An anchorage with obstacles. Departure from Godhavn. Fata morgana. Distribution of icebergs. The shoal off Kasorsoak. A foul channel. At anchor off Upernavik. The colony. Search for Hans. Lack of reindeer due to the immigration of wolves. Exchange of officials. Hans arrives. The ship's crew. The Hanseatics. Buying skins and more dogs. Tasiusaq. Jensen. The natives. The colony's surroundings. Dogs.

Our stay in the colony was approaching an end; on the afternoon of 3 August we weighed anchor to run north to Lievely,[1] where we could expect to meet our supply ship.[2] Four small American vessels were lying at anchor among the skerries; their boats were drifting around on the banks, fishing for halibut (*Hippoglossus vulgaris* Fl.).[3] We spoke to some of the crews and learned that the catch had been rather meagre; the haul had been so small that it was barely enough to meet the needs of the men; hence we had to abandon any hopes of obtaining fresh fish from them.

The halibut are usually to be found on the cod banks near the coast, and their range probably does not extend north of the 70th parallel. Many of the fish, which are about 6 feet long at maturity, reach a weight of nearly 100 lbs. and are a very favourite food for the Danes resident in Greenland, as well as the natives. They fish for them during the summer and fall months using cod hooks in depths of 20 to 50 fathoms; sometimes they are so numerous that, according to Rink, during the summer of 1809 two boats caught more than a hundred in the course of half a day. The two other species of flat fish (*Hippoglossus pinguis* Fabr.[4] and *Drepanopsetta platessoides* Fabr.[5]) which stay close to the coast and in the fiords are smaller in size and of less significance; of these the sole is fished for especially. When fishing for it the Greenlanders often use their traditional fishing lines made from baleen, because it breaks less easily than ordinary fishing line, and because the fish occurs at considerable depths. The fishing season occurs between January and March and generally does not last longer than four weeks.

Proceeding along the coast, around 6.00 p.m. we passed Strømfjord, the political boundary between North and South Greenland, which was drawn only for the purpose of trade and to simplify administration. It divides the Danish possessions into northern and southern inspectorates, which are broken down further into various districts. The former extends from the most northerly settlement to the above-named fiord and encompasses the districts of Godhavn, Egedesminde,[6] Christianshåb,[7] Jakobshavn, Uummannaaq and Upernavik; the latter extends almost to Cape Farewell and consists of the districts of Holsteinsborg, Sukkertoppen, Godthåb, Fiskernæsset, Frederikshåb[8] and Julianehåb. Godhavn or Lievely may be considered the main settlement of the country; it is the residence of the inspector and hence we now headed there.

Shortly before midnight we ran through a narrow belt of pack ice in which there were numerous high floes that were partly dirty-coloured, partly covered with grit and rocks. They had probably come from the nearby coast, under the shelter of which they had probably formed. A small school of beluga[9] that were frolicking in a lead scattered, snorting, scared by the noise of the engine. We fired a few shots at them as they fled but our bullets either went over or fell short and missed the target. Nearby a gyrfalcon[10] was hunting gulls; it later landed, tired, on one of the highest blocks (dead-eyes) in the shrouds, and I was lucky enough to kill it. The bird was an old male, measuring 24½ inches; its wingspan was almost 36 inches. It was almost pure white in colour; only the occasional dark arrow-shaped patch showed on breast and thighs, while the tail bore seven narrow blue-grey transverse stripes with faded outlines. The stomach contained bone remains of a small bird as well as a number of feathers, some of them with a tinge of pinkish-red. Best preserved was the bill; it, along with the integument, might have been those of a linnet (*Linota linaria*?).[11] It is difficult to say whether the raptor had killed its prey on land or over the sea. But in the former case it could not have been far from the coast since many of the bones were still completely undecomposed. When we shot the gyrfalcon the distance from the ship to the closest point of the coast was 153¼ n. miles. The wind was northeasterly at an average speed of 11 miles per hour and the sky was clear. Hence we may assume that the bird (which we must assume came from Greenland and not from Baffin Land) had not strayed out to sea due to fog or high winds but had left the coast of its own volition.

We spotted another driftwood trunk but did not stop to fish it out. While the one we had taken in tow near Fiskernæsset had been worked, this one still retained bark and roots; the branches, however, were missing, or at least those on the part of its surface which protruded above the water. The sky was completely clear; the temperature did not drop below 9° and the coast offered so much of interest that the thought of spending the night on deck was seductively tempting. As the rising sun chased away the brief twilight we made various attempts to make photographic views of the land; but the sea was not calm enough and we found ourselves obliged to reach for pencil and paper. It did not require special attention to perceive that the land was significantly higher here than in the south. The round domes had disappeared; they were replaced by steep, snow-covered peaks. The coast was becoming similar to that of Svalbard between Hornsund and Bellsund.

Around 10.00 a.m. we sighted the outlines of Disko on the northern horizon, at first as a sharp-cut, almost rectangular silhouette and then, once we had got closer, as a high plateau rising in terraces. This sharp contrast in the configuration of the land, which is all the more remarkable when one looks back to see the many-peaked ridges to the south, is caused by the occurrence of a basalt formation that is more massively developed here than anywhere else in Greenland.

This time we obtained a pilot much more quickly than on previous occasions. We were still about two miles offshore when two natives paddled toward us in their skin boats. As we ran into the spacious harbour it was 2.30 p.m.[12] As a result of a misunderstood signal one of the anchor chains parted; we lost the starboard anchor, and in order to recover it we had to drop the other one. The boats were immediately lowered and after several vain attempts they got hold of the end of the chain and made a line fast to it. By this means the anchor was hoisted back aboard.

Hall headed for the settlement to visit the inspector[13] and to seek information about our transport ship, which was nowhere to be seen here either. A women's boat, containing 15 people, laid alongside the ship, but since we were preparing to paint the ship nobody could be allowed aboard. Their leader, shouting, held up a leg of reindeer meat with a view to buying herself access. Others showed us birds that looked less than appetizing and that they swung above their heads, gesticulating. But the first mate,[14] who had the watch, was incorruptible and the boat started back for shore.

These vessels, called umiaks by the Eskimos, like the kayaks are made of a light framework of wood and bone, over which a waterproof skin cover is stretched. Their shape is like that of an ordinary fishing dory (or so-called floating coffin); in common with it they have a flat bottom, but their sides are higher. Depending on their length, which varies between 20 and 30 feet, these boats possess 9 to 12 rowing benches and are used mainly by the women, whereas the kayak serves the purposes of the men exclusively. The oars are short, simple and shovel-shaped, and pivot in loops of untanned hide. If a sail is used it is secured to a low mast in the bow and hence, fairly obviously, can only be of insignificant size. Whether it was invented by the Eskimo or whether the idea was borrowed from Europeans is a moot point; suffice it to mention here that earlier it consisted of mammal intestines sewn together whereas now canvas is generally used.

After a short period Hall returned aboard, but the news he brought was not very encouraging. Thus far there had been no sign of the transport ship, and the inspector, of whom we might expect some assistance in the event that the ship failed to appear, was on his annual circuit through the districts of North Greenland.[15] The season was so far advanced that it would become hazardous to linger much longer in the colonies. But we lacked the coal to make a rapid departure since we had had steam up almost constantly since leaving Newfoundland. Since then 17 days had passed and the fuel was almost exhausted. In the worst case we could take advantage of the coal seams in the Vaigat[16] as Inglefield[17] had done, and hire a number of natives to assist us. Hall immediately formulated a plan, to the execution of which there seemed to be no obstacles. All that was needed was to get permission of the colony administrator who represented the inspector in the latter's absence, and hence we both went ashore, Hall on business, I in order to take a short walk through the colony.

Godhavn (also known as Lievely), located at 69°14' 41"N; 52°34'W[18] on the most southerly point of Disko, is one of the best harbours in Greenland. The first impression the settlement makes on a visitor is less favourable than that of delightful Holsteinsborg, although the buildings here are more impressive. Those belonging to the government lie close to the beach and in terms of design are barely distinguishable from the official residences we had seen earlier in the other colonies. We counted 27 scattered huts, allegedly occupied by about 70 natives, most of whom were away hunting reindeer and fishing for salmon so that it was not possible to take an accurate count.

Disko is the largest of the numerous islands that lie off the west coast of Greenland between Cape Farewell and the 73rd parallel. Its shape is that of an irregular pentagon whose longest side, that lying opposite the Nursoak [Nuussuaq] Peninsula in almost a straight line, runs approximately northwest–southeast. The most northerly point on the island, Iglorpait, lies at 70°18' 5"N; 51°38'W, and the most easterly, Issungoak, at 69°39'N; 51°56'W. The most southerly point is represented by Godhavn and its most northwesterly extremity by Middle Head at 69°40'N; 55°8'W. Thus its two greatest diameters, which are of almost equal length, are about 67 n. miles long. While the coast facing Davis

Fig. 7. Godhavn.

Strait is indented by three fiords, one of which branches repeatedly, the others are almost unindented and are so nearly straight that on a large-scale map (1 mm to the mile) one can easily lay a ruler along quite long stretches of the coast without detecting significant deviation from the straight line. The mean height of the massif, which bears the striking character of a high plateau, is 3000 feet. But there are heights of 4000 feet and probably even more.

As noted earlier, a basalt formation outcrops here; at several places it rests directly on the gneisses which have a controlling influence on the shape of the coast and dictate the straight alignments of the latter. To the east of Godhavn, Nordenskiöld[19] found sand and clay deposits between the basalts, containing numerous fossils; according to Heer, who identified them, they belonged to the Tertiary. From the nature of the deposits the former concluded that the basalts had formed after the start of the Cretaceous and before the end of the Tertiary and suggested that they run right across Greenland near to the 69th parallel, since Scoresby[20] found several specimens of these rocks, containing plant impressions, on the east coast. He even considered it probable that this formation extends under the sea to Iceland, from there northward via Jan Mayen to Svalbard, and from Jan Mayen southward via the Faeroes to the Hebrides and Ireland. What is certain is that these basalts extend westward across the Franklin Archipelago and perhaps even across the volcanic regions of Bering Strait. They probably owe their formation to a chain of volcanoes that were active in the Tertiary, and whose alignment might under certain circumstances offer a means of identifying the boundaries of the vanished Arctis.

The coal deposits we intended exploiting are located on the northeast coast of the island, in the first half of the Vaigat, a strait 9 miles wide separating Disko from the Nursoak [Nuusuaq] Peninsula. Some pieces of the coal that we saw later showed a striking similarity to the jet of the Tertiary formations in Switzerland. The Greenland coal possesses only about half the calorific value of English coal; the ash residue is relatively small and, unlike true coal, it produces little smoke when burning since it lacks the bituminous components.

Hall, whom I met along the way, had consulted with the administrator; the government had no objection to our plans, but Hall preferred to wait till next day before dispatching the boats. Anticipating that our entire crew would then be busy with all the boats, I made arrangements to hire an umiak and a number of Greenlanders, in order to work the fossiliferous strata located near the coal and to accumulate the largest collection possible.

On the adjacent beach a native landed a seal which he had towed ashore; he pulled the animal up onto one of the rounded gneiss rocks, hauled his little skin boat out of the water and set about dismembering the animal. His wife and daughter came hurrying up to lend a helping hand while Hall and I stood by. In a fit of generosity one of the women offered us the liver, which we declined with thanks. By contrast, it was impossible to listen without pleasure to the notes of a piano which floated down from the open windows of the official's residence. Experienced hands manipulated the keys sensitively and expressively. Nothing seemed more natural than to immediately go looking for this virtuoso, especially when Hall told me that this masculine rendition was being performed by a lady. He had lost no time in making the acquaintance of the inspector's wife,[21] and hence we decided to visit the lady together.

In a capital consisting of 27 huts and 2 houses in which two European families live, where even the church does not possess a bell, one could scarcely hope to find a doorbell in a private house. Despite this, for the sake of propriety we looked for a bell-pull when we reached the door of the house. When our investigations turned out to be in vain, we entered the hall, where we were met by a fashionably dressed native servant. She showed us into a room which contained a billiard table, an unheard-of luxury for Greenland. The furnishings were simple and tasteful, betraying the rule of a gentle soul; perhaps the same one that was grieving for Leonora's lost kiss in the adjoining room.[22] As the girl opened the intervening door, the notes died away; before we could rise from our seats, we were confronted by the lady of the house, who had advanced with dignity to the door of the room to meet us.

Mrs. Krarup-Smith, a charming apparition and much too lovely for life in Greenland, bade us enter. We were greeted by a cosy room whose walls displayed good floral arrangements, painted in oils. Blooming heliotropes, carnations and mignonettes stood on the window sills in front of snowy-white curtains. Once we were seated we had to give a report on the news from the civilized world, and then tea was served. When we later returned to the room in which the piano stood, we found wine and cigars; the beautiful lady entreated us to smoke while she herself played to a grateful audience.

After a very enjoyable evening we started on the return journey to the ship around midnight, excusing the length of our visit by the amiability of our hostess. Before we set off we had to promise that we would take at least one meal per day during our stay at the round table at which we had taken tea.

The 5th of August was a rainy day; judging by the racing clouds and the roar of the surf a strong northeast wind was blowing out at sea; hence we postponed dispatching the boats to the Vaigat. Since, given the prevailing conditions, it would scarcely have been worthwhile to make an excursion, we visited the colony's administrator. To the delight of my companions Mr. Lassen proposed that he provide the expedition with coal from the government supply, in the event that the ship did not appear. But since it was necessary to inform the inspector of this step, it was decided to send one of our boats to Jakobshavn in order to get the approval of higher authority. Mrs. Krarup-Smith was kind enough to write to her husband and to describe vividly for him the unpleasant nature of our situation.

Armed with her letter and an official one from Mr. Lassen, next morning the first mate was dispatched to Jakobshavn, about 55 miles away, where he could expect to encounter the inspector. Unfortunately my expedition to the Miocene fossil beds evaporated as a result of this boat journey and the departure from the scheduled programme. Just a brief visit to the Vaigat could presumably not produce the anticipated success, in terms of my aims; a longer sojourn on the site was impossible, however, since we no longer intended digging for coal ourselves, whereby I could easily have managed a few days. Moreover, we could expect the arrival of the transport ship at any time; as soon as this happened the hours of our stay at Godhavn would be numbered.

After the boat had left I had myself rowed to the other side of the harbour, in order to visit the high plateau whose steep slopes begged to be climbed. We landed at a level spot on the beach, and not far above the high-water mark we found a luxuriant vegetation, consisting mainly of low dwarf birch (*Betula nana*) and willow bushes (*Salix glauca*).[23] Innumerable streams meandered down from the foot of the nearby basalt face toward the sea; they saturated the soil and hence we commonly sank to our ankles. The dry talus higher up was covered with lichens; the damp and wet spots were covered with wobbly moss cushions, superb breeding sites for the mosquitoes which pursued us in dense swarms.

During our stay in Greenland we had made our first acquaintance with these importunate insects at Holsteinsborg, near the administrator's house. There they had been less bloodthirsty and we could keep them away from our faces with tobacco smoke, whereas here I could barely protect myself with a butterfly net which I had pulled over my head. My companion, one of the boat's crew, who did not have this protection, emitted vast clouds of smoke from his pipe but he was severely punished on the face. It was no easy task to stay in a good mood since the mosquitoes chose every exposed part of our bodies as their assembly points. One had barely brushed them off one hand when they settled on the other one. They penetrated through the sleeves of our clothes to our arms, and through the neck-openings of our shirts and bit us first on the chest, then on the back, indulging their blood-lust with the recklessness of cannibals.

About half a mile from our landing site we entered a narrow valley which led upward at quite a steep angle and promised to be a good ascent route; here the mosquitoes increased in numbers. It was a charming region but the enjoyment was severely reduced for us. Only when my companion squatted before me on the ground and surrounded me in a halo of tobacco smoke could I get enough peace to sketch the strangely shaped basalt rocks. Shattered by frost and other atmospheric influences, they resembled the shapes of collapsed castles with towers, oriels and bastions. We followed the bed of a mountain stream which probably owed its existence to the neighbouring snow fields since its temperature was only 3° whereas the air temperature had climbed to +12°. When we waded through the water at a shallow spot to reach the other bank, we found an eroded piece of basalt whose numerous cavities were filled with beautiful zeoliths (chabazite?). The birches and willows were now joined by low bushes of Alpine rose (*Rhododendron lapponicum*) and occasional azaleas which, unfortunately, had withered. Near the water's edge sprouted delicate bluebells (*Campanula uniflora*), veronica (*Veronica aloina*) and dandelions (*Taraxacum palustre*), and in the middle of a clump of *Eriophora* I found a cowslip (*Primula stricta*) in full bloom; as far as I was able to determine this may be considered a new discovery for the Godhavn district.

Our search for beetles was almost fruitless; we caught only a few specimens of a ladybug (*Coccinella trifasciata*);[24] its range extends to Canada and the Great Lakes and west via Alaska, the Aleutians and the Kurile Islands to Siberia. A very small staphylin[25] which we found under a rock agilely escaped the murderous grasp of the tweezers and despite the most careful search I was unable to find it again. Our catch of butterflies was more abundant. Two species of moth (*Plusia gamma* and

Agrostis quadrangula) buzzed around the nectar-rich blossoms of the purple saxifrage in rapid flight and we caught numerous specimens of them. A beautiful sulphur-yellow butterfly (*Colias Boothii*) flitted over the heaths (*Erica caerulea*) whose sweet-smelling blossoms coloured extensive areas blue. Glacier fleas were almost as numerous as our tormentors, the mosquitoes; we found them under almost every rock we turned over, wherever the spot where it lay was damp enough.

When we reached a height of 370 feet above sea level (according to the aneroid) the vegetation ceased almost completely; apart from the dark lichens that covered the blackish rock, there were only meagre grasses with here and there a patch of moss or insignificant cushions of purple saxifrage. The region had assumed the character of a desolate boulder field across whose rock-debris we painfully made our way. The boulders lay piled on top of each other in the most fantastic configurations, often so loosely that a foot or a light touch of an arm sufficed to start massive fragments rolling. The torrent had disappeared but one could clearly hear the roaring of the constricted stream as it flowed beneath the scree, loudly dashing against the rocks that confined its course. Apart from basalts we also encountered sandstone rubble and gneisses. While the former derived from the immediate vicinity and had been loosened from the cliffs exclusively by frost action and weathering processes, the sandstones and gneiss boulders had been transported here by running water. Everywhere there were signs that either the torrent had formerly been of greater extent or that annually, at the period of most intense snowmelt, the water level must still rise far above the level at which we saw it—reason enough to eliminate the vegetation from this area. What was spared by the waters must naturally give way to boulders crashing down.

We continued on our way, but only slowly; the situation improved only when we reached a cliff up which a narrow cornice extended, and up which we climbed. But we were forced to proceed carefully. The ledge was barely 3 feet wide and in places it crumbled beneath our feet. We let a flight of ptarmigan[26] pass unmolested over our heads, since we did not have enough room to handle a shotgun. When we reached a height of about 700 feet above sea level, we found a passable terrace, sparsely covered with mosses, amongst which Icelandic lichens flourished, with here and there a clump of yellow arctic poppies or a cushion of purple saxifrage. Only occasionally did we encounter *Draba* or *Andromeda*.[27] In a snow gully we found fresh ptarmigan droppings and near them the most unequivocal signs that the birds had been preening here, since irregular depressions were visible amongst the impressions of their feathered feet, while breast feathers lay scattered around. Barely 5 paces away a hen ptarmigan flew up near a boulder; I fired and missed. It would have been easy to kill the bird with a second shot, but it would have been impossible to retrieve it without wasting a lot of time, since it was below us at the foot of a cliff, and we did not have a dog that might have fetched it. It did not seem to be disturbed when we threw rocks at it, or even when I fired a shot near it, in an attempt to put it up. It pressed itself confidingly against the rock while we admired its sympathetic colouring, which made it almost invisible, and then we continued on our way. Ptarmigan seemed to be far from rare here; we later saw several flights and killed four birds. In the case of one old male the fall moult had either already begun or the bird had not yet completely discarded its winter plumage, since it bore an irregular white patch 3 inches long and about 2 inches wide on its back. The scapular feathers were also largely white.

After an exciting hike along a narrow ravine which formed the bed of a roaring mountain stream, around 3.00 p.m. we reached the top of the plateau, which we determined by aneroid to lie at 2641 feet. With the help of the prismatic compass we determined the location of the spot at which we read the aneroid. A line bisecting the largest of the Whalefish Islands ran S3°, 5°W; a tangent to the western point of the entrance to Diskofjord bore N 65°W.[28] Although the temperature in the shade was only +7° we experienced a feeling of unbearable heat and discarded coat and vest. It was dead calm; a determination of the relative humidity gave a reading of only 40.7%. At the same time, on board ship the temperature was 11.6°; the relative humidity 64.2%, and there was a wind of 9 miles per hour out of the west.

The view was really rewarding. At our feet lay Disko Bugt, bounded on the south by a complex sea of islands and on the east by the dissected coast of the Greenland massif. Behind the latter's blue silhouettes the ice cap showed itself as a white band, separated only vaguely from the wonderfully transparent sky. On the dark sea, which appeared as smooth as a mirror, swam a fleet of shining icebergs, forming a long row stretching from east to west. Using the telescope one could easily recognize the fiord near Jakobshavn, from which the glacier masses seemed to be coming. We looked in vain for our boat which was on its way to the colony; it was probably too small to be seen from this distance, even with the telescope. To the north and northeast rose the Nursoak [Nussuaq] Peninsula, separated from Disko by the Vaigat. Above its dark rock masses towered a long glacier ridge which gleamed in the sun and shut off our horizon. We could overlook almost the whole of Disko, and as far as we could see to the west there stretched the blue sea, covered with ice floes in places.

Contentedly we sat down on a boulder, sketched the panorama and consumed the hardtack and salt bacon that we had brought from the ship. My half-bottle of red wine had long since been drunk; a nearby snowmelt pool contained enough water to quench my burning thirst. The air was unpleasantly dry and we were repeatedly obliged to get up to drink from the pool. My companion looked for some moss while I skinned the ptarmigan. Our hunger was greater than the supply of food we had taken with us; hence we lit a fire and roasted slightly the two mature birds; their skins were carefully wrapped in paper and stowed in the rucksack. After a short rest we started on our return journey; it proceeded quite quickly but involved leaving behind various parts of our nether garments, since at times we were travelling over snowfields and at times sliding on our backsides down slopes that in many places were very steep. On reaching the beach we tried to attract the ship's attention. Since we did not know when we would return, that morning we had sent the boat back to *Polaris* with instructions to keep an eye open for us toward evening. It was now 8 o'clock; through the telescope we could see the officer of the watch striding about the deck, but nobody seemed to notice us, although we were waving a white cloth. Three double shots fired in rapid succession finally produced the desired effect.

Around noon on 10 August we were pleasantly surprised when a horde of Eskimo women signalled the appearance of a steamer by a loud wailing from the top of the adjacent peninsula. When we identified her as our transport[29] by means of the telescope, Hall had himself rowed out to her. It may have been about 2 o'clock when the proud corvette with her crew of 300 men steamed into the harbour and dropped anchor near us. Innumerable times the mountains reflected the long-drawn echo of the thunder of guns as 21 guns were fired for the nation, and as the guns fired the salute for the Greenland inspector. The natives hid themselves timidly in their huts as if terror-struck by the gunfire; they had never seen such a large vessel before.

Shortly after *Congress*'s arrival, with two of our expedition members on board,[30] the inspector appeared. Our boat had pursued him as far as Ritenbenk,[31] since he had already left the colony when it reached Jakobshavn. Without a moment's hesitation he had made his smart yacht ready for sea; a favourable wind allowed him to cover the 90-mile distance in just a few hours. With praiseworthy readiness he offered to do everything in his power for the expedition, and repeated this offer when *Congress*'s commander paid his official visit next morning[32] in order to deliver the dispatches from the American government, which recommended us to the goodwill of the Greenlandic authorities. The warehouse of the Danish Trading Company was placed at our disposal for an unspecified time, as well as a space for storing coal. The corvette's crew immediately began discharging her cargo.

Although it rained heavily and persistently on the 12th, conjuring up memories of milder climates, the work could not be interrupted; the advanced season admonished us peremptorily to hurry. Accepting the inevitable, we laid alongside *Congress*; the two ships were linked by a gangway, and before half an hour had elapsed the combined crews were absorbed in one of those occupations which, despite their obvious benefit and their pressing necessity, are always looked upon on board any vessel with more or less loudly expressed irritation. We were coaling, and the pouring rain faithfully made its contribution toward making an unpleasant task an extremely dirty one, and toward totally countering the efforts of our seamen who only the day before had given the ship a new coat of paint.

A friendly fate provided us with some sunshine for it around midnight and thereby the pleasure of being able to attend an unvarnished native church service. The unpretentious exterior of the church exactly matched the unostentatious prayer hall that we entered around 10.00

a.m. Oblong in shape and barely as high as an ordinary living room, it possessed three windows on each of its longer walls; one of the shorter walls accommodated the door, while opposite it stood the red-draped altar surrounded by a semi-circular balustrade. To the right of the latter was a simple font and to the left the pulpit, whose motif must have developed directly from the form which the unknown inventor of the pulpit had in mind as a model during its construction. Along the two longer walls pews were arranged to the apostolic number of 12, leaving between them a wide aisle that led from the door to the altar. Apart from two blackboards on which the hymn numbers were displayed, a little roundel of Thorvaldsen's "Night" formed the only decoration in the church.[33] The church quickly filled with Greenlanders who chatted noisily among themselves. As the catechist entered the pulpit the men arrayed themselves on the right; the women took their places on the left side of the room. After a short pause he read the words of a hymn in Greenlandic, without any rhythm; it was then sung to the melody "Whoever lets beloved God hold sway" by the congregation with tolerable purity. Then came the sermon, flowingly delivered in Greenlandic; during it exasperated mothers noisily took their offspring outside. The majority of them sang the closing hymn with decidedly divided attention; slapping their books shut, many hurried out into the open before the service had ended.

Later,[34] before a large assembly on board *Congress*, an appeal was made to God to bestow his help on the expedition. Two clergymen shared in the delivery of the sermon, whose length was directly related to the efforts of the two gentlemen,[35] each attempting to exceed each other in verbosity. The natives listened devoutly; the language was just as incomprehensible to them as the expectorations of the catechist had been for us earlier. They joined in the final hymn with unmistakable delight; in many cases the degree of their delight was expressed by a somewhat abnormal alignment of the axes of their eyes.

A further three days passed before we were completely ready for sea. We had taken on as much provisions and coal as the ship could contain, and in the quarters and on deck things were in a state of disorder. On the morning of the 17th we took delivery of seven strong Eskimo dogs which, snarling fiercely, immediately declared war on the Newfoundlanders and behaved in unruly fashion, like a pack of wolves. In a tightly closed phalanx they charged with bared teeth against their civilized cousins; howling, they lunged at them and vigorous applications of the whip were required to separate the bitter antagonists, which rolled around furiously on the deck. In order to prevent the further spilling of innocent blood the new arrivals were tied with lines, but unconcerned as to the possible consequences they chewed through them, and hence the Eskimo Joseph was obliged to inflict the traditional punishment: he immediately tied their mouths shut, which forced them to breathe only through their noses. This they did, with obvious discomfort.

It was only with reluctance that we took our leave of our obliging hostess, the friendly inspector and the colonial administrator's family, in whose midst we had spent many a pleasant hour. Shortly before we weighed anchor *Congress*'s commander came aboard with the two gentlemen of the cloth; as a pleasant distraction pious prayers again rang out; seen in their own right they were neither striking nor entertaining. A further pleasure lay in store for us, one in which one might scarcely expect to participate in Greenland. Instead of alleviating the bitterness of parting with a full glass, the good captain of the corvette found another salve, which he poured onto our stricken hearts in generous doses during the hour of parting. After the entire crew had paraded under arms, including Mrs. Hannah and her lovable little daughter, Captain Davenport took up his position, sure of victory, on the afterdeck and slipped his right hand into his bosom while the assemblage watched him, full of misgivings. And from the depths of his pocket he pulled a roll of paper covered with writing, like a letter. His heinous intention of giving a speech was barely comprehensible, but it became reality as he cleared his throat solemnly, as is the custom of orators. But the words flowed slowly; long pauses for effect separated them and their content was meagre in amount. At a lectern or in a public meeting the speaker would have been effectively shouted down, but here one had to listen with a pleasant expression to the utter nonsense as he admonished us to be well-behaved and virtuous.[36]

A boat that came alongside brought the Eskimo pilot; he was carrying two bundles, one addressed to Hall and the other to me. Mine contained elegant gloves made of snow-white skins. With a mixture of delight and sadness I watched as some of the carnations, grown with such difficulty, and which we had been admiring shortly before, as we took our leave, fell out of the paper. The anchor chain rumbled and the steam boiler hummed dully; the boat moved away, carrying the manuscript of a speech, a corvette captain and two clergymen back to their own vessel. The sound of the whistle rang out shrilly; the ship, free of her fetters, got underway, and a few minutes sufficed to take us to the entrance to the harbour.[37]

Only once did the vessel stop in her course; once we had dropped the pilot she pushed on northward without stopping. Undulating masses of cloud hovered around the tops of the dark basalt cliffs, down whose faces foaming streams roared, rushing down the steepest of the slopes and uniting as a fine spray with the sea which played along the coast in a light green colour. Here the water was almost fresh and its temperature higher than that of the air; it turned out to be poor in pelagic organisms, which avoided it because of its low salinity.

To the west there appeared gullied mountain ranges with gleaming coronets of snow; their shapes possessed a weird savagery. The gullied flanks of the rocks towered menacingly into the milky, hazy air, which shimmered like opals. It took some time before we fully realized that this was not really land but one of those deceptive mirages that have deceived many an explorer into drawing coastlines on a map, only to find them later refuted by influential voices. The distance at which the blue mountain front appeared to lie from us could in the most favourable case have been scarcely more than 30 n. miles at an approximate estimate; despite this, a distance ten times greater than that separated us from the nearest land to the west.

For more than half an hour we were able to contemplate the fluctuating play of this *fata morgana*; then dark cloud masses drifted in front of the sun and cast their shadows on the apparition, which began to pale and disappear. Shortly afterward we spotted the triple reflections of two icebergs which swayed in the sky one above the other. Their movement, following the direction of the current under whose influence these glacier masses were drifting along, could easily be identified since the distance between the ship and the mirage was only a few miles. The mirages changed shape quickly, almost suddenly; now they would rise on massive plinths with almost vertical cliffs; now they seemed to tower boldly on spindly columns that swayed dangerously.

The mirage of the distant land mass again appeared but less clearly than previously and displaced somewhat farther south, as an extensive high plateau with blurred outlines, across which trembling movements ran. As the gentle east wind freshened, the unequal densities of the layers of air swaying over the sea were eliminated; the milky haziness of the atmosphere disappeared and the uplifting panorama of the Greenland coast appeared with wonderful clarity.

As the ship approached the Vaigat the number of icebergs, which thus far had been small, quickly increased; they increased the farther north we went, until we had passed the latitude of Omenak [Uummannaaq] Fjord. Simultaneously their height increased with increasing latitude so that involuntarily the idea of a southward-setting undercurrent obtruded itself. Given the large surface that these ice masses offer, their underwater parts representing about nine times the volume of that rising above the surface, it does not require a very strong current to move them; only a moderate velocity suffices to achieve this effect. It will have to be left to future travellers to confirm the existence of this undercurrent, since under the right circumstances prevailing north winds, which may well have been blowing, might equally well produce this peculiar distribution as the motive power of the water.

Shortly before noon next day we passed the dark headland of Svarte-Huk, thus crossing the 72nd parallel; toward evening we came in sight of the island of Kasorsoak, off which the sea broke foaming on two reefs; they were hidden to the eye and betrayed themselves only by the breakers. As we approached Upernavik harbour, whose entrance is so foul that almost every inbound vessel discovers new rocks, we gazed with concern at a fog bank that rose in the south and drifted toward us. The air quickly became foggy but we reached Sanderson's Hope in good time; this is a dark tower which rises sheer from the sea to a height of over 3000 feet from the western extremity of an island. We were then able to feel our way along between two small islands. After protracted, unpleasant manoeuvring we dropped anchor at 1.30 a.m. on the 19th.

Upernavik is built on a small island located at 72°46'N; 56°2'W, but its location is far from ideal. Like the climate of Lichtenfels, which

Fig. 8 Upernavik.

experiences a unique character due to the fogs of Davis Strait, the cold winds off Baffin Bay lower the air temperature here since the colony lies completely open to the west. The gneiss rocks of the coast are barely covered with vegetation at all; snowdrifts fill the valley troughs until late into high summer, and during the warmest month of the year the thermometer commonly drops below freezing. The houses and huts, 22 in number and occupied by about 60 people, rise about quarter of a mile from the shore. Not one of the government buildings, which are smaller than those in the other settlements we visited, possesses more than one storey. The church is unadorned and unprepossessing.

It was still quite early when Hall went ashore to the colony to arrange for enquiries to be made about Hans. The administrator[38] informed him that he was living in the nearby settlement of Prøven.[39] He had in the meantime exchanged his role as a great lover, which he had readily and successfully played at the time of Kane's expedition, for a more sober one. Whereas then all his senses and endeavours had been directed at winning the daughter of the headman of Etah, with whom he had fallen headlong in love, his ambition had now led him to assume the office of a teacher for the benefit of the population of Prøven. At the risk of robbing such and such a number of hopeful Eskimo children, eager for knowledge, of their source of wisdom, a boat was fitted out to fetch Hans. The administrator was so kind as to compose a long letter in Greenlandic, whereby he hoped to persuade Hans to accompany the expedition. By Greenlandic standards the conditions were extremely attractive; whereas his teaching position paid 25 Reichsthaler annually, his services aboard *Polaris* were to be rewarded at $25 American per month. Armed with this letter the boat left us shortly after noon.[40]

Our efforts to acquire skins were to be almost as unsuccessful here as in the other colonies; most usable skins had already been shipped. Ten sealskins and dog skins were all we acquired. As Mr. Elberg reported, reindeer hunting had ceased to be productive. A few years previously wolves had suddenly appeared, probably immigrants from the American coast that had found their way across Davis Strait, and these now made the grazing areas of the district unsafe. The reindeer had fled north and south. According to Rink, during the 1850s the export of reindeer skins had run on average at 942; now the natives of Upernavik got barely 20, and these they kept.

At the official residence on shore, things looked lively. Dr. Rudolph, who had been the colony's administrator for a long time, intended returning to Denmark. *Julianehaab*, which was to take him back home, was lying in the harbour and signs of packing were still very much in evidence. Mr. Elberg, the new administrator, was just moving in. In the evening Upernavik's people of note assembled at the government building to assist the departing administrator in demolishing various drinks, since the old gentleman's cellar still contained a good number of bottles whose contents, in his view, were too valuable to be exposed to the dangers of a sea voyage.

Next day (20 August) the boat returned from Prøven. It was towing a kayak; Hans was on board, along with his family. As we had suspected, the hero nourished the inconsiderate intention of being separated from neither his spouse nor his offspring; only in exceptional cases does an Eskimo travel without his dependants. Hans did not consider a North Pole journey anything extraordinary, since he had already played a prominent role in two arctic voyages of discovery. He refused to see that his brown wife and their children were extremely unwelcome extras on such an undertaking. Only reluctantly did Hall agree to increase the complement by four useless mouths. But in the worst case Mrs. Merkut could be useful in making winter clothing, the material for which was still protecting reindeer, bears and seals from the cold. One could perhaps guess what the children might be useful for; their round, well-fed faces indicated a very well-developed talent for eating.

Apart from his family Hans had brought the entire apparatus of a Greenlandic household with him. The inevitable soapstone lamp was accompanied by a spacious sealskin tent; then metal pots appeared, a sledge, linen of extremely dubious appearance, lances, harpoons, hunting lines, carpenter's tools, all crazily mixed together. Finally there was a number of young pups that had been hidden in the depths of the kayak. If it had looked quite untidy on deck previously, the appearance of the deck with the new additions was almost comical. Hans, in the midst of the crying ranks, was trying to establish order but his efforts had less than the desired effect. Then Morton,[41] whose devoted companion Hans had been during the Kane expedition, came aboard. "How do you do, Hans. Do you recognize me?" he asked. Hans turned round but immediately resumed his important activities and muttered between his teeth "Me not know you." It was not until Morton reminded him of various events of the expedition that something began to dawn in his memory. But it became full daylight only when he asked the Greenlander to show him his right hand, which bore a large scar, traces of a powder explosion.[42]

With this new addition the ship's complement had been completed. The muster-roll[43] read: C.F. Hall, Commander of *Polaris*; Sidney O. Budington, sailing-master and ice master; H.C. Chester, First Officer; William Morton, Second Officer; R.W.D. Bryan, astronomer; Friedrich

Meyer, meteorologist; George E. Tyson, Assistant navigator; Emil Schumann, Chief Engineer; Alvin A. Odell, Second Engineer; Johannes Booth and Walter Campbell, stokers; John Herron, steward; William Jackson, cook and Nathaniel J. Coffin, carpenter.

To these should be added the seamen: Friedrich Anthing, Noah Hayes, Heinrich Hobby, Gustav Lindquist, Joseph Mauch and Hermann Siemens.[44] In addition there were the hyperboreans: Joseph, his wife Hanna and Pannik and the Hanseatic[45] group consisting of Hans, his wife Merkut (needle),[46] Josephine, beautiful Suschen[47] and the hopeful Tobias.

According to Kane, Hans was a lad of 19 in 1853 and hence he was now 37. Time had changed him; his wide, brown face bore the unmistakable traces of great anxiety. Unless he was totally stupid he was able to conceal his emotions in masterly fashion; his expression remained the same in both grief and joy, and rarely did his features display a smile. He was of average height for an Eskimo and was of powerful, somewhat thickset build, and wore native Greenlandic dress. We could never fathom what had made him play the Romeo in Etah since Mrs. Merkut, as she appeared now, was definitely ugly, small and as filthy as a hoopoe.[48] Perhaps she possessed a beautiful Eskimo soul, appreciation of which was beyond our comprehension; perhaps at that time, when Hans was in his *Sturm und Drang* period, she was an arctic beauty. Now she had faded completely; her expressionless features were devoid of any vitality; the expressionless, almond eyes, above which arched slanting eyebrows, appeared to be cut from black velvet. Her hands and feet were extremely delicate, but all the rest of her components were so angular that she could be expressed in angular degrees with mathematical precision, with only a small probable error.

Josephine, who was about 10 years old, might be seen as a younger version of her mother and perhaps gave one valid grounds for drawing conclusions as to how the latter may have looked in her youth. Six-year-old Tobias, a pretty, lively lad, bore little resemblance to his parents; he was distinguished by a certain cleanliness and was always busy exercising his jaw muscles: hardtack, meat or dried fish seemed to be equally welcome to him. Little Susanne was a different matter; although she was almost three years old she fed almost exclusively on her mother's milk. When she was not suckling she sat happily in the hood on her mother's back and looked out so calmly and innocently on the world that one could have kissed her. The only thing was that Mrs. Merkut's clothing possessed a unique aroma which is hard to describe. Moreover, the mother usually washed her daughter with her tongue instead of with a sponge and the thought of this subhuman cleansing procedure had a definitely repugnant effect.

Every space aboard ship was filled either with people or with dogs, supplies, coal or other items that one needs on a long voyage; hence we really had to rack our brains to think of where the Hanseatics could be accommodated. Chester, who always knew what to do in a difficult situation, had some space cleared in the starboard passageway in the deck house. It was not long before Mrs. Merkut had spread her greasy skins on a sort of podium consisting of barrels covered with planks. The family was to live there for an unspecified time; the spot was beautifully warm due to its proximity to the boiler, and if it was not exactly cosy it was at least more comfortable than the interior of a Greenlandic hut.

Once we had taken 12 powerful dogs on board, we had everything that Upernavik had to offer us. Nearby *Julianehaab* lay at anchor, the last Danish government vessel that would call at the West Greenland coast this year. Dr. Rudolph had taken passage aboard her. He took leave of the population of the colony with tears in his eyes; it was a difficult parting for him, and his hunch did not betray him, when he told us that nostalgia for the North would probably drive him back here again. As I learned from a letter, he could not stand it in Denmark for longer than a year, then returned to Greenland.

In order to respond to the civilities of the authorities as far as we could, given our limited abilities, Hall made an offer to *Julianehaab*'s captain to tow his ship out of the harbour. We had scarcely made fast when the current swung the brig round and her jib-boom crashed across our deck with such force that several dead-eyes tore out. On the rebound it removed several feet of railing as a souvenir and seemed to cherish a strong desire to come in immediate contact with one of the boats. This was avoided purely by accident, although one of the davits received a hefty blow. Apart from a minor scratch *Julianehaab* had received no damage during this collision. Although we were entirely to blame for the collision, the brig's captain apologized with all the courtesy of a European, thanking us and consoling us. Then he set sail and was soon out of sight.

Since Mr. Elberg had promised to accompany us in order to assist us in buying a fairly large number of dogs, we quietly anchored again then went to bed, since it was 2.00 a.m. Almost another day passed before the amiable administrator was ready; at 10.30 p.m. on the 21st we were finally ready to put to sea. This was the most beautiful night that we experienced in civilized Greenland; the air was so calm that the smoke rings from the cannon that marked our farewell salute floated almost to the nearby shore without losing their shape. Whenever the whistle shrilled the low sun produced shimmering rainbows around the escaping steam.

We steamed away across a mirror-smooth sea amongst the confusion of islands, with Mr. Elberg's launch in tow. The crew of the small boat were lying happily on her deck, singing a seaman's song; otherwise all one could hear was the throb of the engine and the churning of the screw. The dark masses of smoke that escaped from the funnel floated almost motionless over our wake; white heaps of cloud that floated in isolation in the sky were reflected in the sea, like ice floes that floated in the deep. As the sun sank lower a clear alpenglow played around the snowy peaks to the south; a light purple bordered the pinnacles of the icebergs and the high faces of the Upernavik Glacier, while a deep, dark indigo blue coloured the rocky cliffs. The clear air made the red appear intense, like burning brands; it blazed so that when one's eye moved quickly to one side, it perceived the extensive snow surface to the east as being tinted beryllium-green.

Occasional petrels cruised around the ship in easy flight; occasionally they landed fleetingly to catch one of the small jellyfish that inhabited the sea in thousands. The shores of the islands that we were passing were terrifyingly barren, but the superb lighting compensated abundantly for the neglect that their shapes had suffered; they appeared with sharply profiled outlines, and the abrupt alternation between light and shadow produced a mood in the landscape which, had some artistic genius conjured it on canvas, would have appeared exaggerated to anybody who had not observed similar effects for himself.

Around midnight the ship stopped near the island of Kingiktok; Hall and the administrator rowed ashore in one of the boats.[49] An umiak full of natives came alongside; they climbed out and visited us on board. Several dozen murres were hanging from the mast, birds we had shot in the course of the afternoon. The Greenlanders took possession of these and ate them as quietly and composedly as if they belonged to them; they barely took enough time to draw or pluck the birds. Nobody prevented them, since we were not greatly disposed to these birds and it seemed to give these sons of the wilderness great pleasure to gnaw the raw meat from the bones.

A figure clambered on deck from a small boat near the bowsprit, unannounced; tall and gaunt, the strange visitor staggered toward the bridge. He wore a top hat on his head, the first one we had seen for months; the coat that enveloped his shaky limbs was threadbare and the wide-striped pants had been frequently and carelessly patched; the heels of his boots had been worn down at an angle. Mr. Petersen—as he introduced himself to us—cherished a desire to examine the ship. Undoubtedly he had seen better days in Denmark; as he now greeted us, with a certain acting talent, he lacked only a brightly-coloured cravat and a stick to play the role of one of the tramps in "Lumpazivagabundus"[50] to great effect. He spoke English badly and smelled of bad tobacco, and once he had finished his inspection he asked for some discarded newspapers. His philanthropic intention of selling us a sleeping bag foundered on the unreasonably high price that he was asking.

Just as he was preparing to leave, Hall and the administrator returned; they brought 11 dogs and a number of sealskins. Mr. Elberg talked to Petersen like a father to his son, explained to him the unreasonableness of his demands, and we got the sleeping bag for a moderate price. Petersen pocketed his money; we continued on our way and at 6.00 a.m. we anchored at Tasiusaq, the most northerly settlement on earth. The position of this uttermost outpost of human civilization was 73°21'N; 56°5' 7"W, about 16 miles farther north than Hammerfest, the Ultima Thule of civilization in the northern hemisphere.

On shore the Danish flag waved in a gentle breeze. As our vessel doubled a steep-to headland we spotted the settlement, which consists of a single one-storey building that can make claim to be a dwelling

Fig. 9. Tasiusaq.

house. Nearby stand the blubber-house and the try-works; off to the side were 10 earth huts which serve as the bolt-holes for 14 Greenlandic families. The colonial tax collector, Mr. Jensen, a former member of the Hayes expedition, met us on the beach.[51] Hall tried to persuade him to accompany us but the two men could not come to an understanding. Jensen was the husband of a blonde Danish woman and the father of several children; if no other reason had persuaded him to decline the invitation his position of head of the family would perhaps have sufficed to keep him by his home fireside, since he and his family were the only Europeans living here.

There are certainly other motives, apart from the prospect of the extremely small financial reward, that are effective in causing people to locate their permanent residence in a zone where the short, raw summer is purchased at the cost of a night that lasts for more than two months and whose continual darkness provokes an almost pathological mood. The power of adaptation of an animal's extremely flexible system to the prevailing conditions is enormous, but the ability becomes less the higher the position of the organism on the ladder of living creatures. Since civilized man has scaled its momentary heights the difficulty of the task becomes greater for him, and must be all the greater, since for weeks and months he is deprived of the sunlight, which has controlled the development of his highest sense that allows him to assess the form and colour of the external world.

A more highly developed plant becomes sickly if it grows in a dark place, and the green of its leaves becomes pale; if animals are forced to live in the dark the sense of sight is the first to suffer; it deteriorates and ultimately may be lost completely. In that case the sense of touch immediately develops to an enhanced level; the function of one organ is partially transferred to another, as in the case of the blind, whose fingertips to a limited degree assume part of the activities of the eyes.

The prolonged darkness which prevents the eye from ranging into the distance has a serious effect on people, who turn in on themselves; everything concentrates on the inner life. Gentle sounds appear accentuated to the ear and a constant degree of tension can easily develop, similar to the prostration provoked after one has observed subjective light phenomena for quite a long time, or if one's hearing has been continually straining to distinguish fine variations in tone. It takes no small degree of mental strength, greater than the personal courage which easily helps one over dangers, to meet this tension and to successfully counteract it. In the case of a man it is perhaps the bent for the adventuresome that moves him to seek the unusual and that keeps him in a good mental mood; but for a woman the dark period must be extremely trying.

But these good people, relying entirely on their own resources, seemed to be living quite happily. They had lived in this remote spot for almost eight years, almost cut off from all communication with the outside world, and limited in terms of personal communication wholly to the Greenlanders.

Among the latter we saw few whose facial features betrayed any admixture of Danish blood; everything appeared closer to nature than in the other colonies we had visited. None of the huts possessed a stove; everywhere they burned blubber instead of the peat and coal that the Greenlanders living farther south used in addition to their lamps. As Jensen informed us, some individuals could still not decide to abandon their religion and their old customs; due to the absence of a missionary the people enjoy their traditional freedom. No church exists here and the way of life appears perhaps much more natural than in any other location in missionarized Greenland.

The area around Tasiusaq is almost more barren than the rocks of Upernavik. The gneiss rocks, which in many places form whalebacks, are generally totally bare; erratic boulders lie scattered here and there but nowhere could we detect glacial striations, perhaps because the rock weathers too quickly. On many of the cliffs, which drop vertically into the sea, almost horizontal bands, devoid of all vegetation, run across the dark crust of lichens that cover the rocks. Their width varied between half an inch and a foot, and unless we were badly mistaken, the lichen cover had been eliminated by icebergs sliding by. The exposed areas seemed to be scarcely older than a few years; perhaps they derived from the last ice breakup, since only the odd plant had begun to stretch its new growth across the edges of the bare patches. If drifting icebergs are laden with rock debris or if there are masses of rock embedded in them, projecting above the ice surface so that they come in contact with the bedrock, the result can easily be, in similar fashion, shallow grooves similar to glacial striae. The fact that the icebergs here often transport significant masses of rock is indicated by an impressive gneiss boulder that lay on the edge of a small plateau near the houses. The natives had suddenly noticed it after a vigorous ice breakup; it was about 15 feet long, 10 feet wide and about 6 feet high at its maximum. It lay almost 25 feet above sea level, was irregular in shape and displayed more-or-less sharp edges all over.

Apart from eider ducks and looms,[52] numerous snow buntings[53] were flitting around on the shore, breaking into flocks of 15 to 20 birds in flight. They were probably preparing for heading for more southerly regions; individual specimens that we killed were as fat as quails in fall. Most of the adult birds were already well into the moult; with the exception of a dark tip their bills were a magnificently vivid orange. It was here that we observed our first puffins,[54] but unfortunately we managed to shoot only one bird, an adult male. The natives reported that the bird was rare; some of them appeared never to have seen it before and nobody knew where it nested.

Jensen was not disinclined to sell us dogs; although he was asking the highest possible price for them one could scarcely grudge him it, since we definitely wanted to acquire quite a large number of sledge dogs and this was the last opportunity that would offer itself. With few exceptions his older animals were well and powerfully built, but many of the younger ones were of mixed parentage; unfortunately their fathers had been representatives of the genus Canis that had come from Newfoundland and that combined in the most unfortunate manner the characteristics of various mongrels. Hayes had left them behind here when he visited Greenland several years before, but he had not contributed to the improvement of the strain. Apart from their dark colour the mixed-breeds had mainly inherited their massive bushy tails from their fathers. Their heads displayed almost the pointed shape of the Eskimo dog but their ears looked extremely strange. Usually the lower third of the ear stood upright, while the upper part hung down slackly. Their legs were definitely too powerful and shorter than the remaining proportions of the body required. About 20 of the best dogs were carefully selected and were immediately taken on board; we took care to focus our attention on powerful bitches in order to achieve good pups.

One of the Eskimos offered to supply us, for a moderate price, with several large purebred dogs whose owner lived on a nearby island. Hall promised to buy them and the native launched his boat to fetch them.

CHAPTER 5

Historical review

Bylot and Baffin. John Ross. Inglefield. Kane. Hayes.

The part that Americans have played in general in polar exploration has already been discussed in passing. It now remains only to examine briefly the various expeditions to the Smith Sound area as they relate to each other in order to do justice to them in full measure. For the flags of two nations meet here and the discoveries of Britain and America abut onto each other.

It cannot come as a surprise that the motives that usually influence the course of the history of discovery only occasionally achieve expression in widespread fashion in the discoveries of the Smith Sound region; the result is a vivid picture of the spirit of enterprise that has inspired the seafaring nations at different times.

Until the middle of the 17th century all expeditions, by sea or land, owed their origin exclusively to those natural lures which in part were concealed beneath the solid crust of our planet, and in part lay openly exposed. The discovery of Smith Sound occurred at the end of this period.

The demand for India's treasures, which provided the impetus for the northern through-passages, induced a number of English noblemen, in conjunction with other speculators, to outfit an expedition to search for the Northwest Passage. Under the command of Robert Bylot, at whose side William Baffin stood as pilot, the little barque *Discovery*, of only 55 tons burden, left the harbour of Gravesend on 26 March 1616. She was to penetrate along the west coast of Greenland through Davis

Strait to the 80th parallel; from there she was to swing southwest to the 60th meridian and then proceed "to the land of Yedzo."[1]

By 14 May the vessel was already in Davis Strait at 75°20'N, and a week later it dropped anchor in a bay in Davis's London Coast at 70°20'N. On the 30th the seafarers reached Hope Sanderson, the farthest point on the coast that Davis had reached in 1587; there they ran into extensive masses of ice which they broke through two days later. A violent headwind forced them to drop anchor in the middle of a group of islands to which they gave the name Women Islands, on account of the Eskimo women who stayed behind there while their men took flight as quickly as possible at the sight of the strangers. Keeping the Greenland coast constantly to starboard they then steered on northward; running into ice again they anchored at 73°45'N in a sound which they named Horn Sound because they acquired numerous "narwhal horns" from the natives there.

When they spotted somewhat more open water on 18 June, they continued their northward course and on 1 July, at 75°40'N, they reached an ice-free sea, the sight of which inspired them with new hope since Baffin now believed he could definitely find the passage he sought. A day later, at 76°35'N, they sighted a high headland, which they named after Sir Dudley Digges; 12 leagues farther north they discovered a wide sound which they named Wolstenholme Sound after another of the enterprise's patrons. On 4 July, at 77°30'N, they ran into a strait which they named Whale Sound because of the numerous whales that frequented it. Seeking shelter from the stormy weather, the ship dropped anchor in a small embayment of the coast but soon had to put to sea again to seek safety and passed the Hakluyt Islands next day. To the north of them they spotted a sound which extended beyond the 78th parallel. According to Baffin this area was very remarkable in one respect since "the magnetic needle displayed the greatest variations ever observed at any point, namely 5 points of 56° westerly variation." The strait was named Sir Thomas Smith Sound and the islands lying on its meridian the Carey Islands.

Since they were faced with ice preventing them from penetrating farther north they swung southwest, favoured by a fresh breeze. When the fog rose on 10 July the ship was close inshore, and they discovered

Sir Alderman Jones Sound, near which a boat attempted unsuccessfully to land; a violent storm thwarted each attempt to reach shore. Hence the discoverers turned south, but since hopes of finding the long-sought passage were disappearing day by day, they prepared to return home and on 30 August they reached England again.

Never before had any seafarer been so favoured by fortune in the Arctic Ocean as *Discovery*'s bold commander; on the memorable 4th of July he had reached the highest latitude attained till then west of Greenland, one which would not be surpassed for centuries.

Unfortunately the memory of this seamanlike feat was besmirched in an irresponsible fashion by the blatant partiality of the geographer, Barrow, who believed only in the discoveries made by officers of the British Navy.[2] Even if Baffin's manuscript reports, still preserved in the British Museum, did not effectively take the edge off the despicable slanders aimed at him and Bylot, as we will see, the next voyage by Englishmen definitely reinstated the good name of English heroes of the sea.

The tumult of war that disturbed all the European nations at the start of this century, or at various times dragged them into direct involvement, had barely died away when exploration of the North was again taken up. The British whalers, who pursued their prey in various parts of the northern seas, for three years in a row brought back such favourable reports on the condition of the ice and the navigability of those seas that the British government took the decision to send out two expeditions. Independently of each other they were to penetrate to high latitudes in order to effect the Northwest Passage, one via Davis Strait, the other via the Greenland Sea.

For us only one of these expeditions is relevant, the one that followed in *Discovery*'s wake and that sailed from England on 25 April 1818 under the command of John Ross.[3] It consisted of two superbly outfitted vessels, *Isabella* and *Alexander*, the former commanded by Ross himself, the latter by Lieutenant Parry. On 1 June the ships entered Davis Strait and made their way along the coast of West Greenland; they crossed the 70th parallel on the 22nd, after having been beset by ice the day before, and penetrated slowly northward. The officers occupied themselves with a quick survey of the coast; they found its longitude in individual spots to be placed almost 10° too far east.[4] They slowly approached the area of Baffin's and Bylot's discoveries. On the evening of 17 August they spotted *Discovery*'s Cape Dudley Digges; the next afternoon they passed Wolstenholme Sound, to which Ross sent off a boat, but fog came down and forced it to turn back before it could reach land. When it cleared up around 9 o'clock the Carey Islands came in sight; they too agreed with Baffin's description. The sea was more free of ice than they had seen previously, and it was only a rising northerly wind that prevented them from putting in to the islands. Cruising in their vicinity during the night, at 8.00 a.m. on the 19th the ships found themselves off the most westerly cliffs of the group and immediately set a northeast course in order to investigate Wolstenholme Sound more closely. Once Ross had convinced himself that he could not penetrate farther in this direction he returned to the islands to take aboard the officers who had been left behind on an ice floe to make astronomical observations.

At midnight they reached the highest latitude attained by the expedition. The most northerly position reported by Ross was 76°54'N at 74°20'W; but since this was not based on an astronomical observation, it may be somewhat too high or too low. Be that as it may, the 77th parallel that Bylot and Baffin boldly sailed across was not passed by Ross despite his two powerful warships. The expedition was touched with a stain of shame which would only be effaced by Parry in a bold deed the following year.

Smith Sound was sighted but Ross described it as a cul-de-sac and on his chart conjured up ghostly mountain ranges which, towering dark and defiant against the sky, barred the way north. Jones and Lancaster sounds suffered a similar fate; both ended in mountainous mirages.[5] The ships returned to England on 30 October.

This inglorious expedition was not totally without result, although it had totally failed to achieve its actual goal. Clearly its greatest success lay in the fact that it caused Britain to set further enterprises on foot that would be epoch-making for the geography of the Far North and would greatly expand our knowledge of the spatial extent of the north coast of America and the islands lying off it within a very short time. In the narrower sense their successes were the discovery of the red snow which gave its name to the Crimson Cliffs,[6] and of the northern band of

Eskimos whose wanderings extend into Smith Sound, various deep-sea soundings and the survey of some stretches of coastline.

To come back to Baffin, his chart has unfortunately gone missing, but Petermann has reconstructed the course of that earlier voyage and has plotted the run of the coast according to the descriptions in the old manuscript.[7] A comparison of this chart with the representation of Ross's survey north of the 75th parallel cannot fail to evoke in us the greatest respect for the achievements of those old seafarers. While the geographical longitudes are uncertain, we should not forget that only the rarely occurring solar and lunar eclipses could be used for accurate determinations; that it was not until 60 years later that the eclipses of Jupiter's satellites were used, and even then they must have been relatively worthless for seafarers in determining longitude; that nautical instruments were of very imperfect quality, and that even the length of a degree of longitude at the equator of our planet had not even been determined with sufficient accuracy.[8]

At any rate, seen in totality the Bylot/Baffin survey gives a much truer picture of the northern inlets of the strait named after the latter than Ross's chart, which is impressively engraved in copper and looks artistic but unfortunately owes many of its interesting details to a monstrosity of the imagination that stuck mountain ranges where Ross scorned to penetrate.

When one compares his work critically with that of his successors, many of the locations he named completely lose their justification, and anybody who takes the trouble to follow the course of history will probably reach the conclusion that the headlands of Cape Isabella and Cape Alexander, flanking the entrance of Smith Sound, for example, certainly cannot be those on which Ross bestowed those names.

Although these latter had now remained the northern Pillars of Hercules for over two centuries, beyond which nobody had attempted to penetrate, they were still to maintain this position for more than a quarter century. In the meantime steam power had come into its own and had attained its rightful place at sea. As a consequence of the Ross expedition, in the late 1840s the British government had dispatched Franklin in order to solve the problem of the Northwest Passage. When anxiety started to develop as to his fate, a number of ships were dispatched to follow in his track and to render assistance. In 1852 Lady Franklin, Sir John's devoted wife, dispatched a small screw-steamer under the command of Commander Inglefield in order to take supplies to the British squadron languishing in Barrow Strait and then to search for the missing seafarers in the northern extensions of Baffin Bay.[9]

On the anniversary of Baffin's and Bylot's feat, on 4 July 1852, the ship left the Thames with a crew of 17 men, including the commander. On 20 August the explorers reached Cape York; next day they landed at an Eskimo settlement near the Peteravik Glacier; and two days later at North Star Bay, and on the 25th at Bardin Bay; from there they pushed on to Smith Sound, where on the 27th they reached the latitude of 78°28' 21".

In so doing Inglefield had surpassed Bylot's and Baffin's highest latitude. Ahead of him lay an apparently ice-free sea, but he felt himself obliged to turn back, since the weather was violently stormy, the season was already far advanced and his small vessel was not equipped for a wintering.

He plotted the most northerly land that he sighted on the east side of the sound at about 79°32'N;[10] he represented it as a projecting cape which he named after Frederick VII of Denmark. His most northerly point on the west side, at about the same latitude and about 79°W longitude, he named Victoria Head. A small island which, in passing, was plotted midway between these two points, but which was never seen again, was named after Louis Napoleon.

If one considers that Inglefield spent barely 14 days in the area of his discoveries, one can only be amazed at the body of valuable material he and his scientific companion, Sutherland, collected during this short time. Geography in the narrow sense, was enriched by the survey of 180 miles of new coastline; geophysics by a complete weather record as well as by hydrographical observations; and the descriptive natural sciences by collections from all three realms.

The discoverers could head for Jones Sound, quite satisfied, on 1 September, and penetrated quite far along it; on the 2nd they ran into Lancaster Sound and by 10 November the little steamer was again lying at anchor at Peterhead.

The first expedition that penetrated into Smith Sound prepared for a wintering, and that wintered at a higher latitude than ever before, sailed under the American flag; its commander was Elisha Kent Kane, an officer of indomitable energy, whose health was so badly undermined by this arctic campaign that he died shortly after his return home.[11]

While Henry Grinnell[12] had covered the costs of the first American Franklin Expedition on his own, the subsequent enterprise took place through his and Mr. Peabody's[13] efforts. The United States Navy, to which Kane belonged, provided 10 men, as well as part of the inventory.

Including the commander, the crew of the brig *Advance* totalled 18; she sailed from New York harbour on 30 May 1853. After a short sojourn in Newfoundland, on 1 July she called at Fiskernæsset and on the 17th at Upernavik in order to buy furs and sledge dogs and to secure the services of a Dane and an Eskimo. Ten days later the explorers had put Wilcox Point behind them, the most southerly bounding cape of Melville Bay, into which they next headed. Along the coast the fast ice was so rotten that it was threatening to disintegrate. Hence Kane opted to swing out toward the middle of Baffin Bay instead of sticking to the usual course along the ice edge until the so-called "Middle Ice" prevented his further progress.[14] Then he headed for Cape York, which he rounded ten days later; on 7 August he was pushing into Smith Sound. As far as the eye could see open water revealed itself to the north, as seen from the masthead; a very promising swell came from the same direction; fresh winds blew alternately from the south and west.

Apart from the tedious work involved in towing the ship through heavy ice masses, the voyage had proceeded splendidly; the sight of the open sea filled the explorers with cheerful hopes. But these high hopes were only of short duration; the wind swung around and blew sharply out of the north; as they reached the Littleton Islands a belt of pack ice appeared a short distance beyond. Kane erected a cairn on the larger of the islands and in it deposited news of the expedition's progress thus far. He had a boat and provisions cached on a headland on the coast, so that they would not be entirely helpless in case the ship lost the battle with the ice.

If they wanted to push on farther they had to force the ice barrier; the first attempt was made during the night (?) of the 7th;[15] the ice was

5: Historical review

117

heavy, apparently several years old, and progress was limited. About 40 n. miles north of the spot where the depot had been left the ship encountered insurmountable obstacles; it was beset in the ice and was saved from being beached on the nearby coast only by an eddy that seized it. During the following three days the explorers were in a serious situation; in constant danger of losing their vessel, on the 13th they finally succeeded in fleeing westward. But here too the ice was closer than had been expected; the days were becoming colder and there was growing fear that they would be overtaken by freeze-up and become beset, defenceless, for the winter.

Under conditions that would have totally discouraged people of less pronounced willpower, on 29 August *Advance* pushed north to a latitude of 78°43'N, the highest latitude she was to reach. The damage she suffered was not insignificant; the railings lay partially in splinters, the bowsprit was smashed, and one of the boats demolished; she had lost more than 600 fathoms of anchor chain as well as one of the anchors. The crew laboured on indefatigably until 1 September, but all further attempts remained fruitless. The brig was steered into one of the bays on the coast; in the meantime, accompanied by some of his seamen, Kane advanced north by boat and sledge in order to reconnoitre ice conditions. From a height of 1100 feet he could scan the sea to a latitude of 80°; it was frozen fast, and numerous icebergs towered above the grey ridges of shattered ice.

With the bitter realization that further progress by ship was impossible, the pioneers started back to the brig. The situation of the harbour seemed quite favourable; Kane decided to make his winter quarters here and had the men start preparations without delay. Later he dispatched a sledge party to the north, whose task was to establish a supply depot at the farthest possible point on the coast, in order to support further journeys which it was planned to undertake in the course of the coming spring. Two further, smaller expeditions were undertaken into the interior in order to reconnoitre the terrain, and to a point on the coast to the north in order to establish an automatically recording thermometer.

Kane named his winter quarters Rensselaer Harbour; an observatory was immediately erected on shore; its position was 78°37' 04"N; 70°52'45"W. Never before had an expedition equipped with instruments wintered at such a high latitude, and the magnetic and meteorological observations that the Franklin searchers made during their sojourn at Rensselaer Harbour could be seen as important contributions to geophysics; equally valuable was their long series of astronomical determinations of position.

The sun disappeared on 10 October; 120 days passed before it reappeared above the horizon, since it was blocked by a chain of mountains. Thanks to the prudence of the courageous commander and of the doctor, the state of health of the crew during the testing period of the darkness was excellent. By contrast, death raged terribly among the dogs, 57 of which died; the magnificent pack was reduced to a few animals. Since the execution of Kane's plan of operations depended almost exclusively on using these draft animals, it was a lucky stroke of fate that in April a band of Eskimos visited the harbour and that they were able to provide a number of powerful dogs.

Low temperatures thwarted the dispatch of the provisions sledges until mid-March; it was not until the 19th that a small party set off northward in order to establish a depot ten days' journey from the ship. In the meantime, preparations for the main expedition were put in hand on board; its aim was to search for traces of Franklin in the northern continuation of the sound.

Three of the men returned unexpectedly on the 31st. Their condition was alarming: they were barely able to speak due to frostbite and hunger, and it was some time before they could explain what had become of their companions. They had left them behind amongst the hummocks somewhere to the north of the brig; four of them were incapable of walking and perhaps had frozen to death. A fifth man, in better condition, had stayed behind to look after them. As they were getting underway to look for help, a violent blizzard had been blowing. This was all the exhausted men would say, having risked their own lives in order to send help to their endangered comrades.

Kane immediately had a sledge made ready; the one man of the three who seemed least affected was wrapped in buffalo robes and lashed to the sledge in order to act as guide. As Kane set off, with nine men on the traces, the thermometer was recording −43°; the utmost haste was necessary if the men's lives were to be saved. Unfortunately

Ohlsen, who lay fatally exhausted on the sledge, began to suffer from hallucinations. He had made a 50-hour march without any food and now he began to ramble and was no longer capable of answering questions directed at him.

The sledge party now moved at random across the waste of ice. Since there was no trace of the tent, when the party had been on the move for 18 hours Kane ordered his men to spread out and to leave the sledge behind. The sharp eye of the Greenlander, Hans, detected a trail. He and Kane followed it; after several hours they spotted a flagpole from which the union flag and the colours of the Freemasons were flying; close by lay the tent, detectable only by these signals since it was completely buried in fine snow. The men were still alive but their hands and feet were frozen and they were unable to move from the spot on their own. After Kane and his party had rested for two hours the four men were sewn into skins & loaded on the sledges, and then they started back to the brig at top speed. The temperature dropped to −48° and the men grabbed handfuls of snow to quench their burning thirst. They were all afflicted by the irresistible desire for sleep, which intense cold usually causes; only the energetic arrival of their valiant leader saved them from freezing to death.

Having allowed themselves no more than four hours' sleep, they reached the ship after an absence of 84 hours. Two of the men died shortly after they got back; most of the others lost parts of their extremities which had to be amputated due to frostbite. They all suffered from disturbing mental symptoms which bordered on temporary insanity and were forced to stay in bed for quite a long time.

It was the end of April before the state of the men's health had sufficiently improved that a new sortie could be attempted. A small supply party pushed on ahead; then on the 27th Kane set off northward with one dog sledge and a single companion. The ice was almost inconceivably impassable and the going was very difficult. On the 29th he caught up with the sledge with the provisions, but instead of improving the going became rougher. Scurvy broke out among the men; one after another they became incapable of walking and the expedition collapsed again. Kane himself was in such bad shape that he had to be carried over the worst sections of the route by the strongest of his men alternately, while he rode on the dog sledge on the passable sections. When they again reached the ship on 14 May the heroically brave leader collapsed, senseless.

Under the prevailing circumstances he had no time to be sick; his keen spirit of initiative was constantly thinking of new ways of attaining the expedition's objective. Since the ice to the north had shown itself to be almost impassable, on 20 May he dispatched a dog sledge to cross Smith Sound south of the winter quarters and to push north along the western shore. Command of the small expedition was entrusted to Dr. Hayes;[16] only one seaman accompanied him.

Instead of following Kane's instructions he set a northerly course and was fortunate enough to approach the coast at 79°24'N on the 25th. After having overcome almost inconceivable obstacles the travellers were afflicted with snow blindness; on the 26th Hayes's companion became incapable of walking; next day the dogs became exhausted; then the sledge collapsed. Combatting these accumulating problems, the explorers continued their journey as far north as their reduced condition would permit. At the 69th meridian they reached their highest latitude on the 27th; according to a noon sun-shot it was at 79°45'. Occupying themselves with a sketchy survey of the coast, they immediately started back and reached the brig again after an absence of 12 days on 1 June.

By this journey they had obtained a glimpse of the disposition of the coast of Grinnell Land as far as the 80th parallel, but the west coast of Greenland still remained to be unveiled. Despite all their efforts it had not been possible to determine the northern limit of the great Humboldt Glacier, that massive wall of ice which, beginning at Cape Agassiz, stretched north beyond the 79th parallel as far as the eye could see in crystalline cliffs several hundred feet high.

On 4 June, Morton was dispatched to solve this problem. Once he had renewed his supplies, on the 18th he left the depot on McGary Island with one dog sledge and the Greenlander Hans. A party which had been detailed to accompany him returned to the ship from that point, while the two men set off northward early in the morning, at 12.30 a.m. They soon found themselves in the labyrinth of icebergs that on previous occasions had obstructed the progress of Kane's parties. They were often obliged to find a way out of the cul-de-sacs into which they had blundered; they often had to bridge wide cracks in order to advance. The difficulties were compounding but the men refused to be discouraged; trustingly they continued on their way. On the morning of the 20th they sighted land to the west, a sign that the sound was narrowing here, since until now they had constantly been moving along within sight of the great Humboldt Glacier without spotting the opposite coast. An observation at noon on the 21st revealed that they had passed the 80th parallel by a mile; on both sides the shores of the channel were still in sight. They had reached the end of the glacier; boldly rising headlands formed the continuation of this picturesque coast.

Once the travellers had cached half their provisions in a rock crevice in order to lighten the weight of the sledge, they continued on their way. Toward evening open water appeared in the distance; flocks of eider ducks, geese and dovekies flew out over their heads; the calls of glaucous and ivory gulls rang out from the nearby cliffs. The ice cover was becoming rotten; it bent under the weight of the sledge; the alarmed dogs refused to go any farther and only with great effort were they able to rescue the sledge from sinking. Heading eastward, after several hours the two men reached the coast and, at the same time, a safer route. During the 22nd they covered 15 miles; they managed to scale the high belt of ice which edged the coast; opposite them the coast of Grinnell Land still appeared to extend north in a straight, uninterrupted line. Delayed by a violent storm, they were unable to continue their journey until the morning of the 23rd. They had barely covered six miles when the fast ice ended. They left their sledge behind; they made their way onward with difficulty across floating pans and floes. Once they had advanced about four miles under these conditions they spotted a projecting cape and an island to the north; then they started back to their sledge.

Early on the 24th they set off to renew their attempts, but the difficulties turned out to be greater than on the previous day: they were able to overcome certain sections only at danger to their lives. The going became increasingly dangerous; finally the two men were forced to battle for latitude step by step on a narrow ice foot along sheer cliffs. The fast ice belt had disappeared completely; only occasional floes drifted around on the dark waves that broke thunderously against the rock faces at the travellers' feet. A heavy swell rolled in from the north, betraying the proximity of extensive areas of open water.

They were unable to reach the headland they were trying to attain and which they named Cape Constitution. Hans became exhausted and stayed behind; near another headland (Cape Independence) Morton climbed an elevation about 500 feet high. Ahead of him lay an apparently ice-free open sea; dark rain clouds hung over the horizon to the northwest. Far to the north, losing itself in the distance, stretched the serrated coast of Grinnell Land; Morton estimated its farthest point, Parry Point, to lie at 82°30'N latitude.

Having once again risked an attempt at rounding the headland, on the 25th the travellers returned to the sledge. Next day a noon sun-shot revealed the latitude of their campsite to be 80°20'N; since, according to Morton's estimate they had advanced a further 20 miles north from there, the highest latitude they had reached was 80°40'N.[17] Near the camp he observed a strong southerly current; a violent north wind swept down the channel, but there was no sign of ice.

Around 4.00 p.m. on 26 June the two men started back to the ship, which they reached on 4 July after a strenuous hike. Had Kane contented himself with unbiasedly publishing Morton's sober report on which the above description is based, the further progress of the exploration history of the Smith Sound area would probably have turned out differently—perhaps even if Rink's excellent article (Rink 1858) had been given the recognition it deserved.

With a pronounced taste for the fantastic, which can be recognized on almost every page of his travel account, Kane clothes Morton's observations, with the inspiration of a poet, in a colourful, fantastic guise, which influenced less critical readers into mistaking the image for reality. If one wanted to belittle his merits, one would be guilty of a flagrant injustice; but it was certainly no benefit to geography that after his return he announced the existence of an open polar sea which, kept open by the warm waters of the Gulf Stream, allegedly washed the north coast of Greenland.

With Morton's sledge journey the geographical results of the expedition came to an end; thereafter there were no discoveries of any significance to report, but there was a new chapter in its history of suffering, rich in examples of bitter strokes of fate and bold deeds. The ship was supplied with provisions for only 1½ years; more than a year had already passed since they had put to sea and June was now drawing to a close, but the brig still lay in the winter harbour surrounded by impenetrable ice.

On 12 July Kane set off on an expedition in an open boat with a small hand-picked crew in order to inform the commanders of the British squadron of his situation. He was aware that a British vessel was stationed in the vicinity of Beechey Island at the entrance to Wellington Channel;[18] under the most favourable conditions the shortest route there was more than 400 n. miles. After a trip filled with hardships he returned to the ship on 6 August, having achieved nothing. Heavy masses of pack ice had prevented him from pushing south of Cape Parry; an apparently solid barrier had barred any further progress.

Since there was no prospect of freeing the ship from her shackles in 1854, they began to prepare themselves for a second wintering. It required more than ordinary courage to reconcile themselves to this idea since provisions and fuel were severely depleted and the resources offered by land and sea were limited. A small party[19] which tried to reach one of the Danish settlements in Greenland returned to the winter quarters several months after they had left it, having undergone indescribable sufferings. Their magnanimous leader welcomed them with open arms and shared the last things he possessed with the exhausted men.

As spring approached, he decided to abandon the brig, since it would have been more than foolhardiness to trust the whims of the ice and to wait for a favourable opportunity to free the ship from its fetters; moreover, the latter had been used as a source of firewood during the winter. On 17 May 1855, the Franklin searchers, equipped with sledges and boats, left their winter quarters. Due to his exertions one of the men died on the trail on 12 June; living almost exclusively from the results of hunting, the survivors reached the colony of Upernavik, 83 days after starting their adventure-filled journey; there they found a Danish brig whose commander agreed to take the shipwrecked travellers on board. In the meantime concern had been raised in the United States as to the expedition's fate. The government dispatched two warships to look for them;[20] they met Kane and his crew at Disko, took them aboard and brought them home on 11 October.

*****

The star that shone on Hayes's enterprise was not a lucky one.[21] The expedition left Boston harbour on 6 July 1860 on board the vessel *United States*, a schooner of 133 tons capacity and with a crew of 15 men, including the commander. It crossed the Arctic Circle on the 30th and next day sighted the coast of Greenland in the latitude of Disko.

The 5th of August found the explorers at the Danish settlement of Prøven, but since they were unable to procure the necessary sledge dogs there they called at Upernavik, dropping anchor there on the 12th. Here Hayes had to undertake the sad duty of burying the ship's carpenter; he had died of a stroke on the night of 11th–12th. Once this was accomplished and once the expedition had acquired a sufficient number of dogs through the offices of the colony's administrator, they signed on a further six men, including three natives. Shortly afterward the schooner was ready to put to sea.

The houses of the settlement were still in sight when the battle against the ice began; it covered the sea, with numerous icebergs of the most varied sizes and shapes. On the 21st the schooner called for a short time at Tasiusaq and two days later reached Melville Bay; 55 hours later it lay astern. The first heavy pack ice was encountered on the 25th, but it allowed the small vessel to pass unharmed, and on the 27th the ship was approaching the entrance to Smith Sound. Cape Alexander was passed without difficulty, but it was no easy task to reach the coast of Grinnell Land. Massive masses of pack ice were drifting down the Sound with the current; some of the old floes rose 10 feet above the water level and the channels between them were very narrow. The pack ice became closer and soon it seemed limitless—as far as the eye could see from the crow's nest,[22] there was no water to be seen to the north. Until now a stiff breeze had been blowing out of the northwest; it now strengthened to a gale, then grew to a hurricane and there was no alternative but to seek shelter under the coast. During the night of the 30th the wind swung into the east; the vessel was driven out of the sound by the force of the storm and dropped anchor near the east coast in 4 fathoms of water. Hayes was able to get a good picture of the ice situation from a cliff which may have been 1200 feet high. Near Cape Isabella a strip of water was revealed along the coast, but north of the cape an apparently solid mass of ice stretched without a break from coast to coast. If one wanted to penetrate through there, one would have to force this barrier; Hayes, intent on advancing, decided to attempt this last and only alternative.

The day was still not over when the ship got into a very serious situation. The anchors would not hold and a violent wind drove the vessel with full force against a grounded iceberg, and before her crew could rescue her the bowsprit and part of the railing had been smashed, one of the masts had snapped and the stern boat totally crushed. They succeeded, with great effort, in getting free of the iceberg; sail had to be set to reach the open sea. One of the sails was ripped by the storm and carried away. Despite this, on the morning of the 31st Hayes made an attempt to reach Cape Isabella, but after a few hours of strenuous work he had to abandon this effort.

The hurricane was again raging and again the battered vessel was driven out of the sound. Not satisfied with these various attempts, Hayes had the damage repaired as best as possible over the next two days, then made a further sortie. A shore lead appeared between Littleton Island and Cape Hatherton; the ship was towed north along it, then immediately penetrated into the first channel that appeared in the pack. After she had covered about 10 miles toward the northwest, the channels closed under the combined influence of a southerly wind and a strong current from the north; the vessel battled valiantly against the driving masses, but with little success. After further fruitless attempts they finally had to concede that the game was lost. On 6 September the ship dropped anchor in a small inlet in the coast which Hayes named Port Foulke, at 78°17' 39"N; 73°00'W, to start her wintering.[23]

If it were exclusively boldness and a spirit of enterprise that crowned polar voyages with success, Hayes must certainly have achieved great things, but fortune did not deign to smile on the explorers and despite all their persistence and sacrifice they did not surpass Inglefield's latitude.

An even crueller misfortune was to befall the expedition. At the start of the winter an epidemic wiped out the majority of the dogs; if new draft animals could not be found any further advance would be thwarted. At Christmas, Sonntag[24] decided to make a trip to the Eskimo settlements of Whale Sound, where he hoped to find replacements. He left the ship by sledge, accompanied only by the Eskimo, Hans;[25] he would return only as a corpse. In an attempt to cross a wide crack in the ice he fell into the water; by the time his companion could pull him out he was already incapable of speech and died before Hans could manage to dig a shelter for him in a snow bank.

If the purely geographical results of the expedition had been severely clouded by the unfavourable elements, the progress of the scientific work received a severe blow from the sudden death of Sonntag, who as astronomer and superb mathematician held great promise. Fortunately, prior to the onset of the winter night he had measured a baseline near the harbour and had begun a trigonometrical survey of the surrounding area; he had arranged a series of valuable pendulum experiments and had set up the instruments for the magnetic observations. The work could probably be continued by Hayes and some of his companions, but the guiding spirit was lacking.

The sun remained below the horizon for 130 days but the men spent the winter without any deleterious effects to their health. They succeeded in procuring new sledge dogs from the neighbouring natives and they were able to start preparations for a further journey north. Hayes left his winter quarters with two sledges on the morning of 16 March in order to investigate ice conditions. The sledges followed the coast for 7 days before they reached Rensselaer Harbour—in fact not very far away. The cold was intense, with the thermometer on one occasion recording −68.5°.

Whereas during the winter of 1853–54 a wide belt of level ice had girdled the coast, they now found only wildly rafted pressure ridges that rose to heights of 30 and 40 feet and significantly impaired their progress. Although Hayes and his native companions covered the entire distance on foot, it was grindingly hard work to get the sledges over the rough hummocks, sharp edges and impassable pressure ridges. The floes were piled mast-high in Van Rensselaer Harbour; there was no trace of the old expedition ship to be seen. Convinced of the need to search for a sledge route along the opposite coast, Hayes started back to the winter quarters, not much the wiser.

The final trip northward was not started until 3 April; persistently low temperatures had made it seem advisable not to start out earlier. All the necessary baggage was first hauled to Cairn Point, which was selected as a suitable relay point; then on the evening of the 3rd the travelling party left Port Foulke. Since the ship could not be left unattended, the crew which accompanied the sledges consisted of only 12 men; two sledges formed the vanguard, then followed a strong, iron lifeboat in which Hayes planned to sail the open polar sea. The men set off inspired by cheerful hopes, but the bad going and the constantly mounting obstacles soon depressed their cheerful confidence. After several fruitless attempts Hayes found himself obliged to abandon the transport of the boat across the sound, and to confine himself solely to the sledges.

The going was indescribably bad; every step had to be calculated ahead of time; unavoidable ice ridges, often over 100 feet high, had to be tediously clambered over. At times the party was unable to find a passage and had to seize axe and shovel in order to cut a route. Commonly tempting-looking cul-de-sacs forced them to turn back after fruitless work, in order to search for another route, which generally did not turn out to be any better. It was particularly discouraging that sometimes after a long, hard day's work the explorers could have fired a shot from the top of an ice pinnacle into their previous night's campsite. 25 days passed and they had barely reached the middle of the sound; this was sufficient cause to sap the energy of even the bravest.

But Hayes refused to be discouraged. If he wanted to push on, he would have to change his strategy. On 28 April he decided to continue the expedition with three of his strongest and most resolute companions, and to send the others back. With these few companions and two dog sledges he then pushed on. But the difficulties grew and the going became worse; it took them no less than 14 days to cover a distance of only 40 English miles. It was not until 11 May that they reached the coast of Grinnell Land, exhausted, and pitched camp at Cape Hawks. They had taken 31 days to cover a distance that, measured in a straight line, was only 80 English miles; they had been obliged to relay their loads, covering the same stretch often three or four times in a row. But now all these efforts were forgotten; the land beckoned here and they could hope for an improvement in conditions.

Of the 8 centners of dog food that Hayes still had in hand when he left the point at which his companions turned back, there were only 300 lbs. left; this could last for another 12 days at the most. The stop near Cape Hawks lasted only long enough to prepare a scanty meal, then the travellers continued on their journey. The ice along the coast was far from level, but incomparably better than out in the sound; in places the sledges were travelling between the steeply rising coastal cliff and an ice barrier about 50 feet high, which bounded a narrow strip of level ice. Without encountering any serious obstacles they continued their journey until the 15th; at that point one of the men, who had injured his leg, could no longer walk. So as not to slow their progress the man had to be left behind; another man stayed with him to look after him. With one companion Hayes pushed on indefatigably, making long marches and granting himself little rest; according to his report on the 19th he reached latitude 81°35'N; 70°30'W. Further progress was thwarted by thin ice. A wide lead, against whose edges dark waves were splashing, stretched out eastward from Lady Franklin Bay, widening like a large delta; it linked up with other leads until it merged with the open water beneath the "water sky" that hung over the northern and eastern parts of the horizon. The white, precipitous peak of a headland (Cape Union) stood out in blurred contours from the dark sky to the north, the most northern known land on earth, which the explorer plotted at 82°30'N latitude. Closer at hand, another bold cape (Cape Friedrich VII) stretched seaward, while south of it there rose another headland (Cape Eugenie) with snow-crowned peaks. Apart from the coast on which they were standing they could see no other land from a cliff 800 feet high.

Once the explorers had erected a cairn, in which they deposited a short report on the journey, at the most northerly point they had reached, they started on the return march; due to the lack of supplies and the rapid onset of the melt they had to make forced marches. On 3 June the small party reached Port Foulke safely, somewhat debilitated by the unpleasant hardships and privations, which had killed eight of the dogs. Hayes intended attempting another sortie with the ship at the end of the summer; but on closer investigation it turned out that the damaged vessel would not survive any further encounters with drifting ice masses. Hence he decided to return to Boston, to have the schooner repaired there and in the following year to penetrate Smith Sound, accompanied by a steamer. The observatory was left at Port Foulke, filled with provisions and ammunition, and the iron lifeboat on one of the neighbouring islands.

On 14 June the schooner left its winter quarters and first set a course for the coast of Grinnell Land, where Hayes himself landed. After a rapid voyage Upernavik was reached a month later; then the explorers called at Godhavn, and on 23 October they dropped anchor at Boston after an absence of 15 months and 13 days. But Hayes's plan to return to Smith Sound was not to be implemented; the Civil War, which had broken out in his absence, meant an untimely end to his hopes. Hayes himself joined the Army and he offered the ship, that had so bravely withstood the battle against the ice of the High Arctic, to the government as a gunboat.

CHAPTER 6

INTO UNKNOWN TERRITORY

Departure from Tasiusaq. Favourable ice conditions. Melville Bay. The coast. Paucity of bird life. Entrance to Smith Sound. Uneven distribution of glaciers. The east shore with a shore polynya. Landing at Cape Fraser. Inaccuracy of the maps. Discovery of a new land. Fog. An unsuccessful sounding. Fog again, and more ice. Repulse Harbour. Strong southerly current. Polaris *reaches her highest latitude. Advice against further progress. Course set to the west. Beset. Ice pressures; ship in danger. Landing of supplies on the ice. Southward drift. Out of the frying pan into the fire. At anchor.*

The history of discovery of the Smith Sound area falls naturally into three periods, which may be termed the Bylot-Baffin, Inglefield and Kane periods. From the early seventeenth century to the time of the Hayes expedition, adventurers and naval officers, philanthropists and men in the service of science had indefatigably gathered material to expand our knowledge of the region; our next task was to complete that knowledge.

Thick fog forced us to lie at anchor longer than we had intended. The weather did not permit us to get underway until 2.15 p.m. on 24 August.[1] Jensen acted as pilot; as soon as the ship was in safe waters, he took his leave of us.

Without having seen any more ice than occasional bergs or drifting floes here and there, which represented no significant obstacle, at noon next day we reached 75°56'N; 69°26' 5"W. We had crossed the dreaded Melville Bay in less than 24 hours; we had accomplished without the slightest effort what most of our predecessors had achieved only after a severe struggle. Thus far our voyage scarcely differed from a pleasure cruise.

At 1 o'clock[2] we passed Conical Rock about 12 n. miles off; it is a steep rock standing totally isolated, which provides evidence of the former extent of the coast. An hour later we rounded Cape Dudley Digges, where, according to our instructions, we were to build a cairn and leave news of the expedition's progress thus far.

Open water extended ahead of us; even a short stop might possibly have serious consequences; acting against our instructions we continued on our way.

To the north the Peteravik Glacier appeared, a gleaming river of ice which, reaching sea level, produces numerous icebergs, about 60 of which were drifting in the vicinity of Conical Rock. Few of them were covered with debris or boulders; over a distance of 12 miles we had noticed only three or four that showed signs of discoloration. Between the glacier and Cape Atholl the land was almost snow-free; the rock was traversed in various directions by white veins (feldspar?) which seemed to attain their greatest development approximately midway between the glacier and the cape.

Wolstenholme Island rises about 6½ miles west of Cape Atholl. If one approaches the cape from the south, Saunders Island, lying north of it, seems to connect Wolstenholme to the mainland in an elongated plateau. One feels that one is looking into a wide bay, until the cape bears about east. Then the separation of the individual massifs, in terms of perspective, eliminates any doubt that they are separate; one can see the entrance to Wolstenholme Sound, on whose north shore a Matterhorn-like tower (Cape Abernethy?) appears conspicuously; its height can probably be estimated at 3000 feet. Its summit is almost horizontally truncated, and round its edge oriel-like formations project; they drop vertically and give the impression of a low, cylindrical structure on the steeply rising cone, which probably consists of metamorphic rock, whereas the slab may be of volcanic origin.

A herd of about 30 walrus[3] was lying on a drifting ice floe. Reducing speed to less than half, we carefully tried to approach them. Even before we were in firing range the dark shapes became restless. A dull bellowing, probably uttered by the lookout, woke the sleeping animals;

they raised their heads, sniffing the air, and raised their clumsy bodies in sphinx-like fashion. When one large animal dived awkwardly into the water, some shots rang out from the ship. The herd humped to the edge of the floe in a wild stampede and hurled itself into the water. One of the stragglers was wounded but it escaped before we had time to launch a boat.

Passing between Wolstenholme and Saunders islands, around 8.00 p.m. we reached the entrance to Granville Bay, off which lie three small islands (Three Sister Bees). To the north a white strip extended east–west across the dark water. As we approached it around 9 o'clock it dissolved into a narrow barrier of rotten ice, which we broke through without any effort. The Carey Islands appeared vaguely to the west like misty apparitions, with grey masses of fog rolling around them; their outlines increased in definition only after we had rounded Cape Wechmar. The distant land to the south had dropped below the horizon; Cape Atholl rose like an island behind the sharply profiled islands we had recently passed.

Around 10 o'clock the ship was off Booth Sound, a multi-branched embayment in the coast whose panorama reminded one vividly of Kongsfjorden in Spitsbergen. The inlet was still bridged by last year's ice cover; dark mountain summits, separated by crevassed glaciers, surrounded the coast. The ice extended almost as far as Fitz Clarence Rock, a needle-like rock which rises approximately in the middle of the entrance. Flat floes drifted slowly by with the northward-setting tidal current. Only here and there did a dovekie, a kittiwake or an occasional eider duck show itself. We tried in vain to find an explanation for this striking poverty of the avifauna. The season was not yet far enough advanced to have driven the birds from this part of the Arctic Ocean. But even in the distance there were no flighting birds to be seen, although the open water could have been a superb congregating spot for migratory visitors.

At noon on the 27th, at a longitude of 73°44'W, we determined a latitude of 77°51'N. The ice still presented no obstacle, although we were within a few miles of the 78th parallel. To the north the outlines of Cape Alexander rose ahead of us while to the northwest Cape Isabella stretched far out to sea, partially enveloped in mist. Around 3.00

p.m. *Polaris* entered the notorious Smith Sound: a pleasant continuation of our pleasure-cruise. The lookout in the crow's nest searched in vain for ice. We pushed on amidst mutual congratulations, at a speed of 6–7 knots.

The Hanseatic corps had been up and about since early morning, moving happily about the deck. We were approaching the blessed land where Mrs. Merkut had first seen the light of day and had spent her honeymoon with Hans, where Augustine[4] and Tobias had been promenaded about in their mother's hood such-and-such a number of years ago, just as little Susanne did now, and hence where all the Hanseatics who then existed, with the exception of the father, had made their first acquaintance with wash-water and soap through Hayes's friendly offices. Mrs. Merkut's excitement clearly betrayed itself by her unusually loud nasal utterances; she revelled noisily in memories of days long past when during a time of famine she had assisted her spouse in consuming the leather cover of his boat. Hans scarcely moved a muscle; he scanned the coast through a telescope, searching with philosophical calm for people, while Tobias wolfed down a piece of meat in order to prepare himself for the sight of his native land.

Polaris passed Port Foulke, Hayes's winter quarters,[5] and Littleton Island, which lay to starboard.[6] At Cape Ohlsen, which projects behind the island, the coast changes its general alignment from northwest to northeast. We followed its direction as far as Cape Inglefield, then set a northerly course as far as possible. From a distance we sighted Rensselaer Bay,[7] where Kane had spent two years, and that same evening we easily surpassed the highest latitude which he had reached by ship, 18 years before.

The more the coast of Greenland dissolved into a blue haze, the clearer Grinnell Land[8] appeared, a magnificent alpine world whose multiformed mountain groups indicated a different geological formation.

It is a remarkable circumstance that the bulk of the Greenland massif lies buried under masses of ice whereas the west shore of the channel, as far as our experience extends thus far, possesses no glaciers north of the 79th parallel. Hayes Sound divides Ellesmere Land from Grinnell Land; its southern shore represents the demarcation line between two areas of land, one of which is still in the Ice Age, while the other, for reasons that still await an explanation, has already laid aside its icy yoke. When once the geological conditions of this complex of land are known more accurately, it may well turn out that the past histories of the different regions have experienced different events and that one area has had a more exciting youth than the other.

Once we had crossed the line of our maximum westerly compass variation (109°W), around midnight[9] we encountered the first extensive ice-masses, apparently blocking the sound in an east–west direction. By way of various detours we reached a lead that led to the shore polynya off the Grinnell Land coast. At the same time a southerly current became apparent.

Everywhere in the Arctic where the east coast of a land mass is exposed to the influence of a current coming from the north, pressure ridges of greater or lesser size appear along it, since by virtue of the direction of rotation of the earth every southward setting current must experience a westward deflection. Greenland and Svalbard may serve as a striking proof of this; under normal circumstances their west coasts are accessible every year whereas their east coasts only rarely permit ships to approach them. Here the reverse applied: the shore polynya stretched darkly to the north, whereas the pack ice gleamed to the east.

Early on the morning of 28 August, a boat landed in a small bay near Cape Fraser to investigate whether it might serve as an anchorage, in the event that the ship might be forced by some accident to seek shelter. Unfortunately I missed the opportunity of taking part in this trip since I had gone to bed late and was still asleep when the boat pushed off. After a stay of less than 15 minutes Hall returned with the men. They had seen only bare rocks; the total botanical collection consisted of a few bunches of withered arctic poppies and several patches of moss. One of the seamen brought back a bag of rock fragments in which interesting fossils were embedded. Apart from three or four erratic pieces of a coarse-grained granite-gneiss and a black-green melaphyr-like mineral, the collection contained numerous examples of a fine-grained grey-blue limestone, some of which were covered by a peach-blossom-coloured sinter (cobalt?). Many of them contained fossils; we identified two types of coral (*Syringopora* and *Favosites*), a small bivalve shell (*Rhychonella*) which was abundant, as well as a severely compressed trilobite (*Illaenus*).

Hall had discovered traces of an old Eskimo camp. Among the bone remains he had bundled together there were several charred vertebrae of the Greenland seal, a left upper-leg bone of a bearded seal, the head of which had been cut off (probably in order to remove the marrow), as well as several fragments of ribs which, judging by their size, probably also belonged to this latter species.

It was rather discouraging that shortly after the ship got underway again, fog descended and concealed the higher parts of the coast. Around 10 o'clock it cleared up somewhat, long enough to permit us to shoot some sun altitudes. Our noon position was 80°3'N; 69°28'W. In its alignment and detail the land seemed different from that shown on Hayes's map. In combination with the poor visibility and the ship's considerable speed, this made orienting oneself doubly difficult; sometimes it was quite impossible to make particular sections of the coast agree with the map. Since under these circumstances there could be no thought of producing a proper survey, and since our main task was to push on without any loss of time, we sketched a panorama on a large scale, so that we could use it later.

Whereas we had glimpsed the Greenland coast only vaguely from the ship's deck since crossing the 79th parallel, or else had completely lost sight of it, around 2.00 p.m. it came into sight again. Semi-transparent banks of fog floated around the grey-blue rock massif; at times they spread out like a wall; at times they clumped together like clouds, giving the coast the appearance of a gleaming glacier, depending as its density varied or the strength of light from the veiled disc of the sun.

The north wind freshened, but it intensified the fog instead of dispersing it. By around 3 o'clock it had attained a speed of 16 miles per hour. With the exception of a brief calm on the day we left Tasiusaq, till now we had experienced constant, light headwinds that blew out of the northerly quadrants. Had we been aboard a sailing ship things would have gone badly for us in terms of our progress.

There was still no sign of major ice masses; full of confidence and anticipation we headed for the open polar sea, which according to Kane's observations allegedly began near Cape Constitution and whose existence Hayes had confirmed.

Around 7.00 p.m. we saw the cape peeping through the fog; in front of it, veiled in grey, lay the Franklin and Crozier islands, which served us as landmarks. Without them we would scarcely have recognized the spot due to the poor visibility. Even before the headland bore east of us, we spotted further land masses north of it and connected to it, but the fog prevented us from determining its full extent. But this much was sure: we were not in an extensive polar basin but in a narrow channel, both shores of which could be recognized with sufficient clarity despite the unfavourable weather. Thus Cape Constitution could no longer claim to be the northern cape of Greenland.

Early on 29 August, at 12.30 a.m., we passed between a small island and the coast of Grinnell Land. A later determination placed this island, which was named Hans Island, at 80°48'N;[10] and still the continuation of the Greenland coast northward could be recognized. Around 4.00 a.m. it cleared up somewhat, but soon afterward the fog descended so densely that shortly after 8 o'clock we had to lay alongside an old floe. At 10.30 we made preparations for making a sounding. We let 300 fathoms of line run out, but got no bottom. As we hauled it back in it broke; we lost about 200 fathoms plus a Brook's sounding apparatus. The negative result of this observation certainly did not justify our assuming a depth of more than 300 fathoms at the spot where we dropped the sounding line, since our proper sounding line was not accessible and we had to use another one, whose thickness was too great in relation to the 36 lb. cannon ball. Evidently the lead and the line had been carried south by the current and had formed a very sharp angle with the water surface, instead of hanging approximately vertical.

At noon it cleared up sufficiently that we could measure a few sun's altitudes, with dubious accuracy, above a rather dubious horizon; they gave a latitude of 81°20'N, while our approximate longitude was 64°34'N. This same position may be taken to be the approximate site of the sounding.

Shortly afterward we again found ourselves underway, feeling our way slowly northward through the foggy atmosphere. Around 3.00 p.m. the land to the east revealed itself for the first time sufficiently clearly that we could think of surveying it. Meyer and I began measuring a series of angles with a theodolite that revolved through a divided circle.

Drifting floes forced us to change course often and suddenly; this greatly complicated our task. We had scarcely begun when we had to abandon it again, since dense fog descended over the low ranges of hills and the lowland which stretched away, barren and devoid of any snow cover, bounded to the north and south by higher hill masses.

Around 4 o'clock we broke through a narrow belt of ice masses which consisted mainly of floes of moderate extent and high hummocks. Since we had crossed the 80th parallel few icebergs had appeared; by contrast old floes, covered with coarse-grained firn, now appeared, rising 3–4 feet above the water surface. From time to time the outlines of the land loomed vaguely and blurredly out of the grey sea of fog, but never for more than a few minutes; it was impossible to get a clear picture of the coast.

During the night too we were moving through fog; toward morning on the 30th it again became so thick that at 9 o'clock we were forced to make fast to a floe about 10 miles long.[11] It must have been 2–3 years old and possessed an extremely uneven surface. Some of the hummocks were 15–20 feet high, but the lowest, level parts of the floe rose no more than 4 feet above sea level.

There was not a bird to be seen; organic life was limited to small ribbed jellyfish that drifted around happily in the cold water amongst the ice debris.

The air was saturated with moisture. The rigging was covered with an ice crust; heavy rime had accumulated on any iron fittings, while a blindingly white layer of frost enveloped the rails and masts. In the afternoon it snowed for three to four hours. The snow fell in two forms. Small hail-like grains, partly composed of irregular spheres, partly of blunt needles, predominated; a smaller proportion consisted of isolated, six-sided prisms, with a rough surface. On the calm water the falling snow particles combined like congealed fat into irregular pans that were caught in a rotating movement and formed centres of attraction for the newly incoming flakes.

When it cleared up at 7.15 a.m., we realized that the snowfall had been only local. The ridges to the south loomed black while the coasts both east and west glistened in their light winter attire. We retrieved our ice anchors and steamed slowly on northward. To starboard, only a few miles away, rose the newly discovered land, in sheerly dropping cliffs; it was indented by a wide bay, the end of which was not visible.

Never before had the keel of a ship furrowed this sea, on whose waves our vessel now rolled amidst tossing ice floes. We avoided the larger ones in tight curves; the smaller ones were pushed aside by our armoured bow. The ice masses often collided noisily with each other; often the ship had to go astern for a short distance in order to be able to ram the floes with sufficient momentum. At 8 o'clock the amount of ice increased, but as far as I could judge from on board it consisted only of pans, old floes and hummocks; nowhere were there icebergs to be seen. Some of the floes were coloured dark with rock debris.

Since the ice was pushing south with increasing speed,[12] at 8.56 Hall[13] rowed ashore with six of the men, in order to investigate whether a small bay which lay ahead of us to the east was suitable as an anchorage. Battling the current, the boat reached the coast in a wide arc, and returned shortly afterward since the spot was not suitable as a harbour. Later a boat was again sent in to the bay, which Hall named Repulse Harbour, because it had not been possible to effect a landing.

Following the navigable channel that ran off among the ice floes in various directions, we steamed on north again at 11.30, but then the fog forced us to heave-to again. Around midnight the current reached its maximum speed of about 2¾ –3 knots. It was the time of the full moon (29 days 18 h. 20 m. 8 s.); it was probably spring tide, and the speed of the constant current was accelerated by the progress of the high-tide wave. The current flowed from north to south, but it was impossible to decide whether the acceleration was the result of the ebb tide or the flood tide since we lacked any fixed observation point. We could not determine whether the tide was rising or falling.

Nearby, some seals were sporting in a polynya, but due to the violent movement of the ice it did not seem advisable to send a boat out to risk an attempt at hunting.

It was not until 6.30 a.m. on 31 August that we got underway again. But our progress was of short duration. At 7.50 the fog again forced us to anchor to a floe. At 9.10 it cleared up somewhat and we again pursued a northerly course. More old floes appeared than previously; the number of hummocks, as against the number of smaller, level floes increased. Soon afterward the navigable leads became narrower.

Unfortunately the much-vaunted experience of Budington, our ice master, was in no way comparable to the courage and spirit that he now displayed. He declared it to be an impossibility to penetrate farther north and wanted to turn south in order to find a harbour. But Hall, whose entire ambition was directed at achieving the highest possible latitude, could not approve this plan, no more so than the rest of the expedition members, who had the success of our enterprise at heart.

Unless circumstances of a special type obtain, the position of the commander of a ship is so totally autocratic that he not only does not need to take anybody's wishes into account but can even dictate as to the life and death of every single person on board. Whether he acts intelligently in asking advice from others in a critical moment, whether it be to diminish his own responsibility or for some other reason, is no longer relevant. It suffices that Hall was the absolute commander of *Polaris*; he ordered the ice master to maintain a northerly course as far as possible; the ice master declared that this order was impossible to execute and Hall asked individual members of the crew what they would do in the situation, in order to best achieve the interests of the expedition.

On the one hand it is both a painful and a thankless task to condemn the efforts of a companion with whom one has shared common dangers; on the other hand the historian must perceive it as his first duty to be able to report an event which led to the turning point of a major enterprise untrammelled by personal preference or aversion. Hence I consider it necessary to quote the later official statements of some of the participants.

Since I myself am one of the participants, I will ensure the greatest objectivity that can possibly be achieved in terms of my representation, in that I will even present my own views, as I uttered them at the time, in the words of the person whose conduct is subject to criticism here. I mean, of course, Budington.

Producing the relevant document, Budington stated:[14] "Hall consulted with the officers—with Bessels, myself and the others—whose views I believe, are recorded here as they were uttered at the time." The document reads:

Council held aboard the steamer *Polaris*[15] concerning attainment of a significant latitude using the vessel, which, with a view to finding a harbour, is located on the east side (of the channel). Present are Messrs. Bessels, Tyson, Budington, Morton and Chester. Bessels wants to cross the strait to search for a harbour, in case it is not possible to penetrate farther north by ship, since he considers the west side to be more suitable for sledge travel, and the east side, by contrast, better for navigation. Morton agrees with Bessels' view; Meyer is of the same opinion. Chester votes for pushing as far north as possible. Budington wants to stick to the east side which promises greater success for ships and hence also for sledging. In view of the pack ice he considers it impossible to push any further north. He proposes turning south along the coast in order to reach a harbour, something we can do in a very short time. The commander decided to cross the strait.

In the presence of witnesses Budington continued: "This document was written at the time and was identical in text to that in Hall's journal, which unfortunately is missing. It was left on the ice."

To the Naval Minister's question as to whether Budington had written the document himself, he replied: "No it was written down on my instructions. It is the record of the council held at that time and of the opinions given at the time; it was committed to paper by Hall's clerk on my instructions, about a week after the event. The same text was entered into Hall's journal by Meyer. Hall once read me the relevant part of his journal and I had the clerk prepare the copy which I have presented here."

It is no business of mine to doubt the accuracy of the text of the above copy. I should like only to stress that we were not *"on the east side with a view to finding a harbour,"* but that it was our intention to try to reach the highest possible latitude.

But let us hear the passages from Chester's official statement, which relate to the movements of the ship and the ice conditions.

> We could see down the channel and to the north we saw a water cloud, a dense water cloud; I mean a cloud that indicates open water. This is a sort of fog that hangs over open water. I believe that from this point we could have pushed further north. It was always my opinion that it would have been possible to push on farther. I was in my bunk that watch and heard the shout of the man in the barrel, reporting a strait of navigable water close under the land, along the east coast. Somebody came to call me; I went on deck where all the officers had gathered.[16]

The man in the barrel was seaman Heinrich Hobby, from whose testimony I will quote the following passage:

> At the time I had the watch in the crow's-nest. To conclude from what I heard all the officers wanted to press north. By contrast Budington and Tyson felt it essential to find winter quarters as quickly as possible. I could hear their every word . . . I could see a channel leading north which extended along the east shore from the north to about northeast. As far as I could observe, I could see open water . . . I shouted down from the crow's-nest to ask where they (Hall and the officer-of-the-watch) wanted to head for. I said there was a lot of open water to be seen to the northeast . . . As far as I could see, the ice conditions were not preventing us from continuing our course northwards.[17]

Morton stated:

> He [Hall] assembled the officers on the deck-house: Budington, Chester, Tyson, Bessels and me. Some of the gentlemen wanted to penetrate further north; others voted to search for a harbour immediately, and I believe Budington opted to turn back in order to run into Newman's Bay.[18]

Although the views reported here do not agree in every respect, they do prove that Budington had little enthusiasm for reaching a higher latitude. But the fact that those who thought they saw frost-smoke or open water to the north were not deceived may be seen from the following table, which contains some meteorological observations that were made on board ship during 30 and 31 August.

Date	Time	Psychrometer		R.H.	Wind		Dist. in 24 hrs.	Weather
		Dry Bulb	Wet Bulb	%	Dir.	Speed (mph)		
30/08	7	−1.23	−1.78	89.2	N	12		Fog
	4	1.56	2.11	88.8	N	7		Fog
	11	0.56	1.67	78.8	N	7	371	Fog
31/08	7	1.78	2.22	91.0	NW	1		Fog
	4	1.56	1.94	92.2	NW	8		Fog
	11	1.78	2.22	91.0	E	0	113	Fog

Unfortunately 10 of the 16 relevant observations are missing, but of the material at my disposal[19] I have quoted quite sufficient to demonstrate that during six hours with fog on five occasions northerly winds were blowing and that according to the psychrometric readings the air was almost saturated. One can barely doubt but that the damp, fog-bearing north winds that were already blowing toward us when we entered Smith Sound must have been passing over open water rather than over a totally ice-covered sea.

I cannot state whether Budington took these conditions into consideration. On the other hand it is certain that he could not have been fully informed about the ice conditions. One can gain a clear view of ice conditions only from the crow's nest, but Budington did not consider it worth the effort to climb to the masthead.

In his view it was not possible to push farther north, and Hall was weak enough to consider this view to be decisive.

Around 2.00 p.m. the ship's head was turned westward in order to cross the strait which Hall had named Robeson Channel in honour of the Naval Minister of the United States. The air became more and more overcast; the insidious fog descended; it restricted our horizon to less than a mile and at 5.30 again forced us to anchor.

6: Into unknown territory

When the ice opened next morning (1 September) at 9.25, we steamed onward; at 10 o'clock our lead closed and we made fast to an old, fairly level floe that was about 5 miles long and rose about 3 feet above water level. During the night a skin of young ice about ¼ of an inch thick had formed on the leads; it rose and fell with the slight swell. The fairly small floes and hummocks were slowly drifting south ahead of a light northerly breeze. In the north dark frost-smoke billowed up on the horizon. The newly discovered land to the east gleamed only vaguely through the foggy air; it was clearer to the west and south.

Around 2.00 p.m. Hall and Chester headed off west across the floe against which we were lying, toward the coast of Grinnell Land. They had scarcely left when the ice began to move, pressing violently against the ship's side; she heeled over slightly to port, toward the floe. For the first time during the voyage the ice chisels came into play. The seamen were sent out onto the ice to round off its sharp corners and edges, in order to prevent any possible damage. The floes towered up to the height of the rail and pressed in on the ship's hull until it shuddered perceptibly. After the tumult had lasted about 40 minutes, it fell calm again. When Hall and Chester returned around 5 o'clock the ice lay almost motionless.

From the top of a hummock the two men had discovered a small embayment in the coast that was fairly ice-free and which might perhaps have served as a temporary anchorage. They regretted that they had not reached any arrangement to send us a signal. Chester climbed to the masthead and found that the navigable lead that he and Hall had spotted during their hike to the west across the floe had disappeared. Even if *Polaris* had been able to turn, it now would no longer have been possible to steam around the floe and reach the spot on the coast that Hall had selected as an anchorage.

Until around 8 o'clock the ice remained quiet, then the pressure began again, just as it had threatened us six hours before. Shortly before 9 o'clock the ice masses surged so violently against the starboard side that the ship was lifted somewhat. At 9.30 the ice rafted toward the bow and probably under the keel. The ship, which was being carried faster by the movement of the current than the large ice floe, heeled to starboard.

Fig. 10. Beset.

6: Into unknown territory

With a loud crack the two strong manila hawsers that till now had secured us to the floe by means of ice anchors, snapped.

The fact that we were lying at anchor again after less than 5 minutes was due only to the presence of mind of Budington who, as soon as the accident happened, himself cast off one of the hawsers and threw it overboard and ordered that the same be done with the other one. Only with some difficulty did we manage to secure the anchors adequately; even then they threatened repeatedly to lose their hold. The pressure renewed itself; the cables stretched as taut as violin strings and could scarcely be slackened off fast enough to prevent them from snapping. Provisions were fetched up on deck from the lower hold with praiseworthy speed; everybody was given orders that his most essential items of clothing were to be lashed up so that in the event of the possible loss of the ship we would each have a spare suit of clothing.

When the pressure relaxed around 11 o'clock, those on the watch below crawled into their bunks fully dressed. Entirely at the mercy of the whim of the ice, it was essential to be prepared for the worst; if further pressure occurred it might be the end of the ship.

Half an hour after midnight the walls of our prison opened; a few small leads appeared east of the ship, their surfaces ruffled by a gentle north wind. Then the floes began moving slowly southward; some bore rusty-red patches from the ship's armour-plating—an indication of how severe the ice pressure had been. Around 1.30 the ice again attacked the starboard side but not violently enough to disturb us.

The north wind freshened and brought dense fog which quickly descended and eliminated any distant view; soon the coast to the east had disappeared from sight. Only the nearby coast of Grinnell Land still appeared vaguely, its outlines blurred; then it too disappeared in the heaving grey masses of vapour.

This problem was now compounded by ice pressures again. Between 9.00 and 10.00 a.m. (2 September) the onslaught became more violent than previously; the deck planks throbbed dully, the masts quivered, the floes rubbed creakingly against the hull. The confused noise lasted for over three hours. From the shattering cover of new ice came sounds like whining and chirping; deeper notes rang out from the floe to which the ship lay moored. A dull humming and roaring carried to us from the drifting floes, at times drowned out by the crash of collapsing ice debris. And mingling with all this was the wailing howl of the dogs.

Hall gave orders to land part of the provisions on the ice. Immediately all hands set to work. A sort of bridge was erected from thick planks between the ice floe and the severely heeling ship, in order to facilitate unloading. One of the Grinnell sledges,[20] which had been quickly assembled, was used to carry coal, packed in sacks, to a raised spot on the floe, far from the reach of the ice pressure. Next to it 1000 lbs. of pemmican, canned meat, several barrels of lemon juice, flour, bread, coffee, tea and other provisions were cached. Rifles and ammunition found room in a box of tools; to it was added a stove and a great assortment of kitchen utensils.

By the time the ship's bell announced noon, the emergency depot lay hidden under several large sails whose edges had been weighted down with bags of coal in order to protect the goods from wind and drifting snow. Later, on board ship, the boats were cleared away and more provisions were brought on deck. We could now await calmly the ice pressures that the next turn of the tide would bring us. If the ship were smashed we at least possessed the means to support life for some time and to get ashore.

It was not until the 3rd that the previous calm was renewed on board. Thick fog still brooded all around us; robbed of any independent movement the ship lay in its icy fetters; we could barely guess the direction in which we were drifting. A solemn church service was held in the cabin;[21] Hall eloquently reminded us of the dangers from which a gracious Creator had protected us. Those who placed more trust in divine omnipotence than in their own powers sent a fervent prayer to heaven.

Over the course of the afternoon two snow buntings flew on deck and settled on the wheel-house; they pecked trustingly at bread crumbs that were thrown to them but they refused to be caught. When we tried to catch them they eluded us and disappeared in the fog. A calm lasting several hours was accompanied by a heavy snowfall; it was not until 8.00 p.m. that we were able to renew the meteorological observations that had been interrupted since the morning of 2 September. But first we had to move the cases and barrels which blocked the way to the instrument screen.

Around 2.00 a.m. on 4 September the fog receded; the coast of Grinnell Land came into view but it was still impossible to get our bearings. Around 4 o'clock the sun showed itself again for the first time in six days, but not clearly enough to allow us to get a celestial position-fix. Bryan later made an attempt with the artificial horizon on the ice but totally without success. We had been able to measure only four latitudes since we had left Tasiusaq; the last latitude that had been determined with approximate accuracy was that of 29 August, namely 81°20'N. Since then fog had prevailed almost constantly; hence all determinations of position depended on the readings of the two patent logs which were streamed constantly as long as the ship was underway and as long as the ice conditions permitted.

When the fog that had been shrouding the east side of the channel cleared, and the land was revealed in detail, we immediately realized that the current had set us significantly southward. The highest latitude we had reached was 82°26' or, taking the current into consideration, probably 82°16'.[22] Never before had a vessel succeeded in penetrating to such a high latitude.

Since the ice had loosened somewhat, we could hope that for the moment we might be spared further ice pressures. Around 9 o'clock extensive leads formed in the vicinity of the vessel; Hall gave orders for retrieving the provisions depot. After three hours of work, in which everyone gave a hand, almost everything was back on board, but it was certainly not easy to catch the dogs. We had hoisted the screw when the ice masses had thrust under the stern, but lowering it again caused serious difficulties.

When we were ready to sail, however, fog descended again at 8.45,[23] accompanied by a heavy snowstorm. In the evening we were able to weigh anchor. Open leads appeared to the east and south and the ship followed their course.

We had barely escaped one unpleasant situation when we landed in another, which might easily have become fatal. A smell of burning made itself perceptible; it seemed to come from the lower hold and raised the fear that fire had broken out. Beginning with the lower cable locker, the compartments were searched in succession. Since there was no smoke visible anywhere it was a long time before we discovered the cause of the smell of burning, which was strongest in the stokehold. The engineers examined the boilers; one of them was completely empty and its glowing fire-bricks had set fire to the felt covering. The water level in the manometer indicated an adequate supply, but since the valve was closed[24] there was absolutely no connection between the tubes and the interior of the boiler; if water had suddenly been fed in it would undoubtedly have given us the shocking surprise of a boiler explosion. The fire was quickly raked out and extinguished and the boiler left to cool slowly.

In the meantime we had approached to within a few miles of the eastern shore of the channel; a level beach promised a tolerably good anchorage for a further advance. At midnight a boat went off to sound the site; Hall planted the American flag and solemnly took possession of the newly discovered land in the name of God and the President of the United States.[25] As the anchor chain went rattling and clanking out, the 5th of September was barely half an hour old; at the latitude at which we were located the sun had started to set briefly, but daylight still prevailed. On the seaward side we were sheltered by a stranded iceberg; to the north and south there were hummocks and floes that were sitting on the bottom Two fulmar petrels circled the ship, harbingers of open water; we had spotted the last ones in the labyrinth of islands between Upernavik and Tasiusaq. A round of drinks in Hall's cabin concluded the ceremony of taking possession; all those not on watch went to their bunks, since it was late. After breakfast Chester climbed to the masthead; open water was visible to the north and west. A further discussion which Hall had with Budington as to reaching a higher latitude elicited from the latter similar expressions of impossibility as previously; as previously, the ice master again investigated the ice conditions from the deck instead of climbing to the crow's nest and taking a look round from there.

Hall gave orders to unload the cargo, thereby tacitly renouncing the chance of making a further advance with the ship during the fall;[26] the honour of the flag and the success of the expedition were sacrificed to the whim of an individual. Fortune, which had accompanied us thus far, became ill-disposed to us and never smiled on us again.

Two boats, lashed together with cross-planks and heavily laden with provision boxes, took us ashore; the distance involved was barely a quarter mile. The ship lay in an open bay about 12 miles long, whose curvature would disappear completely even on quite a large-scale map and would reveal itself as almost a straight line. The beach rose in terraces to a plain, about 10 miles long and barely over 4 miles wide in the centre. To the north of the embayment, which ran almost north–south, rose uplands 900 to 1200 feet high and running east, where their elevation did not exceed 400 feet; the mountains that enclosed the plain on the south may have attained an average height of 2000 feet. The bedrock was a grey, schistose limestone, covered with drift consisting of different materials.

Hall and I went searching for a site to erect the observatory; near the beach we discovered rocks arranged in circles, which undoubtedly had served to secure the summer tents of wandering Eskimos. There were seven of them located close together and three of them were superbly preserved; they were 5, 7 and 7½ feet in diameter. We searched in vain for graves; for the moment we discovered only a fireplace and the half-charred rib of a seal.

Near an erratic boulder of gneiss we spotted several moving points. The telescope revealed them to be ptarmigan that were pecking at the twigs of stunted willow bushes. It was a flock of nine birds; their white plumage made them almost invisible against the snow-covered earth. They let us approach to within a few paces without taking flight; since we were not carrying a gun we did not disturb them any further; we intended returning toward evening to shoot them. Despite the low temperature two mosquitoes buzzed joyfully around us; we were able to catch only one of them and for lack of a suitable container we stuck it between the eye-pieces of the telescope. Flocks of twittering snow buntings enlivened the beach; they were preparing for their southward migration, a sign of approaching winter.

As we hiked homeward along the beach we saw a small horseshoe-shaped bay about three ship's lengths in extent, which promised to provide more shelter than our present anchorage. We just reached the vessel in time to prevent the double-boat from landing a load of coal; but 42 of the dogs had already been landed. Once we had raised steam we weighed anchor and steered for the bay. A bar prevented us from entering and we had to return to the old site, near the iceberg.

Over the period of a few hours a snowfall, accompanied by a calm, transformed the surface of the calm sea into a shimmering, matt-white surface; fine veins of dark water seamed it and gave it the appearance of a fantastic mosaic floor that undulated gently here and there.

Early in the morning the Eskimos were sent out to search for signs of reindeer; they returned in the evening having found neither game nor tracks.

After midnight, at the time of high tide, the ice near the ship came alive; it began to move shoreward and pressed against the ship. We weighed anchor, raised steam and made a few loops to ensure peace and quiet for the rest of the night. These were the last manoeuvres we made before the ship was frozen in.

CHAPTER 7

The first days in Polaris Bay

Unloading the cargo. The observatory. Changes in ice conditions. Survey work. The dogs. The last birds. Fresh muskox tracks. Preparations for a sledge journey. Changed arrangements on board. The population of the saloon reaches its maximum density. The meteorological instruments. The survey party's adventures. Geological and topographic sketch of the bay. Secular uplift. A scene from the past.

A fine custom, rooted in the sailor's attachment to his ship and which makes him bestow his ship's name on newly discovered areas, induced Hall to name the bay which opened before us, Polaris Bay. The anchorage, in the narrower sense, was christened Thank God Harbour, and the iceberg that sheltered us to seaward, Providence Berg.[1]

If one were to describe the anchorage as a harbour, at best one could do so only out of gentle respect, since the floes that formed it, grounded on the seabed all around, were unique symbols of the past, destined for the same fate as the loose snowflake that falls on a blooming violet on a raw March night. As regards the Providence Berg, the generous providence to which it was dedicated seemed not to have allocated it a very long life; having caused all sorts of mischief, one day it disintegrated noisily.

Since these decrepit ice formations no longer exist in the form in which they appeared to us at the time, and since Thank God Harbour thus belongs to the realm of the imaginary greats, in whose possession sober mathematicians, effusive visionaries and religious dreamers share, henceforth we will simply call the anchorage Polaris Bay.

The first period of our stay was devoted to unloading the cargo and to domestic arrangements. The provisions master took a new inventory and sent his boxes, barrels and bales ashore in the double boat. There they were stowed on a nearby elevation, protected from spring tides and ice pressures. Nearby we stowed the coal, packed in sacks containing about 2 centners.

As a result of a further snowfall the young ice cover that extended along the shore rapidly increased in thickness. By the 7th it was already 7 inches thick; it had become so resistant that the laden boat could barely be rowed ashore. Hence after one journey the transport operation was discontinued. The following day, too, the activities of the men were restricted almost exclusively to duties on board. When we were heading ashore in the morning to erect the observatory, it took almost half an hour before we got to land, although the distance involved was scarcely half a mile. A sailor stood in the bow of the boat and strenuously broke a path with an ice chisel; the oarsmen had to push hard with the blades of their oars against the tough ice cover in order to move the boat. Altogether our progress relied more on jerky pushing than on any other movement.

The building which bore the sonorous name of "observatory" was a hut of boards, of Spartan simplicity; it was so unostentatious that it did not even have windows, which would have been of very little use during the long arctic night. We erected the building on a level patch on the plateau, 34 feet above sea level; its component parts had come from the Navy's workshops in New York. It was 10 feet long, 8 feet wide, and the height of the ridge 8 feet 6 inches. The roof slanted down on both sides at an angle of 33° and on both north and south sides possessed two openings that could be closed with shutters. The door, inserted in the north side, opened inward, and was barely 5 feet high. Walls and roof consisted of ½-inch boards, but the floor was somewhat thicker and rested on strong sills. Since we planned to carry out magnetic observations in the hut, as well as the meteorological and astronomical work, no iron had been used in its construction. All the metal work, such as hooks, screws, straps and angles, consisted of copper.

The position of the observatory (as determined later) turned out to be 81°36' 4"N; 62°15'W.

Fig. 11. The observatory.

In the southeast corner of the hut we built a fireplace with bricks we had brought with us. The low temperature immediately turned the mortar into a solid mass; the work advanced rapidly, but our handiwork was not to last long. When we later found ourselves obliged to build special magnetic observatories, we pulled down the fireplace and replaced it with an iron stove.

By the 9th the ice bridge had become so strong that it was able to bear a man standing on a plank. Armed with a boathook, one of the men ventured to make the crossing; he reached the beach without breaking

7: The first days in Polaris Bay

through, but he could not land immediately since the ice right along the shore had been smashed up by the effect of the tides. Once we had cut a narrow channel between the ship and the shore in order to facilitate the boat's progress, the transport of the provisions suffered no further disruptions. Two days later we began using sledges and the work was advanced faster than previously. On the plateau near the observatory Hall, Bryan and Meyer began measuring a baseline to which the coastal survey was to be tied. Later the latter prepared a large-scale plane-table map of the harbour and its surroundings.

Once the ice bridge between the land and *Polaris* became crossable, the dogs frequently came aboard and caused great annoyance. Under the protection of the short period of darkness, they broke into the provisions depot. In the morning several cases that had contained figs and smoked herring were found to be robbed of their contents, as also were some cans of pemmican. Even the instruments which, for convenience, had been hidden under a sail were not spared. The greedy animals had pulled the theodolite out of its case and had purloined an artificial horizon; they had also damaged the vernier on a sextant and had gnawed various leather objects.

When Steller says of the Kamchadals' dogs that "their mores are to be traced to their training,"[2] this applies in equal degree to the Eskimo dog, in which all the virtues that characterize its relatives are dormant. The fact that those character traits that we value in a dog have not attained outward expression is entirely the fault of his master. We cannot expect much more than the achievements of a lap-dog from a hunting dog, even of the most noble pedigree if, like a Bolognese, it is raised largely by female hands instead of growing up under the guidance of a strict teacher. Most of the physical qualities that it inherits from its forefathers and that make it valuable as a hunting dog will remain undeveloped, while to its inherent vices will probably also be added those that derive from its upbringing.

If the Eskimo were to handle his dogs, from the earliest days, somewhat more affectionately than in fact occurs, they would certainly be of a gentler and more sociable nature than under the prevailing circumstances. But he sees his animals only as machines that have to perform a certain job and is only satisfied if their capabilities correspond to his expectations.

The hard school of life begins for the pups when they are scarcely weaned; training begins when they are about six months old. Along with two or three adult dogs five or six of them are immediately harnessed to the sledge, on which the trainer takes his seat. At first they derive definite pleasure from leaning into the traces; but soon following the older dogs runs counter to their independence. They try to veer off to right or left or to hold back so far behind the lead dogs that their traces become slack. On first realizing that this lightens the load, they drop farther and farther behind and finally run along, playing, on either side of the sledge. For some time the trainer will allow them to act like this, but then he begins handling his whip with a merciless severity which borders on cruelty. The more blows rain down on them, the greater their refractoriness becomes. They lie on their backs with dumb resignation and prefer to let themselves be pulled along across the snow than to bend to the will of their master. If the lash of the whip begins to be ineffective, then the driver switches to blows with the handle and continues with the punishment until the pups' defiance is broken; during this severe learning period they receive more blows than food.

Among the inhabitants of the north shore of Hudson Strait and the natives of Williams Land,[3] to whom the use of the whip is almost unknown, training proceeds more gently than in Greenland. There, refractory dogs are punished with snowballs or else the driver uses a heavy stick that he throws at the animal deserving of punishment. This method of training is less advantageous than the one described above and is more commonly used. At the same time it is more tedious since the driver constantly has to pick up the stick again, after throwing it at a dog. If he can't reach it from the sledge he is obliged to jump up, and occasionally this causes the dogs to race off with the sledge.

Since we can presumably assume that the Eskimos already possessed dogs before their range became so extensive as it is now, it is of particular interest to investigate the shouts which different tribes, spatially separated from each other, use in driving their dogs.

The Greenlander Hans used the shout "I! I! I!," a short sound, produced in the fistula. If he wanted the dogs to turn right he accompanied the sound with a whip crack on the snow to the left; if the dogs were to swing left, he dropped the whip lash on the right side. A short whistle meant the dogs should stop. He told me that this mode of dog driving is used by all the inhabitants of missionarized Greenland.

Among the Eskimo group which inhabits the east shore of Smith Sound the shout used is a hoarse "Ha! ha! ha!" The direction in which the animals are to turn is indicated by the whip as reported above. The command to stop is a long-drawn-out "Oh!" that the driver usually utters only once.

According to Joseph the Eskimos in the vicinity of Pond's Bay[4] use the following shouts, uttered in a hoarse voice: Right, "woa-ah-ha-ha-ha!" Left: "ah-woa-wa-ha!" Stop: "Oh!"

For the Cumberland[5] area he reported the following: Right: "woa-hau-ha!" Left: "ach-woah-wit!" or "ach-woah-woah!" The command to start is "Ha! Ha! Ha!," similar to that of the Etah people on Smith Sound. The command to stop is a simple "Oh!" Earlier these shouts were somewhat different, namely, Right: "woa-ha-hu-hua!" and left: "ah-ah-wohak!" The command to stop has not undergone any change with the passage of time.

Among the Eskimos who have taken up residence along the shores of Hudson Strait we encounter simply the command "au! au! au!"

Similarly, the residents of King Williams Land use only a single command: "Kgu! kgu! kgu!."

In the two last-named regions the use of the whip is almost entirely unknown. The animals are either led by a human who runs ahead of the sledge or are guided by a piece of wood that the driver throws to the opposite side to the direction in which the dogs are to turn.

We could not determine with any certainty whether the Eskimos of Alaska lack specific commands. The travel descriptions available to us mention nothing about special calls, and several people who had stayed for quite a long time in Alaska and whom we asked for information could not remember hearing anything but curses, whose colour depended on the refractoriness of the animals and the irritability of the driver. Since here, as in King William Land, a person runs ahead of the sledge, presumably special sounds might not be used.

The number of dogs in a team varies between 4 and 8, the number corresponding to the load on the sledge. Only in exceptional cases does the load per animal exceed 100 lbs. With smooth going, well-fed dogs will cover about 4 German miles[6] per hour and can work for 12 hours per day without suffering any hardship. The harness consists of narrow leather thongs, while the traces, which are 8 to 10 feet in length, consist of undressed bearded seal skin. The traces are secured, by way of ivory rings, along the long axis of the sledge to a strong line that runs through corresponding holes in the runners, in front of the foremost crosspiece. If lead dogs are used they are given longer traces than the other animals; otherwise all the traces are of approximately the same length. Before one can drive a team with any assurance, one has to learn to use the whip, a task involving some difficulty, which can only be overcome by persistent practice. The lash, 15 to 20 feet in length, is controlled by a handle that is barely 2 feet long. A good driver can hit not just the dog that is deserving of punishment but a specific spot on that animal, such as an ear or a flank, for example. He makes the blow from the wrist, with the arm bent, accompanied by a loud crack each time, then immediately pulls the lash back again, so that it does not get tangled in the traces. Despite the apparent ease with which these movements are made, dog-driving is a fairly strenuous activity which, due to the refractoriness of the dogs, often tries the patience of even the most patient person to the limit.

For Steller[7] in Kamchatka, "the greatest annoyance in dog-driving is that as soon as they were harnessed they would raise their muzzles to the sky and howled and complained horribly, just as if they wanted to appeal to heaven for their hard fate. Then there was the further annoyance that one after another the dogs would jump backward, do their business, and while they are resting for this period, they display real cunning in that the whole time, one after the other does its business, sometimes only halfway, and quite often they are only pretending, in vain, to be so occupied."

The Eskimo dogs behave similarly; during a journey they leave no means untried to play malicious tricks on the driver, in order to make him stop. They never run for longer than a few minutes in the original order alongside each other but are constantly jumping to right or left over the heads of their companions; as a result the traces become so entangled that they have to be disentangled at least once per hour. Scarcely is the sledge moving again when two of the dogs start fighting, with such effect that the entire team is thrown into disorder. One of the lead dogs leaps between them to keep the peace, but in so doing he simply gives the signal for a general brawl. Every dog that is not bitten himself bites either his closest companion in misery, or another one whom he considers to be weaker than himself. Finally all the dogs are involved in a single, noisy brawl, at which the driver lets loose mercilessly with his whip handle, swearing and cursing. It often requires a major effort before he is able to restore order, since the enraged animals initially mistake the blows for bites from enemies. If the sledge sticks fast in a snowdrift or between ice hummocks the dogs will throw themselves indifferently to the ground instead of making efforts to get it moving again. Only the whip will immediately cause them to get up and to lean into the traces. When the driver's shout to halt rings out they behave similarly. With their muzzles pressed between their forepaws they throw themselves to the ground; then they get up again to scrape a hole and immediately lie down again. Two of our Newfoundlanders that were harnessed along with the Eskimo dogs gradually adopted their habits, but before they stretched out they always turned around on their beds, something we never noticed in the case of the Eskimo dogs. But if he finds an opportunity to chew through his trace, he will do so readily and run off in the most reckless fashion in order to escape work. Usually he returns to his owner's hut or, if it is too far away, to the most recent stopping place.

Under normal circumstances the dogs are fed daily only when they are working, and as a rule only when the day's work is over. At every feeding each dog is given about 2 lbs. of meat or fish. In general the size of this meal depends on the success of the hunt, which is subject to significant variations. They prefer solid muscle-meat to any other type of food; only in exceptional cases, when their sense of taste has not been developed from birth, will they eat fat. On the other hand they cherish a certain preference for walrus hide, which possesses little nutritional value, and the indigestibility of which makes feedings necessary less often. Dogs that are not working are fed once every two days at most. In periods of need they often have to fast for a week. Scarcely anything is safe from them then. They will not only eat any leather item they can get hold of, but they will also consume wood or other indigestible items that are put in front of them or which are dropped accidentally, as long as they are small enough to be gulped down. Thus one of the dogs on board *Polaris*, that had probably been short-changed at feeding time, swallowed the doorknob from the saloon door which accidentally fell on the deck. The round knob was made of white porcelain, was about 2 inches in diameter, and attached to it was a portion of a four-sided iron bolt, about 1½ inches in length, whereby it had been secured to the lock. It certainly weighed not less than 25 grams and probably not more than 250 grams. When the doorknob fell to the ground, five or six dogs came racing up and fought for a few seconds, and when they were driven away the doorknob had disappeared. We could never determine to whose appetite it had fallen victim. Not till next morning did one of the seamen find it somewhere in the forward part of the ship, covered with sepia-coloured marks that scarcely could be mistaken. Since during the next few weeks there were no deaths among the pack we may assume that we had at least one dog that could perform such conjuring tricks without injury.

Unfortunately we had many opportunities to observe that the dogs could commit all sorts of crimes, even when they were not hungry. Once when some of the pups, barely three months old, fell ill during a sudden change in the weather and suffered from pseudo-prolapsus, they were housed on board in an overturned barrel. During the night two adult dogs sneaked up to the pups' kennel and ate the protruding ends of their intestines. Alerted by the pups' wails the watch-keeper rushed up, but it was too late to save them. In another case one of our bitches killed her five pups which might have been about a month old. She crushed the skulls of all the little animals and left them lying without eating them. Then she courted the favours of a strange litter and suckled it whenever its mother left the kennel.

I learned from Joseph, whose foster-mother always kept some dogs that were never harnessed to a sledge, how an understanding, loving training can transform an animal with a wary, shifty look into a faithful creature whose feeling of honour can become so well developed that all its troublesome thefts cease. One of her dogs usually guarded her hut and her children during its master's absence, and it once rescued from the water a small boy who had fallen down a crack in the ice. The loyal devotion of this animal can only be appreciated in full measure when one recalls that Eskimo dogs are usually shy of water, and that they never bathe in water, whereas according to Wrangel Siberian dogs "spend most of their time in the water in summer, in order to be safe from biting flies."[8] Another dog was so superbly trained that he would catch young seals alive and either guarded them until its master arrived or, if this did not happen, would bring them to the house intact.

In choosing a dog an Eskimo looks more for ability than for physical advantages; his sense of beauty is not sufficiently developed that he can select a regularly proportioned animal from one which is less regularly developed. Joseph listed the following qualities as being those which a good dog should possess: a wide chest, short ears, strong legs, large feet, low hindquarters and a moderately long tail. Dogs with long tails allegedly cannot run so fast as others. If the tail curls too close to the root, this is taken to be a sign of weak loins.

Apart from being a draft animal during the summer, the dog is used for carrying light loads and also for hunting. In the latter case it receives special training. Once it has undergone this training a more friendly fate smiles on him than on his companions, since he is entirely spared the heavy work of hauling a sledge. Usually the strongest dog of a litter is chosen for this training, if its disposition is also good; this training begins in the third or fourth month of life. The Eskimo buries a piece of cooked seal meat in the snow, carefully wipes away his tracks, then brings the animal upwind close to the spot where the meat lies hidden. If the dog does not pick up the scent after quite a long search, its master helps him to find the scent somewhat; he speaks to him and tries to encourage him in the search. When he finally finds the meat he is allowed to eat a piece of it, but the rest is taken from his mouth. Here some blows often have to be applied if he does not release the treat voluntarily. Immediately the teacher leads him to another spot, near which a second piece of meat has been buried, and continues with this training until the animal understands what demands are being made of its abilities.

Another method consists of taking the young dog along with a good seal catcher, whose skills he will adopt after a short time. This is the faster and easier school for both teacher and pupil, but before it can be applied one has to have a well-trained dog that is free of vices as far as possible. During the hunt, when the seal is lying on the ice near its breathing hole, it is the task of the dogs to cut off its retreat route to the water and either to kill it or to hang on to it until the hunter can arrive. If the hunter is too far away from the seal, he releases some of his ordinary sledge dogs in order to assist the other one.

Where geese commonly occur the dogs are used for catching them too, as well as for seal hunting; goose hunting can only be pursued when the birds are incapable of flight during the moult due to the loss of their wing feathers. Training is as follows: the Eskimo catches a goose and brings it to a place where it cannot escape, then sets a dog on it. If the latter succeeds in catching the goose, it is taken away from him; then he is let loose on a second one, and perhaps on a third. Almost without exception the dogs bite through one of their victim's thigh bones; this lames it and it can then be seized without difficulty.

On 12 September Hans shot a kittiwake,[9] the last bird we sighted near the ship. The day before, we saw a solitary sandpiper (*Tringa maritima*)[10] but were not able to kill it. With one wing held low and the other stretched upward it hurried along the beach, then lifted off and flew off in a southwesterly direction.

Two days later, when the natives spotted fresh muskox tracks,[11] everyone on board who possessed a rifle developed a mild case of hunting fever;[12] in Joseph's case it was so acute that he could barely sleep. A few hours after his return to the ship he set off again. He encountered more tracks, fresher than the first ones, but did not run across the animals themselves. It was decided to dispatch a regularly organized hunting party, and Chester set about the preparations without delay. Under his supervision the sailors made a small tent and Joseph and Hans got the sledges ready.

Once the greater part of the cargo had been unloaded we began organizing the compartment beneath the saloon, which till now had been filled with provisions, as living quarters. The middle of the saloon floor was occupied by a hatch, whose cover was removed in order to provide a passage for the stovepipe; the two compartments, which possessed separate entrances, were to be heated by a single stove that, for obvious reasons, was banished to the nether regions. We greatly missed the table that had given way to the stovepipe. At first we had to be satisfied with writing on our knees; the room was simply not spacious enough to allow us the comforts which one would expect aboard a mail steamer.

Fig. 12. *Polaris* in winter quarters.

Hall's self-sacrifice knew no bounds. He moved into the cramped upper saloon,[13] so that the galley could be moved to his small cabin, from which the bunk had been removed to make way for the stove. The hut on deck, where the black cook had been preparing our meals until now, was to serve as the ice house from now on, for during the next nine months every drop of drinking water had to be melted from ice by means of artificial heat before it became water; Providence Berg would provide us with the necessary ice.

Those who, singly or communally with others, had occupied the cabins on deck moved their sleeping places to one of the two saloons, since the temperature began to drop rapidly and reasons of economy did not permit us to heat the entire ship. Apart from in the galley, where fire would be maintained long enough to cook the crew's meals, the only stoves were in the lower saloon and in the men's quarters. Moisture condensed on wooden surfaces inside the ship to form fine frost flowers; around the brass window-mounts, around bolt-heads and anywhere else there was metal, a thick, sparkling ice layer was formed, which hung down from the ceiling in picturesque festoons.

Just as previously, the port passageway in the deck house was used as the dining room; its temperature was regulated by the conditions prevailing in the surrounding ice-covered landscape. For example, if the thermometer in the open stood at −20, inside, where the steward served us with chattering teeth, the temperature was about −15°. Hence it was not at all surprising that we never lingered longer at table than was absolutely necessary in order to satisfy our appetites. Soon after we had moved into our winter quarters, we learned by force of habit to cultivate that celerity in eating which one has to acquire at railway stations, when a train is allowed only a 10-minute stop for its passengers to get refreshments. The food that was served up hot suffered a more significant cooling on its trip from the platter to the plate, and from the latter to the mouth, than the crust of the earth did at the start of the Ice Age; and food that came cold to the table became even colder there, before it could be eaten. Mayonnaise attained the consistency that properly prepared arrow-root ought to possess; English mustard reached the degree of hardness that a sculptor gives his modelling clay, and butter acquired the consistency of air-dried Swiss cheese.

Anyone who had a feeling heart beating in his breast would be moved to deep sadness by the sight of the sour pickled cucumbers. Half a dozen cycles of thawing and freezing which they had experienced in succession had etched massive wrinkles in their youthfully green skins which covered the wrinkled, shrunken flesh in folds. Surrounded by plump onions, slender beans and crisp heads of cauliflower that swam in crisping vinegar, they formed the saddest component that any still-life ever incorporated.

A canvas roof that was spread over the after part of the vessel on the morning of 15 September cast a dreamlike twilight there and raised the temperature in the rooms. Since under these conditions the readings from the thermometers in the weather screen could no longer be reliable, over the course of the afternoon the screen was moved for the meantime onto the deck house and secured to the bridge. Due to this change in height the correction that had to be made to barometer readings in order to reduce them to sea level was increased. It was only a trifling change in the last decimal place and perhaps would have disappeared completely in averaging; despite this we considered it advisable not to neglect it. The thermometers were now influenced to only a minor degree by heat radiated from the ship; the screen that shielded them was far enough away from the location of the stovepipe, and even if it was also in the vicinity of the engine funnel, the proximity of the latter caused no concern, since we had let the steam drop. The engine was put into mothballs, since we did not need it during the winter; the individual parts were carefully overhauled and cleaned; the steam pipes were taken apart to prevent them from bursting.

Up till now the survey work had been proceeding almost without interruption. On the morning of the 16th, Meyer and Bryan left the ship to occupy some trigonometric stations in the south of the bay; Mauch accompanied them to give signals. Around midnight, when none of the gentlemen had returned, we began to be worried about their fate, since the task they had set themselves needed only a short time for its execution. One of the seamen was sent to the crow's-nest, in order to watch out for our companions, but although he used the best telescope he was unable to discover them. Around 1 o'clock two figures appeared in the distance; once they came closer we recognized them as Meyer and Bryan. They approached the ship with a dragging gait; every one of their movements was suggestive of fatigue; ice and rime covered their clothes. Their faculties were so far undermined that several times we had to ask them, by shouting, what had become of Mauch before we got a reply. Meyer was still capable of climbing aboard on his own; Bryan on the other hand needed help in order to ascend the steps. What the two men had experienced could be deduced from the condition of their frozen clothing; only later did we learn about their adventure in a coherent form.

After they had occupied one of the stations they decided to set off for another, the distance to which they greatly underestimated due to the extreme transparency of the air. When they reached the point it was 6.00 p.m.; they set up the theodolite, took a round of angles, then immediately started on their return journey across the frozen sea, in order to reach the ship by the shortest route. As they were crossing a newly formed sheet of ice Meyer broke through and sank up to his armpits; he was barely out of the water when Bryan suffered a similar accident. In order to avoid the danger of freezing they hurried back in the direction of the ship as quickly as their condition and the hummocky nature of the ice surface permitted. In so doing Meyer broke through again; Mauch, who was exhausted, was unable to follow them. Sunk into complete stupidity, he reached the vicinity of our anchorage sometime after 1.00 a.m. He noticed a wide crack which separated him from the ship only when he had soaked one of his feet in the water.[14] Like his two companions in misfortune he was put straight to bed. Hot coffee, laced with some cognac, did not fail to rekindle their prostrated spirits. Meyer recovered most rapidly; Bryan on the other hand needed longer before he was able to smile;[15] a refreshing sleep erased the last traces of the accident, which could easily have been fatal.

Various short excursions in the area surrounding the bay provided us with an insight into the topography of the newly discovered land, as well as its geological characteristics. Many of the erratic limestone boulders which lay scattered over the lowland and the uplands contained Upper Silurian fossils. The lithological character of these erratics completely matched that of the bedrock, but in the vicinity of the bay, at least, it contained no fossils at all. Moreover, at all the locations which we had visited thus far it nowhere occurred in massive form; it was invariably clearly stratified and often schistose, and displayed every conceivable folding and faulting.

Natural outcrops, with a length of 10 m and showing transitions from horizontal bedding right through to almost vertical dislocated dips, are far from rare in the range of hills that runs away to the east of the bay. In general the bedding planes are horizontal; only exceptionally are they gently undulating. In no case are the strata more than 33 cm thick; generally they are much thinner and at times so much so that the thickness of the beds does not exceed that of a sheet of cardboard. Here and there transverse schistosity is displayed, the rock disintegrating into innumerable needles, whose sharp points make the terrain almost impassable in places.

The predominant colour of the rock is ash-grey, with a variety of nuances. Amongst this grey rock one encounters brownish-black strata, whose dark colour derives from bituminous components, which are betrayed by their smell as soon as one rubs one piece against another or strikes them with a hammer. Rock without this admixture consists of an almost pure carbonaceous limestone containing only minor traces of clays and silicic acid. Calcspar veins running through the rock are rare; where they do occur they are always thin and insignificant.

Because of the low resistivity of the rock and dislocations of the bedding, the terrain is highly dissected. The lowland as well as the hill ranges is criss-crossed by narrow erosion gorges that during snowmelt form the beds of raging streams. In the south of the hilly peninsula that we later named Polaris Promontory, there is a stretch of land which represents a canyon region in miniature. The development of these canyons may be followed stage by stage there; alongside shallow furrows, gnawed into the rock by small rivulets, yawn dark gorges with vertical and commonly overhanging walls; with their dislocated bedding structures they resemble disintegrating masonry, grey with age. They run in a meandering pattern, dependent for their general alignment on the original course of the stream to which they owe their presence. They are almost devoid of vegetation since the shattering effect of frost breaks up the rock so quickly that plants barely have time to colonize the surface and their growth is hampered by the unique temperature conditions in any case.

The coast off which we had dropped anchor presented none of the scenic charms that one expects to see in the Far North. But in terms of geology it revealed an interesting transect of earth history.

Almost 100 years ago, in the vicinity of Igaliku in South Greenland, Arctander[16] made the observation that a small, low island, which bore old masonry, was so completely inundated during spring floods that the waves were almost washing the bases of the Viking structures. When Pingel[17] visited the site in the early 1830s he noticed that at high tide the sea level lay right at the ruins. By comparing his own observations with Arctander's he reached the conclusion that the coast had sunk over the course of time. His conclusion was substantiated by the fact that in the interim Leopold von Buch[18] had succeeded in ascribing the changes in level which are perceptible along the Norwegian coast to their true cause, recognizing that it was the coast, rather than the surface of the sea, which had changed its equilibrium.

Pingel assembled his observations and in 1835 presented a brief report to the Geological Society of London, in which he was able to identify several stretches of the Greenland coast as areas of subsidence. He mentioned the storehouses in the Danish colony of Julianehåb, in latitude 60°35'N. These were built in 1776 near the beach on an island; at the time of his visit the remains of the walls projected above the water only at lowest ebb tide. Similar conditions prevailed at Frederikshåb, at 62°, where there were some ruins of Eskimo huts around which the waves broke; in the vicinity of Fiskernæsset, too, he discovered old buildings whose inhabitants had had to abandon them to the waves. And at Lichtenfels he was told that over the course of 30–40 years the Greenlanders had once or twice been obliged to move the stands on which they stored their skin boats on the beach landward, because they were starting to be flooded at high tide. On a peninsula northeast of Godthåb, at 64° 10'N, he also found old huts which had still been occupied in 1736, but which were now underwater at high tide. From the well-substantiated utterances of a Danish official he was able to add to his own observations the fact that near the 67th parallel, north of Nye-Sukkertop, the coast was also affected by subsidence.

Later travellers have added to the evidence of these changes in level. The most northerly stretch of coast that Kane identified as an area of subsidence is located near the Crimson Cliffs; here it was again abandoned Eskimo huts which provided proof of the sinking of the remains; in his view this phenomenon did not occur beyond the 77th parallel.

Although we can frequently identify from carefully compiled maps the protracted victory which the ocean has been winning over the course of time against the solid body of our planet, once a prematurely deceased expert had sharpened our eyes to the phenomenon, losses of land that are occurring or have occurred in many cases reveal themselves only by direct observation. Where climatic conditions are inimical to the existence of reef-building corals, the ruined works of man are the only archives that promise any information to the historian. But the ice-covered sea which washes the Greenland coast offers no sites for those coral structures, and the desolate beach is so sparsely inhabited and so little visited that if subsidence occurs in uninhabited areas it is never discovered. If the land were not slowly rising from the bosom of the sea north of Wolstenholme Sound it would scarcely have been possible to determine the limits of the subsidence so precisely.

Again it is to Kane that we owe this information. At several points on the coast in the vicinity of his winter harbour he discovered rising, amphitheatre-shaped terraces that he recognized as old beach lines; hence the coast there must have risen. Hayes found similar evidence at Port Foulke. He counted 23 steps, the highest of which was 110 feet above sea level, while the lowest lay 32 feet above the extreme high-water mark.

Of disproportionately great interest are the observations that we made in Polaris Bay. There the land displayed the most unequivocal traces of the fact that it had risen from the sea only in the relatively recent past. Just as at Port Foulke and in the vicinity of Rensselaer Harbour, at various points round the bay there were regular terraces, genuine beach formations which consisted partly of small stones whose surfaces had been rounded by the effect of the waves. But we encountered even more unmistakable signs that the sea had once foamed where we now wandered dry-shod. On the lowland as well as on the hill ridges, which rose to 1800 feet, the calcareous remains of marine creatures lay scattered, whose species still live in the sea nearby. Everywhere that the site had favoured organic life there occurred innumerable shells of *Saxicava rugosa, Mya truncata* and other molluscs, embedded in crumbling clay banks and sometimes mixed with leaves of *Laminariae*, which fell to dust as soon as they came in contact with the air. There were also fragments of barnacle shells as well as splinters of wood that the waves had removed from more favoured regions and had cast up here. Later, in a small freshwater lake, 30 feet above the present highest level of spring tides, we discovered a marine crustacean, belonging to the family *Palaemonidae*, living evidence of the massive changes that had occurred here.

Thus, despite the magnificent rigidity with which it has armed itself, this desolate coast is in a stage of youthful movement that embraces the gloomy rock formations of the west coast of Greenland. The main axis of these oscillations lies between the 74th and 77th parallels. Just as the human chest rises with a deep breath, causing a sinking of the abdomen, so the northern part of the coast is straining upward while the main mass of the southern coast is gently sinking below the icy waters.

According to Robert Brown's observations, the bed of the Ilordlik Glacier, at 69°27'N, represents a limited area of uplift that displays clay beds with mollusc remains which lie 500 feet above present sea level.[19] In the case of Greenland too there is meagre evidence to support the idea of secular uplift.

Among the limestone rubble that covers the shore of Polaris Bay we often found minerals and rock fragments of such distinctive lithological character that we could scarcely be in doubt as to their original provenance. We discovered gneisses with garnet secretions similar to those we found outcropping at Fiskernæsset, a basalt similar to one we had seen at Disko, and among the rubble we picked up chabasite crystals and veins similar to those that occur near various of the colonies in North Greenland. Porphyry and syenite similar to those which we encountered later at Port Foulke were far from rare; less common was a reddish-yellow sandstone that contained large, rounded quartz grains; it was barely distinguishable from a beach formation that we saw later south of Cape Alexander. We also found a piece of labradorite and occasional fragments of hornblende and jasper.

This varied collection of minerals and rock types could only have reached its present position due to drifting ice masses; direct transport by glacier ice is entirely out of the question. Since one could scarcely hypothesize that the metamorphic rocks and the basaltic formation that occur south of the newly discovered land along the west coast of Greenland are precisely repeated north of the 81st parallel, the most natural thing is that the source of the erratic material is to be sought south of Polaris Bay.

Although hydrographic conditions in Davis Strait and its northern continuation have not yet been determined with all the accuracy one might wish, there is no doubt that the dominant direction of the current is southward. But since any current can carry any foreign bodies that are floating in it only in the direction of its flow, and since the erratic material that we encountered in Polaris Bay can be traced back to locations lying south of that bay, one can explain the transport of the rock material northward only by the assumption that the direction of the current earlier was totally opposite. But the current could have flowed northward only so long as the archipelago which now extends across the northeast of America formed part of the continent with which Greenland was connected. Since Polaris Bay lies at the northwestern extremity of Greenland and still shows clear traces of a southerly current, the separation of Greenland from America must have proceeded in the original direction of the current, namely from south to north. Only after the land-bridge that existed north of Polaris Bay had been destroyed, and Lancaster and Jones sounds had opened, could the arctic current penetrate into the present Smith Sound and its continuation; but until then the Greenland-American Basin, as I shall call Davis Strait and its northern extension, was under the complete influence of a southerly current.

At that time Greenland connected two worlds, whose flora and fauna it shared. On one side it was linked to America; on the other side with Europe, by way of Iceland. The northern part of the Atlantic Ocean formed a large bay. If we were to venture the experiment of redrawing an idealized pattern of currents for that period, we would have to imagine a current of warm water which flowed along the east coast of America. One of its branches penetrated into Davis Strait as far as the latter extended at the time; the other was deflected to the right of its course and washed the northeastern shores of the Atlantic basin. When the Ice Age began later and the cold air that flowed down across the land to the sea came in contact with the warm current, with its accompanying moist flow of air, abundant precipitation resulted along the then-Atlantic slopes of the European-American continent, first as rain, but later generally in the form of snow.

To pursue the Ice Age in greater detail would take us too far afield; there are already extensive works on it. I should like to restrict myself to letting our eyes sweep across a large detailed map of Greenland and to allow them to linger for a moment on the outlines of the east coast. We immediately realize that its southern part not only possesses more fiords than the northern part, but that those in the south are longer on average than those in the north. Although their coasts consist of hard, metamorphic rocks, they are probably longer and more numerous for the reason that they have had more time for their formation than those that transect the less resistant limestone formation in the north.

We allude to this fact in order to provide further support for our hypothesis that the separation of Greenland and America proceeded from south to north.

CHAPTER 8

The first sledge journey

Inadequate equipment. Departure. A saline interior lake. Old effects of glaciers and icebergs. Lemming tracks. Dissected terrain. Climbing Mt. Chester. Trout. Fossils in a Primary stratum. Salt steppes. Inadequate snow cover. The first muskox shot. Natural history of the muskox. Return to the ship.

The general plan of operations of the expedition, as Hall had designed it, rested largely on using sledges; but our equipment for sledge journeys left much to be desired. The special equipment that the British had used on their various polar expeditions, and at the improvement of which they had worked so successfully, existed only in illustrations as far as we were concerned. The only portable stove which had accidentally found its way on board was a miserable abortion made of galvanized black sheet iron. The craftsman whose hands had produced it was probably a pious man who considered the laws of the Temperance Society to be the Eleventh Commandment, and alcohol a gift from hell; due to the quality of its construction the stove was adapted only for burning wood. But due to its considerable volume and its low calorific value, wood is an extremely inappropriate fuel and on long marches one that is scarcely usable since only in rare cases can supplies be renewed during a journey. Beyond the 81st parallel, which is where we were now, we could scarcely expect to encounter driftwood in large amounts, and the vegetation of the newly discovered land was so sparse that if fate had transported Nebuchadnezzar to the shores of Polaris Bay, he would have been hard put to it to indulge the strange tastes that made him a vegetarian for the latter period of his life. We possessed no alcohol lamps at all, and the few cans of alcohol on board were intended for preserving natural history specimens.

Due to Chester's thoroughness, the equipment for our impending journey was now as complete as circumstances would permit; in the meantime the plan for the intended hunting party had matured. According to Hall's instructions we were not only to supply the galley with game but also to undertake a reconnaissance of the area in order to determine whether it would be possible to head for the Pole overland in case the ice-covered sea turned out to be impassable for sledges during the coming spring.

At 7.30 on the morning of 18 September we were ready to set off. The travelling party consisted of Chester, the two Eskimos and myself; eight dogs, including one Newfoundlander, were harnessed to the Greenland sledge which was loaded with about 3 centners. Two sleeping bags formed the foundation of the load; on top of them lay a bag of split wood; then came the provisions, the dog-food consisting of pemmican and dried fish, as well as four small bags with spare clothing and the cooking utensils. A light canvas tent, lashed with undressed leather thongs, formed a protective covering. On the front part of the sledge sat a box containing the instruments; on the right side lay our rifles, ready for action, and on the left side the tent poles and alpenstocks.

Hall, who was watching us from on board, was kind enough to send several seamen after us to help us manhandle the sledge over the shattered shore ice; once we had reached the vicinity of the observatory we said goodbye to the men. Our course at first lay in a southerly direction. The dogs, long unaccustomed to pulling, could be kept moving only by continued use of the whip. Whenever we reached bare rocky ground, we were obliged to carry the sledge, since the dogs' refractoriness increased as the snow cover decreased. Only when Hans ran ahead of them trailing a fish to which he had attached a line along the ground behind him did we make faster progress. Gradually the traces became more taut and the dogs willingly pursued the unattainable herring that the two natives took turns in dragging ahead of them.

Around 12 the dogs utterly refused to continue. We found ourselves forced to take a little rest and decided to use the resultant pause to brew some coffee. Ahead of us spread a small lake and we were easily able to smash through its 5-inch ice cover, using one of the geological hammers. While Joseph kindled the fire, Hans fetched the water. We had all become thirsty and Chester, who immediately began drinking in great gulps, surprised us with the statement that the water was salty. Hans poured out the contents of the kettle and refilled it with snow, which quickly began to melt over the blazing flames.

Using the aneroid barometer we determined our resting place to lie at a height of 110 feet above sea level. The lake, which was about 1½ miles long, was barely ¾ of a mile wide and lay about 4 miles from the sea. It provided further proof of coastal uplift. Unfortunately neither time nor circumstances permitted us to investigate its fauna and flora, and the cognac bottle that we had intended to use to take a sample of its water on the return journey was smashed when the sledge overturned before it could fulfil that purpose.

After we had rested about 45 minutes we continued our journey, changing from our previous course to an east-northeasterly one. We had barely covered a few miles when we ran across the track of an adult muskox which might have been three to four days old. We followed it for a short distance, then lost it on rocky ground and were unable to pick it up again. Joseph thought he saw a resting herd in the distance, but the telescope revealed the dark bodies to be boulders which, due to the warm air rising, quivering from the ground, seemed to be moving slightly.

Ahead of us lay a small valley, from the bottom of which rose dissected beds of the same stratified limestone that we had encountered near our anchorage. Depending on whether the rock occurred in thicker or thinner strata, the slopes of the limestone descended more or less steeply; rarely were they over 50 feet in height.

Had we encountered any moraines on our hike we might have identified with certainty the occasional beds of clay that we now ran across, and that contained shell remains and the bones of *Mallotus arcticus*,[1] as glacial clays. They reminded us strongly of similar deposits that we had seen at Kongsfjorden, Spitsbergen, where a crevassed glacier descends from the Tre Kroner [Three Crowns] at the back of that bay. But since we had nowhere found incontestable moraines, the mention of the fact, unencumbered by nomenclature, will have to suffice. When we attempted to plot the position of these clay beds roughly on a map, and then joined the points together with a contour line, it turned out that the direction in which the tops of these deposits were aligned was almost parallel to the alignment of the coast.

As on previous occasions, now too we found the ground completely covered with rubble and erratics, amongst which numerous clam shells lay scattered. Here and there were quite large areas, entirely swathed in small, weathered, limestone fragments; groups of granite and syenite boulders projected above them in an irregular arrangement. The idea of ascribing a monumental significance to these groupings was a very tempting one. They probably mark spots where rock-laden icebergs stranded shortly before the coast rose and then gradually melted. From the crushed state of the underlying limestone, however, we might perhaps conclude that these current-transported offspring of a more southerly glacier had taken quite a long time to melt and that they had not undergone this dissolution entirely quietly but rather were constantly disturbed by the rise and fall of the tide.

The valley along which we had been travelling thus far opened to the east into a narrow erosion-gorge whose windings we now followed. The stream flowing through it was covered with a thin ice cover, on which the dogs flew along. We could now sit on the sledge for the first time. Usually three of us enjoyed the pleasure of a ride while the fourth man panted along behind the sledge in order to guide it, since numerous boulders protruding above the ice had to be avoided.

Around 8.00 p.m. we reached a fork in the gorge, in front of which stretched a small spread of alluvium, like a delta; here we pitched camp. The distance we had covered, including all the twists and turns, might well have been 30 miles, although in a straight line it was not more than 15.

Once we had made the pleasant discovery that we had forgotten our tin plates and forks, we prepared our frugal meal, consisting of pemmican soup, salt pork and hardtack. We ate communally from the soot-covered kettle in which we brewed coffee at noon. As our sole luxury we allowed ourselves a swallow of cognac, but even through it there could be no mistaking the aftertaste of the black pemmican soup. Sometimes it assumed the combined taste of dried meat, beef fat, sugar and currants; sometimes these various components came through separately, with varying intensity. Hunger and necessity, those severe pedagogues of the stomach, had to swing their educational rods with great effect before the defiance of our pampered organs of digestion was broken.

It can scarcely be denied that from a physiological point of view the combination of meat and fat is a superb one; but from a culinary point of view it raises much doubt. The minor addition of sugar and currants gives the dish a more pleasant taste, when eaten raw, than the mixture alone possesses; but the latter is definitely preferable when it has been handled by the camp kitchen.

Once the usual meteorological observations had been taken and the maximum and minimum thermometers had been hung up near the tent, we crawled into our sleeping bags; a rounded chunk of limestone, which contained numerous corals, formed my pillow.

At 6.00 a.m. on the 19th we were again ready to set off. We left the tent behind, filled with our possessions and secured by a wall of rocks; by contrast the sledge was loaded with provisions and dog food for two days, as well as with the most essential instruments, our alpenstocks and our rifles. We hoped that, freer in our movements, we might cover a greater distance than previously.

We again followed the course of the stream through the ravine. At many places the ice cover was so thin that we could travel only slowly; one of the natives constantly had to run ahead of the sledge in order to test the treacherous ice cover. After we had travelled about two miles the narrow canyon began to widen and the structure of its walls began to change; instead of the slaty rock there appeared massive cliffs that gradually rose to a height of 300 feet. Absorbed in examining the rock structures, none of us noticed that the sledge had travelled onto thin ice; a crackling noise warned us to watch out. Before we had time to jump up the runners had already broken through and then the ice cover suddenly gave way; we were standing hip-deep in water. The dogs were far from pleased at this ice-cold bath and freely gave vent to their feelings by growling loudly and biting each other's legs and tails. We cut the traces and left the animals to their own devices; they rushed to the nearby shore, howling and shaking themselves. It was not so easy for us to rescue the sledge; its load, like our clothes, was thoroughly soaked; we finally found ourselves obliged to hoist it up and carry it on our heads. Four teeth-chattering, fur-trimmed caryatids, from whose lips issued alternately loud laughter and coarse curses, we limped toward the nearest sandbar. We then wrung out each other's dripping clothes, which were already starting to freeze. Since our spare clothing had been left behind in the tent, we tried to ward off any ill effects with a spoonful of cognac; then we caught the dogs, harnessed them to the sledge and continued our journey.

Around 10 o'clock we reached an oval basin that incidentally may have been a mile long and about 200 paces wide; its main axis ran almost north–south. To the east the walls rose as in an amphitheatre to an apparently sharp crest about 600 feet high. The walls to the west were of similar structure but somewhat lower and severely gullied. The individual steps, whose levels matched on either side of the basin, were on average 3 to 5 feet high, about 10 feet wide, and dropped at a steep angle.

When we ran across some muskox dung, we made a halt; a nearby snowdrift revealed the animal's hoof-prints, but just as before, we lost the tracks on bare ground. We stowed the sledge in a crack in the rock and secured half the team to a rock pinnacle a little distance away. Four of the dogs were taken in hand by the natives. We then shouldered our rifles in order to search for game on the ridges; Chester and Joseph headed west while Hans and I climbed the slopes to the east.

After a 90-minute hike we reached the mountain ridge. We could see our ship clearly through the telescope; long strips of water stretched along the coast of Grinnell Land. A plain about 25 miles wide extended to the north, ending in a blue plateau; as far as could be determined rock outcrops of varying heights were scattered across its surface. Rounded hill masses rose to the east, and behind them stretched a massive glacier, which appeared to connect with a glacier we could see to the south. No further reconnaissance was possible from our present position; on the other hand a conical mountain about 2000 feet high, about 5 miles away, promised a better distant view. Once we had sketched the surrounding area we started back. A flight of ptarmigan flew up close in front of us; Hans and I fired almost simultaneously but both bullets missed their target. Somewhat later we encountered several hare tracks; a snowdrift that had accumulated behind a boulder showed the sinuous track of a small mammal. Since we later found fresh fox droppings that contained lemming bone fragments, we decided that this small track must be that of one of these little rodents. For the moment we had to be content with these few bones; months would pass before we saw a live animal. The occurrence of the species in West Greenland was previously unknown.[2]

Reaching the sledge, we found Chester and Joseph occupied in preparing a meal; their hunting luck had been no better than ours. Joseph had found droppings that were at least one summer old and that he thought were those of a wolf. Since Chester had also selected the nearby conical mountain as the goal of his next hike, we decided to climb it together and to send the natives off hunting in the opposite direction.

By way of a narrow gorge with overhanging walls, and with some detours, we reached a low limestone plateau whose northern slope we ascended; gradually our route climbed at a steep angle toward the mountain peak. Suddenly we were standing at the edge of a deep, vertically eroded chasm that lay transverse to our route; it was of considerable width and there was no possibility of jumping it, while to circumvent it would be too tedious. Hence we selected a likely spot and climbed down into it, with a view to climbing up to the other rim. Having reached the latter, we had barely walked a further half mile when we ran into another similar obstacle; but this canyon turned out to be deeper than the first. The distance we had covered vertically in clambering up and down these slopes was almost greater than the straight-line distance to the sledge. But with hopes that conditions would improve, we continued our trek. We encountered yet another canyon, even deeper than the previous ones; again we reached the opposite lip, but this time barely 50 paces separated us from another gorge. We had barely crossed this one when we were faced with another chasm; the mountain peak seemed unattainable. In three hours of strenuous progress we had not advanced more than a mile. For this reason we decided to walk round the plateau on which we were standing, in the direction of strike of the canyons, with a view to then reaching the foot of the mountain or its vicinity, via one of them. We returned to the spot where the sledge lay hidden; en route we met the two natives, who complained of their failure at hunting; we then headed for the tent.

During our absence a fox had taken advantage of the time to attack our supply of pemmican and to gnaw at one of Joseph's boots which had fallen from the tent ridge. We lit eight stearine candles, and this illumination served the double purpose of lighting up the interior of the tent festively and of thawing out and partially drying our frozen clothes.

A thick fog which had descended during the night did not allow us to set off until 8 o'clock next morning. In the immediate vicinity of our campsite we had spotted a ravine that seemed to lead to the mountain, in the ascent of which our perseverance had been exhausted yesterday. As before, we sent the natives off hunting; Chester and I set off in the direction of the foot of the peak. After we'd followed the course of the ravine for about half a mile, we climbed one of its walls and set off across lightly undulating terrain with a sparse growth of creeping plants; but at many points it was thickly strewn with erratic boulders. Around 10 o'clock we reached a lake which may well have been a mile in length. The thick ice crust that covered it was as transparent as crystal. As we quickly slid across it we spotted numerous fish; later, when we were able to examine a shoal of them close-up, they turned out to be trout. We regretted that we had set off without fishing lines or nets; given the boldness of the fish it would have been possible to make a good haul. As far as we could judge the lake had no outflow in any direction; it was obviously fed by snowmelt from the surrounding hills. Around its shores one could determine that the water level must recently have been about 3 feet higher than at present. Once we'd reached a fairly high point, a second, somewhat smaller lake lay before us; over almost the entire extent its ice cover was clouded a milky colour. The more transparent spots, a dark sea-green in colour, formed almost round, dendritically branching shapes, almost 12 inches in diameter. They commonly appeared closely grouped together in assemblages of 6 to 10 individuals, but we never encountered any whose outer extremities touched each other; they were always separated by a narrow strip of milky ice, which sometimes could be distinguished only with the magnifying glass. We remained in doubt as to their origin; this was the first and only time that we spotted such formations.

After hiking for two hours we reached the foot of the mountain; en route we had encountered two more lakes. We now searched in vain for a suitable place to make the ascent; finally we had to be content with climbing a slope whose angle was nowhere less than 60°. The shattering effect of frost was displayed everywhere; every step forward encountered loose rock debris which yielded underfoot and began rolling noisily. We often ran across vertical cliffs that had to be circumvented by detours. For the first time since we had left the ship the sun was now shining; it lay low in the cloud-covered southeastern sky. Its warming rays lured occasional small wolf-spiders out of their hiding places; they scuttled agilely across the grey limestone rocks and hid in the narrow crevices whenever we tried to catch them. When we turned over several thin slabs of rock, we came across the spiders' webs on their lower surfaces and numerous lens-shaped egg sacs; apparently the eggs overwinter. Otherwise there was no organic life anywhere; every trace of plant life had disappeared. The rapid weathering of the non-resistant limestone could not but be inimical to the development of vegetation.

The higher we climbed, the more dangerous the going; it was 2.30 p.m. when we reached the summit. At 8.00 a.m., shortly before we left the ship, the aneroid reading had been recorded as 28.958"; now it was 27.152." Unfortunately the simultaneous temperature and hygrometer readings, as well as the corresponding barometer readings that were made on board ship, have gone missing; hence the height of the mountain could not subsequently be determined accurately. On a later occasion Hall bestowed Chester's name on this peak, whose height was certainly over 2000 feet. Its summit took the form of a small plateau, in the middle of which we built a low cairn; unfortunately there was not enough material for a larger structure.

From our elevated position it was possible to get an adequate picture of the surrounding topographical relations which thus far had remained obscure. Beyond the plateau that bounded the plain lying before us on the north, mountain ranges now came into view which yesterday had not been visible from the top of the ridge. What appeared to us as a large river covered with icebergs turned out later, during Hall's sledge journey to the north, to be the end of an extensive bay which cut into the land between the plateau and the mountain range lying beyond it. As we had suspected, there was an unbroken connection between the glaciers that we had spotted yesterday to the south and east beyond the rounded hill ranges. They formed a brilliant, slightly undulating high plateau which seemed completely free of crevasses. The ship appeared to the northwest as a dark speck; wide strips of water still glistened along the Grinnell Land coast. Mobile banks of fog hung over them, their edges glowing a pale orange-red. Beneath us, clustered around the foot of the mountain, lay small freshwater lakes; we counted seven of them.

A stiff northwest breeze that occasionally degenerated into violent gusts made our sojourn on the summit less than pleasant. We quickly sketched the surrounding area and Chester chipped off some hand specimens from the bedrock; then we travelled down the first 300 feet of the peak with the speed of a rolling bowling ball, by way of a narrow snow gully. The descent involved more difficulties than the ascent; but the latter required less time than the former, since we slid down the steepest of the slopes. We reached the bottom with scratched hands and with somewhat damaged pants. We repeatedly resorted to the forbidden procedure of eating snow in order to quench our burning thirst, but we were not able to satisfy it completely until we reached the tent.

The natives returned as darkness was falling; they had found tracks but they had been unable to claim the $10 prize which we had offered for the first muskox. The remainder of our task lay clear before us: the next trip must be aimed at exploring the plain that stretched to the north.

Just as on the previous day, on the morning of the 21st the landscape was enveloped in fog; when we stepped outside at 5 o'clock it was barely possible to see even 10 paces. Surrounded by undulating masses of vapour, the dogs lying nearby appeared as big as cattle. For the moment we could not set off. While Joseph made breakfast, I strolled around near the tent in order to chip off hand specimens from the outcropping rocks. In a bed of bituminous limestone I found an Orthoceratid, about 1 foot long. I searched in vain for more fossils: the Orthoceras was the only fossil we had found in situ thus far.[3]

Almost everywhere that there was dry alluvium it was covered with a crumbling, dark, ash-grey layer that seemed to consist of lichens. A microscopic examination of this substance, made on a later occasion on board ship, revealed this conjecture to be false: the crust was composed solely of small salt crystals which quickly dissolved when a drop of water was applied. We later encountered similar salt efflorescences on the shores of Polaris Bay and at various other localities.

By around 10 o'clock the atmosphere had become clearer; we broke camp and searched for a practicable route to reach the plain. At first we were following our old sledge tracks. In the gorge the wind seemed to have been blowing strongly; where we had been travelling over a smooth ice surface only a few days before, there were now inch-deep deposits of sand and gravel, which had originated from the immediate vicinity. In order to be able to set a northerly course without wasting any time, we had to leave the ravines at the first suitable opportunity. Chester and I climbed one of the walls and walked along the edge of the gorge in order to reconnoitre the terrain; Joseph and Hans followed below with the sledge. Reaching an almost vertical cliff, we had the sledge stopped and unloaded; it was then secured to a rope and hauled up, followed by the load. Finally, using a sling, we hauled the dogs up one by one; every jerk on the rope was accompanied by a loud howl from the dog being hauled up; the rest of the pack joined in, duty-bound. Once the two natives had climbed up we carried the bags of provisions up a nearby rocky slope which descended to the plain, packed the sledge and pushed on.

If we'd possessed a small cart or riding horses, it would have been an easy matter to cover considerable distances. But under the prevailing circumstances our progress was extremely meagre. On the snow-free terrain the sledge turned out to be not simply totally useless; it actually impeded our progress. We were no longer able to choose our course but had to follow the individual snow patches that lay scattered ahead of us. As a result we were able to cover only a few miles in the course of a day. An extensive plain extended northward, but we had no other alternative but to cross it on foot. The inadequate snow cover made a mockery of all our efforts, and this in a region which one is only too easily inclined to think of as a wilderness of snow and ice. Very little of the two snow-falls which had occurred since our arrival at Polaris Bay, and which had undoubtedly extended over this plain, was left lying on the ground. The wind had swept the terrain almost clear and had deposited the snow along the slopes and in depressions.

Toward evening we reached a shallow trough, evenly filled with snow. But it stretched in a southeasterly direction and hence could not serve our purposes. We pitched camp near a gently rising limestone outcrop. Just as we were about to crawl into the tent Joseph spotted a muskox on a nearby hill; the shaggy animal gazed at us, half suspiciously, half curiously.

In a moment we were ready to fire; if the distance that separated us from our quarry had not been too great we would have started firing immediately. Inquisitively the animal trotted toward us. Joseph was the only one among us who had hunted muskoxen before. We left the attack to him. He quickly released six of the dogs from the traces; the remaining two he hid behind the tent. The animals had never seen a muskox, but once he had shown them their quarry they immediately hurled themselves toward it; only the Newfoundland cautiously stopped halfway there, in order to respond to that call of nature that seems to whisper to a dog's acute ear from every street corner. Only when he had sufficiently examined and smelled the yellow hieroglyphics that he had drawn on the snow did he join the pack, which their shaggy opponent immediately faced.

The fight was unequal and unusual; we let it proceed for some time without using our rifles. The muskox had received the dogs with lowered head, stock-still, as if carved from stone. They leaped up at it, howling and barking; but it scarcely stirred; a slight turn of the head was all that indicated it was alive. Its long hair flew wildly in the wind.

But the surprise did not last long. Suddenly it began to snort furiously, to stamp the snow, and to turn quickly in a circle. Wherever it turned its head the dogs would be barking at it. They had still not mounted any serious attack; now they began to tug at their enemy's long, trailing hair, to seize him by the legs, and sometimes to make long jumps right over him Its patience was completely exhausted; it was breathing heavily, and in the icy air its warm breath condensed to make clouds. The entire animal seemed to be steaming. Then it again lowered its head, as it had initially when it was waiting for the dogs, agilely caught a dog on its massive horns, and sent it sailing up in a wide arc. The dog that had been tossed writhed whimpering on the ground; the others hurriedly retreated. Standing tall, apparently undecided as to whether to flee or to stand its ground, the muskox eyed first us, then the dogs. Three shots rang out almost simultaneously. The animal collapsed under the shots;

Fig. 13. A muskox hunt.

then it got up in a wild leap and charged at us. The dogs renewed their attack; some of them licked greedily at the blood which reddened the snow. A shoulder shot ended the battle.

The muskox was skinned without any loss of time. We carefully dismembered the still-warm carcass in order to save the valuable skeleton for the collection. The natives ate large pieces of tender meat raw; Chester and I followed their example.[4]

We had barely finished this bloody work[5] when a violent northeasterly storm broke; it confined us to camp for the whole of the next day. Our flimsy tent was often battered so violently by the gusts that we found ourselves obliged to build shelter-walls of snow blocks. Due to the voracity of the dogs we had stowed the fresh meat beside us in the tent; the team repeatedly tried to make assaults on our supplies.

While we were waiting for the weather to improve Joseph told us of his previous muskox hunts and told us of features from the life of the animal that fully deserve to find a place in the following sketch-like description.

In appearance more arctic than any other animal in the Far North, the muskox appeared to us as the original symbol of strength accompanied by harmlessness and dignity. As a contemporary of the Palaeolithic cave-dwellers of southern France, it rouses our interest and sympathy since it is one of the few herbivores of that period that has managed to survive until now. On average it is the size of a large cow. The totally hair-covered, wide head, with horns whose degree of development depends on the animal's age and sex, rests on a short neck. The long hair of the throat is reminiscent of an ox's dewlap. Dark-brown, coarse hair, which in some places on the body may reach a length of over 2 feet, hangs from the thick-set body. Beneath it lies an ash-grey under-wool, which is visible only on the back in the vicinity of the loins and here, along with brownish-yellow guard hairs, interrupts the animal's dark colour. Directly above and somewhat behind the nape of the neck, the coat reaches a massive thickness; as a result this part of the body appears somewhat elevated, like the hump of a buffalo. The hind quarters drop away steeply. The powerful legs which, due to the long hanging guard-hairs, seem much shorter than they are in reality, bear a dense, close deer-coloured coat from the knee downward. In contrast to true oxen the hooves are narrow and asymmetrically rounded on the outside, while they run to a point on the inside.

The name "muskox" is not a felicitously chosen one, since the animal has more features in common with sheep and goats than with true oxen. Jérémie, a French fur trader,[6] who first mentioned it in 1720 in his *Relation du détroit et de la baie d'Hudson*, says that the animals are called "boeufs musqués" because of their smell of musk. More descriptive is the Latin name *ovibos*, which takes account of the combination of the different characteristics. While the exterior, if we include the apparent lack of a tail, resembles a long-haired ox at a cursory glance, the skeleton points in the most indubitable fashion to its relationship to the sheep, and to a subordinate degree to the goat. Probably earlier natural historians, like the great Cuvier,[7] and more recent ones like Richard Owen,[8] let themselves be misled by the shape of the horns into classifying the animals as oxen. In fact the massive horns of the bull, which touch at their bases, have great similarity to those of the African buffalo, but no true ox possesses a hair-covered nose like the muskox; no ox is without a dewlap; and finally no ox possesses such a stunted tail.

Although Kane and Hayes found well-preserved bone remains and hair of muskoxen between 78° and 79° on the east shore of Smith Sound, it was still a surprise to us to encounter the animal alive at such high latitudes. According to the report of the former of these explorers, an Eskimo alleged to have seen a small herd near Rensselaer Harbour in spring 1850, while Hayes informs us that in 1850 a resident of Etah even killed one of these animals in the vicinity of Wolstenholme Sound.

This much is certain: we are indebted to the members of the Second German North Pole Expedition[9] for the first incontestable report of the occurrence of the muskox in Greenland; they found it to be abundant along the east coast. Previously it was excluded from the lists of Greenland's mammalian fauna.

Apart from Greenland one now encounters it distributed widely over the archipelago that extends north from the northeast corner of America, probably as far as the northernmost extremities of Grinnell Land.

If one attempts to plot its range on a map according to the available information, at first it seems striking that the animals are absent from the largest island of that archipelago, namely Baffin Island, whereas they are quite common on the adjacent islands to the west.[10] According to Joseph's report the inhabitants of Baffin Island have a tradition which allows us, with a certain degree of precision, to determine when the muskoxen died out there. Frobisher's landing in the bay named after him, near Meta Incognita, survives down to the present day in the oral tradition of the inhabitants of Baffin Island; although they have no way of calculating time, they certainly remember this indisputable fact, which their forefathers have handed down to them. The last muskoxen were killed about two generations before the Frobisher expedition arrived, which is known to have been in 1576. If we assume that an Eskimo lives to an age of 50 to 60 years, the time of the animal's disappearance would be the second half of the 15th century. Joseph told me in addition that near Lake Kennedy[11] he had found skull fragments and remains of horns, which removed any doubt as to the former occurrence of the animal.

The 60th parallel may probably be taken as the main southern boundary of its present distribution on the American continent, although individuals occasionally penetrate south to the shores of the Nelson; it is still encountered fairly frequently in the vicinity of Fort Churchill. How far its range extends to the west has to remain unresolved for the moment.[12] Murray[13] would have its western boundary coincide with the Mackenzie River, probably on Richardson's authority, although thus far there is no adequate basis for this suggestion.

None of the many animals that we later killed possessed a striking smell of musk. Whether this is to be ascribed to the high latitude at which we encountered them, or to the circumstance that we were not killing them during the rut, is best left unresolved here. Joseph, who had hunted muskoxen at various times on the west shores of Hudson Bay, had never encountered such smell-free meat. He reported that at times muskox meat tasted so repugnant that it was refused even by the natives. We ourselves ate it both raw and cooked, and preferred it to the best beef. When the meat was raw the peculiar taste was always barely noticeable, and if it was prepared skilfully it disappeared completely. It was certainly never strong enough to overcome the aroma of an onion.

Various experienced travellers and hunters consider it difficult to distinguish the track of a muskox from that of a caribou. On hard ground this may well be correct; but on soft ground or on a snow surface, with some practice, the two tracks could scarcely be confused. The track of the muskox is always more widely spread than that of the caribou and the individual hoof impressions are larger; even the hoof of a year-old cow leaves a wider track than that of an old caribou. A caribou track always shows the impressions of the dew-claws, which in the case of a muskox track are only visible if it is travelling over deep snow or very marshy ground. But even then there can be no doubt, since the slender feet of the deer leave smaller tracks than the large feet of the muskox. Even the track of a calf may be distinguished from that of a young caribou by the absence of impressions of the dew-claws.

The animals usually live in herds, which often number 100 head or more.[14] Their food consists mainly of the various grasses of the arctic flora and of arctic willow as well as moss in exceptional cases if no other fodder is to be found. They are, in the truest sense of the word, sedentary animals, which probably winter at the highest latitudes yet reached, and migrate only if the grazing at their present location is no longer sufficient to sustain them. If in so doing they are obliged to cross rivers with strong currents, many drown, since they are poor swimmers and make only slow progress. Joseph reported that only the nose, forehead and horns of a swimming muskox are visible.

The rut occurs between September and November. Between May and June a cow gives give birth to a single calf, which suckles for 3 to 4 months; only exceptionally does she produce twins, corresponding to the number of her teats. The calves are a uniform dark brown; the coat consists of a loose wool, like the coat of a true Newfoundlander. The first moult occurs in the fall; the horns erupt in spring. While in the male calves the back starts to turn a light colour quite early, in the female the yellow-brown patch of hair usually appears only when they grow their summer coat. Both cows and bulls become capable of reproduction in their third year, although they reach full size by the end of the second year.

By far the majority of a herd consists of cows, of which there are about 10 to 20 for each bull. During the rut the latter becomes wild and jealous and fights furiously and vehemently for possession of the cows. Rarely do these fights last longer than a few hours; even more rarely is one of the opponents killed, since the animals charge head-to-head, and even a rifle bullet ricochets harmlessly off their horn bosses. But it often happens that the heavy horns split, or that the combatants become entangled by their horns and remain hooked together for days. During a fight their hoarse voices may be heard, approximately resembling the snorting of a walrus. This snorting, whose utterance may denote various emotions, is the only sound that they emit; their voices never approach a tone reminiscent of the bleating of goats or the baaing of sheep. When danger approaches, the lookout that is posted when a herd is sleeping or grazing never vocalizes but contents itself with stamping the ground or poking the animal lying nearest with its horns, whereupon the signal is quickly repeated.

In its northern home the muskox is threatened by only two real enemies apart from man: the bear and the wolverine.[15] While the latter might be able to overcome and kill a calf at best, the former may attack even an adult bull when driven by extreme hunger. It is not always the winner, since the sharp horns of its peaceable opponent are weapons that can inflict fatal wounds.

Joseph was witness to a fight in which the bear came off second best. As a bear usually does, it had attempted a frontal attack in order to get a good bite at the neck. The muskox, an old animal, awaited it with lowered head. After several vain attempts to scare its opponent, the bear suddenly seized it by the hair; the muskox pulled loose by jumping backward and prepared for a renewed attack. When the assault came, it threw the bear sideways, then attacked it so energetically with its horns that it fled as fast as possible. It had barely covered a hundred paces when it collapsed dead. Apart from several minor wounds in the chest area, its courageous antagonist had smashed two ribs and had slit open the full length of the abdomen.

A similar fate overtook one of our Eskimo dogs which once took it into its head to hunt on its own account. After we had missed the dog for 4 or 5 days on board ship, one of the seamen found it with its flank slit open, lying on the beach a mile from the ship. The wound was so deep that at one point the upper thigh bone was not only laid completely bare, but the pereosteum was even partly removed. Numerous tracks in the soft ground gave evidence of the violence of the battle, which was the last battle that brave Schuhmacher, the gem of our team, was to fight.

The injury turned out to be so bad that it seemed advisable to relieve the poor sufferer from his pain with a revolver bullet.

Depending on the nature of the terrain and the degree of experience of the muskoxen, hunting them may be more or less exciting. If the hunter has a good dog team he is assured of certain success under any circumstances; but if he does not possess a dog or simply hunting dogs that have been trained by the book, he may find it extremely difficult to get within range, especially in open country, without sufficient cover. In terms of its moods the muskox is almost as unpredictable as our fox; amongst muskoxen one finds widely differing characters, which express their various temperaments in various ways, and by all sorts of apparently clumsy movements.

While muskoxen usually see man as an unscrupulous enemy, whose upright gait remains an eternal puzzle, and at whose approach they generally flee, they appear to cherish an insuperable liking for dogs. They gaze at them inquisitively and react in a trusting fashion which presents a comical aspect in view of their ungainliness, until the dogs tearing at their hair begins to make them uncomfortable. If one of the dogs forgets itself so far as to bite the muskox in the leg instead of in the wool, it stamps the ground, lowers its head, snorting, and for the first time tries to make serious use of its horns. If dogs attack a herd it invariably forms a square or a circle; the cows and calves, if there are any, are placed in the middle and the herd moves in this closed formation, with short pauses, from one spot to another, without losing its composure in the slightest. Since the outer animals devote their full attention to the dogs, the hunter can openly approach the animals without any cover at all, to the point that he can calmly shoot them with a revolver. As long as the dogs continue to play their role none of the animals makes the slightest attempt to escape. In this fashion the Eskimo easily overcomes them with bow and arrow; occasionally he simply uses a walrus lance or a seal spear; these latter are secured to a line and after each thrust can be retrieved and then again hurled at the target.

Hunting without using dogs is more sportsmanlike and nobler, since then, in the majority of cases, one has to stalk the game without it catching one's scent. Usually the herd flees after the first shot, but using a bow it is possible to kill several head before the animals run away. In this connection one can make superb observations on individual degrees of development of maternal love. Many cows will use every means to get their less-fleet calves to safety, whereas others will leave their offspring in the lurch in the most inconsiderate fashion. Occasionally even strange mothers will adopt orphaned calves. One of our men fired at a suckling cow; it dropped dead but broke one of its calf's hind legs in falling. Before he had time to reload in order to shoot another cow, one of them trotted up and tried to raise the calf with its horns; it abandoned its efforts only when a fatal bullet penetrated its heart. The calf was brought on board but had to be killed soon afterward because of its injury.

Only in rare cases will a muskox attack a man unprovoked, whereas when wounded it can become an unpleasant enemy. One old bull pursued one of our men so energetically when his ammunition ran out, that he opted to take to his heels. Joseph told me about one of his friends in the Hudson Bay area who received such a bad wound on his right buttock from an animal that had been shot that he was lame in his right leg for life. Joseph himself experienced an adventure of a more lighthearted nature. During the rut he was stalking an old bull harmlessly grazing across level terrain on which occasional boulders lay scattered. Before he got within range the animal spotted him and trotted toward him. When it was about 20 paces away he tried firing but the percussion cap failed. A moment later and the bull was right on him. He took to his heels but his pursuer quickly caught up with him. Reaching a boulder he made a halt in order to reload, but before he could carry out his intention the animal was close enough to touch and he made himself ready for battle. Joseph hopped up onto the boulder, which was about 2 feet high and which his opponent immediately began to attack with its horns. In his excitement the hunter dropped the box with his percussion caps and could not bend down to retrieve it. The bull stubbornly continued its attack on the rock, but never butting high enough to hit Joseph. The latter had to turn constantly so as not to turn his back on his circling antagonist, and when his patience was exhausted he beat the animal about the nose with his rifle stock, but this did not discourage it at all from continuing its efforts. For more than an hour it vented its rage on the rock. When it finally trotted away it received a ball in the loins and a second one stretched it out.

If I have spent rather long on the muskox and its lifestyle, this happened only because I was able to derive the bulk of my material from a man whose major occupation was hunting. Accustomed from childhood to sharpening his gift of observation in this direction, he noticed small details that usually escape the eye of the dull-sensed civilized man, and had had experiences that could only happen to an Eskimo. I record here with pleasure the fact that I owe him sincere thanks for the multifarious lessons that he was always prepared to teach me, both during the long winter night on board ship and on the trips which we made together for various purposes. It would indeed be unjust if I were not to admit that the cursory remarks that from time to time I am able to offer on the lives of animals and Eskimos, insofar as they represent anything new, are largely his contribution. I believe I can vouch for the truth of his statements.

But back to our narrative; I have forged ahead of our experiences by more than six months.

We had patiently let the gale and blizzard sweep over us. At 5.00 a.m. on the morning of 23 September we left the tent and hiked north about 11 miles to try our hunting luck once again. But we saw neither game nor tracks. After a strenuous 12-hour hike we returned to the tent as dusk was falling. Thus our task could be considered to have been fulfilled; we had successfully reconnoitred the terrain, killed a muskox and thus could return to the ship.

Next morning, shortly after 4.00 a.m., we were ready to travel. Because of the darkness we initially found ourselves obliged to travel slowly and carefully; later we moved as fast as the dogs would go. The storm had improved the going and had smoothed out the irregularities. Reaching the coast, we left the land and set a course across the newly formed ice whose level surface allowed us to reach the ship at 2.30 p.m.[16]

*****

We were greeted with loud jubilation. The watch keeper had spotted us in the distance and had announced our approach. It took us two hours to answer the numerous questions with which we were besieged from every side. The saloon had never appeared so cheerful to us as now; never before, or so it seemed to us, had the cook displayed so much talent and skill in making the coffee. As a result of our 7-day absence we had learned for the first time to value the dubious comforts of *Polaris*.

The ship itself had changed its appearance in the meantime. The entire deck lay concealed beneath a tented roof, above whose ridge only the funnel and masts projected. Amidships, on the starboard side, an open staircase of blue, crystal-clear ice led up to a small door leading into the canvas housing. This was the only access route for getting aboard or out into the open. The compartments were in superb order; the starboard passageway beneath the deck-housing had been converted into a skittle alley, the deck cleared and scoured clean.

The favourable results of our trip persuaded Hall to have arrangements made for a second excursion immediately. He wanted to use the few short days which remained to us for a sledge journey to the north, and to travel across the plain which we had discovered. Along with several seamen the carpenter worked on axles and wheels that were to be fastened to the sledge, so as to be able to cross the snow-free stretches of the trail more easily. Mrs. Hannah made ready furs and footwear, while others made a new tent.

During the night of the 28th–29th a violent snowstorm broke,[17] blowing out of the southwest. Combined with the spring tide it set the ice in motion and caused severe ice pressures; the ship groaned and shuddered. Blow after blow could be heard from below. Screwing ice fragments threatened the rudder, which was heaved significantly to starboard. With the start of the ebb tide the pressures relaxed, but not the gale, which whirled massive streams of snow through gaps in the tent roof onto the deck.

On Sunday, 1 October, a new regulation came into force. For reasons of economy, from now on only two meals were to be served per day; breakfast at 9.00 a.m. and lunch six hours later. Anyone who felt inclined could have a cup of tea and hardtack in the evening but it would be everyone's duty to come to the saloon every morning when the clock struck 8.30 for prayers; then, too, the muster roll would be read.

CHAPTER 9

Hall's sledge trip[1]

Instructions for the sailing master. Hans as a messenger. Rough going. Last glimpse of the sun. Topography. Newman's Bay. Distant view to the north. Deficiencies of Hayes's survey. Geographical homology. Poor prospects for success in going any farther. Decided to turn back. A cairn with a document on Cape Brevoort. Definitely turn back. Arrival at the ship. Hall's death.

Accompanied by Chester and the two Eskimos, Hall left the ship with two sledges at noon on 12 October, to start his trip north.[2] He left the following instructions, which can be inserted here as an official expedition document: from them one can see the aim and purpose of his journey.[3]

> Sir, I am about to proceed on a sledge-journey for the object of determining how far north the land extends on the east side of the strait on which the *Polaris* is wintering, and also to prospect for a feasible inland route to the northwest for next spring sledging in my attempt to reach the North Pole, this route to be adopted provided the ice of the strait should be found so hummocky that sledging over it would be impracticable; and furthermore to hunt musk-cattle, believing and knowing, as I do from experience that all the fresh meat for use of a ship's company situated as is that of *Polaris*, should be secured before the long Arctic night closes upon us.
>
> You will, as soon as possible, have the remainder of the stores and provisions that are on shore taken up on to the plain by the observatory, and placed with the other stores and provisions in

197

as complete order as possible. You will have each kind by itself, as near as may be. You will have the ship's housing (winter awning) put up as designed.

Have the night-watch kept up in accordance to my winter instructions of September 23rd, with simply this change, that the watch is to be continued until the cook commences his morning work. Have every light in the ship extinguished at 9h p.m., except from this hour a candle light is to be allowed forward, for the use of the watch.

You will see that no more coal is consumed in any stove of the ship than is actually necessary. I find by thermometers placed in the men's quarters forward and both cabins aft, that the temperature of the air is kept far higher than it should be, both for economy in the consumption of coal and for the health of the ship's company, the thermometer through day and evening ranging from 60° to 70° Fahrenheit; therefore you will require no more coal shall be consumed than is necessary to keep the thermometer, forward and aft, at 50° through the day and evening.

A very small fire to be allowed forward to be kept up from 9h p.m. through the night, but the one aft to be discontinued at 9h p.m.

Have the dogs well cared for, feeding them every other day. Look out some good, warm place in the ship for the puppies, and have them well nursed.

Have Mr. Morton get and open one can of pemmican, and deal that out economically to the puppies. I have great hope of killing many musk-cattle on my sledge-journey, and then we can spare much of our ship's provision to the dogs.

Should any such calamity be in store for the *Polaris* (which I pray God may not be) that a storm from the northward should drive the ice out of Thank God Harbour and the *Polaris* with it during the coming spring-tides, then have steam gotten up as quickly as possible and lose no time in getting the vessel back to her former position. But should the *Polaris* be driven into the moving pack-ice of the strait, and there become beset, and if you should not be able to get her released, then, unfortunately the vessel and all on board must go to the southwest, drifting with the pack; God only knowing where and when, you and the ship's company would find means to escape. It might in this case be that such a drift movement would occur as in the case of the United States Grinnell Expedition of 1851–52,[4] and of the *Fox*, under McClintock in 1857–58;[5] but whenever you should get released, if anywhere between Cape Alexander and Cape York, or between the latter and the Arctic Circle, you will then make your way to Godhavn, Disko Island, and if the *Polaris* remains seaworthy, you will fill her up with coal, stores and provisions, and next fall (of 1872) steam back to this place. If the vessel should become a wreck or disabled from the imminent exposure and dangers of such an ice-drift as referred to, then all possible use of your best judgment must be brought into play for the preservation of the lives of all belonging to the expedition.

You would, at your earliest moment of escape, acquaint the Government of the United States with the whole of the circumstances, and if one of those circumstances be the loss of the *Polaris*, I and my small party, that is about to accompany me on the proposed sledge-journey, will remain here to make discoveries to the North Pole, using Thank God Harbor as our headquarters, and all the time feel that our country would lose no time in sending us aid, in carrying out the great object of the present expedition.

Although I feel almost certain that *Polaris* is safely lodged in her winter position, we know not what a storm may quickly bring forth. A full storm from the south can send the pack of the strait infringing upon the land pack, in the midst of which we are, and within a few moments cast the *Polaris* high and dry on the land. During the spring tides let great vigilance be exercised, especially during any gale or storm at the time of high tides.

As soon as time will allow, have snow-blocks cut from the drift under the lee of the hill by the observatory and sledged over to the *Polaris*, the same to be placed about her as an embankment.

You will have plank and boxes so placed under the poop that the dogs cannot get to the raw-hide wheel-ropes.

The usual routine of the ship that I have established will be gone through with, daily, during my absence. You will see that this is carried out, including church-service on each Sabbath.

The duties that devolve upon Mr. Morton by my appointment are those of paymaster and quartermaster. He has full charge, under my directions, of all the accounts, stores and provisions on board the *Polaris* and on shore belonging to the United States. Whatever relates to the consumption and use of said stores and provisions, Mr. Morton has charge of, and will be made responsible for the same. I am sure that this trust I have committed to Mr. Morton will be carried out with fidelity and to the best advantage of the United States Government and this, its North Polar Expedition.

All the fuel, kindling, and coal, before being used, must pass through the hands of Noah Hayes, who must keep an exact account of the same, which he must render to Mr. Morton, or he may render the account to the Chief Engineer, and the latter to Mr. Morton.

No box, barrel, package, or anything else containing stores or provisions belonging to the *Polaris* must be opened, but by Mr. Morton. This as well as all other orders that I have issued, you will have carried out.

You will keep a journal of all proceedings during my absence, and transmit the same to me on my return. You will not omit to note such violations of orders that are or may be given, and by whom they are made; neither will you omit to note the meritorious conduct of any or all.

Hoping that God will protect you in the discharge of the high duties which devolve upon you, I bid you adieu and all those of my command, trusting on my return to find *"All's well"*; and trusting too, that I shall be able to say that my sledge-journey, under the protection and guidance of Heaven, has been a complete success, not only in having made a higher northing, a nearer approach to the North Pole than ever white man before, but that a practicable inland sledge-route far north has been found, and many musk-cattle have been seen and captured.

I have the honor to be, your obedient servant, and respectfully

C.F. HALL
Commanding U.S. North Polar Expedition

To S.O. Budington
Sailing and ice master
U. S. North Polar Expedition
Thank-God Harbor (lat. 81°38'N; long. 61°44'W),
October 10, 1871

The morning after Hall had left us we were amazed to see Hans bringing his dog sledge to a halt alongside the ship. He was the bearer of a message from Hall, which informed us as to the progress of the trip thus far. The travellers were encamped in a snow house 5 miles east of Polaris Bay; the unfavourable going had not allowed them to penetrate farther. The difficulties had become so serious that they had taken a full 3 hours to cover the first 2 miles; in places the travellers had encountered totally snow-free stretches; in places massive drifts in which sledges and dogs almost sank from sight.

Hall had either forgotten a major part of his equipment or had expanded his travel plan since he had left us, for the requests he included in his note were manifold.[6] He asked for 4 onions, a dozen stearine candles, a pair of bearskin mittens, sealskin pants, a snowshoe, a candlestick, a three-sided file, 3 or 4 pairs of sealskin mittens, 20 fathoms of dog-trace, 8 fathoms of skin line, 3 whip handles, 2 pairs of waterproof boots, a wooden box large enough to hold a pound of coffee, as well as other minor items, which a person could only fully appreciate in the arctic wastes.

A diligent bustle immediately began on board. Mrs. Hannah and the Hanseatic mother tailored a pair of skin pants; the carpenter cut whip handles and the requested snowshoe; traces and thongs were fetched from the lower cable locker; and the steward, a conscientious man, clipped his pince-nez on his nose, so as not to make any mistake in counting the dozen stearine candles and the 4 onions. Once everything was ready every one of the 14 dogs received a treat of 2 lbs. of meat. Hans took his leave of his family and the crew, cracked his whip vigorously, and soon afterward he and his sledge disappeared amongst the hummocks which bordered the coast.

As a result of this mission Hall was condemned to a full day of inactivity; not until 8.00 a.m. on the morning of the 12th was he able to continue his journey. The going turned out to be scarcely better than previously; in 10 hours they covered barely that number of miles in a northeasterly direction. Near a steep, sharply truncated rock cone they built their snow house for the night. Hall named this peculiar mass the Inland Island, since it rose sheer, without any transition from the plain, which had once been covered by the sea.

As the travellers were taking a brief noon rest on the 13th the sun showed itself for the last time.[7] About a quarter of the red disc appeared above one of the glaciers to the south; it formed a halo, with a play of vivid rainbow colours, but it was only partly visible. A reddish-yellow column of light about 15° of arc high next marked the spot where the sun had disappeared. At 1.30 the two travellers reached a small lake from which a river emerged. They followed the ice-covered water course in a northeasterly direction for about three miles; then they came to a tortuously winding ravine. As they were about to build their third snow house it was 3.45.

They did not move camp next day, but the little party dispersed in order to roam the surrounding area on foot and to look for game.

Hall wrote in his journal:[8]

> This afternoon, I took a walk down the river, to see if it was feasible for us to follow it; after keeping along its course for a little over a mile I ascended its right bank, or eastern side, and then also ascended the hills along its border, and from the summit of these I could see the course for two miles farther, the general direction being about northeast. I then walked a little way inland, away from the river-bank, taking sharp looks for musk-cattle. My view was quite extensive but I was not fortunate in seeing any. The banks of the river are very much broken and irregular

and gullied, but in many places cliffy. The cliffs are found 25 to 75 feet high, and are composed of mud—frozen mud. The nature of the land has the appearance of drift-shingle schistose. Lime and slate predominate. I found one large bowlder [sic] of gneiss which, of course, is erratic. Most of the stones are rounded, as if sea-washed. Now and then pebbles of granite are found, which, of course like the gneiss, do not belong here. There is not a sign of vegetation on these hills, save now and then a bit or tuft of grass. Looking to the eastward, I am inclined to think an extensive level country is there. It may be that there we might fall in with musk-cattle, for on the plains considerable grass and other vegetation abound, as we have seen on the plains we have passed over in getting here. Luxuriant lichens are to be seen on rocks here and there.

They left the old snow house at dawn on the 15th. First their route led across the river ice, between the walls of the ravine; then, once the water course had disappeared, over rough rock debris and deep snowdrifts. After six hours of travelling they pitched camp at the north end of the ravine; the route they had covered was extremely tortuous. The distance from camp to camp, measured in a straight line, was only a small fraction over 4 miles, however. Ahead of the explorers lay a large inlet, covered with ice, in which a few icebergs lay scattered, the same inlet whose mouth we had spotted from on board ship before the ship had become beset. Chester and I had spotted the end of it from the top of a mountain on our sledge trip, but we had mistaken the inlet for a river.[9]

Next morning the little company set about crossing the inlet in order to reach the opposite shore. The sledges moved only slowly over the snow cover lying on the sea ice; with every jerk of the dogs on the traces the sledge broke through the thin ice crust, into which alternating thawing and freezing had transformed the surface of the snow. Under these circumstances it seemed advisable to change course and to stick close to the south shore. They travelled on, on a bearing a few degrees west of north, in order to reach a headland, in the lee of which they built their snow house shortly before 3.00 p.m. Despite the unfavourable conditions they had covered about 6 miles.

Things went better on the 17th.[10] The explorers pushed on to the entrance of the inlet across last year's ice. The coasts turned out to be mostly steep mountains which did not exceed 2000 feet in height; almost all the major sinuosities of one shore were repeated in the opposite one. The inlet can be divided into four parts. At its end, the most southerly and most easterly arm has an average width of about 3½ miles; it is about 8 miles long and ends in a seaward direction in two slightly projecting headlands. Next comes an almost oval continuation, about 8 miles long, from the northwest end of which the northern cape at the entrance to the bay is visible. The third section, about 5 miles long, is less clearly demarcated; it gradually widens to the northwest, where it turns out into the entrance. The latter attains its greatest width between Cape Sumner and Cape Brevoort, not exceeding 8 miles.

The travellers' intention of pitching camp under Cape Brevoort was thwarted by the roughness of the ice and by open water. Near the cape the firm fast ice came to an end while the hummocky pack was a mobile mass. They began building a snow house on the fast ice about a mile southeast of Cape Brevoort shortly after 2.00 p.m. It was impossible to round the headland; if they did not succeed in finding a route for the sledges over the mountain ridges to the north their journey would have to be abandoned here. The days were becoming steadily shorter; at 8.00 a.m. a vague twilight still reigned and at 4.30 p.m. one could make out the individual numbers of a watch dial only with difficulty.

While the two natives went hunting on the morning of the 18th, Hall and Chester climbed to the top of Cape Brevoort to reconnoitre the surrounding area.[11] First they followed a steep gully which ran east–northeast for half a mile; then they swung off to the west and climbed the steep slopes. After a strenuous hike they reached the plateau in which the headland ends to the south; it formed only a narrow strip from which a steep cone towered up. Near a massive erratic boulder, Hall took a short rest in order to take a number of compass bearings; then they proceeded to the highest point of the massif, reaching it only with considerable difficulty. But the view was rewarding. The coast atop which the two men stood stretched northeast for a distance of about 12 miles; then it swung sharply east and south and disappeared from sight. A wide sea, covered with hummocky ice masses, extended over the entire northeast quadrant of their field of vision; on the west side of Robeson Channel[12] the land mass extended north and east in almost a straight line and ended in a headland which bore almost north. Hall estimated its distance at 60 to 70 miles. A dark bank of cloud, harbinger of open water, extended along the northern horizon. Beyond it Hall thought he could make out further land masses but the atmospheric conditions did not permit him to be certain about this.

While thus far it had not been easy to reconcile Kane's and Hayes's discoveries with those of *Polaris*, the difficulties inevitably increased once Hall had viewed the surrounding area from Cape Brevoort.

As we have already seen, Kane used Morton's observations to announce the existence of an open polar sea in the north of Kennedy Channel. Instead of contesting this view Hayes not only agreed with it but became its enthusiastic apostle, and by releasing his travel narrative to the world under the title "The open polar sea," he elevated it to the status of dogma. Morton thought he had sighted his open polar sea from the northwest coast of Greenland; Hayes reported his from the opposite coast, the east coast of Grinnell Land. On pp. 349–50 of "The Open Polar Sea" we read:

> Suffice it here to say that all the evidences showed that I stood on the shores of the Polar Basin, and that the broad ocean lay at my feet; that the land upon which I stood, culminating in the distant cape before me, was but a point of land projecting far into it; like the Severo-Vostochnoi-Noss of the opposite coast of Siberia; and that the little margin of ice which lined the shore was being steadily worn away; and within a month the whole sea would be as free from ice as I had seen the North water of Baffin Bay,—interrupted only by a moving pack, drifting to and fro at the will of the winds and currents.

Hayes made these observations on 19 May 1861 at a location which he put at 81°35'N; 70°30'W; in one of the preceding chapters I included the description of the landscape which met his gaze at that point, in the traveller's own words. He thought the range of visibility attained 60 miles. Hence it must appear all the more strange that he did not notice the nearby coast which lay opposite him to the east, the same coast that we had discovered shortly before and off which we had established winter quarters.

Anyone who analyses Hayes's route critically and then tries to check the accuracy of the results obtained using the astronomical determinations of position Hayes made during his sledge journey will run into contradictions which are very difficult to accommodate.

As we learn from the description of his journey, he reached and occupied his most northerly camp on 18 May (p. 348); but the geographical position of that point is alleged to have been fixed astronomically on the 17th.[13]

Should one then believe the date reported in the narrative, or the other one, on which the astronomical determination of latitude is supposed to have been made?

There cannot possibly be any doubt as to when Hayes reached his highest latitude. In a message that he left under a cairn on Cape Lieber, the date is given as 19 May; this is what we learn from the text of that document recorded on p. 351 of the narrative. In addition Hayes reports there: "We arrived here after a toilsome march of forty-six days from my winter harbor." Since the travellers left Port Foulke on the evening of 3 April (p. 295), the 46 days point quite precisely to 19 May.

So much for the narrative. But what do the astronomical observations tell us?

No observation exists for 19 May. On the basis of a determination of latitude, which gave a result of 81°31.5', Hayes estimated the position of his farthest point at 81°35'N. The next astronomical determination of latitude which is recorded is for 20 May,[14] or from the day after Hayes reached his greatest latitude; as can be seen from the calculation quoted here, it gave a result of 79°58.5'N.

If we calculate the latitude difference between Cape Lieber and Camp Leidy, we get a result of 1°36.5'. If Hayes had been able to cover this distance from point to point in a straight line, the length of his day's march would have been 96.5 n. miles. But he did not travel in a straight line, but had to follow the windings of the coast due to the roughness of the ice. If we measure his route as it is laid down on Schott's map which accompanies the "Physical Observations," we get a result of 132 n. miles;

a measurement taken off Hayes's map (*Open Polar Sea*, p. 1) would magnify the distance even more. Assuming that no error has crept in, Hayes must therefore have covered at least 132 miles between 19 and 20 May. All my attempts at finding a plausible explanation for his covering this substantial distance were unsuccessful, and had to remain unsuccessful after I had run across the following passage on pp. 347–48 of the narrative: "With the view of ascertaining how far this course was likely to carry us from the direct line, I walked, while the dogs were resting, a few miles along the shore, until I could see the head of the bay, distant not less than 20 miles. To make this long detour would occupy at least two if not three days—an undertaking not justified by the state of our provisions." Hayes saw himself obliged to make this confession on 18 May, one day before he reached his highest latitude. Hence the going cannot have been very alluring!

If we did not have the volume that contains the astronomical observations that were made during Hayes's sledge journey, we could scarcely state with any accuracy where Hayes was in the second week of May, since the narrative provides very little information on this. But the passages in the popular book that contain precise data are in direct contradiction to the corresponding paragraphs in the scientific publication, as we have seen.

Unfortunately Hayes contented himself with determining his latitudes by means of noon sun altitudes, instead of by measuring circumnoon altitudes; if he had used the latter method perhaps many of the doubts would resolve themselves, doubts with which we are now faced as being unreconciled, and which cast dark shadows over an enterprise that must arouse everyone's admiration.

Certain differences on the journey north might perhaps be explained by the fact that Hayes selected a sun altitude as the noon altitude that was measured before or after the sun's culmination. As a result, due to the low sun position a greater latitude would be recorded than that in reality. But although this, on the one hand, would relieve us of our uncertainty, on the other hand it causes serious problems since, as a result, the latitudes determined on the return journey would turn out to be too great.

If someone were to study the geography of the Smith Sound area, and for this purpose were to use Kane's and Hayes's narratives along with our own observations, without consulting the frequently mentioned determinations of positions he would definitely reach the conclusion that on his sledge journey Hayes overestimated all his distances and did not cross the 80th parallel. A critical comparison of the cartographic material would only strengthen this hypothesis, since Kennedy Channel represents an extremely narrow strait. It would scarcely be possible to travel through it without seeing both coasts simultaneously; but Hayes sighted only the left shore.

I undertook the several days' work involved in producing a map at 1:1,300,000 that showed the routes of the Kane and Hayes expeditions in two different colours. It would exceed the bounds of this work to reproduce it here. Hence I shall simply confine myself to presenting the results that I obtained with regard to the coast of Grinnell Land north of the 80th parallel.

Hayes deviates from Kane's representation only in minor points; he displaces the coast by only a small amount in longitude and draws the various bays deeper than Kane did. Maury Bay, whose northernmost tip is tangented by the 81st parallel on Kane's map, is moved farther north on Hayes' map. Scoresby Bay suffers the same fate, while Carl Ritter Bay retains its original latitude; just as on Kane's map its most northerly cape is cut by the 81st parallel. Between Cape Back and Lady Franklin Bay, Hayes has inserted two shallow bays which do not occur in Kane's rendering, and north of Cape Eugenie, which lies at the same latitude as Kane's Cape Murchison, two further bays occur on Hayes's map which had not been recorded previously.

When I compared the map in Hayes's narrative with that in the *Physical Observations*, it took some time before I could be certain that the two maps do not represent totally different stretches of coast. For the sake of brevity I shall designate the map from the narrative No. 1, and that from the *Physical Observations*, No. 2. On No. 1 the entrance to Kennedy Channel is 85 miles wide, almost twice as wide as in No. 2, where it agrees with Kane's representation, which is more accurate. Although Hayes never spotted the east shore of the Channel north of the Humboldt Glacier, in reproducing it in No. 1, he allows himself various arbitrary ideas that make an unfortunate distortion out of that part of the Greenland massif. In addition, he makes the land at Cape Constitution deviate more than 20 miles to the east. On No. 1, one finds an island in Carl Ritter Bay, and in Lady Franklin Bay two of them; these are missing in No. 2. Where the deep Petermann Bay runs into the land in No. 1, in No. 2 we find the shallow Wrangel Bay, while Wrangel Bay, as depicted in No. 1, is named after Lincoln in No. 2 and appears to have been straightened out.

I've contented myself with mentioning only the worst aberrations. If I were to base my criticism on the fact that the outlines of the coast of Grinnell Land north of 80°N latitude almost exactly agree in both Kane's and Hayes's representations; that Kane's version of that coast is based only on cross-bearings that were made from the Greenland coast; and that the Greenland coast, as Kane has plotted it, is displaced too far north so that as a result, due to the mis-positioning of both the baseline and the sighting points, a displacement of the intersection points must inevitably result, Hayes's discoveries and their graphical representation would appear in even a much more unfavourable light.

I am reluctant to engage here in debates which are probably no less unedifying for the reader than for myself; but I believe I owe it to the honour of the expedition and to the honour of every single expedition member to counter the objections that Hayes raised after our return.

Where Hayes claims to have sighted his open polar sea, there is land; land that is flanked by a narrow strait; land that borders such a narrow channel that we ourselves, at night and by weak moonlight, could clearly discern the opposite coast from the shores of Polaris Bay. This channel, the entire surviving remnant of Hayes's "open polar sea," represents the most northerly outlier of Davis Strait and, in conjunction with that basin, represents a strait of splendid uniqueness.

Where, in a careful search among the various parts of the earth, would we find a similar formation, of approximately the same length, as this arm of the sea that separates Greenland from North America and its complex archipelago?

If Melville Peninsula, a strict mirror-image of the Cumberland (Peninsula), whose northern tip approaches to within 8 n. miles of Baffin Land, did not intervene to disrupt things, the basin between the entrance to

Hudson Strait and the south shore of Lancaster Sound would offer a similar shape, although of more restricted extent. But this would be the only homology[15] that a search of the two Americas would reveal from this point of view.

We will look in vain for a similar configuration on the Pacific littoral of Asia, one whose entrance, like that of Davis Strait, lies on an ocean. If one were permitted for our purpose to move the position of Kamchatka and the chain of islands south of it, as far south as the southernmost outlier of Japan, toward the position of the mainland, we would be confronted with a remote similarity to that arctic basin in the Sea of Japan and the Sea of Okhotsk. But such a comparison would be doubly inadmissible, in that the Sea of Okhotsk is closed to the north.

If we follow the parallel of the southern tip of Japan to the east [sic] we encounter the Red Sea and the connecting Gulf of Aden, where Arabia connects Africa to Asia. Together they may be considered as the only geographical homolog of Davis Strait and its continuation; in addition they alone possess dimensions of similar size.

The distance from the mouth of Davis Strait to the north end of Robeson Channel is, in round numbers, 1300 miles; the length of the Red Sea, including the Gulf of Aden, is about 1600 miles. While the latter attains its greatest width at its entrance, the shores of Baffin Bay lie farthest apart at about 75°30'N; then, in the vicinity of the 78th parallel between Cape Isabella and Cape Alexander, just as at Bab el Mandel, they swing to within about 20 miles of each other. Moreover, by chance in both regions secular uplifts and down-warpings are occurring. As was discussed earlier, the entire Smith Sound region is probably to be seen as an area of uplift, while in southern West Greenland the land is sinking beneath sea level. But we should proceed cautiously before we deny the occurrence of areas of sinking on uninhabited coasts, since it is not revealed in the landscape as is uplift. If we assume that no sinking occurred in Smith Sound because the necessary proof was missing, a comparison would suggest that the movements are reversed on the shores of the Red Sea. Here an upward trend is suggested in the southern part, while in the north the Nile Delta provides evidence of sinking.

We left Hall and his party on 18 October. Chester and Hall had climbed to the top of Cape Brevoort, and I reported earlier on the view that presented itself.

On the 19th they made a vain attempt to round the cape by sledge; finally Hall and Chester found themselves obliged to proceed on foot, but they did not get far. The rocks were steep, almost vertical in many places, hence only the vague beginnings of an ice foot had managed to form, and due to high hummocks it was almost impassable. A short distance out from the coast the ice was not only extremely rough but also extremely mobile. Hence they had to abandon any hope of rounding Cape Brevoort.

It was equally impossible to push on overland, since the mountainous character of the land and the inadequate snow cover presented obstacles which could not be overcome. Moreover, the coast extended only another 12 miles to the northeast, then swung sharply to the east and south. There was nothing to be achieved here. Hence Hall decided to start back for the ship.

But the following day was stormy and the travellers opted to lie up. Around noon, once it had become possible to go outside, Hans headed for the open water in order to shoot seals; Joseph went inland, but his hunt for muskoxen was just as unsuccessful as Hans's assault on the seals. He spotted three, shot at one but missed, and returned to the snow house at 3 o'clock, simultaneously with Joseph.

Hall, too, had been roaming around the area, as reported in his journal:[16]

> As for myself, I have been out now and then looking around seeking specimens of plants, and trying, as I have often done before, to find something of a coal character. I am deeply anxious to find coal in this country, as this mineral would contribute largely to our success in getting the *Polaris* to a far higher latitude next season. Wherever one goes here he finds specimens of stones that look like coal, but on close trial it proves to be slate-stone. This p.m., with my snow knife, in a few minutes I dug my large seal-skin mittens full of a small plant that is quite abundant here and about Polaris Bay; a plant not exactly

Andromeda tetragona,[17] but perhaps of that family. I brought what I had gathered to the encampment to make a trial of it as fuel, but from the fact that it was all full of frost, it could not be coaxed to burn. I think if this plant were gathered in the fall and dried it would make fuel. Any way, if our sealers are successful in the spring and summer of next year (1872), the oil of the seals can be turned to excellent account by saturating the plant I have just alluded to in the oil, and thus a capital combination-fuel for steam-generating on the *Polaris* will be formed. While gathering these plants I found the full stand-droppings of a muskox. They are like those of a reindeer, except the balls are larger – the size of bullets 16 to a pound. Generally the traces of musk-cattle are in mass – like balls all melted together. I gathered a handful of them and brought them to the snow-hut. I found that when crushing one it was completely dry, and that it expanded to almost double its original size. I saturated the crushed mass with melted tallow and I found, as I expected, the substance made excellent wicking.

Toward evening Hall compiled the following document, which is addressed to the Secretary of the United States Navy:[18]

Sixth snow house encampment,
Cape Brevoort,
North side entrance to Newman's Bay
(Lat. 82°3'N; long. 61°20'W).
October 20, 1871.

To the Honorable Secretary of the United States Navy,
George M. Robeson:

Myself and party, consisting of Mr. Chester, first mate, my Esquimaux Joe and Greenland Esquimaux Hans, left the ship in winter quarters, Thank-God Harbor, latitude 81°38'N, longitude 61°44'W at meridian of October 10th on a journey by two sledges, drawn by fourteen dogs, to discover, if possible a feasible route inland for my sledge-journey next spring to reach the North Pole, purposing to adopt such a route, if found, better than a route over the old floes and hummocks of the strait in the event that such a route turned out to be more favourable than the route across the ice floes and hummocks of the strait which I have denominated Robeson's Strait, after the honourable Secretary of the United States Navy.

We arrived here on the evening of October 17, having discovered a lake and a river on our way; the latter, our route, a most serpentine one, which led us on to this bay 15 minutes (miles) distant from here southward and eastward. From the top of an iceberg, near the mouth of said river, we could see that this bay, which I have named after Rev. Dr. Newman, extended to the highland eastward and southward of that position about 15 miles, making the extent of Newman's Bay, from its headland or cape, full 30 miles.

The south cape is a high, bold, and noble headland. I have named it Sumner Headland, after Hon. Charles Sumner, the orator and United States Senator; and the north cape Brevoort Cape, after J. Carson Brevoort, a strong friend to Arctic discoveries.

On arriving here we found the mouth of Newman's Bay open water, having numerous seals in it, bobbing up their heads, this open water making close both to Sumner Headland and Cape Brevoort, and the ice of Robeson's Strait on the move. Thus debarring all possible chance of extending our journey on the ice up the strait.

The mountainous land (none other about here) will not admit of our journeying farther north; and as the time of our expected absence we understood to be for two weeks, we commence our return tomorrow morning. Today we are stormbound to this, our sixth encampment.

From Cape Brevoort we can see land extending on the west side of the strait to the north 22° west, and distant about 70 miles, thus making land we discover as far as latitude 83°5'N.

There is appearance of land farther north, and extending more easterly than what I have just noted, but a peculiar dark nimbus cloud hangs over what seems may be land, prevents my making a full determination.

August 30th the *Polaris* made her greatest northing, latitude 82°29'N; but after several attempts to get her farther north, she became beset, when we were drifted down to about latitude 81°30'N. When an opening occurred we steamed out of the pack and made harbor September 3d where the *Polaris* is. [Corner of manuscript here burned off.] Up to the time when I and my party left the ship all have been well, and continue with high hopes of accomplishing our great mission.

We find this a much warmer country climate than we expected. From Cape Alexander the mountains on either side of the Kennedy Channel and Robeson's Strait we found entirely bare of snow and ice, with the exception of a glacier that we saw covering, about latitude 80°30', east side the strait, and extending east–northeast direction as far as can be seen from the mountains by Polaris Bay.

We have found that the country abounds with life, and seals, game, geese, ducks, musk-cattle, rabbits, wolves, foxes, bears, partridges, lemmings, etc. Our sealers have shot two seals in the open water while at this encampment. Our long Arctic night commenced October 13th, having seen only the upper limb of the sun above the glacier at meridian October 12th.

This dispatch to the Secretary of the Navy I finished at this moment, 8.23 p.m., having written it in ink in our snow-hut, the temperature outside –7°. Yesterday all day the temperature –20 to –23°, that is –20° to –23° Fahrenheit.

Copy of this dispatch placed in pillar, Brevoort Cape,
October 21, 1871.

It was practically still dark when the travellers climbed Cape Brevoort again on the morning of the 21st. Reaching the top they built a cairn, in which Hall had the original of the above-quoted document concealed.

A board with the deeply incised message 10FE (10 feet east) was fastened to the base of the cairn in order to precisely locate the spot where the message, sealed in a copper cylinder, lay buried 3 inches below the surface.[19]

Once the sledges were packed they started for home. They again spent the night in the same snow house on the south shore of the bay, in which Hall had made his fifth camp. On the morning of the 22nd he wrote in his journal:[20]

> It is my purpose to strike direct for the head of this bay, and, from some prominent mountains, try to see the character of the country north, to determine whether sledging in that direction would be feasible; also to look for a route homeward and hunt for musk-cattle.
>
> Every morning now, the first thing that I wish to learn is, whether the stars, or rather Jupiter, can be seen; but generally the heavens are in gloom. Latitude by observation is what I desire, though the elements for determining the latitude of Cape Brevoort I have from post-meridian observations on Jupiter the other morning. We start up the bay, and soon, leaving the new ice, come upon century-old ice, that, commencing from one side of the bay, spreads over to the other. At 10 a.m. I place my tripod on the top of a century-old ridge of hummocks, and take compass-sights to all the prominent points about. At 11, having regained the new ice, stop to examine what appears to be an old floe along which we have been sledging for ten minutes. It is 5 feet above the new upon which we are, and which also extends under it. The upper surface has hillocks, and looks very old. It appears to be fixed. Hans says it is all the same as a glacier.

Shortly after 12.00 they left the ice of the bay and pushed into a gentle valley-trough which extended to the southwest. At 2.57 they stopped to build their snow house for their eighth camp; they had covered 14 miles, the most thus far. Some circum-meridian altitude measurements on Jupiter, which Hall took next morning, revealed the latitude of the camp to be 81°39'N; hence the snow house was located almost due east of *Polaris*'s anchorage.

Although the travellers were moving across completely level terrain, the distance that they covered on the 23rd was less than on the previous day; it was barely 9½ miles. About a mile south of the interior island mentioned earlier, where they had spent the night of 12–13 October, they pitched their ninth and last camp. They broke camp early on the morning of the 24th and reached the ship at 1.20 p.m., after an absence of 14 days.[21]

Seemingly quite well, Hall immediately went to his cabin; without taking time to remove his fur clothing he quickly drank a cup of hot coffee.[22] A few minutes later he experienced extreme giddiness and a severe headache and began vomiting.[23] Unfortunately this indisposition did not pass quickly, as he initially thought it would; rather it was the precursor of a stroke which assailed him in the evening and paralyzed his left side.[24]

He slowly began to recover next day; warm mustard foot baths and cold compresses placed on his head and neck brought him some relief.[25] He had scarcely begun to feel somewhat better when he expressed his intention of undertaking another sledge journey.

He had absolutely no time to be ill, or to allow himself any rest. His restless mind occupied itself with the most minute details; he was constantly asking whether the instructions he had left had been followed in every respect.

These instructions had been followed and everything was in perfect order. The holds had been brought to the condition which he had stipulated; the provisions had been secured; and the ship surrounded with a thick wall of snow to ward off the cold. The men had been using every hour of the short days; after 16 October, once the sun had left us for the last time, they had been working industriously through the period of dim twilight in order to conscientiously fulfill his orders.

Hall suffered temporarily from serious mental derangements which at times degenerated into mild delirium.[26] He believed somebody was trying to kill him; that somebody wanted to stab, poison or shoot him.[27] On 4 November he was on the way to recovery, but his mind was often still obscured. Despite all warnings he ate large amounts of cooked seal meat and drank more red wine than was good for his condition. On the 6th he would not be dissuaded from getting up, walking around the cabin and making an attempt to dictate the results of his sledge journey. Next day he suffered another stroke and early on the morning of the 8th, at 3.25 a.m. he died.[28]

Thus this impetuous heart had ceased to beat before it had brought to fruition the great plans which were germinating in it; the immutable die of fate was cast before he had barely achieved his first success.

While we were dressing the corpse,[29] the coffin was being hammered together in the engine room. The hammer blows reverberated sadly and hollowly through the noiseless silence of the arctic night. With every stroke Hannah let out a violent sobbing. She, her husband and the little girl, Pannick, had lost their best friend; the dead man had been more than a father to them.

Around 9 o'clock the unadorned coffin was brought to the saloon; we laid the corpse in it and then covered it with two flags. The assembled crew stood around with heavy hearts to catch a last glimpse of the dead man's features.

Over on shore a grave was dug; the ground was as hard as rock and it was difficult to find a spot where the coffin could be interred. About quarter of a mile south of the observatory a site was selected. The men dug for four hours but had still penetrated no more than 6 inches into the frozen ground; by next day, with great effort they had produced a grave 2 feet deep.

At 11.00 a.m. on 10 November[30] the funeral procession moved from the ship to the shore. The ship's bell was rung on board. At its sound the dogs began to howl loudly. The coffin, covered with a flag that was lashed securely due to the strong wind, rode on a low dog sledge, hauled by the crew. Men with lanterns walked on either side, while the officers followed the sledge.[31]

Once we reached the grave only a short prayer could be said, since an icy gale was now blowing, whirling up clouds of snow, dimming the light from the hurricane lamps.

The coffin was lowered.[32] Everyone threw a handful of frozen earth on it. [33]

Ognuna in giu tenea volta la faccia:
Da bocca il freddo, e dagli occhi il cor tristo
Tra lor testimonianza si procaccia. (Inferno).

[Each kept his face turned downward; from his mouth, the cold, and from his eyes, his saddened heart provides itself a witness in their midst.][34]

CHAPTER 10

In the realm of darkness

The scientific work. Moving the men. Symptoms of mental derangement. A proclamation from the Governor of the Polar States. Blizzard. The ship's dangerous situation. Repairing storm damage. New dangers. The exodus of the Hanseatics. Celebrating Thanksgiving. Mild weather. Twilight. Christmas. Moisture below decks. The dogs. Toasting the New Year!

We had seen the sun for the last time on 16 October. If a chain of mountains had not blocked the horizon to the south and if the weather had been clear we would have been destined to witness sunrise and sunset within less than half an hour, on the previous day.[1] Now day and night had ceased to be distinguishable here. Only a dim twilight arch still identified the location where the sun passed below the horizon, dropping steadily lower and lower beneath it as time went on. We were at the start of a night which would last for over four months; we were the only people within a radius of thousands of miles.[2]

Hall's death had brought the serious side of life close to us in a brutal fashion. In accordance with the orders from the Navy Department, Budington and I held a consultation, the results of which were recorded. The document, in which we swore to commit our honour toward furthering the success of the expedition, was signed by both of us.[3]

In the meantime the scientific work continued without interruption. On 30 September an apparatus had been erected near the ship to measure the rise and fall of the tide, but the changeable nature of the ice had seriously clouded the accuracy of the results. It was not until 6 November that regular observations began.

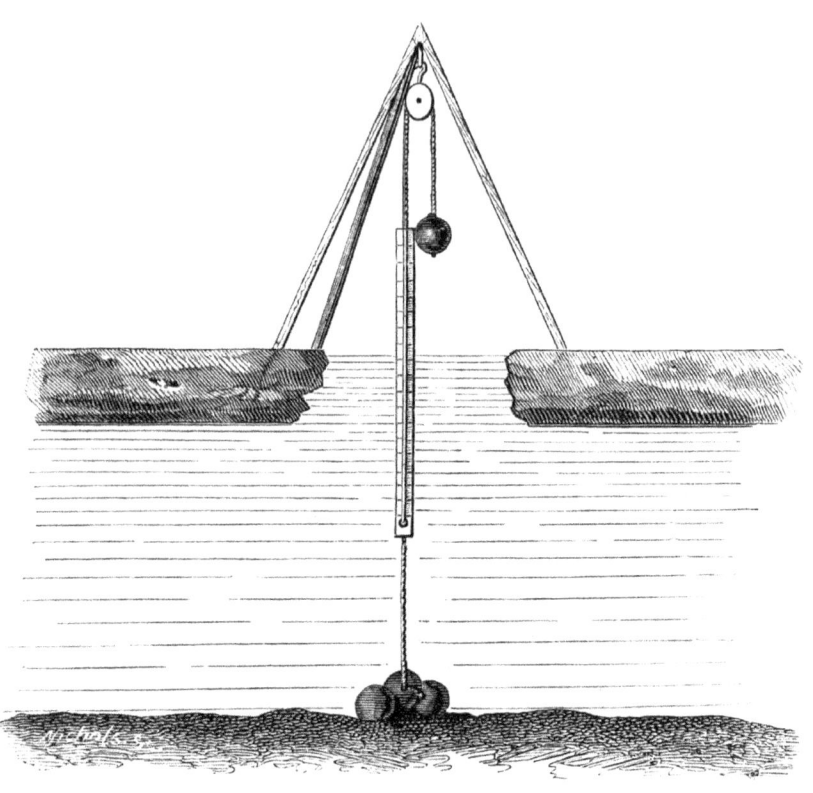

Fig. 14. The tide-gauge.

The tide gauge, built after Hayes's model, was of very simple design. It consisted of three ash poles set up like a pyramid over a hole in the ice and lashed together at the top with cord. A pulley was secured at the point of convergence, over which ran a rope, whose lower end extended down to the sea bed, where it was anchored by four 32 lb. cannon balls. Another 32 lb. ball, with a hole bored through the centre, hung from the other end in order to place the necessary tension on the pulley. A 2-inch lath was secured between the pulley and the anchored end, divided into feet and inches by incised marks. The four cannon balls on the sea bed formed a fixed point. As the tide rose, the ice carrying the tripod rose with it, and the scale began to sink below sea level; as the ebb tide began, a movement in the opposite direction began.

Every hour, despite cold, drifting snow and gales, we would see a man with a lantern emerge from the little door of the ship and wander to the tide hole. On reaching it he would read the position of the sea level against the scale, smash the ice that had formed during the preceding hour, remove it from the water, and clean the moving parts of the tide gauge. Then he would return to the crew's quarters on board and enter the time of the observation and the tide gauge reading in a book that was brought to the saloon every evening in order to be checked and copied.

At the time of full and new moon[4] the man's duties became more difficult. Then he began his readings an hour before each high and low tide and continued them at intervals of 10 minutes for 2 hours. If he believed that he had discovered any sort of irregularity, he lowered the lead and measured the depth of the water. If this did not agree with the corrected reading from the scale, it meant that the gauge had moved along with the ice and was now located at a shallower or deeper location than previously. Such cases were always conscientiously noted, but fortunately they occurred only rarely. Their recurrence was associated with unpleasant consequences; they caused cold hands for the observer and unpleasant work for the calculator of the tidal heights.

Because the tide gauge was a considerable distance from the observatory, two seamen, volunteers, Hermann Siemens and Robert Krüger, looked after the readings. These men were excused from the regular light ship's duties and relieved each other every 12 hours; they carried out their duties with rare loyalty and conscientiousness. When one takes into consideration that if there was heavy drifting snow, they were obliged to change their clothes after every observation, and that they had voluntarily undertaken this unpleasant work, which commonly deprived them of all comfort for 12 hours of the day, one can scarcely praise their patience highly enough. Had it been necessary to initiate observations at intervals of 5 minutes, they would have tackled them without the slightest hesitation.

Shortly before the sun took its leave, the observatory was surrounded with a substantial snow wall, just like the ship. Only on the east wall did we leave a roomy gap to accommodate the screen for the meteorological instruments. The screen consisted of an oblong wooden box with louvred doors and side walls. It was 6 feet high, 3 feet wide

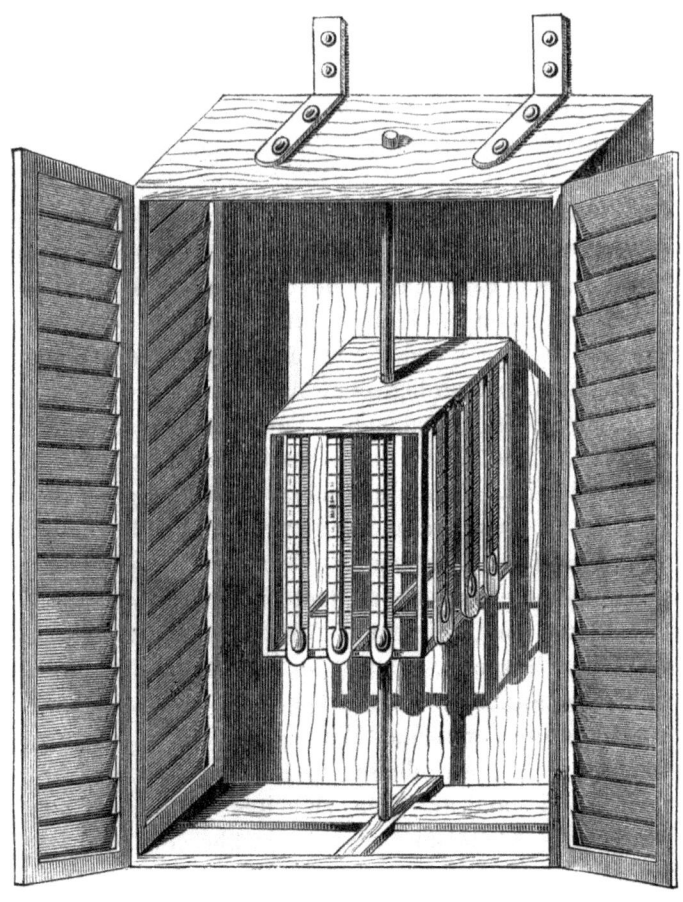

Fig. 15. The thermometer screen.

and almost 2 feet deep. It was fastened by means of iron brackets to the east wall of the observatory in such a way that a space of about 2 feet was left between its back wall and the small building, in order to allow the air to circulate freely. For the same reason there were vents in the floor; a vertical axis ran up through the middle of the floor, extending up to the roof. To it was fastened a four-sided wooden frame which could be turned with minimal friction. The various thermometers were spaced around this frame, their bulbs located a little over 4 feet from the ground. Since this reel revolved, it not only achieved a significant saving in space, but if there were heavy drifting snow we could at will turn any side away from the wind and thus protect the thermometer bulbs from the fine drifting snow. Apart from various thermometers for measuring air temperature, the screen also housed a psychrometer and maximum and minimum thermometers, as well as a double cylinder of fine wire gauze for holding prepared strips of paper designed to determine the ozone content of the air.

North of the observatory, and far enough from it to allow the wind to reach it from every direction, a Robinson anemometer stood atop a pillar about 6 feet high. And near the southern corner of the small building, in the middle of an enclosure of copper wire, various radiation thermometers were located.

The hourly meteorological observations had begun at noon on 6 November. For the moment, Meyer took the observations from 9.00 a.m. to 11.00 p.m., while I handled them from midnight to 8.00 in the morning. The hourly observations were confined to air pressure, air temperature, humidity, wind speed and direction, degree of cloud cover, and cloud drift in both the lower and upper atmosphere. Once per day, at 8.00 a.m., the ozone content of the air was determined and the readings of the maximum and minimum thermometers noted.

Each of us spent his shift in the observatory. Its interior fittings were as primitive as the building itself. The stove stood in the middle of the south wall; to its right was a wooden stand which we called the desk, and a book shelf above it. The middle of the west wall was occupied by the pendulum apparatus; to the right of that hung four mercury barometers. To the left of the door, which was in the north wall, was another stand occupied by the chemistry balance; in the northeast corner stood the stand for the electrometer, while next to it Bryan had set up the tripod for the passage instrument. Two superannuated folding chairs represented our pride and our only luxury. We could not accommodate any more than three visitors at once, since the instruments that had been set up encroached upon the interior, originally only 10 feet long and 8 feet wide, to an almost illegal extent.

Two snow houses, connected to each other by one tunnel and to the entrance to the observatory by another, contained the magnetic instruments. The declinometer was located in one of the domes, the inclinometer in the other. Each instrument rested on a base made of frozen earth and covered with boards that were fastened with copper nails. They had subsequently been cemented together with a mortar of sand and water, and with a temperature below −20° they had attained a solidity as if they were built for eternity.

The same cold that was so useful to us here had driven us out of our mess on board ship. During the past while, it had become more of a torture than a pleasure to sit at table and quickly devour our dinner. One ran the risk of doing an injury to one's stomach and chilling oneself thoroughly from below, while one was burning one's lips and tongue. Such conditions could not possibly lead to any good result. From now on the table was set in the lower saloon. There a comfortable warmth usually prevailed, and even if a cold draught penetrated down the companionway whenever the steward served the next dish, this was a transient calamity, from the numbing effect of which only one's feet and legs suffered, and one could be content.

The carpenter[5] caused us serious concern in that he began to suffer from a mental derangement. One night[6] a loud cry for help rang out from his cabin, right next to the lower cable locker. Several of the seamen went running and found him under the covers in a corner of his bunk. He claimed he had heard a voice from the adjacent provisions room that called to him loudly and clearly, using both his Christian name and surname. He was afraid his life was in danger. In order to reassure him the room was searched, but as one might expect, nothing more suspicious than boxes and casks was found. He was seized by a stupefying terror, which did not slacken even after his quarters were changed, and his bunk was moved to the after saloon. He believed himself constantly surrounded by enemies. An almost iron discipline was required to restrain him from pulling a double fur cap down over his ears before he went to bed; he was afraid someone would pour concentrated nitric acid on his head.[7] At times he had to be closely watched; he even went so far as to set several large fox traps near his bed, in which he hoped to trap his enemies. In his delusions he even later attempted suicide; he jumped into the tide hole but was fished out in time.

The condition in which the Hanseatic (Greenland) mother found herself one night was less serious. Shortly after 1.00 a.m. she came rushing into the saloon, in floods of tears. Her mind was deranged by a black mood of anxiety.

Mrs. Merkut had had a bad dream. She thought somebody was trying to kill Hans and asked that we might protect her spouse from the seamen's murderous knives.

Hans himself accepted the entire scene with the dull-witted indifference peculiar to him. Once he had received a wooden pipe and some tobacco he was as happy as a mole in a heap of grubs. He gargled a few rough words at his better half and, cursing, dragged her back to their conjugal bed.

In the isolated situation in which we found ourselves it might scarcely seem surprising that a proclamation that appeared posted at several places in the ship on 17 November provoked no little stir.[8] After a good American custom it announced a Thanksgiving celebration on the last Thursday of the month. The Governor of All the Polar States had approved it. There was no signature; but there was a coat-of-arms in which a polar bear featured, standing on its hind legs and gazing with melancholy at a setting sun.

Anyhow it was the best thing that could happen to guide the crew's spirits into a cheerful track; the recent past had seen an overabundance of melancholy days and we still had a tough winter ahead of us.

During the night of the 18th a violent blizzard arose out of the northeast and continued for the next two days with raging fury. The pilgrimage to the observatory was attended with loss of time and with obstacles, while even the walk to the instrument screen and the anemometer was often accompanied with serious difficulties. As I was starting my shift on the night of the 19th the wind was blowing at a speed of 45 miles per hour ; it was only with the uttermost effort and patience that I succeeded in continuing the observations. For the first few hours I worked my way to the instruments, bent forward at a pitiable angle. Later, as the wind speed increased, I had to hold the lantern between my teeth and make the journey on all fours. Hurled by the raging gale, the fine ice needles stung my cheeks and forehead, nose and eyes, like hot grains of sand. Sometimes, when I had barely reached my goal, the light would be extinguished and I would have to go back to light it again. Then, having reached the anemometer, I found my eyes would refuse to function; my tears froze; the driving snow became caught in my eyelashes, then turned into ice due to the warmth of my eyelids, freezing them shut, so that I was unable to open them.

Six hours passed under these conditions. From 3.00 a.m. onward I was without coal, since someone had neglected to renew the supply; the fire in the stove had long since gone out; it would have been impossible to get more fuel to the observatory since the unchained storm was raging with ever-increasing fury. My fur boots, which were completely soaked, began to freeze and became as stiff as cardboard. I pulled them on only when I had to leave the cold building to go outside to take the observation. As soon as I got back I wrapped my feet in old newspapers and placed them on the back of my faithful Newfoundlander Nero, who lay sprawled in front of me and happily let himself be used as a footstool. Although the fine animal felt the cold less than I did, it seemed to me at least as hungry as its master, who had eaten nothing for 18 hours. With blinking eyes, he begged as usual for food that I could not give him. I searched in vain in all the corners for a crust of bread.

My ink had long since frozen; the mercury columns in the thermometers attached to the barometers had disappeared completely inside their bulbs.

After Hermann Siemens, who was in charge of reading the tide gauge on board, had been blown over by the gale several times, my companions began to be worried about me.[9] At 9 o'clock Mr. Meyer appeared, breathless and covered with snow and ice, just as I was occupied with scratching my last observation on paper. In carrying out this friendly service the poor man had frozen both hands. He had been so anxious to bring me a few ship's biscuits, which I shared with Nero in brotherly fashion.

Budington now began to be concerned about Meyer and sent out the two Eskimos; they reached the hut as white as snowmen. Joseph had frozen his left cheek; the Hanseatic father was holding his broad stubnose in both hands, like a treasure, in order to thaw it out; on the way over it had attained a serious degree of hardness and had been chilled to below the freezing point. It gleamed in the middle of a brown face like a white rose. He smiled archly, like somebody who was feeling more than he was willing to acknowledge.

If we had had coal and a breakfast we would have been in just as good shape here as on board. But we possessed nothing; we were hungry and cold, and if we wanted to improve our situation we had to get back to the ship.

The lamp had burned down; we scarcely needed to extinguish it. Closely bundled up, we set out. We held each other's hands; we covered the first 30 paces at an irregular gait in order to present maximum resistance to the raging storm. Then we were hurled to the ground. Without respect to inclination, spirit or mood, we rolled down the slope to the beach. After we had picked ourselves up and had reached the sea ice, we suffered from several more accidents, but without rolling as on that first occasion.

To guide us, a torch had been lit at the entrance to the ship; we spotted it only when we were in danger of burning ourselves on it. We were greeted by our comrades as if we had risen from the dead.

Every one of us had frozen some part. Meyer's eyelids and hands were frozen; Joseph's cheek was as white as a tallow candle; the Hanseatic father held his pallid nose with both hands; while my ears were as stiff and cold as marble. We rubbed, thrashed and kneaded, sometimes ourselves, sometimes each other.[10] Then we invited the Eskimos to join us for breakfast. But we were mistaken if we hoped to find a substantial meal. The cook had tried in vain to light the galley stove; the howling gale had persistently thwarted his efforts. The table was laid and a ham lay on it; the plates stood, in rank and file, as if ready for a consecration, but there was no cooked food in sight. It was only after Chester, with one of his pithy oaths, made the miserable cook fetch a pan, that we were able to fry thin slices of ham over the saloon fire.

Down here, in this secure room, the tumult of the elements seemed intensified. With the raging storm roaring round it, the ship, in its icy armour, formed a resonator for the weird noises of the storm. The masts groaned and moaned; and mixed with the groanings and moanings were the rattling of the rigging, the creaking of the yards and the clattering of the stovepipe chains. The blocks rattled; the shrouds hummed like eolian harps. With a hollow roar the tent-roof flapped up and down, swollen enormously like a sail. The planking throbbed; the beams creaked; the hull trembled and shook. From the ice came whining and complaining noises, then a dull howling, sometimes louder, sometimes quieter; a fugue of immeasurable savagery but full of dynamic force.

So it continued in weird, ranting rhythms; hour after hour passed, but the gale showed no sign of ending. After brief pauses it would assault the ship with renewed strength and force a complaining response out of it.

It was not until between 3.00 and 4.00 p.m. that it fell quieter. It now became distinctly possible that the ice was screwing and thrusting against the keel from below.

At midnight the storm was raging more violently than ever. Then the vessel began to rise and fall, as if affected by a swell. The ice seemed to have broken up; open water could not be far away. Outside, the darkness of night reigned and the snow was driving so violently that one could scarcely recognize one's immediate surroundings. Shortly after 2 o'clock we noticed a dull cracking, like distant thunder; the vessel began to roll, heeling heavily first to port, then to starboard. The ship presented an enormous surface to the wind; a pressure of over 46,000 lbs. was being exerted on one side, on the tent-roof and hull alone.

Despite our expectations the night passed without bringing any serious hazards. At 8.00 a.m. we experienced a new movement. The ship suddenly swung from north to west; we could still not determine how things stood outside, since the air was filled with even more driving snow than ever. We were living in painful uncertainty, which was more unpleasant than a settled fate.

Some people thought they could identify Providence Berg through a gap in the tent-roof. The ice surged against the hull, creaking and crashing; a single twist and the worst might happen. We were helplessly at the mercy of the raging elements.

A further glimpse through the opening revealed open water all around; only around the bow did there appear to be floes piled up; we were now very close to the iceberg. Now the ship was grinding against its crystal flanks.

Were we adrift and was the berg drifting with us—or were we still at anchor? The anchor chain was taut, but this gave no assurance as to whether we were drifting or not, since the chain was frozen solidly into the ice and the anchor might still be dragging without our being aware of it.

The storm hit again with renewed force; its howling drowned out the sharp sounds of shouted orders. All hands were on deck, clearing away ropes and ice anchors so that, if it were possible, we might attempt this miserable means of salvation. Everything was at stake; we had to offer some resistance, even if it were vain resistance.

"Cast the lead!" was the order that thundered out.

"Eleven fathoms!" shouted the man on the lead.

There could no longer be any doubt that we were drifting, since the ship had originally been lying in 5 fathoms of water. The lead was cast a second and a third time. The depths were still increasing. "Twelve fathoms; twelve and a half; thirteen fathoms!" came the shouts from the opening in the housing.

Our only salvation now hung on the starboard anchor. Budington gave orders to drop it. Shortly afterward we felt a violent crash; with staccato impacts the ship's hull ricocheted against the Providence Berg.

Now we had to act with circumspection and boldness. It was a joy to see the sterling stuff of which the crew was made. The sailing master called for a volunteer to sink an ice anchor in the side of the berg. William Nindemann immediately stepped forward and volunteered to carry out this risky task; the two Eskimos were to assist him.

One after the other they were lowered with a rope down the ship's side. It was difficult to get a firm foothold on the ice; before they could take a step they had to cut steps with the axe. We followed every movement with growing tension. The anchor had still not been made fast when the gale blew out the hurricane lamps. Burning tar, kindled in a large frying pan,[11] revealed the stress under which our comrades were working. The first anchor was safely secured. They called for a second one and it was thrown down to them, along with a cable. Soon it too had been secured and for the moment we were safe. The men had difficulty getting back aboard. Nindemann's nose had suffered. Joseph had frozen his right cheek and Hans both ears.

It was not until around midnight that the storm slackened; the drifting snow eased; from the top of the Providence Berg we could get a view of our immediate surroundings. The ice around the ship had been completely shattered and carried away by the waves. Only along the coast were a few floes still lying firm. A narrow bridge led from the berg to one of these; we could not determine how things looked on the far side of the strait.

Early on the morning of the 23rd some of the men were sent ashore to look for the dogs. Fortunately most of the animals were on board; only four or five were missing. During the gale we had provided them with a shelter on deck, but they had abused our hospitality; they had managed to get to our reserves of blubber and had consumed a good quantity.

The sailors returned and reported what they had seen; one of them had broken through the ice and arrived back with his clothes frozen; they brought back three of the dogs on leashes. Near the shore they found the tide gauge, which had drifted there, and near it lay one of the Greenland sledges. The other items that had been scattered around on the ice were missing. They reported that the magnetic huts had lost their roofs and that the instruments were buried under the snow.

After an enforced four-day break, on the 24th we returned to the observatory in order to continue the observations. What devastation had occurred here; how changed the terrain was!

The building was completely buried; the tunnel that led to the door was entirely filled with snow; we had to fight our way to the entrance with shovel and spade. The scene inside the walls was very sad. The drifted snow lay knee-deep on the floor boards; it covered the stove and table, the books and the instruments; a white fabric of frost hung from the ceiling. Bryan dug the magnetic huts out; the heavy declinometer had been upset by the wind and lay upside-down near its pedestal; the inclinometer had suffered the same fate. Fortunately nothing was damaged; only the sledge of the magnetic theodolite was missing, but this could easily be remedied.

On the morning of the 25th the crew began sawing a dock in the 8-inch ice cover, by magnificent moonlight. Hour after hour the rasp of the great metal teeth and the ring of the axe rang out, accompanied by the cheerful singing of the seamen. The ship, which was lying immediately behind the berg, was moved away from its dangerous proximity and warped closer to shore.[12] While, the day before, getting on board or off the ship had involved some problems, the situation had now been aggravated by the change in the ship's position. The only access route was via the central porthole on the starboard side, to which a steeply inclined plank led up. Even somebody who was not very corpulent could negotiate the entrance only by crawling on his belly, but a more corpulent person would encounter serious difficulties.

But this too passed; by the evening of the 26th the ice close alongside the ship had become strong enough to bear one's weight. But our joy did not last long. As a result of the spring tide, numerous cracks and leads appeared in the young ice and the water came gurgling up through them to spread across the surface. Next day a storm out of the southwest was added to this.[13] After a brief calm, at 1.00 p.m. the wind had changed; by 7.00 p.m. it was blowing more decisively and two hours later it was blowing at 49 miles per hour .

The ice had started moving in the morning; it had heaved up along the ship's sides and had formed massive hummocks under the stern. Then the floes and ice fields pressed against the berg, which groaned and creaked, rising and falling gently. Under the increasing pressure the colossus suddenly broke up; a massive piece broke away and the floes surged through the breach, threatening the ship.

The berg, lightened, began floating, and moved slowly toward the ship. A dull crash and the trembling of the ship marked the collision; the ice had hit the keel. The berg moved landward with sinister speed, driving the ship before it. If the latter did not rise it must either be hurled completely over to starboard or be sliced into at the waterline.

Until 2.00 a.m. the situation hung in the balance between disaster and salvation. As the tide dropped our persecutor grounded again, at the same time protecting us from the assault of the floes, and the ship came to rest, but with such a heavy list to starboard that one could barely walk on deck.

While we revelled in the comfortable feeling of momentary security, after a few minutes another danger threatened us. A large floe had pushed against the berg from the seaward side and the latter began to lean over; its crest swung closer and closer to the masts. If it capsized, the ship would be buried beneath the disintegrating masses.

It was 6 o'clock before we could breathe more freely. Then the storm slackened and quite gradually the iceberg righted itself again. It really should have ended at that, since the past few days had brought us more ill luck than one would expect in years in other waters. But it seemed that the battle with the elements would never end. As the tide began to ebb, the ship's stern suddenly sank without the forward part being able to follow; finally the bow ended up more than 4 feet higher, and again the vessel heeled over severely.

Having abundantly experienced the unpleasantness of every possible and impossible situation, we were now almost more helpless than ever before. The ship was threatening to disintegrate and it was impossible to relieve her. Once again the wild hubbub of voices arose; every plank groaned and creaked; at times there were loud cracks like nearby rifle shots.

The Hanseatic mother was totally terrified; she had fetched her entire household goods on deck and was waddling around like a winged duck. Hans himself had closed his account with the North Pole; he wanted to leave the ship with his wife and child and build a snow house on land. Without hesitation he was given permission to do so. Thus there occurred the exodus of the Hanseatics.

Instead of immediately tackling the building of the snow house, Hans took care of some other things, and his better half suddenly appeared at the door of the observatory with her complement of children, bedding and a pot, and begged for lodgings for the night. Meyer was on shift and he let her in. The skins were spread around the tripod for the passage instrument, and the refugee Hanseatics lay down on them and slept and snored and filled the hut with the aroma of their furs.

Thanksgiving was celebrated on an inclined plane at a steep angle. The "Governor of all the Polar States" had not prescribed this. There was no word about inclined planes in his proclamation; but if the celebration was not to take place in the open on the newly formed ice, we had to take the angle of the ship in our stride.

Breakfast on this last Thursday of the month differed in no way from that on the previous days; but later, almonds and other nuts were distributed among the men. The Hanseatics had also come aboard; the children cracked the nuts like squirrels and ate the kernels with impressive speed.

The dinner was very ethnic, and would have done even the states of New England proud. Oysters and lobster were served; even the obligatory turkey was present.[14] The cook had done his duty superbly and had made a monument to himself in the form of a three-tiered pudding which, unfortunately, lay like a stone on the stomachs of those who sampled it. By contrast, the activities of which the crew's cellar-master had been guilty were quite reprehensible. He had treated the red wine cruelly; it arrived at the table frozen and rapid thawing would have done serious damage to the juice of the grape. By the time the wine had again attained its normal condition, without any drastic measures, dinner was over; but nobody hesitated to drink it *post festum*. Only Bryan, the hero of moderation and pious man of God, kept the precepts of the Order of Pure Water.

Late in the evening we heard a thumping noise in one of the passageways, then the sound of a fiddle.[15] The noise came nearer. The watch announced official visitors. Then Peter appeared, old Peter[16] who had sailed every sea, and who could tell the drollest stories. He was leading a donkey which strode in with dignity. On the animal's back sat the hopeful Hanseatic boy, Tobias, dressed as a monkey. The donkey was very talented; it hopped and danced to the sound of the music and at times made such violent leaps that the small rider several times was in danger of falling off. But he paid the donkey back with a vengeance. As a reward for its unseemly behaviour he pulled its long ears, or grabbed its tail and beat it mercilessly in the sides with it. Surrounded by the crew, the donkey driver departed again; further merriment was calling, out on the ice.

Thus the Thanksgiving celebration came to an end, and with it the last day of November. During the next few days several attempts were made to get the ship into a better situation, but all efforts were in vain. Whenever the tide began to drop (and this happened twice in every 24 hours) the ship heeled heavily to starboard; and when by chance a low tide coincided with a mealtime our problems at table were serious.

The tidal observations, which had been discontinued since the day the ice broke up, were resumed on 2 December, once a new tide gauge

Fig. 16. Reading the tide-gauge.

had been built. Again we had to go through the entire unpleasant procedure necessary to determine the zero point on the scale.

Had we not been surrounded by deep darkness, the rising temperature might have deceived us into thinking that spring was approaching. On the 5th the temperature fluctuated between −13.4° and −8.5°. It began to melt on deck and large drops dripped from the housing; icicles and frost flowers dropped from the ceilings in the passageways.

A comparison with the November and December temperatures at Port Foulke and Van Rensselaer Harbour, the two meteorological stations located closest to us, reveals that on 29 November 1860 Hayes even recorded −4.44°. There is even rain recorded in his meteorological journal. 1 December at Port Foulke may also be considered a warm day; the sky was clear and blue and the temperature rose to −10.83° with a gentle northeast wind. At Kane's winter quarters in Rensselaer Harbour the maximum in November 1853 was −17.0°; in the following year it even reached -13.89°. On 28 December a temperature of −8.61 was recorded; but in 1854 the same month revealed no temperature higher than −17°.

Since the sun had disappeared the sky had rarely been cloud-free. On 6 December we experienced the first clear noon and we were amazed and pleasantly surprised to sight the matt-white glow of a twilight arc.[17] The sun also sent its greetings on the following day. By 9.00 a.m., between steel-grey banks of cloud in the southeastern sky one could perceive a bright gleam, whose breadth increased until noon. It rose to 3°16′ above the crest of the massif that bounded our range of vision to the south. The sun was about 14.5° below the horizon; as a result twilight should theoretically not have been possible. But there could not be the slightest doubt as to its existence.

In the meantime the spring air had had to give way to lower temperatures; the thermometer dropped to −31.6°; the sky was clear and the gentle, sometimes barely perceptible breeze varied between northeast and southwest. In the strait, open water had formed, over which dark frost-smoke brooded like clouds of steam above the crater of a volcano that is about to erupt.

Prolonged, regulated activity made the time pass more quickly than might be expected under these conditions. The seamen had washed the dog skins we had on hand; Mrs. Hannah and the Hanseatic mother tanned them in Eskimo fashion, and then made them into articles of clothing. There were only a few good skins among the relatively small number; most of them had been skinned in summer and as a result were far from prime.

Where our airy dining room had been located earlier, the carpenter was now housed, still suffering from his *idée fixe*. The fox traps that he had been in the habit of setting for his alleged persecutors had been taken from him and placed in safe storage. With his cap pulled down over his forehead right down to his eyes and his fingers protected by fur gloves, he was now working, with true contempt for death, on large sledge runners for the spring campaign. He was left with little time to think of means of destroying his enemies; his suppressed anger was now focused on the folding table at which we had earlier eaten our meals and which now served as his carpenter's bench. The good qualities of a table were probably never dragged lower in the dust than here. Everyone whose route took him through the workshop had to be an ear-witness to the calumnies which were hurled at the poor piece of furniture. Sometimes it was too large, sometimes too small, sometimes too high or too low; but mostly Nathaniel Coffin Esq. raged against its thin legs. Finally he surrounded them from top to bottom with billets of wood; we could never decide whether it was for reasons of health, in order to keep them warm, or to give them more firmness, since his ill-will continued to seethe, just as before.

The iceberg protecting us disintegrated more and more. The debris falling from it formed a substantial ridge around the unstable colossus and exerted such a significant pressure on the surrounding ice cover that at high tide pools formed to a depth of 1 to 2 feet. They occurred in especially large numbers during the spring tide on the 12th. If a friendly fate had not made the wind drop, the ship would again have been in a serious situation. But we still had to fear the worst; on the morning of the 13th there were again violent impacts against the keel and the bow was raised 3 feet. New cracks appeared in the newly formed ice, and the high tide surged up through them. A wide belt of half-congealed water extended along the coast. On its surface one could see thousands upon thousands of phosphorescent points, which turned out to be small copepods. Their luminescence was barely dimmed by the freezing of the water. Even after the tide had long since dropped, the small animals were still a play of shimmering light, like stars reflected on matt glass surfaces.

The 21st of December had arrived; with this, half the arctic night had elapsed. Thus far we had seen the faint twilight on every clear day; now it formed only a narrow, matt strip; one needed a trained eye to spot it. But the turning point had been reached, and we were glad of it; we experienced a feeling such as is familiar only to someone who for months has had to make do with a dimly burning lamp instead of the sun.

With some dexterity and goodwill we had managed to create a Christmas tree in complete secrecy. It had evolved during the midnight hours over in the little observatory. Wood, wire of different thicknesses, papier maché and green-dyed wax had been sufficient to imitate nature quite deceivingly. Small baskets and chains cut from coloured paper did the rest; our supply of gold leaf, an accessory to one of the electrometers, was large enough to wrap several dozen nuts in shining coats, without making science suffer as a result. The tree was moved secretly to the engine room, in order to be completed later.

An invitation was extended to the crew to assemble in the saloon on Christmas Eve. The room made a fine show, festively decorated with flags. An enormous pennant with the ship's name was wrapped around one of the overhead beams; in front of it stood the large table covered in white sheets, with the tree in the centre. Lights and small coloured lamps shone among the green branches. Whatever the provisions room could offer in the way of luxuries was grouped around the tree; amongst them, piled on plates, were the steward's baked goods, as well as small gifts wrapped in paper and numbered. The crew crowded around the table; lots were drawn from a fur hat; every one of them was worth a prize. The men received their little parcels with childish delight; their seals could not be broken until 10 o'clock.

In the meantime we drank to the success of the expedition, and to the health of relatives at home; whoever had a loved one, or several of them, emptied a number of glasses, corresponding to the size of his heart. If that magical interplay were not a deception, a mysterious ringing must have sounded in the ear of many a fair lady. Toasts were drunk to the health of an Ella, a Marie or a Julie; the girls and wives, about whom our companions were thinking with love, were waiting in every habitable zone. A little light of joy gleamed in many an eye, as if the contact between glass and lip were a surreptitious kiss. The earth's motley array of islands and continents seemed to have become close enough to touch; wherever Byron's or Goethe's languages are heard, there is also a sweetheart, since a seaman's heart is mobile, like the element to which he trusts himself,

By mistake one of the men[18] had undone the string on his parcel prematurely. When, among the trivial gifts, he discovered a watch, whose painted hands pointed to 10 o'clock, the signal was given to break the seals. Joking and laughing, the weather-tanned faces examined the trifling gifts: a trumpet, a clown, a harmonica or some other toy.

The Christmas tree concealed a secret whose unveiling could not be delayed any longer. An inexhaustible flow of aromatic punch flowed from one of its branches. One man after the other stepped forward to fill his glass at this puzzling, red spring; it took only a gentle pressure on a concealed pin to stop the flow or make it flow more freely.[19]

In a cheerful mood the men headed out onto the ice, where a balloon was to be sent up; but the cold and a violent wind produced unexpected difficulties for the aeronauts; finally the balloon fell victim to the flames. A second one became caught in the ship's rigging; before anyone could climb the shrouds to rescue it, it had torn apart. With this the celebrations came to an end.

Next morning "Merry Christmas" rang out from every nook and corner of the ship. Only Joseph opted to deviate from Webster's dictionary of the English language, opting for the softer version of "Kissma." Christmas dinner was a solemn affair, as the occasion demanded. A pig that had been slaughtered five months before, and since then had been hanging in the shrouds, provided our table with pork chops; also served was a quarter muskox, with juicy roasts.

As a result of the various hazards to which the ship had been exposed, it had lost its protective snow wall. As a result, the impact of the cold made itself felt in the cabin in an unpleasant fashion. Moisture gathered between the bedding in the bunks; the condensed water vapour froze to form delicate ice formations, whose melting and refreezing was mainly caused by the warming effect of the sleepers. The ice was removed from the bunks twice per week, and equally often from the skylight, which formed a massive condenser.

The seamen in the crew's quarters were almost spared these unpleasantnesses. There the back walls of the bunks were protected by the coal bunkers; the main hatch, which was closed only during violent blizzards, allowed the water vapour to escape on deck and to condense on the iron fittings and the tent housing. Here everything was enveloped in dense frost flowers and shimmering ice crystals, whose regularity and size depended on the conductive capacity of the object which served as their point of adhesion. Long festoons and rosettes hung from the ropes; the woodwork was covered with moss-like formations; and the ironwork bristled with brittle needles and points. The trembling light from the lantern was reflected a thousand-fold from these fantastic forms; every facet flashed and gleamed. The deck, with its tenting, resembled a cave of immeasurable depth, since the light from the lantern illuminated only the immediate surroundings; the steel-grey half-dark, in which the shadows disappeared, was bounded by blue-black darkness. What lay beyond lay hidden from the eye and lured one's imagination.

We were more fortunate than our predecessors with the Eskimo dogs. Whereas Kane and Hayes had almost lost their packs by Christmas because they had all died, in our case only a few animals had died thus far. The animals were thriving and were becoming as fat as pigs. But the darkness exerted an unmistakable impact on the psyches of the Newfoundlanders. The animals were depressed, subdued, almost melancholy and betrayed an almost pathological sensitivity against even the slightest fondling. Later they developed a skin affliction,[20] which produced almost total baldness on some parts of their bodies. The little Bosun was like a wandering bald head; his nakedness reminded one of Adam and Eve before the Fall. Sympathetic hands made him a coat that buttoned along his back and ended in elegant knee-britches. A bed was made for him in an overturned barrel on deck; in gratitude he would occasionally leap at the legs of careless passers-by and try to bite them. The other dogs were allowed on board only every second day, at feeding time;[21] each animal was given its pemmican separately, and once it had eaten it was taken off the ship again. Many of them developed some remarkable tricks in order to get themselves double rations, but generally the deception was discovered in time and was thwarted. One of the older dogs had studied the mechanism of the ship's door so thoroughly that we had to change the lock because of it. After all attempts to push aside the wooden bar had failed, he assailed the roof until finally he succeeded in reaching it with a great leap. Then he sought out the small opening beside one of the masts and, with a total contempt for death, let himself drop to the deck in order to reach the meat supply that we stowed in the wheelhouse.

In this the ship's inclined position worked superbly to his advantage; the same phenomenon gradually became a torture for us. Ropes had been rigged on the slippery deck, since we did not credit our own limbs with the same degree of unbreakability as our dogs did theirs. It commonly occurred that dishes and plates would go rattling to the floor while we sat at table; that our chairs would give way; that one of us, to catch himself, would grab a corner of the table cloth, and as a result would provoke a lively genre scene, like the representation that glorifies the end result of Zappel-Philipp's deeds in *Struwwelpeter*.[22]

To control this problem, on the 28th several attempts were made at blasting the ice. We chopped through the ice at four points close alongside the ship, close against the keel. A large stoneware jar, filled with powder, and with a fuse leading in through its cork, was sunk in each of the holes. The fuses were lit simultaneously and a dull boom announced the explosion. Only a slight shudder ran through the ship and a gentle crackling through the ice; the ship lay unmoved, just as she was before. A second mine produced no better effect.

As we sat around the steaming punchbowl, the ship's bell rang in the 1st of January; through the crash of rifle volleys a "Happy New Year" rang out loud and long. The crew came aft to the saloon to congratulate us.[23] Out on the ice a balloon was sent up; then followed a procession around the ship.

The year 1871 was now no more than a memory.

CHAPTER 11

The New Year

Pendulum experiments. The crew's state of health. Life on board. Trips to the open water. Magnetic observations. The first term day. Favourable prospects. The open water as a local phenomenon. The mercury freezes.

More than any other zone, the Far North is apt to make a person patient, to dampen the last spark of sanguine hope that may still glimmer in him, and to surround everything with obstacles and difficulties. A person begins to doubt himself, changing from a free will to an irreconcilable skeptic, for his own impotence and the futility of life are revealed to him in every movement of the elements. Anyone striving for higher goals becomes serious, sulky and reserved; but he whose pulse beats only for the normal interests of existence succumbs to a lethargy that may intensify to idiocy. Life becomes a constant struggle against the forces of nature, a struggle that tempers the toughness of the person fighting it and gives the polar man his characteristic stamp.

Gradually we had become accustomed to seeing it as a particularly fortunate accident whenever one of our modest wishes was fulfilled and if the most insignificant of our plans really achieved implementation.

The effect of the November gales, as well as other unpleasantnesses, had prevented us thus far from starting the magnetic observations and the pendulum experiments; further postponement of these projects was no longer possible, however. Since we anticipated that the latter would fully claim our time, we decided to start them and to postpone the magnetic observations for the moment.

The pendulum that was to be used in our observations belonged to Dr. I. Hayes, who had been kind enough to place it at our disposal. It had already been used in Cambridge and at Port Foulke, as well as in Washington.

The instrument was a stable, reversible brass pendulum, absolutely symmetrical in every part, as the diagram shows.[1]

Its dimensions, in British units, were as follows:

total length: 5' 7.75"
width: 1.4"
thickness: 0.7"
distance between knife edges: 39.4"

The steel knife edges, triangular in cross-section, were located 14.2" from the ends of the pendulum rod. They were 3" long, 0.3" in height and 0.27" wide at the base. The pendulum weighed 21.92 lbs. and hence its specific gravity was 8.5. The knife edges, which extended through the rod, rested on steel plates when the pendulum was swung. The latter sat on a brass plate which was screwed onto a block of wood; the block of wood itself was fastened to the back wall of the box in which the apparatus swings. The arc of swing was read off a scale located near the bottom inside the box. The front of the box was closed by a glass door, through which the entire length of the pendulum was visible. Two thermometers were permanently fastened inside the box. One was in the same plane as the wooden block, the other in the horizontal plane of the swinging knife edge.

The relative position of the pendulum apparatus with regard to the observatory and its components is apparent from the diagram, which represents a long profile of the observatory from east to west.

The apparatus stood close against the east wall of the observatory, almost in its centre. Since the floor of the building rested on heavy planks and thus was partly elevated, an opening could be sawed in it, somewhat larger in size than the cross-section of the pendulum box. A plank was pushed beneath this opening, approximately levelled, and then secured to the frozen ground with a mixture of water and sand. The plank was completely isolated from the building; under the influence of the low

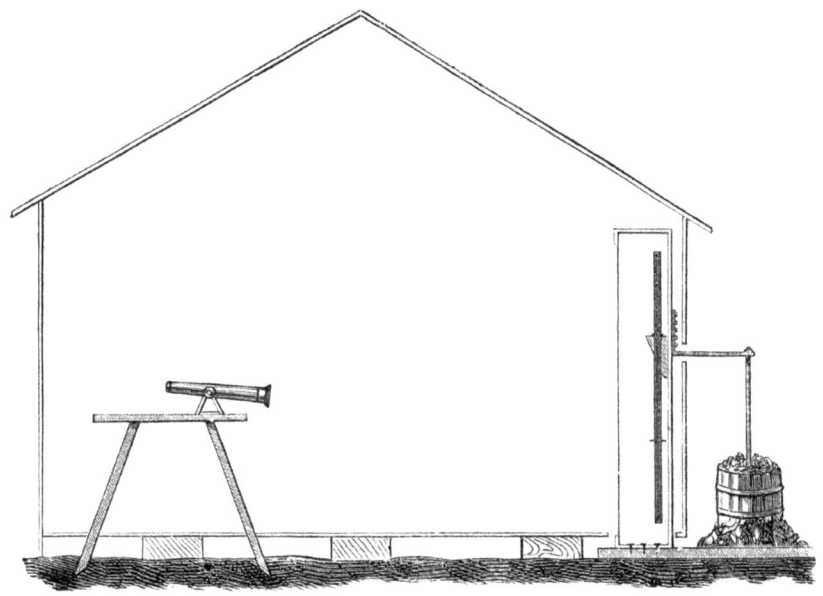

Fig. 17. The pendulum apparatus in the observatory.

temperatures, after 12 hours it had attained such a degree of stability as if it formed part of the ground on which it rested.

The pendulum box was secured to this plank with long screws, in such a way that when the pendulum was set swinging it would do so in a north–south direction.

To increase the stability of the apparatus, we used an upright cask, filled with earth, which stood on the same plank but outside the observatory, and was fastened to it with a mixture of water and sand. From the middle of the cask rose a 3-inch iron rod, the upper end of which bore a thread and matching nut. An opening was cut in the wall of the observatory at the same height as this thread to allow the insertion of an iron rod, bent at right angles. The vertical limb of this rod was screwed against the back wall of the pendulum box; the end of the other limb had a hole bored through it, through which the threaded end of the upright rod was inserted, the nut securing it even more firmly.

Once the pendulum box had been levelled, it was held in the selected position with ropes, and then water was poured over the earth in the cask and was left to freeze.

After two days had elapsed, the ropes were removed. It turned out that the box was not entirely firm; when a 32 lb. ball was thrown against the earth-filled cask, it produced a gentle swaying in a north–south direction. In order to achieve complete immobility, holes were bored through the observatory floor on either side of the box. The holes were 3 inches in diameter; one was located 1 foot north of the centre of the side wall of the box; the other was an equal distance from it, to the south. One-inch iron rods were driven into the ground through these holes and then fastened to the side walls of the box in the same fashion as the rod from the cask to the back wall.

In order to check the stability of this arrangement, a glass beaker filled with sulphuric ether was placed on the plate on which the knife edges of the pendulum sat, and numerous spores of *Lycopodium* were suspended in the liquid. Then a heavy sledge hammer was swung vigorously against the observatory floor. Not the slightest ripple appeared in the glass beaker, which we could observe through a telescope. Hence the box was stable.

Setting up the apparatus had been completed by mid-November, but the actual observations did not begin until 5 January. In the meantime Bryan had been busy observing as many moon culminations as possible in order to check the accuracy of the chronometers. As long as the work continued, two series of observations were made per day, lasting either 4 or 6 hours. Meyer and I made the observations in the morning; at night Bryan took Meyer's place.

The pendulum's swings were observed by means of a terrestrial telescope that was screwed firmly to the passage-instrument tripod, about 8 feet east of the pendulum.

The point of the swinging knife edge served as the target. The swings were observed alternately from right to left (north to south) and from left to right, in order to correct for the eccentricity of the target. Each series began from the right. An arc of a circle, 39.25 inches in radius, was located above the swinging knife edge. From the centre outward, toward each side, it was divided by lines 5° apart; further subdivisions, marked by points, allowed tenths to be read off. The time was noted using a chronometer that ran on star time. Prior to the start and after completion of each series of observations, the chronometer was compared, by means of a pocket chronometer, with all the box chronometers on board.

The vertical hair of the crosshairs in the telescope was aimed at the zero point in the scale, which was located over the stationary knife edge. The pendulum was swung in four different positions, named after the numbers carved in its surface. The number to which the telescope was aimed identified the position. Numbers 1 and 2 were on one surface, 3 and 4 on the other.

The steel plates on which the knife edges rested were levelled before the start of each series of observations using a spirit level; then the glass door of the box was closed and was not opened again until the observations were completed.

In order to locate the stationary knife edge in the same spot for each observation, a thin vertical line was etched in the front of the plate, over which the knife edge lay. To adjust the rear surface of the pendulum, we used a two-pronged brass fork, which was run up and down several times between the pendulum and the back wall of the box, to ensure that the distance between the pendulum and the wall was everywhere the same. The fork was always removed before a series of observations began. The swinging knife edge was located 36.5 feet above mean sea level. The geological formation of the area has already been mentioned.

Although we had to cope with various difficulties, during the night of 13–14 January the work was completed in a satisfactory manner. In connection with other observations, it gave a result for the flattening of the earth of a mean value of 1:299.0.

The ship still remained in its threatening position; a further attempt at blasting, on the 2nd, similarly produced no effect. What our powder could not achieve could be produced in an instant of time, without any warning, by the whim of the wind; but in that case, liberation from our icy fetters must inevitably be followed by certain disaster.

During low tide, living on board was always associated with a constant battle against gravity, which always reminded us of the danger in which we hung. But even this aspect possessed its positive side, since the idea of the uncertainty of our situation brought a certain excitement into our sunless existence, which we probably could never have achieved otherwise.

Thus far, not the slightest trace of scurvy had appeared. Minor gastric upsets, as well as trivial physical injuries, had been the worst problems. The ship's excellent provisioning played no small role in the favourable state of the crew's health. The men daily received fresh bread, abundant quantities of preserved vegetables, dried fruit and lemon juice. Salt meat was completely excluded from the provisions list; by contrast, we were adequately supplied with pickled cucumbers, a cask of which always stood open for general use. The quarters were excellently ventilated, especially the upper saloon, where a fairly fresh flow of air usually prevailed. Anybody who happened to sit beneath one of the ventilators might imagine that his legs were at the equator and his upper body, by contrast, in the polar regions. For the warm air that escaped via a large hatch from the lower saloon, where the stove was located, underwent an abrupt cooling once it had risen about 3 feet above the deck. The two saloons, linked together by this hatch, were divided into an upper and a lower house. Their politics were an abomination, and they were known as the geographical and geological parties. The latter met in the nether regions; it owed its name to its use of coal, which was dictated at any particular moment from the state of the thermometer.

Given the homogenous sedimentary nature of the Silurian limestone, which, at best, offered the variation that the rocks were sometimes bedded and sometimes massive, the effectiveness of a geological party must of necessity remain limited, unless its members could not at the same time become enthused over paleontology. The erratic blocks scattered near the beach contained numerous fossilized shells and corals, which were diligently collected by the geologists. The zeal for collecting degenerated into a real mania and threatened to become quite serious for one of our members, who happened to bring aboard a petrefact embedded in ice. Eager to separate the fossil from its matrix, he laid it on the hot plate on the stove. As ammonia and other fumes penetrated from below into the premises of the geographical group, our attention was drawn to the fossil. But nobody suspected the worst, since at many locations around the harbour the limestone was strongly bituminous and emitted a distinct smell as soon as one rubbed it or struck it with a hammer. Great was the chagrin of the zealous collector when an expert came in, spotted the object and immediately identified it as a coprolite, derived from none of the formations between the Lias and the Cretaceous, but of much younger age, and which provided tangible proof of the excellent metabolism of the Eskimo dogs. This revelation provoked general indignation; only the odd person came to the poor man's defence and tried to excuse the mistake because of the darkness and the intense cold, which later made us all fire worshippers. But the collector was very distressed, since he had been deluded into the fine hope that he had found a rare fossil, and the supports of his infallibility were threatening to totter. In vain, we told him that coprolites, polished and set in gold, had earlier been worn as ornaments by the fair sex and that *album graecum*, the bodily product of the ordinary domestic dog (*Canis familiaris* Linné), not so long before had been used officially.[2] It was all to no avail. Deeply hurt, he went back on deck and thrashed any dog that crossed his path with the rage of a berserk man; even the suckling pups were not safe from this outburst of fury.

It could never be decided whether the activities of the geologists were discontinued due to the increasing darkness or for other reasons. The discovery of the pseudo-fossil remained the first and last exploit of the group, whose numbers now sought to occupy themselves in other ways. Budington used his leisure hours, of which every new day granted him 24, to consume every possible food, and as much of it as possible. When he got tired of eating, he smoked; once he had smoked enough, he went to bed to sleep; and when he slept, he snored so loudly that it rang through the quarters like the rasp of a circular saw cutting through hard wood.[3] Tyson subjected everything that happened on board to a continual, destructive criticism. Apart from this, he stood loyally at Budington's side in all his activities and endeavoured in every possible way to help him bear the strain of his existence to the best of his abilities. Chester, the best man who ever walked a deck, took care of executive matters and kept the log, while Morton administered the provisions with rare faithfulness.

Our gallant engineer[4] displayed an activity of a special type. He collected scraps of paper, cigar butts, candle ends and so forth as diligently as a beaver, thrown away by the members of both groups as they became worthless. Nobody knew what for; but anybody who was forced to spend time in his company was struck by the bitter conviction that the old man's tobacco was sailing under false colours, since the leaves smelled as if they had sprouted from an honest cabbage head. He paid a daily visit to his beloved engine, which had been pensioned off for the winter. Woe to any of his stokers who fell into his clutches during these inspections; he had to be prepared to enjoy a speech about atheism and its effect on the mentality of the nineteenth century. If he managed to assemble a larger audience, he would usually speak about the devil, whom he had allegedly once seen during a hot summer night off the coast of Brazil. When he was discussing these favourite themes, his otherwise dull, grey eyes would gleam, the words flowed easily from his lips, and the pious members of the crew would cross themselves and flee the sound of his voice.

If anybody on board could be called fortunate, it was the ordinary and extraordinary members of the geological group, since they all possessed cabins into which they could retreat in order to be undisturbed. It was a different situation in the upper saloon. Its occupants had at their disposal only bunks, which barely exceeded the length of an adult person. These bunks served not only as sleeping places but also, at the same time, as library and clothes cupboard, arsenal and general lumber room, in which everything was stored that one wanted to set aside for the moment. And there were so many moments when one had to find room for a book, an instrument, a piece of clothing or for some other object that one often had to push aside a complete Chimborazo[5] of untidiness before one was in a position to stretch out one's tired limbs. We had long since given up undressing completely when we went to bed; in the majority of cases, one removed only one's outer clothing. What a pleasure it was to be stretched out on the hard folding bed behind the closed curtains and for a short time to turn to some light reading by the light of a solitary stearin candle, before one fled to the land of dreams, from which one would again be dragged after 5 or 6 hours to start one's shift in the observatory. When there was a gale blowing, it was usually quite impossible to sleep, since the alternating tones of the storm dispelled any slumbers. It was then that the pathological side of life at high latitudes made itself felt in its fullest severity. One would remember the smallest sins that one had committed perhaps years before. One would exaggerate the midge into an elephant and then worry about the grey pachyderm, whose dimensions seemed to expand until they were gigantic. All one's wild tricks would pass in review, but one would not remember the few good deeds one might have done.

Whenever the weather permitted, we made excursions along the coast on moonlit days, either on foot or by sledge. Only rarely did these extend to any great length; Cape Lupton usually formed the objective of the trip. One would make a pilgrimage to the open water, gaze at the grey frost-smoke which hung over the fickle leads, and then return on board, thoroughly chilled. The natives watched for seals, but generally without success; once Hans thought he had heard the call of a walrus, but it was probably his hearing that had deceived him.

On the morning of 24 January, I headed north with two sailors[6] to determine how far the open water extended. We left the ship at 10.30 and covered the distance to Cape Lupton entirely on the sea ice. The going was tolerably level, but near the headland we encountered numerous hummocks that significantly obstructed our passage. After we had rounded the cape, the hummocks ended; in their place there were stranded fragments of bergs, as well as old floes fused firmly together by snow and sea water. The sledge ran crunching across the moonlit surface; both it and the dogs frequently fell into hollows in the snow scooped out by the wind, of which one became aware only once one found oneself in the bottom of one.

Around noon we reached the so-called second cape, a headland that projected only slightly from the general line of the coast, to the north of Cape Lupton. After we had sledged round it, we ran into a high ridge of shattered ice that extended along the steeply rising coast, only 5–10 feet away from it. As we changed course, we moved into the deep shadow of the coast; the moonbeams played on the open water to the west, without touching our route. We were surrounded by a treacherous twilight that completely baffled accurate estimation of distances. The hummocks stood out in vague outline against the dark sky, and the longer one's eye rested on them, the more their shapes seemed to change.

11: The New Year

Thus far we had almost invariably been following an old sledge track; now it suddenly ended. Our predecessors had come this far; we were soon to learn why they had not continued their travels any farther. The going became unconscionably bad; the coast dropped extremely steeply and was bounded by a high ice ridge whose surface was covered by wildly piled heaps of ice rubble. With great difficulty we advanced the sledge about another 50 paces; then we left it behind and tethered the dogs to an ice pinnacle.

The third cape loomed up about half a mile away. Once we had climbed over a long ice ridge, the open water lay close ahead of us, breaking against the wall along which we now pushed ahead, straddling it. At our feet, isolated floes were drifting north at a speed of about 2 knots. Anxious to observe the movement of the ice from a more favourable spot, we made an attempt to get closer to the cape; but after several vain attempts, we found ourselves obliged to abandon this goal. The coast itself was totally impassable; the ice foot had come to an end. To the west and north, the strait appeared to be free of ice; only a few floes were drifting among the dark waves. Unappeased, we started on our return journey. As we rounded a projecting headland and came in sight of the moon again, it turned out to be surrounded by a wide halo, whose diameter decreased amazingly quickly. Fine ice needles were dancing in the air, and if one looked upward, they produced a prickling sensation on one's skin. A little later the moon's disc gave the impression that it was covered with grey gauze; the ice needles were increasing and were obscuring the air.

We had noticed similar phenomena earlier; and later, we also quite often had the opportunity to observe them. At times the crystals were so small that they were perceptible only by feel. Caught on a glass plate and examined under a lens, they revealed the full beauty of their manifold shapes. If the temperature was fluctuating and the moisture content of the air was rapidly changing, they mainly consisted of mulberry-shaped grains; but if temperature conditions were more stable, on the other hand, they appeared as small, delicate stars, whose six points often possessed elegant appendages.

After we had got back on board, Bryan and Mauch hiked to Cape Lupton to check the extent of the open water, and on the 28th, Chester made an attempt to push farther north by sledge[7] and to round the cape that had mocked our efforts. He too found the strait open and found himself obliged to turn back at the point where we had run into obstacles.[8]

It was not until the 26th that we were able to start the magnetic observations, which for the time being would be confined to declination. The instructions that the Academy of Sciences had prepared for the expedition specified that we should make half-hourly observations on three days per month, namely on the 1st, 11th and 21st. But we preferred to ensure a regular hourly series of observations and, in addition, to carry out three term days per month. One of them would coincide with the normal monthly term day which, of course, in February, May, August and November falls on the Friday preceding the last Saturday of the month, and in the other months falls on the Wednesday closest to the 21st of the month.

Bryan, Meyer and I shared this work; we stood 8-hour shifts in turn. The instrument, made available by the head of the Hydrographic Survey, was a unifilar portable magnetometer, whose description I must forego for now. The hourly observations were made at mean local time, simultaneously with the reading of the various meteorological instruments. But on term days we chose Göttingen time;[9] we began the observations at 10.00 p.m. and continued them for 25 hours. The snow house in which the instrument was set up could not be heated, and the joy at serving science near the North Pole was often clouded by the low temperature. It took a certain degree of resignation to sit down in front of the apparatus in that cold chamber with the knowledge that one was in for an 8-hour shift.

The first term day was held on 1 February; a violent northeast wind was blowing outside, its velocity rising to 47 miles per hour. A fine powder snow drifted through the cracks in the snow dome. The two candles set up behind the apparatus cast an unsteady, flickering light on a heavily bundled human figure sitting on a three-legged stool. A sheet of writing paper lay on his knee; he held a pencil in his gloved hand. The glove that enveloped his left hand also concealed a chronometer. From time to time the clock would be pulled out. Finally the observer's eye would rest unswervingly on its second hand, and then it would peer through

Fig. 18. At the magnetometer.

the telescope at the suspended magnet and read off its position at that moment, and a cold hand would record the result. So it would continue for 8 hours; the observations were made at intervals of 6 minutes. Now and then the figure would stand up to turn the upper part of the apparatus to right or left, in case the magnet was threatening to swing out of the field of vision of the telescope. After each turn a new reading of the verniers would be required. While this was being done, the observer had to hold his breath, since the moisture contained in his warm breath would condense on the fine silver divisions of the circle and cover them with an opaque crust of ice. If one's eyelids accidentally touched the metal mount of the magnifying glass during the reading, one would feel a burning sensation, as if a hot object had touched one's skin.

The observer waits longingly for the time when he will be relieved. Ten minutes before that time arrives, a second muffled figure appears in the snow house, exchanges a few words with the hermit, and after the latter has taken a further reading, takes his place, with the prospect that he too will have to occupy it for 8 long hours. This is how life passes, drearily, during a magnetic term day at high latitudes.

On later occasions we sometimes allowed ourselves the luxury of hurrying to the observatory in order to warm up somewhat. But the trip to the stove and back to the magnetometer, even under the most favourable conditions, occupied at least 48 seconds, and since the declination observation recurred at intervals of 6 minutes, there was little time left for socializing. Once we had abandoned the plan of spending the full 8 hours in the snow house, Meyer and I undertook to read the meteorological instruments during our shifts too, although in stormy weather this involved all sorts of difficulties. Since none of the magnetic observations could be missed, we had to go to work fast. Even if one made the barometer reading before one crawled into the snow house and postponed the rest of the observations by a minute, there was scarcely enough time left to collect the rest of the meteorological data. If there was drifting snow, the meteorological observation would be split into three distinct components, the first of which was the pressure reading. After one had read the barometer, one walked to the magnetic hut. On one's return from there, one had to reach for the shovel to dig one's way outside and reach the anemometer, the reading of which fell into the second period. This was followed by another determination of variation, and then it was the turn of the meteorological instruments, the readings from which, along with the sky conditions, were recorded during the final period.

Robeson Channel, which thus far had barely been frozen at all, continued to remain open. If no change in conditions occurred, we could barely cherish any hope of achieving any significant latitude using the sledges, since the ice was fickle in terms of position and infinitely irregular. All signs appeared to indicate that we would probably have to use boats in order to continue the expedition; the prospects that presented themselves were extremely favourable. Already in our minds we were steering our boats north, crossing parallel after parallel and making world-shaking discoveries. Travelling by water we might at any rate hope to attain more worthwhile results than during an exhausting sledge journey over rough ice. In the latter case, we might expect, at best, to make a surficial land survey; in the former case, by contrast, we would be faced with a rich scientific haul.

Until now, the carpenter had been engaged in building small sledges designed to be pulled by one man and to carry his entire travelling outfit since, given the roughness of the ice, a normal-sized sledge could barely be used. In order to be prepared for all eventualities, work now began on construction of a sledge of greater dimensions. It was to be 14 feet long and 2½ feet wide and was to have heavy runners 10½ inches high. It was to be assembled without nails or screws, and simply lashed with tough leather thongs. It was to be used for hauling the boats to Cape Lupton, in the immediate vicinity of which there was open water.

Perhaps this is the place to make the confession that we viewed this open water not as an open polar sea, whose existence was dictated by thermal conditions, but as a local phenomenon provoked by winds and currents. The gales, which blew sometimes from the northeast and sometimes from the opposite direction, kept the sea constantly in motion and prevented the formation of a continuous ice cover. When, occasionally, quite long calms occurred, quite large areas of the sea would probably freeze; but the very next gale would be enough to destroy the work of the frost in a few hours and to pile the shattered masses up in high hummocks.

As a result of the dependence of the open water on the strength of the wind, the effect of calms on the temperature made itself doubly apparent. During the greater part of the year, calms reduce the air temperature, and here they lowered it even more, since under their influence the sea becomes covered with ice, thereby preventing the water from giving off its heat directly to the air flowing over the leads. But quite long calms were a rare phenomenon, and partly for this reason Polaris Bay displayed the distinct character of an island climate, in sharp contrast to Van Rensselaer Harbour. At the same time, it must appear striking that the amount of precipitation is very low. Over the course of November we recorded only 35 hours with snow; in December there were only 7 of them, and in January only 28. The amount of snow that fell during these 70 hours, however, was so insignificant that it could not be measured.

The weather thus far had been extremely mild. The lowest temperature, and at the same time the absolute minimum recorded during our stay in Polaris Bay, was only −46.06°. It was observed at 11.00 a.m. on 9 January. On several occasions, the mercury, whose freezing point we determined to be −39.94°, was a solid mass. We cast balls of mercury, and shot from a pistol at a target with a sufficient charge of powder, they would penetrate 1-inch planks.

CHAPTER 12

Through darkness to the light

Atmospheric electricity. The northern lights. Illumination effects during the twilight. Plan of operations for the spring and fall campaigns. Sunrise. The sun thermometers. Minimum mean monthly temperature. Faunal data. The first willow catkins. Photograph of the ship. Dislocation of the steam engine.

All our efforts at demonstrating atmospheric electricity remained fruitless. A sensitive electrometer with Deluc pillars had been set up in the observatory, together with an electroscope; although these instruments were in excellent order, they never produced the slightest recording. We tried various means, such as suction apparatus and large, spherical collectors, without achieving any better results, and finally reached the conclusion that at the time of our sojourn in Polaris Bay the lower layers of the atmosphere contained no electricity.

Bravais and Lottin had had the same experience at Bossekop in October 1838;[1] by contrast, during February and March of the following year they had succeeded in demonstrating small amounts of electricity.

The results that the Swedish expedition achieved during the winter of 1872–73 on Svalbard were especially favourable.[2] Mr. Wijkander[3] presented a preliminary report on the observations made by himself and Lieutenant Palander[4] in Volume 41 of the *Archives des Sciences Physiques et Naturelles*. During the fall of 1872, the air was slightly positively charged, but the earth negative. In January of the following year, four attempts consistently gave a positive reading. Of the 21 observations made in the course of February, 13 produced the same result; but in the other eight cases, the atmospheric electricity was negative. In March, 32 experiments were recorded; the ratio of positive to negative was 3:5.

As far as these observations go, they appear to point to a certain reciprocal effect between atmospheric electricity and the occurrence of the northern lights. The latter had been almost constantly visible during the months of January and February; they had developed particularly spectacularly between 19 and 26 February. Then they disappeared and did not reappear until 2 March. At the same time, the character of the atmospheric electricity changed; it became slightly positive, as it had been in the previous fall. After 11 March, the northern lights disappeared completely, the temperature dropped and the air was usually negatively charged.

Thus far we too had observed the northern lights frequently, but not with the intensity that one would expect at lower latitudes; the region of their most brilliant display lay behind us. Moreover, the phenomenon was never confined to a specific sector of the sky but appeared sometimes here, sometimes there. The lights occurred most often in the northeast and most rarely in the northwest. If one wanted to attempt to represent their frequency in terms of eight points of the compass, approximately the following pattern would emerge:

N	NE	E	SE	S	SW	W	NW
1.2	3	1,7	1	1,7	1.7	10	0.5

The few instances of northern lights that were observed by Kane and Hayes appeared sometimes in the north, sometimes in the south-southwest, but rarely in the west, as tends to be the case in the northern colonies in West Greenland.

Our own observations can scarcely claim to possess any scientific value since they are too fragmented due to the loss of the journal and of the magnetic record. Moreover, the northern lights as they appeared at Polaris Bay were not bright enough for it to seem worth the effort to investigate them spectroscopically.

The phenomenon usually began with a yellowish cloud forming at some point near the horizon, not unlike a true cumulus cloud. This cloud appeared to maintain its position until a slight flickering developed at its edges. Then it gradually began to expand in height and breadth, and to develop a greater light intensity than previously.

Occasionally such clouds appeared at two opposing points on the horizon, grew toward the zenith and then joined to form an arc. Generally their edges were sharply delimited; more rarely they were blurred. In the latter case, one could usually detect smaller or larger gaps in the luminous area which, due to the contrasting effect, appeared darker than the rest of the night sky. Now and then the arc split along its entire length to form two sharply delineated bands; we never spotted three or more of them at any one time. Sometimes they dissolved into irregularly glowing clouds; sometimes they emitted rays that shot both upward toward the zenith and also, apparently, toward the horizon. Occasionally the arcs appeared so suddenly that it was impossible to account for their formation. The same applied to the rays; sometimes they flared up here, sometimes there; then they would disappear again as quickly as they had formed. But they were generally of more intense colouring than the clouds, sometimes a deep crimson with pale green edges.

Most of the northern lights appeared between midnight and noon. During January the ratio of occurrences during the afternoon to those in the morning was 1:3; in February the ratio was 3:4.

The most brilliant of all the displays was observed from 4 to 5 February; it began between 7.00 and 8.00 p.m. and continued almost without interruption until almost 6.00 a.m. the following morning. Early in the morning of the 4th we noticed severe magnetic disturbances; the declination magnet became more disturbed in its movements than ever before; in one case the disturbance increased to level 9. At 8.00 p.m. the entire horizon was ablaze; the red was most intense in the northwest. Flickering rays shot up restlessly from every direction toward the magnetic pole.

Bryan was stationed at the magnetometer; I myself was observing in front of the entrance to the magnetic hut, sketching crayon sketches and writing descriptions. Each of us was equipped with a chronometer; whenever I pulled on a string that was fastened to Bryan's left arm, he took a reading with the instrument. The changes occurred with such speed that one's pencil could barely record them. Two complete auroral coronae of rare beauty developed; shortly after they disappeared, the most severe magnetic disturbances occurred. Wide arcs of light, the vortices of which appeared to touch the magnetic pole, preceded them. The observations were continued without interruption for over 3 hours; then we had to allow ourselves some rest, since it was strenuous work. But unfortunately the results of our efforts were lost; sketches and notes were lost to the sea.

The first few days of February passed quickly; we looked forward longingly to the return of daylight. The twilight arc had increased in height and brightness; in clear weather yellowish tints appeared on the southern horizon at noon. The twilight glow was visible not just when the sun was at its highest; one could detect it for a considerable time before and after.

As I leaf through the meteorological journal that lies open before me, on 1 February I find 8 hours of twilight recorded, and on the 10th I find 13 hours.

It was an excruciating, tormenting sight to see this brightness develop in the northeast, and then see it move through the south round more than half the circumference of the sky, without being replaced by the long-awaited full daylight, and to observe how, in its progress, it made first one constellation, then another, turn pale. And this game continued for weeks. The landscape was enveloped in contrasts that mocked any attempt at description.

If an artist were to dare to paint this mood, he would have to combine the palette of a Rembrandt with the passionate conception, bordering on boldness, of a Salvator Rosa,[5] each with its mysterious penumbra. What a powerful play of the atmosphere lies in this twilight glow; what strange light effects are displayed by the rocky cliffs, the colossal ice structures and the debris-strewn surface that covers the sea. And yet the tones are nothing but greys—grey against a grey or white background, in varying nuances. Nowhere is there a shadow to be seen. The nearby hills, around whose summits semi-transparent veils of mist are draped, seem flat and disembodied, like silhouettes.

Continually changing their shapes, dark banks of cloud moved across the upper edge of the twilight arch, stretching their multi-shaped limbs menacingly into the bright area. Finely featured cirrus cloudlets, which in warmer zones are confined to the upper layers of the atmosphere,

here swing low, almost on the horizon, and hover around the dark masses that drift along above them. Their colour changes just as quickly as their shapes; it is scarcely possible to find a spot where their colouration remains the same for a single minute. Sometimes the serrated bands of these little clouds are opaquely milk-white, sometimes glowingly golden-yellow or purple, with a reddish glimmer. Here, just before sunrise, one sees the same play of colours occurring directly above the horizon, which at lower latitudes one detects at or near the zenith a short time after the sun has set. All the changes that occur there in less than an hour are distributed here over days and weeks and are strangely distorted.

Only now that the twilight had strengthened were we able to get a complete overview of the state of the ice. The sea was covered with innumerable high hummocks, between which level surfaces appeared only rarely. At only a few spots were the heaps of rubble solidly immobile. Sometimes they moved south with the flood tide flowing from the north, sometimes north with the ebb current. Usually northerly winds, even of low velocity, produced open water that often extended too close to the ship. But if the wind blew from the south, the ice became more closely packed, as far as could be determined.

Since further movements of the expedition depended solely on ice conditions, it was important to observe these changes accurately. The top of Cape Lupton provided a good observation point. Almost daily, odd members of the crew would make for the point to maintain a lookout; usually they would announce "Open water."

On 22 February I sent the following note to Budington:

Sir,
As with the return of the sun the further operations of the expedition must be begun, and as, in regard to all these, a consultation between us should take place, I forward herewith to you the sketch of a plan by means of which, as I think, we may best fulfill the mission upon which we are sent.
    Very respectfully,
    Emil Bessels.

SKETCH OF A PLAN OF OPERATIONS.

As matters stand now, there are two ways of accomplishing the object of the expedition: either by boats and the vessel herself, or, as at first proposed, by sledges. Let us now consider both ways, and the plan of operations for each that seems to offer the most advantages.

The setting out of a boat party will, of course, depend entirely on the area of open water and the improbability of new ice being formed that would interfere with its navigation. Perhaps the party could start during the last of March or in the beginning of April—that is to be seen—if the vessel does not break out before that time, which may occur at any time, as our anchorage does not give us much protection.

If the journey toward the north should be made by means of a boat, considerable time must elapse before it can be safely begun, and the question arises how to employ that time to the best advantage.

As the object of the expedition is a geographical one, and as geography consists not merely in laying down a coast-line, as many may think, but requires much more than that; a sledge-party should be formed, provisioned for twenty days, to penetrate into the interior of the country, to discover if it consists of an ice-plateau, as is supposed by some, but which does not seem probable, or, in a word, to investigate its configuration. This would also give an opportunity for answering some important questions contained in the instructions.

Another party could, at the same time, go to Cape Constitution, to determine astronomically the position of Morton's farthest point, which, in regard to longitude, ought to be verified. Besides that, these points of the coast-line should be connected with the survey of our anchorage.

Regarding the matter of verifying positions, it will also be very desirable to send a party to Grinnell Land, the coast-line of which, although changed a good deal by Dr. Hayes, does not seem to be correct, and ought to be resurveyed. Besides that the party could, perhaps, find out if the land contained any glaciers, as Dr. Hayes stated.

There is no doubt that it would be considered as a very valuable geographical discovery to determine how far Grinnell Land extends from east to west, which might be done by ascending some of the high mountains near the coast. It must be confessed that this party would be subject to many difficulties and much risk, even if open water did not impede their progress, because the ice is rough and hummocky, and liable at any moment to go adrift.

(As matters stand since the day before yesterday, it would be impossible to cross the strait. February 21, 1872.)

It is not impossible that the ice in the southern part of the straits will be better for travelling purposes, so that the Cape Constitution party might cross with comparatively little difficulty; but if you take into consideration how much trouble it cost Dr. Hayes who crossed the strait twice, how it enervated his party, it seems better to give up this plan, especially because next summer there would be very likely a more convenient way of reaching Grinnell Land.

As it has been concerted, the *Polaris* will leave at her anchorage a depot of provisions and a boat. Should the vessel be compelled to leave her anchorage before the sledge parties return, then the party arriving first at Polaris Bay should wait for the other, and upon its arrival proceed to Newman's Bay (the only harbor we know of toward the north), in the most expeditious manner. By all means it would be a good plan, if the vessel breaks out before the return of the sledge parties, to leave also a boat with a patent log and provisions at Newman's Bay, because the boat left at Polaris Bay would be used to carry the united sledge parties, and there should be another to fall back upon, in case of accident.

If the vessel should drift south during the absence of the parties, then documents of the further route they intend to take will be found a few feet to the west of the present site of the observatory. The spot may be known by the iron bar which now holds the pendulum-case.

Let us return, after this digression, to consider a plan for the operations of a boat party toward the north. One of the smaller boats should be taken, with as many provisions as possible, the necessary instruments, and small stores. The party should follow up the eastern side of the strait, surveying the land and making such investigations in hydrography, in regard to currents, sea-atmosphere, and soundings, as may be made without too much delay.

As near each full degree of latitude as possible the party will build a cairn, and deposit a record of its proceedings, in order that the vessel, if necessary, may know where to search for it.

Should we, notwithstanding the favourable prospect we now have, be compelled to use sledges on the journey toward the north, then we should start as soon as possible, by all means by the middle of March, because it is not probable that then the temperature will be much lower than it is now, although we might have more gales.

It cannot be denied that it is a great advantage to use dogs for draught, provided sufficient game can be procured on the way for their food, but as we are compelled to travel over a poor country and make large distances the dogs will prove hindrances rather than help. We must, then, as the English expeditions have done, almost exclusively use men for draught. Two dog-sledges should be taken, loaded with four small sleds, the provisions belonging to them, and besides provisions for the whole party for thirty days. Should the two sledges meet with many difficulties in advancing, which will very likely be the case, then they will establish, at places they may find favourable, small depots of provisions for their return, stay as long as possible with their small sleds, and return when circumstances require it. Then the small sleds will be loaded with the undiminished provisions, and each man drag his own sled, a total weight of two hundred pounds.

By no means can the small sleds expect to return by the same way over the ice, because at that time it will be broken up, and the vessel herself under way for a high latitude.

As has been mentioned in the case of the boat party, the sledge party will also build cairns and deposit records of their proceedings.

Having arrived on their return at a place from which they are unable to travel any farther south, they will keep up a continued watch and signalize by flags and smoke, while the vessel fires a gun several times a day.

Now, a few remarks upon the operations of the vessel. It would undoubtedly be best to use as little as possible of our coal, and to proceed north by sail. If it is possible for the vessel to advance along the coast of Grinnell Land it would be profitable to do so, on account of the running survey that could be made, as there certainly will be someone on board who can conduct a work of this kind.

The determination of the local attraction of the compass before the vessel starts should not be neglected as heretofore, because without this an able survey cannot be made.

It should be considered as a matter of the highest importance to take deep-sea soundings, or soundings in general, whenever practicable; for, except those made by John Ross in 1818, there are but a few taken by Inglefield and two by Kane. If the time will not allow of more, one sounding a day would be valuable and should be taken.

If the water is not very deep, one of the smaller dredges should be used to procure a larger number of specimens than can be obtained by the apparatus of Brooks.

Emil Bessels.

Winter quarters, latitude 81°38'N; longitude 61°44'W. February 10, 1872.[6]

On 29 February I received the following reply from Mr. Budington:

> Thank-God Harbor,
> February 29, 1872
>
> Sir,
> I have carefully examined the contents of your communication, dated Thank-God Harbor, February 10, 1872; and your suggestions as to an early trip to Cape Constitution and the inland meet with my entire approval. Anything to the furtherance of science which can be done before the starting of the final expedition to the north, in pursuit of the principal object of this expedition, I would decidedly advise you to undertake, and you may be assured that all possible aid on my part shall be given to you and your undertaking. The expedition to the north, will, in all probability, proceed by the aid of boats; and it is my decided intention, in such a case, to take command of the boat party. To come to any conclusion as yet in regard to the details of this boat journey and the proceedings of the ship, appears to be useless, inasmuch as circumstances will generally govern our actions.
> Very respectfully, yours,
> S.O. Buddington,
> Commanding, United States Steamer *Polaris*.[7]

In reporting the contents of Budington's letter here, I have anticipated the course of events by a few days, but it seemed to me appropriate to have these two letters follow directly one after the other, since they reveal how unjust and cruel were all the accusations that were heaped upon us after we returned home. They prove that the voices that accused us of having been concerned only with our retreat after Hall's death cannot be made to agree with the true facts.

We cheerfully welcomed 28 February, since now we could hope to see the sun again, which had not showed itself above the horizon for 132 days.[8] Early in the morning some of the men set off for the nearby hills. Others, driven by impatience, climbed either the masthead or the Providence Berg in order to watch the strengthening twilight.

The air was unusually clear. Transparent clouds hung around the mountain crests to the south, the increasing richness of their colours heralding the approach of the sun. When it became lighter, the ice masses that bounded our field of vision glowed a delicate green; the mountain peaks turned red, but the rest of the landscape was still covered in grey tones, shot through with blue-purple tints here and there. The sun was still invisible, but the closer it came to the horizon, the lower in the north the dark shadow of the earth sank and the more distinctly profiled the high hummocks appeared, their snow-covered shapes gradually losing their softness.

Shortly before noon the upper part of the sun's disc appeared as an irregular red patch through a gap in the southern mountain range. From this dark, rocky frame, blinding rays shot across to the snow domes on the coast of Grinnell Land and then to lower elevations. Only fleetingly did the light touch isolated spots on the surface of the sea to the north, and then the sun disappeared below the blue ridge of mountains. Twenty minutes passed before it reappeared. But then it rose completely and brilliantly from behind one of the headlands to the south.

The landscape lay in golden sunshine. The ice formations and rock masses cast long purple-violet shadows that alternated with pink and yellow lights; the changeable play of colours in the thin, translucent frost-smoke over the dark leads was indescribable.

The crew gave vent to their joy in a loud cheer.[9] But the feelings that moved this group of happy people could be read even more clearly in the pale faces, on which the enervating hand of the darkness had left deep traces.

The sun remained visible until about 2 o'clock. It then sank below the horizon as a red, matt disc, distorted by refraction.

The following day was raw and stormy. A violent northeast wind, which rose to speeds of 58 miles per hour, again started the ice moving and again endangered the ship. In the meantime the latter had been pushed up so high that the 6-foot depth mark was already visible above the surrounding floes.

Apart from short pauses, this storm lasted until 3 March. It was still blowing at 25 miles per hour when the mercury began to freeze. Given the low temperatures this relatively light breeze produced an almost intolerable feeling of cold, and due to the cold the wind seemed stronger than it was in reality.

On the 3rd, two blackened thermometers were set up in the middle of a wire enclosure in order to measure the intensity of the solar thermal radiation. One of the instruments was entirely enclosed in an evacuated glass housing; the bulb of the other one was exposed, but the tube, by contrast, was encased in a glass sleeve to protect the scale. Both rested on small wooden stands, the upper parts of which were gently inclined toward the horizon and could be turned easily in terms of azimuth. The bulbs of the thermometers were located about 12 inches above the ground. The latter was covered with oblong pieces of white Canton flannel, to whose surface white cotton wool had been sewn. Due to the strong gales, the edges of the cloths were weighted with small lead weights.

On the 17th, with a lightly overcast sky, the mercury in the evacuated thermometer rose above the freezing point for the first time; but at the same time, the other instrument, whose blackened bulb had free access to the air, read only −19.2°. Two days previously, a few drops of water had appeared on the dark planking of the ship, exposed to the sun. By contrast, the air in the shade was bitterly cold.

Just as in Van Rensselaer Harbour, in Polaris Bay too, March ought to be the coldest month; during Hayes's wintering at Port Foulke it was January. On the 2nd the mercury remained a solid mass for 13 hours; on the 3rd it alternately froze and thawed for 10 hours, and on the 4th for 4 hours. Between the 7th and the 9th it was in a frozen state for 52 hours.

Joseph had spotted the first black guillemots (*Uria grylle*) on 28 February—three young birds with speckled plumage. One can probably assume that this bird occasionally winters in small numbers in the Far North; it appeared quite often during March.

Just as last fall, now too the natives again went out hunting diligently. They spotted the first arctic hare on their journeys on 8 March. But the wary animal would not let the hunters come within range. It had probably wintered in the vicinity of our anchorage and had scraped a meagre existence during the dark period.

The first snow buntings appeared on the 14th, and two days later Chester and Bryan spotted the first gull; we were unable to determine whether it was an ivory gull[10] or a kittiwake.

On land we were encountering lemming tracks almost everywhere; the men set traps and wire snares, but the little animals would not be caught. By contrast, on the 22nd the first arctic fox[11] was trapped. It was of the white variety and was a female; the jaws had caught its left hind leg and shattered it. It had frozen miserably to death while trying to free itself with its teeth by gnawing through its injured limb.

From time to time a track similar to a lemming track was spotted amongst the tracks. By their size they could have been made only by ermine;[12] they were longer than those of lemmings, and occasionally one could discern that the animal which had left them had a long tail. But I must note that we never set eyes on an ermine. Nor did we see any wolves, although the natives claimed to have seen their tracks and droppings. Once, during the latter half of February, two of the seamen announced that they had heard the drawn-out howl of a wolf near the observatory. They set off in the direction from which the sound seemed to come, but without success.

The first ptarmigan were noted by Budington on 25 March.[13] We could not ascertain whether the birds winter in the vicinity of Polaris Bay, but we could report with certainty that they nested in the immediate vicinity. One of the crew found a nest containing three eggs in mid-June.

Just as elsewhere, the females here moult before they start laying. We killed several in the latter part of May that had almost completely finished the moult.

During spring the birds' diet seems to consist almost exclusively of willows, whose shoots, buds and leaves were usually found in the birds' crops in large amounts. Only in isolated cases were there also insignificant admixtures of pieces of stem of purple saxifrage and grass blades. But later, in summer, the birds live on all sorts of seeds and on the leaves and shoots of various plants.

The first willow catkins[14] were brought aboard by Herr Schumann on the 13th. They quickly unfolded and began to produce pollen in the warmth of the saloon. But the other plants still showed no sign

Fig. 19. Ptarmigan.

of growth; no other flowering plant is as undemanding as the willow, which, even in the vicinity of our anchorage, has ensured for itself a growing period of no less than 7 months. Long before the snow starts to melt, when the air temperature is still well below the freezing point, the tips of its dwarf shoots are wakened to new life by the oblique rays of the sun. Independently of the roots, which are encased in the frozen ground, and independently of the main stem, in which the sap is still slumbering, they start growing and producing buds. Weeks and even months may pass before the flow of sap makes its way to the stem and roots. Sometimes the unfavourable conditions may completely thwart this latter process, and the underground parts of the plant wait in this latent state of life until the following year.

On the 14th, with a temperature of −30, an attempt was made to photograph the ship. Since we did not have any dry plates, the operation was attended with no small difficulties. The observatory served as the darkroom. The camera was set up near the radiation thermometers and wrapped in woollen blankets; hot slate slabs were laid on its base in order to warm the air inside the camera sufficiently. The exposure time was 12 seconds. We obtained a good, strong negative, whose only fault was that some of the lighter areas displayed faint wavy lines, produced by the vibration of the warm air inside the camera. As we were bringing the plate on board, it was subjected to such drastic cooling that its surface became covered with frost flowers; as a result, as we were washing the image, the bulk of the collodium became detached.

Over the course of the next few days, the ship was relieved of its housing and was cleaned out. In the process, it turned out that due to the ship's heeling position, the engine had become displaced several inches to starboard. The engineers immediately took the necessary remedial measures to prevent further dislocations; later, as soon as the temperature conditions permitted, the damage would be corrected.

CHAPTER 13

The southern sledge trip

Departure and equipment. Schuhmacher brings a message. Variable going. Geology. Offley Island and Petermann Fiord. The journey through the fiord. Fiord or strait? Return to Offley Island. A two-day marooning. Further progress southward. Bessels Fiord. Atmospheric light phenomena and sensory deception. A bear hunt. Cape Constitution. Return to the ship.

In the meantime, the length of the day had increased so much that it was no longer completely dark. With a clear sky, for the last third of the month one could distinguish the numbers in Vega's logarithmic tables[1] at midnight without effort; and at 2.00 a.m. one could read the finest print in the miniature edition of Musset's *Poésies nouvelles*.[2]

The coldest period of the year had almost come to an end. The depressing monotony of the night had yielded; the new day encouraged us to renewed activity.

That the exploration of the land and sea areas to the north must proceed with the help of the boats was now indubitably established, since the ice debris which covered the sea still formed a mobile mass, traversed by ever-changing leads.

Thus our first task must be to explore the stretch of coast between Polaris Bay and Cape Constitution.[3] The necessary preparations were already in hand. Budington had been kind enough to assist us in this; but our original intention of setting off on the 25th [March] was thwarted by the signs of an approaching storm. We could not leave the ship until the morning of the 27th.

The travelling party consisted of Bryan, the Eskimo Joseph, and myself. Our transport consisted of one of the larger Greenland sledges, fitted with smoothly polished iron runners and pulled by 10 of the strongest dogs. A sextant with artificial horizon, two pocket chronometers, the small Casella universal instrument, an inclinatorium, two prismatic compasses, two aneroid barometers, a psychrometer, and a maximum and minimum thermometer represented our equipment in terms of instruments. We thought we could dispense with a tent especially since we could count with certainty on finding enough hard snow everywhere for building a snow house. For this reason, we equipped ourselves with a short handsaw and several snow knives for cutting blocks; beyond that we relied on Joseph's skills. The amount of provisions was calculated for 3 weeks. Pemmican would serve as the main food item, both for ourselves and the dogs. In addition, we were also provided with hardtack, canned meat, condensed soups, sardines, chocolate, tea, coffee and some cognac.

Our course was determined by the state of the ice. Since the sea was partially open only a short distance from the coast, we set a course directly adjacent to the land. Shortly after we left the ship it began to snow. Soon thereafter the air was so filled with snow that our field of vision was restricted to a few paces. Fog was added to this unpleasant situation; rarely could we distinguish the vague outlines of nearby headlands or ridges. Sometimes the sledge became jammed between rough blocks of ice; sometimes we ran into treacherous areas of young ice and ran a risk of breaking through or of reaching the edge of a lead and of dropping into the water without warning.

When we were about 8 miles from the ship, I noticed that we had forgotten our rubber sheets. The thought of camping without waterproof groundsheets was an unpleasant one. But there could be no thought of turning back to the ship now.

Schuhmacher, who otherwise was the model of a well-trained dog, was not in a good mood that day. Hauling a sledge seemed to give him little pleasure. The bond of friendship that he had established with the galley personnel offered adequate assurance that he would return to the ship immediately if he were set free. While Joseph loosed the trace, I wrote a few lines to Budington on one of our spare whip handles. I asked him to send our rubber sheets without delay to Offley Island, about 25 miles away, where we would be camped for the night. Then the whip handle was lashed to Schuhmacher's back, and our four-legged messenger set off in the direction of the ship in great bounds.[4]

With the snow falling more heavily, we pushed on southward. We groped our way through a labyrinth of hummocks to the coast. It was only when the sledge runners grated, screeching against sharp-angled gravel, that we realized that we had reached terra firma. Around 2.00 p.m. a light east wind got up and cleared the air somewhat; soon afterward the falling snow let up. We found ourselves in a small horseshoe-shaped embayment in the flat beach on which numerous erratic blocks lay scattered. One of the bitches was afflicted with such violent convulsions that we were obliged to carry her on the sledge. When these attacks were renewed later, we cut the animal loose to give her an opportunity to return to the ship.

Around 4 o'clock we reached the entrance to Petermann Fiord and then rounded Cape Tyson. The latter, an imposing headland about 1,800 feet high, is of some significance in terms of its geology. The limestone, which was invariably bedded all along the coast between our anchorage and the mouth of the fiord, changed its character here and became more massive. The steep cliffs of the cape displayed almost horizontal beds of varying width, ash-grey to umber brown in colour.

Once we had knocked off some hand specimens, we set a course for little Offley Island in order to camp there. The southwest coast of the island appeared ready-made for a campsite. A high snowbank, piled up by the wind, promised to provide excellent material for building a house. Bryan and Joseph immediately began carving the hard-packed snow into blocks of appropriate size using knife and saw. I meanwhile prepared the evening meal, since my companions considered me the best cook of the three of us.

Just as we were about to move into the hut, we heard the crack of a whip and the barking of dogs. Shortly afterward a sledge appeared with two men sitting on it. It was at least three-quarters of a mile from us when we spotted it; but although we could not understand the individual words, we could clearly hear the two men chatting. Hence

Schuhmacher had fulfilled his mission; the rubber sheets were arriving just at the right time.

The wide face of the Hanseatic father beamed at us from one of the fur hoods; the second figure was William Nindemann. Among the approaching team we spotted our brave Schuhmacher; but he came running up sadly ahead of the sledge, rather than carrying his tail high like the rest of the dogs. I had clearly treated him basely, since I had asked Budington to send him back to our campsite with the groundsheets. He had been spotted outside the ship shortly before 1.00 p.m. The whip handle on his back caught the attention of one of the seamen, and he had seen that the unique letter had reached its destination without delay. Half an hour later the sledge had set off to take care of our needs.

Nindemann had visited the island some time before and had found beautiful fossilized corals there. After we had finished our frugal meal, I had him guide me to the spot where he had seen the fossils in situ. But he could not identify the exact location since the recent snowfall had changed the topography of the terrain so much that he had difficulty orienting himself. Around 10.00 p.m. the two couriers set off on the return trip to the ship; Schuhmacher stayed with us, as did one of the half-breed Newfoundlanders as a replacement for the bitch that we had set free.

Next morning we continued our wanderings around the island, but all our efforts to locate the fossil site were without success.

The island is somewhat over half a mile in length, while its width does not exceed half that distance. The northeast coast, the highest point, is about 200 feet high and drops steeply to the sea. The back of the island slopes gently down to the southwest, to where the beach extends; the remainder of the coast is more or less abrupt. The rocks display the same character as the cliffs at Cape Tyson. On the steeper, snow-free parts, we noticed the same banding as in them. A certain tendency for these bands to split into strata was clearly displayed in places. As far as could be determined, the bands lay in the same horizons in both locations. Where the rock had withstood weathering, we encountered both whalebacks and deep gouges. The latter, without exception, were aligned in the direction of the fiord. When we were able to view the island from some distance later, whereby the various irregularities of the surface

Fig. 20. Petermann Fiord.

no longer caught one's attention, it resembled a large *roche moutonnée*. Clearly at some earlier time a glacier had filled the entire fiord right to its entrance; traces of its movement could be clearly read in the bedrock of this small island.

We still did not know whether Petermann Fiord was a true fiord or a strait connecting with other sea areas. When Chester and I had climbed a high mountain on our first sledge journey the previous fall, we had been able to see a long stretch of these steep coasts, without seeing any end to them.

With the secret hope of finding an eastern outlet and, in this way, of separating Hall's Land from Greenland as an island, after we had stowed the sledge I penetrated into the fiord along with my two companions.

We selected a route via fairly level, one-year ice along the northeast shore, which formed a small bay with a flat beach between Capes Tyson and Mary Cleland. Behind it rose rows of rounded hills that probably did not exceed 500 feet in height.

After we had covered barely 5 miles, a wide crack in the ice forced us to swing out more to the middle of the fiord. We could now see the shores on both sides equally well and could feast our eyes on the stern magnificence of the wild landscape. Every new bend revealed new beauties. Seen in perspective, the steep walls appeared like giant stage-flats. The stirring impression of the rock banding in the bedrock was pleasantly muted here and there by gently projecting cornices on which bluish snowdrifts were piled. From the ice plateau which lay atop the cliffs, crevassed glaciers forged down to the sea, heaving the grey sea ice up into rough, elongated ridges, a sign that these glaciers do not cease to move even in winter. At other points on the coast, where there were no glaciers, similar ridge-like accumulations of ice debris also appeared. But they were lower than those off the glacier snouts and were exclusively the work of the tide. Seen from a distance they appeared like the snow-covered lateral moraines of a glacier.

The going was so good that we were able to maintain an average speed of 6–7 miles per hour; only occasionally were we held up by deep snowdrifts. At the edge of a wide lead, we spotted a bearded seal the size of a mature walrus. Joseph tried to stalk the animal. But just as he was about to fire, the dogs became restless and the seal dived into the water.

Whereas until now we had seen only a few scattered icebergs, we now reached a real chain of them, stretching across the fiord. After a long search we spotted a route through them near the left shore. As usual, the ice around the foot of the bergs was heaved up and shattered. A few bends brought the sledge to level going again, and we were able to continue our journey unhindered.

But about 25 miles from the entrance to the fiord, we again ran into a row of icebergs. Our problems increased in terms of pushing forward; we often landed in cul-de-sacs and finally found ourselves obliged to stop at the edge of a wide lead. In the hope that the cold would produce a natural bridge for us during the night, we set about building a hut near the water.

When we stepped outside early in the morning of the 29th, we found the lead in almost the same condition as the night before; grey ice floes were drifting on the dark water, but they were too small and thin to bear the weight of a man. A less-than-encouraging prospect revealed itself from the top of an iceberg. Iceberg after iceberg ranged close together on the far side of the lead; as far as we could see, the entire fiord seemed to be filled with bergs.

Since this was the first sunny day since we had left the ship, Bryan began the necessary preparations for making a time determination. In the meantime Joseph and I wanted to try to cross the lead at the narrowest spot and make a reconnaissance on the other side. We hiked along the lead to the left shore of the fiord. But there the lead was even wider than along the rest of its length; the sea was lapping at the bare rocks, which dropped vertically. Finally we entrusted ourselves to a small, drifting floe. Joseph used the widened shaft of his lance as a paddle, and as we approached a projecting tongue on the opposite side of the lead, we jumped across to it, and thus achieved a landing. Behind the chain of icebergs that followed the alignment of the lead, we found a fairly level ice surface, but it too was bounded by bergs. We now hurried to the latter and climbed the highest one. Everywhere we were met by the same depressing sight. There could be no thought of further progress with the sledge. There was so little space between the bergs that it took some effort to win through, even on foot. In order to advance even 50 paces in a straight line, we often had to scale icebergs 70 to 90 feet in height and then climb down the other side of them. In the course of two hours, we advanced barely half a mile.

Under these circumstances it seemed most expedient to abandon our attempt as pointless. We wanted to climb one of the highest icebergs one last time, however, simply to sketch the landscape and take bearings. Once this was done we set off back to our snow house.

We could not decide whether the bergs were aground or afloat. Many of them had clearly capsized in the water since they had broken away from the nearby glaciers. Lines of bedding and veins could occasionally be clearly seen in the smooth fracture planes. Where the latter ran horizontally, one could probably rightly conclude that the berg in question had overturned. But the capsizing must have occurred before it reached the spot where it now lay, since here there was not room for it to overturn.

For the moment we had to abandon any hope of deciding, based on direct evidence, whether Petermann Fiord was truly a fiord or a strait opening to the east or southeast. Thus far our own experience did not admit of a definite conclusion. The massive accumulations of icebergs might have been the outcome of either possibility.

If we were dealing with a fiord, the accumulation of bergs might be explained by the hypothesis that the flood tide running into the fiord was stronger than the retreating ebb tide. If, on the other hand, the channel had an exit, the cause of the icebergs might be explained by the existence of a multi-year ice cover that temporarily made the exit impassable and held the bergs captive. Incidentally this exit might be shallow; and finally one might suggest that the current setting into the fiord from Hall Basin was weaker than the one penetrating from the other side. The mutual interference of two tides, one setting east to west and the other in the opposite direction, would equally cause an impoundment of the ice.

After we had reached our campsite, we took a sounding, but its result was negative in that we obtained no bottom with 90 fathoms of line. During our absence Bryan had taken a number of sun altitudes and had determined the magnetic declination and inclination.

A snowstorm, accompanied by dense fog, confined us to our hut until noon on the 30th. By about 1 o'clock we were ready to set off and set a course for Offley Island, where we had left some supplies.[5] With the exception of a wide lead that we finally succeeded in crossing after several vain attempts, we encountered no obstacles. We again found the depot in the same condition in which we had left it, but the roof of our old snow house had sunk and had to be repaired before we could spend the night in it.

Early on the morning of the 31st, we were ready to set out for Cape Constitution. As Joseph was guiding the sledge over the belt of pressure ice which surrounded the island toward the lower-lying floes, one of the runners broke, forcing us to off-load. During our attempts to repair the damage, our only drill broke. It was impossible to continue our journey with the damaged sledge. We were left with no choice but to send Joseph back to the ship to get the assistance of the carpenter;[6] Bryan decided to go with him. Once all the provisions had been stowed in the snow house, the two men set off. I stayed behind on the island; Schuhmacher, tethered to the shaft of a harpoon, kept me company.

I now had plenty of leisure to wander round the island and to look for the fossil sites. During the first day my efforts were fruitless, but next day I found various corals and brachiopods. Schuhmacher had deemed it expedient to make tracks during the night and to return to the ship. He had hauled the harpoon as far as Cape Tyson, where I later found it.

My companions did not reappear until the evening of 1 April. In a fit of generosity Budington sent me the Hanseatic father and a second sledge, in order to lighten Joseph's work in our future operations. Because Hans had brought assorted supplies as well as a sleeping bag, he represented a not-unwelcome addition, since apart from Morton he was the only person who had seen Cape Constitution close-up. I was also indebted to Budington for a further gift of a long epistle. Little Panik also sent me one, although it was laconically short; it, however, was scribbled on a piece of cardboard.

For that night, the Hanseatic father had to submit to sleeping between Joseph and the wall of the snow house, since the space inside the little structure was just enough to hold three people. Although he was forced to lie on his side and to contort his upper body into a somewhat unnatural bend, he was fully reconciled to his fate by a shot of cognac.

On the 2nd we were finally able to continue our journey south. After travelling for 4 hours we had crossed the entrance to the fiord. We found ourselves off a small bay that runs back gently between Cape Morton and Cape Lucie Marie. Its shores were distinguished by terraces similar to those on the shores of Polaris Bay. The successive uplifts of the coast probably occurred at the same time in both places.

As far as Cape Morton the going was tolerably level. But after we had rounded that cape, we encountered extremely hummocky ice. Numerous leads ran between high hummocks; treacherous young ice alternated with extensive polynyas. Only a short distance from the coast, Kennedy Channel was open. We spotted a wide bear track in the newly fallen snow and also the tortuous track of a fox.

South of Cape Morton the steep cliffs were bordered by a narrow ice foot, whose surface lay buried beneath shattered floes. The farther south we advanced the worse the going became. The level ice had disappeared completely. Often we were able to bypass the open water areas by hauling both sledges up onto the ice foot and by struggling along it step by step.

When *Polaris* had steamed through Kennedy Channel the previous fall, we had rarely been able to distinguish details clearly due to the thick fog. We had noticed that the actual lie of the coast did not agree well with the map, and when we tried to identify Cape Constitution, we ran into difficulties.

From its geographical position, a headland that we could now see to the southwest could scarcely be anything but Cape Constitution. Once we had progressed somewhat farther, we noticed that it was separated by a narrow fiord from the coast along which we were travelling. A small island lay close off the headland. We now set a course for it. The going became even worse than previously. To make any progress at all, we had to cross areas of ice that bent beneath the weight of the sledge. After travelling for 13 hours we reached Johanna Island, exhausted, and built a snow house on its west coast. The place seemed a favourite playground for the local bears and foxes; every level area of ice bore the fresh tracks of these animals.

On 3 April, a cold, sunny day, we devoted our time to determining our position and to exploring the surrounding area. The two natives headed for the open water to shoot seals. They killed several but brought only one back to camp; the rest sank or were carried away by the current.

The longer we lingered here, the stronger the idea grew upon us that the point that we had taken to be Cape Constitution was some other headland. We could have resolved this problem by climbing a high mountain, but the coastal cliffs were so steep that climbing them was quite out of the question. From the top of Johanna Island, we could look into the narrow fiord and survey the coast of Grinnell Land opposite, but to the south, the horizon was concealed by the sheer cliffs of the cape.

Johanna Island, barely a mile in length, forms a sharp limestone ridge covered with debris, whose slopes are partially polished by glaciers. On its highest point we found an erratic chunk of hornblende with scattered crystals of augite. The rock was rounded and was about the size of a fist. Several shells of *Mya truncata* lay nearby. But whether they had been carried here by sea birds, or whether their occurrence is indicative of an area of uplift, is best left unresolved.

If we wanted to fully achieve our goal and to eliminate all doubt as to the identity of the cape before us, we would have to round it. But first we wanted to penetrate into the narrow fiord, the end of which we had not been able to see from Johanna Island.

We chose the following day, 4 April, for this task. Shortly after 6.00 a.m. Joseph and I left the snow house with a sledge, while Bryan and Hans stayed behind. Once we had swung around the island, we hit tolerably level going. Since we did not trust the weather, we stuck to the middle of the fiord, with a view to mapping the coast, given we did not know whether the air would be clear when we returned. In this way, we could survey both sides at once.

The walls turned out to be consistently steep, almost vertical, and did not exceed 800 feet in height. They consisted of a rock similar to that of Offley Island and the cliffs of Petermann Fiord. They too had been glaciated. The ice plateau of the Petermann Peninsula partially spilled over the north coast. Arched ice tongues of the wildest shapes surged through breaks in the cliffs. Small séracs, which hung down free from the upper edges of the cliffs, gave clear proof of the great plasticity of ice.

Whenever the sun's rays broke through the dark snow clouds, refraction played its bizarre games with the more distant cliffs. Now they would appear to float freely in the air; now the mirage swayed atop the swaying pinnacles of boldly towering icebergs that lay well below the horizon. With fluctuating lighting, we often found ourselves deceived in the estimation of distances and heights.

It is well known that light-coloured surfaces, especially in strong lighting, always appear larger to the eye under normal circumstances, while adjacent dark surfaces give the impression that they are smaller than they are in reality. Here, due to the differing densities of the lower layers of air, not only were the effects of irradiation often totally annulled, but dark groups of rocks that rose amidst blinding snow surfaces appeared magnified in a strange fashion.

This observation was made by both Joseph and myself. Our eyes were not yet tired; when we first noticed the phenomenon, it was barely an hour after we had left the snow house. Once one's eyes have become fatigued by the glare off the white snow surfaces, one becomes totally incapable of judging as to distances or size relationships. The irregularities in the surface disappear. At one moment one's foot stumbles over high ice hummocks or snowdrifts whose height one's eye has not registered; next one mistakes deep troughs for level surfaces and is unexpectedly rolling down a slope.

Later we were overcome by an almost irresistible lethargy. Twice we found ourselves obliged to close our eyes for a short time. We slept in turns for 5 minutes.

Although this is rarely a deep sleep, it exerts a surprisingly revitalizing effect on the system. Often, and especially in intense cold, one's hearing becomes affected and is tormented by subjective phenomena. At first, as the sleepiness begins, they resemble the humming that one perceives after taking a large dose of quinine. Later, the sounds become louder and the tones purer; but they soon reach and exceed the maximum degree of clarity. In my own ears, they generally seemed to be interwoven like those of a triola,[7] usually high-pitched and only rarely low. I never succeeded in precisely isolating them and later was never able to exactly recall their pitch.

The effects of replicate images are often added to this phenomenon, to the point that one's eyes, even when closed, scarcely get any rest. Negative images, which often remain clearly visible for 10 minutes or longer, are especially unpleasant.

It is not easy to reject the idea that conditions such as these would have had a significant impact on the development of the religious ideas of the Eskimo. Perhaps these stimuli operate here in a way similar to the way in which the consumption of alcoholic drinks or narcotics affect other peoples. For when the view of strongly lit snow surfaces is accompanied by hunger, under conditions of intense cold, a person could easily be afflicted by vivid hallucinations, which must have an enduring impact on the childish minds of an uncivilized people.

Joseph seemed to be able to combat this lethargy less easily than I. Despite his most honest intentions, he would occasionally close his eyes and drop his whip. It was only when two bear tracks crossed our path that he became really alert. The tracks led to an ice cave where a seal had pupped. The snow was ploughed up and reddened with blood all around. Both mother and pup had probably fallen victim to the bear.

At 3.30 p.m. we reached the end of the fiord, which was about 25 miles long. The shores to both left and right were steep and shattered; by contrast the beach which ran away at the head was so flat that it was impossible to determine accurately the boundary between land and sea. We counted over 20 icebergs, which derived partly from outlet glaciers from the ice cap in Petermann Peninsula, partly from those from the plateau opposite. The ice displayed a striking plasticity. At times the glaciers flowed around steep rock outcrops, then rejoined at a lower spot, without showing the slightest trace of a line of demarcation.

An icy wind blew from the small valley that stretched away in prolongation of the fiord, at times developing into blizzard-like squalls. I finished sketching the area and took bearings on the most prominent visible points, in driving snow.

As we slid down the steep, icy slope of an iceberg in order to return to the sledge, we heard the dull roar of a bear. Confused by the echo, we were unable to determine from which direction the sounds were coming. We quickly threw ourselves on the sledge and allowed the dogs to follow their noses. The excited animals raced off with us between the icebergs and, without stopping, brought us to some level going. The bear was nowhere to be seen. It was only after we had driven around the frontal cliff of a glacier that we caught sight of it. It was about 200 paces from us and seemed undecided what to do. After eyeing us for a while, he took to flight. The dogs raced after him as if possessed. Afraid of losing our quarry, we cut Schuhmacher's trace. Somewhat later we let another three dogs follow him. The animals caught up with the bear almost at the same time. The latter reared up on his hind legs, assumed an extremely comical look and gazed at the dogs playfully.

In the meantime we had approached to within about 10 paces of him. But he seemed not to notice us; his entire attention was focused on the dogs. Schuhmacher, the soul of aggression, circled his quarry in wild leaps, as unpredictable as a goblin, while Bär, a large, shaggy, dark-brown animal, leaped up at his namesake in a very uncivil fashion and

Fig. 21. A bear hunt.

tried to grab its nose. The two other dogs confined themselves initially to making feints.

Joseph was scarcely able to contain his hunting fever. Only my promise that I would leave the quarry to his rifle prevented him from taking a shot. We stood and enjoyed the animal's agile manoeuvres until, with a vicious blow with its left paw, it stretched its poor canine namesake on the ice. The wheezing dog writhed, bleeding on the ice. Two shoulder shots from Joseph's rifle finished the bear's life.

After we had dressed the animal and loaded it on the sledge, I searched for the wounded dog in order to release him from his suffering with a revolver bullet, but the blood trail on the shiny ice surface disappeared behind a barrier of hummocks, and we could not pick it up again. The wind was again driving the snow in dense clouds and erased the last remnants of the trail. Since our repeated shouts produced no result, we continued on our journey.

An hour after midnight we reached the igloo, from whose tunnel the Hanseatic father crawled out to meet us. Our bear was already frozen, and we had to quickly skin and dismember it to ensure that we did not lose the skeleton for our collection. Once the work was finished, we fed the offal to the dogs and roasted a sirloin. We had eaten nothing but two ship's biscuits and a strip of seal blubber during our 19-hour journey. Hence we enjoyed the prerogative of being somewhat hungry and made unrestricted use of that prerogative, since each of us consumed about 4 lbs. of the cooked meat.

When we woke next morning, Hans informed us that the missing dog had returned. The poor animal had a deep head wound, which ran from his forehead over the back of his head to his neck; one of his front legs was also injured. After the sorry sufferer's wounds had been washed, we threw him a large piece of his enemy's haunch, which he consumed with great satisfaction and voracity.

On the afternoon of 5 April, accompanied by Bryan and Hans, I set off to round the dubious cape, which, from its position, ought to be Cape Constitution. When we reached its foot, we realized that it would not be possible to use the sledge to reach it. Hence we left the sledge and dogs behind and clambered onto the fragmented ice foot. The ice in Kennedy Channel was on the move; the short waves of the wind-agitated sea were

Fig. 22. Difficult sledging along the ice-foot.

breaking against the fragments along which we were progressing with such effort. The cliffs dropped sheer. They were 1,200 to 1,500 feet high. After we had covered about a mile with very great difficulty, we reached a somewhat gentler shore, which promised better going. Bryan and Hans returned to fetch the sledge. Until they arrived, I had sufficient time to investigate the terrace formations of the beach, to chip off some hand specimens and to whip off a sketch of the landscape with cold hands.

In the distance a prominent cape appeared, which might possibly be Constitution. After the two men had arrived with the sledge and dogs, we set off for it. We repeatedly had to unhitch the dogs and to carry the sledges over cornices on the sheer face of the cliffs. Our progress was minimal; we could not trust ourselves to the sea ice, since it was sparse in amount and, moreover, was on the move, and the precipitous coast was largely devoid of snow.

At midnight the sun disappeared behind the many peaks on the coast of Grinnell Land. Only a few minutes later it rose again as a deformed red portion of a circle above the mountain ranges that appeared almost black. It was surrounded by a unique halo, the likes of which we had never seen. Its edges dissolved into glowing sheaves of flame, which flickered unsteadily, sometimes lengthening, sometimes shrinking. Dark cloud masses hung above it, fantastic in shape, and received the glowing reflection. Warm and cold tones bordered each other irreconcilably. Bright red lights with orange half-tones lay next to blue-black shadows; the lighting effects were truly demoniacal.

Despite great difficulties we finally reached the headland. But it was not Constitution. Somewhat later we spotted the true cape in the distance. But now we had to leave the sledge behind again, since steep cliffs had reappeared again instead of the low coast. It was only the extremely rough ice foot that allowed us to get within about 25 miles of the cape. Franklin and Crozier Islands, which lay off it, appeared quite clearly. Open water murmured at our feet; open water extended south and west, traversed only here and there by narrow belts of ice.

Of necessity our journey had to be abandoned here. Only a boat could have brought us closer to our goal, but unfortunately we did not possess a boat.

Even Hans recognized the headland. Eighteen years had passed since he and Morton had discovered it. With shining eyes he recounted to us the details of that memorable journey.

"At that time we shot two bears in a small bay that runs in to the south of the cape," he said. "Close by we found the remains of an old Eskimo sledge. And when we made a final attempt to reach the cape we had to crawl along vertical cliffs until open water finally brought us to a halt. Then we hoisted the American flag over a crevice in the rock and left it flying."

Everything he told us agreed with Kane's description. It seemed almost fabulous to me that a homely Eskimo was now relating to me in simple words what I as a boy had read with admiration and that that Eskimo was the same Hans who had accompanied Kane on his journey of discovery.

We were tired and lay down on the ice to take a short rest. Then we started on our strenuous return journey. We had done our duty.

A few miles from the snow house we met Joseph. This faithful soul, concerned that an accident had happened to us, had followed our trail and brought us a bag of hardtack and pemmican. We had been on the move for 23 hours, and we had eaten nothing during that time. Since we thought we were so close to the cape that we were pursuing, we had hoped to be able to get back in a few hours and hence had not thought it worth the trouble to load ourselves up with food.

The miserable snow house now seemed like a stateroom to us. During our absence Joseph had fitted a window in the roof, through which subdued daylight penetrated. A pot of bear soup was simmering over the flickering flames of the blubber lamp, and we were given water to quench our burning thirst.

The cape near which we were camped, and which we had mistaken for Cape Constitution, was named after Bryan; but I had to submit to my name being bestowed on the fiord into which Joseph and I had penetrated.

On the afternoon of 7 April we got ready to set off for the ship; we reached it after a cross-country race of about 20 hours.[8] We had stopped only once, on Offley Island, en route, in order to feed the tired dogs, to rest a little and to grab a hurried breakfast.

CHAPTER 14

Early summer

Preparations for the boat trip north. Scurvy. Hunting trips. Ice conditions. Further excursions. The ship starts leaking. The air temperature rises. The last magnetic term day. The Hanseatics move house. Seals and lemmings. Ethnological finds and remarks. Change in the ice conditions.

During the sledge party's absence, Budington had started preparations for the upcoming campaign. A bustle of activity reigned on board *Polaris*. In the smithy, where the sparks flew constantly, the bellows panted like an asthmatic giant. Under the ringing hammer blows of the engineers and stokers, long rods of iron were converted into bands and bolts. Boat tents and provisions bags were being sewn in the crew's quarters; the carpenter was planing and hammering on his much-maligned work bench, and on the ice the seamen were caulking the boats selected for the trip, singing their seamen's songs as they worked.

The boats designated for the trip were the two large whaleboats, *Ulysses Grant* and *George Robeson*; the former was to be commanded by Chester, the latter by Tyson. Our departure date was set as 1 May. Our own experience, in association with the observations that Hayes had made at Cape Lieber, entitled us to the hope that we would not have to wait long for open water.

In our little observatory on shore, work was continuing uninterrupted. But unfortunately I was not in a position to participate in it again immediately after my return with the sledge party. A severe attack of snow blindness, which befell me on the last day of the trip, had degenerated into a painful inflammation, to the extent that I was forced to spend five days behind the drapes of my darkened bunk. I have to gratefully acknowledge that Meyer willingly stood in for me and took over my work as well as his own.

Once the below-decks and the deck had been thoroughly cleaned, on 15 April work began on removing the ice masses and snowdrifts that had accumulated under the stern over the course of the winter and now held the rudder and the screw captive. On the 16th the sun stayed above the horizon; we now had continuous daylight again, and the temperature slowly rose.

The steward,[1] who had been suffering from mild rheumatic pain, suddenly displayed the worrying symptoms of scurvy. It was indeed striking that it was specifically he who was afflicted with this complaint, in that throughout the entire winter he had been more active than most of the men, who had been sleeping in the saloon and had had no heavy work to do at all. By the 20th the nature of his complaint was unmistakable. A plank bed was knocked together in the observatory, where the air was purer and drier than on board ship, and the sick man was bedded down there. Good care and abundant fresh meat soon helped him recover; he was able to resume his duties on the 29th.

This one case was sufficient to warn us to be careful. We had several casks of barley on board, and since there was a little box of pressed hops in the storeroom, there was nothing more natural than to immediately improvise a brewing operation. The quality of the end product entirely matched the means used in its preparation. The beverage, paler than the blondest "cool blonde" and as turgid as a mountain torrent after a cloudburst, contained no more alcohol than a well-baked mince pie. Hence it could be drunk even on board *Polaris*, where alcoholic beverages were prohibited.[2]

It was a lucky combination of events that between 19 and 25 April our two Eskimos killed seven muskoxen on a hunting trip to Newman's Bay;[3] as a result we acquired a surplus of fresh meat. In addition they had shot several ptarmigan and a hare, and had seen a large snowy owl.[4] A few days later two more muskoxen were killed by a small party led by Chester.[5]

By 1 May sufficient wide leads for the boats had not appeared. During the first half of April the ice had been constantly in motion, but then it seized up, and it was not until the end of the month that it began drifting again.

And this ice was the worst type. I had sailed the open sea between Novaya Zemlya and Svalbard and between Svalbard and East Greenland,[6] but in so doing I had never set eyes on anything like that in Robeson Channel. Here one hummock abutted close on the next. The extent of tolerably level ice was restricted to a narrow belt that extended about from Cape Lupton to Petermann Fiord. The hummocks began at Cape Lucie; everything else was effectively impassable.

Under the prevailing circumstances the sledges were totally useless. The land was largely mountainous and with a very variable snow cover. The ice that extended along the coast of Grinnell Land might perhaps have been favourable for a push north, but it was impossible to cross Robeson Channel to reach the opposite shore.

The idea of having to postpone the solution of the expedition's purely geographical task even longer was very discouraging. But this was only the first of a series of bitter disappointments.

In order to counteract the men's impatience somewhat, small parties were sent out hunting. Accompanied by Joseph, on 7 May, Meyer made a short trip south in order to take bearings on several points on the Grinnell Land coast. Two days later he set off for Newman's Bay for the same purpose. Joseph again accompanied him. Tyson and Hans followed with a second sledge, to hunt.[7]

They returned after five days. They had crossed the bay and had pushed north overland as far as 82°9'N. Favoured by clear weather, Meyer had seen the opposite coast as far as Cape Joseph Henry clearly. He left a report on the general progress of the expedition under a cairn on the south shore of the bay. Tyson and Hans had killed 12 muskoxen: 8 adults and 4 calves.[8]

In order to accelerate the melting process, on the 16th the ice in the immediate vicinity of the ship was covered with a thin layer of ashes. The effect was almost instantaneous. Although the air temperature was still below freezing, the insolation was already so strong that the dark fragments sank visibly into the ice.

While the stokers were engaged in cleaning the engine, on the 24th they made the discovery that there were 3 feet of water in the lower hold.

14: Early summer 293

Attempts to get the frozen deck pumps operating were unsuccessful. Next day, using the smaller hand pump, we managed to get rid of the water; but on the morning of the 26th, there was even more water than previously.

There was no longer any doubt: the ship was leaking. The next step was to locate the damage. The carpenter and one of the stokers[9] were detailed to search for it. Several days were spent in fruitless searches. In the meantime the small boiler was fired up, and the engine was used for pumping.

It was not until 3 June that we discovered that the leak was somewhere forward. At high tide one could clearly hear the water gurgling in. Toward evening we succeeded in locating the leak. It was on the starboard side of the bow, near the stem, somewhat below the 6-foot line, and was 8 feet in length. Due to the violent ice pressures to which the ship had been subjected during the winter, one of the hull planks had splintered, probably damaging the stem. The full extent of the damage could not yet be measured.

The engineers were immediately ordered to remove the iron plates from the damaged area. But when the tide began to rise again half an hour later, this work had to be discontinued. As the ebb tide approached, it was resumed. Before the next high tide rose, the leak had been stopped and sheet lead had been nailed over it.

But instead of decreasing, the surge of water into the ship increased. Further investigations led to the disheartening discovery that there was a leak on the port side similar to that on the starboard side, and perhaps of even greater extent. But due to the ship's list, it was not possible to reach this leak since even at lowest ebb it lay almost 2 feet under water.

Nature was gradually awakening, but due to the depressing worry about the ship, we could barely derive any pleasure from the return of summer. On 21 May the temperature rose above freezing for the first time. The first blowflies appeared at the same time, buzzing around the muskox hides that lay spread out to dry on snow-free spots on shore. The ice stairs that had provided the link between the ship and the outside world began to crumble, and then collapsed, and the snow tunnel in front of the observatory door had to be removed, since it was threatening to collapse.

The start of the melt made the last magnetic term day appear much more unpleasant than during the coldest period of the winter. The snow house was close to melting. Penetrating, cold drips and icy chunks of snow were constantly falling from the ceiling onto the observer and the instrument, not to mention pieces of the filthy soot crust that had accumulated in the dome over the course of time. The panes of glass in the box containing the magnets became steamed up both inside and out, and had to be frequently wiped off. The telescope became wet; the lens for reading the vernier became dim and the pedestal on which the apparatus stood began to sink, so that one could barely take one's hands off the levelling screws. On completing a shift, the individual observers might confidently compete, in terms of the blackness of their hands and faces, with the terrible mulatto who was our cook and who, during unwatched moments, spiced all our food with nutmeg. And the sheet of paper that contained the observations would be in such a state that we immediately had to recopy the results of our work so as not to completely lose the numbers, which had become partially illegible.

The negative aspects of the melt also made themselves felt on board now. The ice that had accumulated in the cracks in the planking and behind the linings began to melt, and soaked our quarters. In the Hanseatics' quarters, where the health authorities had always had difficulty in asserting their control, the filth gained ground to the extent that Budington gladly lent a willing ear to Frau Merkut's request and permitted her to move elsewhere.[10] Hans pitched the old Eskimo tent that he had brought with him from home, on deck between the main hatch and the capstan. Here the entire family lived from now on, in serene bliss. In a certain sense the tent represented a small free state. The Hanseatic mother cooked, stewed and fried the seal meat that was brought aboard, in a soapstone pot over the stone lamp. And when she felt hungry when she became tired of cooking, she ate it raw. Just as previously, the family received the rations due to them, but without tying their meals to specific times. Young and old slept on skins; they had renounced pillows and mattresses. Of the old earthenware dishes, only the sugar bowl had survived, and it was used for a wide range of functions. It rarely contained sugar, since it was kept in a small sealskin bag. On the other hand, it served as a ladle, in order to make the soup palatable to the little one, as well as a wash basin and teapot; and when necessity called for it, it also took the place of that vessel that is a product of our civilization and possesses the shape of a handled cup in folio edition. But one could easily dismiss such minor matters since the Hanseatics were thoroughly good people. The fact that their concepts of cleanliness were somewhat limited was one of those things and was of little concern to us, especially since Frau Merkut never extended invitations to tea. Somebody who cherished an interest in ethnology could make some very instructive studies here, since these good people lived the life of happy, unspoiled children of nature in their tent on board ship. If occasion offered to spend some time on land, they would usually light a fire of blubber and grill the meat of muskoxen and seals on thin limestone slabs.

The latter now appeared more often in the vicinity of our anchorage than during the previous fall. They lay stretched out in a restless semi-slumber along the edges of leads and warmed themselves in the sun's rays. When the natives got tired of lying in wait, they would stalk the animals, usually behind a small sledge, over the uprights of which a white cloth was stretched. In the middle of the latter, there was a hole large enough to accommodate the muzzle of a rifle and to allow the hunter to keep a lookout.

The seal, whose eyes can focus for only short distances, has poor vision; by contrast its nose and hearing are all the more refined. Concealed by the screen on the sledge, the hunter can easily approach them upwind. The slightest noise is usually enough to startle them and to cause them to dive into the water; by contrast true musical notes seem either to affect them sympathetically or to arouse their curiosity. Sometimes animals that have already become restless can be prevented from fleeing by the ringing of a bell or the notes of a whistle. The hunter uses this circumstance and sometimes starts whistling when the seal raises its head and sniffs the air.

Scarcely a day passed now that one or several of these animals was not shot. The wheelhouse, which till now had served as a storeroom for our fresh meat, was no longer usable for that purpose due to the rising temperature. A natural cave in the side of Providence Berg was equipped with a plank trapdoor and was thus converted into an excellent ice cellar. Another cave located below the crest of the iceberg provided us with

Fig. 23. About to fire.

drinking water for a while. But when we discovered that the dogs were contributing to renewing this water source, we opted to melt ice on board ship as we had been doing previously.

The first lemmings were brought in by one of the crew during the last days of May.[11] They were two adult males in winter pelage. Krüger had caught them without any difficulty. They were kept in a spacious tin canister in the saloon to give us an opportunity to observe their imminent moult. The little animals were elegant and trusting; by the second day in captivity, they were taking food from the hands of various people, and rarely tried to bite. But they were so hostile toward each other that they had to be separated. The stronger specimen inflicted several bites on the weaker one. When they were later housed with others in a larger cage, they became more sociable.

Although the plateau where the observatory stood was riddled with numerous lemming burrows, the animals themselves were still quite rare. During our sojourn at Polaris Bay, we caught at most 18 to 20 of them. On 11 August, Mrs. Merkut brought a female and four nestlings on board. The latter were barely a few days old and were still naked and blind and apparently lifeless. When they were warmed somewhat in the hollow of a hand, after some time they slowly began to react to external stimuli. They were then bedded down in cotton wool in a glass that was placed in warm water. Three of the little animals revived and began to produce sounds that resembled the faint cheeping of young chickens. The mother accepted them affectionately and suckled them loyally for two days. But on the third day she decided to mangle one of the little ones. The other two were removed from her and preserved in alcohol since we had no success at feeding them by hand.

It may perhaps be worth mentioning that the distribution of the lemming burrows was concentrated on the erratic blocks that lay scattered across the lowlands. Their holes were always most densely grouped around the erratics, so that the burrows converged on the boulders. In this way the little animals were partially insured against persecution by the foxes, since the chamber in which the tunnels ended usually lay beneath the rock mass. When the melt began, we could observe that, working out from the entrances to their tunnels, these little rodents had undermined the snow in all directions. The exit holes were usually quite a long way from the den. Even after the snow had long since melted, the alignment of their runs was still clearly recognizable from the accumulations of droppings. Later the grass sprouted more luxuriantly in these spots than in less-favoured ones.

Apart from the fox, the lemming appears to have only two real enemies in the high latitudes: the falcon and the snowy owl. According to Joseph, the latter is said to make use of the curiosity of its victim in order to capture it. He told me that the bird settles in front of one of the entrance holes and hisses into it; this allegedly makes the occupants of the tunnels come up to the surface. In so doing they easily fall prey to their enemy. We several times imitated the hissing of an owl, but the lemmings paid not the slightest attention to our enticements.

On 5 June,[12] Bryan set off for Offley Island to take some more bearings on some points at the entrance to Petermann Fiord. Joseph drove the sledge. This trip took barely two days. The going was extremely bad, since the ice was severely broken up, covered by numerous deep pools of water and traversed by leads. The snow had completely melted from Offley Island. Bryan brought back a fine collection of fossils;[13] in addition he had found the remains of an Eskimo camp and had collected a number of valuable objects. These consisted of several worked walrus ribs, parts of a sledge runner carved from the lower jaw of a whale, an extension part of a bone lance point, a few worked bird bones that had probably served as awls, the hand knob of a seal lance, and several other items too numerous to mention. He claimed he could recognize the remains of old houses in occasional heaps of rocks. Joseph, by contrast, thought they were remains of meat caches that the wandering hunters had probably built to protect their kill from predators and the heat of summer.

Since I myself did not have an opportunity to see these remains, I cannot decide which of these two interpretations is the more probable. Perhaps the circumstance that in the vicinity of the heaps of rocks the ground was strewn with bones of killed animals supports the idea of a permanent settlement. But there were no traces of graves anywhere. From this, one may conclude with some degree of certainty that the Eskimos had never spent any long periods on the island. The high latitude of the island would also indicate this. For the constraint applied by nature to man's geographical spread northward is probably not to be sought in the alleged reduction in temperature that comes into play with increasing latitude, but rather in the dark winter night, whose length increases with latitude. The Eskimo are an improvident people, little inclined to live frugally and to lay in large reserves for periods of need. Since at the latitude of Offley Island the sun remains below the horizon for over four months and since, due to the darkness, hunting becomes difficult, this spot cannot be very suitable for providing man with a permanent domicile.

In addition to these discoveries, Mrs. Hannah found an old sledge.[14] It lay about 30 feet above sea level, about 60 paces from the water's edge and was so completely embedded in the fine limestone gravel that one could with justification assume that it had been thrown up by the waves. Hans assisted me in removing the rocks. One of the runners was complete, the other partially so. Three of the crosspieces were still in their original positions, but the lashings were gone. The holes for fastening the latter were large and drilled in Eskimo fashion. It could no longer be determined whether the wood had been worked with stone or metal tools. Its appearance alone identified it as a conifer. The check that was later made under the microscope on board ship confirmed this view. Several sections revealed a total lack of fibres and also the characteristic dots. The wood, which was definitely driftwood, had not grown in the high latitudes, since the width of the individual annual rings was greater than they tend to be in the case of northern trees.

Further finds were made on a level surface near the tent rings. Budington collected half-charred seal vertebrae, the bone handle of a stone knife and a piece of a bone lance head; Schumann found a fragment of meteoric iron that had clearly been used as a fire steel. Joseph found the cast left antler beam of a two-year-old caribou. But I prefer not to make a pronouncement as to whether the antler had been left here by wandering Eskimos. It is noteworthy that we found neither horn nor stone articles, and that there was nothing from which we might have concluded whether these people also possessed boats as well as sledges.

Where had these wanderers, whose traces we had found, come from? Where did they head for when they left the beach at Polaris Bay? These questions can only be partially answered, but in several ways.

It is fairly certain that the settlement of Greenland by Eskimos was not achieved by a real journey of discovery, but that the immigrants were attracted by the proximity of the Ellesmere Island and Greenland coasts. They probably crossed the entrance to Smith Sound, where the shores of the American archipelago lie so close to the west flank of Greenland that occasionally, specifically during a mirage, one might think it possible to fire a bullet across the strait. The wave of migration probably proceeded from Ellesmere Land, across to Cape Alexander. From that nodal point the wanderers spread north and south. Their descendants still inhabit the entrance to Smith Sound, perhaps isolated since that time, unattracted by the civilization of the Whites and undisturbed by the proselytizing of zealous missionaries. They are the most northerly inhabitants of the earth of whom we have knowledge. The traces we had found may have been made by them. In addition, other bands may have crossed the northern prolongation of Kennedy Channel, since Hayes discovered old tent rings on his sledge journey along the coast of Grinnell Land. The possibility that the most northerly inhabitants of East Greenland swung west around the north coast certainly should not be excluded. The German expedition[15] did not encounter any living people when they visited the northern coasts of East Greenland. But they certainly found dilapidated stone houses. Nearby stood heaps of moss-covered boulders beneath which lay bold hunters, sunk in that sleep from which they would be wakened neither by the thunder of the glaciers nor by the rays of the sun that steal into their artless graves during the brief summer.

Thus far only momentary, insignificant changes had occurred in the ice conditions. The two whaleboats lay at Cape Lupton, ready for the journey, but we were still waiting in vain for open water. A northeast gale, which blew on 4 May and which reached speeds in excess of 50 miles per hour, failed in its effect. The same was true for another on the 11th. When finally a gale blew up again from the same direction on the 22nd without the ice opening up, our hopes began to sink. On the 25th a few leads finally appeared, but next day they had disappeared again. On 3 June, Tyson and Mauch were sent off to take a look into the northern continuation of Robeson Channel from the top of Polaris Promontory. They hiked as far as Cape Sumner. They discovered a few openings in the channel, but north of Newman's Bay the rough pack ice formed a tightly packed mass. On the 5th, even the few leads had closed again. When Hans made the discovery that same day that northern Kennedy Channel had opened from shore to shore, we breathed somewhat more easily since now the next north wind could scarcely fail to produce open water. The turning point for the better appeared to be just around the corner. Chester, who had walked to Cape Lupton early on the morning of the 7th, returned with the glad news that the sea was open in the vicinity of that headland.

Hans was now dispatched south with a sledge without delay to fetch part of the crew who were hunting muskoxen about 15 miles from the ship. In the meantime we on board were making the final preparations for our departure. Chester, Meyer, Hermann[16] and Robert,[17] as well as both Big and Little Fritz,[18] were assigned to the boat *Ulysses Grant*, while *George Robeson* was intended for Tyson, Gustav,[19] Heinrich,[20] William,[21] Peter[22] and myself.

In case the boat party could no longer find the badly damaged ship when they returned, Budington had established a depot of provisions, clothing and ammunition on shore.

CHAPTER 15

The boat voyage north

The crews of the Grant *and the* Robeson *leave the ship. Chester returns and reports the loss of his boat. The* Hegemann[1] *canvas boat is made ready to replace the* Grant. *Scene of the shipwreck.* Robeson *departs. Appearance of the coast between Cape Lupton and Cape Brevoort. Robeson's crew lands in Newman's Bay. Unfavourable ice conditions. The arrival and fate of the* Hegemann. *The whims of the ice. Further progress. Hans brings bad news. Return to the ship. Finds of driftwood. Scurvy again.*

Accompanied by their crew, Chester and Meyer left the ship around midnight on 7 June in order to proceed first to Cape Lupton. Next morning Tyson followed with his seamen. Since the ice had closed again in the meantime, I opted to remain on board some time longer, where there were still many things to be done. As soon as open water appeared, Tyson planned to hoist a flag on a slope of the headland, as a signal to me. Instead of the prearranged sign, two of the men appeared on the morning of the 9th to fetch various minor items and to inform me that the opportunity to start on the long-awaited voyage would probably occur in the course of the day.

Shortly before that Chester had returned. His news was less than encouraging. He had lost the boat, *Grant*, along with all its equipment; the crew had barely escaped destruction.

His official report on the accident reads as follows:

On the morning of the 8th, quite a strip of open water leading around the cape; launched the boat and loaded up; pulled up about two miles; the pack closing in again, landed on the fast ice; here we stopped about four hours, watching the movements of the ice from the hill. At the end of that time, the ice began to open again up around the cape near the shore; dragged our boat and provisions over an old floe about one half-mile in extent, and pushed on again. We had proceeded about one mile, when the small drifting ice compelled us to land. We pulled up on a level floe between two grounded icebergs, which we considered to be a safe place to camp. The pack soon set in, and we made arrangements for a short nap before the tide turned again to set the ice off. A good watch was set to observe the movements of the ice, &c., with instructions to call up the crew and to wake us as soon as the ice opened up sufficiently for a passage of our boat up around the cape. At 6 o'clock on the morning of the 9th, the ice began to open again. The mate, who was asleep on a rubber-blanket about one rod[2] ahead of the boat, was called by the man on watch. At that instant the ice broke between him and the boat. Three of the men were with the boat. The piece of ice they were on went off so rapidly that we could not get to them. They soon came in contact with the moving pack, and the boat was crushed to pieces. Everything that was in her was lost, with the exception of three rifles, the box-chronometer, and a few other small articles. The ice soon became still, which enabled the men to get off safely. The pack was moving up the coast to the northwest. A point of an old floe came in contact with the land-ice about a quarter of a mile to the south of us, which broke the ice where our boat was, there being at the time quite a space of open water between our boat and the moving pack.[3]

This accident, that might easily have taken a worse turn, contributed not at all to disheartening the men. Chester asked Budington for permission to use the *Hegemann* portable canvas boat for a renewed attempt. His wish was granted. In the meantime the crew of the *Grant* had arrived and began to get the boat ready without delay and to make the other preparations for the voyage. Meyer had brought the box chronometer with him; as a result of the severe impact, it had lost more than 36 minutes.

He showed me the wreckage of a small, wooden box that belonged to one of the portable anemometers. The wood had been splintered into thin slivers the diameter of a match by the ice pressures.

Around noon Joseph drove me north on one of the dog sledges. The ice was gullied and covered with deep pools of water. Half a mile south of Cape Lupton, we left the sledge behind and then hiked along the steep coast until we reached Tyson's tent. Our men could scarcely wait for the moment to set off; Chester's accident had enflamed their spirit of enterprise rather than dampening it.

Since the ice was still unbroken, we set off to find the spot where *Grant* had been wrecked. Two of the men equipped themselves with boat hooks to retrieve the floating debris for our small cookstove. Our route led over talus slopes that bordered directly on the vertical cliffs and that sloped down to the sea at an angle of at least 40°. At some spots the talus slopes were covered with saturated silts, in which one's foot sank to the ankle. The thaw had loosened the rocks which only shortly before had been welded together by the ice. The snowdrifts, hollowed out by fine water channels, collapsed with a roar beneath one's feet. The water streamed down the cliffs above and accumulated into foaming streams that rushed away from their place of origin, murmuring and splashing. We were now seeing flowing springs again for the first time in over 9 months, and their multi-toned babbling could scarcely have struck the ear of a thirsty desert-dweller more sweetly than it did ours. Along the streams the purple saxifrage had opened its glowing blossoms. Higher spots, which could not be reached by the snowmelt runoff, were so totally desiccated that their surfaces were seamed with gaping cracks. Whitish-grey efflorescences, similar to those on the plain near the observatory, appeared beneath the overhanging cliffs.

When we reached the spot where Chester had lost his boat, the tide was still rising. In the midst of the piled-up hummocks, we spotted part of the shattered stern of the boat; the blade of a broken oar was jammed between two floes and stood vertically. We slid down the steep slope and moved out onto the ice, which was so loose that it moved with every step we took. The sailors made several vain attempts to reach the debris from the *Grant* with their boat hooks. A torn rubber sheet, weighted down with three rifles, lay on a slope; near it was a soaked bag full of clothes. The waves had carried away everything else.

On the way back to the camp, I found a *Maclurea*,[4] which had been washed out, a new species of shell for our collection. Before we had reached the tent our black ship's cook came toward us. He just wanted to pay us a visit and see the place where Chester had been shipwrecked, and to inform us that *Polaris*'s leak had apparently increased.

On the morning of the 10th, the ice situation had experienced almost no change. Only near the tent had a small lead appeared, serving as a playground for a flock of black guillemots. Two well-aimed shots bagged 19 of these birds, and they were immediately roasted, to supplement our breakfast. Shortly after 7 o'clock a light southwest wind rose, and under its influence the ice yielded somewhat. The men got everything ready for our departure. At this point the metal bottle containing the mercury for the artificial horizon fell into the water and could not be recovered. I was left with no choice but to return to the ship immediately in order to make good the loss, since the rest of the mercury was in an inaccessible corner of my cabin. Due to the high tide, the trip back to *Polaris* took a full 2 hours. We had to wade for 20% of the total distance. On our return trip, the going had improved significantly; the tide had begun to ebb, leaving the ice dry. Joseph was driving the dogs, but we had to leave them and the sledge behind before we reached the cape. As we swung round the latter, we spotted the men busy loading the boat. During my absence, Tyson had made a short reconnaissance trip to determine the extent of the open water. He had reached the so-called "Third Cape"[5] without difficulty and had found an open, clear channel extending north along the coast.

Full of cheerful hope we loaded provisions, instruments and bags of clothes aboard the *Robeson*, relayed a final greeting back to those left on board via Joseph, and at 2.43 a.m.[6] pushed off from shore. After we had passed Cape Lupton, the open water lay spread before us, as smooth as a mirror. The few drifting hummocks could easily be avoided. Only at one point did we have to work through loose ice; in so doing we had to haul in the patent log, which we had streamed to measure the various distances. We invariably stayed at a distance of about half a mile from shore, and in so doing travelled along the boundary line of a zone of fresh water that owed its origin to the water draining off the cliffs.

Between Cape Lupton and the "Third Cape," the rock is slaty and displays similar dislocations to those in the ravine near the observatory. The slates dip at every angle from horizontal to vertical. The cliffs are invariably steep, without any beach formation. But somewhat south of Cape Porter the rock becomes massive, like the cliffs of Petermann Fiord, and like the latter it contains eroded cavities, which numerous black guillemots used as nesting sites.

After we had rounded Cape Ammen, a gentle breeze from the south arose, driving the ice before it with disproportionate speed. The channel began to close behind us, but we could still see open water to the north. The breeze soon died again, our sail became useless and the men had to lean into the oars. But the calm was only of short duration. It again began to blow in brief gusts from the same direction, and as a result the ice began to set northward at a speed of at least 3 knots. The safety of the boat was seriously at risk. We could not land anywhere below the perpendicular cliffs. Here and there, certainly, the shore ice lay piled up in belts up to 20 to 30 feet high, from which flat tongues extended, but these spots were far from inviting. The ice came nearer and nearer, but nowhere among the drifting masses was there a floe large enough to haul the boat out upon.

With rapid oar strokes we strained toward the entrance to Newman's Bay. After several vain attempts, with our combined strength we managed to push the boat through a breach in an ice ridge and to reach a solid floe.[7] Even before we had achieved this, the ice had closed up completely. By the time we had pitched the tent, it was 9.30 p.m.

During the 11th there was a stiff wind out of the southwest, resulting in the ice moving northward. Toward evening the wind dropped; the ice masses came to rest; but we searched in vain for open water. Apart from a few black guillemots, an ivory gull and two seals, there was no sign of animal life. The two seals were playing in a lead, but they were too wary to let us get within range. We had installed the meteorological instruments near the tent since we intended to obtain a series of comparable observations between our campsite and Polaris Bay. A psychrometer, a maximum and minimum thermometer and the prepared strips of paper for determining the ozone content of the air were protected from the sun in a small box whose sloping sides were covered on the outside with tinfoil. Nearby, a blackened thermometer, whose bulb was enclosed in a wide, air-filled tube, stood 3 feet above the ice.

On the 12th the flat calm gave way to gentle breezes from the northeast. The ice was moving south at a speed of ½ to ¾ of a mile per hour. Four eider ducks flew off over the bay toward the north. A few isolated leads showed here and there, but they were of very limited extent.

The following day was a repeat of the previous one. We spotted the first fairly large floe in the course of the morning. It was drifting slowly south and collided against the flanks of Cape Sumner; as a result the other masses were dammed up for a period. Deep hollows had developed in the tent where our sleeping bags had lain. The meltwater had penetrated through the rubber sheet; the muskox hides that served as a mattress were completely soaked.

On the 14th conditions had not improved in the slightest. During the night, a gentle, half-liquid snow had fallen; a light breeze was blowing now from the north, now from the northwest, and dense, wet fog hung over the land. An ivory gull and a magnificent pair of glaucous gulls circled the tent, looking for food. The female glaucous gull was so persistent that I managed to kill her at a range of about 30 paces with a pistol ball. Had it not been for this unfriendly attack, she would probably have laid her first egg next day, since she was carrying it inside her, fully formed. In addition, she contained various tape worms, which I immediately preserved in Müller's fluid to add to our zoological collection.

On the 15th, too, the ice was still moving south, but it was not so closely packed as on the day before. Over the course of the afternoon, a gentle breeze from the northwest produced a long lead; we followed its course in the unladen boat as far as Cape Brevoort,[8] to investigate the ice situation. But the latter headland was so closely besieged by hummocks that a landing was totally out of the question. Since, under the influence of the flood tide, the ice was again driving rapidly eastward, we found ourselves obliged to turn back as quickly as possible. Our hopes of making a deep-sea sounding were unfortunately thwarted by the unfavourable conditions. On the return voyage to the tent, we spotted two flights of brent geese, but we had no chance of hunting them.

At 8.00 p.m. Chester arrived in the *Hegemann*.[9] He had hoisted a black pirate sail, and the men were singing a cheerful song as if they were on a pleasure excursion.[10] The capriciousness of the ice had again played them an unkind trick and had delayed them for three days. They had left Cape Lupton early on the morning of the 13th; shortly afterward the boat began to leak, and they had had to pull it up on the fast ice, after covering barely 2½ miles. In the meantime the leads had closed. It was not until the afternoon of the 14th that open water again appeared. They pushed off at 2.20 p.m., but they had had to haul out again at 4.00 p.m. due to the drift ice. During the night, the floe on which they had pitched camp had come adrift and moved 4½ miles southward. The boat could not be launched again until 6.40 a.m. next morning; but then their voyage proceeded without any major obstacles.

We helped the tired sufferers to land their belongings, and since they were hungry, we invited them to join us in our modest meal. They pitched camp on a level floe about a rifle shot from our tent.

The 16th passed without open water appearing. A gentle breeze was blowing from the west, and the ice was moving south again. During the 17th, 18th and 19th, the prevailing wind direction was southwesterly; the ice was drifting constantly northward, sometimes at a speed of 2 knots.

On the 22nd open water appeared again. But in a southerly direction. To the north the rough hummocks lay jammed close together. But when they drifted apart on the morning of the 23rd, we quickly launched the boat, since we cherished the bold hope that we might reach Cape Brevoort.[11] We had barely covered 2½ miles when the pack ice began to close again. The ice mass surged down on us at such a speed that we had to concentrate on saving the boat. After a somewhat exciting but quite fruitless voyage, we landed in the same spot and pitched camp again.[12] Two of Chester's men climbed a hill near Cape Brevoort, but they could not see open water anywhere.[13]

On the morning of the 24th, dark water clouds appeared to the north and northeast; there was a strong wind out of the northeasterly quadrant of the compass, and the ice was setting south without respite.[14]

Each new day now brought us new disappointments. Our hope that the spring tides would break up the ice had not been fulfilled. The floes at the entrance to the bay were covered with pools of water. Despite the rubber sheets, our sleeping bags were completely soaked, as were our furs; anybody who could keep his feet dry was envied by the others. Despite all our economies, the amount of fuel was decreasing alarmingly. Chester's crew was now getting only one warm meal per day, and quite often it was cooked with the skins and bones of the black guillemots they had shot. The inactivity to which we were condemned began to be really irksome; our reserve of untold stories was already so seriously depleted that even Peter, our gallant Norman, who had served aboard a pirate ship, was occasionally tempted to serve up the same old pirate stories to his companions for the second or even third time. The awareness of doing our duty and the hope that we would soon succeed in ending this frustrating existence were, however, quite sufficient to keep the men in a good mood and to make us forget our minor problems.

With a clear sky we could always see a dark cloud bank north of Cape Joseph Henry that was clearly different from the so-called water sky. Its position remained so absolutely unchanged that bearings from our campsite to the eastern and western ends of the cloud rarely varied more than half a degree. The apparent stability of this cloud made us hypothesize that a coast was concealed behind it, and to reach that coast became our most eager wish.

Day after day we waited impatiently for open water. On the 27th our hope was revitalized by the sight of a dark water sky to the north. Wide leads developed near our campsite, extending southward and westward, and the swell that thus far had been barely perceptible broke so impetuously against the ice edge that the hummocks began collapsing noisily. Alerted by this uproar we moved camp somewhat farther east; an old floe wedged firmly between two icebergs provided the necessary protection. We were so confident of finding a favourable channel that Chester sent two of his men[15] overland to the ship to bring back a centner of bread to continue their voyage.[16] The northeast wind, that had blown almost constantly all day, increased in strength toward evening.

At 2 o'clock on the morning of the 28th, we were wakened by the rumble of the ice; the floe on which we were camped began to heave and shake. We quickly hurried outside. A heavy swell was rolling in from the north, and under its assault the ice was disintegrating with uncanny speed. Heavy floes were being split by cracks in every direction and thrown up into wild hummocks. Where our tent had stood at noon, the waves were now foaming.[17] The water was coming so close to our present campsite that we again had to move it. The organization of a regular watch had become an urgent necessity.

The ice continued to drive south throughout the day. On the 29th conditions were generally unchanged. At 2.00 a.m. next morning Hans suddenly appeared with a letter from Budington. According to this message, the ship's situation had become critical; Budington urged us to return to the ship without delay. The strenuous hike overland had quite exhausted the usually robust Hans. After a 12-hour rest he was ready to start back to *Polaris*, accompanying me. Due to the recent gale, the ice bridge to the south shore of Newman's Bay was no longer intact but was seamed by wide cracks that were not always easy to cross. Sometimes we jumped short and landed in the water; sometimes the thin ice crust that had formed on the pools gave beneath our feet; as a result the hike to Cape Sumner became quite unpleasant.

On reaching the shore, I found a piece of driftwood that had been newly washed ashore; this was a pleasant surprise since it was the first such find. We looked for more, but our search was fruitless. Along the way we lost our way in one of the numerous ravines; by the time we reached the ship, we had been on the move for 27 hours.

Meyer had set off almost simultaneously with us, to examine the position of the ice from Cape Brevoort.[18] He reached the shores of Repulse Bay; determined the latitude of his most northerly point, by means of a pocket sextant, the ice horizon and the lower culmination of the sun, to be 82°7'N; and returned to camp at 6.00 p.m. on 1 July, afflicted with snow blindness. He had not seen any open water.

The ice was still driving south. It was not until 3 July that this drift slackened, but despite this the boats could head neither north nor south to the ship. On the 4th the two men whom Chester had sent to the ship to fetch bread returned.[19] At first they had tried hauling their load on a small sledge, but then slung it on their backs and walked for 39 hours to cover the distance of about 23 miles.

On the morning of the 5th, the crews of both boats combined forces to haul the boat *George Robeson* across the ice to Cape Sumner; they hoped to be able to launch it there, in order to travel back to the ship.[20]

When, shortly after midnight, the men began moving the tent and the sleeping bags, the ice had become so impassable that, overcome by exhaustion, they pitched camp on a somewhat raised floe. Each of them had fallen into the water at least once; Little Fritz, never a great hero, would certainly have drowned if Hermann had not grabbed him by the hair just in time and pulled him out. The strong current had already pulled him under the ice, except for his head.

Accompanied by four seamen, Tyson next set off back to the ship on 7 July; but the *Hegemann*'s crew still waited for an improvement in conditions.

In hopes of reaching the ship by water, Chester left the floes in the bay in the *Hegemann* on the 10th. But he had scarcely covered two miles in a southerly direction when he was beset and had to land. Since no opportunity offered of continuing the voyage over the course of the next day either, on the afternoon of the 13th, he lashed his boat to a low sledge, planning to haul it to Cape Sumner. When the men had got to within about a mile of shore, a stiff offshore breeze began breaking up the ice and setting it in motion. They had to abandon the boat and concentrate on saving their own lives. An hour after midnight, after unspeakable hardships, they finally reached the desolate beach and crawled into the tent that Tyson had pitched near the boat. In the meantime the wind had risen to a gale. Before they had time to lie down, the tent had been blown down and carried away by the wind. They were just about to take shelter in the boat when it too was caught by a hurricane-like gust and was carried about 10 paces. In the process, one of the seamen received severe bruises on the thighs, while the boat developed a hole as big as one's hand. Due to the fury of the storm, it was impossible to retrieve and repitch the tent. They tried to weigh the boat down with some boulders, but since they could not find enough of them, they were forced to act as ballast themselves. The gale continued to rage with undiminished strength. By evening they could not hold out any longer in the boat. During a momentary lull, they made preparations to leave it and to secure it with ropes. Then they retrieved the tent, which they hauled to a nearby gully where they spent the night.

Next day, the 15th, a drizzling rain was added to the gale. It was not until evening that the storm slackened and the air cleared; by next morning it was partly fair. A lead that extended along the shore prevented the men from recovering their canvas boat. Chester sent two of them[21] back to the ship, since he wanted to save their strength. He himself stayed with the other two near the cape in order to get his vessel ashore at the first opportunity. This opportunity occurred on the afternoon of the 17th, but it was hard work and took until the evening.[22]

At a flat spot on the shore where they landed, Hermann found several pieces of driftwood that had washed ashore. One of them still retained some bark; the longest of these branches measured 18 inches, and the thickest was 4½ inches in circumference. Unfortunately none of them reached the ship, since the men kindled a fire with them to dry their soaked clothes and to cook a meal. However, under the prevailing circumstances one could scarcely blame them. The piece that I found was the only piece of driftwood of recent age that was recovered. It was a gnarled branch of a conifer; it had closely spaced annual rings, a dark umber-brown colour, and emitted a faint, barely perceptible aromatic scent of resin. The wood that the men found also had the same smell and gave rise to the false idea that they were pieces of *Juglandaceae* wood.[23]

Although at that time I thought I was in possession of facts that appeared to prove that the flood tide wave from the Pacific Ocean penetrated into Robeson Channel from the north, I could not help immediately distrusting that information. The various geographical journals that have cited me as an authority for the occurrence of *Juglandaceae* wood in the Far North were thus in an easily forgivable error. The oft-mentioned official report of the Navy department, published some time after the expedition, should suffice to clear me of this suspicion. It never entered my mind to describe those conifer branches as walnut wood. At a meeting of the Naturforschende Gesellschaft in Halle, Herr Professor Kraus of that city presented a short report on the driftwood from our expedition, including my views, which I had sent him in a letter, along with samples of the wood.

During his return to the ship, Robert collected a handful of splinters of real ancient wood, 3–7 inches in length, at a height of about 1,800 feet on Polaris Promontory; these he gave to me. Even on the basis of a superficial examination, one could not be in any doubt, even for a moment, as to the true nature of this wood; they displayed the characteristics of a conifer very clearly.

On 21 July, Hermann, who was now alone with Chester at Newman's Bay, found a further selection of branches that had drifted ashore in the meantime; since necessity required it, they were immediately burned.[24]

Once the two men had secured the canvas boat and the boat on the 22nd, and had secured the tent and the final remnants of the equipment, there was nothing left for them to do there for the moment. Hence at 2.00 p.m. they started on the return journey and reached the ship next morning.

Chester, with his giant physique, the man of iron will and unconquerable humour, had gone totally to pieces and was crawling about like a shadow. He already carried the germ of scurvy when he returned. After a few days the dreaded disease broke out. In the struggle toward the idealistic goal that we were pursuing, he had always been the first; and now, partially deprived of the use of his limbs, he bore his sufferings with the steadfastness of a real man.

Thus ended a trip that had bidden fair to match our boldest expectations.

CHAPTER 16

The summer

> Polaris's *leak worsens. Clearing out the observatory and sawing the ship out. Unsuccessful forays northward. A dangerous situation. Hall's grave. The flora of the Far North. A return home is deemed to be an urgent necessity. Notes on the fauna. President's Land. The movement of the ice. Lady Franklin Bay.*

Once the boat division had set off northward, the severely reduced crew of *Polaris* had their hands full with regular ship's duties. The leak had become so serious that on 19 June they had to have the pumps going for 12 hours per day.[1] A strong wind that began blowing out of the northeast on the 20th and reached a speed of 40 miles per hour completely cleared the strait of ice to the west and southwest. Hence they had to give serious thought to bringing everything on board that was not to be left on shore, since the ship might now be liberated at any moment. The astronomical and physical instruments were retrieved from the observatory, which was then filled with articles of clothing and provisions; two messages were left on the table. One contained a brief report on the general progress of the expedition; the other contained hints and advice for the still-absent boat division.

By the 22nd the open water had approached to about 10 paces from the ship's stern. Several attempts to blast the ice around the vessel were unsuccessful. Hence they resorted to the saws; but the saws turned out to be too light in the face of the heavy floes and had to be reinforced by the engineers before they could be used to any effect.

The work of sawing the ship free began on the 24th. Nowhere was the ice less than 10 feet thick, but in some places it reached almost 15. By

1.30 p.m. on the 26th, the ship was finally free from its fetters and was rocking on the gentle waves. But in the meantime the leak had worsened so severely that the pumps had to run continually.

Under these circumstances, *Polaris* could scarcely be considered seaworthy any longer; yet Budington was still determined to make a push north without delay. The starboard anchor lay under the Providence Berg, and hence was inaccessible. And since after 3 hours of work we had still not succeeded in weighing the port anchor, the chain was cut and buoyed. At 8 o'clock in the evening the ship set sail, and soon afterward rounded Cape Lupton. Near Cape Sumner she encountered impenetrable masses of pack ice. In order to spot a navigable lead, Budington next followed the ice edge as far as Cape Lieber,[2] but his efforts met with no success. Having spent the entire night in a vain search, toward morning he returned to Polaris Bay and made fast to the Providence Berg.

The amount of water flowing in now seemed to be decreasing since the pumps suddenly began to suck air. Soon afterward one of the men was sent down to the lower cable locker and returned with the news that it was full of water to the hatch coamings. A close examination revealed that several of the other compartments were also completely flooded. Hence the leak had not decreased; instead the water had simply become dammed up behind the swollen timbers and had made its way into the provisions. It was only after we had drilled through the bulkheads that the water began to gush out. All the provisions had suffered badly, since they were not in waterproof packaging; much of it was thrown overboard as being unusable.

A second attempt at pushing north with the ship was made on the afternoon of the 28th. Just as previously, now too near Cape Sumner they encountered heavy masses of ice, whose flanks could not be breached. Budington had learned from the two seamen whom Chester sent on board that the boat division was held up at Newman's Bay, and hence he lingered some time off the ice floes in that bay with a view to embarking the boats and their crews. Since he was unable to push through the ice with the ship, he fired off some shots and let the steam whistle shrill, to catch the men's attention. But these signals were not heard on shore. After spending another night cruising vainly along the edge of the pack, the ship returned to Polaris Bay next morning.

The attempt at breaking through the ice masses was renewed on 1 August.[3] Half an hour after midnight, *Polaris* rounded Cape Lupton but ran into the same old obstacles at 1.50 a.m. off Cape Sumner. From that headland as far as Cape Cracroft, the ice edge along which the ship was steaming formed a solid line. Clearly for this region, the season favourable for navigation had not yet arrived. For the moment there was no alternative but to return to Polaris Bay. By 2 o'clock on the afternoon of the 2nd, the ship was again lying at its old spot near the Providence Berg.

From now on, those left aboard *Polaris* barely had a single peaceful hour, since the ship was constantly threatened by the drifting ice. When large hummocks and floes surged impetuously through the strait, *Polaris* sought shelter behind the southern cliff of the berg. Toward evening a stiff northeast breeze set the fast ice in motion, and they found themselves obliged to put to sea as quickly as possible. Throughout most of the night, the ship was under sail. Everyone was on deck, even the two Eskimo women, and still there were not enough hands.

It was not until around 4.00 a.m. on the 4th that *Polaris* dared return to the vicinity of the Providence Berg and, somewhat later, to make fast to it. The exhausted crew went to their bunks, but they were roused out again at 6 o'clock since the ship was then in serious danger. Hummocks and floes, along with fragments of massive old floes, were pressing at different points against the ship's hull. Many of them could be pushed away somewhat, using strong spars; but even using all their strength, the men were able to achieve little against most of them. Shortly before 10 o'clock an awe-inspiring iceberg came sailing straight for the vessel at hazardous speed, propelled by a strong northeast wind that later strengthened to a gale. The ice masses which lay in its path were shattered and were left bobbing like corks in its foaming wake. It quickly came closer and closer. A single change of direction, and we could fear the worst. When it was within about 15 feet of the ship's stern, the men heard a loud crash. Instantly a swell surged up and the waves dispersed in cold spray along the edges of the floes. But the berg stopped dead in its impetuous advance; a long submerged tongue from the Providence Berg, the same tongue that had holed the ship, had blocked its destructive progress.

When the force of the wind slackened around noon on the 5th, the vessel was warped closer to shore and was anchored in 2 fathoms of water at ebb tide. But at 10.00 p.m., as the tide rose, there was further ice pressure, but they were able to escape it relatively easily by paying out more anchor cable. On the evening of the 6th, she grounded in 11½ feet of water. The ship was being driven steadily closer to shore, and it was not until after midnight on the 7th that they were able to refloat her. But this had barely been achieved when a stiff breeze from the northeast brought further disasters. On the morning of the 9th, the ice pressures became so severe that everyone grabbed for the ice saws. It was not until the following day that they were able to face the future somewhat more calmly.

At 4 o'clock on the morning of the 11th, a polynya about 5 miles across developed around the vessel. But by noon it had disappeared again, and the ice was surging impetuously shoreward. On the 18th there were ice pressures of such ferocity that even the old Providence Berg could no longer endure them. A heavy floe that caught its western flank partially capsized it.

The ship's safety was even more seriously threatened on the 20th. If the sea had been set in an uproar by an earthquake, the tumult in the ice could scarcely have been more grandiose and terrifying than it was now. Even the most dramatic description of the situation (and the non-initiated would probably consider such a description exaggerated) would fall far short of reality. I shall restrict myself here to the simple statement that we began preparations for abandoning the ship; that massive floes were heaved 20 to 30 feet into the air, and that the Providence Berg, too weak to withstand the pressure, disintegrated with a thunder-like roar shortly after midnight.

In the meantime the ship was aground again, lying jammed solidly amongst the hummocks; on the 22nd she heeled over so badly that we had to lash down the barrels of provisions lying on deck. We tried by warping to reach deeper water, but all our efforts were in vain. It was not until early on the morning of the 23rd that we got her afloat again. A sounding revealed a depth of 13 feet. We had gained very little, but we could be content!

We planned to now repeat, under more favourable temperature conditions, the pendulum experiments that we had set up during the winter, but unfortunately these plans could not be realized since in so doing we would have exposed ourselves to the danger of getting cut off from the ship. It was totally out of the question to reach a protective harbour. Newman's Bay, probably the only suitable anchorage north of Cape Constitution, was still blocked. Due to the numerous icebergs concentrated in them, Petermann Fiord and Bessels Bay could scarcely be considered.

If we wanted to leave the ship to make short excursions, this always had to be at low tide, since it was only at low water that we were protected from the onslaught of the ice. Several old floes and high hummocks, which surrounded the ship and which grounded at low tide, prevented the driving ice masses from coming close.

The first part of our brief respite was used to finish off Hall's lonely grave. Before the observatory was cleaned out, the men had surrounded the little mound with rocks and had erected a wooden grave marker.[4] It read:

> To the memory of
> C.F. Hall,
> Late Commander of the U.S. North Polar Expedition.
> Died Nov. 8th, 1871.
> Aged 50 years.[5]

This inscription was written in black oil paint, and since it seemed too transitory, Chester carved the following words in deep letters into a hard board that was fastened to the back of the original "headstone":

> In Memory of
> CHARLES FRANCIS HALL
> late commander of
> U.S. Steamer Polaris, North Pole Expedition.
> Died
> Nov. 8th, 1871—Aged 50 years.
> "I am the resurrection and the life; he that believeth on me,
> though he were dead, yet shall he live."[6]

Moss was stuffed into the cracks in the rocks bordering the grave. The level part of the grave mound was spread with earth that had been

Fig. 24. Hall's grave.

painstakingly scraped together and was planted with saxifrage, young willows and arctic poppies.[7]

Admittedly this was a very meagre floral tribute, but this was inevitable; when the frost keeps the earth frozen rock-hard for 9 months of the year, the munificence of the soil is very limited. The vegetation no longer creates the cheerful impression of the flora of more fortunate zones. The plant has certainly not emerged victorious in its encounter with the elements, but this year-long struggle has not failed to give it a stamp of peace and strength, or even melancholy.

One may observe these small plants, struggling to spread across the sandy lowlands, and the lichens that barely succeed in covering the nakedness of the rock!

In the middle of last year's withered bunch of stalks, a *Poa* raises its brownish panicles, barely as long as one's finger. Nearby dark-headed *Juncus* appear as a fresher green, sprouting from ragged moss cushions, around whose edges a diminutive *Carex* flourishes. If it were not the height of summer, the colour of the little blades might raise doubts as to whether the little plants were at the beginning or the end of their life's course.

The finer talus is covered with a lichen crust that is threatening to expire due to the proximity of the snow fields. When the sky is clear, this meagre lichen cover heats up, reaching a temperature that is probably triple that of the air. Apart from some *Draba*, whose rosette-like circles of flowers stand out sharply from the ground, these areas give refuge to no other flowering plants.

Where snowmelt from the heights saturates the ground, and where small streams spread out sinuously across it and bring their revitalizing influence to play, the scene meeting our gaze is more favourable. The water drops all the fine-grained sediment that it is carrying here, and over the course of time a fertile layer forms, increasing in depth year by year.

The first plants that settle here are usually mosses. Once they have hesitatingly spread their tender green across the alluvium, new arrivals start to join them. Waterfowl that visit these moist areas by choice leave many seeds behind on the new moss cover, seeds that have stuck to their feet, hidden in mud; the wind equally contributes seeds to populate the new colony.

In this manner, green mats of limited extent evolve; seen from a fair distance, they give a false impression of a meadow carpet, but seen close-up, they resolve themselves into discrete patches.

In stark contrast to the communally living plants of other zones, here most of the representatives of the flora[8] appear combined in a patch of ground only a few square metres in area. The dandelion grows here too, just as in the temperate regions. But its yellow blooms are small and inconspicuous. The narrow, serrated leaves barely reach the length of the diameter of the bloom of the species as we know it, and the entire plant, from the extreme tips of the roots to the flower, rarely exceeds the length of one's thumb. And at the same time, at least one-third and sometimes one-half of this length consists of the underground parts.

The flower cushions of the purple saxifrage[9] give the impression of self-contained independence. The flowers, resting on low, moss-like stems, which they often conceal completely with their abundance, are conspicuous from afar by their glowing colour. No less massive in the shape of its clumps is the arctic poppy, while it is almost surpassed in height by the slender *Alopecurae* with their bizarre furred caps. Its growth has suffered less than that of the other plants under the oppressive yoke of the climate. The large, yellow flowers sway on slender, span-long stems that appear almost too weak for their burden. Not uncommonly one sees 30 blooms developing on a single stem, and during the short summer young buds constantly push up from the close rosette of the finely haired leaves; usually only a few days is all they need to unfold.

The contrast between them and the small *Draba*, which occurs in two varieties, distinguishable by white and yellow flowers, is great. The former are so insignificant and small that it requires special attention to recognize them in the general carpet of plants, to the fabric of which they modestly contribute.

The powerful *Oxyria* is a different matter. More sociable than the other plants, it boasts the largest leaves, surrounding the stem in only a limited number. Its stem is topped by a green cluster of flowers. Its root penetrates deep into the soil and thereby balances the lack of leaves, whose activity would scarcely be adequate to nourish the plant.

Spoonworts and *Potentilla* are less common; the same is true of the catch-fly, whose reddish flower petals largely lie hidden in the calyx.

Just as elsewhere in the Far North, only two woody plants are native to Polaris Bay: *Dryas* and the arctic willow. The former forms small, solid swards that crunch beneath the hiker's feet like dry pine or fir needles. Their colour is an indefinite brownish green, and the star-shaped white blossoms, which occur only sparingly, give the impression that they do not belong to the plant above whose scanty leaves they rise.

The flora here offers the strangest contrasts. Few plants provoke joy; by far the majority arouse opposite feelings.

Who would suspect, on seeing the stunted arctic willow, that entire generations of these plants have grown and disappeared; who would detect in its bark, smoothed by driving snow, that it has survived here for centuries? And yet it is perhaps as old as the giant oak in whose shadow stags graze—much older than the slender bamboo whose leaves rustle in the breath of the zephyrs. In it the shrub has dwindled to the barest concept; the stunted branches rise barely a hand-breadth above the ground on which the gnarled, twisted stem spreads. The fresh, dark foliage cannot compensate for the neglect that the plants experience in their main parts; nor can the flowers, beautiful in themselves, compensate, even though their size is in sharp contrast to the rest of the plant.

The main mass of the shrub has taken refuge in the earth. Under the protection of the soil, the roots spread out widely without penetrating to any great depth, which they avoid like the plague. Growth upward and downward is restricted; roots and branches have pulled as close together as possible.

All high arctic plants share this common trait, controlled by temperature conditions. Since the ground thaws only to a limited depth and since under the most favourable circumstances one can barely dig down 2 feet without encountering permafrost, the roots stick to the immediate vicinity of the surface.

Just as the ice has an impact on the underground components, those that project upward are influenced by the air. In summer the atmospheric temperature decreases rapidly with increasing height above the ground, which receives its heat from the sun and conducts it to the layer of air lying immediately above it; as a result the latter usually displays a shimmering undulating motion. Few plants rise above this undulating interface, since the drop in temperature is so great that two thermometers, one hung only a few feet above the other, will record a difference of several degrees. This abrupt temperature differential, however, is not the only control that restricts growth to the ground surface; combined with it is yet another factor that has a determining impact. Plants of the High Arctic can get by only when they shorten their vegetative period to the absolute minimum and run through in the course of a few weeks all those developmental stages which in the case of plants of more temperate zones are spread over the same number of months.

In this situation their miniaturized aerial components offer an advantage that should not be underestimated. Consider the fact that the leaves are the real nourishers of the plants; if one further takes into consideration that a small leaf develops relatively faster than a larger one, and hence is in a position to fulfil its functions earlier, it is quite obvious that those plants that have adapted their leaves to the prevailing conditions will ensure their existence as compared to others and thus will gradually conquer the area.

The plant's growth is often handicapped by local conditions. The small rivulets that develop at the beginning of snowmelt will at the beginning of summer contribute more to thawing the frozen ground than the sun's rays, specifically when they flow across extensive rock surfaces to the lowlands. During their flow they are warmed on the dark bedrock, and when they then come in contact with plants, they deceive them into premature growth. Later when these water courses become swollen and form shallow ponds in hollows in the ground, and when that water cannot percolate downward due to the frozen substrate, the plants are impeded in their growth. For the water not only warms up less than the dry ground but has an even greater cooling effect due to evaporation. For these and similar reasons, the seeds of many plants do not manage to ripen. But the existence of the plant is by no means threatened thereby, since the arctic flora includes just as few annual plants as poisonous ones. All plants are perennials. Flowering plants reproduce by means of seeds only to a minor degree, and even in the case of mosses, the force of the climate has reached such an influence that even they regenerate more commonly by sprouting than by seeds.

Although July was not yet over, most plants were starting to wither. Although they had unfolded just a few weeks previously, they had run through their annual cycle with almost tropical impetuosity.

The weather was becoming more variable than previously. At times the sun would shine bright and clear; at times it was hidden by damp, rising clouds, which gave it a matt, moon-like appearance. Fine, drizzling rain alternated with wintry snow showers; the snow no longer fell in fine crystals but in large, loose flakes. Once a snowfall had ended, usually calm conditions with a few sunny hours sufficed to totally alter the scenery. The swarms of insects[10] left their hiding places and buzzed about gaily. Occasional bumblebees[11] whirred around the yellow poppies and the nectar-rich blooms of the saxifrage in their humming flight. Grey moths[12] of the Bombyx family, having emerged from their chrysalises, sat on their empty cases and waited with trembling wingbeats for their mates. With light wings, yellow butterflies[13] fluttered around the damp moss cushions, and on the scattered snow patches, thousands of small *Poduridae*[14] rushed about with high leaps, pursued by agile birds.

The highest temperature attained at any time of day during the summer did not exceed 9°; the highest mean temperature for a single day turned out to be 2° lower. And yet we felt a sensation of oppressive heat, admittedly provoked purely by contrast, since the difference between the highest and lowest temperatures was 43°. The occasionally dry air made the sun's heat extraordinarily sensible. The rocky ground heated up so markedly that the surface of dark limestone rocks exploded with a clearly perceptible crack, and as a result the bedrock exfoliated in layers. During the first days of July, the ice cover on the small lakes had broken up, and they were now inhabited by vast numbers of small crustaceans[15] and midge larvae, which provided food for flocks of sanderlings. Accompanied by their dainty young ones that still wore their soft down, they would rush about at the edge of the water at a full run, usually in the company of the cosmopolitan turnstone,[16] whose range extends from the southern tip of Africa to the High Arctic.

The saturated ground began to dry out. Occasionally a single windy day would suffice to rob many locations of their moisture so completely that the ground split in wide cracks. Many plants died due to aridity, without their seeds ripening; their leaves turned brown and their stems yellow. The light rains passed them by without any effect.

Small hunting spiders,[17] which previously had been seen scurrying across the warmed lichen surfaces, pursuing their prey, now retreated to moister locations, perhaps less to escape the drought than to follow the flies and other insects that were escaping the drought.

Half-torpid, long-haired caterpillars hung on the withering stems, waiting for a sunny day to spin their chrysalises. But sunny days were rare from now on, and many of these larvae would probably never become butterflies.

During the summer, formation of young ice had rarely ceased completely. While the saline sea water did not itself freeze, the thin layer of fresh water floating on the surface of the sea would freeze during the night while the sun was low. Now new ice formation became more frequent, and it covered the leads almost every night.

In one of these lay a ship whose crew was burning with a desire to set the seal on a disastrous enterprise by one bold deed. But the star of their good luck was sinking rapidly! The vessel, threatened constantly by importunate ice masses, was leaking worse than ever; the reserves of coal had shrunk so much that they would suffice at best to keep the engine running for another 6 days. All available wood had already been burned; even some of the partitions between compartments, as well as the planking from the lower cabin, had found its way down to the stokehold.

Under these conditions there was only one solution: the first favourable opportunity for heading south had to be seized. If one had sacrificed the well-being of the entire crew to the ambition of a few, such a procedure would at best have been unscrupulous. To lose the fruits of months of effort and to leave unfinished an important task whose solution appeared so close was certainly an extremely depressing feeling. But what else could be done? Like many other bitter disappointments, this one too had to be overcome! Turning back without reason after reaching on that August day the highest latitude to which a vessel had ever penetrated; and wintering at a site which was called a harbour and yet which did not offer even the slightest protection against the ice pressures: these two steps had conjured up the fate which now hung over the expedition. These errors might be regretted but could never be expiated.

The small leads were opening and closing so suddenly that until now we had been waiting in vain for a favourable opportunity for sounding the bay. For this reason, too, it was not possible to work successfully with the trawl nets. In total we were able to make only 11 extremely unsatisfactory hauls. Only two of these brought macroscopic creatures to light; the rest consisted exclusively of fine calcareous mud.

Crustaceans were represented by the tail of a *Crangon boreas* with three metamerae clinging to it; by three or four specimens of a Hippolyte; by two specimens of a Mysis species; by numerous *Gammarus locusta* and by two Caprellae that both belonged to the same species. The *Gammarus locusta* were of a significant size, and so numerous that one could fish them out of the tide hole in the hundreds, if one lowered into it the carcasses of seals or birds from which the meat had been surficially removed. An eider duck or a murre was usually reduced most beautifully to a skeleton by these crustaceans in 2–3 hours; a seal over the course of a day.

The only worm that was collected was a small *Priapulus*.

However, these life forms certainly do not provide a picture of the marine fauna, since the site that could be investigated with the trawl net was extremely limited and not at all favourable for the existence of animal life. One may deduce that the fauna is richer than was indicated here, by the fact that occasionally in stormy weather large *Pycnogonidae*[18] were washed ashore. They belonged to the genus *Nymphon* and most resembled *N. grossipes*. However the resources of the ship's library were not sufficient to establish the species definitively.

Whereas the larger and by far the most interesting part of the fauna thus almost totally escaped observation, on our various excursions we were able to assemble almost complete collections of mammals, birds[19] and lower animals. Through the diligence of the hunters and Mauch's efforts, who skinned many of the animals shot, during the absence of the boat division the number of birds had increased significantly. It had not been possible to obtain many eggs, but the small collection concealed an oological treasure, consisting of two clutches of sanderling eggs. During the first few days of July, Bryan and Mauch had shot a male and female Sabine's gull, which is never common in Greenland. Both birds possessed a brood patch the size of a dollar. The female was carrying an almost mature egg and may well have had its nest near the harbour; but they had no success in locating it. By contrast on 14 July, Hans found the nest of an oldsquaw, which was built close to the beach and contained 11 well-incubated eggs. The nesting material consisted of soft brownish-black down, filling a shallow hollow in the ground, about 8 inches in diameter.

This bird was seen only a few times in Polaris Bay, and only two male birds were shot; they displayed great curiosity and naivety. The other species of ducks were extremely shy, however, as too were the brent geese. Only with great care could one get within shooting range of the latter; they had probably been the object of severe persecution in their wintering areas. Even in early August when they were beginning the moult and had lost their flight feathers, it was difficult to get hold of them. Gulls and waders were confiding, without exception, and the terns were even importunate, especially if one was in the vicinity of their young.

On 5 August, since there was still little prospect of our heading south, the two seamen, Robert and Heinrich, were given leave. Budington allowed them to go to Newman's Bay to fetch the belongings they had left there.[20] They returned in the early morning hours of the 9th. They reported that they had spotted various open polynyas north of the bay; by contrast, to the south and west lay close ice. The air was of unusual clarity. The dark cloud that had been almost constantly visible during the boat division's sojourn in the north had disappeared. Instead of it they had spotted high cliffs, which fell sheer and were topped by high peaks. The various details appeared with such clarity that one could make out individual snow features of this distant land with the naked eye.

This land mass was later named President's Land. Both Robert and Heinrich placed it on the site of that "black cloud," on the extremities of which we had repeatedly measured tangents from the camp. While the two men were on the top of Cape Brevoort, the refraction was quite extraordinary. According to Heinrich, Cape Union appeared to have approached to within a stone's throw.

A few hours after these seamen returned, Meyer left the ship accompanied by Hermann and Gustav. They too wanted to go to Newman's Bay, partly to bring back to the ship items of clothing they had left, partly the more valuable instruments. But they did not see the new land since the air was murky and there was fog lying around the horizon. The open polynyas that Robert and Heinrich had spotted had disappeared. As far as the eye could see, they saw only close-packed ice masses.

Hans was now sent daily to Cape Lupton to watch out for open water. Instead of reporting verbally, which he did not always find easy, he usually brought back a small sketch map that illustrated the distribution of water and ice much better than he could have described it. Both he and Joseph possessed the estimable talent of committing such rough drawings to paper with a surprising degree of facility. These situation maps, executed from life, were always sufficiently accurate for practical purposes.

It was not until the 11th that the ice got moving again, and drifted southward. Whenever this had happened previously, we had been able to determine from the masthead or from the higher hilltops that massive floes were pushing into Lady Franklin Bay, without reappearing again later. Since, moreover, with favourable atmospheric conditions the western shore of the bay always gave the impression that it was an island, beyond whose flanks an ice-blink or water horizon appeared, we were inclined to consider the bay an actual strait.[21]

CHAPTER 17

Southward

Departure from Polaris Bay. Charles Polaris. The ice situation. Beset. Protobathybius. Preparations for a wintering in the pack. Analysis of the drift. A night of terror.

The open sea was now only 8–10 miles from the ship. Raised by refraction, the dark water surface often appeared several degrees of arc above the horizon; the smaller polynyas towered up like menacing waterspouts and assumed all sorts of strange shapes as mirages.

Our sojourn in Polaris Bay was now to be counted only in hours. Apart from the inevitable hardships that we had endured, we had enjoyed many fine days at this remote spot—days of pleasant work and of the purest enjoyment of nature, and days that for the most part were days only in name since their beginning and end were no longer marked by sunrise and sunset but just by the dead stroke of the pendulum and the positions of the stars. We had survived a night of longer duration than any people before us. Then we had seen the sun constantly for over 4 months above the horizon, had seen the owl searching for its prey at noon and had listened to the melodious twittering of the snow bunting at midnight.

Now that it was time to turn the ship's bows southward, memories of the hours of adversity began to fade; the pleasant times we had enjoyed passed in glowing colours before our mind's eye and made this departure difficult. The small observatory, whose familiar outline rose from the plain across which we had hiked at all hours of the day and night, had the effect of a powerful magnet. A parting glance fell on the fresh grave which from now on nobody would decorate with flowers.

But we were heading home with the same number of souls with which we had started our voyage. On the morning of 12 August, Mrs. Merkut gave birth to a boy, who, in memory of the expedition, received the name Charles Polaris.[1]

Full of the joys of paternity, shortly afterward Hans climbed to the top of Cape Lupton and returned on board to report that the ice was slackening more and more. Budington and Tyson confirmed this news. The surviving 21 dogs were embarked without delay; the boats were stowed, and all the other preparations for sailing were made. Both anchors still lay buried beneath heavy masses of ice and hence had to be left behind.

At 4.30 p.m. we steamed out of the bay.[2] As the ship was tacking for the first time, the most faithful of our Newfoundlanders[3] jumped overboard and raced toward shore in long bounds. We had to leave the fine animal to its fate, since it would not have been possible to stop without hazarding the ship. All our shouts and enticements remained unsuccessful.

The ice was heavy and lay closely packed; we struggled toward the open water in a tortuous course. Shortly after midnight we reached the entrance to Petermann Fiord. Looking back one could perceive Cape Union as the most northerly visible point on the coast of Grinnell Land. The low shores of Polaris Bay had dropped below the horizon. Like Helgoland,[4] the so-called interior island rose above the plain as a blue silhouette between Polaris Promontory and the ranges to the south. The upland south of Polaris Bay appeared as an island mass.

In the meantime the ice had closed up again. Not until 5.00 a.m. on the 13th did we reach the open water. Favoured by a fresh breeze, we set every serviceable sail and steamed south at full speed. An hour later the wind dropped; thick fog rolled in, and at 9 o'clock we ran into impenetrable masses of pack ice and had to moor to an ice floe.[5]

The ship followed the general movement of the ice and drifted slowly southward. Abeam of Hans Island, we determined our noon latitude to be 80°48'N; our longitude was 68°38'W; Karl Ritter Bay opened to the west.

At 11 o'clock the floes slackened somewhat. Over the course of an hour, we were able to progress only one mile and then had to make fast again. The morning of the 14th passed in several unsuccessful attempts to break through the ice; but around noon a narrow channel opened, and we were able to follow it unimpeded as far as Franklin Island. We passed that island about 3 miles off. Reaching its southwest point, we sighted Cape Constitution as a precipitously projecting massif of the John Brown Coast. At the same time, a rock avalanche roared down close to us; the nearby rocks were hidden in grey clouds of dust; with the fury of the falling talus, the sea foamed and spray flew high up the rock faces.

In a slow, gentle curve we now approached Crozier Island. It, as well as Franklin Island, consists of bedded limestone masses like the cliffs of Petermann Fiord. It might be about 300 feet high. The whole of the John Brown coast appears to be formed of the same rock type.

Shortly before 11.00 p.m. we ran into close masses of pack ice and soon afterward had to make fast to a floe. An altitude sighting of the midnight sun revealed the latitude of the ship's position to be 80°02′N. The ice fields and floes packed together closer and closer. From the crow's nest one could spot open polynyas to the south and west, but they could not be reached; the ship lay as if spellbound.

Not until noon on the 15th did the ice slacken somewhat. With some difficulty we steamed a few miles to the west[6] but then had to moor again. On the 16th various attempts were made to reach the open water; but they were all in vain. The noon latitude of the ship's position was 79°59′N. A light easterly wind opened a small polynya near the ship, which served as a playground for four narwhals. Armed with the heavy hippopotamus gun, Chester crawled to where he could lie in wait; but the animals did not reappear after the hunter had taken up his position. From our experience this is the northern limit of the range of the narwhal west of Greenland.

During the night there were violent ice pressures, and on the 17th these became so unpleasant that we once again made all preparations for abandoning ship.[7] She was listing considerably to port; the list at times reached 30°. The most severe pressures occurred at 10.00 p.m.; while the ice was surging furiously northward, to the south, not more than about 8–10 miles from the ship, a wide channel was visible, extending to Hayes Sound.

At noon on 18 August the latitude of the ship's position was 79°44.5′N. Thus over the course of the past two days the ship had drifted south at an average speed of 7¼ miles. In the meantime the open water had disappeared.

On the 19th it was not possible to obtain an astronomical determination of position due to the overcast sky; on the other hand, we succeeded in taking some soundings, the results of which fluctuated between 90 and 95 fathoms. The bottom consisted of a grey calcareous mud. Since the Brooke sounding apparatus had been left behind at Newman's Bay, we now had to use an ordinary 30 lb. hand lead, which had an armature of soap. With it we obtained smaller seabed samples than if we had coated the lead with tallow, certainly, but the mud brought to the surface could be easily cleaned with sea water, something that would not have been possible had we used a fatty armature.

This mud was so viscous that parts of it remained sticking to the ivory paper knife which was used for scraping the armature. Placed under the microscope with low magnification and without a covering slide, it appeared as a transparent yellowish-grey mass with a low refractive index, in which hung numerous opaque, flake-like formations, as they were similarly suspended in the sea water that surrounded the object. With a magnification of about 800-fold the yellowish-grey seabed mass revealed itself as a net-shaped albumen substance and the dark flake-like formations as small particles of lime, which with the addition of a drop of acid formed gas and disappeared. The main mass of the mud consisted not of lime but of albumen, which with the addition of carmine coloured an intense red but with the addition of iodine and nitric acid coloured yellow.

Once this had been determined, what mattered was to obtain larger seabed samples than could be brought up with the coated lead. Use of a trawl net was thwarted by the thick layer of ice. Hence we used one of the Marcett water flasks, which, secured to a 30 lb. lead, was quickly lowered to the seabed. In this manner we obtained by repeated hauls as much mud with each haul as could be contained in a medium-sized tablespoon.

This mud possessed the same characteristics as that which the lead had brought up. Placed under the microscope in a hollow-ground slide, and left to rest for some time, the albumen-like masses executed unmistakable amoeboid movements, and absorbed from the lime grains as well as the carmine particles that were suspended in the water.

We were undoubtedly dealing here with the simplest species: with clumps of living protoplasm, less differentiated than *Bathybius haeckeli*, the deep-sea ooze that was discovered by the British in 1857 in the northern part of the Atlantic Ocean. While *Bathybius* contained calcareous inclusions, no trace of similar secretions were to be found here. The entire mass consisted exclusively of protoplasm, which represented a previously unknown *Bathybius* shape, without coccoliths, perhaps the progenitor of *Bathybius*. Hence this organism was named *Protobathybius*.

Over the course of the following day, 20 August, we suffered greatly from the importunity of the ice; however we did find the opportunity, by using the Marcett flask, of obtaining more bottom samples, which produced similar results to those we'd brought up earlier. At noon the ship was at 79°42'N. A bottom sample brought up shortly before midnight consisted mainly of calcareous mud, in which protoplasm masses were scattered only sparingly. This was absolutely the last time that we found *Protobathybius*. The depth soundings fluctuated between 90 and 94 fathoms.

A leak in the small boiler, discovered on the 21st, contributed greatly to increasing the precariousness of our situation. To repair the damage that had resulted, the engineers were obliged to draw the fires. Hence during the day the deck pumps were manned. It turned out that the ship's condition had deteriorated; as a result of ramming hummocks and floes, the leak had increased. At noon the ship's latitude was 79°39'N, and hence we had drifted 3 miles over the previous 24 hours. At 10.00 p.m. severe pressures occurred that heeled the ship markedly to port.

On the 22nd a stiff breeze from the southwest impeded the ice so that it almost ceased to move. The bearings from the ship on several prominent points on the coast of Grinnell Land remained unchanged throughout the entire day. At noon on the 23rd the latitude was determined to be 79°37'N; hence the daily rate of drift had dropped to just 1 mile.

Under the influence of a light north wind, on the morning of the 24th the ice began to slacken somewhat. We quickly raised steam, but before the engine could be started, we were again closely beset and were suffering under the brunt of unpleasant pressures.

During the 25th the ship was hopelessly beset. Not until the following morning did the ice slacken. Between 8 and 9 o'clock we raised steam, and the engine was then started. The thickness of the new ice varied between 1 and 2 inches. With great effort we moved slowly west, then back along the same course to the spot where we had been lying previously, and then half a cable-length north to where a lead had opened which led toward the coast. The ice became heavier and mocked all our efforts. The corner of a large floe caught in the screw and bent one of its blades; around 12 o'clock we realized the fruitlessness of our efforts and made fast. To the west, barely 2 miles away, open water sparkled, but we were unable to reach it. From a number of circum-meridian sun altitudes the latitude was revealed to be 79°36.5'N. From the crow's nest, the massive cliffs of the Humboldt Glacier could be vaguely identified; in front of them lay a row of high icebergs which stretched halfway across Smith Sound.

Ice pressures occurred on the 27th with such fury that we again started preparations to abandon ship. Not until the following day did the pressures relax; the ice opened and closed alternately, but without permitting us to move even half a ship's length in one direction or the other. At noon our latitude was 79°35' 47"N; thus over the course of the past 14 hours, the ship had altered its latitude by scarcely ¾ of a mile.

The shore lead that extended along the coast of Grinnell Land was at most 3 miles from the ship on the evening of the 29th, and extended farther south than ever before. An energetic attempt to force a passage with steam advanced us barely 50 paces over the course of 7 hours. At 6 o'clock on the following morning, the fires were therefore dampened down, since the rapidly diminishing stocks of coal could not be reduced further. Unless conditions turned out to be particularly favourable, we were faced with a wintering in the pack. The sun had ceased to circle the sky, and the thickness of the new ice was increasing by the day. We were now placing our hopes entirely on a gale out of the north, or on the imminent spring tide.

The latter occurred on 4 September, but its impact failed to appear. If the conditions of the ice had changed at all, that change had not been to our advantage. Thick fog hung over sea and land all day long, blocking any distant view. When the grey curtain thinned, we were able to see that the ice near the ship was much closer than before; even the shore polynya along the nearby coast had disappeared. Not until the 8th did two small polynyas, barely half a mile in extent, develop in the east; but at the same time the new ice had become so strong that one could stride across it with a firm tread. Thereby our fate was sealed; we were heading for a future, even the best scenario of which did not promise much good. We could never hope to reach a port in the civilized world with our badly damaged ship, since the coal on board sufficed at most for a further 3 days' steaming. In the best-case scenario, we might be driven against the coast somewhere by the ice, to be held fast there, and next summer head for safety in the boats. But an even greater probability was that we would have to abandon our vessel before that. Since the future promised more gloomy shadows than cheerful flashes of light, we wanted at least to enjoy the days we still had on board *Polaris*, in all the comforts that the ship could offer.

Hence, just as a year previously, we now made preparations for an orderly wintering. Two of the forward port cabins were enlarged, the doors of the wardroom opening to the outside were closed off and in their place a new entrance was created which gave onto one of the covered side passages. The lower cabin, the former premises of the geological group, was to serve as galley and dining room.[8] It could no longer be made habitable since the individual transverse partitions and the planking of the bunks had been burned, and at the moment there was no surplus of wood. If anyone found the temperature too low in his own cabin, he moved his bed to the upper cabin; as a result the population there reached its highest density. The cabin on deck was again converted into an ice house; but unfortunately the old tent housing to keep off the wind and the snow could not be stretched over the ship this time, since the uncertainty of our situation required an unobstructed lookout.

On the most secure spot on an ice field lying solidly near the ship between the floes and the hummocks, a structure was erected from spars and sails, half tent, half hut, that offered enough space to accommodate the crew.[9] If an accident now happened to the ship, at least it offered us

Fig. 25. The refuge hut.

shelter. The floor of the hut was covered with boards and sails; on the windward side we stacked up barrels and chests containing provisions.

Provisions were also set in readiness on deck, along with coal, ammunition, weapons and clothing. The two remaining whaleboats, which thus far had stood on the house, were hauled down and slung from the forward davits.

Recently the daily coal consumption had risen to 9 centners; sometimes we even needed 10 centners to keep the pumps working. Since our safety was dependent in no small measure on the coal, it had to be managed with all possible economy. Hence we repeatedly made attempts to stop the leak. First the ice was removed from around the ship's bow, then a sail was hauled under the stem and pulled taut, and the space between the canvas and the planking was filled with oakum and ashes. Later water was pumped over it. This was done in the hope that the resultant ice crust would close the hole. But the results did not correspond to the expectations we had set on it. The attempt to make the after transverse bulkhead of the lower cable locker watertight by caulking it and by then leaving the dammed-up water to freeze was also a failure. On the other hand, Mr. Schumann managed to turn to account a small, previously unused boiler, whereby the daily coal consumption was reduced to 3–4 centners.

The ship continued to drift with the ice movements, sometimes unmolested, sometimes threatened by ice pressures. September was coming to an end and October was approaching and the nights were becoming longer. The birds disappeared. During the early days of September, we were still seeing flocks of turnstones flying south, as well as flocks of eiders, black guillemots and dovekies. On 3 October the last representatives of the avifauna appeared: an eider and an extremely large snowy owl.

Chester had long since recovered from his attack of scurvy; now Meyer was afflicted with this complaint and suffered it for about 2 weeks. Fortunately we now possessed fresh meat in abundance, and it was very beneficial for the sick man.[10] It was only seal meat, certainly, but we had grown accustomed to its taste and had learned to appreciate the antiscorbutic effect of the black, bloody steaks. Its taste is far from being as unpleasant as one might think, provided that one removes most of the fat before cooking. But the fresh blubber, specifically when eaten in a frozen state with ship's biscuits, is reminiscent of butter and is greatly preferable to the oleomargarine which is flooding the market at present.

During the last week of September, the natives had killed 13 seals—a fact of great significance. For these animals provided us not only with food and skins, which served us as clothing, but also with oil, which we required to light the rooms. When the hunters lay in wait for the animals as they surfaced at the edges of the small leads, we usually observed their movements through the telescope from on board. If a shot hit its mark, a sledge was dispatched as quickly as possible to secure the quarry.

The more the ship approached the Greenland coast, the more numerous and bolder the bears became. Joseph had set up a small windbreak of snow blocks behind a row of hummocks; on the 7th one of these animals demolished it and then followed the hunter until very close to the ship. Two days later some of the men pursued a massive animal, but only grazed it without killing it; and during the night of the 12th–13th, a female with two cubs was sniffing around the ship and was scared off by the dogs.

Among the Hanseatics, where it had always been quite lively, since little Suschen had ceased to be the pet, tremendous agitation reigned. Mrs. Merkut's birthplace again came in sight, just as when we were steaming north somewhat more than a year previously. And she stood for hours on deck, staring across at the desolate coast in order perhaps to spot one of her countrymen.[11] The poor woman was filled with nostalgia, and one could easily read it in her eyes. Once when our drifting ice floe came to within 2 miles of land, she even wanted to visit her relatives, to show them little Charles Polaris. The latter usually lay stark naked in his mother's hood; it was a treat to see him growing and flourishing. By a week after his birth, the blue of his eyes had changed to a deep brown; his initial reddish skin colour had become a light tan; and the thick down around his face, shoulders and back had partially been shed.

Thus far I have forborne from describing the ship's drift in detail, in order to present the entire proceedings as a cohesive whole. A brief analysis leads to the following results.

From midnight on 14 August until the evening of the 18th, between latitudes 80°2'N and 79°44'N, the average direction of the current was roughly southwest, or more precisely S42°W. Between the 14th and the 16th, either dead calm prevailed or there was a gentle breeze from northeast, southwest and south; but it probably did not have sufficient strength to influence the drift, whose speed during the first 2 days was 5 miles per 24 hours. During the subsequent 48 hours, it dropped to 1 mile and then rose again between the 17th and 18th to 14.4 miles; this was the absolute maximum of the drift velocity during the entire period. This high velocity can be partially ascribed to a fresh northerly wind, which blew almost continually for 48 hours, and partially to the influence of the spring tide, which followed the full moon on the 18th

(8 h., 53 m., 2 s.). At least we always observed—specifically at the time of the spring tide—that the current of the flood tide coming from the north was stronger than that of the ebb as it ran back north.

A number of sun altitudes measured at 6.00 p.m. on the evening of the 18th in the first vertical revealed the ship's position to be 79°41'N; 70°19'W. Then a sudden change in direction occurred. It changed to about W17°N, and remained there for the next 48 hours, while the average velocity dropped to 2.3 miles.

Between noon on the 20th and noon on the 21st, the direction underwent a further change. It became almost southeast, and the velocity increased somewhat while light northerly breezes were blowing.

A further alteration occurred between the 21st and the 23rd; the direction became E90°S, and the velocity rose from 3 to 6.5 miles, while the resulting direction of the wind formed almost a right angle with the resultant of the current direction.

While previously the current velocity had never amounted to less than 1 mile per 24 hours, between 23 August and 6 September it dropped to about half a mile. During this period the winds were generally light; only twice was it blowing fresh out of the southwest. The total change in latitude of the ship's position during these 14 days did not exceed 5 miles. During the entire period, the current velocity was extremely variable and apparently independent of the wind.

This characteristic of the drift might most easily be explained by the interference of two flood waves, one of which proceeded from north to south, the other from south to north.

In an earlier chapter it was explained that the flood wave at Polaris Bay came from the north. By contrast at Rensselaer Harbour it runs from south to north. These two waves must, of necessity, encounter each other at some spot between these two locations. This probably occurs between 79°30'N and 79°37'N; analysis of the ship's course during the period in question would indicate this with a high degree of precision.

Between 6 and 8 September the drift again acquired a more definite character. The mean direction became W10°S, and the velocity 2.5 miles, where it remained for the subsequent 14 days, although the direction was almost southwest. The winds during this period were on average light and blew from the northerly quadrants.

Between 8 September and 2 October we drifted almost due south; the velocity dropped from 2.5 to 1.5 miles, and between 24 September and 2 October even reached a minimum of 1 mile.

From then on the ship approached closer and closer to the Greenland coast; between 8 and 13 October she was almost following the run of that coast; our velocity increased to 8.5 miles, probably accelerated by the northeasterly winds. The last astronomical determination of latitude, obtained at noon on the 12th, placed the ship in latitude 78°28'N. We lacked positive data for any further determinations of our course. We noticed, not without some unease, that on 14 October we began to drift increasingly to the southwest. If the ship left Smith Sound, whose entrance we had approached to within a few miles, the danger of our situation would increase; for drifting around among the icebergs of the North Water was almost synonymous with certain disaster. Some movement had developed in the ice, probably caused by waves on the sea to the south; the floe to which the ship was made fast slowly began to circle and swung right around the compass.

At 5.00 a.m. on the 15th a stiff wind got up out of the southeast, associated with a heavy snowfall that lasted 3 hours. After the snow had stopped, the wind reached a velocity of 40 miles per hour and swung through the south to southwest. The snow was whirled up in such dense curtains that one could barely see half a ship's length; it was often impossible to determine whether it was actually snowing or whether it was just drifting snow. It was not until the afternoon that the storm slackened.

Around 6 o'clock in the evening—while some of us were sitting happily playing whist in the cabin—there was suddenly an announcement that the ice at the ship's stern was in the process of slackening. We all rushed on deck and noticed that the floe was cut by a crack about 40 feet long, across which one could still have jumped without any effort. In the course of a few minutes, its width had increased 10-fold, and shortly afterward the entire ice mass that had lain tightly against the starboard side of the ship drove off to the east at considerable speed. It was not difficult to see that the entire movement, whose direction did not coincide with that of the wind, had been instigated by the start of the flood tide. There was a full moon, and hence a spring tide, and due to the fact that the sheltering ice mass had drifted away from one side of the ship, our situation now turned out to be more critical than previously. Suddenly the ice stopped driving eastward and became quiescent. But this standstill lasted only a few minutes, since the floes moved immediately with lightning speed toward us, and piled up as high as the rail, and after only a few seconds the vessel heeled over to a very alarming angle to port.[12]

The intensity of the ice pressures increased; the deck planks rumbled and cracked, and the storm howled through the rattling rigging. The order to move coal and provisions onto the ice was executed with feverish haste. Instinctively everyone grabbed whatever lay closest to hand and threw it onto the large floe to which we lay moored, and whose sharp edge was threatening to slice through the ship. Under the prevailing conditions, the ice offered more protection than the ship since the latter might disintegrate at any moment and sink. Larger barrels and cases were lowered onto the edge of the ice with blocks and tackles.[13] There they were received by the crew, the majority of whom were already on the ice, and moved to the more solid centre of the floe, near the emergency hut.[14] The water in the hold was rising with worrying speed, and the snow was being whirled along in dense flurries by the wind, which had now risen to hurricane force, so that it was often impossible to make out one's immediate surroundings. We had great difficulty in keeping the flames in the lanterns burning.

Suddenly the two lines that had held us moored to the floe snapped with a dull thud. The ship righted itself and drifted rapidly away from the floe, on which stood the crew, the women and children, and by far the greater part of the provisions, as well as all the boats

The driving snow ceased briefly, and the light cast by the full moon was almost like daylight. "Farewell, Polaris!" one of the men shouted sadly from the ice.

The apparently solid ice floe had broken into several pieces, across which the men were scattered, shouting loudly for help. Their shouts mingled horribly with the howling of the dogs, the roar of the wind and the thunder of the surf, which broke, hissing against the faces of the floes, whose giant forms now loomed toward us in ghostly fashion out of the darkness. In just a few moments our comrades had disappeared; the sky had again clouded over, and the ship was being tossed around

Fig. 26. Separation of the party.

by the hurricane-like gale on a wild, raging sea between icebergs that threatened its destruction.

In the interim the water had risen so high below decks that it was almost reaching the small boiler. We tried to get the deck pumps working, but all our efforts to get the frozen handles moving were fruitless. The steam pump was no longer capable of handling the ever-increasing inflow of water. The vessel was sinking deeper and deeper beneath our feet, and we hadn't a single boat left for a last rescue attempt. There was not even an ice floe to be seen to which we could have escaped, when the beams of the full moon again broke through the black clouds. The sea was covered with scattered heaps of ice debris, too small to serve as a refuge for even a single person. And even had they been larger, what good would that have been? Without boats they remained inaccessible.

A second attempt to get the deck pumps functioning by means of boiling water finally achieved the desired result. We worked with almost superhuman effort. The water now gushed out in streams, but it froze as soon as it reached the deck. And since the scuppers were heavily iced up, they impeded the water from flowing back to the sea. We were standing knee-deep in the cold, slippery mixture of sea water and ice. But who was worried about this? The pumps were ejecting just as much water as was flowing into the ship through the leak, and we cherished the hope that we could keep the ship afloat for a short time longer, even if it were only until daybreak. Since for the moment the danger of the stokehold being flooded was less, the priority was to fire up the main boiler without delay. We broke up doors and hatch covers, cut down parts of the rigging and threw everything down into the engine room, along with two barrels of seal blubber, in order to raise steam as quickly as possible. After a few hours we had the great satisfaction of becoming aware of the rhythmic clanking of the steam engine and of hearing the pumps gushing water.

For the moment we were saved, but our meagre reserves of coal could last for only a short time. The moon's disc emerged, gleaming from behind the quickly departing masses of clouds, and allowed us to discern the dark outlines of a nearby coast. Where we were, we did not know. The storm had ceased, the sea had calmed down and, gently splashing and murmuring, its rage quickly evaporated. We took it in turns to get some sleep, to rest from our exhaustion.

When the roll was called, the handful of men on board the wreck totalled only 14 men.[15] The missing persons were Tyson and Meyer; the cook[16] and steward;[17] and seamen Peter,[18] Gustav,[19] William[20] and Robert;[21] as well as Fritz senior[22] and junior;[23] and both Eskimo families, for a total of 19 persons.

CHAPTER 18

ON TERRA FIRMA

Daybreak. The missing people are nowhere to be seen. Polaris on the beach. The wreck is unrigged. We proceed to build a hut. Avatok and Mayuk. Chester as building foreman. The Eskimos' contributions. Polaris House. Hunting trips. Scientific projects. Prominent personalities. Arrangement of the hut. The cat, Thomas. Starvation at Etah. Arctic foxes. Lack of wood.

A gloomy arctic day began to dawn, and the sun was still far below the horizon when we wiped the last remnants of a barely refreshing half-sleep from our eyes and went on deck. Gradually as it grew light, we were able to orient ourselves with the help of the map; we were about 40 miles north of our last definitely determined position, approximately midway between Littleton Island and Cairn Point, roughly 5 miles west from the coast.

Chester and Heinrich climbed to the crow's nest to look for our missing companions. Through the telescope the former spotted small, dark objects on a drifting floe, which he thought were provisions bags; Heinrich thought they were rock debris and certainly not people. Since for the moment there was no hope of finding the missing people—we could scarcely guess in which direction they were to be sought—we thought first of saving ourselves. We scanned the ice-girdled coast from north to south and from south to north to try to spot a channel to the coast, but the floes and ice fields lay closely packed.

Around 8 o'clock a gentle northeasterly breeze arose, opening a polynya near the ship. We owed our salvation to this whim of chance. The boiler fires were quickly stoked with new coals; the screw and the rudder were examined and, against all expectations, were found to be in good condition. Slowly we approached the coast, but it was a very difficult task since many large floes had to be moved out of the way, and we hadn't a single boat at our disposal.[1] The seamen on watch would leap onto small floes, which they moved along using their boathooks, and drop ice anchors onto larger floes, so that the ship could be warped up to them through the narrow leads. It would often take us 15 minutes to gain 10 feet; but later the wind freshened and we set sail.

A few minutes before noon, as the sun rose above the mountain peaks to the south for the last time, we reached the coast. The ship was run ashore; we were saved.

But it was too early to celebrate. The fate of our poor comrades wedged itself like an importunate ghost between us and the feeling that one normally experiences after surviving danger. The sight of that disintegrating floe with the wailing people on it could not easily be forgotten; the shout of fear "Farewell, *Polaris*!" was still ringing clearly in our ears. If that scene were to lead to a satisfactory conclusion, circumstances would have to have conspired more favourably than one could have imagined. Unless we were deluding ourselves, those 19 people had to be counted among the dead. Everyone thought so, but nobody expressed it.

While the catastrophe was taking shape, the ice afforded greater safety than the ship. Hence we had stored our most precious possessions: the major part of the scientific records, as well as the journals and collections on the ice floe.[2] They were almost all lost! As I was hurriedly carrying the second of my drawers full of papers out onto the ice—the first one was already hidden there under a rubber sheet—the wind blew away a few sheets of paper. That incident gave me the felicitous idea of carrying them back and of keeping them with me. I therefore packed their entire contents in a bed sheet and laid it at the entrance to the port gangway, so that I could grab it at the last minute as I jumped overboard. Thus it happened that at least the pendulum and tide observations, an almost complete meteorological journal, as well as various natural history and other notes and a number of sketches and drawings, were saved.

At low tide the ship now heeled over so severely to starboard that the water reached halfway up the rail and gushed in through the scuppers onto the deck. The steam engine was working constantly, but it soon had to come to a halt since there was at most only 6 tonnes of coal left. What was to become of us, then? It would certainly not have been possible to spend the winter on board the wreck, since as soon as the pumps stopped working, the men's quarters and the lower cabin would be submerged.

Hence we had no other choice but to build a hut on shore and then to build boats from the ship's timbers, so that we could start for home the following summer. Now that we had lost the greater part of our belongings, we were ill-prepared for a wintering. Anybody who could call more than one suit of clothes his own could consider himself lucky; we possessed scarcely more than the absolute essentials in terms of kitchen utensils, and most of the bedding had been thrown overboard. With the utmost economy, the provisions might just last out; we had a surplus of shot and lead ingots, but our entire stock of powder was limited to the contents of various powder horns and amounted at most to 6 lbs.

With the first gleam of the pale-green dawn on the 17th,[3] we began to make preparations to abandon the ship. The sails had already been taken down; whatever provisions and other items were found in the holds were now hauled out. At high tide we made an attempt to move the vessel closer to shore, but the grounded ice masses would not yield.

As the tide began to drop again, it gave us an opportunity to examine the leak. With the fury of the ice pressures during that fateful night, the ship had completely lost her stem below the 6-foot mark, and hence the water could penetrate unhindered.

The pack ice in the Sound was constantly drifting southward; on 18 October the sea was almost ice-free to west and south; between the spot where the ship lay on the beach and the Littleton Islands, only a few ice floes floated.

Once the topmasts and yards had been sent down, they were hauled across the ice to shore. The hut, which we named Polaris House, was to be erected there on a tolerably level spot on a flat headland. Chester was elected building foreman. He was ready for anything, and no task was too difficult for him. Just as conversant with handling a sextant as with a saw or axe, he could produce a dinner from almost nothing, at a pinch, or could make a pair of pants from a blanket, or gloves from stockings. One of his bad jokes was enough to inject new life into an exhausted boat's crew; one of his colourful oaths could make the ship's carpenter shiver in his shoes.

The hut, which, for lack of planks, had to be roofed just with canvas, was to be 22 feet long, 16 feet wide, 11 feet high at the ridge and 6 feet 6 inches from ground level to the eaves.

On the 19th, just as we were beginning our day's work, we heard the distant barking of dogs; soon afterward two figures appeared on shore. But they were not some of our missing 19 comrades as we assumed at first, but Eskimos.[4] Sitting on their small sledges, they approached the ship without the least fear. One of them introduced himself as Majuk; the other was named Avatok.[5] Kane had already mentioned them in his narrative.

In return for two bayonets, they were prepared to put themselves and their dogs at our disposal. And the services they performed for us were not inconsiderable. They spent the night with us and departed early next morning. Before leaving they promised to return next day with several of their countrymen to help us bring the building materials and other items ashore.

True to their promise, they appeared on the morning of the 21st with four others. The six men brought five sledges and teams; they were willing and obliging and almost tireless.

Under Chester's superb leadership, construction of the hut had advanced so far that all of us, with the exception of the two engineers, whose duties would not permit them, were able to spend the night ashore. He had not only supervised the work but had himself actively lent a hand with it; otherwise it would scarcely have been possible to finish the work in such a short time. Since the coast was girdled by an old ice foot, the sledges could reach shore only at high tide, or when the tide was close to being at full flood. This caused considerable loss of time and added to the work of transporting materials since the sledges had to be unloaded at the vertical front of the ice foot, their loads carried up piecemeal, and then loaded again and hauled to the neighbourhood of the hut. Here the Eskimos were endlessly useful; if we played something for them on a mouth organ, they would work with true zeal. The only unpleasant aspect was that the sea ice between ship and shore was so rotten that we occasionally broke through and became soaked to the skin.[6] Given our scanty wardrobes, these involuntary dunkings gave rise to many a sigh.

Once a porch about 20 feet long and of the same height and width as the main structure had been added to the southwest end of the hut, it could be considered complete. Here we set up the galley and organized the provisions room. Both rooms were windowless. What did we need a window for, since a 4-month-long night was about to start? Twelve bunks extended in double rows along two of the walls of the living room; along the third wall were two single sleeping places, and the fourth was occupied by the door, which one reached via the porch. To the right of the entrance rose a framework for holding dishes and plates; to the left stood a small desk, on the top of which the four surviving chronometers were housed. The upper third of the room accommodated the saloon table.

The Eskimos left us on the morning of the 24th, having been richly rewarded. Over the course of the day, we removed from the tween-decks all the wood that could be torn loose without any great effort and hauled the boards and door jambs up on deck. By 6 o'clock this task, too, was finished; the engineers let the steam pressure drop, the pumps ceased their rhythm and the wreck, secured to the neighbouring hummocks by three cables, quickly filled with water.

One can scarcely deny that one could conceive of more beautiful spots for building a hut than the headland on which we had settled. But when shipwrecked one is generally not particular; and we made efforts to discover very soon the good qualities of our new home and to overlook its drawbacks.

There were historical memories associated with the headland and the small bay behind it. Almost 20 years previously Kane had cached a lifeboat and provisions here, to ensure the retreat of him and his small group; at the time he gave the place the significant name Lifeboat Cove. The immediate surroundings possessed little charm as regards the landscape; the contours of the hills were gentle, almost monotonous, and the beach partly level. But to the west one's eye could take pleasure in the picturesque coast of Ellesmere Island, seamed by glaciers, and at the shapely, gleaming icebergs, which stretched in a wide semi-circle around the wreck.

Fig. 27. Polaris House.

Numerous foxes lived near the hut, and some of them were killed during the first few days. We also encountered, close to the door, the fresh tracks of a superb adult reindeer. This discovery filled us with well-founded joy, for where there are prospects of hunting reindeer, the minor worries of existence can rarely take root in a person's mind.

On the western Littleton Island, Hayes had left an iron lifeboat buried along with its accessories and provisions, before he left Port Foulke in 1861. And why should we not succeed in locating this cache? At any rate it was worth a try. Hence, once the ice was strong enough, on 31 October, Chester, two seamen and I headed for the island. We scoured the entire coastline of the small island but did not find what we were seeking. We learned later from the natives what had become of the boat.

Our scientific projects, of necessity, had been interrupted by the catastrophe; but on 1 November the hourly meteorological observations were begun again. The anemometer stood about 200 paces from the hut; the screen with the thermometers, the psychrometer and the ozonometer was fastened to the southwest corner of the porch. One of the mercury barometers was hung up in the living room; its reservoir was located 8.5 feet above sea level. Mauch, always ready for any task, took charge of the readings from 4.00 p.m. until midnight; I myself took the observations for the remaining 16 hours.

Off to one side from the hut, we erected a small wooden structure to accommodate the passage instrument; the hatch cover formed its roof, with its opening facing south. Unfortunately we were unable to continue the magnetic observations, however, since we had lost both the magnetic theodolite and the inclinatorium. We had also lost other valuable instruments. Particularly painful was the loss of the large, silver concave mirror, with its related thermometers, that we had set up on the ice near the ship. Some dexterity and goodwill made good this loss, in part. With the help of the limited means now at our disposal, we constructed a Pouillet actinometer, similar to that which that great physicist[7] had used to determine the temperatures in space. Instead of the swan's down, which we could not obtain, we used white fox fur, and instead of the silver, we used polished tin-plate.

It would have been of particular interest had we been able to regularly observe the tides, as we had done at Polaris Bay. For such observations would have provided us with a valuable means of identifying more precisely the progress of the flood wave between Port Foulke and Van Rensselaer Harbour. But the flatness of the beach baffled every effort since during low tide the ice masses along the coast regularly grounded. Had we wanted to erect a tide gauge, it would have had to be at least half a mile from the hut in order to produce a usable result. This distance would have frustrated the execution of such a design.

The natives now came to our hut daily. While they had helped us with our work earlier, now they helped us just as loyally in eliminating our provisions. Nine men, three women and eight children arrived together. They represented the entire population of Etah, the small settlement on the north shore of Foulke Fiord. Being in constant communication with them was just as instructive as it was unpleasant in many respects. During the few daylight hours, they usually travelled around in the open; but at night they lay down on the floor of our living room, and the smell of their skins was extremely noticeable and unequivocal even for insensitive noses. If there was insufficient room on the floor to permit everyone to sleep stretched out, some of them rested in a squatting position, leaning their backs against the wall. In this position their heels had to bear the main weight of their bodies, since in the case of all those who slept in this position their toes pointed outward and upward. When I started my watch at midnight, to take the meteorological observations, every hour I had to step through between this sleeping tangle of humanity, taking care not to tread on anyone.

When one considers that the length of our room was 22 feet and its width 6 feet less, one can easily determine that with a population of 34, the average area occupied by one person totalled 10.3 square feet. This constriction of our elbow room was more than illegal and over the long term would definitely have become irksome. Hence we pitched a tent on the leeside of the hut to accommodate our visitors, but the natives always preferred to sleep inside our hut. Ultimately kindness won and we let them have their way; in one case the occupancy increased to 38 head.

My special friend and benefactor was Avatok, the band's shaman. He usually accompanied me as I made my hourly rounds of the instruments. We generally walked arm in arm, and unless there was drifting snow, we would sing the melody of the spirited student song "Was kommt dort von der Höh" [What comes down from on high] to which we sang the words "Bum-bum-bum." After some time he learned to hum it quite decently. His wife was an unpleasant noisy creature; her two half-grown sons bore the stamp of legitimacy on every square inch of their faces.

Later several families settled near us in snow houses. This started with a father about 30 years old, whose fortunes are sufficiently interesting to be noted here. His name is Itokirssuk [Ittukasuk], but we called him Jimmy. He came from Cumberland[8] and was born near Cape Searle, which lies at 67°17'N. As a young man he left his home, along with his father. They headed north, and after wandering for many years, reached

Fig. 28. Snow-houses and Polaris House.

Cape Isabella, where an Eskimo group lived, of whose existence they had no knowledge.[9]

There he married his present wife, Ivalu, a high-belted, intelligent Eskimo beauty with a tattooed face. This marriage produced two children: a young man named Punigkpa and Manek, an extremely pretty girl about two years old, with lively eyes and light brown, velvet-soft skin. Five summers previously,[10] they had arrived here accompanied by an umiak and four kayaks. Jimmy himself could no longer say precisely how many people there were in the group. On that occasion, they landed on little Littleton Island, discovered Hayes's lifeboat and destroyed it. Then they travelled to Port Foulke, visited the observatory that Hayes had left, filled with provisions and other items, and lit a fire to cook some birds. Unfortunately a canister of gunpowder was lying near the fireplace; a violent explosion occurred, the observatory was blown up and several people were injured or killed. Jimmy's father-in-law lost his life on this occasion; Jimmy related these events with a laughing face and indicated with a movement of his hand how the old man had been hurled into the air on this occasion.[11] The survivors, with the exception of Jimmy and his family, returned to the west shore that same summer. A dog that had accompanied Jimmy during his years of wandering was still strong and powerful. Dark brown in colour, it possessed above each eye that yellow patch peculiar to Dachshunds and Rattlers.[12] This distinguishing mark had been inherited by most of the band's dogs.

Jimmy turned out to be a good fellow, who made himself useful at every opportunity. In the morning he hauled ice for drinking water, swept the path from the hut to the meteorological instruments and had a friendly smile for everyone. Ivalu made gloves and fur stockings for us and tanned the skins of the foxes we killed. She accomplished this task with her teeth, simply chewing the fleshy side of the skins. First she carefully bit off the remains of fat or fibres still adhering to the skin. If little Manek was sitting in her hood, after she had accumulated a mouthful, she would press her lips to those of her child and favoured her with this delicacy. Whoever imagined that the group indulged in kissing, must certainly have misinterpreted this behaviour since the attitude was always a beautiful one and the expressions on the faces an extremely affectionate one; but kissing is as alien to the Eskimos as shaking hands.

One of the people of rank in Etah was Majuk,[13] Kane's former companion, a man with a Roman nose but a true Eskimo. He was constantly hungry and begged with the persistence of a barefoot friar, sometimes for himself, sometimes for his wife and children. He named his youngest, who was barely six weeks old, Daktake, which meant no more or less than Dr. Kane. He had bestowed this name on the little one only in order to flatter us and to rise in our estimation, for he was a rogue and, incidentally, an egotist. Sometimes he would bring us a walrus liver or some tongues and would have us give him bread or canned meat in exchange; sometimes he would bring a skin, in order to barter a harpoon for it. In an unguarded moment, he would then eat the tongues himself, and took care to take back the liver he had brought. But one could not dislike him, for he played these tricks with such an innocent look and displayed such innocence when one took him to task that one forgave him it all.

Inuk was a character of a different sort—a lean, quiet young man with a pale face, almost philosopher-like. During the earlier period of our acquaintance, he was always engaged in making love to talkative Munik, who was older than he was, in a dark corner of the porch. Later they became man and wife and lived out a story of passion which might have had the title "Tout comme chez nous." After a few months their marriage gave way to a formal separation, which is to be discussed later.

The handsomest couple in the band were Nanuki and Angulok, a married couple in the prime of life, with two handsome boys. This family was always immaculately dressed, and there was even something dandified in the father's appearance. He was well built and possessed round, almost feminine features, expressive eyes, a mobile play of expressions and light-brown skin. Mrs. Angulok's complexion was only a little darker; her face formed a slightly truncated oval with a low forehead, large almond-shaped eyes and a small mouth, behind whose full, curved lips gleamed the most beautiful teeth. A snub nose, slightly upturned, gave her a somewhat pert look; she was of medium height, well-proportioned and graceful in her movements. When we gave her a little cap, whose red trim brought out her brownish complexion, from Mrs. Hannah's trunk, which was among our salvaged belongings, this small person looked really pretty in it, and was well aware of it.

*****

The daily schedule of our sunless existence was organized similarly to what it had been on board ship. Heinrich Hobby performed the office of cook and John Booth that of steward. However, the former derived little joy from his position, for everyone felt justified to be critical, without taking into consideration that a cook without pots and with very limited provisions cannot achieve anything great. How could one expect that the brown morning beverage, made from burned barley, ought to taste of coffee? And yet everyone seemed to assume this; for everyone sipping this misanthropical brew pulled a long face, or worse. When

Heinrich came running, shortly before mealtime, with a look of dismay on his face, to report that the soup had spilled into the fire, could one really blame him? Anyone whose demands were impartial had to commiserate sincerely with him; for the tin cans which served as soup pots were not intended as such originally. Hence he was not to blame when the bottom of one of these containers suddenly dropped out and the soup was dumped into the fire. In fact the execution of his duties was associated with untold difficulties, the least of which was the cold. Thus it occasionally occurred that after the canned meat had stood for hours in boiling water and on the outside was so hot that one burned one's tongue on it, its centre still consisted of a rock-hard frozen mass.

Breakfast was served at 9 o'clock; we ate dinner at 3.00 p.m. Most of the residents of Polaris House went to bed at 10 o'clock; shortly before breakfast the steward would make his rounds to wake us. During the day most of the people occupied themselves with reading; after dinner, cards, chess or dominos were played by the light of the dimly burning blubber lamp.[14] At night, after everything had fallen quiet, when the keeper of the instruments was sitting at his little desk, calculating the observations, our four-footed companion, the cat Tom, would emerge from his hiding-place and make his rounds, his back arched, then would settle down near the stove, purring contentedly. Tom was a model cat; he possessed deep knowledge of people and was able to draw a sharp boundary between friend and enemy. Tolerated and fed by everyone, suffered by a few, he led a joyless life. His companion of earlier days, the grey Jennie, had stayed behind with the wife of the colony's administrator at Upernavik, and thereby had been permanently separated from him. Since Budington had been compelled to renounce alcohol, he was the only *Kater*[15] in the wide bounds of Smith Sound.

Midwinter came and went, without us really being aware of it. On 20 and 21 December the height of the dull grey twilight arch ranged between 8 and 9½ degrees of arc, but it was completely dark.

We had no Christmas tree this year, and our New Year's Eve celebration consisted of those whose taste had reached the level of civilization of the Eskimos, eating waffles fried in seal oil.

Famine had broken out in Etah. The natives were now living almost exclusively from our limited provisions. Only Avatok scorned to beg for

Fig. 29. Arctic foxes.

himself and his family. We were delighted to find so much pride and self-restraint in a man whose entire outlook on life of necessity had to be very simple. When Budington sent him some blubber and bread by way of Majuk, he had already killed five of his dogs, simply so that his wife and children would not go short. Many of the hunters moved south to watch for walrus and seal during the coming moonlit days. The only land animals that appeared were foxes and two ravens, which remained true to us all winter. The former were extremely trusting, the majority of them being the valuable blue variety. They were usually killed by lying in wait for them and were rarely caught in traps, since it would be hazardous for the Eskimo dogs to set traps near the hut.

By comparison with its cousin the red fox, the arctic fox is an optimist and a philanthropist, an animal devoid of cunning and guile, which scarcely seems to learn even from injury. It commonly happened that when lying in wait when one's foresight was no longer clearly visible in the darkness, we repeatedly fired at one and the same animal without disturbing it in the slightest. Thus Chester fired eight times at a poor little fox, emaciated to a skeleton; after each close miss it turned deliberately in a circle, its tail in the air, until finally the ninth shot took effect. Once while I was walking to the anemometer, a fox ran across my path, but since I did not have a gun, I couldn't do it any harm. I threw one of my gloves just in front of it, walked at a leisurely pace back to the hut, and when I returned to the spot the animal was gnawing happily on the glove, which was made from the skin of one of its own kind. Since I could not have fired without seriously damaging the glove, I fired a shot to scare it; but the fox barely deigned to pay me any attention.

Strangely we never heard the arctic fox's voice during the winter. Only over the course of the spring did we hear its hoarse kha-kha-kha-kha-kha-kha, which sounds like sardonic laughter.

According to the natives, the breeding season coincides with the arrival of the glaucous gulls, which occurred in early May during our sojourn in Polaris House. When the eider ducks begin laying, i.e., late June, the vixen gives birth to six to eight cubs. The den is dug in the frozen ground and is said to possess several escape tunnels, which is in marked contradiction to the innocence of this animal.

The arctic fox is easily satisfied and is certainly not fastidious. In winter when the birds have moved to warmer zones, it often suffers from severe hunger and follows the bear across the ice-covered sea, to appease its hunger on the remains the latter leaves; only where lemmings occur is its existence assured under any circumstances. It enjoys its happiest times in summer, when the gulls, dovekies and murres nest on the skerries and cliffs. Then it finds an overabundance of eggs, eats young birds and wreaks considerable havoc; for it is as bloodthirsty as the marten and kills the young birds without eating them.

Many of the foxes that we killed had either nothing at all in their stomachs or just the food remains that could be ascribed to our meagre kitchen garbage. Without exception they harboured numerous tape worms.

Fig. 30. The abandoned wreck of *Polaris*.

Initially we scorned their meat, but later considered it a delicacy. In a stew it is not to be despised, but roasted it is less to be recommended. Whoever finds himself in a position to eat fox should not neglect to place the meat in boiling water for a few minutes, in order to remove the bitter gamey taste.

Over the course of January we were obliged, for reasons of economy, to let the fire go out at night. As a result it became so cold in the hut, which possessed only a canvas roof, that almost nobody could sleep. The instrument watcher suffered most from the cold, and Tom, the cat, stopped making his nightly rounds. After we had spent some extremely unpleasant nights, the fire was again maintained constantly. But we decided from now on to eat only one warm meal per day and to cook it on the small stove in the living room, rather than in the galley. The first attempts taught us that this plan could not be executed without producing significant drawbacks. The small stove possessed only a single spot for a kettle and hence could not accommodate two pots at once; thus the soup would get cold before the meat was properly cooked. While cooking was underway, dense clouds of steam resulted; in the warmer parts of the room these condensed into a fine drizzle, and in the colder spots fell as snow crystals.

Humidity produced more discomfort for us here than on board ship; our mattresses became quite stiff with ice. If somebody took a bottle of champagne to his bunk in the evening, next morning he would be obliged to warm the wine again to make it drinkable.

On 27 January the last chip of wood was burned, so that it again became necessary to again attack the wreck. But *Polaris* was strongly built, and usually we could count it a good day if, through unremitting work, we could chop off sufficient firewood to last 2 days.

CHAPTER 19

An ethnographic sketch

Origin of the word "Eskimo." The Etah people meet Whites. Their migrations. The Inuit and the paleolithic people of Europe. The physical characteristics of the Etah people. Craniological remarks. Language. Clothing. Dwellings and tools. Weapons. Communism. Marriage and paternal control. Divorce. Burial. Sense of beauty and its manifestation.

The Eskimos on whose coast we had been shipwrecked belong to the most northerly inhabitants of the earth. Like most of their other relatives, they too call themselves "Inuit" or "people"; the term "Eskimo" is totally alien to them.

Apparently this name was first applied to the Labrador Inuit by the neighbouring Naskapi Indians and other groups of Algonquins. Thus, for example, in the language of the Abenaki "eski-mooha^n" means "he eats raw." In the *Dictionnaire et grammaire de la langue des Cris* by A. Lacombe, published in 1874, one finds "aski = raw" and "mowew = he eats it"; hence "askimowew" would mean "he eats it raw." What J.H. Trumbull says in his distinguished work "On Algonkin names for man," published in the *Transactions of the American Philosophical Association* for 1871, complements this. There we learn that the Mohawk branch of the Iroquois was called "Moho-wang-suck" or "Mauquau-og," "Cannibals or man-eaters," by the Algonquins of New England. Specifically, "Moho" means "to eat," and "moohau," according to Elliott's authority,[1] means "he eats what is alive." The form "Esquimantsic," which has found its way into the ethnological texts and manuals, is probably a corruption.

The first information about the inhabitants of Smith Sound derives from 1818 and originates with John Ross.[2] In the report on his voyage, he refers to them as "Arctic Highlanders," a designation that is extremely inappropriate since none of the Eskimo groups known thus far builds their abodes atop hills. Ross and his companions were probably the first foreigners these people had encountered; for the sight of the Whites and of the two warships threw them into tremendous excitement. They thought the latter were living monsters, and the seamen the inhabitants of the sun or the moon. Their clothing consisted of skins; they possessed dogs, sledges made from bones and lances made from narwhal tusks, as well as wretched knives (in Ross's opinion) hammered from native iron ore or meteoric iron.

The next interaction between these people and Whites occurred during the Franklin search period.

In 1849 *North Star*, one of the squadron's tenders, wintered in Wolstenholme Sound,[3] and the other ships of the fleet came in contact with these Eskimos from time to time. Kane was the first to spend a fairly long time amongst them, as did Hayes. Since then they have interacted only temporarily with the British whalers who, on their way to the entrance to the Northwest Passage, occasionally moored to the shore ice near Cape York to wait for open water.

Kane estimated their number at 150, Hayes at 100; our own enquiries suggested a similar result to the latter's estimate. We ourselves saw 102 individuals; the group numbered at most 8–10 more people.

For the sake of brevity we will call these *eschatoi andrōn* [uttermost men][4] Etahners, after Etah, their northernmost settlement on the north shore of Foulke Fiord. But not the entire tribe is resident there; rather they are distributed among several other settlements of varying size and location.

Their northernmost wanderings extend to about the 79th parallel; their southernmost no farther than Cape York. Confined in the north by the massive Humboldt Glacier and in the south by the miles-long cliffs of other glaciers, which so far are still nameless, the range over which they move in a north–south direction is extremely limited. They cannot head east; for there the ice cap confronts them. And apart from this, their fear of evil spirits deters them from venturing far into the interior.

Occasionally it happens that they cross Smith Sound and visit the coast of Ellesmere Land. But such expeditions are rare, for the ice is usually extremely hummocky and barely passable for sledges, in the event that the currents and violent winds in the narrow sound even permit the formation of a continuous ice cover.

Undoubtedly their ancestors had occupied that desolate coast for centuries. When they arrived there can barely be determined; any attempt to do so must lead to pointless speculations that would produce more harm than benefit. Some believe that they are not only qualified to identify the century, but also the year when the Inuit first reached Greenland; but given the lack of reliable data, one naturally has to mistrust such statements.

Only this much is certain: when the Inuit reached Greenland, they were already real Eskimos. And since then, their customs and habits have scarcely changed, except where the influence of the Whites has made its mark. The progress that this people has made over the course of time is so insignificant that the implements of different groups, the contact between whom has been interrupted for many centuries, resemble each other as closely as do the sand grains on a mobile dune. And on the other hand, the primitive weapons used by the paleolithic inhabitants of Europe strikingly resemble the murderous projectiles still used by the Inuit. If one did not know to what a high degree the complicated human organism is to be seen as a product of adaptation to its environment; if comparative ethnology had not taught us how ridiculously similarly peoples' ideas develop—even down to the strangest aberrations, even when they are spatially so far separated from each other that each might just as well inhabit a different planet—one might conclude from this convergence of implements that the Inuit are the nearest blood relatives of paleolithic man.

A prominent British researcher believes that he must unconditionally defend this assumption. He sees such a possible relationship as a certainty, but he still owes us the proof. If one can be sure that the two reindeer antler carvings that were found in the Charente are genuine, and that they represent human heads, the physiognomy of paleolithic man was quite different from that of the Inuit. De Mortillet[5] informs us that "L'ensemble de la tête paraît intermédiaire entre le type conventionel de Mephistopheles et la tête de François I."

The physical type of the Etah people is so absolutely similar to that of other Eskimos that we believe we can dispense with its description here. May we be permitted just the remark that we saw several men, full brothers, who were almost 6 feet tall? This stature had been inherited from the mother, who was 5 foot 6 inches, while the father was below medium height.

Through the obliging benevolence of various corporations, institutes and private individuals, I was able to examine critically and draw more Eskimo skulls than anybody previously. Specifically, the Academy of Natural Sciences in Philadelphia and Dr. Hayes made available to me the skulls collected by the latter in the neighbourhood of Etah for examination.

The number of usable Etah skulls amounted to 101 specimens. Of these, 100 could be used in order to determine the mean width index, which was 71.37. The mean height index, derived from the measurement of 99 skulls, was 76.91. The maximum width index was 79.8, and the maximum height index was 81.8, while the minimum width index was 63.4, and the minimum height index was 70.8.

The detailed measurements of these skulls are reported in Volume 10 of the *Archiv für Anthropologie*.

The following table contains a number of means for width and height indices from other Eskimo groups:

LOCATION	WIDTH INDEX	HEIGHT INDEX	NUMBER SKULLS	SOURCE
?	70.4	73.7	24	Welcker [6]
West Greenland	71	75	10	Davis [7]
Northeast America	72	75	6	Davis
West Greenland	71.8	70.5	5	Virchow [8]
East Greenland	72.9	74.2	4	Pansch [9]
Northwest America	72	75	4	Davis
West Greenland	72.6	73.7	21	Bessels

Samuel Kleinschmidt,[10] one of the most accomplished experts on the Eskimo language, distinguishes two main dialects in West Greenland, a northern and a southern one. "The former is the harder and at the same time the purest in pronunciation, especially that of the vowels; the southern one is softer, but also less intelligible." From this, the dialect of the Etah people would be closer to the southern one. Their vocalization is extremely sharp, and the accent is singing, undulating slightly up and down, while the consonants, especially at the end of a word, are almost swallowed.

The clothing of the Etah people is similar in cut to the garments of the Danish Greenlanders. In winter both sexes wear underclothes of bird skins, with the feathered side turned inside. The jacket, equipped with a hood, and the short pants are made from the skins of seal, reindeer, bear or dog; less commonly one sees jackets made of fox skins. Over two or three pairs of fur stockings, watertight boots of sealskin are worn; occasionally the outer footwear is made from bear skin. In the case of the men, the boots are tied somewhat below the knee by means of a drawstring over the lower hem of the pants.

The women's boots are higher and reach almost to the groin. Herein lies the main difference between the men's and women's dress. While the man's hood is rounded, that of the woman runs to a point, and in the case of married women is of a considerable size because the children are carried around in it until they are three or four. Gloves are made from either sealskin or from furs; mittens are most common.

In summer the heavy jackets of bear skin are exchanged for those of sealskin, while the underclothes of bird skins are either discarded or are worn alone without the outer garments.

Domed snow houses or stone-built houses provide shelter, as well as skin tents. Snow houses are used during the cold season, stone-built houses less commonly; but tents are used exclusively in summer.

Invention of the dome, which probably occurred independently in three different areas of our planet, perhaps redounds to even greater fame for the Eskimo than the construction of the sledge. The Etah Inuk is a master of building this hemispherical or beehive-shaped snow house. Its size depends on the number of occupants; the average floor diameter is about 12 feet and the height about half that. The length of the snow

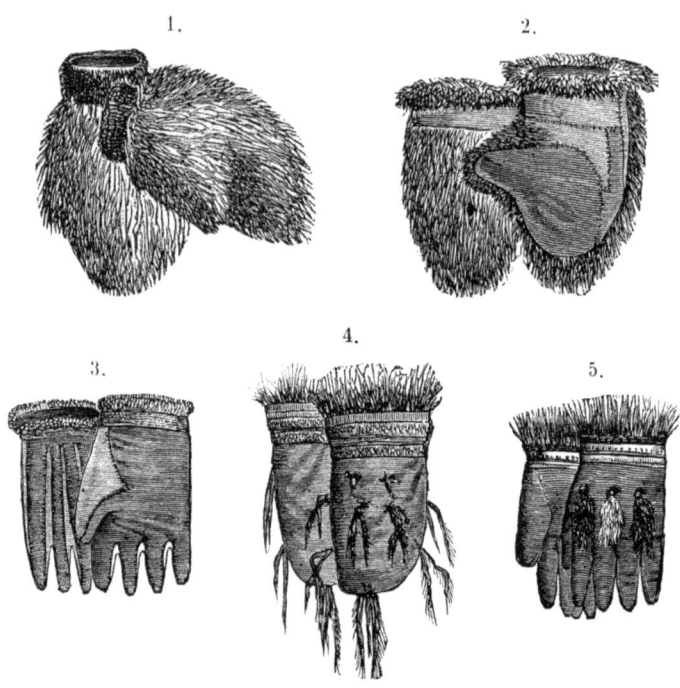

Fig. 31. Inuit gloves: figs. 1 and 2 from Etah, the rest from the North American Arctic.

blocks varies between 2 and 2½ feet; their height between 10 and 12 inches and their thickness between 8 and 10 inches. In long section they have three shapes. The dominant one is a parallel trapezium with two slightly diverging sides; then there is a long rectangle and finally a trapezium, whose largest angle is rarely more than 109° and whose smallest never drops below 70°.

A sabre-shaped snow knife is used to cut the blocks; it is cut from wood, from the lower jaw of a narwhal or from a long walrus tusk.

Two people are usually involved in building a snow house; one cuts the blocks and the other fits them together. The bottom layer consists of upright rectangular blocks which are arranged in a circle. The

Fig. 32. Inuit boots and shoes from various locations.

Fig. 33. Inuit at home.

remaining layers form a spiral which becomes most pronounced in the dome. Each successive circuit is set at a greater angle of inclination than the preceding one.

Finally the door opening, in the shape of a pointed arch, is cut out; in front of it a short arched passageway is built, as represented in Figure 28. Occasionally several houses are connected together.

The interior furnishings of these dwellings are extremely simple. Opposite the door there is a low platform made of snow, covered with skins, which serves as the sleeping place. In the stone-built domes this raised platform consists of the same material as the building itself.

The most important item of household equipment is the stone lamp, which provides light and heat. Depending on the size of the room, one or two of these are present. They rest on blocks of rock or snow, directly beside the sleeping platform. The stone cooking pot usually hangs above it from thongs. Small frames made from bones serve for drying clothing.

What was said about the lamp and cooking pot of the southern Greenlanders also applies here. The wick consists either of moss fibres or of the dried catkins of the arctic willow. These also serve as tinder to catch the sparks that are produced by rubbing two pieces of stone together. The widely distributed fire drill also occurs here. The spindle, held firmly between a bone mouthpiece and a rotten fragment of wood, is set in motion using the well-known bow, and is kept spinning until the dry wood starts to smoulder. The other contents of the house can quickly be enumerated. We need mention only some shallow vessels made of waterproof sealskin; a few women's knives, not unlike our half-moon-shaped chopping knives; the housewife's primitive sewing implements; and finally a few scrapers made of bone, ivory or stone for preparing skins. The main part of tanning soft skins is achieved with the teeth.

Although the temperature inside the dwelling rarely rises above the freezing point, when one enters the room, coming from outside, the heat seems almost oppressive. Hence the adults usually discard their clothing with the exception of the short pants; the children commonly run around stark naked.

As long as starvation does not threaten, home life offers much that is appealing. The people are carefree and happy, and every emotion finds a reflection in their faces. For everywhere there prevails a total freedom of action—action and behaviour devoid of malice or guile.

The only vehicle which these most northerly people now use is the sledge. Prior to their encounter with Whites, this conveyance consisted of pieces of bone skilfully lashed together; now wood is commonly used for making it.

Figure 2 on p. 372 represents one of these old sledges, borrowed from Ross's narrative; Figure 3 on the same page represents another one, made of wood.

The Etah resident owns neither boats, nor bow and arrow, although the words for these items still exist in his language. However, this is

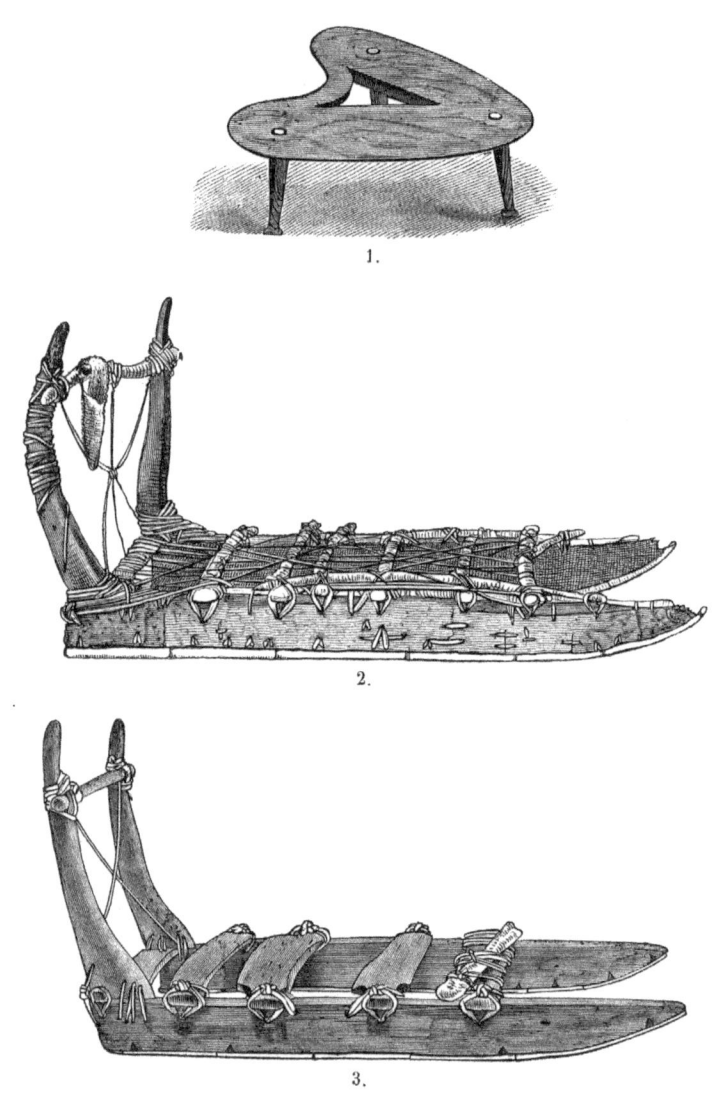

FIG. 34. 1. Inuit stool. 2. Old Inuit sledge (after Ross).
3. Modern Inuit sledge.

a significant circumstance in a hunting people, a circumstance which indicates a definite retrograde development. Everywhere else the Inuit impress us as bold seamen with enviable proficiency, who can handle their delicate skin boats with the greatest skill; everywhere else they are superb archers, or where the more primitive weapon has been superseded by the introduction of firearms, they can handle a gun with eminent assurance.

Only Jimmy owned arrows and a bow, which he had brought with him from his southern home. Frequently repaired and little-used, these weapons were in a wretched condition; moreover their owner was a poor shot. The bow consisted of four pieces of reindeer antler, lashed together with sinew, and had little curvature; it was 33 inches long. The bowstring was woven together from four-ply sinew from the ligaments at the nape of the reindeer's neck and was fastened to the ends of the bow around charmingly carved small bear heads. The arrows—of which he possessed only three—had iron heads. The shafts were made from pieces of wood glued together and were feathered with raven wing feathers. The length of the arrows ranged from 18 to 20 inches, including the heads.

Weapons are limited to the lance; the harpoon with its float, which, however, was used without the spear-thrower that the other Inuit use; and the bird dart.

Next to the illustration of a lance that I copied from Ross's narrative, on p. 374, Figure 5, I have illustrated another one, whose shaft consists of wood, about one-tenth of life-size. Figure 6 represents the upper part of that weapon at a somewhat larger scale.

As soon as the harpoon has struck its target, the shaft, in the terminal hollow of which the ball-shaped base of the head rests, slips away from it and drops to one side. But since it is secured by two leather thongs, it is prevented from becoming totally separate. This ingenious mechanism, which rests on the principle of the ball joint, which could not remain concealed for long from a hunting people, is illustrated in Figure 7, as, too, is the fastening of the head of the shaft. Figure 8 shows a more perfected version.

Two separate harpoon heads are represented in Figures 3 and 4. The basal opening of the latter is broken and has been repaired with thongs

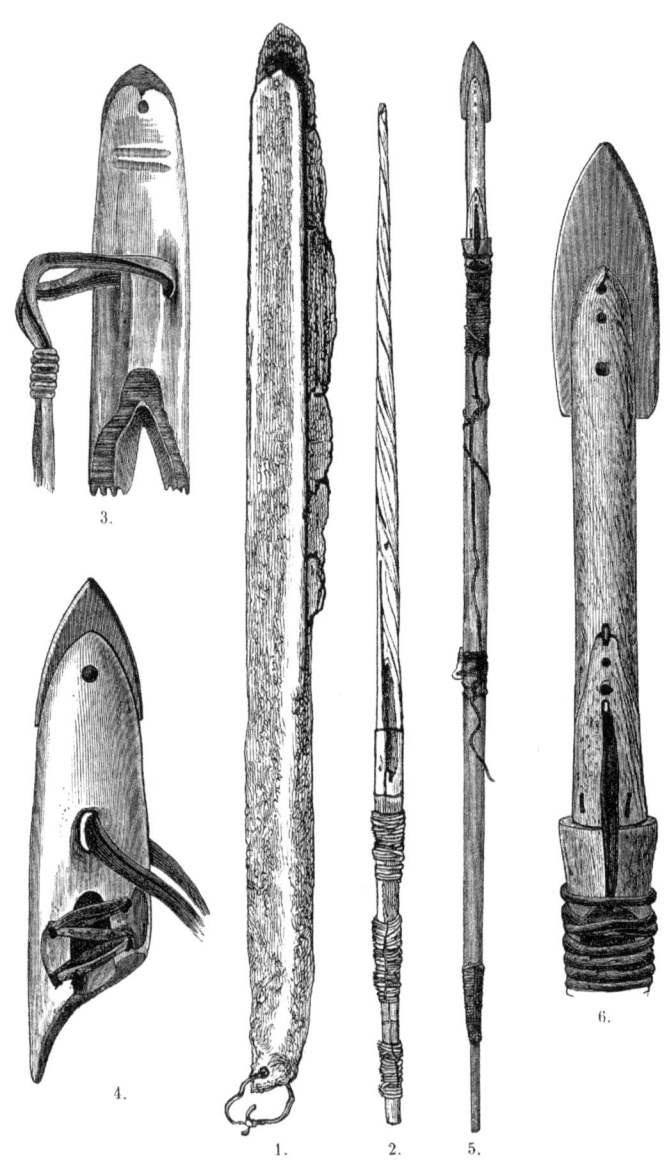

FIG. 35. Inuit weapons from Smith Sound.

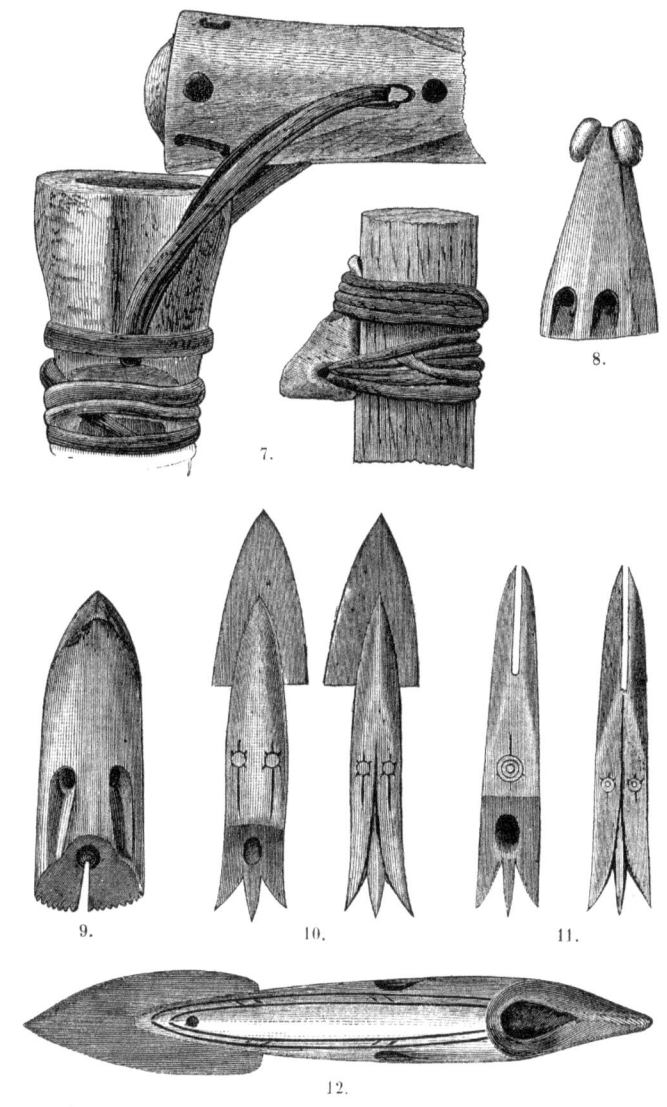

FIG. 36. Inuit weapons from Smith Sound and elsewhere.

to prevent an accidental separation of the shaft and the head. In both illustrations the long line has been cut away near the loop. In the first of these figures, one can notice two horizontal grooves below the rivet, i.e., rough ornamentation. These resemble the lines that one finds on many of the paleolithic arrows from the Dordogne, and which were thought to represent marks of ownership.

Probably those "marks of ownership" are also ornamentation. Perhaps they fulfilled at the same time the purpose of representing certain events numerically, perhaps the killing of a reindeer, a bear or some other game animal.

A primitive people does not require special marks to identify its property; for when each man makes his own weapon, he will endow it with a certain individual stamp which possesses unmistakable characters, similar to a person's handwriting. The senses of an Eskimo who was accompanying me on a sledge trip were so sharpened in this regard that he could tell me when we encountered 11 criss-crossing sledge tracks, whose sledge had produced each of the impressions in the hard snow. And this man was in no way distinguished from the others as regards intelligence. Somebody who can achieve this can certainly distinguish his own weapon from those of another band member or hunter.

Figures 9, 10, 11 and 12 are reproduced here solely on account of their ornamentation and represent harpoon points from western Eskimo groups. The illustration of a stone point, taken from an old grave in North Greenland, is presented on the right at two-thirds life-size.

With these primitive lances, supported only by his dogs, the Etah Inuk fearlessly battles the bear, which often becomes a dangerous opponent. Several of the older hunters in the band bore scars of terrible lacerations on shoulders, backs and hips. He intrepidly goes to battle with walruses, kills the massive bearded seal and waits for hours and days, despite cold and blizzard, at the breathing holes of the smaller seals.

What the individual kills belongs to the entire community. The hunter keeps only the skin of his kill exclusively for himself. With the blubber and the meat, he first looks after his own family, as well as those who occupy the same hut as himself; then the rest get their share. As long as supplies last, the table is set for everyone.

During the winter the Etah Inuk lives exclusively on the meat of the various marine mammals, as well as bears and foxes; during the summer various species of sea birds and their eggs form a not inconsiderable part of his food. He obtains fish only by accident, since angling for fish is alien to him. Sometimes meat is eaten raw, sometimes boiled, but without any salt being added. A hunter who returns home hungry from hunting can consume 8–10 lbs. of meat without suffering any harm. And he finds nothing unusual in this. With his left hand he grabs a large chunk, shoves as much of it in his mouth as it can hold, and then cuts off this enormous bite-sized piece close to his lips. Then he starts chewing lustily, smacking his lips as noisily as possible while so doing.

In contrast to the western Eskimos, who frequently possess several wives, the Etah Inuk is monogamous. Only as a result of free-thinking passion is the bond of marriage powerfully loosened.

The average number of children in a family is two. If hard times occur, babies are often killed. Sometimes the mother lays the little one out at some remote spot and abandons it to starvation and the cold; sometimes she kills it by suffocating it. It seems to make little difference whether it is a boy or a girl.

When Majuk, already mentioned several times, died, leaving behind three children, the youngest, a boy, was throttled by the mother and buried with his father. Two of our men tried to rescue the little one. They even managed to prolong his life by a few hours; but when they left the mother unguarded for a short time, she completed the deed.

Otherwise the children are treated affectionately, occasionally with excessive tenderness. Thus we saw a mother who not only was carrying her six- to seven-year-old boy around in the hood, but even from time to time would give him the breast and let him suckle. The Etah Inuit never have recourse to corporal punishment. The little ones grow up like lapdogs. Once when I gave old Avatok's half-grown son a well-deserved thrashing, my good-natured friend became downright angry.

The only method of punishment that I ever saw applied was really original. The shrieking urchins, barely able to walk and stark naked, were placed on the snow by their mothers until they stopped crying. And this happened several times when the temperature was some 30° below freezing.

Given the children's undemanding nature, it is easy to make them happy. The boys usually play with small sledges and practice throwing harpoons once they can run around. The girls are given dolls carved from walrus tusks and clothed in skins, or small toy animals. Puppies that are tormented with a boundless lack of consideration are a favourite toy.

Among many western Eskimo groups, girls are tattooed in their youth. But here this custom is not embraced. Jimmy's wife, the lady from the country to the west, whose face bore a simple pattern of tattoos, was therefore often laughed at by the other women. When I painted the face of a pretty 10-year-old girl with water colours and then held a mirror in front of her, she began to weep bitterly. The little girl's mother, thinking that the design could not be removed again, almost attacked me. She calmed down again only when I washed the lines off again.

When a boy reaches the age of 12 or 14, he follows the hunters when they go hunting seals and learns to drive sledge dogs with voice and whip. When a girl becomes a woman—at the age of about 15 or 16—she has already acquired sufficient dexterity that she can assist her mother in making articles of clothing. In this, and in bearing children, lies the main task of the woman among this most northerly people. Cooking requires no great knowledge, nor do the other household chores, with the exception of handling game.

A young man takes a wife as soon as he is in a position to take care of the needs of the body. Generally a marriage is contracted out of affection, more rarely out of convenience. In the event that a marriage takes place against the wishes of his parents, the man requires only the approval of the girl's parents to consider her his spouse. The widespread, age-old custom, to pretend to carry off the chosen one apparently by force, also prevails here.

Among a people whose lifestyle is as totally communal as that of the Inuit, there can seriously be no question of a dowry. The husband's entire property, in terms of major items, is limited to his sledge and dog team and his simple weapons; the wife's possessions consist of a lamp, a pot, a knife and a few needles. Their meagre clothing should also be mentioned. Here, above all, the physical advantages must also be placed in the balance, as well as those qualities that best enable the individual to wage the struggle for existence. Our knowledge is still too incomplete for us to dare to attempt to fully characterize the ideals of the human form as these may exist in the minds of the various so-called peoples of nature. Differentiation of this ideal will, of necessity, go hand in hand with the division of labour between the sexes; for where there is little differentiation, the man's physiognomy will differ only little from that of the woman.

In general the Eskimo appears to prefer round, full features. To what extent individual taste has an impact still has to be determined. In addition the woman expects that the man should be a good hunter, while the latter aims at bringing home a life partner who possesses sufficiently the skills to handle her domestic duties.

The marriage bond, so easily contracted, can be dissolved only through certain formalities. Some of our men[11] had occasion to be present at a divorce. A brief description of the procedure follows.

Manik had become Inuk's wife through her father's coercion. But her heart belonged to somebody else. After her union she granted the latter those privileges that were due only to either her spouse or to the other married hunters in the group. In a fit of jealousy, Inuk stabbed her with a knife and wounded her slightly in the side. This incident induced the father to give Manik's inclination free rein. From now on she was to belong totally to the man of her choice. Hence she was separated from the husband, to whom she could not extend her love. While Inuk lay weeping in one snow house, stubbornly refusing food and drink, in another Manik had to go through the actual ceremony of divorce. With her knees drawn up she lay on her back on the sleeping platform of a neighbouring dwelling. A leather thong was fastened around her head, its end held by one of the oldest women in the band. While the latter uttered incomprehensible words in a soft, monotonous singsong, for somewhat over 2 hours she continually pulled at the string so that Manik's head alternately rose and fell. Of her countrymen, Manik's brother-in-law was the only spectator. Once the procedure was finished, the latter took the woman on his sledge to a neighbouring camp. Her beloved, who was waiting for her there, enfolded her in his arms and immediately took her to his igloo.

Inuk visited us a few days later. He had completely got over his loss. At worst his face had become a shade paler. When I enquired about his former spouse, I received the unexpected answer: "Manik is a very bad person."

Soon after this divorce had occurred, Majuk's funeral took place.[12] The dead man was wrapped in skins, loaded aboard a sledge, and then buried in the snow with his face facing west. Once the corpse was covered, the sledge was laid over it, and the dead man's hunting equipment laid beside it. Hereupon the men stuck a small wisp of hay in their right nostrils; by contrast the women stopped up their left nostrils. These plugs were worn for several days and only set aside when the people entered one of the snow houses.

But corpses are not always so carelessly covered as happened here. Certainly a real grave is never dug in the frozen ground, but it is the custom to pile a heap of stones over the corpse, unless frost or deep snow make this impossible.

The Etah Inuit believe in the survival of the soul after death, but for various reasons it is really not possible to discuss their religious views in greater detail. We also have to abstain from discussing other questions in case we considerably exceed the bounds of this unassuming ethnological sketch. Anyone who would like to delve deeper into Eskimo folklore will find a rich source of pleasure in Rink's "Eskimoiske Eventyr og Sagn."[13] Anyone who reads those traditions will immediately recognize that the imaginations of these primitive people are far from sluggish. Their imaginations are sufficiently active to endow solid rock and moving air, the circling stars and the glowing aurora, and all the various cosmic and telluric phenomena with genius and life.

Since one of the main aspects of beauty is rooted in this psychic phenomenon, it is not without interest to investigate in passing in what way the sense of beauty reveals itself among the Eskimos.

Discussion of this question gains in significance when we recall the great similarity prevailing between the weapons and tools of the reindeer people of Europe and those of the Eskimo. It becomes of even great significance when we consider that that extinct race lived under similar conditions as many of the Inuit do today. And certainly nobody can doubt that similar causes produce similar effects.

The question of whether those paleolithic engravings and carvings that have been found in southern France and Switzerland are genuine has now become a burning issue. For since it has turned out that some of the Thaying finds are counterfeit, one is inclined to consider debatable whether these so-called peoples of nature possessed a sense of beauty and to deny them the proficiency to represent animal shapes artistically in characteristic fashion. One is reluctant to comprehend why people on the one hand should make only rude stone weapons, while on the other were carving animal figures on reindeer antler and bones, which one cannot deny possess a certain freedom and originality in execution.

Such a remark may be partially justified, especially since the proficiency in figurative representation in prehistoric time apparently arose suddenly, then totally disappeared. But one should not ignore the fact that thus far only a small part of such finds has been uncovered and that one has only just begun to find them.

The degeneration in this so-called prehistoric art is not strange in itself and is not without parallels.

It is a well-known fact that over the course of history figurative representation of various natural objects experienced a one-sided development. Are there not numerous paintings by the old masters where, next to the most superb human figures, the landscape part is treated in childish, even rough fashion? Do we not see in impressive composition, alongside human figures whose features betray the most secret emotions of the soul, at the same time animals that, seen only in outline without the redeeming interference of colour, would cause even a zoologist some perplexity?

When one takes such circumstances into consideration, the gap between a stone knife and a decorated piece of bone becomes not insurmountable.

If the sense for beauty among the Etah people is less developed than among the more favoured, more southerly Eskimo bands, this should not surprise us. For where man's existence is threatened by concerns about food of the most pressing nature, where the strength of the individual and of the community has to be directed solely to satisfying bodily needs, little time remains for taking pleasure in the sight of beautiful forms, or for creating them.

Yet here we find various ornamentation on clothing, combinations of differently coloured furs and skins that would please even a jaded eye. The illustrations that accompany this chapter may serve as proof of this.

During the winter, in our presence, some of the hunters carved animal figures and human shapes that were extremely characteristic. With limited means they succeeded in representing the typical features of the Inuit physiognomy, as well as expressing the European cast of features. Many of the animals were unrecognizable.

Moreover, the aptitude of the Greenland Eskimos for plastic representations is less than that of the western Eskimo. Specifically, among the Bering peoples there are superb ivory carvers, whose products—this may not remain hidden—occasionally clearly reveal the influence of the neighbouring Indians. It would be of great interest to ascertain how far one primitive people influences another in this regard.

The National Museum of the United States in Washington possesses numerous carvings from these northwestern Indian groups. Among much that is barbaric and mediocre, there is much that is superb. Anyone contemplating the facial expression, reflecting great spiritual refinement of the wooden human statues, Nos. 713 and 714, would no longer find anything extraordinary in the execution of the "grazing reindeer."

I have illustrated at life-size an ivory torso that Dr. Hayes collected from an old grave near Etah. Unfortunately, however, woodcuts are not very suitable for reproducing such items. Moreover, during this technical execution various parts have been distorted to their disadvantage; many of the indispensable half-tones have been totally lost. Despite this, the total impact of this small carving is not at all unfavourable. The left side of the original, seen in profile, in fact displays beautiful features. Admittedly, the back surface is devoid of any detail, but there is little with which to find fault in the area of the loins and the lower extremities.

Once I myself had contrived various attempts to carve ivory with stone and metal, I reached the conviction that the torso illustrated here was not produced with stone tools.

Among a hunting people who betray a sense for the beginnings of music, and possess bows and arrows, one should expect right away to find primitive stringed instruments; for the sharp noise of the whirring sinew must inspire the hunter to make such instruments.

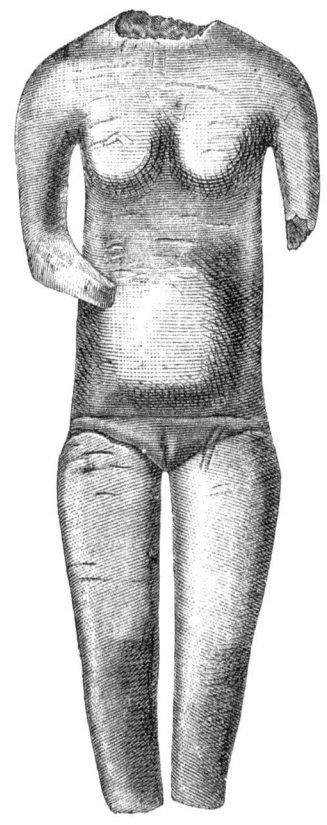

Fig. 37. Ivory carving of human torso.

But no such instruments have been encountered among any of the various Eskimo groups who use this weapon. Everywhere only the drum has been found: a rough, bone hoop covered with an elastic membrane. A small bone is used as a drumstick: usually an upper thigh bone whose head naturally possesses the necessary curvature. One of the earlier illustrations (Figure 33) demonstrates how the instrument is played.

There is little praiseworthy to be said about the musical accomplishments of the Etah Inuk. He beats relentlessly at irregular intervals on his instrument, moves his upper body first to the right and then to

FIG. 38. Inuit song.

the left, and in addition sings a melody that sluggishly winds around a varying keynote.

The variations in this singsong may be represented roughly in the above manner.

But this rendering is only partially correct; for many of the intervals amount to less than a half-tone and hence cannot be expressed by the usual system of notation.

A very similar singsong is found among the Bering Strait Eskimos. A sergeant in the federal army who was stationed near Norton Sound sang their melody for me; even the meaningless text is the same, except that the *a* in *ah ya* sounds as a^n, i.e., very nasal. The songs of the southern Greenlander appear also to have been similar. Also Joseph sang a similar strain for me whose nuances, analyzed with the help of various resonators, undoubtedly could be established. On p. 542 of his *Second Voyage for the Discovery of a North-West Passage*, Parry[14] reproduces the songs of the inhabitants of Winter Island. Although they are extremely melancholy, some of these phrases move through 2½ tone intervals. The text is as follows: *Amna Aya Aya Amna ah*; thus it is similar to that of the Etah people and of the other Greenlanders.

It emerges from these cursory remarks that from West Greenland to the shores of Bering Strait the Inuit possess a common ancient song that over the course of time has suffered smaller modifications than their language.

CHAPTER 20

FURTHER PROGRESS

The crew's state of health. Effect of the winds. High tides. Freezing point of mercury. Sunrise. The natives. Chester makes preparations for building boats. Pendulum attempts. Actinometric observations. Plan for a sledge trip northwards. My companions. Charting the harbour. Equipment for the sledge trip. Postponement of our departure. Setting off. Underway. Turning back due to the insubordination of the natives. Trip to Sorfalik. Second departure for the north and turning back again. The third attempt also fails! Arctic hares. Bryan's trip to Rensselaer Harbour. Foulke Fiord and Brother John Glacier. The ice cap. Port Foulke. The dovekies. Preparations for returning home.

In the case of most of the men, the consequences of the double wintering at high latitude were starting to make themselves apparent. Minor physical effort caused fatigue and shortness of breath; scorbutic symptoms were showing themselves in several cases. Hot lemonade, made from citric acid and syrup—sugar had ceased to exist for us—did little to check the scurvy. Fresh seal meat and walrus liver had greater effect, except that the consumption of the latter occasionally led to attacks of dysentery, similar to the effects of bear liver but without causing vomiting.

Here at Polaris House the storms were neither so frequent nor so violent as at Polaris Bay. Yet in connection with the very pronounced tidal current, their force was sufficient to keep the sea open. Here, too, northerly winds generally produced open water; if, on the other hand, a southerly wind blew, the ice usually became solidly packed. If calm prevailed all around, one could clearly hear the noise of the surf inside the hut; occasionally the surf broke barely half a mile from the beach on the piled-up ice floes. As a result of these conditions, frost-smoke was extremely frequent. It billowed up higher here than at Polaris Bay and robbed us of the view of the nearby coast of Ellesmere Land. We spotted its ridges for the first time since we had landed only on 9 February and then only for a few hours.

These southerly storms were welcomed by the natives since there were usually walrus hauled out on the drifting floes, and they could hunt them.

Although we did not have the pleasure of making regular tide observations, it did not escape us that the height of the spring high tide was extremely variable. The highest high tide that we experienced here occurred on 29 January. Around 11.00 a.m. that morning a black bank of fog rose over Littleton Island, completely obscuring the twilight arc. It was a flat calm. Yet it spread rapidly northward; about 10 minutes after it first appeared, it had reached the headland where our house stood. Half an hour before noon the rising tide broke through a weak spot in the ice foot and flooded the lowland. Some of the men were hauling firewood from the wreck; in order to ensure their return, we had to rig a temporary bridge. A torrential stream was flowing northeast of the house, turning the headland into an island. It took an hour before the high tide subsided. The temperature was raised noticeably near the water. A thermometer secured to a post 3 feet above the waves recorded −37.2°C, yet the instrument in the screen read −40.9°C.

The mercury was frozen, and we again had an opportunity to establish the fluctuations to which the freezing point of this material is subject. In the box sheltering the thermometer, there was a shallow glass dish containing about 2 oz. of chemically pure mercury. This remained entirely fluid while the contents of one of the thermometer bulbs was so solidly frozen that I could smash it and peel the metal out as a hard ball.

The brightness of the twilight had increased so markedly that on 7 February a window that was let into the roof of the hut made the lamp redundant for 2 hours. Ten days later the northeastern mountain ridges were reddened by the reflection of the sun, but it was only on 2 March that its rays hit our desolate headland.[1]

The wanderlust now became very keen among the natives; they came in crowds from near and far. Some of them had never seen any other people than their own group. Gradually they became more communicative. We learned that they had set fire to Kane's ship;[2] that Hayes Sound was a strait;[3] and that Hans, the faithless husband, had a wife and two children in one of the neighbouring settlements.

There was not a single person in the entire band who could have represented the run of the coast graphically. The western Eskimos are excellent cartographers; Erasmus York,[4] that famous Greenlander, even drew the entire stretch of coast from Cape Alexander to Cape York for Captain Ommanney;[5] but our friends were completely helpless as soon as we put a pencil and paper in their hands. We often repeated the experiment but always with the same result. It made absolutely no difference as to whether we began the delineation at Etah, at Cape Alexander or at any other locality. They seemed to understand the idea of representation, but they were incapable of adding anything at all to our drawings.

Chester, under whose leadership Polaris House had gone up so quickly, was also to build the boats for our homeward voyage; we could not count on the half weak-minded carpenter.[6] We had collected and hoarded every screw we had found up till now, and every nail that came our way; for our entire resource in these items was limited to what could be removed from the planks and spars of the wreck.

At the end of February, in bitter cold, Chester, assisted by the carpenter and the stoker Booth, began carefully taking apart the planking of the saloon. The boats would have to be built from this timber—weak, half-inch boards. To achieve this one needed a man like Chester who never shrank from any difficulty.

We could scarcely count on starting our voyage before the beginning of June. But we had to get to work quickly, for the storms were becoming stronger and more frequent, and the wreck was at the mercy of the treacherous waves, whose vagaries might rob us of the only source of timber available to us.

Among the few instruments we had saved was the pendulum. Hence it was our duty to set it up and to obtain a series of observations. Since we lacked a proper observatory, the general living and sleeping room had to serve that purpose. The instrument was set up on the north wall of the room, between Budington's and Chester's bunks, as it had been previously in our dear hut at Polaris Bay. But this time the pendulum did not swing north–south but in a direction approximately northeast–southwest. The swinging blade lay about 11 feet above mean sea level, and the telescope for observing its passage was screwed firmly to the lid of a box about 3 feet to the right of the instrument. To ensure that there were no disturbances, we selected the morning hours from 1.00 to 5.00 a.m. This work, carried out by Bryan and myself, lasted from 5 to 13 March.

Since the sun had risen, we had neglected reading the actinometer which I had constructed shortly after we landed. A series of observations revealed the temperature in space to be –206°F. Pouillet in Paris had recorded it to be –142°C; our observations at Polaris Bay had produced a result of –174°F. The mean of our own observations was –190°F or –123°C, i.e., 19° warmer than Pouillet's result. A further determination of this temperature, using different equipment and calculated using a different formula from Pouillet's, would probably produce a more reliable value. For this method is basically extremely crude and less satisfactory than the determination of the thermal radiation from the sun using thermometers, which we had begun again on 2 March.

A plan that had matured over the winter was now to gradually approach its execution. Chester was the only person who knew about it. I wanted to make an attempt to reach Polaris Bay, in order to achieve the highest possible latitude from there, in the event that conditions allowed it. Two of the natives were to accompany me. For the moment my movements had to remain a secret. I identified the Humboldt Glacier as the goal of this trip, and its purpose was the investigation and survey of that glacier.

We had gradually accumulated 10 of the best dogs; all that was missing now were skins for making stockings and a sleeping bag. Hence on 26 March, I sent Jimmy to one of the southern settlements to barter needles and three large snow knives that Chester had made for this purpose from hoop iron for a number of reindeer skins. He returned after an absence of 11 days, but brought only a single skin. But this was no reason for abandoning the trip; we had learned to be satisfied.

The day of my departure was set for 12 April, for the natives wanted to accompany me only on condition that I waited until the sun's noon altitude was higher. I was very impatient but I had to yield. Jimmy, invariably called Zimme by his wife, declared himself ready to go with me. Pointing to one of the nearby icebergs, he told me: when the shadow of this berg is so short that it no longer falls on that rock cliff, we can set off. My second companion rejoiced in the name Avatok [Arrutak]. He owned a superb team of dogs, as well as a wooden leg with a hinged joint which he had invented and manufactured himself,[7] and was of a sanguine temperament. It was this above all that prompted me to hire him; also, despite his wooden leg, he was much more agile and nimble than most of his companions. When he was young a rock falling from a cliff had shattered his left leg a little below the knee. His own mother had carried out the amputation of the severely injured limb.

While Jimmy and Avatok made themselves at home and enjoyed our hospitality, Chester assisted me in measuring a baseline, from which I effected the detailed survey of the surroundings of Polaris House over the course of the next few days. Once the work was finished, he travelled to Etah with Nanuki, the Bear, who usually went by the name of Sorkak or Baleen, in order to hunt reindeer. Also Bryan and some of the men shouldered their guns and headed out, some eastward, some southward.

I had been ready to start for a long time; but my companions, whose concepts of punctuality suffered from a regrettable imprecision, still wanted to deal with all kinds of tasks. I could scarcely expect that they would grasp the purpose of my sledge trip. For this reason and also partly to arouse their curiosity and hunting lust, I pretended that my trip was to be a muskox hunt, at a location lying 10 days' travel from Polaris House. They had seen several skulls of that animal on board the wreck, and they were eager to acquire some hides.

On the day before I was to set off, Jimmy suddenly took it into his head to go to Etah to fetch moss for his spouse's lamp. It would have been totally impossible to dissuade him from this purpose. But he promised to return in the evening. Since he wanted to visit Chester, who in the meantime had sent a reindeer and two hares, on his way back, I gave him a letter to take to the latter. I called upon him to send the bearer of the letter to the house as quickly as possible, under the pretext of carrying some urgent news.

The evening came, and then the following morning, but not Jimmy. To shorten the period of his journey, I had let him have my 10 dogs and had told him not to spare the animals. Now the dogs were gone, as well as the driver. Just as I was about to send another native after him, he drove up. He had not delivered the letter to Chester—as the latter informed me—until 6.00 a.m. Instead of breakfast Chester then gave him hell and sent him on his way, and told him I would give him his breakfast. This had its effect. His empty stomach spurred him to hurry; but when I now looked around for my second companion, he had vanished. Believing that Jimmy would not return before the following morning, he had gone out to hunt seals.

The 12th of April was a lost day, in terms of travelling; we were not able to set off until early on the 13th. The equipment for our journey was simple in the extreme. Only the two sledges, pulled by eight and 10 dogs respectively, were faultless; I would gladly have exchanged the rest of my equipment for better items. For my companion and me, the rations were calculated for 6 weeks, but for the dogs for a month. Otherwise we were counting on hunting and on the provisions at Polaris Bay. Our provisions consisted mainly of salt pork and hardtack,[8] as well as some canned meat, 30 lbs. of oatmeal and 20 lbs. of peas. For reasons of economy, the latter were cooked before we started, mixed with chopped bear meat and pork, and then allowed to freeze and sawed into cubes. As dog food we took walrus hide, and seal blubber as fuel to cook our food. Our supply of coffee had been exhausted months earlier, but the tea was so wretchedly bad that I preferred not to take any at all. Instead I provided myself with citric acid crystals, which, dissolved in hot water with brown syrup, produced a revolting lemonade that served as an antiscorbutic morning drink.

The only fairly serious problem to which I was exposing myself on this trip was that of being cut off from Polaris House by a premature break-up of the ice. At the end of March, I had handed Chester a letter to the sailing master, Budington, which contained a detailed explanation of my plans. I called upon the latter to take advantage of the first favourable opportunity to start for home with the crew, to take my sealed papers with him, but to leave Chester behind. The latter had made the generous proposal that he would wait for me. He wanted to build a small boat, sufficiently large for the two of us, in order to reach one of the Danish settlements in it. I conveyed all this to Budington. As soon as the ice opened, Chester was to give him my letter.

Thus we cheerfully left the house at 10.00 a.m.[9] A flat calm prevailed. The sky was overcast, and the temperature fluctuated between −19° and −20°C. Following a beaten sledge track produced by the natives on their various hunting trips, we travelled in a gentle arc to Cape Hatherton. The going was tolerably good. Then we set a course that was close to due north. After we had passed Cairn Point, a light breeze arose that began increasingly to freshen the farther we went. Finally a gale-force wind was blowing in our teeth. Jimmy and Avatok didn't like this much; they began eloquently to praise the great advantages of Polaris House, where they received food without having to work for it, and earnestly pleaded with me to pitch the tent. But for the moment there could be no thought of this, for we had covered barely 12 miles from the hut, and I had resolved to cover the entire distance to Polaris Bay in forced marches. I sweet-talked them into travelling on. But later, when we reached a half-collapsed snow house that Nanuki had built a few weeks earlier, my exhortation ceased to have any effect. Hence we had to make camp here. In 5 hours of travelling we had covered about 20 miles, a day's work on which I could not look back with any satisfaction.

While my companions were repairing the snow house, I climbed a high iceberg to examine our route. A tolerably level ice foot stretched north along the steep coast; I intended continuing our journey along it after a short rest. A row of hummocks, about half a mile in width, separated our snow house from the fast shore ice; the sledges and the loads could easily be hauled across to it.

Around 10.00 p.m. the wind dropped; there was light snow falling, and fog billowed over the coast. I woke the natives. Avatok required some more sleep, as did Jimmy. At 11 o'clock I shook them again, held a pot of hot syrup-water with oatmeal stirred into it under each man's nose and told them to drink and to get ready.

Shortly after midnight the sledges were packed and the dogs fed and harnessed. But my companions did not want to take the route via the ice foot as I intended, preferring to travel by the sea ice this side of the hummocks. I agreed, for basically it was of little significance whether I followed the coast now or later. If I wanted to direct these two men at all, who had to be treated like spoiled children, it was necessary to yield to them in insignificant matters. It certainly wouldn't do to use force; I had to see my orders more as suggestions. It was bad enough that I had to rely on these Eskimos for my purposes. But there was not a single good dog driver among our entire crew, and moreover I could not have called upon any of the seamen to accompany me under the prevailing circumstances. For even under the most favourable case, the provisions I could offer were far from good, and a European needs warm clothing, which I could not have provided.

We pushed on in a northeasterly direction through a thick snowstorm. Now little could be seen of the coast; apart from a few mountain tops everything was hidden in fog. At 9.00 a.m. on the 14th the snow stopped; the air became clearer, and we could get a better overview of the route we had started on. This generally led over hummocks and rarely over level ice. Whenever we reached the rugged barriers, sloth got the upper hand over my companions. Then I had to encourage them with sweet talk, and when this had no effect, I gave them a spoonful of frozen syrup, which they liked passionately. Admittedly this was a somewhat strange discipline, but conditions required it. While I otherwise would have resorted to some strong curses, now I had to have recourse to persuasion.

But given the prevailing blizzard even this was pointless, as I was now to learn. At noon a southwesterly wind arose, and by 1 o'clock it had developed into a sharp wind, accompanied by storm-like gusts which whirled the snow up in dense clouds. Although we had the storm at our backs, the natives still wanted to make camp. Avatok had been whining to me for half an hour as to how much he was freezing. Hence I had to decide to make a halt.

We dug a cave in a high snowbank, covering its roof, formed by the two sledges and the light hunting tent, with snow. Two lances served as supports. Of the 14 hours that we had been on the way, the natives had spent about 2 hours hunting. They had stopped at almost every seal hole that we had passed, until Avatok finally succeeded in harpooning a seal about 5 feet long. While I prepared our meal, the other two skinned the seal. In the floor of the cave, they made a shallow hollow which they lined with the sealskin, with its hair side turned down. On it they dismembered the carcass, scooped the blood with both hands into the raw trough and mixed it with the pounded brains. After we had eaten, Jimmy asked for my kettle in order to cook for Avatok and himself. He filled the vessel with snow, and once he had melted enough of it, he cut a piece of blubber into small cubes, which he chewed into a mush and spat into the pan. To the boiling liquid he then added a handful of the blood, which had frozen in the meantime, and threw in large chunks of meat until the pan was full to overflowing. In less than half an hour, this first round of about 6 lbs. had been consumed; a second one followed quickly. This too was devoured, and my companions could not understand why I refused their invitation to participate in their meal.

A violent blizzard was raging over our heads. Only when our excavation was half buried did the temperature in it start to rise; previously the minimal heat that the lamp gave off was whisked away by the wind. At midnight, when I wanted to continue our trip, the wind reached its maximum strength. Until 6 o'clock on the morning of the 15th, I had to lie still and wait patiently. In order to leave our cave we were obliged to start shovelling; during the night one of the dogs had broken loose and had devoured a piece of the walrus hide.

Now we could see the coast clearly for the first time. The snowbank in which we had spent the night was about 5 miles from it; Cape Leiper, the northern headland of Rensselaer Harbour, bore east. Pressure ridges stretched northward, as far as the eye could see. Hence I chose a northwesterly course; but even here the going was extremely bad. Old floes, jammed tightly between the upthrust ice masses, represented the only passable routes. Often we first had to move one of the sledges forward by our combined strength, and then bring the other one up; in this the dogs were more a hindrance than a help. Covering the first half mile demanded considerable effort. My companions were despairing; they suggested that it was easier to shoot seals than muskoxen and wanted to turn back. During our last rest stop I had spread some pieces of hardtack with syrup; whenever we reached a difficult stretch, I would hand them some of this bread-and-syrup. This helped. In addition I gave Avatok a knife, and I promised Jimmy that if he really persevered, I would make him a gift of my rifle when we got back to the house. After 5 hours of heavy work, we had overcome the horrible pressure ice. A level ice surface stretched ahead of us; we changed course and headed north. The sea here had frozen only very recently; the ice was as smooth as a mirror and so thin in many places that we had to travel warily. Whenever we approached a seal's breathing hole, the natives would stop and walk carefully up to it, to investigate it. Yet we still made rapid progress since the going was good and remained so until we had covered about 12 miles on our northerly course.

It was totally impossible to advance any farther in a northerly direction; we swung wearily westward through a chaos of less rugged ice hummocks, combined with numerous icebergs. Six hours passed in strenuous work, but then I had the satisfaction of seeing the route north clear.

We pitched the tent at 8.00 p.m. on a mirror-smooth ice surface. A wave-washed hummock sheltered us from the north wind that had sprung up shortly after we had pitched camp. Around midnight it strengthened to a gale and brought the snow that the southwest wind had previously swept north, back again with interest. Around 2.00 a.m. on the 16th, I was wakened by a rattling noise that differed clearly from the roar of the wind. Soon afterward I thought I felt a slight movement in the ice. I woke the natives, and they noticed the same thing. We rushed outside. Through the driving veils of snow we spotted a dark patch close beside the tent. The wind had played a nasty trick on us and had shattered the ice cover. We quickly packed up our belongings, harnessed the dogs and fled southward, and resumed our interrupted night's rest among the hummocks. It was blowing too hard for us to be able to pitch the tent. We therefore leaned the sledges against the vertical face of an iceberg, spread the tent over them, lashed it securely and weighed it down with chunks of ice and, overcome with fatigue, fell into a deep sleep.

By 4 o'clock the gale, which reached a speed of 30 miles per hour at Polaris House, had almost died; an hour later it was calm. I therefore lit a fire, cooked oatmeal for breakfast and woke the natives. They complained about my importunity and wanted to sleep longer. A 2 lb. can of veal that I gave them made them so willing that by 7 o'clock both sledges were packed, and we were able to set off.

We travelled across the shining cover of young ice to the crack that had formed during the night and which had now frozen over again. Until 11.30 we were able to travel on unhindered in a northerly direction. Then we again ran into hummocks, which stretched across the Sound in closely ranked rows. We took a short rest to have a bite. A noon sun altitude gave a latitude of 79°16.5'. After I had completed this observation, we continued our journey across the young ice, following the strike of the pressure ridges. Over the course of the next two hours, we covered about 18 miles.

When the west coast now came in sight, my heart beat faster. I intended to head for the shore ice and then push onward on the ice foot. Under favourable conditions I might reach Polaris Bay in a further 5 days. The dogs stepped out so smartly that we were rapidly approaching our goal. At 4 o'clock in the afternoon we were about 6 miles east of Bache Island,[10] off the entrance to Hayes Sound. A chaotic row of hummocks stretched from here to the coast. My companions again refused to go farther. By presenting Jimmy with a saw and Avatok with an axe, I succeeded in making them more cooperative. From now on they were happy to follow me without grumbling. But as soon as we were among the hummocks and had to lift and push the sledges laboriously, they seemed to regret their promise. The prospect of an impending muskox hunt had lost all appeal; they even wanted to give back the gifts I had made them.

In a whining voice Jimmy said: "It is impossible for us to travel across this rough ice; if you insist on continuing your trip to the north, you may do so without me, since I shall return to my wife. The dogs are your property," he continued, "and your companions gave me the wood for my sledge; but I will hand the sledge over to you; you can push on with it unhindered."

Avatok wanted to give me the pleasure of his company somewhat longer, if only I turned south. He hoped to find a life partner among the Eskimo bands who inhabit the coast south of Cape Isabella. I should now follow him there.

I still had one expedient: the observatory that we had left filled with provisions, clothing, weapons and ammunition at Polaris Bay. Hence I promised the two men that I would make them and their band richer than ever before. I told them that in 4–5 days, we would reach a place where a house stood, filled with all sorts of valuable items. It, and its entire contents, would become their property if they accompanied me there.

They consulted for a few moments, but their decision to turn back held fast. All enticements were in vain. I asked them to consider my proposal once again, but they stood by their refusal.

I then told them that I was prepared to turn back with them, but that we would not sleep until we reached Polaris House. Only in this way could I force them to hurry, and I needed to hurry since I intended making a new sortie. They agreed; but before we started back, they demanded that we stop for a brief rest.

In order to strengthen the dogs for the impending forced march, we fed them generously with seal meat and walrus hide; then we stretched out in the open on the loaded sledges and slept for about 90 minutes. At 6.00 p.m. we were ready to start. We travelled south along the coast, about 8–10 miles offshore. We made rapid progress on the new ice; the going was generally as level as a parquet floor. We frequently came across extensive polynyas, over which hung dark banks of fog. It was my intention to follow the coast until we were opposite Polaris House and then to cross Smith Sound at its narrowest point. But the open water thwarted the execution of this plan.

Shortly before 6 o'clock on the morning of the 17th, we took our first rest, which lasted 15 minutes. We ate some bacon and biscuit; there was not time to prepare a meal. Before we'd started on the return trip, I had filled a rubber 1 L bottle with meltwater and kept it in my bosom. We now drank from this meagre supply for the first time; it had to last until we reached the house.

Despite his promise to cover the route to the house in a forced march, shortly after we had set off, Avatok tried to persuade me to pitch camp. Circumstances did not allow me to comply with his wish. I told him that he could certainly stay behind but that Jimmy and I would continue our journey. At the same time I offered him two rations of bread and bacon since we had thrown the seal that he had killed to the dogs.

But he refused to abandon his demand, and when I positively asserted that I could not agree to this, he tried to make the loyal Jimmy desert, and finally became aggressive.

Driven to the extreme, I levelled my rifle and stated that I would shoot him if he would not yield to my demands. He made a leap toward the sledge to grab his harpoon, but I blocked his route and aimed at him until he promised to obey me. My firm behaviour made him seem like a different person, since from then on he was obliging and polite.[11]

When we were about 15 miles from Baird Inlet, we headed east; but we were unable to reach the Greenland coast in this direction since open water that extended as far as Force Bay forced us to detour. We had to swing north until we managed to circumvent it. On reaching Cape Inglefield, I buried the greater part of my travelling equipment near a high iceberg; with the lightened sledges we then made rapid progress.

Now, for the first time this year, we saw half the sun above the horizon at midnight. Almost lustreless and badly distorted by refraction, the deep red disc glowed only dimly through the billowing frost smoke that rose before us.

We reached the hut at 2 o'clock on the morning of 18 April. Noah Hayes, who had been looking after some of the meteorological readings during my absence, came to meet us, astonished. The rest were sleeping.

We too were urgently in need of rest. Our last march, discounting the short rest stops that were indispensable, had lasted 32 hours; but during the past 45 hours we had slept for only 2 hours. The dogs were worn out; some had critically injured paws; I myself was suffering from snow blindness.

Jimmy was prepared to accompany me again; but I could not persuade any of the other natives sojourning near Polaris House to follow me. Avatok, who now played the role of the martyr with great skill and natural charm, told everyone of my assassination attempt and declared me to be an extremely dangerous fellow.

If I wanted to reach my goal quickly, there was only one solution. I would have to make a further forced march to Sorfalik, the small Eskimo settlement that lay about 40 miles from the hut; for I needed not only a companion, but I also had to procure dog food.

I began this journey in the early morning of the 19th. A native had let me have his dogs in return for a trifle; I could not overwork my own animals, which had not completely recovered yet. The good Jimmy, whose confidence in me was still unshakable, drove my sledge. We headed south along the coast, keeping Littleton Island on our right.

The reddish gneisses and brown syenites which form this island and the area round Polaris House disappear somewhat south of the island. In their place an overlying sandstone appears, which probably does not exceed 1,500 feet in thickness. In many places it assumes the character of a distinct beach formation with an undulating surface and scattered embedded cobbles of blinding white quartz that occasionally attain the size of a walnut. This sandstone, whose age cannot be determined for the moment, is here and there cut by bands of trap rock and basalt; as a result the coast has acquired an extremely picturesque appearance.

Near Port Foulke our team spotted a fox. We cut off its route to the coast, loosed one of the dogs after him, and raced after him with the sledge in a wild chase. The dogs behaved as if they were mad. They charged at the high hummocks and roared down the other side so that we became worried about the safety of the sledge and that of our own bones. When the lead dog finally caught the fox and seized it by the neck, the others fell on it. The chase ended with a free-for-all of such violence that Jimmy's whip was totally useless and I had to lay into it with the butt of my gun to help him bring the raging pack to its senses. On this occasion I burst the rubber bag of meltwater that I carried on my chest; as a result about a litre of cold liquid found its way into my stockings and boots, and chilled me thoroughly for the rest of the trip.

At low tide we climbed onto the ice foot at Cape Alexander since open water stretched almost to the southern cliff of that headland, which presents an imposing massif about 1,500 feet high. It consists of a dirty yellow sandstone, cut by dark basalt bands, whose columnar structure stands out sharply from the horizontal strata of the sedimentary formation.

The width of the ice foot varied. Depending on the water depth it fluctuated between a ledge barely wide enough for one's foot and a route about eight paces in width. A few miles north of Radcliff Point, we reached overhanging sandstone cliffs against whose faces the waves were breaking. Jimmy immediately knew what to do. He travelled back a short distance and then turned off into a narrow gorge which brought us past the worst spots. Frost and streams had powerfully shattered and eroded the bedrock; here and there strangely shaped stone men rose above the talus-covered ground.

When we reached the small settlement, its inhabitants came to meet us, shouting. They welcomed us rousingly and asked for all sorts of gifts. Avatok, my old friend [the shaman], invited me to rest in his hut. Before I followed him I entrusted Jimmy with negotiating for someone to accompany us; provisionally the payment would consist of a long snow knife from Chester's factory.

But such filth prevailed in Avatok's hut that I escaped as fast as possible to look for better accommodations and to dry my clothes. An elderly little mother, who occupied a spacious snow house in common with two families, received me hospitably. When I told her what I needed, she immediately busied herself to remove my wet moccasins and stockings, to wring them out and to hang them up on a small framework over the lamp. Then she rubbed my cold feet with both hands and in so doing looked at me so solicitously that I felt really grateful. She cleared the best spot for me on the sleeping platform right next to the lamp and invited me to make myself comfortable. But this was more easily said than done, for with the exception of my fur jacket I had nothing dry on my body. When she saw this, she wanted to lend me the only pair of pants she could call her own. But I could not put her kindness to an even more severe test, and declined her offer. My friend Avatok helped me out of this embarrassment and lent me his pants while my own were hung up to dry. I improvised stockings from two strips that I cut from my blanket, since I wanted to expedite the negotiations that Jimmy had started.

I had scarcely crawled outside when a violent uproar developed nearby. Two of the natives came running up breathlessly, shouting "Auvik, Auvik," and grabbed their lances. Avatok, pantless, suddenly appeared at my side and impetuously demanded his pants. He wanted to help the others kill the walrus that had appeared out there at the open water. But, repaying his kindness poorly, I grabbed my gun and ran off with the crowd.

On reaching the spot I was witness to an exciting scene. Six natives were engaged with two walruses (Figure 39). One of them lay already half skinned on the ice; the other, whose blood was reddening the sea, had just been harpooned. It was a violent, almost desperate struggle. A harpoon was embedded in the animal's left side, its line held tight by two hunters, while a third was trying to plant a further weapon in the neck of the tormented beast. The hunters were sprayed all over with blood.

A few thrusts with the lance, a dull roar of rage—a suppressed rattling snorting—then a loud shout of joy, and the animal was dead and was hauled onto the ice. The work of butchering it began immediately.

In return for a trifle, they let me have both hides for dog food; but it was more difficult to obtain a driver. Finally I succeeded in this too. Ivnarssuk, one of the first people we had come to know, agreed to accompany me for an unspecified time, at least 40 days. He was a good-natured, athletic fellow, called Sharky by the men; for he possessed a mouth of such a size that one might have shoved the cartridge for a 60-pounder easily into it.

Next morning, as I was wanting to depart, I encountered unexpected difficulties. Mrs. Shark did not want her spouse to go and was crying like a child. Sharky ordered her to go away, in a rough voice. But instead of this the excited wife rushed at me and implored me not to take away the head of her household. Then her tears touched the Shark himself, and he appeared to be giving way to gloomy thoughts. To prevent him making the wrong decision, I offered his contrite spouse a string of beads. She rejected this gift angrily. But their faces brightened, and I noticed that she was not unsusceptible. Hence I pointed to my sledge and told her to select anything from among my belongings. She smiled sadly and asked for my chronometer which I was carrying in my pocket. I shook my head and said no. A silver fork, as well as the ruptured rubber bottle, whose contents had soaked me so thoroughly, now found favour in her eyes and offered her the necessary consolation. Both the Shark and his spouse were now happy, and we headed off quickly.

Just before Sutherland Island, an insignificant sandstone mass about 200 feet high, the ice had broken up. The open water cut off our route back. Hence we again turned southward, travelled with the sledges through a narrow ravine and then climbed up to the glacier plateau of

Fig. 39. A walrus hunt.

Cape Alexander. On the crevasse-free blue ice of the glacier, we struck northward. I estimated the altitude of our route at 1,500 feet; but to my regret I had to do without a direct measurement since I had no instruments. At Port Foulke we headed down via steep slopes, whereby the dogs often had to run backward behind the sledge, since the descent was extremely steep.

Immediately after we reached Polaris House, Sharky's sledge, which was somewhat dilapidated, was strengthened and improved. Various modifications to our equipment delayed us for a further day, but early on the morning of 22 April, we got under way.

We travelled north following our old sledge tracks. This time I wanted to turn east between Cairn Point and Cape Inglefield and to get onto the ice foot at the first favourable opportunity, and intended following it as far as the southern ice cliff of the Humboldt Glacier. The belt of pressure ice that bordered the coast was narrowest at Cape Inglefield. I now chose this spot, in order to reach Force Bay next. Immediately we were engaged in hauling the heavily laden sledges over the ridges of shattered ice. Our progress was slow, but we overcame one obstacle after another.

In view of the variety of uphill and downhill travelling we would be doing, in loading the sledges I had taken care not to locate the centre of gravity at the centre as occurs under normal circumstances, but farther back. Hence when we now travelled down a steep slope, the danger of smashing the sledge was considerably reduced. We had just overcome a bad spot when the horrible Sharky made an awkward turn and his sledge and dogs dropped about 15 feet. The animals howled, the driver was rubbing his back, and the right runner of the sledge was irreparably broken.[12] In an attempt to repair it, I broke my dagger, which I was using as a drill. I cursed the Shark and the entire clan of selachians,[13] since there was only one solution to this mess. We had to head back home quickly and make a new sledge runner. The distance involved was about 20 miles. If everything went according to plan, we could be back there in 8 hours.

We quickly stowed the load in a snow hollow between two hummocks; harnessed all 21 dogs to the undamaged sledge, on which we lashed the damaged one; and once we had reached the level ice, raced home at a wild gallop, arriving there at 4.00 p.m.

Chester and the carpenter were immediately prepared to help us. The sledge was in working order again within an hour. To my great irritation the Shark now refused to go back with me. He wanted to give me back the snow knife, and I was to release him.

All persuasion was in vain especially since Avatok declared the area to be unsafe and told everyone of my attack on him. Jimmy also now became disloyal; he alleged that he was not up to the heavy work among the hummocks.

After living and working like a galley slave, under constant stress, I was now no further ahead than before and had lost valuable time. Not a very encouraging thought!

Next morning I sent Jimmy to Cape Inglefield to fetch my belongings. He was to bring the 3 centners of dog food only as far as Cape Hatherton and bury it there.

My resources were almost exhausted; but one last resort was still open to me. Among the greatly reduced crew there was only one man who had some experience at driving dogs. This was the seaman Heinrich,[14] who now filled the position of cook. Hence I informed Budington of my plans and requested of him that he let me have Heinrich. In view of the peculiar conditions and the meagreness of my means, I promised the latter a bonus of $100 for reaching the latitude of Polaris Bay and a further $200 for attaining the latitude of 82°45'N.

The matter was settled. We intended setting off on the following morning. Our personal equipment was limited in the extreme, since I wanted to take the undiminished supply of dog food with me.

But during the night, without any external cause, the ice began to move and the waves carried off the walrus hides that Jimmy had brought to Cape Hatherton. It was a bitter disappointment.

There was now no alternative but to send Jimmy to Sorfalik to acquire further dog food. Accompanied by another native who had been our guest for the past few days, he immediately set off. The open water forced the two men to travel over the Cape Alexander Glacier. Hence they could not bring back heavy loads. In order to enable Jimmy to hire several sledges to transport the dog food, Budington had given him some harpoon irons.

On the 26th there was a gale out of the northwest. The ice in the sound was drifting constantly southward, and the open water extended from Littleton Island to the southwest point of our headland. During the following days, too, the wind blew with devastating force.

It was not until the 28th that the storm subsided; but in the meantime the water had increased so considerably in extent that it was lapping the cliffs of Cape Hatherton; the belt of ice bordering the coast was at most only 300 paces wide. Around noon Sharky drove me to that headland. Wide cracks in the ice forced us to detour; we had to stick close in to the land, and occasionally had even to drive across the rocky beach. Off the cape the ice foot was scarcely 3 feet wide. In order to move the sledge ahead, we turned it on its side and soon afterward found a route upward. From a height of 800 feet, a good view over the sound was offered: to the northeast the ice lay solid, but to the north, west and south the sea was open.

In the evening Jimmy returned home. He had not been able to obtain any dog food. The failure of his mission, the rapid break-up of the ice and the advanced season now made the execution of my plan impossible.

By contrast, preparations for our homeward journey were now pursued with all diligence. Chester had started building both boats on the 19th and was making rapid progress. His resources were limited, even wretched; often the most essential items were lacking, but he was never at a loss for advice.

After the day's work was finished, the men usually went out to hunt small game. Hares appeared in large numbers, but the animals were wary, and anyone who did not have enough patience to lie in wait for them generally came home empty-handed.

In the Far North, once the sun is constantly above the horizon, this sort of hunting demands endless perseverance; for then the animals no longer go to feed at specific times of the day and moreover change their routes with inconsiderate persistence. But they are such graceful creatures that one can easily overlook this bad habit.

During a short stay in Foulke Fiord, I had occasion to watch a group of 15 animals for almost a whole day. The old lateral moraine of a glacier, sparsely covered with lichens and mosses, was their playground; further down was a luxuriant growth of saxifrage species and arctic willows. It was mating time, and the animals were extremely restless. Whenever I looked around, I could see one or several of them running awkwardly down the slope to feed. Sometimes they would crouch down to sleep for a few minutes; sometimes they would chase each other.

Suddenly I heard the hoarse barking of a fox, and soon afterward the predator appeared amidst the harmless group. They scattered. Only one old infatuated hare, which had distinguished itself from all the others by its wild upright posturing and leaps, found its retreat route cut off and began to complain loudly. I grabbed my gun, aiming to kill the disrupter of the peace; but it was a long shot and I missed. Both the fox and the hare disappeared, and the animals did not return.

During the first few days of May, a female hare was shot that was carrying seven young that were barely half grown. Whether the female hare gives birth once or several times, I was unable to learn from the natives. Given the large number of young, one can probably assume that this does not happen more often than twice; for our common hare, which has three or four litters in the course of a year, never produces more than three young in the first litter.

For High Arctic conditions there was a lot of snow in May. During the entire month we recorded 117 hours with snow; the amount of water this produced, as water equivalent, was 0.374 inches. The natives informed us that it snows heavily every year at the time of arrival of the glaucous gulls. The first of these birds arrived on 9 May; occasional dovekies had appeared on 5 March.

On the morning of 13 May, Bryan travelled to Rensselaer Harbour[15] to establish the difference in longitude between that location and Polaris House on the basis of determinations of the time at each. Jimmy accompanied him as dog driver. On reaching Cape Hatherton they climbed up onto the ice foot and followed it as far as Cairn Point. But then they selected a route across the fast ice and reached the coast at 11.30 at Anoetok. From here on they again had to continue their trip along the ice foot, although there the snowdrifts, softened by the sun's heat, were difficult to wade through.

After a strenuous journey which took almost 16 hours, they reached their destination at 10.00 p.m. On the shore, to the west of the small island where Kane's observatory had stood, they built a snow house in which they spent the night.

Unfortunately the sky was heavily overcast during the 14th; and since it had still not cleared by noon next day, Bryan sent his companion home with a letter to Budington, since the agreed period for the trip had elapsed. He himself stayed behind with one of the dogs, to wait for the sun to appear. It showed itself between 4 and 5 o'clock that same day. He then measured some angles to determine the time and started on his return trip at 7.30 in the evening.

A hike lasting 20 hours brought him to the hut at Anoetok, where he rested for 2 hours. Reinvigorated, he then continued his lonely trek. While attempting to leap across a crack in the ice, he jumped short and fell up to his armpits in the water. Fortunately it was calm. He wrung his clothes out and again shouldered his gun and the case with the instruments.

Along the way he found a large chunk of seal meat, left behind by one of the natives.[16] A fight then ensued between man and dog, for they were both hungry and each looked upon the find as his own property. But Bryan was the winner; after he had his fill of the foul-smelling meat, he left the rest for his four-legged companion.

Shortly after 2 o'clock on the morning of the 17th, he reached Polaris House and had to endure all the agonies of snow blindness. But he had accomplished a minor feat, having covered a distance of 60 miles.

The sun's rays were now strong enough to melt the ice between the rocks in sheltered spots. Small rivulets snaked across the lowlands and loosened the snowdrifts. On the 16th the temperature had risen above freezing point for the first time.

Since I intended measuring the valley of the Brother John Glacier and getting a glimpse of the ice sheet, on 24 May I had Jimmy drive me to Foulke Fiord, at the head of which that glacier reaches sea level, but without itself reaching the water.

Due to the advanced season we had to take a route overland. We drove about 2 miles north, then struck east and via a gorge reached the plateau, whose mean elevation averages 1,200 feet. It was a difficult route, since the ground was largely totally free of snow. As a result I was presented with my much-desired opportunity of studying the impact of the ice sheet, which had retreated over the course of time.

Everywhere that the rock was visible, traces of the effect of the glacier were revealed—in places as glacier polish and whalebacks, in places as rock debris that represents the remains of ground moraine.

On the north shore of Foulke Fiord, near its entrance we headed downhill. The snow-free slopes, often covered with moss cushions and saturated with snowmelt, were extremely steep so that Jimmy needed all his skills to handle the dogs. This route, the only one leading here from the north, is travelled by the natives only when it is totally impossible to travel along the sea ice.

The cover of one-year ice on the fiord seamed with small leads here and there, spread before us as a level surface; a low row of hummocks extended from Jensen Point to Radcliff Island. Along the precipitous coast, too, the ice was heaved up into irregular ridges.

The fiord, whose maximum width is barely 3 miles, is about 6 miles long; its walls reach a height of 2,500 feet. The gneisses that we have mentioned several times outcrop here only in a few places; the sandstone overlying them, with its bands of basalt and trap rock, is involved almost exclusively in the formation of the cliffs.

A short journey brought us to Lake Alida, a small basin that is partially separated from the waters of the fiord by a quite low frontal moraine that has been left behind by the Brother John Glacier during its retreat. Over the course of time the waves have eroded through the dam in its centre so that the lake connects with the sea. Hence its water is salty.

By twice pacing the distance I determined that the front of the Brother John Glacier lay 2,409 feet from the eastern arm of Lake Alida. In a similar fashion I later established the width of the strongly convex glacier snout to be 3,120 feet.

On the left side of the glacier we unloaded the sledge, and laden with the instruments and other items, we climbed up a gully which rose at a steep angle between the side cliff of the glacier and its bed. At a height of 180 feet we suddenly found our route blocked; here the glacier butted directly against the red sandstone rocks and dropped vertically. Once we had chopped some steps, we were able to reach the surface of the glacier via one of the side-crevasses; we hauled the baggage up with a rope.

With the exception of the lateral crevasses, the ice was almost crevasse-free, with only a scanty snow cover and fairly rough. Ogive lines could be distinguished only vaguely. Judging by the steepness of our ascent, the glacier appeared to be flowing over a very steep drop, but despite this it had broken up only slightly. Even higher up where a small sandstone outcrop projected above the ice, where the glacier split and the two arms then rejoined, the line of demarcation between the two was only vague and was indicated only by a weak and almost smooth depression. But on the west side of the outcrop, a narrow crevasse had formed, its edges bristling with fantastically shaped needles.

I reached my station somewhat above this gorge. Jimmy had agreed only to get me onto the glacier; once this had happened he wanted to turn back. I did not attempt to persuade him to stay with me, and he left.

Given my lack of suitable instruments, in order to measure the glacier's rate of movement, I had to adopt a somewhat unusual method. Namely I used a large camera, equipped with a 5-inch lens, with a 19-inch focal length. I replaced the opaque plate by an ordinary glass plate to the back of which oiled tissue paper was stuck.

The camera was set up on a tripod on the left side of the glacier. I set up two rows of thin wooden laths right across the glacier and at right angles to its direction of movement, their narrow surfaces facing the camera lens. There were five laths in each row. For the sake of clarity, the laths in one row may here be identified as A, A_1, A_2 ... A_5, those in the second row as B, B1, B_2 ... B_5. The distances between A and B, A_1 and B_1, etc., were determined accurately by two-fold measurements.

Once the camera was adjusted, the images of the laths which were projected on the oiled paper in the camera as lines of varying thicknesses were fixed by means of a fine needle point under a 10-fold magnification.

Thirty hours later this process was repeated. In the meantime the images had moved, since the laths stuck into the surface of the glacier had followed the movement of the glacier. Using a pair of hair compasses and the magnifying glass I had used earlier, I measured the distances between laths A and B, and A_1 and B_1 on the first image and between the same laths on the second image. And using the scale of a field barometer, whose divisions allowed readings to within 0.002 inches, I converted these into absolute measurements. Since the distances of the

Fig. 40. Measuring glacier flow on Brother John Glacier.

laths in the first row from those in the second row were known, the rate of movement of the glacier could be determined by a simple calculation.

The mean from all the laths revealed an advance of 8.6 inches in 30 hours. However this result applies only to the left side of the glacier.

Undoubtedly it would have been better to select equivalent points on both sides for the insertion of the laths. But I had to forego this since this would have required changing the position of the camera, which would not have been possible without running the risk of losing the original azimuth of the camera.

Unfortunately I was denied the possibility of measuring the advance of the centre of the glacier, since the considerable distance from the camera to the laths would have introduced an excessively large probable error.

Once the first image had been fixed, I made camp for the night. My entire personal equipment consisted of a rubber sheet, some canned meat, hardtack and tobacco. I had not taken a cooking apparatus to avoid increasing the weight of my pack unnecessarily. Hence, apart from tobacco smoke, I could not enjoy anything warm. However, this smoke emanated from the terrible chewing tobacco which the colonial administrators at the Spanish settlements sell to the natives by the ell. Before we had left Christianized Greenland, we had taken aboard a cask of this tobacco. When we were shipwrecked, it was saved, guarded like a treasure and later washed out with hot water in order to remove the admixed syrup.

I slept for several hours beneath my rubber sheet, which served as a tent; at 2.00 a.m. on the 25th I got ready for the road, planning to hike inland up the glacier. My instruments were limited to a mercury barometer, a small aneroid, a prismatic compass, a clinometer and a pocket psychrometer. A rucksack contained a military pistol with six shells, 2,000 feet of thin silk cord, and a pair of binoculars, as well as a few pounds of meat. An axe and an alpenstock completed my equipment.

Between the sandstone massif mentioned earlier and the Dodge Mountains, I crossed the glacier in a northeasterly direction, and then swung east. The recent storms had swept the ice clear and had piled the snow in deep accumulations beneath the mountain faces. After I had covered about 5 miles on the smooth, gently rising plain, the ice became hummocky, but not at all broken up. Nowhere was there the slightest trace of a moraine to be seen, and the eastern horizon was exclusively limited by ice, above which not a single mountain spire rose. At a height of 1,100 feet above sea level, about 8 miles from my station, the rugosities disappeared, and only here and there was the ice covered by insignificant patches of snow that bore the mark of the wind. The first crevasses occurred here, narrow cracks with sharp edges, running predominantly from north-northeast to south-southwest. Somewhat higher up and more toward the interior, they became more common and wider, and forced me to make unpleasant detours. When I sounded one of these chasms, the small lead bullet fastened to the end of the string encountered resistance at a depth of 42½ fathoms, and I was unable to obtain any deeper depth. On both sides, both the lines of stratification and veining were clearly developed, but the characteristic bands of dirt were lacking. To examine the interior of the crevasse better, I lay down flat at one of its rims and threw my handkerchief into the depths, having first rubbed it in powder and ignited it. It fell barely 30 feet before it became hung up on a projecting ledge, and the strong draft extinguished the flame. Beyond the crevasse-seamed belt, which was at most half a mile wide, the ice became more level than previously. The snow cover was variable, but it was never deeper than 5–6 inches and occurred in isolated patches. At a height of 3,181 feet above sea level, about 27 miles from my station, I encountered the lower boundary of the firn zone; the ice became cut by numerous crevasses, but without being chaotically broken. I made another sounding in one of these crevasses which was somewhat more than 5 feet wide; this revealed a depth of 95 fathoms. Since I was alone, I felt obliged to turn back here. After an almost continuous march of 29 hours, at 7 o'clock on the morning of the 26th, I again reached the spot where I had set up the camera. After a short rest I repeated my measurements and then went to sleep.

At 4 o'clock in the afternoon I packed up my effects and descended into the valley. I left the valuable portable camera behind on the glacier; it had fulfilled its purpose and no longer was of any importance to us, since we were soon to start on our homeward journey. On reaching the marginal crevasses where we had chopped the steps, in trying to climb down, I slipped; I fell and unfortunately smashed the barometer.

In the lonesome fiord, where until now the silence of the grave had prevailed and where at most only the hoarse bark of an arctic fox had been heard, it had become quite lively in the meantime. The dovekies had arrived, the smallest and most elegant of all the arctic seabirds. Thousands of these creatures had occupied the cliffs and filled the air like dense swarms of locusts. Their calls were deafening. They streamed to and fro, flying out to the polynyas to fish and returning to the cliffs where they settled noisily, and then they whirred off again as fast as an arrow toward the open water. It was endlessly exciting to watch their cheerful activity. They appeared as a harbinger of the short summer, the summer that was to make an end to our imprisonment. The cliffs were now no longer barren, and the ice-covered sea had lost its rigid ice cover.

I devoted the morning of the 27th to a more precise study of the structure of the glacier front. Around noon Bryan and my friend Avatok arrived with his dog sledge.[17] Once they had rested for a while, we travelled together to the mouth of the fiord to visit Port Foulke. On reaching the vicinity of this harbour, Avatok refused to accompany us any further. He pointed to a low saddle and indicated that we should cross it to reach the old winter quarters of the Hayes expedition; he himself wanted to stay with the dogs and wait for us to return.

When we reached the small bay, the reason for our companion's strange behaviour immediately became clear. His refusal to follow us to the harbour was now explained. His countrymen had exhumed Sonntag's corpse for the sake of the wooden coffin. The bleached bones of the astronomer, who had died prematurely for science, lay scattered along the desolate beach. We collected the remains, buried them and re-erected over them the overthrown stone slab, in which the dead man's name, age and date of death had been chiselled.

Nothing remained of the Hayes observatory. Apart from the rude gravestone, a few glass shards and splinters of wood, there was nothing to indicate that this spot had once served as the winter harbour of an exploring expedition.

At midnight I parted from Bryan, who was staying behind at Port Foulke to make some time determinations. Avatok was prepared to take me to Polaris House; once I'd arrived there, another sledge was immediately to be despatched to be at Bryan's disposal.

On the north shore of the fiord, where the dovekies nested most densely, we stopped and climbed the cliffs, since my companion wanted to catch a few dozen birds here. Equipped with a net, he took up his post on a ledge and began a cruel war of annihilation against the harmless creatures that whirred confidingly around our heads.

Often three or four birds would be entangled in the meshes of the net. He would take them out cold-bloodedly, cold-bloodedly bite into their skulls, and throw the still-fluttering little birds, their wings crossed, onto a lower ledge on the sandstone cliff.

Fig. 41. Netting dovekies.

Apparently Foulke Fiord is the most northerly point in Smith Sound where these birds nest communally; according to Jimmy they are almost totally absent on the opposite shore, in Ellesmere Land. Extremely elegant and agile, they are barely bigger than a quail. Their plumage is a smoky black in colour; the back and wings are even darker and shiny, while the plumage of the underside, from the breast down, is completely white. The tips of the secondary flight feathers, the edges of the long shoulder feathers, and a small, narrow half-moon above the dark-brown eye are also white. Bill and feet are a brownish-black.[18]

In less than half an hour, Avatok caught around 50 of these birds. Then we set off for home overland, arriving there at 4.00 a.m. Heinrich cooked a bird soup for us—the first warm dish, apart from tobacco smoke, for 4 days!

Seven hours later Bryan returned accompanied by an Eskimo whom Budington had sent to fetch him with a sledge. Favoured by a clear sky, he had successfully carried out his task, although, by mistake, I had kept the mercury trough from the artificial horizon in my pocket, instead of leaving it at Port Foulke.

In the meantime Chester had given the boats their last coat of oil paint, and had also built a small boat of which he made a gift to the faithful Jimmy. In order to complete the boats, it had been necessary to dismantle part of the hut and to remove the boards from the bunks, since there was a dire shortage of wood.

Everyone now worked diligently at his personal equipment for the trip home,[19] since the date of our departure was quickly approaching. On 31 May the meteorological journal was closed; with that our regular scientific activities at Polaris House came to an end.

CHAPTER 21

The start of the ice floe drift

The scene on the ice after the parting. Polaris *appears again under sail and steam. Vain attempts to reach the ship or the coast. Discovery of the old emergency hut and provisions. Life on the floe. Hans is mistaken for a bear. Tough times. Thanksgiving. Christmas. The valuable services of the natives.*

While our preparations for our homeward voyage were approaching completion at Polaris House, the news flew around every civilized country that a small group of shipwrecked people, clad in rags and almost dying of starvation, had reached the capital of Newfoundland.

Through the terrors and torments of a Dante-esque hellish struggle they had survived for weeks and months, drifting on frail ice floes, surrounded by the darkness of an arctic night, battling threefold threats of death: at the mercy of freezing, starving and drowning.

"Pure a noi converrà vincer la punga!" ["It is appropriate that we should win the fight"] [1] was the watchword for them too; but this victory had to be dearly bought, and the time till it was finally won seemed endless.

The situation on the ice appeared worse than on board the wreck on that night when the catastrophe occurred. We had been driven off over the mountainous waves in a sinking ship by the furious storm; the flood of water that poured in through the major leak was increasing by the minute; but we possessed at least some light and could apply the wretched means that seemed to promise our salvation. But the others who had sought refuge on the treacherous ice were enveloped in total darkness.

Dense veils of snow, whirled up by the raging gale, billowed around them in a wild, stormy dance. Barely able to open their eyes or to draw breath, they were scarcely able to step forward or backward on the creaking floe that was now hurled down into the depths of a wave trough, now thrown from wave crest to wave crest, the furious sea raging and foaming all around them.

Gradually the wind dropped; the driving snow abated and the moon's light transitorily illuminated the scene of devastation. Only now could one get a general view of the floe. The ice fragment was roughly circular and might measure four miles in circumference. The crying children, wrapped in skins, lay very close to the water; near them the mothers huddled, wailing and wringing their hands in despair. Other groups appeared scattered here and there. Several dark figures were standing on a detached chunk of ice, barely large enough to find a foothold on, begging the others to help them.

The boats were still intact. Tyson launched the small skiff. Just as he was about to push off, a mountainous wave broke over him. The skiff filled and sank; Tyson barely had time to leap back onto the floe. An attempt with the large whaleboat was more successful; it rescued the cook and two seamen and brought them to join the others. Then both boats[2] were hauled to the middle of the floe, where everyone now lay down. But nobody was able to sleep.

When the dismal day began to dawn on 16 October, they climbed one of the numerous ice pinnacles that littered the floe. Searching eyes swept every sector of the horizon, but not a trace of the ship was to be seen. The emergency hut, the boxes, casks and bales that contained the provisions—all had disappeared. All there was on the floe was some pemmican and hardtack—and 19 hungry people, shivering with cold.

Some leads extended toward the coast. Reaching them was the first task. The floe's position was still unknown.

After everyone had had some food,[3] they hauled the boats in the direction in which the open water appeared. They were able to cover short distances only at the cost of great effort and expenditure of time. When they reached the water, it was 9 o'clock. They had travelled barely a mile when the ice closed up again. The boats had to be hauled onto a floe to prevent them from being crushed.

Nobody had expected that the boat trip would end so quickly; instead of improving, the situation had deteriorated; now they could neither reach the coast nor return to the floe they had left a few hours before.

Large icebergs were drifting along with the current. As they pushed and thrust through the sea ice, the floe on which the 19 people were camped was heaved upward, and when it dropped back down again heavily, the surrounding brash ice yielded. Another slight oscillation and it moved landward, circling as it did so.

Suddenly the ship appeared from behind a headland on the coast. To attract its attention they hoisted the flag and a black rubber sheet. A gentle north wind unfolded both signals. But nobody on board seemed to notice them; the ship calmly followed its set course. Dense clouds of smoke billowed from the black funnel, and sails were set; the vessel now swung to starboard, now to port, then disappeared as suddenly as it had appeared.

Some of the seamen now made an attempt to return to their old floe. Along the way they spotted the ship, which lay with reefed sails, apparently beset, behind an island that some thought was Northumberland Island, others Littleton Island. In their exasperation they thought the ship was refusing to come to their aid and began to grumble and curse.

If they could have suspected how anxiously we were watching for them, without detecting any trace of them, they certainly would have made a second attempt to catch our attention by means of flags or other signals. But their discontent left no room for such thoughts; since they had spotted clouds of smoke, as they saw it, the ship must still be seaworthy. But in reality she was a helpless wreck, whose crew had only barely escaped destruction.

The floe on which the 19 people found themselves, held fast between immobile ice fragments, had scarcely changed its position. Now it began to drift again. If one had wanted to make another attempt to reach the ship, this would have to be without delay. Some leads that ran northward appeared to promise success; but before they could get close to them, they had closed again. Over the course of the afternoon several more futile attempts were made, during which some of the men landed in the water.

Tired, cold and hungry, they lay down on the highest point on their floe as the short day came to an end. A violent wind arose, and it was combined with a heavy snowfall; the sea was in a wild uproar and the darkness was impenetrable. Shortly before dawn the sleepers were awakened by a loud crack. They struggled to their feet, but due to the darkness they were unable to locate the cause of the noise. All too soon they realized that the floe had split; the second whaleboat had drifted away into the night on one of the fragments. Before they could even try to save it, it had disappeared from sight.

As day began to dawn, all hope had vanished of ever reaching the ship again. The northeasterly storm had become a gale. The white-crested waves broke seethingly against the floes and ice fields which under the force of the swell had separated, leaving wide leads between them. One breaker followed another; broken ice fragments were severed with a crash from the edges of the floe; and by noon its circumference was reduced by half. Still there was no sign of the storm abating. The surf raged angrily around the weird raft, working unremittingly to destroy it. By nightfall it had become so small that it could barely accommodate the shipwrecked people any longer. But then the storm slackened and they could breathe more freely again. However, there could be no thought of sleeping; for anybody who lay down would have run the risk of being washed away. Everyone hung on tightly to the boat.

It was a long time before the new day grew light. Dense fog lay around the horizon and veiled the dim dawn arch. Joseph and Hans had the good fortune to kill two small seals and they were devoured voraciously. One of the hides was cut into strips and given to the dogs; they had received no food since the separation from the ship. When the fog lifted, land appeared. A glittering cover of new ice, which would not bear a man's weight, extended to the coast; the sojourn on the floe was becoming more precarious by the hour.

It was not until the 21st that they succeeded in moving to a larger floe near to which their floe had drifted; on this occasion Joseph discovered the other whaleboat, which had gone missing a few days before and which was now recovered.[4] The natives built three snow houses. The crew members were accommodated in the largest one; another housed Hans and his family; and a double house, split only by a snow wall, but provided with a common entrance, was occupied by Tyson and Meyer and also by Joseph, Mrs. Hannah and little Pannik.[5]

During the next few days the wind was almost constantly out of the southeast. Yet on the 23rd Joseph went off to hunt seals. He didn't get any shots, but he spotted a fragment of the old ice field with the emergency hut. It was about three miles from the camp.

Due to the lack of food a general debilitation had begun, and the run-down state of the crew made a strenuous hike, such as that to the hut, almost impossible. Hence, with the exception of women and children, everyone received a double ration; the dogs were fed the remaining seal skins, and soon thereafter they set off for the floe with the emergency hut.

Covering the first mile took over an hour. At times the route led across young ice that was so thin that it bent beneath one's feet; at times they had to clamber over high barriers of chaotically piled ice blocks; or else they had to cross wide leads, where the dogs caused major delays. Later the situation improved and after a fatiguing march they reached the floe. Apart from the hut, everything else was buried under drifted snow which they quickly dug away. The boat and the provisions were revealed to be in excellent condition; only some of the pemmican cans had been gnawed by the dogs, which had devoured their contents.

First the crewmen cleaned out the boat and loaded it; then the dogs were harnessed to it and they started back to the camp. Next day the work continued. The low temperatures had strengthened the ice so that they could follow a shorter route and were able to reach the emergency hut in about an hour. The natives filled their kayaks with small items that lay scattered around, and hauled them on their backs, while the seamen removed the stiff-frozen tent-roof from the hut; they also knocked together a rough sledge from its poles. In this way they were able to haul considerable loads to the camp. Robert and William, who were heavily laden, broke through the thin ice layer covering a lead on their return journey. Half frozen, they were hauled out onto the ice. Their loads were placed on the sledge, and they themselves reached the camp running non-stop, without further accident.

Through this expedition they had acquired a large number of valuable items. They had found a boat's compass as well as a sextant, and thereby an awkward dilemma had been removed.

Only a number of planks and poles, part of the tent-roof and several sacks of coal were left on the floe. During the night the rough sledge was strengthened; the remainder of the material was to be hauled back on the following day.

But since a heavy fog rolled in it was not possible to execute this plan. They were obliged to remain in the snow houses or near them, and this enforced leisure was used for arranging the houses somewhat more comfortably. Floors were made from the planks; the sail-cloth was used to line the roofs. The natives built another small adjoining room, which was to be used as a kitchen; a large, silver concave mirror was adapted as the stove.

Once everything had been brought to the camp a list of the provisions was drawn up. The sum total of supplies was limited to 14 cans of pemmican, 10 dozen cans of meat and soup, 14 hams, 1 can of dried apples, about 20 lbs. of cocoa and 11½ bags of hardtack—in total about 800 lbs.

Thus 14 adults and 5 children possessed at most 800 lbs. of food. They were faced with a long, cold winter, and the natives were well aware that it would not be possible to hunt successfully during the dark period. Fuel was limited almost entirely to the two bags of coal; but since there was no suitable fireplace they could not be seriously considered; the silver concave mirror had served the purpose to which it had been assigned, superbly; but it was totally useless as a stove. When they would succeed in reaching shore could not be guessed at. With the uttermost economy the provisions could last for only a few months; but fuel, even with the most modest consumption, barely a week. Hence it was decided to have only two meals per day; and to be fair to everyone in sharing the slim rations, Meyer made a rough wooden scale, and weights from lead shot.

Thus far it had not been possible to determine the floe's position astronomically. However, it must have been driven significantly southward since the ship had been lost from sight; for on 27 October the upper edge of the sun appeared above the horizon, whereas previously only twilight had prevailed at noon. To the east, about 40 miles away, rose the well-known outlines of Northumberland Island, and somewhat farther south from it the cliffs of Hakluyt Island appeared, enveloped in a blue haze. A dark lead ran off to the west; Joseph and Hans followed it to look for seals. They returned as night was falling, but empty-handed. Over the next two days their luck at hunting was no better; not until the 30th did Hans manage to shoot a small seal.

In the meantime the floe had again approached the coast to the point that a faint hope was again wakened in the hearts of the shipwrecked people. The coast lay almost close enough to touch; they were just waiting for a favourable opportunity to reach it. When the two natives returned from a reconnaissance on the following day, bringing good news as to the state of the ice, the next morning was fixed for that purpose. Everyone went to bed early, to strengthen themselves for the impending hardships; but the welcome prospect of an imminent deliverance scared away sleep from many a bed.

Pitch darkness still reigned when on the morning of 1 November the sailors pulled down the recently built snow houses and stowed the few possessions in the boats. The planks and poles, along with both kayaks, were left behind for the moment. With the exception of the children everyone was harnessed to the boats, which moved only reluctantly over the rough ice surface; they often had recourse to axe-work to level the route; quite commonly high ice hummocks forced them to move the load forward in stages. When the approach of night made it impossible to continue the journey, they camped in the open on an old ice floe. The distance they had covered was scarcely a German mile![6]

Early next morning the natives set off with the sledge for the old campsite to fetch the items that had been left behind; two of the seamen and the cook had hurried on ahead of them.

A dull rumble suddenly made them stop. The floe beneath their feet began to shake and crack, then it fell calm again. Hans dropped to the ground, his ear pressed hard against the ice, to listen to the weird sounds. The noises now became louder than before. Close in front of Hans a wide crack suddenly opened; he had barely jumped up when he found his retreat route already cut off; innumerable cracks seamed the ice in every direction. Joseph was adrift with the dogs on a small fragment of a floe. He tried in vain to reach a larger floe with the frightened animals, which were howling and whining loudly; but they were so refractory that he finally left them, to save himself by reaching a larger floe.

The two seamen and the cook, who were already close to the remains of the hut, wanted to hurry to the assistance of their comrades. Only when they reached the edge of their floe did they notice that they themselves were in danger. They were standing on a drifting ice island, and their combined voices were not sufficient to make themselves understood by Joseph and Hans, each of whom was marooned on a small floe.

Several hours of desperate effort followed. In the meantime the two natives had succeeded in taking refuge on a more solid floe, which they were trying to paddle toward the hut using a pole. But a light breeze that had arisen in the meantime was offering them so much resistance that all their efforts were fruitless. Only when the flood tide began and the wind dropped were they able to reach their companions; they then hurried to the camp along with them. They were able to take only the two kayaks with them; all the rest had to be left behind since the gathering darkness urged them to hurry.

A violent blizzard that broke shortly after they arrived and continued raging until the following evening thwarted any further attempt at setting off for the land. It blew so extremely violently that they did not even dare to fetch the remainder of the planks and poles from the hut. And as a result the poor people were as good as shelterless. During the excitement of the day that had passed it had not been possible to build snow houses. But this now had to be tackled without delay.

During 4 November the weather was scarcely better than on the day before, and on the following morning a violent northwesterly gale was added to the snowstorm, putting the ice in motion again. It was not until the 6th that the force of the gale relented; the air became clear and on the southern horizon a dull dawn-arch rose to the monotonous grey clouds.

The floe had again moved farther offshore; thereby the last hopes of delivery died for the shipwrecked people.

From a nearby iceberg a pretty unfavourable sight was revealed. Open water appeared all around, strewn with massive banks of ice; here and there was a reflecting cover of young ice. As a result of the excessive efforts, Tyson's health was so badly strained that he was not capable of leaving the snow house.[7] The floe on which the collected timber was stowed was nowhere to be seen. The seamen repaired the storm damage and the natives went hunting. Joseph killed a small seal; Hans returned empty-handed. But he had located the old floe and brought some of the poles back to camp.

Next morning Tyson had recovered somewhat, but nobody dared to leave the houses since there was a powerful gale again. It was not until the 19th that the bad weather improved. The natives went off hunting and some of the seamen travelled with the dog sledge to the old floe where the debris of the hut lay scattered.

On reaching the open water Joseph and Hans separated. When it began to get dark Joseph returned to camp. Hours passed, but Hans did not come back. Accompanied by Robert, Joseph left the house around midnight to search for the missing man. The moon was almost full, but only occasionally did its rays break through the dark clouds covering the sky. The two men followed several tracks that appeared to have been made by Hans. To get a wider view they then climbed a high iceberg, but without success. The variable lighting and the cloud shadows, which moved from place to place, teased one's eye and one's imagination. Once they had started for the camp, Joseph casually turned round and ordered Robert to quickly drop to the ground and to behave calmly. He himself kneeled down in the shadow of an ice hummock and prepared to fire; the other man did the same, for a bear was moving slowly but deliberately toward them. Joseph, the better shot, exchanged his pistol for Robert's rifle. Reaching a snow bank the animal stopped; it stopped short, then moved off in a different direction, away from the hunters. The two men crawled carefully after it; when they came to a level ice surface they lay down, ready to fire in the shelter of a hummock. The bear was moving off again and again the two men followed it, hidden by a low ice ridge. Finally the animal came within range. With the rifle pressed to his cheek Joseph began imitating the growling of a bear. The animal stopped dead for a moment. Impatiently the hunter raised his rifle. Just as he was about to squeeze the trigger he saw the long barrel of a gun glinting, just in front of the presumed bear, which was in fact

Hans. A moment later and Hans would have been relieved of the painful life that he was facing on the floe.

Unable to find his way to the camp, the poor man had wandered around for hours; the driving snow had lodged in the fur of his clothing so that he appeared completely white. As a result of this and due to the peculiar gait of the exhausted man, even the experienced Joseph had been deceived.

The two men cheerfully brought the rescued Nimrod to the houses, where Mrs. Merkut looked after her man and took care of his physical well-being. Exceptionally, he was granted a double ration—under the prevailing circumstances an extraordinary event. For since the hunting had ceased to be productive, it had become necessary to be satisfied with only one meal per day. But even had more provisions been available, it would scarcely have been possible to prepare it properly due to the deficient facilities of the kitchen. For understandable reasons they had had to discard the silver concave mirror as useless; and since they possessed neither rocks nor usable metal to build a fireplace, they were unable to use the two sacks of coal. The only cooking vessels consisted of two old frying pans and a few empty tin cans, which generally began leaking after they had been used for a short time; all the plates had gone missing, as too had the forks.

The food was heated over a blubber lamp, made from a pemmican can; it was impossible to cook it properly since there was not enough blubber. Lint teased from canvas served as a wick; only the small flames that flickered around the edges of this rude lamp spread only minimal heat and even less light. And yet they possessed no other source of light, since the sun had long since dropped below the horizon and the gloomy twilight, often obscured by fog and drifting snow, was too weak to penetrate through the small ice windows into the interior of the houses. The lack of cleanliness was especially serious. Nobody could wash since there was barely enough water to quench the burning thirst caused by the cold.

The hours passed slowly for these poor people, particularly when they were unable to leave the houses because of darkness or blizzard conditions. And at the same time the hungry children were constantly begging for food that was simply not available. Meyer made a deck of cards from old packing paper. Big-bosomed queens and armed jacks, depicted with lamp soot and fat more energetically than artistically, adorned the cards. Even the hearts were a shiny black, and since they commonly could be distinguished only with difficulty from the spades, many a jocular altercation ensued.

To add to the accumulated distress that prevailed on the floe, on 13 November Peter also fell ill and the faces of the others became more gaunt day by day. The roof of one of the houses began to sink. Hence they began building another snow house, and from now on they worked at it every day as long as the weather and the twilight illumination permitted. The natives continued to go out hunting but they always returned empty-handed. On the 15th, with the full moon the tide rose unusually high; added to this was a stiff wind from the southeast that produced open water all around the floe, threatening the houses once again. Next day the men completed the snow house they had begun, inserted a large ice window into its roof, and immediately attended to moving into it. The dogs, which, like their masters, had seen better days, were having great difficulty in adjusting to the meagre rations. They made a united attack on the provisions, and caused a lot of damage and annoyance. Five of the animals were shot and eaten; the pack now numbered just four animals, and maintaining them was difficult enough.

More stormy days followed; during the 17th and 18th nobody could leave the houses. Violent squalls out of the north and northwest assaulted the houses and buried them almost completely under fine driven snow. The sky was heavily overcast and prevented any distant view. But it could be inferred that there was open water nearby since the ice floe began to rock and to move irregularly.

After a brief calm on the 19th the wind swung round to the north. It was magnificently clear and the twilight glow remained visible for four hours: an infallible sign that the floe had been driven a considerable distance southward. The natives discovered two fresh bear tracks. The animals had made the same rounds as the two hunters and had enlarged some seal holes; but their tracks disappeared on the young ice.

In the meantime Peter's health had improved so much that he could leave the house again. But on one of his first excursions he had the misfortune to break through the young ice, and as a result brought unpleasant rheumatic pains upon himself, that again put him back in his sickbed. Tyson was suffering from the same complaint; but given the low temperatures, their inadequate clothing and the scanty food, this could scarcely be remedied. It was not until the 21st that the natives' hunting was again successful. They killed three seals; but the largest was lost to the waves. The young ice on which the animal was lying gave way beneath its weight and, in his efforts to secure the valuable booty, Hans almost came to grief himself.

Again two of the dogs had to be killed.[8] It was with a heavy heart that Joseph seized his gun, but urgent necessity gave them no choice. There were now only two of the animals left, those that had stood the test best.

On the 22nd Joseph managed to shoot another seal, and on the following day Hans brought in a slim year-old animal. Now, for the first time since the separation from *Polaris*, they could satisfy their hunger again. The blood-rich meat quickly gave the half-starved men new strength; the new supply of blubber allowed them to light another lamp, and as a result the temperature inside the house rose somewhat and checked the spread of the rheumatic ailments.

A two-day calm, combined with low temperatures, resulted in the leads becoming still and covered with a skin of ice. As a result the natives were obliged to make longer trips to reach the spots where they lay in wait; but seals were not appearing at all now. Only a thin fox circled the houses from time to time, but the hunters sympathized with it and spared its life since it was so bold and trusting.

Thanksgiving, celebrated everywhere in the United States, was also celebrated on the ice. The 28th of November, the day on which it fell, was extremely stormy; the sky was covered with black clouds and the dim twilight arch was barely visible. But the shipwrecked people tidied themselves up and for this occasion tried to banish their cares.[9]

On the 30th a high coast appeared as a dim blue-grey silhouette far off to the south-southeast. But without a map it was impossible to get their bearings and the sky was too gloomy for one to have been able to get an astronomical position fix.[10] On 1 December the ridges had disappeared again. One of the sailors discovered a fresh bear track near the house and followed it until he came up with the animal. Since his gun misfired, the hunt almost became disastrous; finally the bear turned on the hunter, who took to his heels and raced back to camp in great bounds. On the other hand, a few days later the little fox atoned for its boldness with its life. Apart from the dense white pelt the rest of it was barely worth the powder; the little animal was as thin as a rake, and provided just a few bites.

It was not until 6 December that the coast again appeared, but this time less clearly than before. During the night a glowing aurora rose above a dense-black segment of cloud; it moved from east to west and at times covered more than half the sky. The brilliant rays shot up to half the height of the zenith and poured their soft light over the desolate icy wastes which, as far as the eye could see, were not broken by a single lead.

On the following day the first determination of position was achieved. Under favourable conditions Meyer obtained some altitudes for stars in Cassiopea; but since he did not possess a nautical almanac, the declination of the constellation could be determined only approximately, with the help of a star map that by chance had found its way onto the ice. The calculated latitude was 74°4'N; longitude 67°53'W. If one places the approximate position of the separation of the ship from the ice floe drifters at 78°10'N; 75°W, since 15 October the floe had moved south about 4.9 miles per day. But the drift was certainly not steady, rather at times had been more rapid, at times slower, depending on the strength and direction of the prevailing winds that had influenced it.

The darkness had increased; the weak twilight did not even contribute enough light to tempt the natives to go out hunting, and the moon had barely reached its first quarter. The rations were now doled out even more niggardly than before. From now on the adults received daily only 6 ounces of bread, half a pound of meat and 1 ounce of ham; but the children only half of this. Under such circumstances the general debilitation rapidly increased, and the state of health of the crew, which previously had not been good, deteriorated. The next man who was banished to his sickbed was unfortunately Hans, whose services could not easily be dispensed with. Nobody moved more than was absolutely necessary; for the hunger, which could not be sufficiently appeased, was not something that one would willingly conjure up. The blubber ran out, and they were now usually without fire and light. They had long since sacrificed one of the two whaleboats. All means of procuring fresh food were fruitless; only one scrawny fox was caught in a trap that Joseph had set.

Christmas came, but they could not enjoy the day; their worries about existing were becoming more pressing and more serious, and the mood of the floe drifters was as gloomy as the surrounding environment.

Nineteen half-starved people, coated with filth, sat in the cold, meagrely lit snow huts to celebrate a festival such as probably had never been celebrated under similar circumstances. A pound had been set aside from the last ham of their provisions. Somewhat over half an ounce of it, along with an ounce of hardtack, 2.5 ounces of pemmican and some frozen seal blood formed the servings for this festive meal.[11]

In the meantime Hans's health had improved; he again went out hunting with Joseph, but no game of any kind appeared. After the slightest physical effort everyone felt as exhausted as a convalescent. The poor wretches had reached the stage where they were eating frozen sealskin and old scraps of leather, and were devouring the bits of charred connective fibres from the blubber, which stuck to the bottom of the greasy lamps, which were no longer burning.

During the 29th a gale-force north wind was blowing and it opened up the ice. Joseph killed a seal in one of the leads. That this priceless booty was not lost was thanks only to the hunter's nerve; he entrusted himself to a drifting floe and paddled after the kill with the butt of his gun since it was rapidly drifting away, carried by the current. He reached the seal, passed a leather thong through its jaws and secured it to his frail vessel. When he tried to turn back he found it impossible to make any headway against the current. Quickly coming to a decision, he paddled to a larger floe and landed on its slippery surface. Only when he shouted loudly for help several times did Hans arrive in his kayak to rescue him.

The seal was brought to the camp and dismembered, always an unpleasant task given the low temperatures. Division of the prey followed firmly established rules, from which there were only exceptional deviations. The skin with the adhering blubber was laid in a shallow hollow in the snow, into which the blood was ladled to let it congeal. The liver and heart were consumed raw, while still warm; the brain and the kidneys belonged to the hunter and the eyes to the youngest child, while the intestines were hung up and allowed to freeze, then to be stored in the provisions house. One of the women cut up the carcass into the appropriate number of equal parts, laid them in a row and gave each person the appropriate portion as his or her name was called out. In this way it was hoped that personal favouritism would be prevented.

CHAPTER 22

Between hopelessness and optimism

The new year. Distress increases. Intense cold. Sunrise. Land in sight! "Shipboard tasks." Narwhals. The provisions depot at Disko. The rate of drift diminishes. Unreliable geographical longitudes. The first birds. The decision to set off for the coast. The floe breaks up. Northern lights.

The good wishes that were exchanged on New Year's Day sounded like bitter mockery. The only good fortune in which one could take pleasure was life itself; but this seemed worse than death, since it consisted of an endless sequence of very painful torments. Dismal reality smothered any hope for a more friendly future and smothered the gentle lingering notes of better times; no rosy glow interrupted the gloomy shadows of the present which, heavy and pregnant with malice, confined the narrow range of ideas.[1]

Just as previously the natives would go out hunting; but no open water appeared anywhere and hence the seals stayed away. The blubber ran out and the men had to have recourse to planks that separated their sleeping places from the floe, just to procure drinking water. Two meandering bear tracks ran around the houses, but the darkness thwarted any attempt at pursuing the animals.

On 6 January Meyer measured the noon altitude of Polaris and Cassiopeia above the ice horizon. The latitude, derived from the altitude of the North Star, was 72°3'N, while Cassiopeia gave 72°11'; the average of these two observations was hence 72°7'; the longitude, calculated from

431

the altitude of the latter star, was 60°40.7'. The declination and also the right ascension of these stars were taken from the star-chart mentioned earlier. According to this determination the rate of drift, which between 15 October and 7 December had been about 4.9 miles per day, had increased to 5.2 miles. Assuming that the longitude was correct, although legitimate doubts were raised about it, since in the meantime the west coast had been in sight, the floe was now about 80 n. miles from the west coast of Greenland, roughly west-southwest of Upernavik. The surrounding area was covered with ice, which in the west towered up in high ridges.

Since hunting was producing no prey, the distress increased day by day. The only sledge had already been burned; the thwarts of the boat, from which shavings were cut, were becoming steadily thinner. Only with difficulty was Tyson able to persuade the desperate men to spare the boat, on which the last hopes had been pinned.[2]

On the 13th the temperature dropped so low that the mercury froze in the bulb of the thermometer.[3] Due to the cold nobody could leave the houses. A light northeasterly which started during the night, in association with snowfall, brought some relief. The thermometer rose, but the breeze developed into a violent storm, which only abated on the evening of the 15th. Given the lean rations, the dogs could rarely be fed. For some days they had stayed well away from the houses, and when they now returned they displayed deep, bloody wounds on various parts of their bodies, from an unequivocal fight with a bear. Joseph followed their tracks and reached the spot where the attack had occurred; the bear had sought safety in flight and had dived into the water.

In the very bleak existence of the floe drifters 19 January brought a critical juncture in that it transported them from the gloomy shadowed zone of the polar night. For 83 long days the sun had not risen above the horizon; now it rose again bright and brilliant and illuminated the stark ice wilderness. With thankful hearts the severely tested men gazed steadily southward. Many lips, which otherwise had uttered only curses and blasphemies, now uttered a whispered prayer.

An astronomical determination of position that Meyer obtained on the 20th revealed a latitude of 70°1.7'N and a longitude of 60°0.6'W; the daily drift had thus increased from 5.2 to 8.5 miles. On the same day the first bird appeared: a young black guillemot with spotted plumage. It sat innocently on the top of a rounded hummock, where it fell victim to a ball from Joseph's gun.

The cold had now intensified again and the open water disappeared. From now on one had to lie in wait for the seals at their breathing holes, a hunting technique that demands a lot of practice and great endurance, and that can only be practised by people who are completely tempered against the hardships of an arctic winter. The hunter must wait for hours, almost motionless at the small hole in the ice, his face turned into the biting wind, so as not to alarm the surfacing seal; for the slightest careless movement is enough to scare away the sharp-eared animal. But Joseph was persistent and success did not elude him. On the 23rd he harpooned a small one-year animal and Hans got another the next day, so that the cruel lack of oil for feeding the lamps was remedied. And this was seen as good fortune, since it became so cold that the mercury again froze and remained solid for five days. It could not be determined how low the temperature sank; but it must have been bitterly cold, for the natives were repeatedly forced to return home, having been away from the houses for barely half an hour. The rest of the crew, as well as the women and children, remained inside the houses, near the warming lamps, which could not be allowed to go out, for high winds were now added to the low temperatures, making the cold even more sensible.

On 27 January, according to Meyer's observations, the floe was located at 69°32'N; its longitude was 60°3'W. The rate of drift, which between the 5th and 20th of the month had still been 8.5 miles per day, thereafter had dropped to less than half that; the ice had probably become congested due to the intense cold. No land was visible either to east or west; hence there were justifiable doubts as to the determination of longitude. According to Meyer's observations and calculations, over the course of January the floe had been moving roughly along the 60th meridian, about 80 miles off the coast of West Greenland. If this longitude had been accurate the high land would certainly have come into sight occasionally.[4] If one considers that the chronometer was exposed to significant temperature fluctuations, and that during the constant struggle for bare existence, of necessity it was often handled roughly, one could scarcely expect anything more precise; but up till now no opportunity had offered itself for measuring lunar distances.

On the other hand the latitudes were approximately correct. Assuming this, the floe was now about 20 miles north of the latitude of Disko. The expedition had left an abundant depot of provisions there. Hence the men proposed to Tyson that he and they should set off for that island. But, being older and more experienced, he could not approve such a plan and depicted for the crew the serious consequences of such a risky enterprise in the most lurid colours. Tackling the journey to the coast with the women and children could certainly never have a good outcome; the marooned party did not even possess a sledge to transport their boat, and it could not have been hauled across the rough ice without suffering damage.

This difference of opinion caused a bitter mood in the camp; but the men ultimately came round, since they realized that this dreadful adventure could have a satisfactory conclusion only by maintaining the strictest unity. In the meantime they had forfeited the last dog. Hans, who had taken Jennie hunting, had lost the dog among the hummocks and all attempts at finding it had been in vain.[5]

Violent storms swept over the houses; hunting had ceased to be productive, and the prostrate men greedily devoured the last remnants of the sealskins, which they now no longer had to share with the dogs. There was no sign of the better times for which they had been hoping; moreover, the steward was afflicted with scurvy and it was impossible to control this terrible illness.

It was not until 5 February that the tireless Hans succeeded in killing a small seal, whose blood was set aside for the sick; Joseph shot a splendid animal, but it landed in a crack running between two floes, and sank before the hunter could race up to grab it.[6] An observation gave a latitude of 68°50'N. Hence since 27 January the floe had been moving south at a rate of 4.7 miles per day, an acceleration of almost half a mile since the last observation.

During the 6th there was a constant gale blowing from the northwest; then toward evening, with rising temperatures the wind swung into the south, and on the following day it blew impetuously from the west. This rapid change in wind direction resulted in the formation of numerous extensive polynyas. A pod of narwhals gambolled happily in the largest of them. Snorting loudly, the animals shot spouts of water high into the cold air.[7] Joseph shot a large male but it sank noiselessly without surfacing again. The rest swam off to the north; but after a short time they returned since, judging by the ice-blink, there was probably no open water there.

The season was so far advanced that it began to grow light by 8 o'clock, but by 4.00 p.m. a deep twilight prevailed again. The lack of cleanliness made itself doubly perceptible with the increasing light which penetrated the interior of the houses and illuminated the filth that had been accumulating there for months. They still could not wash themselves; but on 8 February a regular duty roster was introduced, and by virtue of the orders that were issued, from now on the houses had to be cleaned weekly at least as far as could be achieved without using water. The canvas that lined the domes was thick with ice and soot; the people's warm breath as well as the steam produced during cooking had condensed as thick frost-flowers on the muskox skins that were used as bedding; the old canvas that covered the floor was completely saturated with the blood and fat of the animals they had killed. The success of this first cleanup lasted only a short time; for during the night a violent blizzard arose, filling the interiors of the houses with fine drifted snow, and buried the houses so that on the following morning they had to dig a tunnel out to the open air. The water was now washing the southern edge of the floe, and the narwhals were approaching so close that one could fire at them from the camp. Several were killed, but they all sank before the natives could reach them in their kayaks.

It was a bitter feeling, to be surrounded by superabundance, to make more than a thousand pounds of meat lifeless with every shot and then to see the prey sink. With a strong harpoon one could easily have secured the animals, but all the stratagems of the natives to produce such a thing failed from the lack of suitable materials and appropriate tools.[8] Over the course of the afternoon the westerly wind again attained gale force; it again began to snow so persistently that on the 10th they again had to have recourse to the shovel in order to get out of the houses.

The joyful shout: "Land in sight!" wakened the sleepers on the morning of the 16th earlier than usual. Illuminated by the rising sun, the snow-crowned, jagged mountain range of the west coast glowed a light red; encircled by thin wreaths of fog, steep foothills stretched their dark rocky slopes far out into the frozen, debris-covered sea and threw long shadows across the entrances of deep bays from which translucent veils of fog rose, chased away by the sun. Tyson, who was familiar with the coast from earlier voyages, thought he could recognize Cape Seward;[9] natives lived there and the distance separating the camp from the land was not more than 38 to 40 miles. The ice lay in mast-high ridges, and if it had been more traversable they might have set off immediately on the trip to the coast, but under prevailing conditions it seemed advisable to wait before setting off.

Since the 10th they had procured only a single small seal, since in the interim it had been stormy or foggy; and distress was again threatening to make itself felt when Joseph succeeded in taking by surprise a scrawny yearling, which was sunning itself sleepily on the ice. The dovekies, which thus far had appeared only singly, now arrived in quite large flocks; 11 of these birds were shot on the 20th. Of the old provisions only three cans of pemmican and two bags of hardtack were left now; they were considered inviolate since the winter was still not over and there were still many stormy days ahead. If they did not succeed in reaching land in the near future, in the most favourable case weeks might still elapse before the long-cherished rescue arrived.

On 21 February the temperature rose to an unbelievable level; the thermometer recorded −14.5° in the shade; this was the warmest it had been since they were separated from *Polaris*. Despite the good intentions that had been adopted, the provisions now had to be rationed in a more modest fashion; the dovekies and the last remnants of seal meat were eaten, and the natives roamed the whole of the surrounding area without getting a shot. To quiet the gnawing hunger they were again eating the frozen refuse of hides, since pemmican and bread could be doled out only by lot.

Since conditions could scarcely get worse the people decided to grasp the first opportunity to reach land and to risk everything to do so. Hence some damage that the boat had suffered was repaired, firearms were put in order, and powder and shot were packed in oiled leather. They intended setting off on the 24th. But execution of this plan was thwarted by a heavy snowfall that began on the evening of the 23rd and lasted until the following afternoon. The soft snow now covered the rough surface of the frozen sea knee-deep and made marching extremely difficult.

The floe, which had again moved farther from the coast on the 25th, was now drifting rapidly south. Several headlands that the day before had been sighted to the west now bore northerly. Apart from a small polynya which lay about three miles from the camp, no open water was visible; but dark clouds that lay over the northern horizon seemed to indicate ice-free areas in that direction. During the following two days the cold again intensified to −32°; to this was added violent winds that made it so unpleasant to stay outdoors that the hunters felt themselves obliged to stay in the houses. On the 28th they discovered a fresh bear track that led from the camp to a nearby smooth ice surface, where it disappeared. They searched for the animal but their efforts were unrewarded. By contrast, toward evening they killed 30-odd dovekies, to which they added a further 60 next day. The old supplies could now again remained untouched.

March had arrived, and with it the intense cold peculiar to the start of that month. On the 2nd, Joseph shot a gigantic bearded seal 8 feet in length, whose meat and blubber removed all cares about the existence of the ice drifters. The monotony of life now became little interrupted; the people compensated themselves for the difficult times that they had suffered, and ate and slept to their hearts' content.[10]

In the meantime the floe had approached the latitude of Cumberland Sound. There were gales from every point of the compass, and on the 10th a hurricane raged out of the north; its fury broke up the ice during the dark, starless night. Beneath the floe the sea raged ferociously; like a cork it was hurled from wave to wave, crashing thunderously against crumbling brash ice. Occasionally there was a pause. But the calm would last for only a few seconds. Then the dreadful noises would rise again: groaning and moaning, creaking and cracking. And through it all mingled the howling of the wind and the thunderous roar of the waves, sometimes dully, as if from a great distance, sometimes like thunder from the immediate, terrifyingly close proximity.

It might have been about 9 o'clock[11] when they noticed a loud crash. The floe rocked, the houses shuddered; then came a crunching sound, like the sounds caused by the keel of a ship sliding over rocky ground.

Under the effect of violent impacts from the side, the snow tunnel leading to the houses suddenly collapsed. Joseph and Tyson hurried outside. They had scarcely left the house when the combined fury of the gale and of the waves hurled them to the ice. The waves were breaking only 10 paces from the camp at most. With driving snow whirling around them they reached the edge of the ice on hands and knees. The floe had disintegrated; the last impact had split it apart; they could not form any idea of how much was left of it, since the violence of the hurricane forced the two men to return quickly.

The gale continued all night without intermission; morning came, but due to the wild blizzard nobody dared leave the hut for longer than a few minutes; but this was not sufficient time to get a clear idea of the present extent of the floe. Either it was now blowing more strongly than yesterday, or the floe on which the house sat had become significantly smaller, since the swaying, lurching movements, which were now making the women seasick, were coming more frequently and more impetuously.

The events of the following night were a repetition of those of the previous one, only at a more impressive level. The weird voices of the ice roared louder; the rage of the howling storm seemed to have increased; and the wild surf of the massive seas surged more noisily and more violently around the floe, which they treated as a plaything.

When the storm finally died after lasting 60 hours, and the shipwrecked people were able to leave their damaged houses, they found massive changes in the character of the ice. The massive floes and ice fields had been ground into small fragments; bergs whose mass had previously been on an overpowering scale were now disfigured till unrecognizable; but all around them their own floe had disintegrated, now covering scarcely more than a third of its original extent. There was not a floe in sight to which they could have moved; far and wide there was nothing but unsafe debris, scarcely large enough to serve as the place of refuge for a single person.

A noon sun altitude gave the floe's latitude as 64°32'N; the longitude could not be determined, but it seemed to be significantly farther east than previously, since the coast was no longer visible.

During the 13th the storm damage to the houses was repaired. Next day Joseph shot another bearded seal which, however, was much smaller than the first. It was a female, carrying a pup, the length of a normal adult ringed seal, and when one squeezed its mammary glands one obtained a considerable amount of milk. In addition three Greenland seals[12] were shot, although one of them was lost. According to a noon sun-shot the floe was at a latitude of 64°19'N; hence during the previous two days it had moved 12 miles south.

On the 15th there was a strong wind out of the east and the ice was again under pressure, but not with sufficient violence to become dangerous. With the temperature rising, the wind swung into the southwest next morning, bringing a light mist, so that it was not possible to make a determination of position; Meyer did not succeed in this until the 17th. The result was a latitude of 63°47'N; the current had become stronger, and for the past three days had attained a speed of over 10 miles per day. A bear was spotted near the houses, but to the hunters' regret it escaped unscathed. Attracted by the smell of the seal meat, it had cautiously examined the camp and vicinity, and had scarcely vouchsafed Joseph a glance when he stepped outside without a gun. It was only when the native emerged again, armed, that it pricked up its ears and set off at a rolling gallop, with an agility that one scarcely would have credited, across the loose brash ice where nobody could follow it.

Over the course of the month scarcely a clear night had passed that aurora borealis was not seen. A particularly brilliant example appeared on 18 March; but as usual it was followed by a storm that began blowing with great violence out of the northwest. It then swung into the north and, with associated drifting snow, raged almost continually for two days with such force that nobody could leave the houses. Occasionally, when the noise of the wind fell silent for a short time, whales could be heard, their snorting penetrating clearly into the interiors of the houses. But the natives' hunting ardour was not strong enough to tempt them into the open and to cause them to exchange the warm camp for a windy lying-in-wait.

CHAPTER 23

Spring on the floe

The rate of drift increases. Hooded seals. An importunate bear. Storm and spring tide. The floe is shattered. A life-and-death boat trip. Landing on the pack. The boat beset. Dreadful days. A sail is sighted!

The sun had reached the equinox but spring was still delayed in starting. The desolate chaos of ice covering the sea extended wintry and stark into the remote distance and glittered in the treacherous sunlight, whose warmth was barely perceptible.

Although the floe drifters had already crossed the Arctic Circle and were moving steadily farther away from it, they were still not going to escape the raw days of an arctic March; indeed, ahead of them lay even more fearful times than the worst they had experienced during the dark winter.

On 22 March the floe was at a latitude of 62°56'N and its speed had dropped by only a small fraction of a mile. The following day was stormy again; the temperature dropped and nobody could leave the houses. Once the weather had improved on the 24th the natives headed out to the limited polynyas, which were now about 5 miles from the camp. Joseph killed a fat seal; and the next morning produced another three of the animals. From a number of sun altitudes that Meyer measured at noon, it turned out that since the 22nd the floe's daily movement had increased to 19 miles; it was now 1 mile north of the 62nd parallel.

Whereas until now only two species of seals had been shot, Greenland and bearded seals, on the 26th the first hooded seals[1] appeared; their geographical distribution is more limited. The hooded seal is only a little smaller than the bearded seal and is distinguished from all other seals by the fact that the male possesses a large sac of skin on its head, which is connected to its nose. The animal can, at will, fill this balloon-like extension of the skin of the head with air; when extended it assumes the shape of a hood, and it is to this that this species of seal owes its name. Like the other representatives of the family it has no external ear; the ear opening is so small that at first glance it is barely visible. The body is long and heavy; the background colour of the upper body varies from a light to a dark chestnut brown, with even darker patches, whose distribution resembles the markings of a leopard. The underside is dark grey, and in animals that have just emerged from the water, it reveals a shiny silver nuance.

Unlike its relatives, the hooded seal defends itself furiously when attacked; it bites, scratches and hisses, and there are cases where one has wrested a club away from a sealer by seizing it in its teeth, swinging it from side to side by rapid rotary head movements, and thus forcing the disarmed enemy to retreat. Hunting it with a rifle is completely safe and neither easier nor more difficult than hunting other species of seals. During the mating season violent fights occur over the possession of the females; the incensed animals are so noisy that the sounds are audible for great distances.

Having assembled into small herds and sharing the area with no other species, the hooded seal gives birth to a single pup in March or April, either on the pack ice of the open sea, or on the ice fields that border the coast. The mother suckles the pup for 20 to 25 days. It is a slightly yellowish-white in colour and when it exchanges its sojourn on the ice for the water, it gradually gives way to a dirty grey.

The hooded seal probably does not cross the 76th parallel;[2] it is nowhere numerous and has now completely disappeared from many regions where it once occurred. Most of them are killed along the southwest coast of Greenland and the Labrador coast; only exceptionally do they occur in the vicinity of Jan Mayen; farther north and east and in Svalbard waters they are rare. Occasionally they occur on the coasts of Scandinavia and England when they have been driven there by storms; some are even encountered near New York.

From now on these animals provided the floe drifters with food. Three were killed on the 26th alone,[3] and next day a bear appeared in the camp and paid with its life.

Shortly after twilight began Tyson heard a noise in front of the house, as if the ice was moving, just as he was planning to go to bed. He sent Joseph out to check. After a few seconds the latter returned with the exciting news that a bear was gnawing at his kayak, which was lying barely 10 feet from the entrance to the house. But Joseph's rifle was stowed inside the kayak, while Tyson's was leaning against it. Apart from one of the pistols they had no weapon to hand. Once Tyson had hurriedly pulled on his footgear, the two men carefully crawled outside. Reaching the end of the snow tunnel, they could clearly hear the bear gnawing. Another step and they spotted the animal, which was now occupied with one of the hooded seal pelts. While Joseph crawled toward the crew's house to fetch help, Tyson crept carefully toward the kayak, closer to his rifle. Just as he was about to grab it, it fell over and banged noisily against a double-barrelled gun that lay near it. Disturbed by the noise, the bear turned and growled; but Tyson had already seized his rifle and got the bear in his sights. He tried to fire but the rifle misfired; he cocked the hammer a second and a third time, but it still wouldn't fire. Inquisitively the bear now toddled toward the hunter, who in the meantime was not polite enough to wait for the visitor but hurriedly retreated to the house to fetch shells. Sticking the muzzle of his newly loaded rifle out of the bolt-hole of the tunnel, he spotted the bear close in front of him. He brought the rifle to his shoulder, aimed as well as the darkness permitted, and fired. His shot was followed in rapid succession by two more from Joseph's rifle and pistol; the bear made a desperate leap in the air, then ran off for a short distance and collapsed.

Since it was already too dark, they buried it in the snow; when the natives dressed it next morning, it was revealed that Tyson's bullet had drilled through it from the direction of the left shoulder to the right and had penetrated its heart. One of Joseph's shots had penetrated its left haunch, but the pistol ball had smashed one of its neck vertebrae.

There was a full moon on the 28th, and the following spring tide, which was accompanied by a gale-force north wind at times attaining hurricane force, again did not pass without having some effect. The ice again broke up and the heavy surf of the high, swelling seas caused great devastation. Under the violent impact of the waves, the smaller floes and fragments were shattered; the bergs, which numbered in the hundreds, were now free of their shackles and were rocking in the wild waves. Whenever one of them capsized, the small floe rocked and heaved, to the point that they feared that it would disintegrate. During the night of the 29th it came into conflict with one of the giants; the collision was announced by a dull crash; everyone rushed to the boat in order to launch it in the extreme emergency.

When day finally began to dawn a violent blizzard rose. Toward noon the wind dropped, but the snow was still falling in dense flakes. A fragment of ice appeared vaguely near the floe; on it lay a dark object that looked like a seal. Joseph fired. The dark object made a slight movement but then remained quiet as before. The boat was manned and when the men reached the floe, they found an old hooded seal with her pup. The wounded mother defended herself angrily but after a brief, fruitless resistance it was killed and pulled into the boat along with the pup. The pitiful call of the little animal attracted the male and a bullet from Hans's rifle went through its head.

At noon on 31 March a meridian altitude reading on the sun placed the floe at 59°41'N latitude; hence the daily rate of drift had risen from 19 to 23 miles since the 25th. A storm began to blow up again; again the wind whipped up a heavy swell and again there followed a tense night, but much more stressful than the previous one. The floe had separated from the rest of the ice and was drifting toward the open sea; the seas grew higher and with them the heaving and pitching of the strange craft, against whose crumbling edges the waves broke constantly.

By morning the floe had disintegrated as far as the periphery of the houses and could no longer serve as a refuge, since the waves were already lapping at the snow walls of the houses. But where were they to turn? There wasn't a single piece of ice in sight.

The floe became steadily smaller; and in order to sell their lives as dearly as possible the unfortunate wretches decided to launch their boat and to search for the pack ice that must lie somewhere to the west. Nobody knew how far, but certainly it was a substantial distance since no ice-blink appeared on the western horizon, where dark clouds rose threateningly.

The boat, originally intended for 6, now had to hold 19, and the seamen who handled the oars could scarcely manoeuvre enough to combat the wild seas. Although they took only the essentials, leaving behind all the skins and the entire supply of meat with the exception of the bear hams, the boat was so badly overloaded that it could not possibly survive the seas for long. It threatened to fill and of necessity had to be lightened, if it was to be prevented from sinking almost immediately.

First the bedding was thrown overboard and, somewhat later, the meat. But the boat was still riding too low and necessity demanded that the bulk of the pemmican also be jettisoned. Shortly afterward they had to sacrifice almost the entire remainder of the pemmican.

Now everything was dispensable and much that would be badly missed was thrown overboard; but little good came of this, since the seas had increased. Water had to be bailed out continually, but the amount of water in the boat refused to drop. The oarsmen battled tenaciously against wind and seas; the appearance of the pack ice edge gave them new courage and fresh strength.

It was late in the evening when they reached it; a lot of ice appeared, but they had to search for a long time before they found a floe which was suitable for a campsite. The boat was assigned to the women and children for the night while the men sought shelter in a tent that they had made from old canvas over the course of the winter.

After a sleepless night, on the morning of 2 April the shipwrecked party took to the oars again, since during their uncomfortable stop the floe had broken into several pieces, all too small to offer safety. But they had covered barely two miles when a violent south wind blew up and grew into a gale. In the meantime the boat had developed a leak and had to be hauled up onto a small floe as fast as possible. The gale continued to blow; night fell, and was passed under similar circumstances to the preceding one.

At daybreak the men began repairing the damaged boat, but this took over three hours.[4] Around 9 o'clock they launched it, and fled south along the outer edge of the pack. Around 2.00 p.m. the wind forced them to haul the boat up on a floe. The ice was packing together; they were beset, and had no alternative but to camp. It was only with great effort that they succeeded in pitching and securing the tent and in protecting it from the fury of the storm. Several hooded seals appeared in the immediate vicinity. The natives killed a young male, which provided both food and fuel, both of which were urgently needed.

The 4th of April passed scarcely better than the preceding day. Around 9.00 a.m. the shipwrecked party succeeded in freeing themselves from the fetters of ice, and in reaching open water. Again they rowed south along the edge of the pack ice. They might have been underway for about two hours when floes and fragments came driving toward them and jammed their boat tight. Before they had time to find a campsite, they were again beset. They hauled the boat up on the nearest floe and pitched the tent. According to Meyer's observation this new home was located at 56°47'N latitude. The site looked quite uninviting; but they counted themselves lucky to have found it, since it was starting to blow impetuously out of the northwest and a short, wild sea came rolling in from the east.

As it began to grow dark the storm broke with desperate fury. The wind chopped round through north to northeast; the sea became rougher and white flecks of foam flew into the camp in thick masses, like snow. The light tent provided little shelter, and its occupants huddled with chattering teeth around the lamp. The children cried and the women wailed. To put an end to the general suffering, the irreplaceable Joseph built a snow house in which the party might have felt more comfortable if only the roaring surf were less violent.

It might have been about 5.00 a.m. when the floe began to crackle in a high-pitched noise. Then came a weird crack, then a dull groaning, a boisterous shaking and a loud crash; and the ice had split quite close to the tent. A short pause that followed next was interrupted by noises similar to the previous ones. The floe was splitting again. The snow house was quickly evacuated and the tent was struck and brought to the middle of the ice. The children had barely been taken to safety when another piece of the floe broke away; the snow house collapsed and drifted away with that fragment.

The day passed amidst increasing anxiety. Nobody knew where the floe would split again; the very next moment these poor people, who for six months of suffering and despite the most bitter disappointments had remained unflinching, might end up in a cold grave in the foaming waves.

The increased cold caused Joseph to build a new snow house, since the tent barely provided any shelter for the children from the icy wind. Posting a guard during the night was superfluous, in that everyone was awake; nobody dared yield to sleep, although they had been deprived of it for so long. The wind swung from northeast to northwest without decreasing in strength. It was a terrifying night, but it passed without any further danger.

Morning dawned again (it was 6 April) but conditions refused to improve. The sea rose and became more tormented than previously, and the wind rose to a hurricane. Toward noon a wide crack appeared, running through the house that Joseph had built. There was now only a small fragment of the floe left, but due to the violent seas they were unable to leave it.

The shipwrecked party placed their meagre possessions in the boat, in which the women and children then took their places. The rest kept watch by the side of the boat, so that they could launch it at a critical moment. And thus they spent another night.

But the day that followed was even worse. At 6.00 a.m. the floe split again. Only with great difficulty and in the most serious danger were they able to save themselves on the larger of the two pieces, and in so doing almost forfeited their precious boat. They now possessed neither blubber for the lamp nor meat for food; but most of all they lacked drinking water, since the snow on the greatly diminished floe had become completely brackish due to the breakers.

Toward midnight the tumult of the elements rose to a climax. A further piece broke away from the floe, and with it Meyer drifted helplessly away, clinging to the gunwale of the boat.[5] The others gazed after him in dismay; it was impossible to help him, and he could never manage to handle the boat alone.

Joseph's kayak was in the boat. Meyer now launched it, in the hope that the wind would carry it to within reach of the natives. But the little craft was carried off in a different direction and finally drifted back to him in a wide arc.

At this moment of extreme crisis the Eskimos showed their composure and selflessness. Neglecting their families and hazarding their own lives, they deliberately and cheerfully climbed aboard two pieces of ice that were just drifting past, as if going for a pleasure trip, and using the shafts of their lances they paddled toward the helpless man on the floe.

Their companions stared after them fearfully, since the two men were having to battle strenuously against the driving waves and the brash ice. With their powerful arms they worked away steadily for over an hour. Then they disappeared from their companions' view; it began to snow; the flakes fell thicker and thicker and the matt twilight grew fainter.

At 3.00 a.m., when dawn broke and the snowstorm ceased, Meyer and the natives were spotted along with the boat on the shattered floe, near which the kayak was still floating. The two parts of the floe, about a mile apart, were separated by small fragments of ice that heaved in the short waves. Along with the rest of the crew, Tyson now set off to rescue the Eskimos and Meyer and to bring the boat to safety; only two men who were too faint-hearted stayed behind. They all reached the boat safely, although totally soaked, but their progress across the heaving brash ice had exhausted their strength.

On the return trip Meyer and a seaman landed under the ice. The former would have drowned if the alert Joseph, risking losing his own footing, had not pulled him out.[6] Once the boat had been landed, the natives pulled out the kayak, which was still drifting around. It was not until late in the afternoon that they were able to pitch the tent; Joseph immediately built a new snow house.

The night passed quietly; when the party went to sleep a guard was posted, and relieved every two hours; next morning everyone felt invigorated by the refreshing sleep.

The wind began to blow violently again; but the sky was clear and Meyer measured some sun altitudes, which placed the latitude of the camp at 55°51'N. Toward evening the wind and seas were rising again. A large breaker smashed the snow house and swept Mrs. Hannah to the edge of the floe. Once again Joseph's agility and presence of mind saved a human life.

The boat was kept constantly ready to be launched in case the situation deteriorated even more. There was not a single dry spot left anywhere on the entire floe. The waves rolled impetuously over the treacherous refuge floe; the men clung to the gunwales of the boat in which the women and children had been placed to weigh it down.

It was not until after midnight that it became calmer. The ice began to pack, and the people pitched the tent and threw themselves down exhausted in their wet clothes on the slippery, cold surface.

The next day, 10 April, passed more pleasantly. The sky was completely overcast; a total calm prevailed; the ice was close-packed and held the shipwrecked party captive.

On the 11th and 12th things were similar. During the 11th, dense fog brooded over the immediate surroundings. Since a raven and several small land birds appeared, they decided that the coast could not be far away; later a fox visited the floe, but it cleverly knew how to stay out of range of Joseph's rifle. There were never any seals to be seen now, and hunger again became as rampant as previously. When it cleared on the 12th, Meyer made a determination of their position, which placed the latitude at 55°35'N. According to this the floe's daily rate of drift had dropped to 5 miles, and the land that they had hoped to see was nowhere in sight.

On the 13th, around 1.00 a.m., the ice slackened; but an hour later it had closed up again. Now their sweeping gaze searched in vain for open areas; all around there rose nothing but desolate ice debris, lit by the red glow of the flashing northern lights. At noon the latitude of the floe was 12 miles less than on the previous day. A small seal surfaced from time to time behind a floe, but it stayed out of range.

Five days slowly passed in constant excitement and the torments of gnawing hunger. In the meantime some seals had been seen but they had not allowed anyone to approach them. When some open water appeared on the afternoon of the 18th about half a mile from the camp, Joseph went hunting and killed a fat seal. Somewhat later the dark banks of cloud above the southwestern horizon dispersed. Finally the long-sought land appeared in clear outline; but the prospects of reaching it were less favourable than ever. Another raven appeared, and some smaller birds and a flock of ducks passed over high in the sky.

Black storm clouds rose ominously next morning, and spread menacingly across the sky from the northwest. The rapidly rising sea heralded the approach of the wind, and as it began to grow dark it began raging at gale force. Around 9 o'clock the hurricane was raging with full fury, driving hissing breakers across the floe, which was spinning like a top.

The tent was blown down and Joseph, who was trying to hold it up, was hurled to the ground under the impact of a wave. Everything that the waves had not carried away was hurriedly stowed in the boat, in which, as before, the women and children had to take their places.

Of all their nights of terror this one took the prize![7] The fury of the elements was more terrifying than ever before; the unchained hurricane raged more violently than during the devastating winter storms, and the waves were higher than they had ever seen before. Everyone clung frantically to the boat, which had been anchored down in the middle of the disintegrating floe in order to make it more secure. Despite all the strength expended by the men, the boat was carried toward the edge of the piece of ice by every breaker; often a second one was approaching before they had time to push it back again. Every successive wave seemed to rage more wildly than the preceding ones; and each wave carried away a chunk of the floe on whose slippery surface one could barely maintain a footing.

The arms of the harassed men were growing weak, yet nobody dared to let go the boat. If anybody had flinched he would have been irreparably lost. The waves broke thunderously around the floe and the storm howled horribly. Its weird voices even drowned out the shouted orders, despite the fact that the area on which the crew were standing was frighteningly small and was still shrinking.

In the meantime dawn had broken; but several hours passed before any moderation began. Around 7 o'clock the floe split under the boat; the smaller piece was carried off by the waves, which licked hissingly at the keel of the boat and broke over the bodies of four unfortunates who clung grimly to its sides. Their legs were half swinging with the movements of the waves, which boisterously pulled them first in one direction, then in another until finally, during a favourable moment, they could be rescued.

But they could not stay on the floe any longer; the dangers that threatened the boat in the stormy waves were no greater than here on the treacherous chunk of ice which, under the weight of the people, barely rose above the water level any more. When a larger floe appeared nearby the boat was safely launched. The cook, who fell overboard and received some severe contusions, was fished out again only after repeated vain attempts.

Reaching the new floe required endless effort; clambering onto it was even more difficult, since at one moment it was wallowing in the trough of a wave, and at the next it had been heaved up and was teetering on the crest. The men pursued it persistently with the boat, handling the oars with exhausted arms, until they finally succeeded in throwing out the ice anchor. But they still had not won the gamble; an anxious hour passed before the boat was secured.

By evening the storm had certainly slackened but not the waves and breakers that still broke, foaming, on the floe. Everyone was soaked; nobody could sleep. They spent the night shivering and with chattering teeth.

The next day appeared more friendly, since during the early morning hours the ice had closed. The people now tried to sleep in turns in the boat; but the cold and their gnawing hunger would not permit them the rest that they sought. It was only the sunny afternoon that provided some relief; clothes were spread out to dry, and also the tent, which could not be pitched since it was frozen hard. The natives searched for game, but all their searches were in vain.

On the 22nd the weather was indescribably bad. It had snowed heavily during the night; then came hail and then a softening downpour of rain that persisted until the afternoon.

The entire reserves of food now consisted only of 12 small ship's biscuits, and these were completely soaked in sea water. They had already eaten the last remnants of the pemmican several days before and now they again had to fall back on old scraps of leather and shreds of sealskin, to avoid dying of hunger. Meyer could barely stand any longer due to exhaustion; some of the others were not much better, but he seemed to be suffering most.

Three times already Joseph had ventured out over the heaving brash ice, but each time he had returned empty-handed. Setting off again, he got lost in the fog and found his way back to the boat only with great difficulty. When the fog descended he climbed on to a disintegrating iceberg.[8] He had left his rifle behind since, after the various disappointments he had experienced, he scarcely expected to find any game.

Scarcely three rifle shots away from him a bear suddenly appeared; it raised its head, sniffing the air and then headed toward him. He quickly headed for camp, or as quickly as the unsafe footing allowed. The bear approached quite close, then stopped and keenly eyed the handful of men on the floe. The natives told the others to throw themselves flat on the ice and to imitate the movements of a seal with their heads and legs, in order to fool the animal, which was upwind.

Now followed some minutes of great tension. The bear had become suspicious and had turned away. Under the cover of up-heaved ice hummocks, Joseph and Hans crawled close to it. The bear turned back, sniffed again, then continued on its way, ambling straight toward the supposed seals that lay closest to him. Crouched behind a hummock the hunters lay in wait for him. Two shots rang out together and the animal was rolling in its own blood.

The prey was quickly torn apart by the half-starved men. Only once they had somewhat appeased their hunger on the raw meat did they start cutting the bear up and cooking individual parts.[9]

Despite the rain that fell for the next two days, the shipwrecked party was in high spirits and cheerful; perhaps they guessed that they had survived the cruellest strokes of fate. Occasionally the land appeared in faint outline through the fog, but always just for a short time. In the meantime the ice slackened, but the narrow leads disappeared again just as fast as they had appeared.

Early on the morning of the 25th the wind, which thus far had been blowing constantly from the northeast, again rose to gale force. Pouring rain and the pounding of the waves had already contributed powerfully to diminishing the floe, whose strength was quickly decreasing. Its edges were beginning to crack and split. When the swell became even heavier around 5 o'clock, and when the breakers again began to break over it, the party again had to put their trust in the boat, which was leaking and hence in a poor condition.

Emergency repairs were made on the boat and it was launched. But just as before, it had been overloaded this time too, and the party was forced to part with its food reserves. With heavy hearts they threw the bear meat overboard. After they had been rowing for eight hours, putting every effort into it, their strength gave out. They hauled the boat onto a fairly large floe and pitched camp; late in the evening Joseph killed another seal.

Shortly after 6 o'clock next morning they continued their voyage; but two hours later they again found themselves beset in the ice. Hence they pulled back to a floe and stopped the leak in the boat. Then half the crew went to sleep, while the rest spread out their soaked clothing to dry.

The 27th was a Sunday. During the night it had begun to snow; it was not until noon that it became clearer. Meyer measured some sun altitudes since the sun now appeared in vague outline. This rather unreliable determination indicated the latitude to be 53°30'N. Dark leads appeared far away to the south, but it was impossible to reach them, since they were unable to haul the boat over the brash ice. But toward evening the rising swell heralded the approach of a storm, which broke with full fury as it was beginning to get dark. By midnight the camp was completely inundated; it began to snow again and the situation became extremely serious.

Since this floe, too, was disintegrating, the boat was launched again at first light. It was not until 6 o'clock that they succeeded in reaching another floe. The people lay down to grab some rest finally, but their sleep would only be of short duration. Wakened by the watch, they hurriedly evacuated the tent. Three icebergs had collided close to the floe; one of them was heaved up, and when the pressure slackened it collapsed back into the sea with a noise of thunder; the surface of the water was covered with debris, several fragments of which were hurled into the camp and threatened to shatter the floe. There was real danger, and it was only exacerbated by the fact that the berg lost its equilibrium, capsized noisily, then drove straight toward the floe, grinding up the smaller ice debris which surrounded it.

The only hope of salvation lay in immediate flight. The boat was quickly manned and the crew rowed toward a more extensive polynya. After some time the seas subsided and Joseph killed three young hooded seals. The ice slackened, the leads became wider, and the harassed party was able to continue its journey. But dense fog reduced their visibility to less than a ship's length, and they had to wend their way very cautiously through the tortuous channels.

For a few hours they slowly pursued their southerly course. When the fog lifted they spotted the outlines of a steamer at a distance of a few miles.[10]

All their worries were now forgotten; their spirits lifted and a loud shout of joy rang out.

But their joy was premature. The vessel, which previously had been heading for them, suddenly altered course. The party hoisted their flag; they screamed and yelled and fired off a volley. Their shouts were carried away on the wind. The ship turned completely away from them, then steamed out of sight.

The ice floe travellers, who had thought themselves so close to being rescued, felt this disappointment doubly bitterly. Despondently they again pulled the boat up onto a floe and pitched their tent. They were all tired and worn out, but the resentment that they harboured, and the excitement, kept them awake. For a long time they tossed and turned, unable to sleep on their cold bed; occasionally they left the tent and stared expectantly in the direction in which the ship had appeared and disappeared so unexpectedly.[11]

It was not until late into the night that nature asserted itself and let them forget their sorrow.

CHAPTER 24

The seals

The Newfoundland seal hunters. The seals' pupping areas and their habits. The movement of the ships. Cruel wars of annihilation. The pelts and the fat. Accidents.

Shortly before the snow starts to melt, lively activity begins to reign in the larger ports of Newfoundland. The seagoing population of the island switches from the inactivity of the cheerless winter to a busy life; for now work begins on fitting out every ship that is intended for the seal hunt.[1]

Since the Newfoundlanders have realized the value of this industry their sails have annually swarmed around the shores of Labrador. In 1807, when the first seals were harvested, the number of ships was only 30; 50 years later, by contrast, there were almost 400 of them. This bloody trade had reached its climax at this point. No fewer than 13,600 men participated in this murderous war of annihilation; during a two-month voyage they killed around 500,000 seals, the value of which at that time was about £425,000 in round figures. But it was not long before this spirit of enterprise was dampened, since the reckless pursuit of the hunt had so seriously depleted the previously numerous seal herds that the owners' profits became extremely dubious.

When the seals later appeared in larger numbers, the extinguished zeal of the Newfoundlanders blazed up anew; and when the 19 shipwrecked people were drifting off the coast of Labrador, they were surrounded by over 100 ships, among which were 20 superb steamers. Within a small circumference were scattered almost 8000 men, exposed to the same rigours of the rough weather as the ice drifters, although under different circumstances.

Certainly in good years the profit from the seal hunt is a substantial one, but the life of the seal hunter while he is pursuing his trade is an unenviable one, richly spiced with danger, and he has to earn his bread the hard way.

When the gales of early March and the associated storm tides break up the ice covering the harbours of St. John's, Catalina, Harbour Grace and the other sealing ports, the ships weigh anchor and put to sea without delay; for now the seals are hauling out to give birth to their pups.[2] Nobody knows where they come from or where they have been for the last months before their arrival. They just suddenly appear. But not singly or in hundreds; no, they are to be counted in thousands, for they cover the ice, tightly packed, for miles.

Usually the females seek out large floes for their pupping sites, strong enough to withstand the gales and the pounding of the waves. For although predominantly aquatic, the young seal will inevitably perish if it is forced to exchange its sojourn on the ice for a life in the water before a specified time, an old legacy from ancestors which first saw the light of the world on land, and ended their days there too.

The seal hunter always bears this peculiarity of the animals in mind. It takes years of practice and a sharp eye to locate the spot where the seals have hauled out. Whether the seals are close to the outer edge of the pack or farther away from it depends entirely on the nature of the ice. If an extensive surface of younger ice lies in front of the main mass of the pack the ships will bore through it, since the hunters expect to find their prey beyond it. But if they immediately run into older floes they follow their edges, since the seals like to find peninsula-like tongues of ice from which the pups can easily reach the water later.

From the first gleam of dawn to the fall of night there is always a lookout in the crow's nest; equipped with a superb telescope, he carefully scans the ice. Despite the most favourable signs, occasionally there is scarcely a seal to be seen and the seal hunters spend the best and longest part of the season in cruising vainly. Commonly the success of the hunt depends even more on the interaction of fortunate accidents than on the judgment and keen eyes of the ship's captain. Thus over the course of a few days a vessel can kill a full cargo while another, only a few miles away, heads home completely empty or makes only a minimal cargo. Commonly a ship is beset in the ice and the crew can see the herds of seals in the distance without being able to approach them, and have to calmly accept the fact that others, whose luck is better, are killing the animals.

In stormy weather the ships generally seek shelter in the middle of the pack ice, where the sea is less violent than off the ice edge. Then it may well happen that next morning the ships are totally besieged by seals whereas the night before there was not a seal in sight.

In such cases it is necessary to act quickly and carefully. With the exception of the captain and a small crew, everyone grabs his sealing gaff, a heavy pole about 5 feet long, with a heavy double hammerhead at one end. Filled with a wild killing lust, hundreds of men scatter in all directions across the ice, in order to annihilate a poor defenceless creature with every blow.

The seals, which are usually so wary that it takes a skilled hunter to shoot one, and an even more experienced hand to harpoon them, have suddenly lost their fear, due to concern about the pups, and let themselves be killed without resistance.[3] Only in exceptional cases, if the pup begins to cry, uttering noises resembling the bleating of a lamb or the crying of a baby, will the mother protect its pup with wild desperation. She snaps furiously about her and scratches; and there are even cases when her efforts are successful and she manages to put the hunter to flight.

But the hunters know no pity. They are motivated only by the desire for profit, which in some cases makes them blind to the suffering and torments of the poor creatures, and in others give their eyes the sharpness of a telescope, so that they can spot their prey when they are still far away from them, appearing only as dark spots on the icy horizon.

One cannot watch this unsportsmanlike hunting (that barely deserves the name) without the deepest repugnance, for it is lower than the lowest extermination, carried out in a manner that arouses horror. The hunter approaches to within a few paces of the mother animal, which slowly raises its head, looks at him piteously with its big shining eyes. Its gaze is undoubtedly human-like. Anybody who spotted this expression on the face of a human would start back at the infinitely deep torment of the soul that was reflected in it with awful clarity.

But these eyes, that legend says are weeping tears of sorrow, do not influence the seal hunter. He only grips his implement of death more firmly, raises it quickly for a furious stroke, and smashes the skull of his victim. The latter quivers in its grim death throes or, if it is not badly injured, tries to escape from its persecutor in flight, by means of clumsy movements. But he just reverses his weapon, raises it again, and slams the sharp point of the gaff into the back of the tortured animal. Thus bringing it to a halt, he gives it another blow on the skull, and a third, till the skull is smashed. At that moment, tormented by a double pain, the mother seal often gives birth. And the little animal which has scarcely breathed the air that surrounds it, scarcely seen the light whose beams break quivering on the masses of ice, dies at the moment when it enters life, while the beating of its heart is practically still controlled by the beats of its mother's quickly fading heart. A boot to the still-soft skull usually brings a quick end; the slaughterer rarely uses his gaff; lifting it requires more strength and time than lifting one's foot. He must not expose himself to fatigue to no end, or squander his time pointlessly; a great deal of bloody work still awaits him.

Each time that he swings his gaff up for a blow, he kills another seal, if he does it properly. And he is not alone in this cruel war of annihilation, since his numerous companions are working furiously in just the same manner. In the space of a minute every one of them can kill three or five seals; and the number of minutes in an hour is substantial; and the day is long at these latitudes; and the slaughter does not end until it grows dark. The ice is soaked in blood, like a battlefield; for miles the snow is reddened from the footprints of the butchers, as they return to the ship at nightfall. On board the captain follows every detail of the cruel massacre, telescope in hand.

Piled up in enormous heaps, the motionless seals cover the surrounding area.[4] But it is a treacherous environment. A gentle wind can set the ice in motion and a high tide can shatter the floes, and then thousands of poor creatures will have been murdered pointlessly and will revert to the sea from which they originated.

All too frequently the crew of a ship kills more seals than it can carry. In order to guarantee their right of ownership against other vessels, in such cases a pennant with the ship's flag number is planted on the heaps of carcasses. But these markers are often blown away by the wind and another ship takes possession of the seals.

Occasionally even the coastal residents take possession of them. Thus in the spring of 1872 about 5000 seals that drifted ashore with the ice were seized by the population of Bonavista, near the cape of the same name. The evening before, the usual pennant had fluttered over each heap of carcasses (there were 13 of them). But when the ice grounded during the night several of the flags were carried away by the wind, and next morning the local residents hurried out to secure the valuable booty. A few days later more piles of seals appeared, which until then had been buried under the floes, but the animals had already started to decompose and hence were unusable.

Assuming that the seal hunters can take possession unhindered, once they have killed a fair number of seals, at daybreak they immediately start skinning their haul.

The crew again hurries out onto the ice, but now, instead of the gaff, each of them carries a knife and steel in his belt, as do our butchers, and the butchery now continues with undiminished zeal.

The animals are laid on their backs one after the other; then the sealer makes a long incision from the neck to the root of the tail and some more incisions round the flippers. A few adroit movements of the hand and the knife separate the pelt and the layer of blubber adhering to it from the underside of the carcass; the carcass is then turned over and the pelt is simultaneously pulled off from the back. After a sufficient number have been skinned some of the crew haul the pelts on board. About three or four pelts, depending on the man's physical strength, are attached to a line and hauled to the ship, in the holds of which they are immediately stowed, piled with the fat side on the hair side in order to retain the blubber between the pelts as it becomes liquid.

Their further processing occurs only after the vessel has returned to its destination, which is usually the same port from which it sailed. As soon as the ship has dropped anchor the unloading of the cargo begins. The pelts are spread out, hair side down, on small tables whose surfaces are slightly inclined. To remove the layer of fat the worker uses a long blade that can best be compared to a Turkish scimitar. Holding the blubber with his left hand, he separates it from the pelt with a few cuts. In the course of an hour a good worker can clean 35–40 of these pelts without effort; they are then packed, interlayered with salt, which results in an incomplete tanning process. After three to four weeks this has proceeded sufficiently that the pelts can be exported.

In order to extract the oil, in earlier times the fat was boiled in large iron or copper kettles over open fires; but nowadays for this purpose one uses either superheated steam or the heat of the sun. If one uses the former, extraction of the liquid oil is not only achieved significantly faster than by the old method, but the oil produced is also better; it smells less strongly and it is said to provide more illumination and less soot. The fat of young seals is prized more highly than that of the adults, since in the latter the residue of connective tissues is greater than in the former.

The wages received by the sealing captains and their crews are not fixed but are controlled by the size of the catch and the market price of the cargo. A third of the value of the total belongs to the owner, who pays the ship's captain a bonus, the size of which depends on the number of pelts. In this manner the owner of the ship receives the bulk of the profit, since he is the only person involved who risks real pecuniary losses. He is responsible not only for fitting out the ship but also for provisioning it; the crew's meals are all provided throughout the voyage, and in the case of an unsuccessful year they lose at most the hypothetical wages they might have made at other employment.

Not uncommonly a ship obtains a full cargo in the course of two or three weeks and can then undertake a second voyage, which is often just as productive as the first. But sometimes many of the ships return almost totally clean or are crushed by the ice. Thus in the spring of 1871 the brig *Confederate* left the harbour of Harbour Grace and was immediately beset in heavy ice in Bonavista Bay, and was driven ashore. According to the St. John's newspaper, for 10 days the ice was so close that not the slightest lead was visible anywhere around the ship. After that period had elapsed the floes began to slacken; but a few hours later the water had disappeared again; the floes nipped the ship and screwed themselves under her keel. Nobody suspected any damage, until the lower compartments were underwater, and it rose so rapidly that the crew were obliged to flee to the nearby shore.

This is one of the numerous accidents such as occur almost annually, and to which steamers seem to be susceptible to a greater degree than sailing ships, whose design is more appropriate to the ice conditions. Fortunately, heavy losses of human lives are rare events since, at a pinch, the crew of a damaged vessel can usually reach the coast.

When westerly winds blow in early March, the pack ice invariably moves seaward and the ships can easily reach the fast ice near the shore. But if periods of calm begin, the temperature generally drops so low that the sea becomes covered with new ice that holds the ships beset. When the latter are finally freed after a lengthy besetment, they rarely manage to make a successful voyage since, as the season advances, the seals leave the ice and are difficult to kill because they are increasingly vigilant.

As a result the hunt becomes more noble; the hunter now scarcely finds any opportunity to use his murderous gaff, and it is the bullet that either hits or misses its mark.

CHAPTER 25

Salvation

Another steamer in sight. Another ship appears, but they shout in vain. The shipwrecked party on board Tigress. *The reaction. Gales. Among the seals.* Tigress *anchors in Bay Roberts. Arrival in St. John's. The news is telegraphed to the United States. The warship* Frolic. *Arrival in New York.*

The sail that had turned away so shabbily from the shipwrecked party was one of the Newfoundland sealers. When it again hove in sight next morning the people quickly launched their boat and rowed toward it. After they had been struggling successfully against the ice for over two hours, the ice closed and held them beset. Their boat lay as if riveted to the spot; all efforts to free it were unsuccessful.

They clambered up one of the highest hummocks in the vicinity, hoisted a flag and fired three volleys, to which the steamer replied with the same number of cannon shots. It turned and immediately seemed to be steering toward them. It changed course from north to east; from east to west, and then to southwest, but it was held fast by the ice and could not get close to them.

They again fired three volleys but there was no reply. The vessel remained in the vicinity till late in the afternoon, then dense clouds of smoke belched from her funnel and an hour later she was out of sight.

With an unwavering gaze the shipwrecked party stared after the black smoke that curled up on the distant horizon; a gentle west wind erased the last trace of it.

In the direction opposite to that taken by the steamer, a second ship appeared somewhat later; but this one did not bring the salvation for which they were hoping either.

As the sun sank, the land appeared to the southwest as a vague, dark silhouette. The day was coming to an end and the severely tried men saw themselves cheated out of another hope. But they had not yet given the game up for lost. Before they went to sleep a lookout was posted who maintained several signal fires using the fat of the seals they had killed.

The fires flickered only dimly through the thick fog that had descended on the sea and the ice, but they were spotted by the vigilant eye of a ship's captain who was cruising at the edge of the pack. Suspecting an accident, he stuck close to the flickering points of light all night; and when the fog cleared on the morning of 30 April the ice drifters spotted a steamer almost right on top of them.

Fearing that this ship, too, would swing away from them, Hans began paddling toward it in his kayak. But the vessel was steaming slowly toward their floe even without this. When it came within hail the people fired a salute, hoisted the flag and cheered with joy!

On board the crew climbed immediately into the shrouds and replied to this greeting; then two boats were lowered to pick up the shipwrecked party. But they launched their own boat, which had borne them so faithfully this far, and with rapid oar-strokes sped toward the ship.

The ship, *Tigress*, was also a Newfoundland sealer from Conception Bay; her skipper, Captain Bartlett, was an old, trustworthy seaman.[1]

The feelings that surged through the hearts of the shipwrecked party when they stepped on the deck of the rescuing vessel can be understood and empathized with, but not described. For 196 long days their lives had been constantly threatened and now—now they were finally safe.

As they related their experiences during their dreadful voyage to the men, the latter listened almost incredulously and were inclined to consider it impossible that creatures of flesh and blood could have defied such dangers. The story of these ragged people sounded like a fairy-story, a terrible fairy-story, in the details of which death and destruction recurred in almost endless sequence. Even the hardened sealers experienced a slight degree of awe. They praised the steadfastness of the men, admired the heroic courage of the women, and felt pity for the poor children, who in their childhood had seen all the suffering and horror of a lifetime.

They were all given the best of care. The brave skipper invited Tyson and Meyer to share his cabin with him, while the men adopted the crew, the women and children, who for the moment were accommodated in the crew's quarters.

Since *Tigress*'s captain intended to spend a few more weeks at sea, the rescued party still had to curb their impatience to set foot on shore. When the ship picked them up she was near Grady Harbour,[2] on the Labrador coast at latitude 53°35'N; now she set a northward course in order to follow the fleeing seal herds.

Next day, 1 May, a few steamers hove in sight. Some of the captains, to whom the trustworthy Bartlett had spoken during the night, came aboard *Tigress*, and soon afterward the majority of the sealing fleet was informed of the expedition's fate.

With the rest that followed the hardships they had suffered, reaction set in for the party. Everyone, with the exception of Joseph and Hans, was affected to a greater or lesser degree. Scorbutic symptoms appeared in some of the sailors; almost everyone suffered from rheumatism; Meyer, whose frozen hands were causing him great pain in addition, was in a critical condition.

During the 3rd there was such a violent storm out of the northwest that *Tigress* sought out the pack ice, in order to escape the wild seas. Toward evening she was beset.[3] Then came such fierce ice pressures that the ship was creaking in every joint; but she was strongly built and withstood the violent assault without suffering damage.[4]

It was not until the morning of the 5th that the ship got free again. At the same time the lookout spotted some herds of seals, lying on the floes, 5 to 6 miles away. Immediately over 100 men were ready to start the hunt; they hurried toward the harmless animals across the heaving brash ice.

The crew returned after sunset. They had killed between 700 and 800 seals, piled them in three piles and flagged them in the usual way, so as to begin skinning next morning. But in so doing they had not taken account of the needs of the others. When they hurried back to the spot at daybreak to bring home their pelts, only a few of the seals were left.

Despite the flags the crew of another vessel had appropriated the seals they had killed and had gone off with them in the darkness and fog.⁵ A gaff had been left behind, with the name of another ship on its haft; this betrayed the miscreants, who later were to be brought to trial.

Since a stiff breeze had sprung up in the meantime, *Tigress*'s commander attempted to break through the ice in order to take aboard the people and the remaining pelts; in this he finally succeeded after many vain assaults. The rest of the day was spent in a fruitless search; not a seal showed itself anywhere, and the best part of the season had passed. Since the prospects had not improved next day and since, in addition, the storm had blown up again, the skipper decided to run for home. Several days earlier one of the boilers had started to leak. This defect had now become so serious that *Tigress* had to reduce her speed by half, and later conditions dictated that the engines be stopped completely. Given the heavy seas, progress became extraordinarily slow as a result, and the shipwrecked people could barely restrain their impatience to set foot on terra firma.⁶

The increasing storm came to their assistance; on 8 May the vessel dropped anchor in Bay Roberts⁷ in order to let the gale blow itself out.

This meant that they had survived all the dangers of their journey. The people were welcomed with jubilation by the residents of the little place where Captain Bartlett lived;⁸ and when the steamer *Walrus* reached St. John's harbour next day to discharge her cargo, her captain informed the United States consul of the fate of the expedition.

That same day the following telegram could be read in the evening papers in the major cities of North America, its defective composition slightly excusable given the uniqueness of the event. It read:

St. John's, Newfoundland, 9 May 1873.

To the Secretary of State, Washington, D.C.

The English whaling ship *Walrus* has just arrived, and reports that the steamer *Tigress* picked up on the ice at Grady Harbor, Labrador on the 30th of April last, fifteen of the crew and five of the Esquimaux of the steamer *Polaris* of the Arctic expedition.

Captain Hall died last summer. The *Tigress* is expected hourly at St. John's. Will report further details.

F.N. Molloy, United States Consul.

Although this telegram was quickly followed by several more, the latter were unable to clarify the entire circumstances, and hence the excitement grew by the hour. Through the efforts of the Navy Department, the authority to which the expedition was alone accountable, the various doubts were soon resolved, however, and the cloud with which the press had been doing its best to surround the event was removed.

In the meantime the ice drifters had spent some pleasant days under the hospitable roofs of the Newfoundlanders. At 8 o'clock on the morning of the 12th, *Tigress* left Bay Roberts harbour and, favoured by the most superb weather, steamed round the mountainous headland whose most northerly point is formed by the feared Cape St. Francis, and 12 hours later she reached St. John's.

More than half the residents of the capital were assembled on the quayside, since everyone wanted to see the people who had made the adventurous ice-drift. Once the first surge of curiosity had been satisfied, the seamen, women and children were led through the narrow streets to the dwelling that the consul had selected for them. Only Meyer and Tyson remained behind on board, to await the arrival of a tailor.

The number of steamers that keep Newfoundland in contact with the rest of the civilized world is very small, especially during the first months of spring, as long as the numerous icebergs make navigation dangerous. Hence the warship *Frolic* was ordered to put to sea without delay, in order to bring the rescued group home, where friends and relatives were waiting for them.[9]

At the time, this steamer was lying at New York; only a few hours were needed to ready her for sea. She sailed from the Navy Yard under the command of Commander C.N. Schoonmaker on the evening of the 16th.

Until the 19th the weather held fair; but then dense fog rolled in and hence, as she approached Sable Island, the vessel had to reduce speed to a few knots. When it cleared at noon on the 21st, Cape St. Mary and

Cape Pine came into view; numerous icebergs appeared at the same time and at 6.00 p.m. *Frolic* was rounding Cape Race.

Unfortunately it had not been possible to obtain a pilot in New York, and this lack now made itself distinctly felt. The number of icebergs increased; in the course of the night the ship passed no fewer than 120 of them, and since, moreover, many large floes were drifting with the current, the ship could make little progress. It was not until the morning of the 22nd that she dropped anchor in St. John's harbour. But it was a religious holiday[10] that day, and since a national holiday was celebrated on the 24th,[11] *Frolic*'s commander had to contain his patience until the 26th before he could take on coal. By the morning of the 27th the bunkers were full, and in the afternoon the 19 people boarded the ship; due to foggy weather, however, she was unable to put to sea until early next morning.

Shortly after noon *Frolic* was again rounding Cape Race; then came 53 unpleasant hours of fog; the sea rose; a gale got up and homeward progress became very slow.

It was not until 5 June that *Frolic* reached New York,[12] where the warship *Tallapoosa* lay ready to take the ice drifters to Washington. There they gave detailed statements about the events during their voyage before a judicial committee, which consisted of the Naval Minister, a Rear-Admiral, one of the heads of the Smithsonian Institution, and a Captain in the Federal Army.

Anyone who leafs through the stenographer's reports that emerged from this hearing, and which contain an incredible history of suffering in the simple words of the homely seamen, will perceive one of those unique facets of the seaman's changeable life, which cast only sombre shadows. But almost every page bears evidence of the devoted self-denial of the two Eskimos, whose patience alone saved the little party from death.

CHAPTER 26

The boat voyage in arctic waters

The route of the voyage. The boats and their equipment. The tom-cat Thomas. Departure from Polaris House and the natives. Sorfalik. Vain search for the Gulf Stream. Hakluyt Island. Bad weather. Northumberland Island. Ornithological notes. Unfavourable ice conditions. Beset. In memoriam. The boats' drift toward Northumberland Island. The glacier system of that island. Voyage to Cape Parry. Blackwood Point. Narwhals. Dalrymple Island. Conical Rock. Slim rations. A dangerous situation. On the land ice in Melville Bay. Unfavourable prospects. "Water pants." Off Cape York. Hoping and waiting. Ship ahoy!

Thus our companions, for whom we had long since given up hope, were restored to the civilized world earlier than we were, due to a favourable interaction of events.

Between our draughty hut and the nearest Danish colony lay a distance of about 360 miles, measured in a straight line, and at least three times that, following the coastline. In order to save the results we had obtained we had to sail across a stormy, ice-infested sea and strike across the dreaded Melville Bay, and the length of such a trip could not be anticipated in advance. The meagreness of our supplies made such a coastal voyage an urgent necessity. If we wanted to bring the adventure, into which that fateful October night had changed our scientific voyage of discovery, to a satisfactory conclusion, we could not move very far from the edge of the fast ice. Chester had done everything in his power to make usable boats for us; but they were not seaworthy, and suitable only for a river voyage at best.

These flat-bottomed skiffs, without any keel and with square-cut bows and sterns, had the shape of a kneading trough; they were 25 feet long; maximum width 5 feet, but they were only 2 feet 4 inches deep. A spare oar served as a mast; a bedsheet as a sail, once it had been soaked in oil in order to make it wind-tight. Each of the boats was provided with a light tent-roof which, it was intended, could be erected during rest stops. Schumann had made two small stoves from old coal buckets; tarred rope had to serve as fuel, although unfortunately we were unable to take enough with us. The provisions consisted of hardtack, canned meat, bad tea and some syrup; with utmost economy it might last 75 days. Beyond that we were relying on our hunting success. We were adequately provided with gunpowder since we had subsequently found a chest containing 12 grenades in the wreck; we had ground down the coarse-grained powder they contained.

The journals and the scientific sketches were packed in waterproof canvas and the most valuable of the smaller items in the collections in a box. But the bulk of them had to be left behind.[1] We took the most essential of the instruments: namely, for each boat a sextant and a chronometer; one of the latter, of which Bryan took charge, was only a pocket instrument. For my personal use I had put together a fairly complete travelling meteorological kit, since on the return journey across Melville Bay I wanted occasionally to try to find the Gulf Stream, which we had sought in vain two years earlier. In addition it seemed to me advisable to complete an extensive sequence of observations for the chart of our voyage.

To eliminate any doubt as to the accuracy of the observations on air pressure that we had made thus far, it was necessary to bring back one of the Fortin standard barometers for purposes of comparison. This was neither an easy nor a pleasant task, since the instrument had to be carried on one's back the whole time.

Each boat was designed to hold seven men and their equipment. Budington, Morton and Bryan, along with Odell, Mauch and Hayes,[2] formed the crew of one, which was unnamed. The other, which we had christened *Hopes dashed*, accommodated Chester, Schumann, the two stokers, Booth and Campbell, seamen Heinrich Hobby and Hermann Siemens, and finally myself.

Even the poor, orphaned cat, Tom, was taken care of; in his arctic sanctuary he had completely forgotten how to catch mice. It would have been heartless to abandon him; and cruel and thankless to shoot him. He had stuck with us so loyally in every situation that we saw it as our duty to make his lot as happy as possible. A bed of soft bearskin was made for him in a small, barred box that the men had knocked together for him; the bond of affection tied him to Budington and he was accommodated in his boat.

The day of our departure, originally set for 1 June, had to be postponed due to the stormy weather. On the 2nd the wind was still blowing with unabated violence; shattered floes pushed noisily against the ice foot and thwarted every attempt at pushing the boats toward open water. Over the course of the morning Chester and I carried three boxes of books and smaller instruments, as well as the pendulum apparatus and the passage instrument to a low elevation near the hut. The natives helped us with this and brought boulders with which we covered the boxes, after we had lowered them into a fissure in the rock. Somewhat later we also buried three of the Negus box chronometers that I had removed from their mounts and packed in a box in order to take them with us; but the very limited space in the boats meant that I had to abandon the idea. Our loyal Jimmy was given our dogs. He promised to keep an eye on the boxes and to watch over them, as being our property, against any intrusions by strangers. In one of the boxes we left a message giving a brief history of the expedition and information as to its future movements.

Shortly before noon the wind dropped; around 3 o'clock a light fog rolled in and an hour later a welcome soft breeze arose out of the southwest. If conditions did not change we could put to sea on the next high tide.

The Eskimos, who had gathered in large numbers, were looking forward to the moment of our departure with perhaps even greater anticipation than we ourselves. For everything we left behind must ultimately fall to them; and the most trivial items were enormous riches in their eyes. Admittedly we had told them that we would return at the end of the summer and that any thefts would then be strictly punished; but they knew very well that these expressions were not to be taken literally. They asked us constantly: "When will you be leaving?" Day after day we had consoled them with "Tomorrow"; but by now our "today" had become infinitely long and their impatience was boundless. Avatok and the Shark had already set up their tent poles with a view to covering them with the old canvas roof of our hut as soon as our backs were turned; total disorder now reigned inside the hut's rooms. Although all our preparations had been finished long before, everyone could still find something to do. Here bundles were being tied up and reorganized; there a worn boot or torn fur stockings were hurriedly being repaired; hauling belts were being shortened and lengthened again, or people were trying to stuff yet another small memento of the voyage into their clothes bags, whose weight was not to exceed 8 lbs. The cook was delighted at having prepared his last dinner and the steward was happy at finally being rid of his duties. Anyone who intended sleeping had to go to bed early, since we were to embark at 1.00 a.m. next morning. The boats and the provisions had already been moved to the ice foot near the water.

At the prearranged time everyone was assembled on the beach. The red midnight sun, which glowed through billowing frost smoke, illuminated nothing but happy faces. An ice-free horizon lay to the south and southwest; but it was barely seven miles away, and by climbing a nearby height we had established that after only quite a short time we would run into close ice masses. Several of the natives were standing on the shore, to see us off. For loyal Jimmy and his family this was a sad occasion; but the rest displayed no more affection than a butterfly and could scarcely wait for the moment we left. When I took my last walk to the hut, in order to bring the box chronometer on board, one of the Eskimo beauties had already settled in and set up house there. Her youngest offspring was sitting, stark naked, in our old syrup cask, the bottom of which was still sticky; she herself and two other children were standing in front of it. As I walked up to her she pulled the child out and licked the sweet liquid off his body, without being put off in the slightest by the "topography" concerned. Then she placed him back in the cask, and once she had pulled him out again, his little brother was allowed to lick him, and then his little sister too.

FIG. 42. The boats setting off.

At 2.30³ we pushed off from shore with the *Hopes dashed* in the lead. The natives ran around on the ice foot, loudly shouting "Ho!" and "Aie!" and holding their arms in the air.

Favoured by a good breeze, we set sail. The boats, which had been made in damp weather, leaked somewhat; but against all expectations they were easily manoeuvrable and sat in the water so superbly that we gave Chester three cheers. We sailed through between Littleton Island and the mainland and at 3.40 rounded Cape Ohlsen.

Eighteen years before, when Kane passed here with his little party, after he had had to abandon his ship, the sea was still so covered with ice on 17 June that the boats could be moved only with the greatest effort, on runners. Christian Ohlsen, one of his men, died from the hardships of the journey and found his last resting place on the headland that now bears his name. Morton, too, was among those strugglers who had to fight their way back, step by step; and now, at the age of 50, he was sailing past the same spot under similar circumstances, indulging in gloomy thoughts.

We made such rapid progress that by 6.25 we were already rounding Cape Alexander. To the west the sea was open, but in the direction in which we were heading the yellowish shades of an ice-blink rose into the deep-blue sky. Around 11 o'clock, near Cape Saumarez, we ran into thick masses of pack ice, which our boats were incapable of tackling. Hence we turned back and rowed to Siorapaluk, where we hoped to encounter natives. But we found only abandoned snow houses that were half collapsed and thick with dirt. At 1.50 we landed with the rising tide on a grounded floe and with some effort carried our effects ashore; not until full high tide were we able to haul the boats up onto the ice foot.

Immediately after we had put ashore we climbed a cliff about 300 feet high in order to make an interim examination of the ice. It stretched close-packed from Cape Saumarez to Herbert, Northumberland and Hakluyt islands; the meridian of the latter formed its western boundary. A chain of grounded bergs, almost black in colour in the peculiar light, bordered the ice edge and seemed to hold the floes and ice fields captive.

Hence for the moment we had to be patient, particularly since the ice was setting landward with the rising tide. If we succeeded in breaking through the pack ice at some point and in reaching its western edge, we could set a course for Hakluyt Island. Later several of the men climbed the highest of the neighbouring hills but similarly returned with an unfavourable report.

When we wanted to push off, shortly after midnight, the ice was lying closer packed than ever. To pass the time we strolled around the surrounding area and shot dovekies, which swarmed around the beach in small flocks; among them an occasional turnstone appeared from time to time, while on a steep cliff a dignified pair of ravens enjoyed their brief weeks of courtship. A quarrelsome glaucous gull tried to contest their nesting site and displayed an admirable audacity in its attacks. He circled the birds in tight loops, then would swing upward and occasionally swooped on them like a sparrow hawk. The two ravens bravely defended their territory and repaid the pecks of their attacker with interest.

The vegetation was meagre and still very backward. The flowers of the purple saxifrage had not yet opened; the *Draba* and the arctic poppy had scarcely begun to turn green. Only the willow showed fresh sprouts, but even these were extremely small and less developed than those we had encountered the year before in Polaris Bay.

Unbounded filth reigned in the houses that we visited. Majuk's snow-covered grave-mound had been unable to withstand the sun's rays and had partially melted and partially collapsed. We caught a glimpse of our deceased friend's corpse, wrapped scantily in a bear skin. He was in a sitting position and looked as if he was asleep; decomposition had not yet started.

Right next to the grave a clear stream babbled; a knot (*Tringa canuta*)[4] ran busily up and down its banks. It was a male, its breast already brightly coloured. Grey salt crystals stood out against the dark syenite rock faces; in some places they extended up to a height of 30 feet. Along with this syenite the sandstone, previously mentioned several times, also occurred here; it included white quartz inclusions of substantial size. This rock, which is commonly foliated and not very resistant, is highly susceptible to weathering and the generally rounded pebbles could easily be broken out of it.

At 5.00 a.m. on the morning of the 4th we hauled the *Hopes dashed* over shattered ice and immediately landed on quite a large floe, a little off the coast, in order to sun ourselves, since the entire beach still lay in deep shadow due to the high hills. Budington was still not ready to travel; hence we decided to use the time until we pushed off very usefully. Since we had not yet had breakfast we cooked a stew from the dovekies we had killed. There were 40 of them, but this was certainly not too many for seven hungry people.

The two boats pushed off shortly after 6 o'clock. We steered through close masses of pack ice, first southward, then southwestward, and after much toing and froing we reached the western edge of the pack. From here we set as straight a course as possible for Hakluyt Island, which rose on the distant horizon like a dark, sharply delineated cloud. It was a fine, sunny day but there was a gentle southerly breeze blowing against us, and if we wanted to make any progress at all we had to row energetically. The distance between the boats and the coast averaged 20 miles.

Hourly, and occasionally even more frequently if the colour of the water changed, I tried to locate the Gulf Stream, but it made itself apparent neither by its temperature nor by its specific gravity. The ice we were passing consisted of one-year fields and floes and of low hummocks. Bergs were extremely numerous, often of enormous extent, generally ending at the top in quite level surfaces that represented the natural surface of the glaciers from which they originated. If they had been floating for any length of time in the warmer water of the Gulf Stream they would have displayed different shapes. For when icebergs are floating in a medium whose temperature exceeds the freezing point they melt from below and finally capsize; they then display extremely dissected and often fantastic shapes.

Apart from the wind, until about 3.00 p.m. the tidal current coming from the south worked insidiously against us. While the tide was ebbing we made faster progress. We usually broke through narrower belts of pack ice, especially when they extended far to the west; it would have been too time-consuming to row around them. If on such occasions we encountered extensive floes we hauled the boats out and pulled them across the obstacle.

Covering the last three miles of our journey was especially difficult since we were moving through close ice masses that, driven south by the ebb current, were jammed against the north coast of Hakluyt Island; nonetheless we landed there at 9.25 in the evening. We could be pleased with our day's work this time. We had gained about 45 miles, although we had been at the oars for 15 hours practically without a break. Since we could not immediately haul the boats up on the ice foot since it was low tide, we pitched a temporary camp under the shelter of the nearby cliffs and cooked a meal.[5]

The southwest wind had blown almost continually all day, and the more it strengthened, the more overcast the sky became. High water appeared to occur at 2.30 a.m.; on the basis of a rough measurement on a grounded iceberg, the tidal range was 7.3 feet. The tidal current was extremely confused, sometimes setting northwest, sometimes south. In the former case the velocity rose to at least 1½ knots, but in the latter case it attained barely half that speed. After the water had ceased to rise, the tidal current continued to flow for a further 20 minutes; but now it was toward the east, but no faster than half a knot at most. We were unable to determine what influence the wind exerted on these conditions, since the wind blew almost constantly as long as we stayed on the northwest end of the island. A needle-shaped rock that we had passed produced a local diversion of the drifting floes. It was about ¾ of a cable-length from shore and rose from water so deep that we were unable to reach bottom with an oar, even at low water.

We spent an unpleasant night under the boats' canvas housings.[6] On the morning of the 5th there was such a strong wind that we could not risk leaving the island. Toward evening the wind became a gale and lashed the spray from the waves as far as the spot where our boats lay; we had to haul them farther inland. Several projecting tongues of the ice foot split away and collapsed. The cold completely robbed us of sleep; shivering, we ran around on the snow-covered beach and waited longingly for conditions to improve. But next day was much worse, since a heavy snowfall was added to the gale. Moreover, dense fog prevailed so that the nearby cliffs, which rose in terraces to a height of about 1400 feet, were totally hidden from view.

It was not until early on the morning of the 7th that the wind dropped, but it continued to snow. Around noon the sky cleared; soon afterward the sun appeared and compensated us for the rigours we had suffered. The sandstone faces acquired an appearance as if they were glowing in the magical light of Bengal lights.[7] Their blazing colours produced transitions from the delicate shades of a peach blossom to the deepest crimson; and the snow drifts lying on the terraces and the projecting ledges sparkled like facetted crystal.

Out to seaward it looked less encouraging; the ice lay close-packed. There could be no thought of leaving for the moment, and the dreadful inactivity became all the more painful when our hearts imbibed the fragrances of home in the silence.

Some powerful change also seemed to be developing in the gentle soul of the cat, Thomas. But neither then nor later were we able to determine what sort of feelings set his soul in an uproar, since he slipped quietly away. All our searching, enticing and calling were in vain; his tracks disappeared on a bare slab of rock which was bounded by mirror-like ice surfaces. Our good cat had vanished for good. A noon sun altitude revealed the site of his desertion to be at 77°24'N.

After midnight some open water appeared, but shortly afterward the narrow channels closed again and it seemed as if the time of our liberation would never come. At 7.45 on the morning of the 8th, the *Hopes dashed* finally made an unsuccessful attempt at rounding the southwestern point of the island. We then turned back and, accompanied by the other boat, set a course for the northwestern tip of Northumberland Island. It was a time-consuming crossing and not without danger, since a stiff southwesterly breeze set the close-packed ice in motion. But after a 3-hour trip we got across safely and quickly hauled the boats up on the ice foot to save them from damage.

In the vicinity of our landing place the dovekies were swarming in such vast flocks that we killed over 300 in a short time. Our gunfire seemed to alarm them greatly since next morning they had all disappeared.

We followed their example and at 8 o'clock[8] we continued our journey. But only an hour later a stiff southwest breeze arose, associated with heavy snowfall; this again forced us to haul the boats up onto the ice foot. We had barely covered four miles and all around the ice now lay close-packed and apparently impenetrable. Around noon it stopped snowing, certainly, but no leads appeared anywhere. Only to the south did a solitary, small opening appear; a pair of gulls (*Larus leucopterus*)[9] lounged at its edge.

This is probably the northernmost limit of the range of this bird; this was the first time we had seen it north of Upernavik. In terms of other gull species we spotted occasional examples of the ivory gull, as well as a number of glaucous gulls which were already paired. Apart from several ordinary brent geese,[10] a solitary white-fronted goose appeared, but I could not decide whether it was *Anser albifrons* or *A. Gambeli*,[11] since the bird was extremely wary and never came within range. The proximity of the American archipelago would probably favour the latter form.

Apart from these we observed several flights of common eiders as well as a pair of king eiders, and the cliffs at the northwest point of the island were occupied by murres and black guillemots. Turnstones and sanderlings appeared on the beach; the latter settled only temporarily and seemed to be on migration toward the north. We also noticed several ravens and snow buntings. Some of the men saw a swallow, not a common event in the midst of this world of ice. The species to which the bird belonged again had to remain in doubt, since the individuals who saw it did not know the difference between a barn swallow and a house martin. According to Reinhardt a single specimen of *Chaetura pelagica*[12] is said to have been killed near Sukkertoppen, at 65°25'N. Single specimens of *Hirundo horreorum*[13] were also shot at Nanortalik, near the 60th parallel, and at Fiskernæsset; and Parry observed a pair of *Cotyle riparia*[14] on Melville Island.

The following report appears in Heuglin's "Reisen nach dem Nordpolarmeer":[15] "According to Captain Ulve[16] he encountered a pair of barn swallows near Cape Nassau on the northwest coast of Novaya Zemlya in July 1870. Gillett saw the species on 22 July 1870 in a small bay at 76°10'N but no specimens were killed. Perhaps both reports refer to one and the same observation, and this still needs further confirmation."

In 1869 I myself saw a specimen of *Hirundo rustica*[17] in the vicinity of Jan Mayen. I quote the following note about it from one of my journals:

> June 7; position at midnight 71°19'N; 8°40'W on the basis of reckoning from the log; a stormy wind out of SEbW that has been blowing for the past 9 hours; foggy; cruising among loose pack. At 00.30 on the morning of the 8th we spotted a specimen of *Hirundo rustica*. The bird flew around the ship several times then, probably exhausted, settled on the topsail yard. One of the men tried to catch it, but it escaped. When it reappeared I fired at it; the gun hung fire; the bird wheeled, then disappeared in a northerly direction and was never spotted again.

The swallow seen by our men, like the white-fronted goose mentioned earlier, was a lost American bird, however. Unfortunately I omitted to find out later whether the southwest storms to which we were exposed had also prevailed in Davis Strait; and now, as I write these lines, the

American weather charts that represent the conditions in the United States during that period are not available to me.

Some of my ornithological friends, to whom I reported this case, are inclined to think the bird was *Hirundo horreorum*. Robert Ridgway[18] would prefer to totally exclude the possibility of it being *Cotyle riparia*.

Although the ice conditions were not at all encouraging, early on the 10th we pushed off and followed the west coast of the island. But after barely two hours of travelling we were again obliged to haul the boats up on the ice foot at 11.20. Our supply of tarred ropes was so significantly reduced that from now on we commonly ate the birds we killed raw. Certainly we ran across small peat deposits here and there, but it was frozen and burned so badly that it barely repaid the effort of gathering it.

Everything now depended on our reaching Cape Parry; but to achieve this, of necessity we had to leave the coast, and in the direction in which we were heading the ice still lay close-packed. Chester, who had climbed a high cliff, returned in the evening with the news that a narrow lead extended across the entrance of Whale Sound to the headland that was the next goal of our journey. At 8 o'clock we cheerfully set off; initially we followed the coast, then set a southerly course.

After we had been battling the ice successfully for somewhat over two hours and had covered a third of the distance, a light southwest wind sprang up and under its influence the fields and floes were pushed violently together. The areas of open water shrank with disturbing speed. Suddenly we realized that Budington's boat, which had been left astern, had been nipped. The crew leaped onto the ice in great haste and rushed to save the threatened boat; they succeeded only after several vain attempts. The *Hopes dashed* was also beset, and then it was our turn to look for a solid floe. We had barely reached one when the ice all around us closed and we realized that we were thoroughly beset. We could move neither forward nor back, and had to let ourselves be carried along involuntarily by the tidal current. For a period our floe spun like a top, then came to a brief standstill, accompanied by severe ice pressures. Before we could get a full overview of our situation, the floe had split; there was scarcely enough room left on the larger of the two pieces for the boat; all around there was only brash ice, across which we could not have escaped.

The wind strengthened and, with the help of the current, drove us north. We were again faced with a sleepless night. Even if the cold had been less sensible we still would not have dared to go to sleep, since we had to be constantly on guard.

The old, worn playing cards were brought out and preparations were made for a game of poker. But all too soon we grew tired of the brightly coloured cards and laid them aside again. Then we looked across at Budington's floe, where the people were jumping around like grasshoppers to keep warm. Through the telescope we examined their faces, which mostly looked long, comical and red. Oh, those faces! We had seen them so often, too often, and with the best will in the word they could not hold our attention for long. Our situation was such that we would have found reading a logarithmic table exciting. In addition we were tortured by thirst and we had no water. The men were uttering all sorts of crazy wishes, revolving around beer, wine or even stronger drinks, but without exception they were totally unattainable.

Then one man, a model of moderation and piety, said, in an admonitory voice, words worthy of notice: "Think of poor Tom, who only a few days ago was still a living cat, and who now lies dead in one of the snowfields on Hakluyt Island. For my part I would much rather be a freezing sailor, who in addition is suffering from thirst, than an old tom-cat, whose tail has stopped wagging forever."

Most of us recognized and sympathized with the tenor of this speech; we were amazed that we could have forgotten the fine animal so soon, and dedicated some respectful words of acknowledgment. Those of us who were keeping a diary did so in writing.

On a water-stained, crumpled sheet of paper that dates from that period are the following lines, reproduced just exactly as they flowed from somebody's pen at that time. The words are as follows:

In memoriam

Er ist dahin mein Tom! beklagt von Allen,
    Die ihn gekannt, den Abgott aller Katzen:
    Den Kater Tom mit seinen weichen Tatzen,
Den Kater Tom, der von uns abgefallen.
Er endete sein glanzvoll Erdenwallen
    Auf ödem Eiland, fern von Maus und Ratzen;
    Ein Katerheld in Knurren und im Kratzen,
Soll dies Sonett als Nachruf ihm erschallen!
Durch Sturm und Schiffbruch mit uns im Vereine
    Ging Tom und theilte die Gefahr der Reise;
    Auf dem Verdeck, im rothen Nordlichtscheine,
Spann er vernügt die alte Katerweise,
    Nun ist er todt mein armer Tom! Ich weine, --
Die Thräne rinnt, doch sie erstarrt zu Eise.

[In memoriam.

My Tom is gone! Mourned by all
    Who knew him, the idol of all cats:
    Tom-cat Tom with his soft paws,
Tom-cat Tom, who abandoned by us,
Ended his splendid earthly pilgrimage,
    On a desolate island, far from mice and rats;
    A hero of a cat, at growling and scratching.
May this sonnet be an obituary!
United with us by storms and shipwreck,
    Went Tom and shared the danger of the voyage;
    On the deck, in the red light of the aurora,
He purred happily in old tom-cat fashion.
    Now my poor Tom is dead. I'm weeping and
The tears are flowing, but they are turning to ice.]

Budington's floe was drifting in almost a northward direction, and faster than ours, which was heading somewhat east of north. Around 8.00 a.m. on the 11th we and our *Hopes dashed* were near our old campsite on the northwest coast of Northumberland Island. Several quickly executed manoeuvres released us and at 9 o'clock we hauled the boat up on the ice foot. It was a different story for Budington, who was less fortunate. He and his men had to work hard before they reached open water, from which they were separated by a belt of ice a mile wide. At 7.30 they began carrying their provisions and the rest of their baggage in manageable loads to the edge of the water; to do this they had to cover the same route a good ten times. Only then could they haul their boat to the water; but a major part of the route was so hummocky that they were obliged to use ice axes in order first to remove the obstacles from their route. When they landed near us it was almost noon; they were all snow-blind, without exception, and their faces and hands were peeling like dried onions. Their snow blindness could be treated; but their rags of skins could not be stuck on again.

Hence we again found ourselves at the same spot on Northumberland Island that we had left the day before; we had set off healthy and cheerful and had returned half-exhausted.

But this time our stay was to be as short as possible; we hoped that we could put to sea on the next high tide. Hence we could not move away far or for long from our campsite, an aspect which we deeply regretted, since it would have been of the greatest interest to examine more closely the magnificently developed glacier system on this small island. A close study of it would without doubt produce valuable results, and a small vessel specially equipped for the purpose could solve, over the course of a few summer months, many important questions, which would compensate generously for the expenditure of time and money.

The island, whose length on the map is shown as 11 miles, and whose maximum width is about 7, is about 800 feet high, and completely glacier-covered. To a certain degree the coastal cliffs consist of the boundaries of a small ice cap which sends out five ice streams that all reach the sea or at least sea level. As far as we could determine, the firn line of this glacier system extends down extraordinarily low. Its mean height is probably less than 100 feet. As we travelled along the west coast of the island I spotted the most unequivocal traces of markedly intermittent movements on the middle glacier. Specifically, the glacier was in a stage of regeneration. The main mass of the glacier, which dropped over steep cliffs, had melted back and had almost isolated the ice which filled the valley bottom; but in the middle of the cliffs the ice steps had again reached the ridge of the lower part.

The more I examined the island on the map, the more strongly the conviction impressed itself upon me that probably most of those heavily glacier-covered islands in the arctic region that lie near the coast in regions where precipitation is low owe their glacial system to an earlier time—specifically, to the time when they were still connected to the adjacent mainland, from whose firn region they were nourished. If it were possible to identify an actual increase or reduction in the ice masses on such islands over time, this would either disprove or confirm this hypothesis.

The night high tide, which reached a height of somewhat over 11 feet, inundated the ice foot and surged into our camp, so that we had to move it. On the morning of the 12th we spotted much open water to the north from a hill near our camp, and hence we quickly launched the boats and pushed off from shore. Around 11 o'clock, in a flat calm, we reached a narrow belt of pack ice that consisted of fairly small, rotten floes and eroded hummocks. The tidal current set these ice masses moving rapidly, and the leads were so changeable in their extent and position that we often had to turn back from a spot which, as we rowed toward it, had been occupied by a polynya. Generally the lanes of water closed immediately after we had passed; once the *Hopes dashed* was caught in a nip, but she got free again in a short time. The other boat, which, as usual, was somewhat behind us was less fortunate. On reaching a lead that we had negotiated unscathed, it was surrounded by ice and had to head eastward along the south coast of Northumberland Island before it could again reach the open water by means of a detour.

Once we had put the belt of pack ice behind us, a light northerly breeze sprang up and filled our sails. We immediately set our course for Cape Parry and arrived off its cliffs at 5.45, despite the fact that the flood tide had been running constantly against us. We made fast to a grounded hummock close inshore, to wait for the other boat to arrive and have a bite to eat. During this brief rest I made a sketch of this headland.

A rough ice foot, covered with vast snowdrifts, was welded to the cliffs of this cape, which was probably not less than 1400 feet in height. At low tide the water here is so extremely shallow that we grounded repeatedly in our flat-bottomed boat, about 6 cable-lengths from shore. About 2 miles from land we noticed a chain of 14 grounded icebergs whose alignment followed that of the coast. This line probably marks the boundary between deeper and shallower zones, since not a single iceberg lay between it and shore. The seabed was overgrown with large *Laminariae*, whose green tops projected almost a yard above the water, so that one could easily believe oneself in one of those subtropical *Nelumbium* lakes,[19] if only the cold and the nearby icebergs had not quickly destroyed this illusion.

Budington's boat made rendezvous with us at 6 o'clock. In the meantime the wind had dropped, and in order to continue our progress we had to take to the oars. Hakluyt Island had partially dropped below the horizon, and gloomy rags of fog floated around the eight sharply-delineated mountain masses of Northumberland. From the former of these islands an ice-blink extended westward as a low segment of a circle. It was yellowish in colour and its intensity increased as the sun sank lower. When a dark bank of cloud arose and concealed its lower part, its upper part, elevated by contrast effects, resembled a faint aurora borealis.

Repeatedly, large flights of eider ducks and brent geese passed ahead of us, but they always stayed out of range. We now also spotted the first fulmars, which followed our rushing wake with easy wing-beats, in almost dreamlike fashion. A dense flock of oldsquaws, consisting entirely of males, rose calling, pursued by two wedge-tailed jaegers. Later we spotted three puffins, while all along our route murres, black guillemots and dovekies were quite common.

Battling the strong tidal current, at 8 o'clock we reached Fitzclarence Rock and landed on the ice floes for an hour to wait for the ebb tide flowing back. Booth Sound was still bridged by last winter's ice cover, on which lay deep snowdrifts that had in part metamorphosed to coarse-grained firn. Half an hour after we had landed, Budington's boat arrived.

Morton's and Odell's snow blindness had deteriorated. The latter had lost his sight completely and had to be led around.

After the current had slackened we set a course for Blackwood Point, and around 10 o'clock we stopped at the spot marked Tasiusaq Hat on the chart.

It looked more wintry than at any of our previous stopping places; the area was even more desolate than the shores of Polaris Bay in the first months of spring. We searched in vain for running water in order to quench our thirst.

Next morning at 11.45 we continued our voyage. During the first hour we were favoured by a light westerly wind; when it dropped we had to reach for the oars. Sometimes we were breaking through narrow belts of pack ice; sometimes we had open water. Occasionally a small herd of walrus would surface nearby, or some narwhals which, with strong exhalations, spouted vaporizing jets of water into the air, then fled warily in dolphin-like arcing rolls. Toward evening we made fast to a fairly large floe for half an hour and melted some snow to obtain some drinking water. Then we continued on our way through close pack ice to Dalrymple Island, whose barren shores we reached at 9.30.

Due to the numerous eider ducks nesting on it, the island is often visited by the whalers; it consists of a cone-shaped rock of syenite gneiss, whose height we estimated at 700 feet. Once the boats were secured, the men scattered to collect eggs, but the birds had not yet started to lay. We spotted a few small flocks which suspiciously kept their distance; only the terns were more trusting and swarmed around us, screaming, in elegant curves.

We left Dalrymple shortly before 1.00 on the afternoon of 14 June and steered through loose pack for the northwest end of Wolstenholme Island, where we landed an hour later. Bryan and Odell climbed the steep cliffs, which were formed of a metamorphic rock similar to that at our previous stopping place. From a height of 700 feet they got an overview of the disposition of the fast ice that extended to distant Conical Rock in an obtuse triangle whose apex extended seaward. This forced us to make an unpleasant detour, since we now had to swing around this ice tongue, and in so doing found ourselves 30 miles offshore. Fighting a strong breeze, we set off rowing at 12.30 a.m. The wind increased in strength and the waves rose dangerously, and hence at 4.00 next morning we had to haul the boats up on the ice. But this was not the landfast ice, as we had initially thought, but a drifting floe whose treacherous movements we escaped some six hours later. After an exciting voyage we reached the southern cliff of metamorphic Conical Rock and hauled the boats up on the ice foot. A wide bear track, barely a few hours old, immediately set the hunters' blood coursing. They followed the wide tracks across the snow-covered floes till they reached a mirror-like ice surface where they lost them; they then returned to the boats.

The weather became extremely bad: it stormed, rained and snowed, and hence we had to spend a large part of the time under the roof-canvasses of the boats. Moreover, the ice lay close-packed, holding us prisoner.

It was not until 6.30 a.m. on 18 June that we were again able to set off; but only two hours later, after we had covered barely six miles, the ice was again closing in on us and we saw ourselves obliged to haul the boats up on the fast ice. The ice was extremely level here, with high icebergs towering above it here and there; the ice everywhere was covered with snow that had already begun to get brackish.[20]

When small polynyas appeared here and there, walrus usually appeared in herds of 8–10 animals and gazed inquisitively at us. We would have liked to kill one of the walruses in order to renew our limited supply of fuel, but they constantly stayed out of range; but even if we had succeeded in hitting one, this would probably have been of little use, since the walrus would probably have sunk. Bryan's tall rubber boots became shorter by the day, since he had been cutting the uppers away, from the top, in strips, in order to use these strips as fuel. Since we had left Wolstenholme Island the dovekies had become rarer; hence we also had to reduce our rations and for breakfast could allow ourselves only a can of water in which we had softened the four ship's biscuits that were carefully and conscientiously measured out to each man. Our taste had sunk so low that we considered it a delicacy if we could sweeten this terrible mixture, which even a hungry hunting dog would have scorned, with some treacle. We had no tobacco left. Only one man in Budington's boat still possessed a large pouchful of tobacco; but he took great care to keep every single strand for himself; to his credit it should be said

Fig. 43. A narwhal hunt.

that the old miser was not a seaman. After some of the seamen had made several vain attempts to steal this little bag of tobacco, we called on its heartless owner to give us half of his tobacco in return for a high price. If we had been in a position to offer him cash, he would happily have sold the tobacco to us; but since, in our view, they were totally worthless, during the long winter night we had hammered our last gold and silver coins into thin plates and used them to decorate small ivory carvings, and hence we had to content ourselves with the aroma of his tobacco smoke, which was far from aromatic. Thus in our stubby pipes we smoked the terrible tea that the Naval Minister's avaricious bosom-friend had saddled us with, and consoled ourselves with the thought of being better people.

On the morning of the 19th an extensive polynya developed close to the camp, but to the south the ice still lay close-packed. Panting herds of narwhal played in the open water and occasionally approached to within a few paces. We fired at them frequently and successfully; our bullets were hitting the animals but we were not in a position to take possession of them.

Repeatedly I had been struck by a bird with light plumage that was drifting around with five ivory gulls in the distance. It was somewhat smaller than them and its movements were strange, reminiscent of those of a tern. When the ivory gulls snatched up food, one would see it cruising over the narrow leads too, occasionally picking something up. But when it dropped it did not flutter down or dive, but descended as quietly as a petrel. The longer I watched it, the more inclined I was to think it was a rare *Rhodostethia rosea*,[21] since I could clearly distinguish the wedge-shaped tail and the black neck ring. It might, at the outside, have been an albino *Stercorarius pomarinus*,[22] but its behaviour refuted this. It was also smaller than a jaeger and in addition had a small bill. When we were cooking, its companions approached very close to watch for the scraps from our meagre meal; it flew away, however.

*****

A brief calm followed a light westerly breeze; the ice slackened and a channel opened. We pushed off at 7.25,[23] but an hour later we were met by drifting fields and floes and we again had to secure the boats. It was not until about noon that we were able to continue our voyage. We sailed south for two hours before a light wind; after we had covered about 12 miles the foul conditions forced us to land again. The tongue of ice on which we had pitched camp suddenly broke away from the fast shore ice and we drifted west for quite a long time, without being able to get free. It was not until midnight that we had an opportunity to turn east again, and after two hours of fighting impenetrable ice masses, we again hauled our boats out again. But the ice on which we were standing was rotten and unsafe. Three hours later, at 3.00 a.m. on the 20th, we

Fig. 44. In a tight spot.

again had to flee. We followed a narrow lead that extended northward and rowed for seven hours without a break. But here our progress ended; the ice ahead of us lay close-packed and the open water behind us was disappearing extremely quickly. Once we had hauled the boats out, to our annoyance we realized that we were not on fast ice but that we were again adrift and were quickly being carried west.

Robbed of any independent movement, we travelled with the drift of the floes until around 8.00 a.m. on the 21st; then we launched the boats, but soon afterward we hauled them out on a floe again since it was impossible to force a passage. When the ice slackened somewhat we continued our voyage, but we had barely covered a few miles when dense fog rolled in; to this was added snow-squalls, and we ran the risk of being separated and getting lost.

Despite great difficulties, once the weather had cleared we reached the fast ice of Melville Bay at 3.30 p.m. Cape York bore about northeast. Favoured by a gentle wind, we set sail and followed the ice edge, sometimes eastward, sometimes southwestward, until we came to an involuntary halt around 7.00 p.m. A wide tongue of ice extended ahead of us; closely surrounded by smaller floes and hummocks, it stretched westward in a wide arc. To avoid undergoing the unpleasantnesses of a major detour we hauled the boats out of the water and across this ice bridge, which barred our way in the direction in which we wanted to head. Reaching the southern edge, we spotted a narrow channel, but it closed so quickly that by 9.00 p.m. all hope of pushing on had vanished. Only a northerly wind could liberate us now.

Under the influence of the flood-tide current, the floes and hummocks packed even closer together and were jammed against the fast ice on which our camp was located. The ice pressures were repeated, and during the night they recurred with such violence that we had to haul the boats closer to shore since they were under threat. This had barely happened when a massive piece of the fast ice broke away. For the moment there could be no thought of any peace. Budington's crew caulked their boat since its seams were gaping in some places; the rest scattered in various directions to find drinking water.

When some leads appeared on the morning of the 22nd we continued our voyage, but the difficulties became so serious that we covered barely half a mile in 45 minutes. By 9 o'clock the open water had disappeared and we again hauled the boats up on the ice, which displayed unmistakable signs of severe pressure here. At some points the floes had been rafted under each other into multiple layers, although they did not project higher above sea level than the rest of the ice, where conditions were normal and where the ice formed an unbroken cover. We did not have the means necessary to measure these rafted ice masses, but we estimated that they were 5 fathoms thick. Estimating the dimensions of bodies that are underwater is somewhat uncertain, admittedly, but I think I can state that the value just reported is too small rather than too large.

Fig. 45. A campsite near Cape York.

We had left only a few pieces of the tarred rope that we used as fuel; they were deemed inviolable and were to be kept for a later period. We had recourse to an unusual method in order to produce drinking water. I possessed a pair of rubber riding breeches; we had cut them down the middle and Chester and I used them as clothes bags. The two parts were now taken apart and carefully sewn together again lengthwise and secured between four short posts stuck in the ice. The black surface of the material was spread with snow that slowly melted in the rays of the sun. The resultant water was caught in a tin-can and satisfied our needs for the moment.

All day we waited in vain for a favourable opportunity to continue our journey. It was not until midnight that the floes began to slacken. At 1.00 a.m. on 23 June we pushed off and steered southeast through close ice masses. But half an hour later we were again obliged to haul the boats out, and to haul them in the direction in which we were heading. Around 3.00 a.m. we reached open water; we pushed off, but after we had covered a few miles we were solidly beset. Budington's boat developed a bad leak.[24] We took refuge on the ice and hauled the boats out; Budington's crew repaired theirs by nailing sheets of lead and canvas over the planks that had been holed.

We made a halt in the vicinity of an eroded iceberg and were lucky enough to find fresh water, with which we filled the casks. Since the ice pressures had started again, a watch of two men was organized; the rest went to sleep under the tentings in the boats.

It might have been about 10 o'clock when the fog hanging over the southern horizon dispersed. Chester, who was on watch, suddenly shouted in a loud voice: "Ship ahoy!"

"Ship ahoy!" The cry rang out throughout the entire camp as if from one voice, and everyone jumped up and dashed outside.

About 10 miles from us a three-masted vessel lay beset in the ice with her sails clewed up and with the air quivering above the hot column of smoke from her funnel.

Our people hoisted the flag on two oars that had been lashed together, the old historic Grinnell flag that had flown over the ice fields of the South Pole, and which now had been carried to the arctic regions by *Polaris* for the fourth time.

Almost simultaneously the colours went shooting up on board the bark, but since they were hanging slack we could not identify them immediately. Somewhat later we saw that it was the British flag.

CHAPTER 27

WHALING

The walk to Ravenscraig. *Beset. Westward. Search for the Gulf Stream. In* Lancaster Sound. Arctic. *The bird cliffs at Cape Hay. The Greenland whale and the fishery. Navy Board Inlet and the Wollaston Islands. A wandering Eskimo band. Elwin Inlet. In Prince Regent Inlet. Fury Beach. The North Capers. Trip ashore. Old Eskimo houses. Reindeer. Return aboard.*

The joy that the appearance of the ship had caused us was not a general one. For now that we had suffered so many hardships, we were not to owe our rescue to our own efforts but to a strange ship under a strange flag.

When the first expression of surprise had passed, Budington sent Chester to the bark accompanied by the seaman, Hobby, in order to inform its captain of our situation and to ask him to pick us up.

Halfway there, ten of the Britishers came to meet our two men. Hobby continued on his way with two of them, while Chester turned back to guide the rest of them to our camp. Around 2.00 p.m. the nine figures emerged in front of us from the confusion of icebergs. We gazed at the men through the telescope and spotted that some were armed with sealing gaffs. Hence the ship whose captain had sent them was probably a whaler.

Chester was walking at their head. While still some distance away he shouted that our 19 companions, whom we had lost on that stormy October night, had been saved.

We hurried to meet the men and besieged them with questions, since people who have lived in isolation for two long years, far from any contact with the civilized world, have many things on their minds. Even the taciturn ones were talkative, talking with feverish haste.

The men could not tell us much that was new. Without exception they were residents of the Shetland and Orkney islands, an honest, ingenuous race that, in its fortunate seclusion, concerned itself little about the weal and woe of the outside world. Most of them, if they could read at all, probably never opened any book other than the bible or a hymn book.

The ship, to whose crew they belonged, was *Ravenscraig*, a Scottish whaler out of Kirkcaldy, commanded by William Allen and owned by Mr. Ninian Lockhart.[1]

The seamen had filled their pockets with hardtack since they thought we would be suffering from lack of food. We had been spotted from the bark's crow's nest early that morning and had been assumed to be wandering Eskimos. Our boats had been mistaken for sledges and the items of baggage lying scattered around for dogs. Once the ship had got closer and the outlines of the boats had emerged more sharply, they thought we were shipwrecked whalers, since they could not make out the colours of our small boat's flag.

Laden with our minimal provisions, we set off at 6.00 p.m. on the walk to the bark. Our two boats were left behind. We reached our goal at midnight and were welcomed on board with that pleasant warmth that forms a prominent trait of character of seamen of all nations.

In our outward appearance we resembled degenerate bandits; our fur clothing was torn and dirty and our faces were tanned as if we had been in the tropical sun. Our beautiful and stimulating gypsy life was now at an end.

While the men were taken to the crew's quarters, Dr. A.D. Souter, the ship's doctor, led us to the saloon. The bark's captain was indisposed and could not welcome us himself, but he requested that we make ourselves at home on board his vessel.

The kindness and self-sacrifice of these good people was limitless. They shared their clothes and linen with us, and invariably wanted to give us the best of everything.

Under these circumstances we immediately felt at home. The rather dark cabin was extremely cosy. The entire ship, a former merchant vessel that only later had been fitted with a steam engine, made a solid, almost antiquated impression. Even the speech of the crew, the broad Scottish dialect, with a strong mixture of sonorous Gaelic expressions, reminded one of past times.[2]

Our encounter with *Ravenscraig* had occurred only because she had lingered too long in the area of the southwestern whaling grounds, and had then found the so-called North Water closed. She was now beset and was waiting for the ice conditions to improve so that she could head westward to Lancaster Sound. Her lot had become ours and we did not see it as a cruel twist of fate that we would be ending our voyage of discovery with a three-month whaling voyage, and that we were to visit and get to know the area of the Northwest Passage.

Two days after we arrived on board the bark, Captain Allen was fully recovered and personally bade us welcome. Since there was still no prospect of getting free, he sent 20 members of the crew to our old camp to fetch the boats; our carpenter and two of the seamen also accompanied this expedition.

After they had been gone about 18 hours they returned, but bringing only the *Hopes dashed*, and it had been damaged in transit.[3] They had had to leave Budington's boat behind because of the difficult, rough going.

When the floes slackened on the morning of 26 June *Ravenscraig* steamed a few miles northwest. On the following day she gained a further short distance in the same direction. Then the ice surrounded us again and appeared to never want to yield.

Captain Allen had spent the past few days almost exclusively in the crow's nest. On 4 July he spotted a wide lane of water that extended northwest. Hence he decided to force a passage. The crew was sent out on the ice to remove the larger hummocks crowding the ship's bow. Then the ship charged at full steam against an extensive, rotten floe that lay in our way, and literally bored its forward part into this ice mass. Backing up, it again rammed the same spot which, after a few more charges, began to crumble, and a gaping crack at least 100 yards long had appeared.

The ship's charges followed each other quickly and violently. The shattered debris was pushed up, crackling, in high barriers on either side of the ship, then sank back roaring into the foaming water. Every inch of progress had to be fought for, but every turn of the whirling screw had an effect. Whenever the forward part of the keel stopped on the ice, the entire crew would run stamping from the port side to starboard and back again until the ship was finally swinging from side to side and the ice finally collapsed under her weight.

For hours one could hear nothing but the spirited sound of words of command, sometimes interrupted by the captain's shrill whistle as he stood on lookout in the crow's nest, sometimes by the penetrating clangour of the bell that controlled the activities of the personnel in the engine room.

Toward evening we were approaching open water. A quickly executed flanking movement finally overcame the last obstacle and we pushed on westward at top speed.

Hourly, and sometimes even more often, we measured the temperature of the sea and determined its specific gravity. If the Gulf Stream actually existed here, it could not remain hidden from me, since we crossed Baffin Bay from coast to coast and of necessity we had to traverse the alleged current, which could only be a surface current.

On the basis of these numerous observations I believe I can state that the Gulf Stream, as such, does not occur anywhere in the continuation of Davis Strait, north of latitude 75°30'N.

Of necessity it follows from this that the Gulf Stream cannot reach Smith Sound and hence cannot wash its eastern shores. The current that Captain Inglefield first detected, and that is said to flow at a velocity of 72 knots per day, is intermittent, i.e., it is the flood tide current that is so conspicuous only because the returning ebb current is less powerful.

During our unsuccessful search for the Gulf Stream the ship was approaching the west shore of Baffin Bay. On the evening of 5 July snow-crowned mountain ridges came into sight, and early next morning we swung into Lancaster Sound.[4] These waters were practically ice-free; only rarely did we pass rotten floes or shattered hummocks. A short Mediterranean swell came from the west, but the wind blew from the northeast over the gloomy cliffs and filled our sails.

The lookout in the crow's nest watched in vain for whales. But on the morning of the 7th a sail hove into sight on the western horizon, steering eastward. At a distance of five miles Captain Allen recognized her. He told us she was the *Arctic*, a whaler out of Dundee. People launched into all sorts of suggestions, trying to guess at the ship's success from her draft.

"The ship is full and bound for home," was the mate's suggestion. "She appears to have taken a whale quite recently," shouted another, "since her sides are still glistening with oil." "You'll probably get an opportunity to get home quickly now," said the captain.

Off Cape Crawford we approached to within hailing distance of each other. Instead of the usual question "How many fish?" the worthy Allen shouted to *Arctic*'s captain that he had the shipwrecked crew of the American North Pole expedition on board.

A boat was immediately launched from *Arctic* and her captain came alongside. A few moments later he was standing on deck, a blonde giant whose face bore an expression of boundless good nature. Captain Allen introduced us in turn to his friend William Adams; then, despite the early hour, we went below to the cabin to have some wine. We had scarcely sat down when two more gentlemen appeared: Captain Markham,[5] an English naval officer and passenger on board *Arctic*, and Mr. Graham, the ship's doctor.

Arctic had already taken 20 whales, but nonetheless her captain planned to cruise near the whaling grounds until the end of the season in order to fill his ship completely if possible. He wanted to take us all on board. But our skipper would not hear of it; he wanted to take us to Scotland himself.

Now there arose a noble competition between the two captains; the one wanted to have us; the other didn't want to relinquish us. Captain Adams asked *Ravenscraig*'s captain at least to bring our crew to meet him. While the men entered the cabin in twos, Captain Adams quoted from *Coriolanus*:[6]

> Here come more voices --
> Your voices; for your voices I have fought;
> Watch'd for your voices, for your voices. . ."

And he had really intended searching for us, since he had heard of the rescue of the 19 in Greenland. Now he wanted to translate his good intentions into deeds and asked Captain Allen that he transfer at least half the crew and their officers to him. Ultimately the latter could not but accede to this selfless request.

Adams again had a quotation from Shakespeare ready, but from *Julius Caesar* this time. He recited in a loud voice:

Let me have men about me that are fat;
Sleek-headed men, and such as sleep o' nights:
Yond' . . . has a lean and hungry look!

If he believed literally in the words of the great bard, whose works he knew almost by heart, we were really in trouble, since Budington was the only one among us who could really be called fat. Which of us was to go? Moreover, each of us saw it as a matter of honour to continue sharing the fate of the old *Ravenscraig*, and it was difficult to reach a final decision.

Chester and Schumann, the engineer, could not withstand the friendly manner of the blonde captain for long. I too was won over, especially since he promised me the prospect of landing at various interesting points on the coast. Of the crew members, we took with us Hermann Siemens, Noah Hayes, Heinrich Hobby and Walter Campbell the stoker.

We took our leave of Captain Allen, of *Ravenscraig* and of our companions who were staying behind, and climbed down into the small boat that was tossing on the waves alongside; the crew members were to follow in another boat. During the brief trip across to *Arctic*, her captain delivered another Shakespeare sonnet, and on later occasions he entertained us for many pleasant hours with his lively recitations.

On reaching the other ship we were welcomed wildly. Here, too, we had to reiterate the story of our adventurous voyage and undergo a crossfire of questions that was kept up in lively fashion even during breakfast.

The ship continued her voyage eastward. Off Cape Hay, which we reached shortly after noon, we hove-to in order to plunder the bird cliffs, since the steward's supply of eggs was exhausted. Since the sea here was extremely deep, even close under the sheer cliffs, probably not less than 150 fathoms, there was no point in dropping anchor. Hence the ship was eased to within about 15 paces of the land and made fast to the ice foot that girdled the cliffs in a ledge 3 to 15 feet wide.

The cliffs of the cape consist of a limestone similar to those of Petermann Fiord and contain no fossils. The vegetation was extremely meagre, finding little room to grow here. Only in a few spots, where the talus that had been split off by frost then tumbled down had already become quite weathered or was covered with guano, did a few stunted specimens of purple saxifrage and withered arctic poppies appear. By contrast the bird life was extraordinarily rich. Everywhere, even where the cliffs ended only in narrow ledges, one saw nothing but closely packed birds. On the highest buttresses nested screaming glaucous gulls, whose mates sat tight on their eggs and huddled down carefully to escape notice. Next to them kittiwakes nested, quite widely spaced, along with innumerable murres in rows, gazing down at us unswervingly. They made almost a comical impression in their black-and-white plumage. They turned their heads deliberately first to one side then the other in order to see us clearly, then with outstretched necks, closed both eyes, as if in meditation.

The first shots sent the residents of Cape Hay into such wild excitement that they flew up, calling loudly, swarming around the cliffs in dense clouds. The hubbub of their jarring voices and the roar of their wing-beats drowned all other sounds; even the shrill clamour of the steam whistle was overpowered.

The hunters killed several hundred murres without any trouble, as well as a number of black guillemots and dovekies. Once the availability of our omelettes for the next month was assured, the ship was warped farther out to sea; in the meantime the men had been plundering nests from the topmasts. In the interim the tide had begun to rise; the floes began to move and were rubbing and grinding against the ship's sides. Finally Captain Markham and I took another stroll across the ice foot and bagged about 50 birds, then returned aboard heavily laden with our haul of birds and with hand specimens of the bedrock. Then the boats were hoisted in; the ice anchor was retrieved, and we steamed eastward.

Captain Adams was so kind as to allow me to continue the meteorological observations that we had been making almost without interruption thus far. To shelter the thermometer and the psychrometer the carpenter made a special box that we set up on the after deck; we installed the aneroid in the cabin. Captain Markham and I shared the work of observing; the former took the period from 4.00 p.m. to midnight, while I took the rest of the day. This routine was strictly adhered to until we reached Scotland; and when we made minor excursions on shore, we always took pocket instruments with us, so as not to interrupt the sequence of observations.

At midnight we rounded Cape Byam Martin, then swung south toward Pond's Bay. The ice masses were increasing; on the morning of 8 July we were surrounded; only to the northeast was open water to be seen. Over the course of the day we organized our accommodations on board. A bed was organized for Chester in the captain's cabin, on the large sofa-chest, whose interior was filled with port. The engineer found a sleeping place in the chief engineer's corner, and the crew in the men's quarters. Markham insisted on sharing his bunk and cabin with me and I accepted this generous offer with thanks, although not without pangs of conscience since, as a result, I was depriving him of every comfort. When I got up to start my watch, he usually went to bed; and if he found his bed already warmed, he could certainly look upon this as a special sort of labour of love.

But we lived happily and in harmony. The captain, for whom Shakespeare's works replaced the Bible, had brought a small library of *belles lettres* with him, and Captain Markham a choice of travel works. We were also given newspapers, whose contents were only intelligible to us, however, once we had been informed of the political and other events that had occurred during our absence.

With our arrival the total complement on board *Arctic* had increased to 62. About one quarter of the crew derived from the Shetland Islands; the rest, with the exception of an Englishman and a Norwegian, were Scots, generally stalwart lads from the Highlands.

One of the most remarkable personalities around us was a deaf-mute, bluntly known as "The Dummy." He expressed his feelings by means of a dull grunting, from the tone of which one could determine his degree of happiness. When Markham put his arms across his chest and made motions as if he were rocking a baby, the "Dummy," who had become a father shortly before joining the ship, grunted in his highest tones. By contrast, if somebody reminded him, by way of a gesture, of the debtor's prison, he uttered deep noises, like the gabbling of a courting blackcock. Despite his regrettable condition, he missed none of the orders issued on board; his practised eye understood the slightest gesture, and he worked happily and smartly. Two of the other men enjoyed the privilege of being named Webster; one of them was short and the other, by contrast, tall. Recalling the prominent role that both editions of Webster's dictionary of the English language had played on board *Polaris*, we named the former the *abridged* and the other the *unabridged* Webster.

Both were great whale hunters, and on the third day after our arrival they found an opportunity to prove their mastery. Over a period of 12 hours two massive whales were killed.[7]

In order to avoid repetition, I shall here make an attempt to describe very briefly the operations of the hunt and the dismemberment of the prey. In so doing I shall make an effort to use technical expressions, which generally derive from Dutch, only when a circumlocution is not possible.

The whales are not hunted from on board the ship, but from small boats, manned by six oarsmen. Every boat designed for whaling contains five lines, each 120 fathoms long. These are coiled in the line tubs, spacious containers, the larger of which sits in the boat's stern, the smaller one amidships.

The harpoon gun is secured to the bow; this is a weapon with a barrel almost 2 feet long and a little over 2-inch bore; like an antiquated swivel-gun it sits in a swivel and can swing in any direction.

The gun-harpoon lies to the right of the gun: a missile made from soft iron with a widened, arrow-like head and a split shaft, along which a ring runs loosely, to which a line about 12 fathoms long is spliced. This line, called the foreganger, is also stowed in a small tub, and is located close behind the gun.

On the port side of the boat lies the hand-harpoon, of a similar design to the gun-harpoon, but with a long, wooden shaft. It too has a foreganger spliced to it, but it rarely exceeds 3 fathoms in length. The shaft of the harpoon rests on the so-called "mick," a wooden rest whose shape is reminiscent of that of the frog of a violin bow.

The boat also contains four lances, an axe for cutting the line in an emergency, and also a long knife called the fluke knife. With the exception of the ammunition box and several towing lines, the rest of the inventory is not directly relevant to the hunt and hence does not merit any special attention here.

As soon as the shout "A fish! A fish!" rings out, the engine is stopped as quickly as possible so that the noise of the screw does not alarm the animal. The men dash on deck in a wild rush and tumble into the boats; the watch-below are often only half-dressed; here one of them is still carrying his boots in his hand; there another is carrying a bundle of clothes on his back.

The boats quickly push off and follow the direction that the skipper indicates. They charge through narrow belts of ice but are hauled over others that would have offered too much resistance. The boat steerer handles his oar with sinewy arms. He constantly gazes around, his gaze following the wake of the dark monster that surfaces sometimes here, sometimes there, in order to take a panting breath.

Now the boats separate to surround their quarry. A dull splashing like the thrashing of the paddlewheels of a steamer slices through the waves; a massive spout of water shoots upward, the sun glistening on the water droplets; and the clumsy body of the whale appears on the surface. It has still not noticed its enemy. And it lies there for a while, apparently motionless.

> Men roeit'er recht op ann, geen roeyer durft omkyken,
> Om niet door Visch of Staart, de schrik baart, te bezwyken,
> Dus roept hen moedig toe, de Harpoenier vol vuur,
> 't Sa Mannen wakker aan! hy is ons, binnen 't uur.
> Pas op nu Stuurder, zoo, zoet, sachjes, zonder schreeuwen.
> Haal uit! Courage, Sa! als Turken en als Leeuwen.
> Dat's braaf! nu zyn we'er by: zitvast: de riemen in,
> De Lynen kant en klaar, dat's weer een nieuw begin.
> De Harpoenier schiet toe - - - -
> [One rows straight ahead; not a soul looks round,

> So that the baleen monster doesn't vanish, fins and flukes,
> Then the harpooner shouts, fresh and full of fire:
> So, men, bravely now! We have the fish now,
> So, steersman, better stand up, gently, quietly, no shouting,
> Get ready to throw! Boldly, just like that. Like Turks or lions.
> Oh, great, now we have him; sit tight, in oars.
> Get the lines prepared, so that they are ready again.
> The harpooner lances it. . .]8

A shot cracks out, evoking a long-drawn, confused echo from the icebergs. The whale is hit and lashes the sea with its powerful tail, until it foams white. It dives, tortured with pain; but no blood marks the wounded animal's route, only the boat, which shoots away as fast as lightning.

The crew hoists a flag as a sign of victory, and the joyful shout of "Whale! Whale!" quickly flies from mouth to mouth and is repeated from on board the ship. But the victory is only a half-victory. The animal might still escape. The line, like a furious grey snake, runs out at such a speed that the eye can scarcely follow its movements; it smokes, as too does the bow of the boat; it has to be constantly wetted to prevent it from catching fire. Woe if the line should become tangled; it would haul the boat under with it into the icy waves.

Then a spout of water shoots up again: a blood-red gush; and the noise accompanying the spout has a rattling note to it. The giant's dark body shows itself again. Another boat that has been waiting for it to appear rows toward it. The harpooner stands high in its bows, and fires off a second shot.

The wounded whale dives again; the lines and boat start smoking again, and again the red flag waves to the resounding shout "A whale! A whale!" The second line also runs out; and both boats are now towed along by the wounded animal, just as the single one had been previously. But the speed of their progress diminishes. The whale surfaces, exhausted. Its warm life-blood pours in streams from its gaping wounds and spreads in a trembling network of veins across the gently rolling waves, standing out strangely from their deep dark green colour.

Now the real battle begins; a battle that calls on a man's courage; a battle one on one. Noiselessly, propelled only by the boatsteerer's long oar, the boat approaches its prey. It avoids the vicinity of the powerful tail, a blow from which would smash it. Instead it runs in close to the giant head; the harpooner hurls his lance and buries the sharp iron in the animal's flank; it twists and turns and, enraged, dives deeply again.

But then it surfaces and receives a second thrust. The boats close in to within a smaller radius and now the attacks come from both left and right. Lance after lance whizzes through the air; the streams of blood gush faster and the fatally wounded animal, its eye glazed, rolls onto its side. Even a dying hare is permitted the gift of complaining, but the giant of the oceans dies in silence.

The privilege of securing the animal is reserved for the crew of the boat whose harpooner fired the first shot. A cut is made through the middle of each fin and through it a rope is rove, hauled tight through both holes, and tied in a knot across the body; this is so that the wide, paddle-like extremities lie tight against the sides, so that the resistance will be reduced when it comes to towing. Once this has been done the towline is fastened round the tail and secured to the bow of the boat. Then, to a cheerful song, the boat proceeds toward the ship, on whose starboard side everything is standing ready to receive the whale.

Part of the railing has already been removed; the whale, with its tail lying forward, is rolled on its back and secured by lines. The head-line is passed through an incision made along the throat; another line is passed around the spinal column just ahead of the flipper-like tail and led to the middle of the body, and there it is secured by a loop that is passed around the body. A block and tackle secures the whale to the foremast and a second one to the mainmast. A chain, secured to a suitable spot on deck and hauled tight, is passed around the right fin.

Only now can one examine the blue-black colossus at leisure.[9] It lies stretched out by the ship's side, a plaything of the waves, through which it had been plunging only a few hours before. It measures almost 50 feet in length; an elephant would appear a dwarf compared to it; but its relative the sperm whale is much larger. Its massive form reminds one of a prehistoric creature. Such an animal can live only in water, can only be borne up by it, can find enough food only there, in order to satisfy the needs of this giant body.

Almost a third of the total length of the body is accounted for by the enormous head, the cranial part of which recedes markedly toward the face; indeed, the latter consists only of a mouth and jaws. The edges of the upper jaw are arched upward. The thick, fleshy under-lip fits into these arches. The eyes lie behind the lead-coloured corners of the mouth. They are extremely small. The length of the almond-shaped orifice probably rarely exceeds 4 inches. Due to the lack of distinct eyelids they appear expressionless. The pupils are elongated transversely; the whites are barely visible, and the blue-black iris can be distinguished only by its moist sheen from the colour of the skin. The ear, which is devoid of an outer ear, is a minute opening lying somewhat above and behind the eye and has undergone all the changes demanded by a life in water. The nostrils, 2-foot-long slits, open in the middle of the projecting forehead, in front of the eyes and the corners of the mouth. The nose itself has completely lost all significance as such, and serves only as an air passage; the smelling nerves have completely atrophied. To what end would such a giant creature still require a sense of smell? It lives in groups and hence the two sexes can easily find each other. Apart from man it has only one enemy, the North Caper,[10] whose approach it can detect by hearing, and which is unable to follow it under the ice due to its large dorsal fin. It needs neither to see or smell its food, since the sea is full of it; the minute winged-snails, jellyfish and small crustaceans are so numerous here that they give the water their own colour. It needs only to open its mouth and close it again in order to capture thousands of these creatures in its mouth. The baleen plates set into the gums prevent them from escaping: a few swallowing movements and they are carried via the narrow throat into the gullet. With this diet even teeth become superfluous; on their initial appearance they are diminutive and disappear long before the calf leaves its mother's body. They are simply historical evidence in which part of the genealogy of this giant species is preserved, a species whose closest terrestrial relatives are the ungulates, and the elusive reindeer involuntarily comes to mind as the representative of the latter.

In keeping with its aquatic lifestyle the whale has the shape of a fish, and in the whaler's usage is succinctly referred to as just that. The actual neck can no longer be identified externally; head and body merge directly into each other. The front extremities take the form of fins that externally display no articulation; but the hind legs lie completely hidden in the mass of meat as insignificant small bones. The cylindrical-shaped body tapers rearward into a transversely-set flipper-like tail that is over 20 feet in width.

Beneath the dark skin, which feels as smooth as leather, lies the massive blanket of blubber. I will now describe how this is removed.

Before the actual flensing begins, the crew all receive a drink. In the meantime the captain has taken his place at the rail in order to supervise the work; he passes his orders to the first mate, who relays them onward. Two boats, the so-called mollymok boats, are placed alongside the whale; the two mollymok boys man them, ready for any task. The harpooners, led by a specksioneer, stand on the animal's belly, which rises high above the water level. They all wear ice-spikes on the heels of their boots, to prevent them from slipping off the slippery carcass.

The work begins. Just behind the front fins a strip of blubber, 2 to 3 feet wide, is cut free using a blubber-spade, a sharp spade fastened to a long handle; this strip is called the canter piece. But it is only partially separated from the carcass. A line is rove through its free end, then led to the capstan, so as to be able to roll the carcass over as required. First the belly is flensed, the blubber being hoisted aboard in strips weighing 2 to 3 tons. All the cuts run transversely around the whale. The boat-steerers, assembled on deck, cut the masses of blubber, which are 12 to 14 inches thick, into smaller pieces. These are immediately hauled away by several seamen using sharply honed hooks, and thrown down the *flensgat*. Down below they are received by the blubber-king, who stows them temporarily.

The harpooners continue their work with undiminished diligence. At every stroke the blood flows. The water around the ship turns red and is covered with liquid oil, on which play the delicate colours of the rainbow.

Flocks of fulmars approach in headlong flight and settle impudently among the working men. Scorning the dark meat, they peck greedily at the blubber, trying to tear small pieces from it, or fish up the drifting scraps. Full of high spirits, the mollymok lads in the two boats grab them, slip collars of blubber around their necks, then release them again. Barely are they freed when they are pursued by their screaming companions and stripped of their collars. But they soon return again to continue gorging with the greed of a harpy. Their feathers are dripping with oil and blood; they can no longer fly and, flapping, regurgitate the half-digested food.

From time to time a shrill call rings out, high in the air, like the distant call of a sparrow hawk. This is the voice of the ivory gull. The birds come prowling over in pairs, their heads turned downward; they settle on the blood-soaked floes and peck timidly at the reddened spots. All their movements are calm and full of endless grace; whether they sit there with necks drawn in, moving their heads slightly to look across at the busy crew, or whether they are walking across the ice surface in a short, tripping walk, they invariably assume positions whose beauty one has constantly to admire. Their brilliant plumage is as white as new snow. Even now, when they have sated themselves on the flows of blood that the current carries toward them, they appear unsullied and as clean as the moment when they first landed.

Suddenly the whole flock disperses, screaming; the fulmars rise flapping and clumsy, the gulls easily, in bold sweeps. The chains slung around the whale's fin are unfastened; with a rattle they slide away; some of the harpooners leap into the boats, others on deck; some of the lines are hauled tight, others loosened, and to the loud cheers of the crew, the bloody carcass is rolled over.

The rest of the animal is now flensed in a similar fashion to the belly. Then the flensers begin removing the baleen plates with sharp knives. These radiate out from the centre line of the gums toward both sides of the jaw, and decrease in size from back to front. They are rarely fewer than 300 in number and are said not to exceed 470. The longest measure somewhat over 10 feet and are about 14 inches wide. They are embedded in the mass of the gum to a third of their width. Once hoisted on board they are split into sections of 8 to 15 plates with iron wedges. These are later cut up even further, to the point that not more than 3 to 5 of the brownish-black plates remain attached to each other.

Once the baleen has been extracted the lips are removed; they are almost 2 feet wide. But their structure is looser, with an abundance of connective tissue, and their value is less than the rest of the blubber layer.

Most of the harpooners climb back aboard and the two mollymok boats move to the area of the tail. The latter is separated from the spinal column close to its root; for this both long flensing knives and axes are used. Once this has been achieved the lines are cast off, and to the cheers of the crew the carcass of the whale sinks into the depths.

As soon as time permits, making-off begins; this consists in the two harpooners cutting the blubber into small pieces weighing about 20 lbs. and removing the muscle fibres. The cubes thus produced are then transferred to another group of harpooners and are placed by their assistants on vertical iron frames whose shape resembles that of a double trident. Here, once the outer skin has been removed, the blubber is piled up in front of the blubber trough. The latter consists of a wooden gutter about 20 feet long and 2 feet wide and deep. In the middle of the trough there is a circular opening into which a canvas chute is fitted, whose free end extends down through the main hatch into the hold. The lid of the trough is folded back and used as a table. On this, rectangular blocks, cut from the whale's tail, are laid, and on them the boatsteerers cut the blubber into quite small cubes that are then thrown down the canvas chute into the hold. Down below, the blubber-king and his companions are waiting for them and supervise the filling of the barrels and tanks.

In keeping with an old custom, a meal is always served after a whale has been flensed, whether it be morning, noon or night. When we sat down to eat on board *Arctic* on 10 July after the two whales had been flensed, the witching hour had already struck. Delighted with the day's work, our good captain recited the witch scene from Macbeth and made Banquo's ghost appear. When the first witch asked of the second "Where hast thou been, sister?" he put these words in her mouth: "Killing whales," whereas in reality only homely pigs had been massacred. The remaining lines were also recited with corresponding modifications.[11]

*****

14 July was a rainy day, such as is rarely encountered in the arctic zone. We stood on deck and caught the large drops in our hands, the first we had seen for a long time. During the night two sails hove in sight; like *Arctic* they were cruising for whales. Next day fog forced us to heave-to and make fast to a large floe. A sounding, whereby 200 fathoms of line

were run out, produced a negative result in that no bottom was reached. The temperature at depth was 0.0° and at the surface 1.9°, whereas the air temperature had risen to 5.5°.

Since for the moment no more whales appeared in Baffin Bay, we steamed back to Lancaster Sound. We passed Cape Byam Martin at 8.00 p.m. on the 18th. The captain was kind enough to reduce the ship's speed somewhat to allow Markham and myself to make a running survey of the coast, whose delineation on the available charts revealed significant errors. The hours passed like minutes; when I'd finished my sketch of the panorama it was 3.00 a.m.

On the evening of the 19th the first opportunity presented itself of going ashore. While several of the boats were waiting for a whale, Markham, Chester, the ship's doctor and myself rowed to the north-easternmost point at the entrance to Navy Board Inlet and to the small Wollaston Islands. The low coast, which consists of fossil-free Silurian limestone, reminded me strikingly of the shores of Polaris Bay. In both cases the land is experiencing a general uplift; in both cases numerous erratics lie scattered about the lowlands. The nature of the bedrock is surprisingly similar in both places, and this similarity extends even to the shapes of the hills and mountains. Limestone predominated among the erratic boulders. In addition there were coarse-grained red syenite, various gneisses, diorite sandstone, quartzite and hornblende. Close to the beach I picked up several crystals of tourmaline that were scratched and partially rounded.

The vegetation was poor; indeed one could scarcely expect otherwise on a limestone substrate. Just as elsewhere we found the purple saxifrage most abundantly represented here; by contrast the arctic willow was strikingly rare; *Saxicava caespitosa* and *S. nivalis* were in full bloom. The alpine poppy grew less luxuriantly than at Polaris Bay, and the few clumps of sticky catch-fly[12] that we were able to dig up were quite stunted. There were no insects to be seen.

Of the birds, apart from the numerous fulmars, only some murres and dovekies showed themselves, along with a king eider drake at which we fired in vain. In a rock crevice on the western cliff of the largest of the Wollaston Islands we found the nest of a snow bunting, with three young and an addled egg. The nest consisted of dried grass stems and was less artistically constructed than usual; arctic poppy leaves and old feathers were worked through it. To my great astonishment I found the breast feather of a starling on the bottom of the nest.[13] After my return, when I found an opportunity to compare this feather, I convinced myself quite definitely that there was no mistake. As far as I was able to discover, only a single specimen of the starling had been killed in southern Greenland.

Midnight had long passed. A few hours later we encountered the *Narwhal*, another Scottish whaler, whose captain sent us the latest newspapers. They were over two months old but we fell on them greedily and were delighted to find the first detailed news of the rescue of our 19 companions. As a result of a vague suggestion, the American government was said to be about to send out a warship to search for us.

Narwhal made fast to the fast ice which extended across the entrance to Admiralty Inlet. *Arctic*'s captain did the same. Shortly afterward the boats were lowered. Each of the ships killed a whale. Just as our whale was flensed, numerous dark figures appeared on shore: a wandering band of Eskimos with women, children and dog sledges. Their agile teams soon brought them to our side. We counted 10 men, 9 women, 3 girls and 5 boys, distributed among seven sledges.[14] They brought fox pelts and walrus tusks and a minor barter-trade immediately began.

Two of the women were tattooed. The design consisted of double blue-black lines. Two ran in a steep arc from the forehead to the upper part of the temple area; two others, convex downward, from the nostrils across the cheeks to the middle of the cheek bones. A further seven lines were grouped around the mouth, six of them being arranged in pairs. The odd one ran from the middle of the lower lip to the point of the chin; the others, diverging outward, extended from the lower half of the mouth across the lower jaw.

In contrast to the Greenland women, all the women here had their hair parted in the middle; it fell over the shoulders in two strands, loosely tied with leather thongs. In every case the short skin jacket ended at the back in a narrow, undivided, frock coat–like tail that reached almost to the heels.

A gale that broke around midnight and churned the sea up so violently that the ice disintegrated forced the Eskimos to head for land as fast as possible. We ourselves sought shelter in Elwin Inlet,[15] where we dropped anchor in the early morning of the 21st.

The small bay was swarming with narwhal. It was an enormous school that certainly numbered at least 500 animals, mainly females and young males. In a short time we harpooned 7 of them; the rest, disturbed by the shooting, fled from the area.

After a rest of a few hours I accompanied Markham ashore, in order to collect the necessary data for a chart of the harbour. The limestone shores of the harbour reach a height of about 1200 feet and are steep almost everywhere. The rock is similarly stratified to that in the walls of Petermann Fjord. On the most northerly point of the harbour, where erratics are quite common, I spotted indubitable traces of relative uplift. We were unable to discover much about the depths. Markham took a sounding from on board ship that gave a depth of 190 fathoms. The bottom consisted of grey calcareous mud. The air temperature was 2.8°; that of the water at the bottom 1.4° and at the surface 1.1°. No definite tidal current was recorded in the bay during our stay.

At 10.00 a.m. we weighed anchor and left the harbour in order to follow the edge of the ice in Admiralty Inlet. When the *Tay*, another of the whaling fleet, hove in sight, Adams sent a boat away and it returned with letters and newspapers. The latter were of a later date than those for which we were indebted to *Narwhal*'s kindness and contained equally sensational news on the rescue of our comrades.

At midnight we returned to Elwin Inlet in order to take on water.[16] Once the casks had been filled we again began cruising along the fast ice as before; the latter had disintegrated only a little under the fury of the storm. Shortly afterward dense fog arose and enveloped both sea and land for five days, at times depriving us of any distant views.

When the fog dispersed the ship was just off the entrance to Prince Regent Inlet. At 1.00 a.m. on the morning of 28 July we pushed into that strait under steam. The air had suddenly become wonderfully clear; but at the same time we encountered such a heavy swell that the foam from the long, regular waves was wetting the decks. Not until we had broken through a wide belt of ice did we reach calm water. Toward evening the engineer received orders to let the steam pressure drop since the captain was definitely counting on encountering whales here. Next day a whale appeared close to the ship. The smaller Webster fired but missed. When the whale surfaced again the captain shouted to the harpooner to hurl the hand harpoon. The latter did so but unfortunately the line became tangled so that the crew of the boat was in mortal danger for a moment.

"Save yourselves! Abandon everything!" thundered the words of command. The boat was already heeling over and the men were just about to jump into the water when the harpoon suddenly pulled free.

While this whale was lost, shortly afterward another one was harpooned, but its unruly behaviour quickly exhausted the men's strength. Chester volunteered to give the animal its coup-de-grace. When he fired, the wounded whale dived so abruptly into the depths that its tail struck the boat's stern and hurled Markham into the water.[17] The boat was close to capsizing, and the ship's doctor, one of the oarsmen, jumped overboard to swim to a nearby floe. Once the men had gathered their wits, the two soaked hunters were hauled out, but almost two hours passed before an opportunity offered of changing their clothes. Chester pursued the whale courageously and finally gave it several fatal lance-thrusts. Before midnight had passed we had its blubber and bone on board.

The whales were extremely numerous here; at times they appeared in schools of 30 to 50 animals, but they were wary and rarely let the boats come within firing range.

During the 30th we were cruising off Port Bowen, Parry's former winter harbour,[18] and on 1 August near a large ice field that extended from that harbour to Batty Bay, watching for whales. But the latter had departed. Next day at 6.00 a.m. we sailed past Fury Beach at a distance of about four miles off. The cases, barrels and other items that Parry had saved from the shipwrecked *Fury* in August 1825 and had landed here were clearly recognizable. We were burning with the desire to step ashore, but the captain cherished other plans. He wanted to follow the fast ice to Fury Point, then to penetrate through the Gulf of Boothia, Fury and Hecla Strait and Foxe Basin to Hudson Bay.[19] Markham and I greeted this plan with delight. The area lying along that course was, in part, not yet accurately enough surveyed, and we immediately organized ourselves to be ready for a running survey. But things were to turn out differently; the whims of our blonde captain were as changeable as the ice situation.

After several unsuccessful chases *Arctic* steered back north again, rather than south, and on the morning of 3 August we again reached the area of Fury Beach; and this time we actually landed.

The beach was covered with barrels and chests, with cordage, fishing gear and other items that in part still lay in the same arrangement as Parry had left them almost half a century earlier. Some of the flour casks had been gnawed and smashed by bears. Their contents had suffered due to damp; by contrast the sugar and rope-tobacco had survived excellently. We took some powder from an open magazine that was still half full. It had completely retained its granular nature, but it burned slowly when it was put in contact with fire, and with a bluish flame since the saltpetre had largely been leached out. We later took some of the numerous cans of meat and vegetables aboard and had the contents cooked. The various dishes tasted neither better nor worse than canned food ever does; they behaved like most such foods; if thoroughly salted or peppered they tasted predominantly of those condiments.

One of *Fury*'s two boats had disintegrated; but the other, a 22-foot jolly-boat, was in such good condition that only a few hours would have sufficed to make it seaworthy again.

The hut that the two Rosses had erected here in the fall of 1832,[20] after they had had to abandon their ship, was a total ruin. A more luxuriant flora had taken root on the canvas of the former roof, which now lay flat on the ground, than at other locations. The oldest arctic willow that we found on it possessed 14 annual rings. Other phanerogams we collected here included *Ranunculus glacialis, Lychnis apetala, Dryas octopetala, Saxifraga caespitosa, S. oppositifolia, S. Nivalis, S. flagellaris, Pedicularis hirsuta* and *Pleuropogon Sabini*. All of these plants were huddled together in a space of only a few square metres.

Close by on the shore Markham and I spotted a cairn almost simultaneously and raced each other to it since we hoped to find some documents in it. We quickly removed the rocks but our expectations were disappointed. It was only a grave: that of Chimham Thomas, *Victory*'s carpenter, who died here on 22 February 1833 during Ross's wintering.

Once we had collected some mementoes we climbed the plateau-like upland that rises terrace-like to a height of about 600 feet and extends westward in slightly undulating terrain. Even on the highest points that we visited we encountered shells of *Saxicava rugosa* and *Mya truncata*, which clearly indicated a relative uplift. Erratic boulders of metamorphic rocks were common everywhere. On one of the steeply dropping grey limestone cliffs we found a substantial number of typical Upper Silurian fossils.

Around noon it began to rain gently and the visibility became so reduced that we were robbed of all distant prospects. Hence we returned aboard ship, which we reached at 3 o'clock. Next day, 4 August, we were again cruising in the vicinity of Fury Beach, and on the 5th we crossed Creswell Bay, whose shores are laid down inaccurately on the charts. This is specifically the case with regard to Cape Garry, its southernmost point, which lies farther north and west than Ross and McClintock indicate. Parry's original survey appears to come closest to the truth.

A sounding made 6 miles east of Cape Garry revealed a hard bottom in a depth of 30 fathoms. Later a boat was sent off to sound. The sea bed shoaled significantly toward the land; 3 miles east of the cape the depth was only 4 fathoms. The bottom samples that were brought aboard were very small, but they were sufficient to allow us to determine that the bottom consists of coarse-grained reddish sand. A few days later several whales were killed in this area. When the harpoons were removed we discovered in one of the shafts a piece of red sandstone about 3 inches long and 2 inches wide. In association with the results of the various soundings, this find appears to prove that the Silurian limestone of Creswell Bay rests directly on sandstone.

At midnight on the 6th we again found ourselves at Fury Beach, but instead of whales we now sighted only their bitter enemies, voracious North Capers. When the latter appear in an area one can count with certainty on the fact that the former will disappear. The captain allowed the intruders to be hunted, but they shot through the water so impetuously that the boats were unable to follow them. The seamen call them swordfish. I estimated their length at 20 feet; the height of the dorsal fin, which looks like a boat-sail from a distance, is about one third of the animal's total length. All the individuals that we spotted were of one dark colour. We were unable to determine the species of Orca to which they belonged.[21] They appeared in schools of from six to eight animals and made very characteristic movements. They usually came so close to the surface that the entire upper half of the body was visible, then followed each other in dolphin-like rolling dives.

Near Cape Garry a further three whales were killed on the morning of the 10th. Markham convinced the captain to let him have the jolly-boat for a more detailed investigation of the coast. We began our journey at 8.00 p.m. Hermann,[22] one of our own seamen, accompanied us; the provisions were calculated to last a week. We planned to follow the west shore of the entrance and to push on as far as Bellot Strait, where we were to rendezvous with *Arctic* again.

With a favourable breeze we sailed toward Fearnall Bay, a minor embayment somewhat south of Cape Garry. The latter extends out in a low headland that merges with the horizon, even when seen at close range. When we had approached to within a mile of land we grounded several times. The shoalness of the water finally obliged us to set a southward course. Only after various vain attempts did we succeed in landing about 5½ miles south of Cape Garry.

Hermann stayed behind with the boat while Markham and I hurried to a small lowland that had attracted our attention for some time. What we had mistaken from a distance for the stranded skeleton of a whale now turned out to be a complex of very old, collapsed Eskimo huts. We counted 34 of these structures. Nine of them had originally consisted of stone, the rest of whale bones: ribs, lower jaws and skulls. We found no fewer than 60 of the latter. Originally they had been arranged in a circle, standing on the rearward part of the head, with the centre of the building as the point of convergence. The largest number in a single hut was nine. In three of the structures individual rocks had also been used as well as bones.

The longer I examined these ruins, of which I cannot provide a more detailed description here, the more strongly I was tempted to ascribe to them a significance in terms of history of development as well as their actual historical significance. Specifically, they reveal the way in which the Inuit were led to build a dome.

It is a known fact that Roman architecture is based upon Greek architecture; but to the Romans is reserved the recognition for discovering the dome in the old world. Originally the Eskimos also erected their buildings only with flat roofs. Hence in both areas the dome dates to a later period. The unsupported, freely arched snow domes that have been described in detail in one of the previous chapters occur only among the eastern bands. If, apart from the older style of building their dwellings among Alaska's Inuit, older forms of speech than on this side of the Mackenzie River were also to be encountered among them, this would lead one to certain conclusions of considerable significance.

The age of the ruins that we found here could not be determined. Once we had drawn a site plan by eye, we returned to the boat. An hour after midnight we continued our voyage southward and landed on the most northerly point of a small bay that is still unnamed on the map. While Markham measured a few sun angles, I drew various sketches and took astronomical bearings to prominent points. The compass was totally unreliable and hence had become useless since we were in the immediate vicinity of the North Magnetic Pole.

By the time our work was finished the tide had almost reached its lowest point. The boat lay completely high and dry, and since it was impossible to launch it we used this involuntary leisure period for an excursion.

We wandered inland across boggy lowlands to a row of hills that consists of a limestone similar to that of the other stretches of coast that we had visited. Here, too, the lowlands were thickly strewn with erratic boulders. Most of the limestone erratics contained animal remains from the Upper Silurian. Nine old beach-lines that extended along a hill-slope indicated that this was an area of uplift, but sub-fossil shells such as we had collected at Fury Beach were nowhere to be found here.

On reaching a boggy plateau we spotted four reindeer at a distance of about 500 paces: a bull, two cows and a calf, grazing unconcernedly. Markham, who was carrying a rifle, carefully crept closer and fired at the bull, which dropped at the second shot. We gutted the animal with a pen-knife and hauled it to a neighbouring hilltop. Then we set off on the shortest route to the boat, in order to bring it closer to our kill. When we reached it the tide had still not risen high enough to allow us to carry out our plan. It was only with the high tide, which occurred at 2.50, that we got the boat afloat, and then sailed south.

Near our second landing place Markham again got a shot at a bull, barely half a mile from the coast. The first bullet missed and thudded into the bog close in front of the animal. The latter ran off a little but then trotted toward us in friendly fashion and finally stood still. It was obviously surprised. At the second shot it dropped.

Both this and the other reindeer had disproportionately small antlers. In one case the velvet had already partially come off the bez-antlers;[23] in the other case the tines were showing the first signs of forking. The smallness of their antlers seemed all the more striking in that the young calf that had fled along with the two cows already had points of substantial length.

A reindeer specimen which is to be found in the National Museum came from Great Slave Lake and carries antlers of unusually large dimensions.

It was hard work carrying the first bull we had killed to the boat, since the treacherous, saturated ground forced us to make major detours.[24] Despite all our care we sank to our knees at times.

When we reached the boat we spotted the ship in the distance, flying a red flag, the signal that we should come aboard. We immediately started back and at 8.00 p.m. stepped onto *Arctic*'s deck after an absence of only 24 hours. In the meantime the crew had succeeded in killing another whale that had already been flensed. The captain had again changed his plans.[25] We had to abandon our planned boat trip to Bellot Strait.

The strait was clearly visible from the masthead with a telescope. It appeared as a dark stripe in the land masses, separated in perspective; it was bounded on one side by North Somerset and on the other by Murchison Promontory, the northernmost cape of the American continent, which we had left two years before.

CHAPTER 28

The search

Resolutions of the Navy Department. Purchase and refit of Tigress. *Movements of* Juniata. Tigress *leaves New York. Voyage of* Little Juniata. Tigress *reaches Polaris House.* Tigress *returns to the Danish colonies and her voyage to Cumberland Sound. Iviktut and the cryolite mine.*

The brief hints that we had gleaned from the Scottish newspapers that the American government was in the process of making preparations for our rescue were more than just rumours.

After the arrival of our 19 companions the Navy Department had immediately taken active steps to organize an expedition to search for us. Since the Federal Navy did not possess a vessel that might have been used for such an operation, the government purchased *Tigress*, the Newfoundland sealer that had taken our comrades aboard so hospitably.[1] She was taken to the Navy Dockyard in Brooklyn and there was strengthened, altered and equipped for an arctic cruise that, if necessary, could last for a year.[2]

While these preparations were underway, the Department was fitting out the warship *Juniata*, a vessel of 828 tons burden.[3] She was commanded by Commander D.L. Braine, and on 24 June she left New York harbour;[4] she was to call first at St. John's, Newfoundland, then proceed to Greenland. *Juniata*'s main task was to support *Tigress*'s operations by providing her with provisions, coal and sledge dogs. She was also to search for *Polaris* and her crew, but without exposing herself to the hazards of ice; she was not built for arctic waters and was not adequately strengthened.

On 14 July *Juniata* encountered the first extensive ice masses near Fiskernæsset and next day anchored at Sukkertoppen, where Commander Braine hoped to purchase a number of sledge dogs. But he was disappointed in these hopes and hence on the 18th he put to sea again. But at Holsteinsborg, which he reached at midnight that night, through the kindness of the colony's administrator, he obtained 18 strong sledge dogs and 150 sealskins.

The next harbour at which *Juniata* called was Disko. Here 70 tons of coal were brought ashore, as were the dogs, whose numbers gradually rose to 30 through further purchases. On 29 July the ship put to sea again and two days later she reached Upernavik. Braine immediately made contact with Dr. Rudolph, the colony's administrator, in order to win him over to his plans. The sealskins were given to the Eskimo women in the settlement, for them to be worked up into items of clothing for *Tigress*'s officers and men.

The latter had not been able to leave New York until the evening of 14 July.[5] Commander J.A. Greer had been selected to command her. Among the crew, which numbered 15 men, were 5 of our companions from *Polaris*, namely Tyson as Lieutenant and ice pilot, the Eskimo Joseph as interpreter, and Krüger, Nindemann[6] and Lindquist as seamen. The Hanseatics, who were to be brought back to their homeland, were the sole passengers.[7]

Like *Juniata*, *Tigress* also called at St. John's to take on coal. She left that port on 27 July after a stay of barely 36 hours, and then proceeded directly to Greenland where her field of operations began. The steep coast came in sight on 4 August on a cheerless, rainy morning;[8] two days later the ship was lying at anchor off Disko. Here the dogs were taken on board, as well as the coal that Commander Braine had left behind, while some repairs were made to the engines.[9] These tasks kept the crew busy until the 8th. Toward evening the vessel put to sea again; she next called where *Juniata* was lying and where the Hanseatics were to be disembarked.[10]

In the meantime *Juniata*'s commander had been active to the best of his abilities. His original intention to send an umiak manned by Eskimos northward to inform us of the ship's arrival, had been foiled by the recalcitrance of the natives, who could not be persuaded to tackle such an undertaking. Hence it had been necessary to think of another scheme, and since his own ship was scarcely suitable for a voyage in ice, he had assigned the larger of his two steam-launches to proceed to the entrance to Smith Sound. This boat, *Little Juniata*, was provisioned for two months and bunkered for two weeks.

On 2 August she left Upernavik harbour, commanded by Lieutenant De Long;[11] he was assisted by Lieutenant Chipp[12] and Midshipman May. Also on board were an ice pilot, an engineer, a bosun, two seamen and an Eskimo who was to serve as interpreter. The launch was towing one of the ship's boats, laden with 12 centners of coal; it and the boat were left at Tasiusaq, which was reached at 11.00 p.m.

Delayed by thick fog, De Long was unable to put to sea before 10 o'clock next morning. At 8.00 p.m. the launch passed Cape Shackleton; abeam of it De Long found an opportunity to take an astronomical observation that gave a position of 77°42'N, 57°W. At 4.00 a.m. on the 4th the launch was a few miles northwest of Baffin Island.[13] At the same time a strong wind out of the north and west blew up; when fog was added to the wind, *Little Juniata* made fast to an iceberg close inshore at 3.00 p.m. The current sometimes set northward, sometimes southward. At 5.00 p.m. progress was renewed. The launch was so overloaded that casting the log line involved major difficulties; hence the accuracy of the calculations was seriously compromised.

Like others before him, De Long found the charts of Melville Bay extremely inaccurate. He described the delineation of Allison Bay inadequate in that it is choked with islands that do not appear on the map. These islands extend southward almost 15 miles from Cape Seddon toward Wilcox Head, and had probably only been overlooked previously because they barely rise above sea level.

When the fog became so thick at 10.00 p.m. that it veiled the land to the point that it could not be recognized, the launch turned back. But she had steamed barely a few miles back south when the pack closed around her and *Little Juniata* was beset. Once she had been freed again De Long carefully set a course westward. Progress in the fog was dangerous; but it would have been even more dangerous to heave-to since young ice was forming continually, threatening to freeze the launch in.

Open water was finally reached at 10.00 a.m. on the 5th, although the increasing swell had already heralded its proximity an hour before. De Long set a northwesterly course and at 2.00 p.m. the Sabine Islands were sighted. From here on the pack extended to the coast, solidly close; Melville Bay was filled with numerous icebergs. Constrained by the unfavourable conditions, De Long decided to head for the coast, the nearest point of which was about 50 miles away.

At 11.00 a.m. on 6 August, Peaked Hill hove in sight; it is a mountain with a cleft summit, whose position is shown on the chart as being 76°18'N; 62°W. At the same time a narrow lead appeared, cutting through the pack in a westerly direction. Before *Little Juniata* succeeded in getting close to this channel, the fog descended again, and the launch had to anchor in the lee of an iceberg.

The coal was almost half exhausted and the distance to Cape York was still about 40 miles. The launch continued her voyage under sail, before a gentle wind. Around 10.00 a.m. on the 7th she reached more open water and at 8.00 p.m., when the south wind began to freshen, she headed west.

It was not until after 1.00 a.m. on the 8th that Cape York hove in sight; an hour later the launch had managed to close to within 8 miles of its cliffs. It was impossible to penetrate any farther due to the ice; all efforts to find a lead were in vain. At noon the launch's position was 75°48'N; 66°50'W. During the afternoon the southeasterly wind grew to a gale, producing a wild sea, and *Little Juniata*'s situation became extremely dubious. De Long's official report reads as follows:

> The wind had swept the pack away from the land to the north and west, thereby producing a small bay, in which we lay. We had to set sail in order to be able to control the launch. Steam would have been totally useless since *Little Juniata* was not in a position to battle against such a gale. We could not think of keeping underway without exposing ourselves to the danger of driving against the pack and seeing the launch smashed. Our prospects were terrible. Nearby icebergs, 100 feet high, were being totally swept by spray. As we approached the edge of the pack we were confronted by a scene of wild devastation. The ice along

the pack-edge was being smashed and heaved up and hurled furiously against the floes lying farther back. The fate of boat and crew seemed sealed. At times we were half-buried by the waves; breakers crashed over us, soaking everything on board. If the sail had torn or the mast split it would have been impossible for us to raise a finger. Fortunately everything held together and we were still able to control the launch to some degree. The fog was extremely thick; it was extraordinarily difficult to spot the drifting masses of pack ice soon enough to avoid them. We frequently had to change course without knowing whether we would succeed in escaping the capsizing hummocks.

And so it continued until the morning of 9 August. At 10 we were finally pleased to experience a calm. The gale had lasted for 30 hours and we were frozen and exhausted. Everything was totally soaked. The water level in the boat was so high that we were afraid she was leaking. *Little Juniata* had behaved superbly, much better than we could have expected of such a small craft. The stoke-hold was under water; the coal bunkers were half submerged. The matches were damp and hence were useless; the tinder was totally soaked. Once Ensign May had dried some matches by placing them on his chest for several hours, we succeeded in lighting a candle, but shortly afterward it was blown out by a gust of wind. Once we had again produced light in the same manner we tried to light a fire, but the wood refused to burn. Only when we had soaked a handful of oakum in oil was this problem solved.

My orders instructed me to start back when the fuel was half consumed and under no circumstances to endanger the boat in the pack. The fuel was half exhausted and what was left was in extremely poor condition. As far as we could determine the ice extended close-packed to the north and east and our course lay precisely in those directions. I did not know how close we had come to the Middle Ice during the gale and I was afraid of becoming beset. Even if we had succeeded in steaming to the coast we would not have been able to steam back, for lack of fuel; a northwest wind would have sufficed to beset us forever.

Under these circumstances it was imperative that they turn back. Hence at 4 o'clock on the afternoon of 9 August the launch's bow was turned south.

At 1.00 a.m. on the 12th *Little Juniata* ran into the harbour at Tasiusaq and there rendezvoused with *Tigress*, whose task it now was to push north herself.[14] De Long gave her commander the necessary information on ice conditions, took aboard the coal that he had left here, then returned to Upernavik, which he reached on the evening of the 16th.

Tigress, which had put to sea at the same time as *Little Juniata*, passed Cape York at 10.00 a.m. on 13 August, but was unable to close with the cape. The pack that had defied De Long's efforts was now closer than ever and extended farther south and west. Only once *Tigress* had run past the cape some distance offshore did Commander Greer succeed in following the run of the coast. At 9.00 p.m. he reached North Star Bay, which he searched carefully.

Netilik, the Eskimo settlement, was reached on the morning of the 14th, but the natives had departed. As the ship approached Northumberland Island, its mastheads were crowded with zealous lookouts, since the 19 men had erroneously identified this as the spot where they had seen *Polaris* for the last time. From here Greer headed farther north; he was firmly convinced of the error that had arisen, especially since Tyson and the rest of our former companions who were aboard *Tigress* now considered it more probable that the larger Littleton Island was the site of the separation.[15] At 9.00 a.m. *Tigress* was lying just off that island. The watch officer discovered the hut that we had built on the headland in front of Lifeboat Cove and spotted some people who were running up and down the shore. A boat was launched immediately and rowed ashore.

Greer learned from the natives[16] that we had headed south in two boats at the time when the eider ducks were nesting. The hut with its 14 bunks and the remains of a primitive carpenter's bench explained the rest.

The wreck had disappeared.[17] A short time after we had left on our boat voyage, the ice had started moving due to a violent storm and had driven the ship's hulk seaward. Our old friend Avatok showed one of the officers the place where the remains of *Polaris* had sunk; two grounded icebergs seemed to hold the wreck fast. In this area the water depth varied between 7 and 11 fathoms.

Greer examined the hut and its surroundings, since he hoped to find some hidden documents that might give him some information as to our intended movements.[18] Unfortunately he overlooked the heap of rocks beneath which lay several boxes of instruments and books, as well as the reports for which he was looking.

Smith Sound was filled with heavy pack, slowly drifting southward, and *Tigress* could not expose herself to the danger of becoming beset in the ice. Hence Greer decided to turn back. Once the more valuable items that we had left behind in the hut had been taken aboard, the ship set a course for the south and reached Tasiusaq again on the afternoon of 19 August.[19] Since in the interim nothing had been heard of us there either, *Tigress*'s commander conjectured that we had headed west. He now headed first to Upernavik and then to Disko, which he reached on 25 August. From here he reported to the Navy Department on his movements thus far. His dispatch ended:

> At 2.30 p.m. on 19 August I met with the colony administrator, Jensen, in Tasiusaq, but I could learn nothing as to the whereabouts of the missing men. At 9.30 I dropped anchor at Upernavik; here too there was nothing to be learned concerning *Polaris*'s crew. I stayed at Upernavik until 2.00 p.m. on 23 August to repair the engine;[20] then I set sail and reached here at 2.00 a.m. on 25 August. I, personally at least, am quite firmly convinced that *Polaris*'s crew is aboard a whaler.[21]
>
> In accordance with my instructions, which direct me to search thoroughly for the missing men, I will now proceed to the west side of Davis Strait and head north along the ice edge until I succeed in closing with the eastern shore. I will then look for the whalers that usually follow the run of that coast on their homeward passage. I shall continue the search as long as the ice conditions and my supplies of coal permit. Later I shall head for St. John's.

The next dispatch from Commander Greer to the Navy Department was written on 15 September at Niantilik in Cumberland Sound. This message reads:

> We set a northward course and on 26 August, at 67°30'N; 60°15'W we ran into the pack which extended north and east. I followed its edge southward and eastward and ran into every lead that seemed to promise a through-passage to the coast. As I reached the vicinity of Cape Searle I found that the coast was totally ice-bound. I then tried to reach Exeter Bay but my efforts were in vain. Since I had learned that the Scottish whalers occasionally visit Cumberland Sound I decided to call at this place since my coal supplies were running very low.
>
> We arrived here on 4 September[22] and immediately took on ballast. I intend putting to sea again tomorrow, in order to call at Ivigtut [now Ivittuut] in West Greenland.

After an extremely stormy passage, *Tigress* dropped anchor in that harbour on 27 September and Commander Greer immediately took the necessary steps to procure coal. The agent for the cryolite company obligingly met his wishes, supplying him with 190 tonnes from the company's supplies; these were immediately taken aboard.

Since cryolite has started to be used for the production of alumina and soda, Ivigtut, which lies at a latitude of 61°N, has become one of the most important settlements in West Greenland. The site where this rare mineral is exploited covers an area of, at most, 40,000 square feet and is the only deposit in Greenland. So far only one other deposit is known.[23]

We are indebted to Mr. J.W. Taylor for a detailed description of the cryolite works; his observations were published in Volume 12 of the *Quarterly Journal of the Geological Society of London*. Rink also mentioned them in his various works, but the geologist Giesecke had already studied the area thoroughly in 1806.[24]

At Ivigtut the cryolite occurs in the granitic bedrock in the form of a body that is about 400 feet long and that varies in width between 50 and 100 feet. Its depth is still not known; but the miners have penetrated about 100 feet downward without encountering the granite in which

Fig. 46. Ivittuut: from a photograph.

the mineral lies embedded. At the surface it is predominantly white; at a depth of 10 feet it appears in brown masses, while farther down it assumes an almost black appearance.

The workings lie close to the beach, and as a result the shipping of the raw material is greatly facilitated. In 1856 the output was not more than a single shipload of 343 Danish tons; in 1862 this had already risen to 24 shiploads of 11,045 tons; the total production during these six years was 29,275 tons, which represented 60 shiploads.

Mr. von Hegermann-Lindencrone, the Danish ambassador in Washington, was kind enough to provide me with these and other data on the cryolite workings; the most interesting of these have been compiled in the following table:

YEAR	OUTPUT		TONS SHIPPED TO	
	SHIPLOADS	TONS	EUROPE	AMERICA
1863	10	5498.3		
1864	10	4261.1		
1865	25	19891.7		
1866	23	19582.4	8895.3	10957.1
1867	30	24908.8	8635.1	16273.7
1868	25	18890.2	17800.4	1098.9
1869	28	22847.0	6764.8	16082.2
1870	21	15522.6	4801.1	10721.5
1871	22	21177.9	7609.1	13568.8
1872	31	26607.3	11673.9	14933.5
1873	23	17358.6	11124.0	6234.6

According to Rink, 100 people are employed in the mines during the summer, on average, but in winter scarcely more than 30. In 1857 the workings were leased by a joint-stock company that still operates them.

Copper, tin and zinc, as well as silver-bearing galena, also occur here in association with the cryolite; but these ores do not occur in sufficient amounts to make it profitable to work them. Ivigtut is probably richer in different minerals than any other place in Greenland. Rock crystals 1 foot long are far from rare here; fluorspar too is common, as too are molybdenum, tantalium and zircon.

Tigress's officers made a valuable collection of most of these minerals, and this was later entrusted to the National Museum in Washington. On 4 October the ship put to sea again and swung west.[25]

CHAPTER 29

Homeward bound

Arctic leaves Prince Regent Inlet. Changed ice conditions. A bear and her cub. Stormy days. Slow progress. Arctic's *catch. Rendezvous with* Ravenscraig. *Vain attempts to reach the East Water.* Arctic *crosses the Arctic Circle. Arrival in Scotland.* Juniata *and* Tigress. *The crew returns to the United States.*

At the same time as *Little Juniata* reached Tasiusaq again after her unsuccessful voyage north, *Arctic*'s captain decided to head for home and informed his crew of his intention.

On the evening of 12 August the ship's bows were turned north; the engineer received orders to raise steam, and in a very zig-zag course we headed for the entrance to Prince Regent Inlet.

In the interim, ice conditions had changed drastically. Where we had encountered open water previously, we now ran into impenetrable pack. Thus it came about that on the 13th when we wanted to set a course from Fury Point for Cape York[1] we were obliged to make a wide detour that took us to the vicinity of Cape Leopold. Only from here were we able to swing east and to cross Prince Regent Inlet. Barrow Strait was now open; the northerly winds had probably driven the ice south.

Around 8.00 p.m. we passed Cape York; near it a bear and her cub were playing on the ice. The captain ordered one of the boats lowered; this caused the animal to dive into the water and try to escape. She swam off in a desperate effort to escape her pursuers; the mother's head was stretched up and her hindquarters were elevated but there was nothing visible of the cub but the head and part of its neck. When the mother saw that her cub was in danger she made an attack on the

531

boat and only abandoned it when Markham sent a bullet through her brain. The cub was caught with a lasso and hoisted aboard. It was the size of a half-grown Newfoundlander and expressed the pain caused by the death of its mother in a heart-rending howling wail. As some of the seamen skinned its mother, it watched sadly. It was almost callous to throw it a piece of the still-steaming meat. But it ate it greedily and later begged for more. It hissed at anyone who came near it, and it became so refractory, vicious and mean that it had to be locked up. Placed in a large barrel, fitted with bars, it soon came to its senses; but one could never play with it with impunity. Its favourite food was oil. Whenever the engineer approached it, oil can in hand, it would crawl agilely out of its corner to the bars and licked greedily at the spout of the can. But it showed a strange aversion to water, probably because the seamen often splashed it when they were washing the deck.

When we left Lancaster Sound on the evening of the 14th there was such a strong south wind that one sail had to be reefed after another. The barometer dropped lower and lower; the wind rose to a gale; and the ship began to roll and pitch so much that here and there a face turned green with seasickness. Even the little bear fell ill and lay apathetically in his barrel. In the tween-decks the tanks started moving; the seamen's chests and the baleen were rolling from starboard to port and back to starboard; and everything that was not nailed and tied down formed a variegated mobile heap. During the night the waves even smashed one of the whaleboats and the small jolly-boat.

Under these conditions we were making little progress. On the afternoon of the 16th the ship was off Cape Liverpool, the same location that we had passed 48 hours before. The gale did not drop until the 17th. We sailed through several belts of close-packed floes, but once we had these astern of us, we reached smooth water. Heavy snow-squalls now alternated with fine sleet and the latter with drizzling rain and grey, billowing fog. When the sky cleared on the 18th we discovered to our dismay that we were farther offshore than our reckoning had indicated. The sea here was completely open; it was not until the latitude of Cape Adair, lying about 30 miles to the west, that more extensive ice masses appeared, as well as numerous icebergs. On a drifting floe an old bear was happily consuming a beluga that it had hauled out of the water in order to be able to eat undisturbed. When one of our boats approached it, it immediately fled and finally, after a hot pursuit that lasted over half an hour, it escaped. As a substitute for the failure of their hunt, the hunters flensed the whale, which was about 18 feet long, then brought the blubber on board.

The farther south we came, the closer packed lay the ice. On the afternoon of the 19th we spoke *Victor*, and a little later we sighted *Herald*, a Norwegian, the only whaler in Davis Strait that did not sail under the British flag. Over the course of the evening we received the unwelcome news from *Tay*'s captain that it would probably be impossible to gain a passage to the open East Water in the south.

But neither this fact, nor the other unpleasantnesses with which we had to contend soon thereafter, was capable of banishing the captain's good mood. His holds were full; not only had he been more successful than the other captains, but his ship was carrying the largest cargo that had ever been brought home from any part of the Arctic seas. *Arctic* had killed no fewer than 28 whales, which had produced about 5300 centners of blubber and about 300 centners of whalebone, for a total value of about £19,000.

On 20 August we again met *Ravenscraig*, which so far was still totally clean. Captain Adams was kind enough to place the jolly-boat at our disposal and we went on board to satisfy a pleasant debt of gratitude. Four of our companions returned to *Arctic* with us. They were Budington, Morton, Odell and the carpenter. Bryan, Mauch and Booth had transferred to *Intrepid* on 17 July, and the latter ship appeared either not to notice our signals or not to understand them. Given the changeable ice conditions Captain Adams could not risk deviating from his course. Hence he had to abandon his intentions of bringing the entire *Polaris* crew to Britain.

The ice lay so extremely close-packed that all our attempts to force our way eastward were totally fruitless. On 24 August we were at the latitude of Cape Bisson, at 69°14'N; 65°39'W. From the masthead, as far as the eye could see there was not the smallest lead to be seen either to the south or east. Hence the captain decided to head north again. But since in the meantime several whales had appeared, he was in no particular hurry to get home.

Battling constantly against obstinate ice masses, on the 27th we again crossed the 70th parallel, which we had left astern on our passage south a week before. Every ship's length had to be strenuously fought for; in addition the fog now hampered us more than previously.

It was not until the 30th that it seemed advisable to set an eastward course. The open areas became more common; the floes rotten and friable. In the course of the afternoon a gentle swell rolled to meet us out of the east, making us suspect that the open water could not be far away. But only too soon we were to realize that this surmise was incorrect, since for several hours we had to bore through enormous masses of ice and escaped the threat of being beset only with great difficulty.

An exciting hunt provided us with a welcome change. No fewer than five bears appeared in rapid succession; we pursued them stubbornly but not once did we get within range. By contrast, before midnight our persistence was rewarded when we got into the open water to the east. But next day, the last day of August, again brought thick fog and we were again surrounded by ice, but without being subjected to the noisy ice pressures that we had suffered earlier. We used this involuntary leisure to take several tonnes of glacier ice on board to produce drinking water.[2] At noon we finally got free; thereby the last barrier between us and the civilized world had fallen. We could still see one solitary iceberg, i.e., shortly before midnight near 70.5°N; 61.3°W.

During the night of 2–3 September we crossed the Arctic Circle and on the 9th we rounded Cape Farewell. A northerly wind blew several small land birds on board: a linnet,[3] a Lapland bunting[4] and a white wagtail;[5] they were all totally exhausted and all died shortly afterward.

The ship's appearance was gradually improving. The men stowed the whalebone; they scrubbed the oil-soaked decks, polished the cannon, and gave the woodwork and the funnel a new coat of paint.

After a stormy voyage, at 3.00 p.m. on the 17th the small islands of Barra[6] and Rona came into sight, at first as cloud-like silhouettes, then as colour-drenched rock masses with rocky, cliffed coasts. At nightfall we spotted the lighthouse on Cape Wrath; and by 1.00 a.m. on the 18th we were at the entrance to the Pentland Firth. There was a strong west wind blowing and a high sea running; but the wind was fair and *Arctic* was running at 10–12 knots. The long-missed sight of the lighthouses was so alluring and the night air so mild that we stayed on deck till sunrise. An hour before noon we dropped anchor in Peterhead roadstead.

It was a sunny day; the trees were displaying their magnificent fall colours; sheep and cattle were grazing in the green meadows, and blue clouds of smoke wafted over the little town, from whose church spires the clear sound of bells rang out.

Our first destination once we stepped ashore was the telegraph station. Then we hurried to a green wood to breathe the fresh scent of the woods and to escape from the importunate people who besieged us in the most inconsiderate fashion, trying to interrogate us. Our appearance was far from prepossessing; anybody who did not know where we had come from would probably have taken us for vagabonds, since even in the best case the state of our clothing was lamentable. Months before, Markham had given me a coat; the good captain and one of the boat-steerers had given me the rest of my outfit, and over the course of time it had not improved with constant use. Most of us owed everything we wore to the generosity of others.

After those of the seamen who lived in the Shetland Islands had been paid off, *Arctic* put to sea again, and on the morning of 18 September she dropped anchor in Dundee harbour.

News of our return had preceded us, and it was difficult to avoid the various demonstrations that, without exception, were well-intended but that, under the prevailing circumstances, were not pleasant. We urgently needed rest and isolation and tried to satisfy this need at any price.

On the same day that we reached Scotland, *Juniata*, which on 10 September had returned to the Newfoundland capital from Greenland, received orders by telegraph from the Navy Department to continue her search for us. But a few hours after she had left St. John's, news of our rescue arrived there and the American consul immediately chartered the steamer *Cabot* in order to inform *Juniata*'s commander of the news. At midnight on the 18th *Cabot* overtook *Juniata* 70 miles north of St. John's, and then they returned to Newfoundland together. Next day *Juniata* again set sail and on the 25th was back in New York.

We too wanted to sail for the United States without delay. The directors of the various British steamship companies, as well as the directors of Norddeutsch Lloyd, relayed to us via the American consulate a generous invitation to use any of their ships for the crossing. On the 23rd we put to sea from Liverpool on board *City of Antwerp*, a steamer of the Inman Line, commanded by Captain Laver, and reached Sandy Hook on 4 October. Here we were met by a small naval steam-tug which ferried us to the warship *Talapoosa*, whose commander was detailed to transport us to Washington.

The bad luck that had pursued us thus far still prevailed even now. During a dark night we ran down a schooner in Chesapeake Bay and *Talapoosa* reached Washington on 7 October with two shipwrecked crews on board; there we were summoned before the same commission as the ice-floe drifters previously.

Our three comrades who were still on board *Intrepid* when *Arctic* started for home transferred to *Erik* on 13 September. The latter ship, commanded by Captain Walker, was delayed so long by foul winds in Davis Strait that it was not until 12 October that she managed to round Cape Farewell. Ten days later *Erik* reached Dundee. Two men were given passage on board *Georgia*, a steamer of the State Line that left Glasgow on 24 October and reached New York on 7 November. By contrast, Bryan had requested and been granted a short leave by telegram and did not return home until the 13th.

Tigress, which had put to sea again from Ivigtut on 4 October, had continued her search for a short time longer. But the harbingers of winter urgently warned her to turn back. On the 8th the ship turned south again and sighted Bonavista lighthouse early on the 16th.

When one of the Newfoundland pilots came aboard during the afternoon and informed Commander Greer of our rescue, he could consider his task fulfilled. Having replenished its supplies of coal at St. John's, *Tigress* too returned to New York. With this the expedition was over.

Epilogue: Motive for Murder

While working on his excellent biography of Charles Francis Hall, *Weird and Tragic Shores*,[1] Dr. Chauncey Loomis became intrigued by the mysterious circumstances of Hall's death and especially by the suspicion that he might have been poisoned. On the basis of the documentary evidence he concluded "that murder was at least possible and plausible."[2] His curiosity was sufficiently aroused that he applied to the Danish government's Ministry for Greenland for a permit to visit Thank God Harbour, to disinter Hall's remains (in the hope that they had been relatively well preserved in the permafrost) and to conduct an autopsy. His application was referred to the archeologist Count Eigil Knuth, who acted in an advisory capacity to the ministry. Count Knuth's initial reaction was quite negative, in that he felt that the idea of disturbing the grave was repugnant. Loomis visited the Count in Copenhagen and, on Loomis's assuring him that he would leave the grave exactly as he found it, the Count gave his approval and official permission was granted.

Loomis then assembled his team: pathologist Dr. Franklin Paddock, outdoorsman William Barrett and ex-Marine Tom Gignoux. In August 1968 they flew north by scheduled airline to Resolute Bay and from there the renowned bush pilot Weldy Phipps, owner of Atlas Aviation, flew them in a de Havilland single-Otter to Thank God Harbour. They easily located the grave from the commemorative plaque erected to Hall's memory by members of the Nares expedition, and having found Hubbard Chester's headboard lying face-down on the ground, they began examining the remains of Bessels's observatory. Next day the task of disinterring Hall's remains began. On opening the coffin they found the body wrapped in an American flag. On removing it they found Hall's face only partly preserved: there was still some flesh and most of the hair and beard, but the eye-sockets were empty and the nose was almost gone. The skin was tanned and stained by the dyes from the flag.

From the waist down the body was encased in ice, although Hall's stockinged feet stuck out rather incongruously at the end of the coffin. The upper part of the torso was clear of ice, and hence Paddock was able to start the autopsy, although this involved him straddling the coffin in an awkward position. Unfortunately the internal organs had almost totally disappeared. The best samples he was able to remove were samples of hair and fingernails and a triangular section of skull. After Paddock's three hours of painstaking work, the corpse was reclosed, the coffin lid replaced, the earth shovelled back and the rocks replaced.

On the team's return to the United States, for a preliminary investigation the skull sample was submitted for analysis to the Massachusetts Department of Public Safety Laboratory.[3] Analysis revealed an unusually high level of arsenic in the bone.

Next the samples of a fingernail and hair were submitted to the Centre of Forensic Sciences in Toronto, along with two chips of bone and two samples of soil from around the grave. The overall conclusion from the neutron-activation tests to which the samples were submitted was that they indicated "an intake of considerable amounts of arsenic by C.F. Hall in the last two weeks of his life."[4]

The best evidence had come from the fingernail sample. Dr. A.K. Perkons sliced the fingernail into small segments, each of which was submitted separately to the neutron-activation test. The results revealed an increase in the concentration of arsenic from tip to base, namely from 24.6 parts per million at the tip to 76.7 ppm at the base. Given the normal growth rate of fingernails this would indicate a large intake of arsenic in the last two weeks of the individual's life. The soil samples from around the grave yielded quite a high level of arsenic (22.0 ppm), and while some arsenic might have migrated from the soil to the body this would not explain the increase in arsenic concentration from tip to base of the fingernail.

Many of the symptoms which Hall exhibited—the initial gastro-intestinal pains and vomiting, difficulty in swallowing, dehydration, stupor, delirium and mania and, shortly before his death, skin eruptions on his face—are consistent with the symptoms of acute arsenic poisoning.[5] But this raises the questions of how the arsenic was introduced into Hall's system, and who was responsible.

There is the possibility that Hall may have been unwittingly responsible (at least in part) for his own demise. Arsenic was commonly used as a medication, in the form of arsenious acid, in the nineteenth century. In a popular remedy, "Fowler's Solution," it would have been present in any comprehensive medical kit, and such a kit would undoubtedly have been on board *Polaris*. It is conceivable that during the period when Hall was refusing Bessels's ministrations, he might have been taking such a medication, and thereby, if it were in large doses, accidentally poisoning himself. But this does not explain the initial symptoms of which he complained prior to that point.

Two individuals stand out as possible candidates for having tried to poison him. Budington had made it no secret that he disliked Hall intensely and was determined to ensure that *Polaris* did not go farther north. He had tried to persuade Hall to winter much farther south, at Port Foulke. But there is no evidence that he was even near Hall for any length of time after the latter first fell ill. Moreover, while he might have somehow obtained arsenic from Bessels's medical supplies, it seems unlikely that he would have had the knowledge or the skill to administer it in appropriate doses over such a lengthy period as to simulate the effects of "apoplexy," i.e., a stroke.

Bessels is a more obvious candidate, in terms of opportunity, medical knowledge and skill. Significantly, during the period when Hall refused to let Bessels treat him, Hall's condition improved noticeably. Also, at the start of Hall's illness, when others had suggested administering an emetic, Bessels had refused. In this context, while an emetic would have been dangerous if Hall had suffered a stroke, an emetic would have purged the system of any arsenic, if it had been administered. When Budington offered to take the medicine which Bessels was prescribing, in Hall's presence, to demonstrate that it was not poisonous, Bessels refused to allow him to do so; if it had contained arsenic, Budington would have been poisoned too. And while Bessels claimed that he was injecting quinine, it might equally well have been arsenic.

The main drawback to the argument that Bessels might have poisoned Hall is the lack of an obvious motive. While he may have harboured a degree of contempt for Hall as being uneducated and unrefined, unlike Budington he was keen to continue to push north and, indeed, made attempts to do so, even after *Polaris* was aground and effectively abandoned.

Loomis's considered and cautious appraisal of Hall's death is as follows:

> Perhaps Bessels murdered Hall. Perhaps. The only certain truth that can be found in this case is a knowledge of the inevitable and final elusiveness of the past. What happened aboard the USS *Polaris* between October 24 and November 8, 1871, can never be entirely known. What went on in the minds of Hall, Bessels, and the others aboard that ship, and what they did furtively, on their own, is done, gone, past. The questions that the Board of Inquiry did not ask can be asked today, but many of them cannot be answered.[6]

Elsewhere Loomis wrote:

> Bessels had the opportunity, the skill, and probably the material [to murder Hall], but why would he do it? He had no apparent rational motive; he would gain nothing concrete by Hall's death.[7]

But now, some 45 years later, a potential and very credible motive has surfaced. At an online auction, arctic historian Russell Potter spotted an envelope that was for sale. It had been sent from *Polaris* at Upernavik and bore Hall's name, and was addressed to Miss Vinnie Ream, 726 Broadway, New York.[8]

Vinnie Ream, aged 22 or 23, was a young sculptor/singer/musician, who is probably best known for her statue of Abraham Lincoln which stands in the Rotunda of the Capitol building in Washington. She had a reputation for cultivating influential older men (usually 20 years or more her senior) to her own advantage.[9] A measure of her success in this is that she is probably the only artist to be provided with studio space in the Capitol, rent-free. She met Hall in Washington while *Polaris* was being fitted out, and gave him a photo of her statue of Lincoln, which had only recently been unveiled.

While *Polaris* lay at the Brooklyn Navy Yard, more than once Hall had dinner with Vinnie, who was organizing a studio in New York. On several occasions Bessels accompanied Hall. While Hall probably was simply enjoying the company of an attractive young woman, Bessels was infatuated with her. On 28 June, on the eve of their sailing from New York, he wrote to her:

> While thinking of you all the time and anticipating the pleasure of seeing you tomorrow we received very unexpectedly an order requiring us possibly to leave early tomorrow before starting our perilous and uncertain voyage. Send by the reply vessel, which leaves shortly, a few words to one who will cherish your memory, dear Vinnie, and who must now, however unwillingly, bid you a long farewell.[10]

We do not know what Vinnie's feelings for Bessels were, but Hall had evidently made quite an impression on her, and in addition to a photo of her statue of Lincoln, after *Polaris* had sailed she also sent him a bust of Lincoln and other items via the steamer *Congress*, which caught up with *Polaris* at Upernavik. On 21 August, at Upernavik, Hall wrote to her:

> Your notes, flags and other valuables all quickly and safely received by the US steamer *Congress*. You should see my sweet little cabin. As you enter it our great, noble-hearted statue of Lincoln strikes the eye while beneath it hangs the photograph you gave me of the statue of Lincoln. Today I resume my voyage—the Smith Sound remarkably open—never known to be more so. You may expect that when you again hear from me and my company, that the North Pole has been discovered. How true is your faith that we are going to conquer.[11]

It is not inconceivable that Bessels, pathologically jealous of Hall as competition for Vinnie Ream's affections, grasped the opportunity to eliminate him. Men have been murdered for much weaker motives. It would be fascinating to know whether Bessels tried to renew his relationship with Vinnie on his return to the United States. But if, as seems likely, he made such an attempt but simply received the brush-off, neither is likely to have retained any relevant correspondence.

— William Barr

Appendix 1

Scientific Appendix (outline)

Bessels's scientific appendix, dealing with the marine and atmospheric environments, covers 113 pages. In that all the data presented here are also available in the Scientific results which were published in English (US Navy Department 1876), only the main headings will be listed here, to give some idea of the scientific scope of the expedition's work.

I Hydrographie (Hydrography)

1. Ebbe- und Flutbeobachtungen (Tidal observations) (pp. 530–48)
2. Aräometer-Beobachtungen (Observations of specific gravity of sea water) (pp. 548–51)
3. Meeres-Strömungen (Sea currents) (pp. 552–60)
4. Bemerkungen über die Eisverhältnisse (Sea ice observations) (pp. 561–65)

II Erdmagnetismus und Nordlichter
(Terrestrial magnetism and aurora borealis)

1. Erdmagnetismus (Terrestrial magnetism) (pp. 566–70)
2. Nordlichter (Aurora borealis) (pp. 570–71)

III Meteorologie (Meteorology)

(The meteorological data are for both Thank God Harbor and for Polaris House)

1. Die Temperatur der Luft (Air temperature) (pp. 573–86)
2. Die Winde (Winds) (pp. 586–601)
3. Der Luftdruck (Air pressure) (pp. 602–13)
4. Hygrometrische Beobachtungen (Hygrometric observations) (pp. 613–29)
5. Die atmosphärischen Niederschläge (Precipitation) (pp. 629–32)
6. Die Bewölkung (Cloud cover) (pp. 632–36)
7. Die Wärmestrahlung der Sonne (Solar radiation) (pp. 637–41)
8. Der Ozon-Gehalt der Luft (Ozone content of the air) (641–43)

Appendix 2

Hall's Instructions[1]

Navy Department, June 9, 1871

Sir: Having been appointed, by the President of the United States, commander of the expedition toward the North Pole, and the steamer Polaris having been fitted, equipped, provisioned, and assigned for the purpose, you are placed in command of the said vessel, her officers and crew, for the purposes of the said expedition. Having taken command, you will proceed in the vessel, at the earliest possible date, from the navy yard in this city to New York. From New York you will proceed to the first favorable port you are able to make on the west coast of Greenland, stopping, if you deem it desirable, at St. John's, Newfoundland. From the first port made by you, on the west coast of Greenland, if farther south than Holsteinberg [sic], you will proceed to that port, and thence to Godhaven, (or Lively), in the island of Disco. At some one of the ports above referred to you will probably meet a transport, sent by the Department, with additional coal and stores, from which you will supply yourself to the fullest carrying capacity of the Polaris. Should you fall in with the transport before making either of the ports aforesaid, or should you obtain information of her being at, or having landed her stores at any point south of the island of Disco, you will at once proceed to put yourself in communication with the commander of the transport, and supply yourself with the additional supplies and coal, taking such measures as may be most expedient and convenient for that purpose. Should you not hear of the transport before reaching Holsteinberg you will remain at that port, waiting for her and your supplies, as long as the object of your expedition will permit you to delay for that purpose. After waiting as long as is safe, under all the circumstances as they may present themselves, you will, if you do not hear of the transport, proceed to Disco, as above provided. At Disco, if you hear nothing of the transport, you will, after waiting as long as you deem it safe, supply yourself as far as you may be able, with such supplies and articles as you may need, and proceed on your expedition without further delay. From Disco you will proceed to Upernavik. At these two last-named places you will procure dogs and other Arctic outfits. If you think it of advantage for the purpose of obtaining dogs, &c., to stop at Tossak, you will do so. From Upernavik, or Tossak, as the case may be, you will proceed across Melville Bay to Cape Dudley Digges, and thence you will make all possible progress, with vessels, boats, and sledges, toward the North Pole, using your own judgment as to the route or routes to be pursued and the locality for each winter's quarters. Having been provisioned and equipped for two and a half years, you will pursue your explorations for that period; but, if the object of the exploration require it, you will continue your explorations for such a further length of time as your supplies may be safely extended. Should, however, the main object of the expedition, viz., obtaining the position of the North Pole, be accomplished at an earlier period, you will return to the United States with all convenient dispatch.

There being attached to the expedition a scientific department, its operations are prescribed in accordance with the advice of the National Academy of Sciences as required by the law. Agreeably to this advice, the charge and direction of the scientific operations will be intrusted, under your command, to Doctor Emil Bessels; and you with render Dr. Bessels and his assistants all such facilities and aids as may be in your power to carry into effect the said further advice, as given in the instructions herewith furnished in a communication from the president of the National Academy of Sciences. It is, however, important that objects of natural history, ethnology, &c., &c., which may be collected by any person attached to the expedition, shall be delivered to the chief of the scientific department, to be cared for, under your direction, and considered the property of the Government; and every person be strictly prohibited from keeping any such object. You will direct every qualified person in the expedition to keep a private journal of the progress of the expedition and enter on it events, observations, and remarks, of any nature whatsoever. These journals shall be considered confidential and read by no person other than the writer. Of these journals no copy shall be made. Upon the return of the expedition you will demand of each of the writers his journal, which it is hereby ordered he shall deliver to you. Each writer is to be assured that when the records of the expedition are published he shall receive a copy; the private journals to be returned to the writer, or not, at the option of the Government; but each writer, in the published records, shall receive credit for such part or parts of his journal as may be used in such records. You will use every opportunity to determine the position of all capes, headlands, islands, &c., the lines of coasts, take soundings, observe tides and currents, and make all such surveys as may advance our knowledge of the geography of the Arctic regions.

You will give special written directions to the sailing and ice master of the expedition, Mr. S.O. Buddington, and to the chief of the scientific department, Dr. E. Bessels, that in case of your death or disability—a contingency we sincerely trust may not arise—they shall consult as to the propriety and manner of carrying into further effect the foregoing instructions, which I here urge must, if possible, be done. The results of their consultations, and the reasons therefore, must be put in writing, and kept as part of the records of the expedition. In any event, however, Mr. Buddington shall, in case of your death or disability, continue as the sailing and ice master, and control and direct the movements of the vessel; and Doctor Bessels, in such case, continue as chief of the scientific department, directing all sledge journeys and scientific operations. In the possible contingency of their non-agreement as to the course to be pursued, then Mr. Buddington shall assume sole charge and command, and return with the expedition to the United States will all possible dispatch.

You will transmit to this Department, as often as opportunity offers, reports of your progress and results of your search, detailing the route of your proposed advance. At the most prominent points of your progress you will erect conspicuous skeleton stone monuments, depositing near each, in accordance with confidential marks agreed upon, a condensed record of your progress, with a description of the route upon which you propose to advance, making caches of provisions, &c., if you deem fit.

In the event of the necessity for finally abandoning your vessel, you will at once endeavor to reach localities frequented by whaling or other ships, making every exertion to send to the United States information of your position and situation, and as soon as possible to return with your party, preserving, as far as may be, the records of, and all possible objects and specimens collected in the expedition.

All persons attached to the expedition are under your command, and shall, under every circumstance and condition, be subject to the rules, regulations, and laws governing the discipline of the Navy, to be modified, but not increased, by you as the circumstances may in your judgment require.

To keep the Government as well informed as possible of your progress, you will, after passing Cape Dudley Digges, throw overboard daily, as open water or drifting ice may permit, a bottle or small copper cylinder, closely sealed, containing a paper, stating date, position, and such other facts as you may deem interesting. For this purpose, you will have prepared papers containing a request, printed in several languages, that the finder transmit it by the most direct route to the Secretary of the Navy, Washington, United States of America.

Upon the return of the expedition to the United States, you will transmit your own and all other records to the Department. You will direct Dr. Bessels to transmit all the scientific records and collections to the Smithsonian Institution, Washington.

The history of the expedition will be prepared by yourself, from all the journals and records of the expedition, under the supervision of the Department. All the records of the scientific results of the expedition will be prepared, supervised, and edited by Dr. Bessels, under the direction and authority of the president of the National Academy of Sciences.

Wishing for you and your brave comrades health, happiness, and success in our daring enterprise, and commending you and them to the protecting care of the God who rules the universe,

I am, very respectfully, yours,

GEO. M. ROBESON
Secretary of the Navy.

CHAS. F. HALL.
Commanding Expedition toward the North Pole.

Appendix 3

The Board of Inquiry

On the same day that *Frolic* reached Washington (5 June 1873) with Tyson and the other ice-floe survivors on board, an official Board of Inquiry was hurriedly convened on board *Talapoosa* at the Washington Navy Yard. In the chair was Navy Secretary George Robeson, and the other members of the Board were Commodore William Reynolds, Professor Spencer F. Baird of the Smithsonian Institution, and Captain H.W. Howgate of the Signal Service Corps.[2] The remainder of *Polaris*'s complement, including Bessels, reached Washington from New York on board *Tallapoosa* on 7 October. The Board of Inquiry, still with the same composition, reconvened, again on board *Tallapoosa*, and resumed its questioning on the morning of 11 October. On 16 October, by special invitation from Robeson, Surgeon-General W.K. Barnes of the United States Army and Surgeon-General Joseph Beale of the United States Navy were also present for Bessels's testimony.[3]

Even before the Board met for its first session to question Tyson and the other survivors on 5 June, the newspaper accounts, and simply the fact that the expedition had split into two groups, one of which had barely survived, and the fate of the other of which was still unknown, must have given George Robeson, as Secretary of the Navy, enormous cause for worry. That this expedition, outfitted by the US Government at such great expense and dispatched with such great fanfare, had clearly disintegrated without even starting to achieve its objective was a cause for acute embarrassment.

And once the survivors started to give their testimony, Robeson's level of worry and embarrassment must have risen exponentially. First of all there was the disturbing revelation that Budington (sailing master, and, after Hall's death, expedition leader), on the way north had openly expressed his preference that they should winter at Port Foulke (some 500 km south of the latitude which *Polaris* ultimately reached). This, of course would have been impossibly far south to be the starting point at any attempt at reaching the North Pole. When questioned on the subject Budington insisted, "I did my best to get the ship north. I never said anything about never going any further north."[4] Various members of the expedition testified that Budington clearly had no interest in the expedition's primary objective, namely trying to reach the Pole. For whatever reason Tyson opted not to reveal the plan which Budington had disclosed to him in January or February 1872, namely that after the ice breakup he would take the ship south to near Upernavik, deliberately run it aground and then take to the boats as far as Disko (where a substantial depot of provisions and fuel had been left). From there he proposed travelling by whaler to Europe, then home by steamer at government expense. He anticipated that his (and the crew's) pay would continue as if still actively engaged on the expedition.[5] One can only guess as to why Tyson decided not to reveal this astonishing plan to the Board of Inquiry; Budington undoubtedly would have denied it.

Another accusation levelled against Budington by both officers and crew members was that he was frequently drunk, having helped himself to Bessels's supply of alcohol for preserving specimens or, after Hall's death and after he (Budington) had inherited Hall's keys, to the limited supply of alcohol on board, intended for celebrations. Probably the worst of his bouts of drunkenness (in terms of its ultimate results) occurred during the night of 14–15 August, as *Polaris* was steaming south in open water in Kennedy Channel. Budington, who had the helm, was drunk, and in this condition allowed the ship to stray from the open channel until she was solidly beset.[6] This led, subsequently, to the disastrous night when half the ship's complement was left on the ice, which led in turn to their remarkable ice-drift for the full length of Baffin Bay, Davis Strait and the Labrador Sea. When confronted by the accusation of drunkenness by Robeson, who asked, "Were you in the habit of drinking alcohol?," Budington replied, "I make it a practice to drink very little. I did take too much twice during this voyage, that I recall."[7] With respect to one of these occasions (when Bessels had caught him stealing alcohol), Budington told the Board of Inquiry, "I did not consider, however, that I was not in a condition to do my duty. I merely felt the liquor. I do not think a stranger would have seen it on me at all. I had drank occasionally before but not to any excess."[8]

Possibly even more damning was Tyson's accusation that Budington had been a "disorganizer." When asked for clarification Tyson replied that "he [Budington] associated himself with the crew very much, cursing his commander, and blaming him, and speaking slightingly of him.... His ground of complaint was that the captain was not a seaman. On the most frivolous things he would be among the crew and complaining of Captain Hall."[9]

Any one of these three deficiencies—lack of enthusiasm for the main objective of the expedition, repeated drunkenness, or belittling his superior officer to the crew—would normally in the United States Navy have been grounds for a court-martial, and probably dismissal. But Budington was a civilian. Partly because of this, and partly to avoid the scandal of further "washing of dirty laundry" in public, the Board of Inquiry made no recommendation to punish Budington.

Nonetheless Robeson's summation as to Budington's character and capabilities was more than somewhat damning:

> The facts show that though he was perhaps wanting in enthusiasm for the grand objects of the expedition, and at times grossly lax in discipline, and though he differed in judgment from others as to the possibility, safety, and propriety of taking the ship further north, yet he is an experienced and careful navigator, and when not affected by liquor, of which there remained none on board at the time of the separation, a competent and safe commander.[10]

Potentially an even more scandalous topic which emerged when the Board started to probe the details of Hall's death was the fact, revealed by various witnesses, that Hall believed that he was being poisoned.

Apart from his having the means and the opportunity, if Hall was indeed poisoned, various aspects pointed to Bessels as being the culprit: for example, his refusal to administer an emetic—which would have cleared his system of any poison—or the fact that Hall experienced a noticeable recovery during the several days when he refused to be treated by Bessels, but then suffered a serious and fatal relapse when Bessels started treating him again.

If Surgeon-General Barnes and Surgeon-General Beale had any suspicions, however, they clearly decided that it were best for the Navy's reputation that any such suspicions not be publicly aired. After listening to Bessels's testimony (which differed only minimally from what he would later state in his book[11]), they submitted their own, separate assessment of the circumstances of Hall's death:

> Washington, D.C., December 26, 1873
>
> Sir: We, the undersigned were present by request of the honorable Secretary of the Navy, at the examination of Dr. Emil Bessels, in regard to the cruise of the *Polaris* and the circumstances connected with the illness and death of Captain Hall. We listened to his testimony with great care and put to him such questions as we deemed necessary.
>
> From the circumstances and symptoms detailed by him, and comparing them with the medical testimony of all the witnesses, we are conclusively of the opinion that Captain Hall died from natural causes, viz. apoplexy, and that the treatment of the case by Dr. Bessels was the best practicable under the circumstances.
>
> Respectfully, your obedient servants
>
> W.K. Barnes
> Surgeon-General of the United States Army
>
> J. Beale
> Surgeon-General of the United States Navy[12]

The Board, as a whole, recommended that no action be taken against anyone among the officers and crew of *Polaris* and that no further investigation be undertaken. Undoubtedly embarrassed by the disastrous outcome of its expensively outfitted and equipped expedition, the United States Navy was clearly keen that no further scandalous revelations should emerge.

Appendix 4

Biographical sketches

EMIL BESSELS was born to Jewish parents in Heidelberg on 2 June 1847. His father ran a boys' boarding school and his mother was the principal of a girls' boarding school.[13] French and English were used almost as much as German on a daily basis at home. His first choice was to pursue a scientific career, but since she had three young children to consider, his mother insisted that he leave high school at the age of 15. He was then apprenticed to a banker. But while pursuing a banking career he devoted his evenings and weekends to studying, improving his artistic skills, and expanding his knowledge of the sciences, especially zoology.

Fortunately for him, after two years his family recognized that he was not suited for the banking profession, and, with his boss's approval, he left his job and devoted himself full-time to his scientific studies. He entered the University of Heidelberg, but since he had not graduated from high school, he had no prospects of being accepted to a medical programme. His solution was to enter a prize competition in which he won first prize. He not only was allowed to enter the programme but submitted his prize-winning essay as his doctoral dissertation. And at the age of 18, in 1865, he became the youngest doctor that the Ruprecht-Karls Universität Heidelberg had produced until then. He then published his dissertation, titled *Studien* über *die Entwicklung der Sexualdrüsen bei den Lepidopteren* (Studies on the development of the sexual glands in lepidoptera).[14]

Thereafter, having developed an interest in Africa, Bessels started to learn Arabic, as well as pursuing medical and natural history studies at Jena and Stuttgart. At the age of 20 he became curator of the Natural Sciences Museum in Stuttgart. But then, some 18 months later, he got in contact with August Petermann, well-known geographer and promoter of geographical exploration. The latter persuaded him to change his geographical focus, and in 1869 at Petermann's recommendation he took part in the combined sealing and exploring expedition mounted by ship owner Albert Rosenthal on board *Albert* (Captain Hashagen).[15] *Albert* put to sea from Bremerhaven on 23 May. The aim was to round Spitsbergen on the north, but the ship reached her highest latitude at 80°14'N; 9°52'E, where she was blocked by close, heavy ice. Two attempts at reaching Hinlopenstretet, from where a search for Gillis Land was contemplated, were foiled by heavy ice. An attempt to reach Gillis Land by running south around Spitsbergen was no more successful, reaching only Tusenøyane. Swinging south, Bessels was able to determine the position of Hopen more accurately than previously, fixing its southern tip at 76°35'N; 25°47'E. From there *Albert* ran east until Mys Nassau at the northern tip of Novaya Zemlya loomed through the fog. From there the ship started south, reaching Bremerhaven on 22 September. Bessels carried out meteorological observations and soundings throughout. One of his more important achievements on this voyage was to confirm Petermann's hypothesis that the warm waters of the North Atlantic Drift (the continuation of the Gulf Stream) penetrated north to between Svalbard and Novaya Zemlya.

In the following year, once again at Petermann's initiative, Bessels began preparations for a further arctic expedition, on this occasion aiming for the area northeast of Svalbard. But when a possible financial contributor withdrew his promised support, and when the Bremen Committee, which had organized the First German North Pole Expedition, led by Karl Koldewey, refused Petermann's request to use that expedition's ship *Grönland*, the plans for the expedition collapsed

It was partly on the basis of Bessels's arctic experience that Petermann was able to convince the American authorities that he was the ideal candidate for the position of Chief Scientist on the *Polaris* expedition.[16] At the time Bessels was fulfilling his military service during the Franco-Prussian War, but Petermann was able to obtain his release.

On his return from the expedition Bessels settled in Washington and, from an office at the Smithsonian Institution, worked on the first volume of the scientific results, namely "Physical Observations."[17] Thereafter he continued to work intermittently on further scientific results of the expedition. But by 1883, with no sign of further volumes appearing, Spencer Baird's patience was exhausted. Bessels's salary was cut off and he received a blunt note from Baird's secretary that he must vacate his office since the space was required for a visitors' toilet.[18]

Bessels's delay in publishing further expedition results was undoubtedly due in part to the fact that he was involved in at least one further expedition. In 1875 he was dispatched north by the US government, this time to the Chukchi Sea, with instructions to collect ethnographical material for the Centennial Exhibition in Philadelphia in 1876.[19] Bessels sailed on board USS *Saranac* (Lieutenant Commander Sanders), a side-paddle steamer of 2100 tons. Heading north, Sanders chose the Inside Passage between Vancouver Island and the mainland but had the misfortune to hit notorious Ripple Rock in Seymour Narrows, while steaming at 14 knots with a 7-knot current, on 18 June 1875. Sanders managed to beach his ship on the Vancouver Island shore, but she later sank completely. All on board got ashore safely and set up a camp. Sanders and a party of men made their way overland to Victoria.[20]

Returning to Washington and to his office at the Smithsonian Institution, in 1881 Bessels started planning for a further arctic expedition, to take place in 1882 and funded by private contributions, but the plan fell through. However, in 1881 Bessels was voted $10,000 by the 46th United States Congress for his contribution to Arctic science.[21] In the early morning of 25 December 1885 he suffered the serious misfortune that his house near Washington burned down and he lost all his books, manuscripts, sketches and collections.[22] He himself escaped only by jumping from the third floor. Thereafter he suffered from insomnia and convulsions. Early in 1888 he returned to Germany to visit his aged mother, and for some rest and recuperation. After an evening among friends, he died of a heart attack at his home in Stuttgart on 30 March 1888.

SIDNEY O. BUDINGTON (1823–1888) was a native of Groton, Connecticut. Like so many of his relatives he went to sea at an early age on board whaling vessels sailing out of New London. By 1860, when Charles Francis Hall came to New London in search of a ship which could take him to the Arctic, Budington offered to take him on board his ship; by then he was captain of *George Henry* owned by Messrs. Williams and Haven of New London.[23] This offer appealed especially to Hall in that Budington had brought an Inuk, Kallarjuk, south from Baffin Island the previous year and would be taking him back north in 1860. Hall saw this as an opportunity to learn Inuktitut. Unfortunately Kullarjuk died off the Greenland coast on 1 July.[24] *George Henry* wintered in Cyrus Field Bay, and with Hall on board, returned to New London on 7 September 1862.

In July 1863 Budington headed north again, again in command of *George Henry*, but this time bound for Hudson Bay, where the ship ran aground and sank.[25] In the meantime Hall had had a serious disagreement with Budington. Nevertheless, when the former returned from his second expedition (to northwestern Hudson Bay and King William Island) in December 1869, accompanied by Ebierbing and Tookoolito, who were to stay with the Budingtons, Hall visited them there, evidently with a view to also patching up his friendship with Budington. In this he was successful, and Budington was Hall's first choice to command *Polaris* in 1871.

After the expedition, and after the revelations as to his conduct which emerged at the Board of Inquiry, Budington never went to sea again. He is buried in the Starr Burying Ground in Groton, Connecticut.[26]

EBIERBING (more correctly IPIIRVIK) and TOOKOOLITO (TAQULLITUQ). Ebierbing, known to the whalers and the members of the *Polaris* expedition as Joe or Joseph, was born at Qimmigsut, off the south shore of Cumberland Sound, probably in 1836. At some time prior to 1853 he married Tookoolito according to Inuit custom.[27] She (otherwise known as Hannah) was born at Cape Searle on the east coast of Baffin Island in 1838. In 1853 they were taken to England by John Bowlby, who was in Baffin Island hoping to develop a cod fishery.[28] There they spent two years, during which they converted to Christianity, acquired a command of English (Tookoolito more so than Ebierbing), and on one occasion were presented to Queen Victoria and Prince Albert. They were also "exhibited" on numerous occasions in Hull and London.

In the fall of 1860 Tookoolito met Hall on board *George Henry* at the mouth of Frobisher Bay, and she and Ebierbing accompanied him as interpreters and, in the latter's case, as hunter and dog driver for the remainder of his travels around southern Baffin Island. They and their infant son travelled south with him on board *George Henry* in the fall of 1862. Once again they were exhibited in public, for example at Barnum's Museum in New York,[29] and appeared at Hall's numerous lectures, aimed at raising funds for his next expedition. Stressed by the rigorous schedule and by the relatively hot climate, Tookoolito was frequently ill, and their young son died in the spring of 1863. When not travelling with Hall they stayed with Captain Sidney Budington and his wife in Groton, Connecticut.

They once again accompanied Hall on his second arctic expedition (1864–69), aimed at searching for possible records left by the Franklin expedition, and during which they roamed from Depot Island to Repulse Bay, Melville Peninsula and, briefly, southern King William Island. During this expedition Tookoolito gave birth to, and lost, a second baby. She then adopted a daughter, Isigaittuq, in Igloolik. In his writings Hall refers to her as Punna, his rendering of Panik, the Inuktitut word for "daughter."[30]

After returning to Groton in 1869, Ebierbing bought a house on Pleasant Valley Road. He worked as a carpenter and Tookoolito as a seamstress, making fur clothing. Their daughter, known as Sylvia Ebierbing, attended the local school.[31]

Following the *Polaris* expedition, the ice-floe drift—during which few of their companions, if any, would have survived without their skills, he as a hunter and she as a cook and seamstress[32]—and then the Board of Inquiry, the small family settled down again in Groton. But Ebierbing soon headed north again, this time as interpreter on board Sir Allen Young's *Pandora* in 1875. Young's aim was to try to relocate the North Magnetic Pole and, if possible, to continue west through the Northwest Passage. After running south through Peel Sound, *Pandora* was blocked by ice in Franklin Strait and was forced to turn back.[33]

Tookoolito died on 31 December 1876 and is buried in the Starr Burying Ground in Groton, her grave marked by a substantial headstone.[34] Also buried in this grave are Panik (Sylvia) and Tarrilikitak, the son who had died in 1863.

In 1878 Ebierbing headed north once again, this time on Frederick Schwatka's expedition, whose aim was to investigate reports that records from the Franklin expedition might have survived.[35] After landing from the whaler *Eothen* near Depot Island, the expedition made contact with the local Inuit and, travelling with some of them, headed north. Schwatka searched the south and west coasts of King William Island and discovered numerous skeletal remains and artefacts. When the expedition started back south from Depot Island on board the whaler *George and Mary* on 1 August 1878, Ebierbing elected to remain behind, on Marble Island. He died in the Arctic soon afterward, although his name appears on the family headstone in the Starr Burying Ground in Groton.[36]

CHARLES FRANCIS HALL (1821–1871) was born in Rochester, New Hampshire (although possibly in Vermont, moving to Rochester with his family at an early age).[37] After only a few years of schooling he was apprenticed to a blacksmith. A few years later he moved west and, possibly after a few stops along the way, and having married his wife Mary, had settled in Cincinnati, Ohio, by 1849. Initially employed in a seal-engraving business, after three years he struck out on his own as an engraver. But then in 1855 he started publishing a small, single-page news sheet, the *Cincinnati Occasional*, and in 1859 he graduated to publishing a daily newspaper, the *Daily Press*.

By this time Hall's interest in Arctic exploration had been kindled, possibly by his having witnessed the transfer of the body of Elisha Kent Kane from a riverboat to a train at Cincinnati, on its long journey from Havana to Philadelphia, on 7 March 1857. Thereafter Hall began reading intensely about Arctic exploration. His interest was probably further sparked by reading that Lady Franklin was about to dispatch Lieutenant Francis Leopold McClintock on board *Fox* to search for survivors or news of her husband's missing expedition.[38] As a result he decided to mount his own expedition to search for documents or relics from the expedition. Frustrated in his attempts to persuade Henry Grinnell to provide him with a ship of his own and to find a captain, in 1860 he set off north on board the whaling ship *George Henry* (Captain Sidney Budington), and taking his own small boat.[39] To his immense good fortune, off Frobisher Bay he encountered Tookoolito (Hannah) and her husband Ebierbing (Joe), who would act as his guides and interpreters on this and his subsequent expeditions. His plan was to head west to King William Island via Frobisher Bay (then still thought to be a strait). This plan was thwarted when his boat was wrecked and when he discovered that Frobisher Strait was a bay, not a strait. This discovery and the discovery, guided by local Inuit oral tradition, of the site of Martin Frobisher's mining activities on Kodlunarn Island in 1558, represented the most important results of Hall's expedition.

On his return south (along with Ebierbing and Tookoolito), Hall did not return to his own family in Cincinnati but lived either with Sidney Budington and his wife in Groton, Connecticut, or, after he had quarrelled bitterly with him, in New York. Apart from writing his account of his expedition and lecturing, over the next few years Hall was fully engaged in preparing for a further expedition, again aimed at solving the mystery of the fate of the Franklin expedition, but tackling the problem from the south, from Hudson Bay, rather than from the east. Again accompanied by Ebierbing and Tookoolito, in 1864 he shipped aboard the whaling ship *Monticello* (Captain Edward Chapel), bound for Roes Welcome Sound. The arrangement was that he would be landed at Wager Bay, with the aim of wintering at Repulse Bay, but by mistake he was landed some 60 km further south, near Depot Island. He wintered among local Inuit there, but this error may well have cost him a year. Over the next few years his plan to reach and search King William Island was frustrated by the reluctance of the Inuit to guide him there, although he did manage to push north to Igloolik. There were several American whalers wintering near Depot Island, and in the hopes that members of their crews might be more cooperative, Hall hired five of them to accompany him on his further searches. Hall had a disagreement with one of them, Patrick Coleman, and shot him.[40] On his return south he asked Henry Grinnell for advice on the matter, and the latter contacted the British ambassador in Washington. His reply was that since the incident occurred beyond the boundaries of Canada (which at the time extended barely beyond Lake Superior), Canada, and hence Britain, had no jurisdiction over the matter. In 1869 Hall finally reached the south coast of King William Island, but his Inuit companions refused to accompany him any farther; he found a few relics and skeletons from the Franklin expedition, and during his sojourn in the general area he recorded several oral accounts of the Inuit's interactions with the Franklin expedition members. On 13 August 1869 Hall, Ebierbing and Tookoolito were on board the whaling ship *Ansel Gibbs* when she sailed from Repulse Bay, southward bound for New Bedford.[41]

Hall was not finished with the Arctic, however. But now his attention was focused on trying to reach the North Pole. Remarkably, through his persistence, luck and his influential contacts, especially Henry Grinnell, his ambition resulted in a major expedition, sponsored and funded by the United States government. Unfortunately, as Bessels's account reveals, the expedition did not live up to expectations but ended in dissension, acrimony, disaster, and in Hall's death, and might well have resulted in the loss of life of most of its personnel.[42]

AUGUST HEINRICH PETERMANN (1822–1878) was born on 18 April 1822 in Bleicherode, Thuringia, the son of August Rudolf Petermann, the local registrar. From an early age August showed a keen interest in maps and a remarkable talent in drafting maps. After he attended the high school in nearby Nordhausen, having recognized his talent his father enrolled him in Heinrich Berghaus's "Geographische Kunstschule" (Geographical Art School) in Potsdam. Berghaus also spotted that he had exceptional talent as a cartographer and "adopted" him as a sort of a foster son. Having mastered a wide range of cartographic techniques, on graduating from Berghaus's establishment in 1845 Petermann moved to Edinburgh, where he worked for cartographer Alexander Johnston. Then in 1847 Petermann moved south to London. Initially he worked as a reporter for the periodical *Athenaeum*, but then in 1854 he established his own cartographic business: "The Geographic Establishment: Engraving, Lithography and Printing Office." He published a wide range of maps and atlases, including maps for the Royal Geographical Society. He had become a member of the latter as soon as he moved to London, and in 1850 he became Under-Secretary of the Society. In London he got to know a wide range of scientists and explorers, and his later interest in polar exploration evolved from this, especially during the period of intense searches for the missing Franklin expedition in the early 1850s.

In 1854 Petermann moved back to Germany, where he joined Wilhelm and Bernhardt Perthes's publishing company in Gotha; he was also appointed professor at the University of Göttingen. In 1855 he published the first instalment of his *Mittheilungen aus Justus Perthes Geographischer Anstalt* über *wichtige neue Erforschungen auf dem Gesamtgebiet der Geographie von Dr. A. Petermann.* Under the much more convenient title of *Petermanns Geographische Mitteilungen,* this publication continues to the present.

Petermann was very active in promoting geographical exploration, especially polar expeditions, from the very first German polar expedition in 1865 onward. And it was his strong recommendation that resulted in Bessels being hired to participate in Hall's expedition.

Petermann retired from the Perthes's establishment in 1876, but was subject to manic-depressive problems and committed suicide on 25 September 1878.

GEORGE E. TYSON (1829–1906) was born in New Jersey, but at an early age moved with his parents to New York. On leaving school he worked in an iron foundry.[43] Determined to see the Arctic, in 1850 he shipped aboard the New London whaleship *McLellan* (Captain William Quayle), for a voyage to Davis Strait and Baffin Bay. At the close of the following whaling season, along with 11 others, led by first mate Sidney Budington, he volunteered to winter ashore in Cumberland Sound, in order to be able to start whaling early in the spring before any ships could reach that location. In 1855 Tyson shipped as boatsteerer aboard the bark *George Henry* (Captain James Budington). Late in that season Tyson was one of the party which went aboard the derelict HMS *Resolute*, abandoned by Captain Henry Kellett off Cape Cockburn, Bathurst Island, in May 1854).[44] Thereafter Budington put a crew aboard her, who took her to New London. She was purchased by the US government, refitted, and as a gesture of goodwill donated to Queen Victoria.[45]

In 1860 Tyson headed north as captain of *Georgiana*, his first command, and encountered Charles Francis Hall, on his first arctic expedition, on board *George Henry*, in Cyrus Field Bay, although he had met him earlier in New London. He met Hall again in the winter of 1865–66 in Hudson Bay, when Tyson was commanding the bark *Antelope* and Hall was on his second arctic expedition. In 1867–68 Tyson was back in Hudson Bay again, this time aboard the topsail schooner *Era* and again encountered Hall, who was still trying to reach King William Island. In 1869–70, again on board *Era*, Tyson wintered in Cumberland Sound. Soon after he returned home to New London in October 1870, Hall came to see him to invite him to come on his North Pole expedition on board *Polaris* as sailing master or ice pilot.[46]

Having survived the winter (1871–72) on board *Polaris* at Thank God Harbor, the harrowing experience of the ice-floe drift over the winter of 1872–73, and finally the pointed questioning of the Board of Inquiry, Tyson returned to his life as a whaler. But in 1877 he headed north on board the small schooner *Florence* on a special mission, known as the Howgate Preliminary Arctic Expedition. Captain Henry Howgate of the US Signal Service had proposed establishing a colony of some 50 men at Lady Franklin Bay on northern Ellesmere Island. As a support party he proposed including a number of Inuit families. Tyson's task was to spend a winter in Cumberland Sound, where he was to acquire fur clothing from the local Inuit, recruit a party of Inuit for the main expedition, and in the summer of 1878 take them across Davis Strait to Disko, to rendezvous with the main expedition ship, on its way north to Lady Franklin Bay. Along with two scientists, Tyson wintered on board *Florence* at Anarnitung in Cumberland Sound and managed to recruit four Inuit men, along with the wives of two of them and four of their children, and transported them across to Disko. But when the main expedition did not materialize since the plan was voted down by Congress, Tyson waited at Disko until 22 August, then returned the Inuit to Cumberland Sound, and then headed back south.[47] Tyson died in Washington, DC, on 18 October 1906.

Notes

Notes contributed by Bessels are indicated by E.B.

Foreword

1. Loomis 1971:263.
2. Anonymous 1873.
3. Blake 1874.
4. Davis 1876.
5. Blake 1874:110.
6. Ibid., 134.
7. Ibid., 142.
8. Loomis 1971:265.
9. Parry 2001:57–60.
10. Blake 1874:74.
11. US Navy Department 1876.
12. Loomis 1971.
13. See biographical sketch, p. 556.
14. Krause 1992:17–18; Murphy 2002: 21–22.
15. Koldewey 1871:4.
16. Freeden 1869.
17. Koldewey 1874.
18. Krause 1992; Hegemann 1993.
19. Smith 1830.
20. See biographical sketch, pp. 555–57.
21. *Petermanns Geographische Mittheilungen* 1869.

Dedication

1. This dedication is in English in the original.
2. In 1873 Captain Albert Markham had shipped aboard the whaling ship *Arctic* (Captain William Adams) on a cruise to Baffin Bay in order to gain experience for his later participation in George Strong Nares's British Arctic Expedition

(1875–76), and thus was on board *Arctic* when that vessel rescued Bessels and one party of the survivors from the *Polaris* expedition (see p. 495) (Markham 1874).

3   Markham was leader of a sledge party from HMS *Alert*, which had wintered near the site of the present station Alert on northern Ellesmere Island and which reached a record high latitude of 83° 20'26'N on 12 May 1876 before being forced to turn back due to an outbreak of scurvy (Markham 1878; Nares 1878).

PREFACE

1   In fact the natural history results were never published.
2   Bessels reached Dundee, Scotland, on board the whaling ship *Arctic* and then travelled by train to Liverpool to catch a passenger steamer to New York (see p. 495).
3   Also referred to as Joe or Ebierbing in contemporary accounts, or more correctly Ipiirvik. See biographical sketch, p. 558-60.
4   Davis 1876.
5   Ibid.
6   US Navy Department 1876.
7   By this term Nares was referring to the Lincoln Sea or the Arctic Ocean in general.
8   Captain James Cook, on board HMS *Resolution*, reached his highest southerly latitude of 71°10'S in the Southern Ocean, where he was stopped by ice on 30 January 1774 (Beaglehole1961)
9   Bessels is possibly referring to James Weddell, who, in the *Jane* of Leith, reached a record high southerly latitude of 74°15'S in the Weddell Sea on 20 February 1823 (Weddell 1825). But Weddell was a sealer, not a whaler.
10   The term "ice cellar" was coined in 1838 by academician Karl Maksimovich Ber, who had made a voyage to Novaya Zemlya and had reached the east end of Matochkin Shar in 1837 (Solov'ev 1934).
11   The reference is to A.E. Nordenskiöld's ship *Vega*, in which he completed the first transit of the Northeast Passage in 1878–79. Having been blocked by ice, he was forced to winter at Kolyuchinskaya Guba, only a short distance short of Bering Strait, and emerged from that strait on 20 July 1879. He then returned to Stockholm via the Suez Canal (Nordenskiöld 1881).
12   Cape Dezhnev, the easternmost tip of Eurasia.

1: ORIGIN OF THE EXPEDITION AND ITS OUTFITTING

1   The reference is to Sir John Franklin's expedition, whose aim was to complete a transit of the Northwest Passage from east to west. His ships *Erebus* and *Terror*, with combined crews of 129 men, disappeared into what is now the Canadian Arctic Archipelago in 1845, giving rise to an intense search for them which continues to the present (Cyriax 1939). The sunken wreck of *Erebus* was discovered in eastern Queen Maud Gulf by underwater archeologists with Parks Canada in early September 2014 (Geiger and Mitchell 2015). The search for *Terror* continues. The wreck of H.M.S. *Terror* was found by the Arctic Research Foundation's *Martin Bergmann* in Terror Bay on the south coast of King William Island on 3 September 2016.

2   In 1850, *Advance* (Captain Edwin De Haven) and *Rescue* (Samuel Griffin) pushed north through Baffin Bay and west along Lancaster Sound to Beechey Island, where their crews joined those of three British expeditions in examining the traces of the Franklin expedition, which had wintered there in 1845–46. The two American vessels then became beset in the ice and drifted with the ice north up Wellington Channel, back south again, east out of Lancaster Sound and south through Baffin Bay throughout the winter, finally being released in June 1851 (Kane 1854).

3   The graves of John Hartnell and William Braine of *Erebus* and John Torrington of *Terror*, who had all died during the winter of 1845–46. Their bodies (amazingly well preserved in the permafrost) were exhumed and samples of tissues taken for forensic investigation by an expedition led by Dr. Owen Beattie of the University of Alberta in 1984 and 1986 (Beattie and Geiger 1989).

4   Remarkably, despite extensive searches no messages were found as to intended further routes—in contravention of standard arctic expeditionary procedure.

5   This geographical name has not survived; now Inglefield Land.

6   Pushing north through Baffin Bay and Smith Sound into Kane Basin in 1853, Kane wintered twice at Rensselaer Fiord on the Greenland coast of the basin at 78°37′N. In the spring of 1854 several sledge trips were made farther north. When there was no sign of the ship getting free of the ice in the summer of 1855, Kane and his men started south by sledge and boat, reaching Upernavik safely (Kane 1856; Villarejo 1965; McGoogan 2008).

7   In his schooner *United States*, Isaac Hayes pushed north through Baffin Bay, hoping to reach "an open polar sea" and the North Pole. Encountering heavy ice in Smith Sound, he was forced to winter in Foulke Fiord near the Inughuit settlement of Etah. In the spring of 1861 he sledged across Kane Basin to the coast of Ellesmere Island and headed north. He claimed to have reached 81°35′N, but this claim is now disputed. *United States* got underway again on 14 July 1861 and returned safely to Boston (Hayes 1867; Wamsley 2009).

8   Strangely, Bessels has reversed Charles Francis Hall's Christian names. For his background and two earlier arctic expeditions (in 1860–62 and 1864–69) see the biographical sketch, p. 560–62. Most importantly, during the first of these he had met Ebierbing (Ipiirvik) and Hannah (Tookolito; Taqulittuq), who would accompany him on all three of his arctic expeditions (Hall 1865; Nourse 1879).

9   By invitation, on 5 March he gave a lecture in Lincoln Hall, which was attended by the President, Ulysses S. Grant, and by Vice President Schuyler Colfax, on "Arctic expeditions, past and prospective" (Davis 1876:25–26; Henderson 2001:15).

10   Congressman Job Evans Stevenson.

11   Ulysses S. Grant. Hall had met privately with the President on 3 February, only three days after his arrival in Washington (Loomis 1971:233; Henderson 2001:15).

12   Senator John Sherman.

13   Chaired by the Hon. Charles Sumner of Massachusetts (Blake 1874:100).

14   Isaac Hayes was a serious contender for the position of expedition leader (Loomis 1971:238–39; Henderson 2001:17–18).

15   But it barely passed the Senate; it was a tied vote, broken only by the vote of Vice President Schuyler Colfax (Loomis 1971:240).

16 Hall had requested $100,000.
17 The Statutes at Large and Proclamations of the United States of America from December 1869 to March 1871. Boston 1871, Vol. XVI, Chap. 251, Sec. 9, p. 251 (Davis 1876:27; E.B.)
18 That commission read as follows:

Executive Mansion, Washington, D.C., July 20, 1870.

Captain C.F. Hall:

Dear Sir,

You are hereby appointed to command the expedition toward the North Pole. To be organized and sent out pursuant to an Act of Congress approved July 12, 1870, and will report to the Secretary of the Navy and the Secretary of the Interior for detailed instructions. U.S. Grant. (Blake 1874:101).

These "detailed instructions" signed by George Robeson, Secretary of the Navy, are presented in full in Appendix 2.

19 She was a screw tug, built in Philadelphia in 1864 and originally named *America* (Henderson 2001:29).
20 Bessels must have been misinformed; she operated as a gunboat on the Potomac, Chesapeake Bay and especially the Rappahannock (Henderson 2001:29). After the Civil War she was based at Norfolk, Virginia, which is where Hall found her.
21 Her timbers were extensively replaced and additional ice-strengthening installed; she was also caulked and coppered. She was rigged as a topsail-schooner. The bow was strengthened with iron plates for 40 feet aft from the stem (Henderson 2001:29–30).
22 Always keen to save money, Hall had organized a free passage for Bessels through a German shipping company, Oelrichs & Co. (Loomis 1971:252).
23 Of interest is the fact that Bessels was not the first choice as chief scientist. At Lady Franklin's suggestion, Dr. David Walker had offered his services (Loomis 1971:247). Walker had served as medical officer on board McClintock's *Fox* on his 1857–59 voyage, when the only message, and many relics and skeletal remains, from the Franklin expedition had been discovered. At the time he wrote, Walker was serving in the United States Army. Hall, accepting Lady Franklin's recommendation, wrote to Dr. Spencer Fullerton Baird at the Smithsonian Institution, responsible for engaging the scientific staff, to propose Walker as chief scientist. This proposal was accepted, in principle. But then August Petermann, the distinguished German geographer (see biographical sketch, p. 562–63), proposed as his candidate Dr. Emil Bessels. Like Walker, Bessels already had arctic experience, having participated in Petermann's 1869 expedition on board *Albert*, and Baird and Professor Joseph Henry felt that Bessels's scientific credentials were stronger than Walker's (Loomis 1971:252). Thus it was Bessels who was hired.

Hall's instructions included the following order: "The charge and direction of the scientific operations, will be intrusted, under your command, to Dr. Emil Bessels; and you will render Dr. Bessels and his assistants all such facilities and aids as may be in your power" (Blake 1874:108).

24 Joseph Henry, Secretary of the Smithsonian Institution and President of the National Academy of Sciences.

25   Dr. Spencer Fullerton Baird; then Assistant Secretary at the Smithsonian, he would succeed Henry as Secretary on the latter's death in 1878.
26   Rear-Admiral Benjamin F. Sands.
27   Commodore (later Rear-Admiral) Daniel Ammen, then Chief of the Bureau of Yards and Docks.
28   Although later promoted Commodore and later Rear-Admiral, in 1873 Robert H. Wyman's rank was Captain; he was the head of the Hydrographic Office.
29   Julius Erasmus Hilgard (1825–1890), a German-American engineer with the Coast and Geodetic Survey.
30   Carl Anton Schott (1826–1901), a German-American engineer with the Coast and Geodetic Survey.
31   In late May President Ulysses S. Grant, Secretary of the Navy Robeson and various other officials had visited the ship. On that occasion the Reverend Dr. Newman had led a brief service (Loomis 1971:255; Henderson 2001:30–31).
32   For further details of the ship, and of the modifications to prepare her for work in ice, see Blake 1874:102–3.
33   A summary of the scientific observations which were to be pursued is to be found in Blake 1874:109–10.
34   1 centner = 50 kg approximately.
35   Tookolito (Taqullituq) and her husband Ebierbing (Iviirvik) (also named Joe or Joseph by the whalers: see biographical sketches, p. 558–60).
36   Her first child, a son, Tarrilikitak, had died at Groton on 28 February 1863 (Nickerson 2002:28). She gave birth to a second son on 16 September 1865, during Hall's second expedition; Hall called him "Little King William," but his true Inuit name appears not to have been recorded. He sickened and died on 13 May 1866 during one of Hall's attempts to reach King William Island from Repulse Bay (Nickerson 2002:34). It was probably this son to whom Bessels was referring.
37   Only when her face became screwed up when crying did her brows, which arched above somewhat expressionless dark eyes, acquire a slant and her features changed completely, assuming an unmistakably Japanese cast. E.B.
38   The speakers included Captain William Morton, Bessels and of course Hall. The latter was introduced by Judge Daly, President of the American Geographical Society (Loomis 1971:258). For a summary of Hall's presentation see Henderson 2001: 22–23.
39   The Cooper Institute for the Advancement of Science. The building, erected in 1859, still stands on Cooper Square in Manhattan.
40   The United States Exploring Expedition of 1838–42, led by Lt. Charles Wilkes, consisted of six vessels, and its focus was exploration of the Antarctic. The flag was presumably on board the flagship, *Vincennes*, when Wilkes completed a coastal survey of Terre Adélie, Wilkes Land and Queen Mary Land (i.e., in the southern Indian Ocean), in the southern summer of 1839–40 (Stanton 1975). This flag was a somewhat ill-omened symbol, in that the Wilkes expeditions had been riven by dissension, and ended in Wilkes being court-martialled.
41   See p. 567, n.2.
42   See p. 567, n.7.

2: From New York to Newfoundland

1. Now Roosevelt Island.
2. The Renwick Smallpox Hospital, opened in 1856; the ruins of the building are still standing.
3. The Blackwell's Island Penitentiary was closed and its inmates moved to Rikers Island in 1936.
4. Blackwell's Island Insane Asylum was New York's first mental hospital and the first municipal mental institution in the United States. The building Bessels saw was completed in 1839.
5. Hell Gate is a narrow strait in the East River between Wards Island on the west side and Astoria, Queen's. The Army Corps of Engineers made repeated efforts at removing underwater hazards from 1851 onward. Bessels is perhaps referring to preparations for a major underwater explosion which took place on 24 September 1876.
6. Completed in 1777 and named after Governor Jonathan Trumbull, Fort Trumbull was captured by the British under Benedict Arnold in 1781 during the Revolutionary War. It is now a state park.
7. Fort Griswold, captured, then abandoned by Benedict Arnold in 1781, is now the centrepiece of Battle of Groton Heights State Park.
8. It was the assistant engineer, Wilson, who had deserted in New York; his replacement was Alvin Odell (Blake 1874:453; Loomis 1971:258).
9. William Jackson (Loomis 1971:258)
10. For Tyson's earlier career see the biographical sketch p. 563. Tyson had made a very good impression on Hall on the basis of their various past encounters, and he was his first choice as sailing master on board *Polaris*, but by the time he made him an offer Tyson had already committed himself to a whaling cruise and had to decline. But the whaling voyage was cancelled, and Tyson contacted Hall. By then, however, Hall had hired Sydney Budington as sailing master. Having cleared the unusual appointment with George Robeson, Secretary of the Navy, Hall then appointed Tyson "assistant navigator" (Henderson 2001:27).
11. For the exact wording of that communication see Blake 1874:102.
12. The clergyman who conducted the service on board was Dr. Foster of New London (Davis 1876:47).
13. John Cleve Symmes (1780–1829); in 1818 he circulated a pamphlet in which he argued that the Earth was hollow and that the interior was habitable.
14. John Philip Newman (1826–1900), Chaplain to the US Senate (1869–74).
15. Rave Rock pilot station, off Fisher Island at the mouth of the Thames River.
16. Off the east end of Nantucket Island.
17. More correctly, the Labrador Current.
18. Unless otherwise indicated, temperatures are always given in Celsius and longitudes from Greenwich. E.B.
19. Possibly Leach's storm-petrels (*Oceanodroma leucorhoa*) (Sale 2006:76).

20 The northern bottlenose whale (*Hyperoodon ampullatus*) has a range which extends from the Gulf of St. Lawrence to Davis Strait and the Barents Sea (Sale 2006:440–41).
21 St. John's harbour.
22 There were two fair-sized icebergs in the harbour (Blake 1874:142).
23 Fort Amherst Lighthouse, on the south side of the harbour entrance.
24 Not the present tower, Cabot Tower, which was completed only in 1900. It, however, was preceded by a series of other towers from 1704 onward, which served the same purpose, i.e., to inform the city, by a system of flags, of the details of approaching vessels.
25 During World War II anti-submarine nets were stretched between the two rocks.
26 Known as "flakes."
27 Thomas N. Molloy, US consul at St. John's.
28 The Basilica-Cathedral of St. John the Baptist, still the most prominent building on the skyline of St. John's.
29 Governor of Newfoundland 1825–34.
30 Now the residence of the Lieutenant-Governor for Newfoundland and Labrador.
31 Richard Edwards (ca. 1715–1795), Governor of Newfoundland.
32 Charles Pedley,*The history of Newfoundland from the earliest times to the year 1860* (London: Longman, Green, 1863), 155.
33 Lying between the town centre and the sea, this small lake is the site of the annual Royal St. John's Regatta, a rowing regatta and the oldest sporting event in North America.
34 The most easterly point and the most easterly lighthouse in North America.
35 Sir Stephen John Hill (1809–1891), Colonel in the West India Regiment, was Governor of Newfoundland from 1869 until 1876. In fact Captain Hall and all his officers were invited to lunch at the Governor's residence on the 13th. In return the Governor and his entourage were entertained on board *Polaris* (Davis 1876:48).
36 One presumes Bessels is referring to an outhouse. Perhaps an "O" cut in the door was a German or European tradition. In North America the tradition of the crescent-moon on outhouse doors has an extremely long history.
37 A reference to Don Quixote's broken-down old nag in Miguel de Cevantes novel *Don Quixote*.
38 The Hospital for Mental Diseases, on Waterford Road, now known simply as Waterford Hospital, was opened in 1854. It seems a strange destination for a casual visitor to St. John's.
39 Cormack 1928.
40 In terms of agriculture Newfoundland is still not a major producer. According to Statistics Canada's Census of Agriculture, in 2006 there were only 22,571 acres of cropland. The main crops were hay, potatoes, turnips, carrots, beets, cabbage and broccoli. There were 558 farms, averaging 160 acres in size, and 710 farm operators, 45.8% of whom also worked off-farm. The main sources of farm income were poultry, eggs and dairy products, the farms producing these being mainly

clustered around St. John's; other significant agricultural areas were around Deer Lake and in the Codroy Valley.

41   According to the Economic Research and Analysis Division of the Department of Finance for Newfoundland and Labrador, the population (including that of Labrador) on 1 January 2014 was 526,896.

42   By contrast, mining is now a major component of the economy of Newfoundland and Labrador, but mainly in the Labrador section of the province. Of major importance here are the iron mines at Wabush and Labrador City and the nickel mine at Voisey's Bay on the Labrador coast.

43   The Tilt Cove copper mine continued to operate until 1920. It re-opened in 1957 but closed again a decade later. Most recently it has been functioning since 2011.

3: From Newfoundland to Greenland

1   29 n. miles north of St. John's.

2   William Scoresby Jr. (1789–1857), English whaler and arctic scientist, published a remarkable treatise (Scoresby 1820) on the arctic environment, to which Bessels is here making reference.

3   Bessels appears to be a little confused as to terminology. Sea-lice are parasitic crustaceans of the order Cyamidae which infest the skins of whales. *Limacina arctica* (also known as *Clione limasina*) is a free-swimming pteropod (common name: naked sea butterfly) which inhabits the North Atlantic and North Pacific oceans.

4   Kane 1856.

5   Present name: Qeqertarsuatsiaat.

6   Hans Hendrik.

7   August Sonntag (1832–1860) participated as astronomer in Kane's Second Grinnell Expedition and as astronomer and second-in-command on Isaac Hayes's North Pole Expedition. While travelling with Hans from the expedition's winter quarters at Port Foulke (Foulke Fiord) south to Northumberland Island to buy dogs to replace those which had died of disease, Sonntag fell through thin ice and, although able to struggle out of the water with Hans' assistance, died soon afterward (Hayes 1867:231; Wamsley 2009:281–82).

8   Hayes 1867:66.

9   Tyson describes it as "a heavy piece of ship's timber" (Blake 1874:143).

10   On 27 July (Davis 1876:49).

11   They probably obtained the cryolite from the deposit at Ivigtut (Ivittuut), where the mine, now abandoned, operated for many decades, as the only known commercial source of the mineral, essential in the production of aluminum.

12   "Schönheit" means "beauty" in German.

13   *Eriophorum vaginatum* —Tussock cotton-grass.

14   Most probably *Draba lactea* (Lapland or milky whitlow grass), a small white, circumpolar flower.

15   Present name Akunnat.

16 Like almost all the settlements in West Greenland, Lichtenfels was founded by the Herrnhuter Brüdergemeine, commonly known as the Moravian Church, which operated in Greenland between 1733 and 1800.
17 The capital (present name Nuuk).
18 Present name Ilulissat.
19 Emil Schumann; the seamen were Nindemann and Mauch (Davis 1876:50).
20 I.L. Starick, Moravian missionary.
21 J.-W. Uellner, who spent 38 years at Lichtenfels.
22 Rothspohn, or Rotspon: a red wine produced in Lübeck, but a French wine in origin, which has been transported in barrels and stored in barrels until bottled.
23 Bessels appears to be referring to china figurines; Neuruppin now supports several manufacturers of semiconductors, which have evolved from a ceramics industry.
24 The reference is to Anthony van Dyck's painting "The Virgin and child with repentant sinners" (1625).
25 *Corvus corax principalis*, occurring throughout northern North America, including the Canadian Arctic Archipelago and the ice-free areas of Greenland, except the extreme north and northeast coasts (Sale 2006:310–11).
26 The heathen Eskimos at the entrance to Smith Sound displayed an unmistakable abhorrence of the same perfume (Jockey Club); by contrast they had an expressed preference for asaphoetidae and butyric acid. E.B.
27 Northern fulmar (*Fulmarus glacialis*), ranging throughout the North Atlantic and North Pacific (Sale 2006:72–73).
28 Holboell, *Ornithologischer Beitrag zur Fauna Grönlands*. Leipzig: Ernst Fleischer, 1854. p. 58. E.B.
29 Present name Qeqertarssuak, on Disko.
30 During his voyage on board *Albert* in 1869.
31 Present name Sisimiut.
32 A.E. Nordenskiöld had found large metallic blocks at Blåfjeld (Uifvaq, southwestern Disko), and believed them to be meteorites (Nordenskiöld 1872). They later proved not to be meteorites.
33 Frederik Wilhelm von Otter, later Prime Minister of Sweden, 1900–1902.
34 In the recently published hydrographic reports of the British Admiralty, produced by that country's Hydrographic Office (Hydrographic Notice No. 36) it states, with regard to Holsteinsborg (p. 2): "The tide in the harbour is barely perceptible." In fact Holsteinsborg possesses the only harbour in the whole of Greenland where the tidal range (10 feet at springs) is sufficiently large to permit careening of a ship. In the same notice the position of the flagstaff at the harbour (cf. the figure in the text, p. 74) is given as 66°54'14"N; 53°40'W, whereas on the chart which appeared somewhat later (British Admiralty Chart No. 2266, May 1876) it is recorded as 66°55'42"N; 53°42'W. According to Hall's observations, made 6 paces west of the flagpole, its position is 66°57'N; 53°53'45"W. I shall refrain from offering any explanation for the difference in latitude; on the other hand I must note that our chronometric determination of longitude is totally reliable. It is based on a time-transfer from St. John's Newfoundland. Our six box-chronometers kept perfect time and suffered no disturbances; this was

confirmed by a second time-transfer from the same location to Godhavn made by the corvette *Congress* on 10 August. E.B.

35 Professor Theodor Magnus Fries (1832–1913), Lund University, lichenologist.

36 Botanist.

37 The Swedish expedition was now southward-bound. Von Otter reported that they had been as far north as Upernavik, and had encountered little ice, although there had been occasional bergs between Disko and Upernavik (Blake 1874:134). He had taken 30 deep sea soundings and water temperatures, which Blake presents in an appendix (Blake 1874:457).

38 Dr. Hinrich Johannes Rink (1819–1893), a Dane, first arrived in Greenland to study geology in 1848. From 1857 until 1868 he was the Royal Inspector for South Greenland and from 1871 until 1882 the Director of the Royal Greenland Trading Department.

39 In the meantime nickel has been discovered in the basalts of New Mexico and Arizona, in association with cobalt (0.03%). Cf. Low's geological section in *Report upon Geographical and Geological Explorations and Surveys west of the hundredth Meridian*, Vol. III, pp. 646–47. Washington: Government Printing Office, 1875. E.B.

40 Loch Shin, Sutherland, is a narrow lake some 27 km in length in the northwest Highlands of Scotland.

41 The Royal Greenland Trading Department (Den Kongelige Grønlandske Handel) held a trading monopoly with all the Greenlandic settlements from 1774 until 1979.

42 Governor Lowertz Elberg (Loomis 1971:271).

43 Hans Egede, a Dano-Norwegian Lutheran minister, arrived in Greenland in 1721, in search of traces or survivors of the earlier Norse settlers. He founded the capital, Godthåb (now Nuuk).

44 Present name Qaqortoq.

45 Some individual lamps in the American National Museum in Washington are very remarkable; they were found on the Aleutians, and must be ascribed a very great age, from their shape and where they were found. They represent the Eskimo lamp in its most original form and consist of beach cobbles in which the water has eroded hollows. Some of them clearly show traces of fire, and microscopic analysis of the foreign particles adhering to them allows one to deduce their earlier use without any doubt whatsoever. E.B.

46 Cranz 1820.

47 See the picture of Fiskernæsset on p.55, in the foreground of which one of these boats is shown. E.B.

48 Greenland shark, now *Somniosus microcephalus*.

49 Hall had also hoped to obtain coal here, but had no success. Although the governor, Elberg, had only 15 tonnes on hand, he offered two thirds of it to Hall; the latter understandably declined this generous offer, counting on replenishing his stocks from his supply ship at Disko (Blake 1874:135).

50 Nindemann.

51 According to Davis (1876:51) he was rescued by a boat from the Swedish vessel *Ingegerd*.

4: From Holsteinsborg to the northernmost settlement on Earth

1   An alternate name for Godhavn (Qeqertarssuaq).
2   Governor Elberg accompanied the expedition as far north as Tasiusaq (Loomis 1971:271).
3   Atlantic halibut: now *Hippoglossus hippoglossus*.
4   Now *Reinhardtius hippoglossoides* (Greenland halibut).
5   Sole.
6   Now Aasiaat.
7   Now Qasigiannguit.
8   Now Paamiut.
9   White whales (*Delphinapterus leucas*): circumpolar in distribution, and even frequenting such southerly locations as James Bay and even the Saguenay and St. Lawrence rivers (Sale 2006: 436–47).
10 The gyrfalcon (*Falco rusticolus*), the largest of the falcons, is circumpolar in distribution (Sale 2006: 156–57).
11 A former name for the Hoary redpoll (*Carduelis hornemanni*) (Sale 2006:335–36).
12 On 4 August (Blake 1874:144).
13 Sophus Theodor Krarup-Smith (1834–1882), Inspector for North Greenland, 1867–82.
14 Hubbard C. Chester.
15 In his absence Hall was received by his deputy, Governor Lassen, with Mrs. Krarup-Smith acting as interpreter (Davis 1876:54).
16 Now Sullorsuaq Strait—between Disko and the mainland of Greenland; the coal seams outcrop on Disko on the west side of the strait.
17 Captain Edward Inglefield, on board *Isabel*, searching for Franklin in the summer of 1852 (Inglefield 1853).
18 From our observations taken 10 paces northwest of the flagpole that is visible on the adjoining illustration between the inspector's house and the administrator's. E.B.
19 N.A.E. Nordenskiöld, during his expedition in 1870 (Nordenskiöld 1872).
20 The English whaler William Scoresby Jr. during his voyage aboard *Baffin* in 1822 (Scoresby 1823).
21 Mrs. Krarup-Smith.
22 Leonora was the heroine of Beethoven's opera *Fidelio*.
23 More likely *Salix arctica* (Arctic willow).
24 Three-banded ladybug.
25 Rove beetle.
26 Rock ptarmigan (*Lagopus mutus*); circumpolar in distribution, including all coastal areas of Greenland (Sale 2006:162).
27 Probably *Andromeda polifolia* (bog rosemary).
28 If there is no indication to the contrary all bearings are corrected for compass variation. E.B.

29   USS *Congress*, (Captain H.K. Davenport) (Davis 1876:55).
30   One of them was Richard W.D. Bryan, the third member of the scientific group (Henderson 2001:44). Also on board as passengers were Rev. E.D. Bryan, Richard Bryan's father, and Captain James Budington, Sydney Budington's uncle (Davis 1876:57). *Congress* also brought Tyson's commission as assistant navigator; since his appointment to that position had been made so late, there had not been time to make it official before the ship left the United States (Blake 1874:136).
31   This had involved Chester and his crew in a trip of 175 miles, mainly under oars (Blake 1874:135).
32   On 11 August. Davenport was accompanied by Captain Hall; they were welcomed by a gun salute, which was returned by *Congress* (Davis 1876:55). Inspector Krarup-Smith arranged for a depot of stores intended for the expedition to be stowed in a government warehouse.
33   Bertel Thorvaldsen (1770–1844) was a famous Danish sculptor, for whose considerable output of work the Thorvaldsen Museum located next to the Christiansborg Palace in Copenhagen was built, and opened in 1848. The original of his roundel "Night" ("Nyx"), sculpted in 1815, hangs in the Museum opposite the matching roundel "Day," each representing female figures.
34   On the 13th.
35   Dr. Newman, who had come north on board *Congress* specifically to give the expedition his blessing (Loomis 1971:266) and Rev. E.D. Bryan.
36   Dr. Newman then led a prayer, the exact words of which may be found in Blake (1874:145) or Loomis (1971:268). Loomis surmises that this part of the prayer might have been in response to the dissensions which Newman had observed even during his brief presence on board.
37   At 2.00 p.m. on 17 August (Blake 1874:136, 145), while *Congress*'s crew manned the yards and gave three cheers (Davis 1876:56–57).
38   Dr. med. Christian Nicolai Rudolph (1811–1882).
39   Present name Kangersuatsiaq.
40   Again under the command of first mate, Hubbard Chester; his crew, rowing, covered the 100 miles to Prøven and back between noon on 19 August and 8.00 p.m. on the 20th (Blake 1874:137).
41   William Morton, second mate.
42   From an accident during the Kane expedition (Davis 1876:60).
43   Bessels has modestly excluded himself from this list.
44   But Bessels has omitted the following seamen: Friedrich Jamka, Peter Johnson, Robert Krüger and William Nindemann.
45   A play on the Hanseatic trading cities of the Baltic and North Sea coasts, such as Bremen, Hamburg and Lübeck. Bessels employs this play on Hans Hendrik's name regularly to denote him and his family.
46   Bessels's rendering of "Mirquiti," Inuktitut for "needle."
47   Diminutive for Susanne.
48   This is a literal translation of the German simile. "As ugly as sin" would be the English equivalent.

49 To try to buy dogs and furs (Davis 1876:63).
50 The reference is to the farce *Der böse Geist Lumpazivagabundus* or *Das Liederliche Kleeblatt*, written by Johann Nestroy and first performed in the Alttheater in Vienna on 11 April 1833.
51 Peter Jensen, who served as interpreter and dog driver on Hayes's expedition in 1860–61. For a photo of Jensen see Wamsley 2009, p. 258.
52 Either thick-billed murres (*Uria lomvia*) or common murres (*Uria aalge*), more probably the former (Sale 2006:264–66).
53 *Plectrophenax nivalis*.
54 Atlantic puffin (*Fratercula arctica*), which breeds both farther south (in the Uummannaaq area) and farther north (Sale 2006:277–78) but not in the Tasiusaq area, and hence would be relatively uncommon there (Sale 2006:264–6).

5: HISTORICAL REVIEW

1 For further details see Markham 1881.
2 The reference is to the book by Sir John Barrow, Second Secretary at the Admiralty (Barrow 1818). But even greater damage had been done to Baffin's reputation much earlier. Samuel Purchas (1905–7) published Baffin's journal but not his chart or hydrographical observations.
3 For complete details see Ross 1819.
4 This improvement to the chart has not been mentioned by any historian, although Ross plots the course of the coastline according to his predecessors' surveys and according to the results of his own survey. Cf. Ross 1819, frontispiece. E.B.
5 In that Lancaster Sound would subsequently prove to be the entrance to the Northwest Passage, Ross's error in that case was extremely unfortunate. He was so convinced that the strait was blocked by a range of mountains that he even named them—the Croker Mountains. Nobody on board Parry's ship, *Alexander*, some distance astern, saw these "mountains."
6 This was the name Ross gave to snow-covered cliffs just west of Cape York, coloured red by the snow algae *Clamydomonas nivalis*.
7 Dr. A. Petermann. Das nördlichste Land der Erde. *Geograph. Mitt.*, 1867, Tafel VI. E.B.
8 Perhaps the accuracy of the positions is to be ascribed to the fact that for measuring the sun's altitude Bylot and Baffin used an astrolabe instead of the cross-staff, then more common. Since the ship was commonly beset by ice, there was nothing to compromise the reliability of the former instrument on board, since the ice dampens the swell so completely that a beset ship lies almost motionless. But on firm ground a good astrolabe, according to a report by Tycho Brahe, allows readings to within a sixth of a minute of arc. [Tycho Ottesen Brahe (1546–1601) was a renowned Danish astronomer, famous for, among other things, the fact that he wore a false nose, having lost the original in a duel.] The higher latitudes which the two seafarers attained meant sun's altitudes which did not exceed 45°. Hence if in calculating their observations they used Tycho's refraction tables, which proceeded from the false assumption that altitudes over 45° were not influenced by refraction (Delambre, *Histoire de*

l'Astronomie moderne, Tome 1, p. 151), they would have avoided the then widespread source of error, which could easily amount to one minute of arc.

In order to recognize the superbness of the Baffin/Bylot observations in their full significance it finally should also be mentioned here that important astronomers such as Regiomontanus and Peuerbach recorded many latitudes with errors of 26» (Venice) or even 27» (Nurnberg) (*Alfontii Regis Castellae Tabulae impr. Erhardus Ratdolt*); and their instruments were no more imperfect than those of the English seafarers, since until the invention of Hadley's octant the same means were used, as those used by the Greeks and Arabs. E.B.

9 Unfortunately I am unable to find a copy of Inglefield's *Summer search for Sir John Franklin* here in Washington. Instead of trusting to memory I opted, in compiling the above lines, to use the brief overview of the Inglefield expedition that Petermann published in the previously mentioned article, "Das nördlichste Land der Erde." I hope this fact explains the brevity with which I have treated this epoch-making voyage. E.B. The full details of Inglefield's voyage may be found in Inglefield 1853.

10 These coordinates are based on a measurement taken from Petermann's map. E.B.

11 For full details of Kane's voyage see his account: Kane 1856. E.B.

12 Henry Grinnell (1799–1874), an American shipowner, was the major financier of a series of arctic expeditions, including Edward de Haven's in search of the missing Franklin expedition (1850–51), Elisha Kent Kane's (1853–55), Isaac Hayes's (1860–61) and Charles Hall's (1860–62 and 1864–69).

13 George Peabody (1795–1869), American merchant, banker and philanthropist.

14 Ice conditions in Baffin Bay and the adjacent sea areas will be discussed in greater detail in a later chapter. E.B.

15 Perhaps not until the 8th; here there is clearly an error in Kane's journal. Unfortunately I am not in a position to clear up this and other errors, since when the Smithsonian Institution burned down [in 1865] the log was a victim of the flames. Also the descriptive part of the journal, which was in Kane's estate, could not be found by the heirs. E.B.

16 Isaac Israel Hayes, the expedition's medical officer. For details see Wamsley 2009.

17 Kane plotted Cape Constitution, which rises only a few miles north of Cape Independence at 81° 22'N, almost 22 miles farther north than it was confirmed by Morton's astronomical determination and by the latter's estimated distance. Instead of viewing the astronomically determined point as decisive, he incomprehensibly based the construction of his published map on the mean position derived from the estimate of distances covered and the astronomically determined positions. Five years after the appearance of Kane's work the Smithsonian Institution in Washington published the observations made by the expedition (*Physical observations in the Arctic Sea, reduced and discussed by C.A. Schott*. Washington 1859–60), whereby the map underwent significant modifications. The accuracy of these final positions will be discussed later. E.B.

18 This was HMS *North Star* (Captain William Pullen), the depot ship of Captain Sir Edward Belcher's squadron.

19 The party was led by Dr. I.I. Hayes; for details see his account: Hayes 1860.

20 These were USS *Release* (Captain Henry Hartstene) and *Arctic* (Captain Charles Simms). For details see: Laws 1967.

21 For full details see Hayes's own account: Hayes 1867. See also: Wamsley 2009.

22 All fairly large vessels that visit the high latitudes carry a barrel at the main mast-head (called a crow's nest by the old whalers), in which the lookout maintains a watch. The bottom of the barrel consists of a trap door through which the lookout slips in and out. The time at which he is relieved depends on the temperature, the wind strength and the ice conditions. E.B.

23 A latitude of 78°18'30"N is more correct than that quoted by Hayes, as our expedition's later observation revealed. E.B.

24 August Sonntag (1832–1860), astronomer and second-in-command on Hayes's expedition.

25 The same Hans Hendrik who later took part in Hall's expedition.

6: INTO UNKNOWN TERRITORY

1 Governor Elberg left the ship at this point, taking Hall's dispatches with him and promising to ensure that they would ultimately reach the American ambassador in Copenhagen. They included Hall's report of events thus far to George Robeson, Secretary of the Navy, quoted in full in Blake 1874:138–40.

2 On the 26th (Davis 1876:71).

3 *Odobenus rosmarus*; with bulls weighing up to 2000 kg, and with tusks up to 75 cm long (longer in the Pacific subspecies) (Sale 2006:427), a herd of walrus hauled out makes a spectacular sight. This herd was lying on the ice between Wolstenholme and Saunders islands (Davis 1876:72)

4 Bessels alternates between "Augustine" and "Josephine" as the name of this girl.

5 Budington tried to persuade Hall to make Port Foulke his winter quarters, and to continue north by sledge from there (Henderson 2001:54). Hall refused.

6 At 5.00 p.m. on the 27th (Davis 1876:75).

7 At 8.00 p.m. on 27 August (Loomis 1971:275).

8 The name then applied to the northern half of Ellesmere Island.

9 On 27–28 August (Blake 1874:147).

10 Recently the subject of a fairly amicable dispute between Canada and Denmark, as to which country possesses sovereignty over the island, since it lies exactly midway between the two.

11 This would be the highest latitude which *Polaris* would reach; to quote the report of the later Board of Inquiry, chaired by George Robeson "the ship. . ., on the 30th of August, attained the highest northern latitude reached by the Expedition, in latitude declared by Captain Hall to be 82°26'N., but afterward found, by the careful calculation of Mr. Meyer, to be 82°16'N" (Davis 1876:85). At this point *Polaris* had reached the point where Robeson Channel opens into the Lincoln Sea, i.e., into the Arctic Ocean.

12 Carrying the ship with it.

13 Accompanied by Tyson (Blake 1874:149).

14	Anonymous 1873:447. E.B.
15	This meeting was held on the afternoon of 31 August (Davis 1876:91–92).
16	Anonymous 1873:480–81.
17	Ibid., p. 556.
18	Ibid.,p. 498.
19	US Navy Department 1876, Part IX, p. 6.
20	Donated by Henry Grinnell; it had been used by Lt. Henry Hartstene on board USS *Release* during his search for the missing Kane expedition in 1855 (Davis 1876:100).
21	Led by Bryan (Davis 1876:102).
22	We can probably claim a higher latitude than 82°26′. Another calculation of the relevant day's run gave 82°29′, but for well-known reasons the results of a log calculation cannot be very accurate. On a later occasion the latitude of the bay, which Hall named Repulse Harbour, was determined to be 82°9′N; from all appearances, when *Polaris* reached her highest latitude she was more than 9 n. miles north of that point. The mean of the three observations, 82°24′, may well have come closest to the truth. E.B.
23	On 4 September (Davis 1876:103).
24	It had been accidentally closed by one of the seamen who had hung something on it to dry (Davis 1876:104).
25	This flag raising occurred on the night of September 4–5 (Blake 1874:150; Davis 1876: 104). After searching for a more suitable site, Hall decided that this was the best he would find, and returned there several days later. At this point he named the bay Thank God Harbor.
26	This decision, i.e., to settle in to winter quarters, was not made until 7 September according to Tyson (Blake 1874:150).

7: The first days in Polaris Bay

1	This berg, the largest the expedition had encountered since entering Kennedy Channel, was aground in 13 fathoms, i.e., nearly 80 feet of water; it was 450 feet long, 300 feet wide and 60 feet high (Blake 1874: 151; Davis 1876: 110).
2	Steller 1774.
3	King William Island.
4	Pond Inlet, northern Baffin Island.
5	Cumberland Sound, southern Baffin Island.
6	A German mile varied in length from one part of what is now Germany to another, but was generally around 7.5 km.
7	Georg Wilhelm Steller (1709–1746), naturalist on Vitus Bering's Second Kamchatka Expedition. The reference is to Steller's account of the expedition (Steller 1774).
8	Wrangel 1840.
9	Black-legged kittiwake (*Rissa tridactyla*) (Sale 206:253).
10	Probably a purple sandpiper (now *Calidris maritima*).

11   Historically, in terms of its distribution in Greenland, the muskox (*Ovibos moschatus*) was confined to the ice-free coastal strips of north Greenland (north of the Humboldt Glacier) and northeast Greenland (south to Scoresbysund). Recently, however it has been introduced to two locations in West Greenland.

12   A hunting party consisting of Bessels, Chester, Joe and Hans, set off immediately (Blake 1874:152).

13   Which he shared with Bessels, Bryan, Meyer, Schumann, the cook, William Jackson and steward, John Herrod (Loomis 1971:277).

14   He was found by Morton and Siemens, who had set out to look for him, quite close to the ship, staggering as if drunk, and barely conscious (Davis 1876:130).

15   He had passed out soon after coming back aboard, and regained consciousness only some time later, after he had been manhandled into his bunk (Loomis 1971:278).

16   Aaron Arctander, the assistant on Andreas Bruun's expedition (1777–79), whose mandate was to investigate the economic potential of the Julianehåb area. For details see Ostermann 1944.

17   Peter Christian Pingel, who mounted a private expedition to the Julianehåb area in 1828–29. For details see Pingel 1841.

18   Christian Leopold von Buch (1774–1853) a well-known German geologist who spent two years (1806–8) in studying the geology and natural environment of Norway and Sweden.

19   Brown was the naturalist on Edward Whymper's 1867 expedition to the Ilordlik Fjord area (near Jakobshavn) aimed primarily at investigating the Greenland Ice Cap (Holland 1994:271).

8: The first sledge journey

1   More correctly *Mallotus villosus* or capelin, a small fish of the smelt family.

2   Bessels is referring to the northern collared lemming (*Dicrostonyx groenlandicus*) the only lemming species occurring in Greenland, and only in the extreme northern and northeastern coastal areas (Sale 2006:363).

3   A Silurian nautiloid cephalopod.

4   Eating the raw meat caused two of my companions violent diarrhea; Joseph and I were spared this affliction. On later occasions, due to lack of fuel we often found ourselves obliged to eat large quantities of raw meat, but none of us was afflicted by the state of weakness that some polar travellers mention as the result of an exclusively meat diet. Even after my return from the polar regions I lived for a full year exclusively on animal food without my health suffering in the slightest. I would enjoy a standard breakfast of raw oysters, baked fish, beef steak and eggs; during the summer a few raw tomatoes replaced the oysters. My noon meal consisted of soup, fish and several meat dishes, as well as some olives; only on rare occasions would I eat bread or vegetable. E.B.

5   They took most of the meat back to the ship with them; Tyson reported it "was good, and did not taste of musk in the least—very much like other beef" (Blake 1874:154).

6   Nicolas Jérémie (1669?–1732), a Quebec-born employee of the Compagnie du Nord, participated in d'Iberville's expedition against the English at Fort York, and in his account describes his experiences and the Hudson Bay region and of the customs and activities of the Indians (Jérémie 1720).

7   Baron Jean Léopold Nicolas Frédéric Cuvier (1769–1832), naturalist and paleontologist; his best-known work was *Le règne animal* (The animal kingdom), 1817.

8   Sir Richard Owen (1804–1892), British naturalist and paleontologist, probably best known for coining the word *dinosaur* [terrible lizard], and for his opposition to Charles Darwin's theory of evolution by natural selection.

9   The expedition on board *Germania* and *Hansa*, led by Karl Koldewey and Friedrich Hegemann, 1869–70. While *Hansa* became beset in the ice and was ultimately crushed, without ever reaching the coast of East Greenland, *Germania* wintered off Sabine Ø and Koldewey and his men made extensive sledge trips, exploring large sections of the coast (Koldewey 1874).

10 Muskoxen are still absent from Baffin Island.

11 A former name for Nettilling Lake, southern Baffin Island.

12 For a detailed discussion of the variations in the range of the muskox, see Barr 1991.

13 Andrew Dickson Murray (1812–1878), Scottish naturalist and author of *The geographical distribution of mammals*. London, 1866, p. 140. E.B.

14 This is somewhat of an exaggeration; rarely does a herd of muskoxen exceed 10–12 in number.

15 Muskoxen (especially solitary animals) are also commonly attacked by wolves.

16 Earlier that day, during his usual Sunday service, Hall had complimented the crew on their behaviour. In response they sent him a letter of thanks:

"The men desire to publicly tender their thanks to Capt. C.F. Hall for his late kindness, not, however, that we were suffering want, but for the fact that it manifests a disposition to treat us as reasonable men, possessing intelligence to appreciate respect and yield it only where merited; and he need never fear but that it will be our greatest pleasure to so live that he can implicitly rely on our service in any duty or emergency. H. Siemens and others." (Davis 1876:132).

In his reply he wrote, in part: "The reception of your letter of thanks to me of this date I acknowledge with a heart that deeply feels and fully appreciates the kindly feeling that has prompted you to this act" (Davis 1876: 132–33; Blake 1874:154).

17 According to Tyson the storm broke on the morning of 27 September and continued until the evening of the 28th (Blake 1874:154).

9: Hall's sledge trip

1   It is perhaps significant that Bessels did not think it relevant to mention Hall's death in this chapter title.

2   The two teams each consisted of 7 dogs. The date of 12 October is an error for 10 October; see Bessel's later report that Hall could not continue his journey after Hans had returned, until the morning of the 12th. Davis (1876:141), Loomis (1971:278), Tyson (Blake 1874:155), Henderson (2001:71) and Nickerson (2002:47) all place the initial departure from the ship on the 10th. Tyson and some of the men initially accompanied the sledge party to assist them up the first steep climbs (Blake 1874:155).

3   See Davis 1876:141–47.

4   The reference is to the drift of De Haven's ships *Advance* and *Rescue* – in 1850–51, not 1851–52. From near Beechey Island they drifted north up Wellington Channel, back south again, east along Lancaster Sound and then south through Baffin Bay (Kane 1854).

5   *Fox* became beset in the ice of Melville Bay in mid-August 1857 and drifted south through Baffin Bay and Davis Strait, getting free only on 25 April 1858 (McClintock 1859).

6   The note is quoted in full in Blake 1874:156–57. Parry (2001:99) would interpret the fact that Hall had forgotten so many items as a measure of his incompetence, and a reminder to Bessels to wind the chronometers daily, from a man with no scientific qualifications, as a deep insult.

7   It was last seen on the 17th at the ship (Davis 1876:148; Blake 1874:157).

8   See Davis 1876:152–53.

9   Hall now named this inlet Newman Bay.

10 That morning Hall read a prayer, prepared by Dr. Newman (Davis 1876:154).

11 Hall's own description of this climb may be found in Davis 1876:156–57.

12 This was the coast of Ellesmere Island.

13 *Physical Observations in the arctic seas by Isaac I. Hayes. reduced and discussed at the expense of the Smithsonian Institution by Ch. A. Schott.* Washington: Smithsonian Institution, 1867, p. 20.

In view of the importance of the matter I shall present the relevant observations here:

Northernmost camp, Kennedy Channel

Observation to determine the latitude of the camp,

17 May 1861

Sun's noon altitude, Dr. I.I. Hayes, observer.

$$2\odot$$

Pocket sextant   56°52'
Index correction   −1 31
55 21
Temperature = +22°F
Altitude   27 40.5
Barometer 30.0' at 53°F approx.
Refraction par.   −1.8
Approx. longitude = 4 h. 35.5 m.

Semidiameter	+15.8
Max. Altitude	27 54.5
Decl. at apparent noon	19 26.0
	81° 31.5' EB.

14   Ibid., p. 20; the following observation is recorded:
Leidy's Camp, Smith Sound,
Observation to determine the latitude of the camp,
20 May 1861.
Noon altitude of the sun, Dr. I.I. Hayes, observer.

2☉

Pocket sextant	61° 14"
Index correction	–1 30
59 44	
Temperature = +22°F approx.	
Altitude	29 52.0
Barometer = 29.7 at 52° approx	
Refraction, par.	–1.7
Approx. longitude = 4 h. 44 m.	
Semidiameter	+15.8
Maximum altitude	30 06.1
Decl. at apparent noon	20 04.6
	79° 58.5" EB.

15   It is only with reluctance that I use the word "homology," as it has been proposed by Louis Agassiz in the geographical sense and has been introduced by Peschel into science, since this expression is not strictly correct. Agassiz, who as a zoologist borrowed it from comparative anatomy, would probably never have seen the wing of an insect as a homology for a bird's wing. E.B.

Jean Louis Rodolphe Agassiz (1807–1873) was a Swiss geologist/zoologist, probably best known for his deduction that the Swiss glaciers had once been much more extensive, coalescing into a massive ice-cap—an important step toward the concept of the Pleistocene glaciations.

Oscar Ferdinand Peschel (1826–1875), a German geographer and anthropologist, probably best known for his classification of the various human races as set out in his book. *The races of man and their geographical distribution* (1876).

16   Davis 1876:160–62. Here, and elsewhere, quotations from Hall's journal have not been re-translated from Bessels's German translation.

17   *Andromeda tetragona* was not found in the newly discovered land. What Hall collected was evidently *Dryas octopetala*. E.B.

18   Davis 1876:163–66.The original is reproduced in Davis 1876:70–71.

19 A diagram and description of the establishing of this cairn and location of the messages may be found in Davis 1876:162–63.
20 Davis 1876:167–68.
21 Tyson, who was engaged in banking up the ship with snow, saw them coming and went to meet them. He recorded the meeting as follows: "Captain Hall looks very well . . . Captain Hall seems to have enjoyed his journey amazingly. He said he was going again, and that he wanted me to go with him. He went aboard, and I resumed my 'banking'" (Blake 1874:159).
22 Which was handed to him by the steward, John Herron (Nickerson 2002:47).
23 Bessels announced that Hall had had an apoplectic attack (Davis 1876:173). He administered a powerful laxative, consisting of castor oil and a few drops of croton oil (Henderson 2001:78).
24 Tyson has described the onset of Hall's illness as follows:

"*Oct, 24, evening.* I kept at work till it was too dark to see, and then came aboard. Captain Hall is sick; it seems strange, he looked so well. I have been into the cabin to see him. He is lying in his berth, and says he feels sick at his stomach. This sickness came on immediately after drinking a cup of coffee. I think it must be a bilious attack, but it is very sudden. I asked him if he thought he was bilious, and told him I thought an emetic would do him good. He said if it was biliousness it would. Hope he will be better tomorrow.

"*Oct. 25.* Captain Hall is no better. Mr. Morton and Mr. Chester watched with him last night; they thought part of the time he was delirious.

"*Evening.* Captain Hall is certainly delirious; I don't know what to make of what he says. He sent for me as if he had something particular to say but—I will not repeat what he said; I don't think it meant anything. No talk of anything in the ship but Captain Hall's illness; if it had only been 'the heat of the cabin,' which some of them say overcame him, he could have got out into the air, and he would have felt better. I cannot hear that he ate anything to make him sick; all he had was that cup of coffee." (Blake 1874:160–61).

According to Henderson (2001:77), in response to Tyson's and Hall's conversation about possibly administering an emetic, Bessels disagreed, saying, "No, that will not do. It will weaken you."

25 Bessels also injected him with what he said was quinine (Davis 1876:174).
26 From 30 October until 4 November Hall refused all medical treatment, afraid that he was being poisoned (Davis 1876: 174–75) and his condition improved noticeably. Tyson describes Hall's last few days as follows:

"*Nov. 1.* Captain Hall is a little better, and has been up, attempting to write; but he don't act like himself—he begins a thing and don't finish it. He begins to talk about one thing, and then goes off to something else; his disease has been pronounced [by Bessels] paralysis, and also apoplexy. I can't remember of any one dying of apoplexy in the north except Captain M'Clintock's engineer [George Brands, engineer on board *Fox*, who died 6 November 1858], and he died very suddenly . . . Hope the captain will rally.

"*Nov. 4.* Captain Hall very bad again. He talks wildly—seems to think someone means to poison him; calls for first one and then another, as if he did not know who to trust. When I was in he accused — — and — — of wanting to poison him. When he is more rational he will say 'If I die, you must still go on to the Pole,' and such like remarks. It's a sad affair; what will become of this expedition if Captain Hall dies, I dread to think.

"*Nov. 5.* No change for the better—worse, I think. He appears to be partially paralyzed. This is dreadful. Even should he recover his senses, what can he do with a paralyzed body?

"*Nov. 8.* Poor Captain Hall is dead; he died early this morning. Last evening Chester said the captain thought himself that he was better, and would soon be around again. But it seems he took worse in the night. Captain Buddington came and told me he 'thought Captain Hall was dying.' I got up immediately, and went to the cabin and looked at him. He was quite unconscious—knew nothing. He lay on his face, and was breathing very heavily; his face was hid in the pillow. It was about half-past three o'clock in the morning that he died." (Blake 1874:162).

27   Hall was convinced that it was Bessels who was trying to poison him, and banned the doctor from his bedside from 29 October until 4 November (Henderson 2001:82).

28   Morton, who was sitting up with him, suddenly noticed that Hall had stopped breathing (Henderson 2001:87). Davis cites several instances during Hall's 1864–69 expedition when he had experienced severe cardiovascular and gastric attacks, and attacks, including severe vertigo, during the preparations immediately before the start of the North Pole expedition. He describes them as "sudden attacks, not unlike the one of which Hall died" (Davis 1876:178).

29   According to Henderson (2001:89–90), it was Tyson and Morton who laid out and dressed the corpse.

30   On the 11th according to Tyson (Blake 1874:162), but on the 10th according to Davis (1876:184).

31   The flag on the flag-staff above the observatory had been lowered to half-mast (Blake 1874: 165).

32   Bryan read a brief burial service (Davis 1876:184).

33   Tyson makes the prescient comment: "But with his death I fear that all hopes of further progress will have to be abandoned" (Blake 1874:165). By contrast, two weeks later Bessels remarked to Noah Hayes, "You know, Hayes, Captain Hall's death was the best thing that could have happened to this expedition." (Henderson 2001:94).

34   Dante's *Inferno*, Canto XXXII, terzina 13:37–39.

10: In the realm of darkness

1   Astronomically the upper edge of the sun should have disappeared at 0 h. 11 m. 6 on 17 October at the latitude of Polaris Bay. The adjustment for refraction is based on a barometric pressure of 29.9" and a temperature of –24.4°C. E.B.

2   Bessels is overlooking the Inughuit of northwest Greenland, who would later play a major role in the survival of him and his group.

3   This document reads as follows:

Consultation.
THANK-GOD HARBOR
November 13, 1871.
First consultation held between Messrs. S.O. Budington and E. Bessels. Through the mournful death of our noble commander, we feel compelled to put into effect the orders given us by the Department, viz.:

"Mr. Budington shall, in case of your death or disability, continue as the sailing and ice master, and control and direct the movements of the vessel; and Dr. Bessels shall, in such case, continue as the chief of the scientific department, directing all sledge-journeys and scientific operations. In the possible contingency of their non-concurrence as to the course to be pursued, then Mr. Budington shall assume the sole charge and command, and return with the expedition to the United States with all possible dispatch."

It is our honest intention to honor our dear flag, and to hoist her on the most northern part of the earth, to complete the enterprise upon which the eyes of the whole civilized world are raised, and to do all in our power to reach our proposed goal.

S.O. Budington.

Emil Bessels.

(Davis 1876: 227–28).

4   In other words during spring tides, when the tidal range was greatest.
5   Nathaniel Coffin.
6   On the night after the funeral for Hall, i.e., 11–12 November (Henderson 2001:95).
7   Carbonic acid, according to Loomis (1971:285).
8   According to Davis it appeared on 16 November (Davis 1876:231).
9   On his way to the tide gauge at 4.00 a.m. on the 20th, Siemens was blown off his feet and hurled about 39 m, ending up in water which had surged up through a crack (Davis 1876:233; Henderson 2001:96)
10   One of Bessels's ears was also frozen (Blake 1874:167).
11   This was a rope soaked in kerosene (Loomis 1971:282; Henderson 2001:97).
12   *Polaris* was warped ahead some 80 feet, where, 50 feet from the berg, it was hoped that she would be frozen in solidly, sheltered by the berg, but a safe distance from it (Davis 1876:241)
13   On 28 November (Davis 1876:243).
14   Also various other meats, vegetables (including green peas), apple and cherry pies with an excellent plum sauce, nuts, raisins and wine punch. The entire crew was invited to the lower cabin for the Thanksgiving dinner (Davis 1876:247).
15   Played by Noah Hayes (Davis 1876:248).
16   Peter Johnson.
17   But in the early hours of the 6th a severe blizzard had been blowing. Bessels became disoriented on his way to the observatory and wandered about until about 6.00 a.m. Thereafter a rubber-coated wire was strung from the ship to the observatory to act as a guide in poor visibility (Blake 1874:169; Davis 1876:256).

18 Friedrich Jamka, known as Big Fred (Davis 1876: 263).
19 This ingenious arrangement had been devised by Bessels (Davis 1876:262).
20 *Favus* occurred almost simultaneously in the Newfoundlanders. Only the pure-blooded animals were afflicted with this ailment; the smooth-haired ones were spared entirely. E.B.
21 I would recommend to future expeditions that they take dried horse meat with them for the dogs, since in the majority of cases pemmican might be too expensive. Each animal received a ration of 2 lbs., costing $1. E.B.
22 *Struwwelpeter* [Shock-haired Peter] was the title of an illustrated children's book by Heinrich Hoffmann (1845) which included ten stories, one of which, *Zappel-Philipp* [Fidgety Philip] deals with a young boy who would not sit still at table at meal-times, the ultimate result being that everything on the table landed on the floor.
23 And were rewarded with hot spiked punch, brewed by Bessels (Davis 1876:269).

11: The New Year

1 The diagram and the description of the apparatus have been taken from Schott's discussion of Hayes's observations, since we had to leave the pendulum behind when we began our retreat. Cf. *Physical observations in the arctic seas*, by Isaac I. Hayes, [Washington, DC: Smithsonian Institution, 1867], p. 29. E.B.
2 It was used for dressing leather and also used medicinally.
3 This is as close as Bessels comes in his book to outright criticism of Budington, whom he despised.
4 Emil Schumann.
5 An Ecuadorean volcano, 6,268 m in height, inactive at present.
6 And a sledge team (Blake 1874:172).
7 With 4 men and 12 dogs (Blake 1874:172).
8 They set off at 10.00 a.m. and were back by 4.00 p.m. (Blake 1874:172).
9 Johann Carl Friedrich Gauss (1777–1855) had established a magnetic observatory in Göttingen in 1833, and Göttingen time became the standard for magnetic observations worldwide.

12: Through darkness to the light

1 A. Bravais and V.C. Lottin were members of the French scientific expedition on board *La Recherche* (Captain Jean-Jacques-Louis Fabvre) in 1838–40. The expedition leader was Paul Gaimard. The expedition operated in northern Norway (Bossekop is on Altenfjord) and on Svalbard. For details see Marmier 1844–47.
2 The reference is to Adolf Erik Nordenskiöld's expedition to Svalbard on board *Polhem*, *Gladan* and *Onkel Adam*; the expedition wintered at Mosselbukta in northern Spitsbergen. For details see Kjellman 1875.
3 August Wijkander, geophysicist and astronomer.
4 Louis Palander, captain of *Polhem*.

5   Salvator Rosa (1615–1673), a Baroque Italian painter and artist whose work is generally considered unorthodox and extravagant.
6   Davis 1876:305–11.
7   Davis 1876:314–15.
8   With an unobscured horizon, we would have sighted the upper edge of the sun on 25 February at 11.30.4 a.m. The refraction, which lies at the base of this calculation, is 39.7′. EB
9   To mark the occasion, each man was given a half-bottle of wine and 100 cigarettes (Davis 1876:313–14).
10 The ivory gull (*Pagophila eburnean*) is a spectacular, pure white gull; it is an exclusively High Arctic species, circumpolar in distribution (Sale 2006:255).
11 *Alopex lagopus*; Bessels's reference to a white variety is based on the fact that there are two forms of this species, a white morph (grey-brown in summer, white in winter) and a blue morph (dark chocolate-brown in summer, pale blue-grey in winter) (Sale 2006:385)
12 In Greenland the ermine, also known as the stoat or short-tailed weasel, is found only in the coastal zones of extreme northern and northeastern Greenland (Sale 2006:401–2).
13 Two ptarmigan (probably the same birds) were also seen by Robert Krüger and Friedrich Anthing on an iceberg the same morning (Davis 1976:328).
14 From the arctic willow (*Salix arctica*), which adopts a creeping form, rarely exceeding a height of 15 cm.

13: THE SOUTHERN SLEDGE TRIP

1   Baron Jurij Bartolomej Vega (1754–1802), a Slovenian mathematician, physicist and artillery officer, published his *Thesaurus Logarithmorum Completus* [Complete treasury of logarithms] in 1794.
2   Alfred de Musset (1810–1857), French Romantic poet, dramatist and novelist, published his *Poésies nouvelles* in 1850.
3   The intention was to link up with Kane's survey (Davis 1876:332).
4   It reached the ship at 1.00 p.m. (Davis 1876:332).
5   Along the way Bryan tried practising with his whip and accidentally hit Bessels in the face, "which caused great pain and called forth some remarks of a significant character; but the doctor's equanimity was soon restored, and it was mutually agreed that whip-practice should be deferred to a more fitting occasion" (Davis 1876:346).
6   According to Henderson's mistaken version (2001:117), it was Hans who was sent back to the ship. On arrival he allegedly reported that the broken runner was caused by Bessels being too lazy to get off the sledge while tackling rough ice.
7   A children's harmonica.
8   On his return Bessels was aghast to find that his stock of 48 bottles of spirits had been stolen from his locker (Henderson 2001:120). Parry (2001:147) assessed the results of Bessels's trip south, namely the crucial achievement of tying his own and other surveys to those of Kane, as having little to show for his efforts.

14: Early Summer

1. John Herron.
2. The end product was sour and bitter, but the men seemed to enjoy it, and it was deemed to be beneficial (Davis 1876:357).
3. They had left three of them in a snow house, since the dogs could not haul more than four (Blake 1874:179). They found a fœtus in one of the cows and brought it back for Bessels (Davis 1876:353).
4. *Bubo scandiacus*; in terms of its breeding distribution in Greenland, it is confined to the extreme northwest and the northeast of the island (Sale 2006: 283–85).
5. During a trip to recover the three muskoxen left in the snow house by Joe and Hans (Blake 1874:179). They had travelled to the head of Newman's Bay to where a glacier discharged at its head. On their return Chester and Jamka were suffering from snow blindness (Davis 1876:355).
6. During his voyage on board *Albert* (Captain Hashagen) in 1869.
7. This was a serious attempt to get as far north as possible, i.e., not just a hunting trip (Davis 1876:356; Blake 1874:180).
8. They had killed eight on the first day they encountered the herd and, on following the herd, a further four next day (Blake 1874:181).
9. John Booth.
10. Some of the crew had complained to Budington since the Inuit were housed just forward of the men's quarters (Davis 1876:361).
11. By Robert Krüger on the 26th (Davis 1876:360).
12. In the interim, on 20 May one of the boats was sent to Cape Lupton on a sledge, this being the closest open water in which to launch it, with a view to attempting an advance northward by sea. A second one was transported to Cape Lupton on 24–25 May. Despite his conviction that Budington's plan for an expedition northward by boat so early in the season was bound to fail, Tyson had agreed to participate (Blake 1874:182).
13. Fossils of fairly large tropical trees (Davis 1876:372).
14. Near Cape Lupton (Davis 1876:360).
15. Karl Koldewey's expedition of 1869–70.
16. Hermann Siemens.
17. Robert Krüger.
18. Friedrich Anthing and Friedrich Jamka.
19. Gustav W. Lindquist.
20. Heinrich Hobby.
21. William Nindemann.
22. Peter Johnson.

15: The boat voyage north

1. Probably named after Paul Hegemann (1836–1913), captain of *Hansa* on the Second German North Pole Expedition, 1869–70.
2. 1 rod = 16½ feet.
3. Davis 1876:375–77.
4. A large spiral gastropod.
5. We had got into the habit of calling three small headlands north of Cape Lupton, the First, Second and Third capes. They remained unnamed on the map. E.B.
6. On 10 June (Blake 1874:186).
7. The boat was hauled up on the floe. Bessels was suffering severely from snow blindness (Blake 1874:186).
8. Over a distance of about 2½ miles (Blake 1874:679).
9. He and his crew had rowed 23 miles that day (Blake 1874: 675). Tyson was not greatly impressed by their vessel: "Chester's party are not very comfortable in their canvas boat. She is not fit for such rough sailing as we have to encounter; it is square fore and aft, and the slowest craft I ever saw. She would do for a party of children to paddle about on a calm and placid lake; but you might as well put an egg-shell in the way of an ice-pack as this patent contrivance" (Blake 1874:188).
10. The opening line was "We are going to the Pole" (Davis 1876:3678).
11. Chester and his men also launched their boat, but having covered only 2½ miles, they were forced to retreat some distance and haul the boat out onto the ice (Blake 1874:675–76).
12. Meanwhile Chester's party was "camping" under the overturned canvas boat with rubber blankets draped over the front (Blake 1874:676).
13. These men were Siemens and Krüger. Meanwhile Meyer buried a cylinder with a message recording Hall's death and the coordinates of the location, and then built a cairn over it (Blake 1874:187).
14. Chester and party had no cooking equipment or fuel and that evening heated some coffee by burning some worn-out boots (Blake 1874:676).
15. Siemens and Krüger (Blake 1874:676).
16. Tyson, however, was proposing to make an attempt to push north overland on foot, but could not persuade anybody to join him. But Budington, who was determined to take the ship south, told him that "if he got a chance he would not wait"; this put paid to Tyson's plans (Blake 1874:188).
17. Chester and party were forced to pack up and retreat 200–300 yards (Blake 1874:676).
18. He set off at 3.00 p.m. on the 30th (Blake 1874:676).
19. At 5.00 a.m. (Blake 1874:676). They relayed Budington's message (now more urgent) that both parties should return to the ship (Blake 1874:681).
20. According to Tyson the plan was to haul the boat ashore at a secure spot, and then to walk back to the ship; it took them almost 48 hours to reach a suitable ravine near Cape Sumner (Blake 18874:189).
21. Jamka and Krüger; they were followed by Meyer at 2.00 p.m. (Blake 1874:677).

22   The canvas boat was cached beside Tyson's boat (Blake 1874:191).

23   *Juglandaceae*: trees of the walnut family.

24   One of these branches was about 4½ inches in diameter and about 18 inches long (Blake 1874:678).

16: THE SUMMER

1   On the 25th there was a sudden increase in the inflow of water. Budington divided the crew into two watches, so that pumping could proceed continuously; once the water level had been reduced to a manageable level, pumping for only 2 to 4 minutes per hour kept the situation under control (Blake 1874:191).

2   On the Ellesmere Island coast, just south of Lady Franklin Bay.

3   On this occasion Tyson ruefully assessed the expedition's accomplishments—or lack of them: "What opportunities have been lost! And the expedition is to be carried back only to report a few geographical discoveries, and a few additional scientific facts. With patience we might have worked up beyond Newman Bay, and there is no telling how much farther. Someone will someday reach the Pole, and I envy not those who have prevented the *Polaris* having that chance" (Blake 1874:192).

4   It was erected by Emil Schumann (Loomis 1971:288).

5   This inscription is in English in Bessels's account.

6   Chester added this additional inscription (also in English in Bessels's account) on 27 July (Davis 1876:395).

7   A copper cylinder containing a brief history of the expedition, was also buried in the grave mound (Davis 1876:386).

8   The following vascular plants were observed: *Ranunculus nivalis* L. var.; *Papaver nudicaule* L.; *Vesicaria arctica* Br.; *Draba alpina* L. var. *algida*; *Draba alpestris* Br.; *Cochlearia fenestrata* Br.; *Lychnis apetala* L.; *Cerastium alpinum* L.; *Dryas octopetala*; *Potentilla nivea* L.; *Saxifraga oppositifolia* L.; *Taraxacum palustre* DC.; *Polygonum viviparum* L.; *Oxyria digyna* Campd.; *Salix arctica* Poll.; *Juncus biglumis* L.; *Eriophorum vaginatum* L.; *Alepocurus alpinus* Sm.; *Carex dioica* L.; *Dupontia psilosantha* Rupr.; *Poa arctica* Br.

Professor Asa Gray of Cambridge, Mass., was so kind as to verify the above identifications. The identification of *Dupontia* was entirely his. I should like to add a *Peducularis* sp. conditionally to the above list. Mauch and Bryan found a plant that from their description was probably *Pedicularis*. E.B.

9   *Saxifraga oppisitifolia*.

10   These swarms consisted mainly of *Chironomus polaris* Kirby. Among them Mr. C.R. von Osten-Sacken [Baron Carl-Robert von Osten-Sacken (1828–1906), Russian-German entomologist], who was so kind as to identify the diptera we had collected, found a new species: *Tipula bessels* n. sp. *Grau*. Thorax and abdomen with dark stripes; wings with dark brown stigma; antennae black; ovipositor of the female very short. Body length, male, 9–10 mm; female, 12–13 mm. Wing length, male, 12–14 mm; female, 15 mm. E.B.

11 *Bombus kirbyellus* Curtis. Among the Hymenopterae, Dr. A.S. Packard, Jr. [American entomologist, 1839–1905)], who identified some of our insects, found a new ichneumon [wasp]: *Microgaster hallii* n. sp. E.B.

12 *Laria rossii.* E.B.

13 *Colias boothii* Curtis. E.B.

14 *Podura humicola* Fabr. One of the *Poduridae* [springtails] that we collected was new to science. Packard named it *Isostoma besselsii* n. sp. E.B.

15 *Daphnia rectispina* Kr.; *Branchinecta groenlandica* Verrill. E.B.

16 Ruddy turnstone (*Arenaria interpres*). While Eurasian birds may migrate south as far as South Africa, the Greenland birds migrate south as far as Chile and Argentina (Sale 2006:222).

17 *Lycosa glacialis* Thor. Dr. T. Thorell of Genoa [Tord Thorell, 1830–1901], Swedish expert on spiders, was so kind as to undertake the identification of the spiders. Apart from the above-named species, our collection also included *Erigone psychrophila* Thor., *Erigone pensa* n. sp. Thor., *Trochosa* inc. spec. E.B.

18 Sea spiders.

19 The following list contains the names of those mammals which indubitably occur abundantly north of 81°N:

Ursus maritimus L., polar bear; *Canis lagopus* L. [now *Alopex lagopus*], arctic fox; *Phoca groenlandica* Müller, harp seal; *Phoca hispida* Erxleben [now *Pusa hispida*], ringed seal; *Phoca barbata* Müller [now *Erignathus barbatus*], bearded seal; *Lepus glacialis* Leach [now *Lepus arcticus*], arctic hare; *Myodes torquatus* Pallas [now *Dicrostonyx torquatus*], lemming; *Ovibos moschatus* Zimmermann, muskox.

By contrast the occurrence of the following mammals is problematic:

Mustela erminea L., ermine. Several times we encountered the tracks of a small mammal that had not been made by lemmings. They had probably been left by ermines.

Canis lupus L., wolf. Some of the seamen asserted that they had seen a wolf; others, however, thought this animal was a dog. The natives were inclined to identify various tracks that they encountered as wolf tracks.

Cervus tarandus L. [now *Rangifer tarandus*], reindeer. Joseph found a cast reindeer antler. Since traces of nomadic Eskimos were discovered in the vicinity of where it was found, the antler might have reached Polaris Bay through human means.

The following species of birds were observed:

Falco arcticus Holb. [now *Falco rusticolus*], gyrfalcon. Spotted by Hall during his sledge trip in the vicinity of Newman's Bay. During spring some specimens were also seen. Probably nests in the Far North.

Strix nyctea L. [now *Bubo scandiacus*], snowy owl. Seen by Hall near Newman's Bay and by some seamen during the spring. During the last days of July, Joseph and I heard the call of this bird in a ravine near the anchorage, but did not see it. On a later occasion I found freshly cast-up pellets that consisted of lemming bones and hair. In assuming that these pellets were produced by a snowy owl, I can scarcely be mistaken. The smallest of them was the size of buckshot. During the first days of August, I found a shed breast feather with brownish-black speckles. Probably nests in the vicinity of Newman's Bay.

Corvus corax L., raven. A solitary specimen of the bird was seen by Mrs. Hannah near the ship on 19 June. During our sojourn on the ice fields of Newman's Bay, we several times heard distant bird calls, which resembled the croaking of a raven. It is certainly not a permanent resident as it is at somewhat lower latitudes.

Emberiza nivalis Naum. [now *Plectrophenax nivalis*], snow bunting. Was spotted in flocks during fall. The first specimen appeared on 14 March. Nests near Polaris Bay; however, we found only young birds, but no nests.

Stresilas interpres L. [now *Arenaria interpres*], turnstone. Appeared in large flocks in late July and early August, consisting of adult males and females as well as young birds. Hence the bird nests in the Far North.

Tringa maritima Brünnich [now *Calidris maritima*], purple sandpiper. The only specimen of this bird was seen soon after the ship's arrival.

Tringa canutus L. [now *Calidris canutus*], knot. A single male specimen with extremely bright plumage was shot at the end of June. The circumstance that the bird was in full breeding plumage might indicate that this species of shorebird nests in the vicinity of our anchorage.

Calidris arenaria, L. [now *Calidris alba*], sanderling. Common in the vicinity of Polaris Bay. In mid-July two of its simple nests were found. One clutch contained three, the other four, of its extremely rare eggs.

Lagopus spp., ptarmigan. Probably a permanent resident. Fairly common. Nests in the Far North. No eggs found.

Sterna macroura Naum. [now *Sterna paradisaea*], arctic tern. Nests on the shores of Polaris Bay. Very common.

Xema sabini Sabine, Sabine's gull. Spotted at the beginning of July in company of *Sterna macroura*. Not common. Only two specimens of this bird were killed, a male and a female. Both possessed a brood patch. There was an egg with a soft, chalky shell in the female's oviduct.

Larus glaucus Brünnich [now *Larus hyperboreus*], glaucous gull. Not common, but undoubtedly nesting.

Larus eburneus Phipps [now *Pagophila eburnea*], ivory gull. Somewhat more common; also nesting.

Larus tridactylus L. [now *Rissa tridactyla*], kittiwake. Was encountered in flocks in Newman's Bay in June; less common near *Polaris*' anchorage. Nesting?

Stercorarius parasiticus Brünnich, parasitic jaeger. Was seen often and several specimens were killed. Probably nesting.

Stercorarius longicaudus Briss, long-tailed jaeger. Less common than the preceding species. Probably nesting.

Procellaria glacialis L. [now *Fulmarus glacialis*], northern fulmar. Sighted once during the fall. Non-nesting.

Bernicla brenta Pall. [now *Branta bernicla*], brent goose. Very common. Nesting.

Harelda glacialis L. [now *Clangula hyemalis*], oldsquaw. Rare, but nesting.

Somateria mollissima L., common eider. Fairly common. Nesting.

Somateria spectabilis L., king eider. In flights with the previous species; fairly rare. We were unable to determine if this bird nests north of the 81st parallel.

Uria grylle L. [now *Cepphus grille*], black guillemot. The commonest of all birds. Probably winters sporadically. The first individuals noted on 28 February. Nesting. However, the eggs were never collected.

Uria arra Naum. [now *Uria lomvia*], thick-billed murre. Fairly common and nesting.

Mergulus alle Sabine [now *Alle alle*], dovekie. Only two individuals seen in Newman's Bay. E.B.

20   But he admonished to start back immediately if the wind became northeasterly, since that would release the ship and he planned to take the first opportunity to start south (Davis 1876:404).

21   Despite these observations, it is in fact a bay.

17: SOUTHWARD

1   Many of the crew had not even realized that she was pregnant, deceived by her normal substantial girth and the loose-fitting fur clothing she wore (Henderson 2001:135).

2   On 12 August 1872.

3   Named "Tiger" (Davis 1876:407).

4   The isolated, steeply cliffed and flat-topped island in the North Sea, about 80 km northwest of Bremerhaven.

5   According to Henderson (2001:139–40), the ship had become beset as a result of Budington's orders to the helmsman while drunk.

6   And managed to pass Cape Constitution (Blake 1874:193).

7   This involved piling provisions, clothing and bags of coal on deck, ready to be thrown overboard onto the ice at a moment's notice (Blake 1874:193).

8   The stovepipe from the galley stove was led up through the upper cabin, providing a source of heat (Davis 1876:418).

9   Over several days, starting from 16 September. This house, measuring 27 by 24 feet, was built by Tyson, assisted by Morton, Bryan, Mauch and Joe (Davis 1876:418).

10   Despite his initial reluctance at drinking fresh blood and eating the meat raw (Davis 1876:421).

11   The ice-drift carried the ship past Rensselaer Harbour on 4 October (Blake 1874:195).

12   Two men had already been manning the pumps, but now the leak became much worse, gaining on the pumps (Blake 1874:197).

13   As, too, were all the boats.

14   Bessels presents a much better organized picture than the reality—which was a confused, panic-stricken operation. To quote Tyson: "[Budington] threw up his arms, and yelled out to 'throw everything on the ice!' Instantly everything was confusion, the men seizing everything indiscriminately, and throwing it overboard. These things had previously been placed upon the deck in anticipation of such a catastrophe; but as the vessel, by its rising and falling motion, was constantly breaking the ice, and as no care was taken how or where things were thrown, I

got overboard, calling some of the men to help me, and tried to move what I could away from the ship, so it should not be crushed and lost. . ." (Blake 1874:198).

A measure of the confusion that prevailed is provided by the following incident, as related by Tyson: "We did not know who was on the ice or who was on the ship; but I knew some of the children were on the ice, because almost the last thing I had pulled away from the crushing heel of the ship were some musk-ox skins; they were lying across a wide crack in the ice, and as I pulled them toward me to save them, I saw that there were two or three of Hans's children rolled up in one of the skins; a slight motion of the ice, and in a moment more they would either have been in the water and drowned in the darkness, or crushed beneath the ice" (Blake 1874:201).

15   They were Budington, Chester, Morton, Bessels, Bryan, Schumann, Odell, Coffin, Booth, Campbell, Mauch, Hayes, Siemens and Hobby (Davis 1876:439).
16   William Jackson.
17   John Herron.
18   Peter Johnson.
19   Gustav Lindquist.
20   William Nindemann.
21   Johan W.C. (Robert) Krüger.
22   Friedrich Jamka.
23   Friedrich Anthing.

18: On terra firma

1   It was at about this time that Tyson, marooned on the ice, spotted the ship about 8 or 10 miles away, travelling under sail and steam, smoke belching from her funnel. He hoisted a flag, and a piece of waterproof cloth—but to his amazement and intense disappointment, *Polaris* disappeared behind Littleton Island (Blake 1874:204).
2   Meyer's and Bryan's records, which were all placed on the ice, are listed in detail by Davis (1876:430–33).
3   To complicate the situation, the sun had disappeared for the winter on the 16th (Davis 1876:444).
4   They both wore polar-bear-skin pants (Davis 1876:445), still invariably worn by the Inughuit, the Inuit of northwest Greenland.
5   From previous encounters with Inuit during his career as a whaler, Budington had at least some knowledge of the Inuit language, sufficient when supplemented by sign language to make some communication possible (Davis 1976: 446).
6   Bessels fell through the ice twice and Mauch once (Davis 1876:447).
7   Claude Servais Mathias Pouillet (1790–1868), a professor of physics at the Sorbonne and a member of the Académie des Sciences, famous for having calculated the solar constant in 1837–38 as 1,228 watts/m^2.
8   Cumberland Sound, southern Baffin Island.
9   Unless his was a slightly later migration, he was thus the son of Qitdlarssuaq, who led the remarkable migration from southern Baffin Island to northwestern

Greenland in the mid-nineteeth century. During its progress north, the group was encountered by Commander Inglefield of HMS *Phoenix* at Dundas Harbour on 29 July 1853 (Inglefield 1853), and by Captain McClintock, in command of *Fox*, at Cape Horsburgh on 11 July 1858 (McClintock 1859:144). The migration is described in great detail by Mary-Rousselière (1991).

10   If they had arrived with Qidtlarssuaq, given McClintock's encounter with the group at Cape Horsburgh in 1858, they may well have reached Etah earlier than 1865, i.e., this may be an example of the Inuit's well-documented vagueness in determining the dates of events.

11   This incident was described by Ivalu (Davis 1876:463). It is discussed in some detail by Mary-Rousselière (1991:63–64).

12   The Prager Rattler typically has tan or yellow markings on its head and legs.

13   In the event that the word "Majuk" reveals itself to be a dialectal variant of *Maujôk*, which is extremely probable—naturally the final decision must be left to the linguist—this might provide very significant clues as to the former wanderings of the residents of Smith Sound. In the *Grønlandske Ordbog, omarbeidet af Sam. Kleinschmidt: udgiven paa Foranstaltning af Minsteriet for Kirke- og Underviisningsvæsen et og med det kongelige danske Videnskabernes Selskabs Understøtelse ved H.F. Jørgensen. Kjøbenhavn. L. Klein. 1871* one finds on p. 205: Maujôk = "an unknown animal." And in parentheses "formodenlig en Gnaver af Musefamilien." This unknown animal can scarcely be anything other than the lemming, whose occurrence in West Greenland is confined only to the extreme uninhabited north, where we discovered it. E.B.

14   It was during this period that an incident occurred, the description of which certainly represents the clearest example of Davis's whitewashing of relations during the expedition: "On the 7th [December] a serious violation of discipline occurred – the only one during the voyage. An engineer and a seaman quarreled about the possession of a shelf, and made use of threatening language and gestures" (Davis 1876:460).

15   *Kater* may mean either a tomcat or a hangover.

19: AN ETHNOGRAPHIC SKETCH

1   An apparent reference to Church of England missionary Adam Elliot's *Vocabulary of Mohawk* (1846). Reprint: *American Language Reprints*, Vol. 20, 2000.

2   Ross 1819.

3   Cyriax 1964.

4   Homer, *Odyssey*, Book 1, line 23.

5   French anthropologist Louis Laurent Gabriel de Mortillet (1821–1898). The quotation may be translated as: "Overall the head appears to be intermediate between the conventional representation of Mephistophele and the head of François I."

6   Hermann Welcker (1822–1897), anatomist and anthropologist, Professor, University of Halle.

7   Joseph Barnard Davis (1801–1881), English medical doctor and phrenologist.

8   Rudolf Carl Virchow (1821–1902), German medical doctor and pathologist, Professor, University of Berlin.
9   Adolf Pansch (1841–1887), medical doctor and anatomist, Associate Professor, University of Kiel, surgeon on board *Germania* on the Second German North Pole Expedition 1869–70.
10 Samuel Petrus Kleinschmidt (1814–1886), born in Greenland of German missionary parents, published his grammar of the Greenlandic language in 1851.
11 Hayes and Campbell, who happened to be visiting the settlement (Davis 1876:484–85).
12 On 3 May. The funeral was observed by Hayes and Campbell (Davis 1876: 484).
13 Rink 1875.
14 Parry 1824.

20: Further progress

1   Astronomically the upper edge of the sun should have disappeared at 00 18 min. 6 sec. on 25 October and reappeared at 11 11 2 on 16 February. For the day of its disappearance, I took a refraction of 38.4' into my calculations; for the day of its reappearance, by contrast 41.3'. E.B.
2   *Advance*, which Kane had abandoned at Rensselaer Harbour (Kane 1856).
3   In fact it is a multi-branched fiord.
4   Qalasirssuaq, alias Erasmus York, so named by Captain Erasmus Ommanney, joined the latter's ship HMS *Assistance* when she called at Cape York in 1850, and after spending the winter on board, was still on board when she returned to England in the fall of 1851. There he was known as Erasmus Augustine Kallihirua.
5   Captain Erasmus Ommanney (1814–1904) was captain of HMS *Assistance* in 1850–51, and led a complex sledging operation to search Prince of Wales Island for any traces of the missing Franklin expedition.
6   Nathaniel Coffin.
7   While he may have designed and fabricated the hinged joint, the wooden leg had first been made by James Rae, assistant surgeon on board HMS *North Star*, wintering at Wolstenholme Fiord in 1849–50 (Mary-Rousselière 1991:65) and later had been repaired by Hayes (Davis 1876:474).
8   50 lbs. of pork and 100 lbs. of hardtack, as well as 2 gallons of molasses (Davis 1876:476).
9   Bessels was accompanied by Jimmy and Avatok; the latter hoped to find a wife on Ellesmere Island, which Bessels was planning to reach after visiting the Humboldt Glacier (Davis 1876:479).
10 In fact a peninsula, rather than an island.
11 Bessels appears to have been completely unaware of how dangerous his action was. The murders of the American explorers Harry Radford and Thomas Street by Inuit near Bathurst Inlet in 1912 (Anderson 1972) and of the priests Father Jean-Baptiste Rouvière and Father Guillaume LeRoux on the Coppermine River in 1913 under almost identical circumstances, i.e., a Kabluna (a non-Inuit) threatening Inuit in

an attempt to persuade them to travel against their wishes (Moyles 1979), clearly demonstrate the risk Bessels was running.

12 Sharky later confessed that he had broken the sledge runner deliberately, since he did not wish to go any farther (Davis 1876:481).
13 Selachians: cartiliganous fish including sharks and rays.
14 Heinrich Hobby.
15 The longitude of which had been accurately determined during Kane's wintering there in 1853–54.
16 The dog spotted it first, and reached it first (Davis 1876:490).
17 En route Avatok had given Bryan a demonstration of his skill at catching dovekies out of the air, using a small net fastened to a long pole (Davis 1876:494–95).
18 This is an impressively accurate description. See Sale (2006:262).
19 Each man was allowed only 8 lbs. of personal belongings (Davis 1876:495).

21: The start of the ice floe drift

1 Dante's *Inferno*, Canto IX, l. 7.
2 Eight-man whaleboats (Nickerson 2002:58).
3 In fact, despite Tyson's pleadings the men had insisted on cooking and eating a meal and even, in some cases, changing their clothes, before they agreed to help (Blake 1876:203).
4 But only through the efforts of Tyson and Joe and 5 or 6 dogs which hauled the boat across the ice (Blake 1896:208). Both kayaks were also discovered by Joe, but since most of the men refused to try to recover them, only one was saved (Blake 1896:209).
5 Joe and family had a snow house of their own according to Tyson (Blake 1896:209).
6 German mile = 7.5 km.
7 He was laid up for three days (Blake 1876:218).
8 They had gobbled down some of the provisions (Nickerson 2002:70).
9 For Thanksgiving dinner Tyson, Hans and his wife and daughter shared 6 hardtack biscuits, 1 lb. of canned meat, a small can of corn, and a small can of mock-turtle soup—all mixed together and warmed over the lamp (Blake 1876:223–24).
10 Also on the 30th, Bessels, accompanied by Herron, Jackson, Johnson and Lindquist made a trip to the old hut to salvage the canvas, which was then used to line Hans's snow house (Blake 1874:225).
11 Along with a few mouthfuls of dried apples (Blake 1876:233).

22: Between hopelessness and optimism

1 The temperature on New Year's Day was –29°, the coldest day thus far during the ice-drift (Blake 1876:237).

2 With the exception of John Herron (English) and the black cook William Jackson (American), all the men were German and generally conversed in German, a language Tyson could not understand.

3 This would indicate a temperature of around −40° or colder.

4 Due to Meyer's consistent errors as to longitude, especially since he was also German the men believed him and repeatedly insisted that they should head east, hauling the boat across the ice, in order to reach Disko, where they knew a large depot had been left. Such an attempt would, of course, have been suicidal (Blake 1876:247; 255–56).

5 On 30 January, almost at the end of his tether under the stress of hunger, cold, and the responsibility he felt for keeping the entire group alive, despite the machinations and lack of cooperation from the men, Tyson wrote a sort of last will and testament:

"Now as death is liable to all men and especially to one in my situation I wish here to make a few remarks which, whether I live or die I sincerely hope will come to light. I here brand Sailing Master and Ice Pilot Sydney O. Budington as a villain, a liar, a thief, a coward and a drunkard and now has, I fear, added murder to his many crimes" (Nickerson 2002:95). This last accusation is to the effect that Budington had murdered Hall; a few days before Hall set off on his last sledge trip Budington had predicted: "the damn old son of a bitch will die soon..."

6 Tyson's account differs somewhat from this: the seal had stuck its head up through young ice, and it remained visible after Hans had shot it. To reach it he had "paddled" his kayak across the thin ice, which would not have borne his weight if he had tried walking (Blake 1876:270).

7 As with all cetaceans the "spout" is the moist exhalation from the blow-hole, the water vapour in the exhalation condensing in the cold air.

8 The group had initially had one of the ship's whaling harpoons, but one of the men had cut it down into a spear—useless for harpooning a narwhal (Blake 1876:275–76).

9 This name is no longer current, but must be in the area of the Henry Kater Peninsula, eastern Baffin Island.

10 Despite Tyson's warning the men all ate the liver of the bearded seal, and were all seriously sick for most of a week (Blake 1876: 298–99). Like the liver of the polar bear, this seal's liver is toxic due to the high concentration of Vitamin A.

11 On 11 March (Blake 1876:301).

12 *Phoca groenlandica*; also known as harp seals.

23: Spring on the floe

1 *Cystophora cristata*.

2 This is correct with regard to Baffin Bay, but in the Svalbard area, its range reaches 80° (Sale 2006:422).

3 According to Tyson 9 hooded seals were shot, but only 4 recovered (Blake 1876:307). Tyson calculated that they had enough meat for 18–20 days.

4   The work included fitting washboards to the top of the gunwales to prevent waves breaking inboard (Blake 1876:311).
5   This occurred in the early hours of 8 April (Blake 1876:313).
6   But it was discovered that Meyer had frozen some of his toes during his ordeal (Blake 1876:315–16), and his condition deteriorated rapidly thereafter.
7   This was the night of April 20–21 (Blake 1876:320).
8   On the afternoon of the 22nd (Blake 1876:323).
9   Having eaten his share of the bear meat, Meyer soon showed signs of recovering (Blake 1876:324).
10 Tyson later learned that this was the sealing vessel *Eagle* (Captain Jackman), of St. John's (Blake 1876:333).
11 In case another ship approached during the night they lit fires with seal blubber on the ice (Blake 1876:326).

24: THE SEALS

1   For the best comprehensive history of the Newfoundland seal hunt see Ryan 1994; and for one of the worst losses of life at the seal hunt, involving the crew of the *Newfoundland* in 1914, see Brown 1972.
2   The main species involved is the harp seal (*Phoca groenlandica*).
3   Bessels's account of the seal hunt is somewhat inaccurate. The mother seal would invariably take to the water as a sealer approached, and few adults were killed. The main quarry was the white-coat pup, which was killed for its skin and the underlying layer of blubber, known as a "sculp."
4   Here again Bessels is mistaken; it was the sculps, not the unskinned carcasses, that were piled up, to be picked up later by the ship; the piles, known as "pans," were then flagged. The skinned carcasses were abandoned.

25: SALVATION

1   Captain Isaac Bartlett, an uncle of Bob Bartlett, who accompanied Robert Peary on his various attempts at the North Pole, and who was captain of Vilhjalmur Stefansson's ill-fated *Karluk*, crushed by the ice to the north of Ostrov Vrangelya [Wrangel Island] in January 1914.
2   About 50 km northeast of the present-day town of Cartwright and only some 120 km north of the Strait of Belle Isle.
3   To Tyson's surprise and delight Captain Bartlett held a church service that evening (Blake 1876:334).
4   If the *Polaris* survivors had still been on the ice floe, they would almost certainly have perished in this gale (Blake 1876:334).
5   Misappropriation of each other's pans of sculps in this fashion was a common feature of the seal hunt throughout its history. For details see Brown 1972.
6   Several of them were in poor health; two of the men as well as Joe and Hannah were ill; Meyer and Tyson had swollen feet and ankles, and Meyer's hands were

badly frostbitten. Almost all were suffering from colds, sore throats and rheumatism (Blake 1876:335).
7. In southwestern Conception Bay.
8. On shore Tyson and Captain Bartlett met the American consul from Harbour Grace, who then telegraphed the news of their arrival to Mr. Molloy the consul in St. John's (Blake 1876:336).
9. *Frolic* was a side-wheel paddle steamer of 880 tons (Henderson 2001:227).
10. Pentecost or Whit.
11. Victoria Day.
12. Bessels is in error here; *Frolic* took Tyson and his party directly to Washington, arriving there on 5 June (Henderson 2001:227; Loomis 1971:297).

26: The boat voyage in arctic waters

1. On 2 June these were cached, along with Hall's extensive arctic library, the pendulum, the transit instrument and three chronometers, in a cairn about 400 meters ESE from the house (Davis 1876:499).
2. Also Nathaniel Coffin (Davis 1876:495).
3. On 3 June 1873.
4. Now *Calidris canutus*.
5. A soup made from dovekies (Davis 1876:500).
6. Although Bryan, Hayes and Mauch made themselves remarkably comfortable, in the lee of a large rock and on a bed of moss with one blanket below them and two on top (Davis 1876:501).
7. Emergency blue flares.
8. On 9 June (Davis 1876:502).
9. Iceland gulls—now *Larus glaucoides*.
10. *Branta bernicla*.
11. Bessels is distinguishing between *Anser alvifrons flavirostris* (the Greenland white-fronted goose) and *A. a. gambeli* (the Pacific white-fronted goose), which breeds in the Mackenzie Delta and farther west (Sale 2006: 92).
12. Chimney swift.
13. Barn swallow.
14. Sand martin; now *Riparia riparia*.
15. Theodor von Heuglin, 1872–73. *Reisen nach dem Nordpolarmeer*. Braunschweig: Georg Westermann.
16. Erik Ulve, captain of *Samson* on a walrus-hunting voyage (Holland 1994:283).
17. Barn swallow.
18. Robert Ridgway (1850–1929), American ornithologist and artist, curator of birds at the Smithsonian Institution.
19. The reference is to the lotus *(Nelumbo nucifera)*.

20 Bryan's observations at midnight revealed a latitude of 76°02'30"N (Davis 1876:507).
21 Ross's gull.
22 Pomarine jaeger.
23 On 19 June.
24 One plank had been stove when the boat was caught in a nip before her crew could haul it up onto the ice (Davis 1876:510).

27: WHALING

1   The ship's position was 75°38'N; 65°35'W (Davis 1876:512).
2   Shetlanders and Orkneymen would not have been Gaelic speakers, but would have spoken a dialect of English influenced by Norn, the language spoken in these islands until gradually replaced by English after they became Scottish in 1468–69.
3   Captain Allen had his carpenter repair it, however. Arriving with the ship at Dundee, the owner, Mr. Lockhart, presented it to the Smithsonian Institution. It was transported to the United States by the steamer *Georgia* of the State Line free of charge, and on 10 May 1876 it was exhibited at the International Exhibition in Philadelphia alongside Kane's boat, *Faith*, as part of the Arctic collection exhibited by the United States Naval Observatory (Davis 1876:514–15).
4   Initially the ship followed the Devon Island coast until past Cape Warrender, then crossed to Admiralty Inlet (Davis 1876:515).
5   Albert Markham, R.N. (1841–1918), who was on board *Arctic* to gain experience prior to serving on board HMS *Alert* during Nares's expedition of 1875–76. He reported that Bessels was "the only man of scientific attainments in the ship, and the only man besides Hall and Chester, who felt any enthusiasm for the objects of the voyage" (Markham 1875:188). He further noted that while Budington was paid $120 per month, Bessels was initially offered only $75. He asked for an assistant, to whom he proposed handing over his salary. At this his salary was raised to $100 per month.
6   A tragedy by William Shakespeare, written between 1605 and 1608.
7   On 10 July off Cape Graham Moore, Markham and Chester contributed to one of these successes: hiking across the ice with a harpoon gun, they managed to kill a whale which had already been harpooned but was seeking safety among the ice (Markham 1874: 202).
8   This is a translation from Lindeman's German translation of Cornelis Gijsbertsz Zorgdrager's original Dutch version. See Lindeman 1869:55.
9   The description which follows is of a bowhead whale (*Balaena mysticetus*).
10 The orca or killer whale (*Orcinus orca*)
11 Markham and Bessels had been taking the specific gravity of the sea water every two hours, but on 13 July their hydrometer broke. Next day Bessels manufactured a replacement from a small bottle, a quill and a little mercury—which turned out to be a great success (Markham 1874:204).
12 *Silene viscaria.*

13   This is possible but seems unlikely. The common starling (*Sturdus vulgaris*) is a European species, introduced to North America (in Central Park, New York) only in 1890 and now common throughout North America.

14   In striking contrast to Bessels non-judgmental comments, Markham wrote, "They seem to me about the lowest specimens of humanity I have ever come across, not excepting the Solomon Islanders" (Markham 1874:213).

15   On the east side of the entrance of Admiralty Inlet.

16   From streams flowing down the cliffs (Markham 1874: 218).

17   Chester, Markham and Dr. Graham were in the same boat. Markham describes his misadventure as follows: "The dingy failed to get clear of the brute's tail, which it had thrown up out of the water on receiving the contents of our gun and which, descending with tremendous violence, just caught the gunwale of our boat, knocking me over the stern. Before coming to the surface, I imagined the dingy had been smashed to pieces, which would have been rather a bad case for us, as the other boats were some way off, and, also, fast to fish, and no loose boat being near us, and with the temperature of the water only a few degrees above freezing point, I don't think that I for one could have kept up long, accoutered as I was in a heavy monkey jacket and sea boots. However, on rising to the surface, I had the satisfaction of seeing the dingy a couple of boats' lengths off, and the doctor (who had taken to the water, imagining that the tail was coming right down upon us) and myself were soon hauled in. If the boat had been one foot nearer the fish she would most assuredly have been dashed to pieces and we should all have been killed before having time to jump overboard" (Markham 1874:223–24).

18   Parry had wintered here in *Fury* and *Hecla* in 1824–25. For details see Parry 1826.

19   If Captain Adams had achieved this, his would have been the first ship to negotiate Fury and Hecla Strait.

20   And which they had named Somerset House (Ross 1835).

21   There is only one species of Orca.

22   Hermann Siemens.

23   The second branch of the antler.

24   The distance involved was about 5½ miles. To make the task easier they quartered the animal; Siemens took the hind quarters and the other two a fore quarter each (Markham 1975:253).

25   *Arctic* was now a full ship and Captain Adams had decided to head for home (Markham 1875:255).

28: THE SEARCH

1   The US government paid the Newfoundland owners $60,000 for the ship. Built in Québec in 1871, she was a strongly built vessel of 350 tons, with engines of 1200 hp, rigged as a barkentine (Blake 1874:344–47).

2   The cabin was enlarged and two deck-houses were added to accommodate the number of officers involved (Blake 1874:344).

3   *Juniata* was a screw-steamer (Blake 1874:342).

4   On board, serving as ice pilot, was Captain James Budington, uncle of Sydney Budington (Blake 1874:342).

5   Following a visit by the Secretary of the Navy, George Robeson, on the 12th and a brief sortie to the buoys off Sandy Hook to correct the compass deviation on the 12th–13th (Blake 1874:356).

6   Wilhelm Nindemann was clearly a glutton for punishment; having survived the ice-floe drift, and this search expedition on board *Tigress*, he would later serve on board the ill-fated *Jeannette* and would be one of the only two survivors from De Long's boat, and even thereafter, helped Melville in the search for De Long's party (see note 11 below).

7   Significantly, the ship's engineer, George W. Melville, would later (in 1878–81) serve in the same capacity on board the ill-fated *Jeannette*, and, having reached the Lena Delta safely, would mount a search for the only other boat's crew which reached land, but of which only two men survived, one of them being Nindemann (Melville 1884).

8   Abeam of Sukkertoppen (now Manniitsoq) (Blake 1874:362).

9   A dance was held on shore in honour of the American visitors (Blake 1874:363).

10 At Upernavik, arriving on 10 August (Blake 1874: 364).

11 George W. De Long, who would later command the ill-fated USS *Jeannette* which, having become beset in the ice near Wrangel Island, drifted north and west to a point north of the New Siberian Islands. De Long died of starvation and exposure after reaching the Lena delta. For further details see De Long 1884.

12 Lt. Charles Chipp, who also served on board USS *Jeannette*, and along with the crew of one of the three boats heading south across the Laptev Sea, disappeared in September 1881 (De Long 1884).

13 Evidently a small island off the Greenland coast and not the much larger Canadian island on the opposite side of Baffin Bay; the name has not survived.

14 *Tigress* had arrived only on the previous day from Upernavik (Blake 1874:364).

15 Greer and Tyson had had an exchange of letters on the topic, Tyson affirming that the separation from *Polaris* had not occurred off Northumberland or Hakluyt islands but rather off Littleton Island (Blake 1874:365).

16 With Joe acting as interpreter (Blake 1874:353.)

17 But Tyson spotted one of the hawsers by which she had been moored, one end made fast to a rock, the other end trailing in the water (Blake 1874:366).

18 He found that the interior of the hut had been thoroughly trashed, but it was not clear whether this was the work of the *Polaris* party or of the Inuit (Blake 1874:354). Tyson salvaged books, tools and manuscripts, which he gave to Greer (Blake 1874:366).

19 She had put to sea on the 16th; on the way south a fire in a coal bunker had caused some anxiety but was quickly extinguished (Blake 1874:368–69). Then on the 18th a bear was sighted and shot; roast bear was served for dinner. And that evening a collision with an iceberg in thick fog was narrowly averted (Blake 1874:370).

20 Here too, on two evenings in succession the Americans were invited to a dance on shore (Blake 1874:372).

21   He had learned at Godhavn that *Arctic* and 8 other whalers had gone north, and hence there was a high probability that one of them would have picked up the *Polaris* party (Blake 1874:355).

22   Having experienced a very severe gale on the 1st and 2nd (Blake 1874:374–75).

23   This deposit became of crucial importance in the manufacture of aluminum, and was a major factor in prompting the occupation of Greenland by the United States during World War 2. The mine was abandoned in 1987 and the town soon afterward.

24   Karl Ludwig Giesecke (1761–1833) led an extended geological expedition to southwestern Greenland from 1806 until 1813, investigating the geology from Cape Farewell as far north as Tasiusaq (Holland 1971:172).

25   Having loaded 190 tonnes of coal (Blake 1874:381). Having experienced several days of severe gales and fog, *Tigress* reached St. John's on 16 October, to learn for the first time that Budington, Bessels and party were safe. On 9 November *Tigress* reached New York (Blake 1874:386).

29: Homeward bound

1   Northern tip of Brodeur Peninsula, Baffin Island.

2   From an iceberg rather than from a glacier (Markham 1874:272).

3   Common linnet (*Carduelis cannabina*), normally confined to Europe, western Asia and northern Africa.

4   Lapland longspur (*Calcarius lapponicus*), occurring in both Baffin Island and west Greenland (Sale 2006:326–28).

5   *Motacilla alba*—generally a Eurasian species, although it does occur in Iceland and in a small area of east Greenland (Sale 2006:295–96).

6   Bessels is almost certainly mistaken; Barra is the southernmost of the larger islands of the Outer Hebrides, whereas the small, rocky neighbor of Rona is Sula Sgeir.

Epilogue: Motive for Murder

1   Loomis 1971.
2   Ibid., 338.
3   Henderson 2001:282.
4   Loomis 1971:344.
5   Ibid., 345.
6   Ibid., 353.
7   Ibid., 348–49.
8   Potter 2015.
9   Cooper 2004.
10   Ibid., 159.
11   Ibid.

APPENDICES

1. Full title: *Instructions for the Expedition towards the North Pole from Hon. Geo. M. Robeson, Secretary of the Navy.* Washington: Government Printing Office, 1871. Bessels included these instructions in English.
2. Henderson 2001:229.
3. Ibid., 270.
4. Loomis 1971:304.
5. Henderson 2001:110–11.
6. Ibid., 140.
7. Loomis 1971:302.
8. Henderson 2001:263.
9. Loomis 1971:305.
10. Parry 2001:275.
11. See p. 217.
12. Loomis 1971:329–30.
13. *Allgemeine Zeitung des Judentums,* 1888.
14. Bessels 1867.
15. *Petermanns Geographische Mitteilungen* 1869.
16. See p. 563.
17. US Navy Department 1876.
18. Parry 2001:310.
19. *Allgemeine Deutsche Biographie* 1902.
20. *Sidney Morning Herald* 1875.
21. *Deutsche Rundschau für Geographie und Statistik* 1882.
22. Letter, Emil Bessels/Franz Boas, Washington/New York, 13 January 1886. Franz Boas Papers, American Philosophical Society, Philadelphia, PA.
23. Loomis 1971:52.
24. Harper 2013.
25. Loomis 1971: 170.
26. Harper 2013.
27. Loomis 1996b.
28. Harper 2005.
29. Davis 1996.
30. Harper 2005.
31. Nickerson 2002.
32. Ibid..
33. Young 1876; 1879.
34. Nickerson 2002:162.
35. Gilder 1881; Klutschak 1987.
36. Nickerson 2002:162.

37 Karpoff 2005.
38 McClintock 1859.
39 Hall 1865.
40 Nourse 1879.
41 Ibid..
42 Davis 1876; Loomis 1971; 1996a; Henderson 2001; Parry 2001.
43 Blake 1874:77.
44 De Bray 1992:171.
45 Ibid., 184–85.
46 Blake 1874:99.
47 Tyson 1879.

Bibliography

Allgemeine Deutsche Biographie. 1902. Bessels, Emil, *Allgemeine Deutsche Biographie.*

Anderson, I.S. 1972. Bathurst Inlet patrol, *The Beaver* 302(4):20–25.

Anonymous. 1873. *Annual report of the Secretary of the Navy on the operations of the Department for the year 1873.* Washington DC: Government Printing Office.

Barr, W. 1991. *Back from the brink: The road to muskox conservation in the Northwest Territories* (Komatik Series 3). Calgary: Arctic Institute of North America.

Barrow, J. 1818. *A chronological history of voyages into the Arctic regions: Undertaken chiefly for the purpose of discovering a North-east, North-west, or polar passage between the Atlantic and Pacific.* London: John Murray.

Beaglehole, J.C., ed. 1961. *The journals of Captain James Cook on his voyages of discovery.* Vol. II: *The voyage of the Resolution and Adventure, 1772–1775.* Cambridge: Hakluyt Society.

Beattie, O. and J. Geiger. 1989. *Frozen in time: Unlocking the secrets of the Franklin expedition.* Saskatoon: Western Producer Prairie Books.

Bessels, E. 1867. Studien über die Entwicklung der Sexualdrüsen bei den Lepidopteren, *Zeitschrift für wissenschaftliche Zoologie* 17:545–64.

———. 1879. *Die Amerikanische Nordpol-Expedition.* Leipzig: Wilhelm Engelmann.

Blake, E.V. 1874. *Arctic experiences: Containing Capt. George E. Tyson's wonderful drift on the ice-floe . . .* New York: Harper and Bros.

Brown, C. 1972. *Death on the ice: The great Newfoundland sealing disaster of 1914.* Toronto: Doubleday.

Cooper, E.S. 2004. *Vinnie Ream: An American sculptor.* Chicago: Academy Chicago Publishers.

Cormack, W.E. 1928. *Narrative of a journey across the island of Newfoundland in 1822.* London: Longmans, Green.

Crantz, D. 1820. *The history of Greenland: Including an account of the mission carried on by the United Brethren in that country.* London: Longman, Hurst, Rees, Orme & Brown.

Cyriax, R.J. 1939. *Sir John Franklin's expedition: A chapter in the history of the Royal Navy*. London: Methuen.

———. 1964. The voyage of H.M.S. *North Star, 1849–50, Mariner's Mirror* 50(4):3307-318.

Davis, C.H., ed. 1876. *Narrative of the North Polar Expedition, U.S. Ship* Polaris, *Captain Charles Francis Hall commanding*. Washington D.C.: Government Printing Office.

Davis, R.C. 1996. Ebierbing. In R.C. Davis, ed.,*Lobsticks and stone cairns: Human landmarks in the Arctic*, Calgary: University of Calgary Press, pp. 52–54.

De Bray, E.F. 1992. *A Frenchman in search of Franklin. De Bray's arctic journal 1852–1854*, W. Barr, trans and ed. Toronto: University of Toronto Press.

De Long, G.W. 1884. *The voyage of the Jeannette. The ship and ice journals of George W. De Long..., 1879–1881*. Boston: Houghton Mifflin.

Deutsche Rundschau für Geographie und Statistik. 1882. Dr. Emil Bessels, *Deutsche Rundschau und Statistik* 4:139–40.

Freeden, W. von. 1869. Die wissenshaftlichen Ergebnisse der ersten deutschen Nordfahrt, *Petermann's Geographische Mittheilungen* 15: 2011–219.

Geiger, J. and A. Mitchell. 2015. *Franklin's lost ship. The historic discovery of HMS* Erebus. Toronto: HarperCollins.

Gilder, W.H. 1881. *Schwatka's search. Sledging in the Arctic in quest of the Franklin records*. New York: Charles Scribner's Sons.

Hall, C.F. 1865. *Arctic researches and life among the Esquimaux*. New York: Harper & Bros.

Harper, K. 2005. Ebierbing, Hannah (Tookoolito) and Joe. In M. Nuttall, ed., *Encyclopedia of the Arctic*. New York and London: Routledge, I:520–521.

———. 2013. Inuit graves in Groton, Connecticut, *Taissumani/Around the Arctic*, 8 March 2013.

Hayes, I.I. 1860. *An arctic boat journey in the autumn of 1854*. Boston: Brown, Taggard and Chase.

———. 1867. *The open polar sea: A narrative of a voyage of discovery towards the North Pole*. New York: Hurd and Houghton.

Henderson, B. 2001. *Fatal North: Adventure and survival aboard USS* Polaris. *The first US expedition to the North Pole*. New York: New American Library.

Hegemann, P.F. 1993. Journal of Captain Friedrich Hegemann of the ship *Hansa* during the German expedition to East Greenland 1869–1870, *Polar Geography and Geology* 17: 264–329.

Holland, C. 1994. *Arctic exploration and development, c. 500 B.C. to 1915: An encyclopedia*. New York & London: Garland Publishing.

Inglefield, E.A. 1853. *A summer search for Sir John Franklin with a peep into the polar basin*. London: Thomas Harrison.

Jérémie, N. 1720. Relation du détroit et de la baie d'"Hudson. In J.F. Bernard, ed.,*Recueil de voyages du Nord*, Amsterdam, No. 6. (Reprinted in *Bulletin de la société historique de Saint Boniface*, 1912. And in English as *Twenty years of*

        York Factory, 1694–1714, R. Douglas and J.N. Wallace, eds. Ottawa: Thorburn and Abbott, 1926.

Kane, E.K. 1854. *The U.S. Grinnell expedition in search of Sir John Franklin. A personal narrative*. New York: Harper and Bros.

———. 1856. *Arctic explorations; the second Grinnell expedition in search of Sir John Franklin, 1853, "54, "55.* Philadelphia: Childes & Peterson.

Karpoff, J.M. 2005. Hall, Charles F. In M. Nuttall, ed., *Encyclopedia of the Arctic*. New York and London: Routledge, pp. 826–27.

Kjellman, F.R. 1875. *Svenska polar-expeditionen år 1872–1873 under ledning af A.E. Nordenskiöld*. Stockholm: P.A. Norstedt.

Klutschak, H. 1987. *Overland to Starvation Cove: With the Inuit in search of Franklin 1878–1880*, W. Barr, trans. and ed. Toronto: University of Toronto Press.

Koldewey, K. 1871: Die Erste Deutsche Nordpolar-expedition im Jahre 1868. *Petermann's Geographische Mittheilungen, Ergänzungsheft* 28. Gotha: Justus Perthes Verlag. Reprint 1993: Gotha: Justus Perthes Verlag.

———. 1874. *The German Arctic Expedition of 1869–70, and narrative of the wreck of the "Hansa" in the ice*. London: Samson Low, Marston, Low and Searle.

Krause, R.A. 1992. Die Gründungsphase deutscher Polarforschung 1865–1875, *Berichte zur Polaforschung* 114. Bremerhaven: Alfred-Wegener-Institut für Polar- und Meeresforchung.

———. 1997. Zweihundert Tage im Packeis. Die authentischen Berichte der "Hansa"–Männer der deutschen Ostgrönland-Expedition, *Schriften der deutschen Schiffahrtsmuseum* 46.

Laws, J. 1967. Dr. James Laws' journal of the Kane relief expedition, *Polar Notes* 7:1–24.

Lindeman, M. 1869. Die arktische Fischerei der deutschen Seestädte 1620–1868 in vergleichender Darstellung, *Petermanns Geographische Mittheilungen, Ergänzungsband* VI, No. 26.

Loomis, C. 1971. *Weird and tragic shores. The story of Charles Francis Hall, explorer.* New York: Alfred A. Knopf.

———. 1996a. Charles Francis Hall (1821–1871). In R.C. Davis, ed., *Lobsticks and stone cairns*. Calgary: University of Calgary Press, pp. 49–51.

———. 1996b. Ebierbing (ca. 1837–1881). In R.C. Davis, ed., *Lobsticks and stone cairns*. Calgary: University of Calgary Press, pp. 52–54.

McClintock, F.L. 1859. *The voyage of the "Fox" in the arctic seas: A narrative of the discovery of the fate of Sir John Franklin and his companions*. London: John Murray.

McGoogan, K. 2008. *Race to the Polar Sea: The heroic adventures of Elisha Kent Kane*. Berkeley CA: Counterpoint.

Markham, A.H. 1874. *Whaling cruise to Baffin's Bay and the Gulf of Boothia. And an account of the rescue of the crew of the "Polaris."* London: Sampson Low, Marston, Low & Searle.

———. 1878. *The great frozen sea: A personal narrative of the voyage of the "Alert" during the Arctic expedition of 1875–6*. London: Daldy, Isbister & Co.

Markham, C.R. 1881. *The voyages of William Baffin, 1612–1622*. London: Hakluyt Society.

Marmier, X. 1844–47. *Voyage de la Commission scientifique du nord, en Scandinavie, en Laponie, au Spitzberg et au Feröe, pendant les années 1838,1839 et 1840, sur la corvette la Recherche . . . Relation du voyage*. Paris: Arthur Bertrand.

Mary-Rousselière, G. 1991. *Qidtlarssuaq: The story of a polar migration*. Winnipeg: Wuerz Publishing.

Melville, G.W. 1884. *In the Lena delta: A narrative of the search for Lieut.-Commander De Long and his companions*. Boston: Houghton-Mifflin.

Moyles, R.G. 1979. *British law and Arctic men: The celebrated 1917 murder trials of Sinnisiak and Uluksuk, first Inuit tried under White man's law*. Saskatoon: Western Producer Prairie Books.

Murphy, D.T. 2002. *German exploration of the polar world, 1870–1940*. Lincoln NE: University of Nebraska Press.

Nares, G.S. 1878. *Narrative of a voyage to the polar sea during 1875–6 in H.M. ships* Alert *and* Discovery. London: Sampson Low, 2 vols.

Nickerson, S. 2002. *Midnight to the North: The untold story of the Inuit woman who saved the* Polaris *expedition*. New York: Jeremy Tarcher/Putnam.

Nordenskiöld, N.A.E. 1872. Account of an expedition to Greenland in the year 1870. *Geological Magazine* 9:289–306; 355–68; 409–27; 449–63; 516–24.

———. 1881. *The voyage of the Vega around Asia and Europe*. London: Macmillan, 2 vols.

Nourse, J. E., ed. 1879. *Narrative of the second arctic expedition commanded by Charles F. Hall*. Washington DC, Government Printing Office.

Ostermann, H., ed. 1944. Dagbøker av Nordmenn på Grønland før 1814. 2. Andreas Bruuns og Aaron Arctanders dagbøker fra undersøkelsesreisen i Julianehaab district 1777–1779, *Norges Svalbard-og Ishavs-Undersøkelser, Meddelelser* 58.

Parry, R. 2001. *Trial by ice: The true story of murder and survival on the 1871* Polaris *expedition*. New York: Ballantine Books.

Parry, W.E. 1824. *Journal of a second voyage of the discovery of a North-West Passage from the Atlantic to the Pacific performed in the years 1821–22–23*. London: John Murray.

———. 1826. *Journal of a third voyage for the discovery of a North-West Passage from the Atlantic to the Pacific, performed in the years 1824–25*. London: John Murray.

Petermanns Geographische Mitteilungen. 1869. Rückkehr der Rosenthal'schen Dampfer "Bienenkorb" und "Albert" und der Lamont'schen Expedition..., *Petermanns Geographische Mitteilungen* 15: 350–55.

Pingel, P.C. 1841. "Om sænkning af Grønlands vestkyst," *Skandinaviske naturforskeres Møde. Forhandlingar* 2:353–63.

Potter, R. 2015. A motive for the murder of Charles Francis Hall, *Visions of the North*. http://visions.north:blogspot.ca/2015/07/a-motive-for-murder-of-charles-francis.html.

Purchas, S. 1905–7. *Haklutus posthumus* or *Purchas his pilgrims: Contayning a history of the world in sea voyages and lands travels by Englishmen and others*. Glasgow: James MacLehose & Sons, 20 vols. (First published 1625).

Rink, H. 1858. On the supposed discovery by Dr. E.K. Kane, U.S.N. of the north coast of Greenland, and of an open polar sea..., *Journal of the Royal Geographical Society* 28:272–87.

———. 1875. *Tales and traditions of the Eskimo*. R. Brown, trans. Edinburgh/London: Blackie & Sons.

Ross, J. 1819. *A voyage of discovery, made under the orders of the Admiralty, in His Majesty's Ships* Isabella *and* Alexander, *for the purpose of exploring Baffin's Bay, and inquiring into the probability of a Northwest Passage*. London: John Murray.

———. 1835. *Narrative of a second voyage in search of a North-West Passage, and of a residence in the arctic regions during the years 1829, 1830, 1831, 1832, 1833*. London: A.W. Webster.

Ryan, S. 1994. *The ice hunters: A history of Newfoundland sealing to 1914*. St. John's: Breakwater.

Sale, R. 2006. *A complete guide to arctic wildlife*. London: Christopher Helm.

Scoresby, W. Jr. 1820. *An account of the arctic regions with a history and description of the northern whale fishery*. London: Constable, 2 vols. Reprint: Newton Abbott: David & Charles, 1969.

———. 1823. *Journal of a voyage to the northern whale fishery, including researches and discoveries on the east coast of West Greenland, made in the summer of 1822, in the ship Baffin of Liverpool*. London: Constable.

Sidney Morning Herald. 1875. The wreck of the *Saranac, Sidney Morning Herald*, 15 September 1875.

Smith, J, ed. 1830. Journal of a voyage to Spitzbergen and the east coast of Greenland in His Majesty's Ship *Griper, Edinburgh New Philosophical Journal, New Series* 9:1–30.

Solov'ev, M.M. 1934. *Ber na Novoy Zemle*. Leningrad: Izdatel'stvo Akademii Nauk.

Stanton, W. 1975. *The Great United States Exploring Expedition*. Berkeley CA: University of California Press.

Steller, G.W. 1774. *Beschreibung von dem Lande Kamschatka. Reise von Kamschatka nach Amerika. Ausführlicher Beschreibung von sonderbaren Meerthieren*. Frankfurt/Leipzig: J.G. Fleischer.

Tyson, G.E. 1879. *The cruise of the Florence; or Extracts from the journal of the Preliminary Arctic Expedition of 1877–"78*. Washington D.C.: James J. Chapman.

US Navy Department. 1876. *Scientific results of the United States Arctic Expedition. Steamer* Polaris, *C.F. Hall commanding.* Vol. I. *Physical observations.* Washington D.C.: Government Printing Office.

Villarejo, O.M., ed. 1965. *Dr. Kane's voyage to the polar lands.* Philadelphia: University of Pennsylvania Press.

Wamsley, D.W. 2009. *Polar Hayes: The life and contributions of Isaac Israel Hayes, M.D.* Philadelphia: American Philosophical Society.

Weddell, J. 1825. *A voyage towards the South Pole in the years 1822–24.* London: Longman, Hurst, Rees, Orme, Brown and Green.

Wrangel, F. von. 1840. *Narrative of an expedition to the polar sea in the years 1820, 1821, 1822 & 1823.* London: James Madden.

Young, A. W. 1876. *Cruise of the "Pandora." From the private journal kept by Allen Young.* William Clowes & Sons.

———. 1879 *The two voyages of the "Pandora" in 1875 and 1876.* London: Edward Stanford.

INDEX

A

Aasiaat, 675n6
actinometric observations, 353, 388
Adamello-Presenella Mountains, *xxvi*
Adams, Captain William, 499
    heads for home, 604n225
    quotes from *Coriolanus*, 499
    quotes from *Julius Caesar*, 500
    quotes from *Macbeth*, 510
    shares his cabin with Chester, 502
Admiralty Inlet, 512, 604n15
Advance, 10, 117, 118, 567n2, 583n4
    abandoned at Rensselaer Harbour, 598n2
Agassiz, Jean L.R., 584n15
Akunnat, 572n15
Albert, *xxvii*, 573n30, 590n6
Aleutian Islands
    lamps from, 574n45
Alexander, 113, 577n5
Allen, Captain William, 496
    repairs survivors' boat, 603n3
Allison Bay, 523
Alopecurae, 322
alpine rose, 90
Alttheater, 577n50
American Geographical Society, 11
    special meeting of, 25, 569n38
American National Museum, 574n45
Ammen, Daniel, 569n27
Andromeda tetragona, 92
    as potential fuel, 212
Angulok, 357
Anoetok, 405, 406
Antarctic, 569n40

Anthing, Friedrich, *xiii*
    sees ptarmigan, 589n13
    assigned to *George Robeson*, 302, 590n18
    member of ice floe party, 346, 596n23
antiscorbutics, 246, 385
Arctander, Aaron, 581n16
Arctic, *xxiii*
    a full ship, 604n25
    crew of, 502
    meets *Ravenscraig*, 499, 533
    season's catch of, 533
    starts for home, 531
    takes half the shipwrecked party aboard, 500
Arctic (USS), 579n20
Arctic Circle, 67, 125, 441, 534
Arctic Highlanders, 364
Arctic Ocean, *xxvi*, 566n7, 579n11
arctic fox, 352, 359–60, 426, 449, 593n19
    den of, 360
    depredations of, 182
    food sources of, 360
    killed and eaten, 427
    meat of, 361
    tracks of, 281
    trapped, 269, 428
    two morphs of, 589n11
arctic hare, 268, 404–5, 593n19
    shot, 292
    tracks of, 180
arctic poppy, 56, 92, 475, 501, 511
arctic willow, 56, 89, 475, 511, 575n23
    adaptations of, 322–23
    catkins of, 269

early growth of, 270
  height of, 589n14
  oldest found, 515
Ardencaple Fjord, *xxvii*
Arizona, 574n39
Army Corps of Engineers, 570n5
Arnold, Benedict, 570n6, 570n7
arsenic
  in Hall's hair and fingernails, 538
  possible accidental ingestion of, 539
Assistance, 598n5
Astoria, 570n5
astrolabe
  accuracy of, 577n8
Atlas Aviation, 537
atmospheric electricity
  studies of, 257–58
Augustabukta, *xxv*
aurora borealis, 48–49, 258–60, 427, 439, 449, 543
  relation of to magnetic disturbances, 260
Austro-Prussian War, *xxiv*
Avatok (Arrutak), 350, 354
  accompanies Bessels on northward trip, 389, 598n9
  Bessels threatens to shoot, 397
  catches dovekies in net, 412, 599n17
  declares Bessels to be dangerous, 397, 403
  disgusting state of hut of, 399
  harpoons seal, 392
  hopes to find wife on Ellesmere Island, 598n9
  independence of, 359
  lends Bessels his pants, 399
  refuses to go to site of Sonntag's grave, 412
  wooden leg of, 389
azaleas, 90

B

Bab el Mandel, 210
Baccalieu Island, 48
Bache Island, 395, 598n10
Baffin, 575n20

Baffin, William, 111–13,
  accuracy of observations of, 577n8
  reputation of damaged, 577n2
Baffin Bay, 117, 210, 498, 511, 567n2, 567n6, 578n14, 583n5
Baffin Island, 190, 209, 582n10
Baffin Island (near Greenland), 523, 605n13
Baird, Spencer F., 549, 568n23, 569n25
Baird Inlet, 397
Barents Sea, *xxvii*, 571n20
Bär (dog)
  severely wounded by bear, 287
Bardin Bay, 116
barn swallow, 479, 602n13, 602n17
Barnes, W.K., 549, 552
Barra, 534
  Bessels's confusion over, 606n6
Barrett, William, 537
Barrow, John, 113, 577n2
Barrow Strait, 531
Bartlett, Bob, 601n1
Bartlett, Isaac
  captain of *Tigress*, 464, 601n1
  holds church service, 601n3
  shares cabin with Tyson and Meyer, 465
basalt, 84
  distribution of, 86–87
Basilica-Cathedral of St. John the Baptist, 571n28
Battle of Groton Heights State Park, 570n7
Batty Bay, 514
Bay Roberts, 466
Beale, Joseph, 549, 552
bear, polar, 340, 439, 593n19
  attacked by dogs, 285–86
  cub captured, 532
  eating beluga, 532–33
  hunted, 427, 487, 534
  killed by muskox, 192
  shot, 287, 443, 452, 532, 605n19
  tracks of, 281, 425
bearskin pants, 596n4
Beattie, Owen, 567n3
Beechey Island, 124, 567n2, 583n4
beer
  brewed on board, 292, 590n2
Beethoven, Ludwig van, 575n22

Belcher, Edward, 578n18
Bellot Strait, 517, 519
beluga, 82
　range of, 575n9
benthic mud, 334–35
benthic protoplasm, 335
Ber, Karl M., 566n10
Bergen, *xxv*
Bering, Vitus, 580n7
Bering Strait, 6, 87, 566n11
Bessels, Emil, *xiii, xx,* 140, 555–57
　almost freezes in observatory, 226
　almost reaches Cape Brevoort on boat trip, 309
　ascends Brother John Glacier, 407–8
　assigned to *George Robeson,* 302
　attends church-service at Godhavn, 94–95
　becomes disoriented in blizzard, 587n17
　biographical sketch of, 555–57
　breaks through ice, 179, 596n6
　brews punch, 588n23
　bunk of, 248–49
　climbs Mount Chester, 181–84
　climbs to plateau above Godhavn, 89–93
　compares Kane's and Hayes's maps, 208–9
　compiles map of Kane's and Hayes's routes, 208
　consults with Budington, 587n3
　continues ascent of Brother John Glacier, 410–11
　continues weather observations on *Arctic,* 502
　cramped cabin of, 24
　death of, 557
　dedicates book to Albert Markham, 1
　describes Greenlandic settlements, *xxiii*
　devises punch-dispensing Christmas tree, 588n19
　diagnoses apoplexy for Hall's death, 585n23
　discourteous to Hall, *xxi*
　discusses sources for book, 3–5
　disinters old Eskimo sledge, 300
　disoriented in blizzard, 587n17
　earlier arctic experience of, *xxvii,* 555

　eats raws muskox meat, 188
　encounters arctic fox, 360
　explores Offley Island, 276
　explores Petermann Fiord, 277–80
　finds Orthoceras fossil, 184
　finds piece of driftwood, 313
　finds snow bunting's nest, 511
　finds stock of alcohol stolen, 589n8
　first reaches New York, 14
　first sees *Polaris,* 14
　forced to abandon sledge trip off Bache Peninsula, 396
　forbids emetic for Hall, 539, 552
　forgets plates and forks, 178
　freezes ears, 227, 587n10
　goes ashore at Elwin Inlet, 513
　Hall's potential murderer, 539–40
　helps Hall look for observatory site, 150
　hit in face with whip by Bryan, 589n5
　in charge of scientific investigations under Hall, 546, 568n23
　includes details of whaling cruise, *xxiii*
　includes scientific details, *xxiii*
　injects Hall with quinine, 585n25
　investigates colour of sea water, 49–50
　investigates timing of noon gun at St. John's, 39–41
　joins muskox hunting party, 581n12
　joins Tyson and boat's crew, 305
　lands at Fury Beach, 515
　lands at Peterhead, 535
　lands on Wollaston Islands, 511
　lands south of Cape Garry, 517
　later failed arctic expedition, 557
　leaves *Arctic* at Dundee, 566n2
　leaves depot at Polaris House, 471
　loses journal and papers, 4
　loses mercury, 306
　makes boat-trip to Lichtenfels, 62–65
　makes excursion ashore at Fiskernæsset, 56–57
　makes first sledge journey, 176–95
　makes hydrometer, 603n11
　makes sledge trip to Cape Constitution, 274–90
　makes sledge trip to Foulke Fiord, 406–7

makes sledge trip to Sorfalik for dog
    food, 397–402
makes winter trip to "Third Cape",
    249–50
measures Eskimo skulls, 366
measures flow of Brother John Glacier,
    408–10
measures specific gravity of sea water,
    603n11
member of crew of *Hopes dashed*, 471
member of party left on board ship,
    596n15
not first choice as chief scientist, 568n23
possible motive for murdering Hall,
    541–42
place of in German arctic exploration,
    xxiv–xxvii
plans to sledge back to Polaris Bay,
    388–91
presents plan of future operations,
    261–65
reaches Washington on *Tallapoosa*, 536
receives salary of $100 per month, 603n5
recommends route to North Pole, 6
reinters Sonntag's bones, 412
relationship with Vinnie Ream, 541
relies on Tyson's account, *xx*
reminded by Hall to wind chronometers,
    583n6
returns to ship to replace mercury, 306
rich scientific content of account of,
    xxiii
sails from Liverpool, 536
salvages canvas from old house, 599n10
saves scientific data, 348
searches Littleton Island for Hayes's
    lifeboat, 352
second unsuccessful attempt at sledge
    trip north, 402–4
sets trap for Budington, *xxii*
shares cabin and bunk with Markham,
    502
shares magnetic observations, 251–53
shares pendulum observing duties, 244,
    388
shoots birds at Cape Hay, 501
shoots reindeer, 518

shoots glaucous gull, 308
shoots gyrfalcon, 83
shares cramped upper saloon,
    581n13
shares weather observing duties 223 ,
    353
sketches aurora borealis, 259
speaks at American Geographical
    Society, 569n38
suffers snow blindness, 291–92, 591n7
surveys coast from *Arctic*, 511
suspected of poisoning Hall, 552
takes bearings, 137
takes part in consultation after Hall's
    death, 587n3
takes weather readings in gale, 225–26
threatens to leave expedition, *xxii*
threatens to shoot Avatok, 397, 598n11
transfers from *Ravenscraig* to *Arctic*, 500
traveling provisions of, 390
treatment of sick Hall, 585n23
treatment of Hall approved by Board of
    Inquiry, 552
tries carving ivory, 382
tries to photograph interior of
    Greenlandic house, 72
visits administrator at Upernavik, 100
visits catechist's home in Fiskernæsset,
    60–62
visits Thule culture ruins, 517–18
visits Mrs Krarup-Smith in Godhavn, 88
visits Elberg's home in Holsteinsborg, 71
visits *Ingegerd*, 68
visits Schönheyter's home in
    Fiskernæssset, 58
wants to find harbour on west shore, 141
within sight of Cape Constitution, 289
Bessels Fiord
    exploration of, 283–87
birds observed at Polaris Bay, 593n19
bird-spear, Inuit, 75–76
black guillemot, 75, 268, 306, 307, 339, 432,
    478, 485, 595n19
    shot, 501
Blackwell's Island, 28
    Insane Asylum, 570n4
    Penitentiary, 570n3

Blackwood Point, 486
Blåfjeld, 573n32
blasting ice, 240, 245, 315
blowflies, 294
bluebells, 90
blueberry, 56
blizzard, 225–28
Board of Inquiry, *xx*, 549–53
bog rosemary, 575n27
Bonavista Bay, 460
Booth, John, *xiii*
    as steward, 357
    crew member of *Hopes dashed*, 471
    member of party left on board ship, 596n15
    searches for leak, 294, 590n9
    transfers from *Ravenscraig* to *Intrepid*, 533
Booth Sound, 133, 485
Börgen, Carl N.J., *xxvi*
Bossekop, 257
Boston, 11, 130
Bosun (dog)
    skin condition of, 239
bottlenose whales, 34, 571n20
Brahe, Tycho O., 577n8
Braine, D.L., 521
    buys dogs, 522
Braine, William, 567n3
Bravais, A. 257, 588n1
Bremen, 14, 576n45
Bremerhaven, *xxvi, xxvii*
brent geese, 308, 327–328, 478, 594n19, 602n10
Brevoort, J. Carson, 213
Brodeur Peninsula, 606n1
Brook's sounding apparatus, 137, 334
Brooklyn, 28
Brother John Glacier, 406–11
Brown, Robert, 171, 581n19
Bruun, Andreas, 581n16
Bryan, E.D, 576n35
    arrives on board *Congress*, 576n30
    shares in sermon, 576n35
Bryan, Richard W.D., *xiii*
    arrives on *Congress*, 576n30
    boots of cut up for fuel, 487

    breaks through ice, 167
    climbs cliffs on Dalrymple Island, 486
    collects fossils and artifacts, 299
    comfortable in lee of rock, 602n6
    cuts snow blocks, 275
    determines latitude, 603n20
    digs out magnetic huts, 230
    fights dog for meat, 406, 599n16
    finds probable *Pedicularis*, 592n8
    goes hunting, 389
    granted leave in Britain, 536
    is teetotal, 233
    helps to build house on ice, 595n9
    helps to measure baseline, 156
    hikes to Cape Lupton, 250
    in Budington's boat, 470
    joins Bessels at Brother John Glacier, 412
    joins Bessels on trip to Cape Constitution, 274–90
    joins ship at Godhavn, 575n30
    leads church service, 580n 21
    lives in cramped upper saloon, 581n13
    manhandled into bunk, 581n15
    measures sun altitudes, 280
    member of party left on board ship, 596n15
    needs help to come aboard, 167
    observes moon culminations, 244
    occupies trigonometric stations, 166
    reads burial service at Hall's grave, 586n32
    records of left on ice, 596n2
    returns to ship with broken sledge, 281
    sets up instruments in observatory, 223
    shares magnetic observations, 251, 259
    shares pendulum observations, 388
    shoots Sabine's gull, 327
    sledges to Offley Island, 299
    stays at Port Foulke, 412
    spots first gull, 269
    takes charge of chronometer, 470
    transfers from *Ravenscraig* to *Intrepid*, 533
    travels to Rensselaer Harbour, 405–6
    tries handling whip, 589n5
    tries to determine position, 148
Buch, Christian L. von, 581n18

Budington, James, 576n30
  ice-pilot on board *Juniata*, 605n4
  salvages HMS *Resolute*, 563
Budington, Sidney O., *xiii, xviii*, 101
  admits faults, *xxi*
  affection of towards cat, 471
  battling ice in boat, 483
  biographical sketch of, 558
  casts off hawser, 146
  collects old Inuit artifacts, 300
  commands one boat, 470
  concerned about Meyer, 26
  consults with Bessels after Hall's death, 19, 587n3
  damning characterization of, 551
  determined to push north, 316, 550
  did not check ice from masthead, 143, 149
  drunk, 550–51, 595n5
  eating, smoking and sleeping, 247
  escapes punishment, 551
  establishes depot on shore, 302
  first meets Hall, 558
  forced to give up alcohol, 358
  gives Jimmy harpoon irons, 403
  grave of, 558
  has some command of Inuit language, 596n5
  hired as sailing master, 570n10
  his boat nipped, 480
  instructions to from Hall, 197–201
  instructions to from Robeson, 587n3
  is fat, 500
  is trouble-maker, 551
  leads wintering party, Cumberland Sound, 563
  member of party left on board ship, 596n15
  not interested in reaching Pole, 550
  offers to sample Hall's medicine, 539
  plan of for new season, 266
  plans to sabotage ship and escape south, 550
  possible poisoner of Hall, 539
  predicts Hall's death, 600n5
  pushes north to Cape Lieber, 316
  pushes north to Cape Sumner, 316
  prepares for boat-trip north, 291
  records minutes of council meeting, 141, 586n3
  repairs boat, 493
  reports ptarmigan, 269
  reprimanded by Hall, *xxi*
  reluctant to push north, 140, 149
  salary of, 603n5
  sends blubber and bread to Avatok, 359
  stealing alcohol, *xxii*
  transfers from *Ravenscraig* to *Arctic*, 533
  urges Bessels and others to return to ship, 311, 591n19
  wants to winter at Port Foulke, 142, 550, 579n5
  wants to follow Greenland coast, 141
  wants to turn back, 142
bumblebees, 325, 593n1
Bueau of Yards and Docks, 569n28
butterflies, 91, 325
Bylot, Robert, 111, 113, 577n8

C

Cabot, 535
Cabot Tower, 571n24
Cairn Poin, 128, 347, 391, 402, 405
California, 10
Campbell, Walter, *xiii*
  member of crew of *Hopes dashed*, 471
  transfers from *Ravenscraig* to *Arctic*, 500
  member of party left on board ship, 596n15
  observes Eskimo divorce, 379, 598n11
  observes Eskimo funeral, 598n12
Cape Abernethy, 132
Cape Adair, 532
Cape Ammen, 307
Cape Agassiz, 121
Cape Alexander, 115, 125, 126, 133, 171, 210, 214, 300, 387, 398, 402, 474
Cape Atholl, 132
Cape Back, 208
Cape Bisson, 533
Cape Brevoort, 204, 205, 211, 213, 214, 308, 309, 311, 328

Cape Bryan, 290
Cape Byam Martin, 502, 511
    sledge trip to, 273–290
Cape Constitution, 123, 136, 137, 209, 262, 263, 266, 273, 280, 282, 287, 319, 333, 578n17, 595n6
    almost reached by Hall, 290
Cape Cracroft, 317
Cape Crawford, 499
Cape Dezhnev, 566n12
Cape Dudley Digges, 112, 114, 132
Cape Eugenie, 129, 208
Cape Farewell, *xxvi*, 82, 534, 536
Cape Franklin, *xxvii*
Cape Fraser, 135
Cape Frederick, 116, 129
Cape Garry, 516, 517
Cape Graham Moore, 603n7
Cape Hatherton, 126, 391, 403, 404, 405
Cape Hawks, 128
Cape Hay, 500–501
Cape Horn, 10
Cape Horsburgh, 597n9, 597n10
Cape Independence, 123, 578n17
Cape Inglefield, 134, 397, 402, 403
Cape Isabella, 115, 126, 133, 210, 355
Cape Joseph Henry, 6, 293, 310
Cape Leiper, 393
Cape Leopold, 531
Cape Lieber, 206, 291, 316, 592n2
Cape Liverpool, 532
Cape Lucie Marie, 281, 293
Cape Lupton, 249–250, 293, 301, 303, 306, 316, 317, 328, 332, 590n14
    boats transported to, 590n12
    ice observed from, 261
Cape Mary Cleland, 278
Cape Morton, 281, 282
Cape Murchison, 208
Cape Nassau, 479
Cape Ohlsen, 134, 473
Cape Parry, 124, 480
    reached by retreating party, 484
Cape Pine, 468
Cape Porter, 307
Cape Race, 468
Cape Saumarez, 474

Cape Searle, 354, 528
Cape Seddon, 523
Cape Seward, 436
Cape Shackleton, 523
Cape Spear, 39, 571n34
Cape St. Francis, 467
Cape St. Mary, 467
Cape Sumner, 204, 213, 301, 308, 311, 316, 317
Cape Tyson, 275–76, 278, 281
Cape Union, 129, 328, 332
Cape Warrender, 603n4
Cape Wechmar, 133
Cape York (Baffin Island), 531
Cape York (Greenland), 68, 116, 117, 364, 387, 491, 524, 526, 577n6
capelin, 581n1
carbonic acid, 587n7
Carey Islands, 112, 114, 133
Carex, 321
Carl Ritter Bay, 208, 209
Casarini-Wadhams, Maria Pia, *xv*
Cassiopea, 427, 431
Catalina, 456
catechists
    Greenlandic, 60–61
caterpillars, 325
Cathay, 9
Centre for Forensic Sciences, Toronto, 538
cephalopods, 581n3
Cevantes, Miguel de, 37, 571n37
Chain Rock, 35
Chesapeake Bay, 536, 568n20
Chester, Hubbard C., *xiii*
    abandons *Hegemann*, 314
    accompanies Bessels on hunting trip, 176–95
    accompanies Bessels to Littleton Island, 352
    accompanies Hall on sledge trip, 197–216
    attends council meeting, 141
    builds boats, 387, 404, 414, 469
    builds Polaris House, 349–50
    carves inscription on headboard, 319, 592n6
    climbs cliff on Hakluyt Island, 480

climbs Mt. Chester with Bessels, 181–84
commands *Hegemann*, 304, 309, 591n9
commands *Hopes dashed*, 470
commands *Ulysses S. Grant*, 291, 302
develops scurvy, 314
eats raw muskox meat, 188
enthusiastic about voyage, 603n5
felt ship could have pushed further north, 142
finds space for Hans and family, 103
given bed in captain's cabin, 502
harpoons a whale, 514
heads across to Grinnell Land, 144
helps Bessels measure baseline, 389
helps Bessels establish depot, 471
is applauded as boat-builder, 473
keeps vigil over Hall's body, 585n24
kills a whale, 603n7
loses the *Grant*, 303–304
makes snow knives, 388, 399
member of party left on board ship, 596n15
member of muskox hunting party, 580n12
multiple talents of, 349
praised by Bessels, 247
reaches Cape Brevoort, 204
recovers from scurvy, 339
sees first gull, 267
sets off for *Ravenscraig*, 495
shoots fox, 360
shoots two muskoxen, 292
spots ship, 493
suffers from snow blindness, 590n5
surveys ice from masthead, 144, 149
takes boat to Prøven, 576n40
takes boat to Ritenbenk, 576n31
transfers to *Arctic*, 500
travels to Etah, 389
tries to shoot narwhal, 333
tries to sledge beyond Cape Brevoort, 251
walks to Cape Lupton, 301
Chimborazo, 248, 588n5
chimney swift, 479, 602n12
Chipp, Charles W., 523
  serves on board *Jeannette*, 605n12

dies in Laptev Sea, 605n12
Christiansborg Palace, 576n33
Christianshåb, 82
Christmas
  celebrations, 237–38
  gifts for crew, 589, n.9
  on the ice floe, 428
chronometers, 17–18, 573n34
Chukotka, *xxv*
Cincinnati, *xix*
City of Antwerp, 536
Civil War, 13, 130
Clavering, Douglas, *xxvii*
Clavering Ø, *xxvii*
coal
  deposits in Vaigat, 87
  shortage of, 326
coaling, 94
Coast and Geodetic Survey, 569n29, 569n30
cobalt, 574n39
Cochrane, Thomas, 36
Codroy Valley, 572n40
Coffin, Nathaniel, *xiii*
  anger of at table/work-bench, 236
  builds sledges, 254
  becomes mentally deranged, 24, 235, 387, 587n5, 598n6
  in Budington's boat, 602n2
  makes axles and wheels for sledge, 196
  makes box for met. instruments, 502
  makes whip handles and snowshoes, 201
  member of party which remained on board ship 596n15
  repairs Bessels's sledge, 403
  searches for leak, 294
  transfers from *Ravenscraig* to *Arctic*, 533
Colfax, Schuyler, 567n9, 567n15
Committee on Foreign Affairs, 13
Compagnie du Nord, 582n6
comparative coastal movements
  north Greenland, 170–71
  south Greenland, 169
Conception Bay, 602n7
Confederate, 460
Congress, *xxii*, 93–96, 576n29, 576n35
  church service on board of, 95

crew of mans the yards, 576n37
continental drift
    Bessel's ideas on, 172–73
Cook, James, 6
    reaches highest southerly latitude, 566n8
Cooper Institute, 25, 569n39
Copeland, Ralph, *xxvi*
copepods, 50
    luminescent, 236
coprolite
    mistaken, 246–47
Coriolanus, 603n6
    Captain Adams quotes from, 499
Cormack, W.E., 41
cowslips, 90
Crantz, D., 74
Cresswell Bay, 516
crevasses, 410–11
Crimson Cliffs, 114
cross-staff, 577, n.8
crow's nest, 125, 134, 143, 149, 333, 336, 347, 456, 496, 497, 498, 579n22
Crozier Island, 137, 289, 333
crustaceans, 326–27
cryolite, 528–29, 572n11
Cuba, 9
Cumberland Peninsula, 209, 354
Cumberland Sound, 437, 528, 580n5, 596n8
currents, 543
Cuvier, Jean L.N.F., 582n7
Cuxhaven, *xxiv*

D

Dalrymple Island, 486
dandelions, 90, 321
Danmarkshavn, *xxvii*
darkness
    impact of, 107
Davenport, H.K., *xxii*, 576n29
    gives speech, 96
    visits Krarup-Smith, 576n32
Davis, C.H., *xx*, 4
    white-washes expedition, 597n4
Davis, John, 112
Davis, Joseph B., 597n7

Davis Strait, 43, 111, 113, 114, 210, 479, 527, 536, 571n20, 583n5
Deer Lake, 572n40
De Haven, Edwin J., 25, 567n2
    drift of ships of, 583n4
    expedition of, 578n12
Delaware River, 13
De Long, George W., 523
    commands *Jeannette*, 605n11
    dies in Lena Delta, 605n11
Denmark Strait, *xxv*
depot established on ice, 147
Devon Island, 603n4
diatoms, 49–50
Director of the Coast Guard, 17
Discovery, 111
Disko, *xxii*, 68, 83, 85, 93, 125, 171, 522, 527, 550, 574n37
    dance held at, 605n9
    men on ice-floe plan to reach, 600n4
Disko Bugt, 92
Dodge Mountains, 410
dogs, 332
    attack muskox, 186
    bought at Godhavn, 95–96
    bought at Kingiktok, 105
    bought at Tasiusaq, 109
    bought at Upernavik, 103
    chase and rip apart a fox, 398
    control of with whip, 159
    details of harness for, 159
    depredations of, 156, 160–61, 425
    faeces of, uses for, 588n2
    feeding of, 160, 239
    fight with a bear, 432
    fighting, 159–60
    Inuit training of, 157, 162–63
    killed and eaten, 425, 426, 599n8
    Newfoundland, 37–38
    protective instincts of, 161–62
    qualities of selected by Inuit, 162
    recommended food for, 588n21
    suffering convulsions, 275
    uncooperative, 175
    variations in commands for, 157–58
Don Quixote, 571n37
Dovebugt, *xxvii*

dovekies, 133, 339, 411, 413, 485, 511, 595n19
  caught in net, 412
  shot, 436, 437, 474, 475, 478, 501
Draba, 56, 92, 322, 475
Draba lacteal, 572n14
driftwood
  floating logs examined, 53, 83
  found washed ashore, 311, 313, 314, 592n23, 592n24
Dryas, 322
Dundas Harbour, 597n9
Dundee, 534, 536, 566n2
dwarf birch, 89

E

Eagle
  spotted by ice-floe drifters, 601n10
East Greenland, 301
East Greenland Current, *xxvi*
East River, 28, 570n5
Edwards, Richard, 571n30
  ordnance of about dogs, 38
Egede, Hans, 71, 574n43
Egedesminde, 82
eider, 109, 133, 308, 339, 360, 485, 486
  common, 478, 594n19
  eggs of collected, 327
  king, 478, 511, 594n19
Elbe River, *xxiv*
Elberg, Lowertz, 71, 72, 78, 100, 574n42, 575n2
  accompanies *Polaris* to Kingiktok, 105
  accompanies *Polaris* to Tasiusaq, 575n2
  garden of, 71
  offers Hall coal from own stocks, 574n49
  takes Hall's dispatches south, 579n1
Ellesmere Island, 579n8, 583n12
Ellesmere Land, 134, 300
Elliot, Adam, 597n1
Elwin Inlet, 513
Erebus
  wreck of discovered, 566n1
Erik, 536
ermine, 269, 593n19
  range of in Greenland, 589n12

Eriophorum, 56, 90, 572n13
Eskimo
  derivation of the name, 363
Etah, 353, 567n7
  population of, 364
Etahners (Inughuit), 364
  clothing of, 267
  lacking in skills as cartographers, 387
  physical appearance of, 366
  preferences of about perfumes, 573n26
  skulls of, 366
  traveling range of, 364–65
Exeter Bay, 528

F

Fabvre, Jean-Jacques L., 588n1
Faeroe Islands, 87
favus in dogs, 588n20
Fearnall Bay, 517
Fidelio, 575n22
fire narrowly averted, 148–49
First German North Pole Expedition, *xxiv*
First Grinnell Expedition, 10, 117
first flowing water, 305
Fisher Island, 570n15
Fiskefjord, 54
Fiskernæsset, 50, 82, 83, 117, 169, 171, 479, 574n47
  dance at, 57
  details of houses at, 58–59
  details of native huts at, 59
  expedition arrives at, 55
  middens at, 59–60
  reached by *Juniata,* 522
Fitzclarence Rock, 133, 485
flakes, 571n26
Fligely Fjord, *xxvii*
fog, 136–47, 184
Force Bay, 397, 402
Fort Amherst Lighthouse, 571n23
Fort Churchill, 190
Fort Griswold, 29, 570n7
Fort Townshend, 37
Fort Trumbull, 29, 570n6
Fort William, 37
Fort York, 582n6

fossils, 135, 167, 184, 590n14
    above Fury Beach, 516
    on Offley Island, 281, 299
fossil wood, 313–314
Foster, Dr., 570n21
Foulke Fiord, 353, 404, 406, 567n7
Fowler's Solution, 539
Fox, 568n23, 583n5, 597n9
Foxe Basin, 514
Fram Strait, *xxv*
Franklin, Jane, 116, 568n23
Franklin, John
    last expedition of, *xix*, 9, 566n1
    no messages left by at Beechey Island, 567n4
Franklin Island, 137, 289
Frederikshåb, 82, 169
Frederiksdal, *xxvi*
freeze-up, 154–55
Fries, Theodor (Thore) M., 68, 574n35
Frobisher Bay, *xix*
Frolic, 602n9
    dispatched to St. John's, 467
    reaches St. John's, 468
    reaches New York, 468
    reaches Washington. 549
    takes Tyson and party to Washington, 602n12
frost smoke, 386, 397
Frying Pan Shoal, 28
fulmar petrels, 66–67, 149, 485, 508–509, 511, 594n19
    range of, 573n27
Fury, 514, 604n18
Fury and Hecla Strait, 514, 604n19
Fury Beach, *xxiii*, 514–56
    condition of Parry's depot at, 515
Fury Point, 514, 531

G

Gaimard, Paul, 588n1
Gauss, Johann C.F., 588n9
Geestemünde, *xxvi*
geographical homologies, 209–10
geological features of Polaris Bay, 167–68
Geological Society of London, 169

George Robeson (boat), 291, 302, 311
    abandoned on shore, 314
    voyage of, 306–307
Georgia, 536
Germania, *xxvi*, *xxvii*, 582n9, 598n9
Germaniahavn, *xxvi*, *xxvii*
Germanialand, *xxvii*
Giesecke Karl L., 528
    geological expedition of, 606n24
Gignoux, Tom, 537
"Gillis Land", *xxv*, *xxvii*
Gladan, 67–68, 69, 588n2
Glasgow, 536
glaucous gulls, 308, 360, 405, 474, 478, 501, 594n19
Godhavn (Lievely), 67, 82, 84–97, 130, 575n1
    church service at, 94–95
Godthåb, 60, 71, 82, 169, 574n43
Göttingen, 588n9
Governor's Island, 28
Grady Harbour, 465
Graham, Mr., 499
Grant, Ulysses S., *xx*, 567n9, 567n11
    visits *Polaris*, 569n31
Granville Bay, 133
Gravesend, 111
Gray, Asa, 592n8
Greenlanders
    dialects of, 54
    men's dress, 58
    women's dress, 57–58
Greenwich, 570n18
Greer, J.A., 522, 526–28,
    exchanges letters with Tyson, 605n15
Griffin, Samuel, 567n.2
Grinnell, Henry, 10, 14, 117, 578n12, 580n20
    presents flag to Hall's expedition, 25
Grinnell Land, 121, 122, 123, 125, 128, 130, 134, 137, 144, 180, 184, 208, 209, 262, 263, 265, 335
Griper, *xxvii*
Grönland, *xxiv*, *xxv*
Groton, 29, 569n36
groundsheets
    missing, 274

Gulf of Aden, 210
Gulf of Boothia, *xxiii*, 514
Gulf of St. Lawrence, 571n20
Gulf Stream, *xxvii*, 33, 123
　Bessels's search for 476, 498
gyrfalcon, 83, 575n10, 593n19

H

Hadley, John
　octant of, 577n8
Hakluyt Island, 112, 421, 474, 475, 481
　retreating party lands on, 476
halibut, 82, 575n3, 575n4
Hall, Charles Francis, *xiii, xix*
　addresses American Geographical Society, 569n38
　appointed expedition leader, 12–13
　appoints Tyson, 570n10
　arctic library of, 602n1
　arranges free passage for Bessels, 568n22
　arsenic in system of, 538–39
　autopsy of, 537–38
　background and earlier expeditions of, *xix*, 558
　believes he is being poisoned, 216, 551, 585n26, 586n27
　biographical sketch of, 560–62
　buys dogs at St. John's, 37
　buys dogs at Upernavik, 105
　"buys" Pannik, 22
　climbs Mount Chester, 181–84
　commission of, 568n18
　compliments the crew, 582n16
　death of, *xviii, xix, xx*, 217, 586n26, 586n28
　dispute with Meyer, *xxii*
　earlier expeditions of, 578n12
　eats raw muskox meat, 188
　employs Joe (Ebierbing) and Tookoolito, 559
　establishes emergency depot,147
　establishes coordinates of Holsteinsborg, 573
　exhumation of, 537–38
　explores Newman Bay, 203–204
　falls ill, 216, 585n24
　financed by Henry Grinnell, 578n12
　finds Inuit tent rings, 150
　first meets Tyson, 564
　flowers planted on grave of, 320
　funeral of, 217
　gives mail to Swedish expedition, 78
　gives speech at New London, 30
　goes aboard *Congress*, 93
　goes ashore at Holsteinsborg, 68
　grave markers of, 319, 537
　hikes towards Grinnell Land, 144
　hires Budington, 570n10
　initiates expedition, 12
　instructions to from Navy Department, 542–48
　investigates Repulse Harbour, 139
　is delirious, 216, 585n24
　lands at Cape Fraser, 135
　lands at Godhavn, 84–85
　lands at Upernavik, 99
　instructions of for Budington, 201
　leaves message at Cape Brevoort, 214
　lectures in Lincoln Hall, 567n9
　makes sledge trip, 197–216, 583n2
　measures baseline, 156
　meets President Grant, 567n11
　message buried in grave of, 592n7
　moves into upper saloon,165
　names Mount Chester, 183
　names Newman Bay, 583n9
　names Polaris Bay, 153
　names Robeson Channel, 143
　official cause of death of, 552
　overrides Budington, 140–42
　plans to mine coal in the Vaigat, 85
　possible motive for murder of, 540–42
　potential murderers of, 539–40, 552
　presidential commission of, 568n18
　raises American flag, 149, 580n25
　reaches Cape Brevoort, 204
　received by Governor Lassen at Godhavn, 575n15
　refuses medical treatment, 585n26
　refuses to winter at Port Foulke, 579n5
　relations with Bessels, *xxi*
　relations of with Budington, *xxi*, 558
　returns to ship, 216

sees gyrfalcon, 593n19
sees snowy owl, 593n19
tows *Julianehaab* out of Upernavik, 103
tries to recruit Jensen, 106
unloads cargo, 149
visits Schönheyter, 56
writes to Vinnie Ream, 541
Hall Basin, *xx*, 280
Hamburg, *xxiv*, 576n45
Hansa, *xxvi*, 582n9, 591n1
Hanseatics, 102, 134, 576n45
  accommodation of, 103
  crew members complain about, 590n10
  move ashore, 232
  passengers on *Tigress*, 522
Hans Island, 137, 332
  dispute between Canada and Denmark over, 579n10
Harbour Grace, 456, 460, 602n8
harpoon 435
  cut down to a spear, 600n8
Hartnell, John, 567n3
Hartstene, Henry, 579n20, 580n20
Hashagen, Captain, *xxvii*, 590n6
Hayes, Isaac, 11, 25, 262, 364, 578n19
  as contender for expedition leader, 567n14
  expedition of, 125–30, 567n7, 577n51, 578n12, 578n16
  falsely reports open polar sea, 205–207, 209
  leaves dogs at Tasiusaq, 109
  observations of, 583n13, 584n14
  on Kane's expedition, 121
  recognized by Hans, 50
Hayes, Noah, *xiii*
  in Budington's boat, 470
  in charge of fuel and coal, 199
  member of party left on board ship, 596n15
  observed Eskimo funeral, 598n12
  plays fiddle at Thanksgiving, 587n15
  takes meteorological readings, 397
  transfers from *Ravenscraig* to *Arctic*, 500
  witnesses Eskimo divorce, 598n11
  washes Hans's family, 134
Hayes Sound, 395

Hebrides, 87
Hecla, 604n18
Hegemann, Paul, *xxiv*, *xxvi*, 582n9, 591n1
Hegemann (canvas boat), 304, 591n1
  abandoned on shore, 314
  reaches Newman Bay, 309
  Tyson's assessment of, 591n9
Hell Gate, 570n5
Hell Gate Shoal, 28
Helgoland, 332, 595n4
Hendrik, Hans (Suersaq), *xiii*, 120, 121, 579n25
  almost accidentally shot by Joseph, 423–24
  appearance of, 102
  brings missing groundsheets, 276
  climbs Cape Lupton, 332
  commands of for dogs, 157
  delivers Budington's recall message, 311
  Hall looks for at Fiskernæsset, 56
  fails to recognize Morton, 101
  fails to shoot ptarmigan, 180
  fetches water from lake, 177
  finds Kennedy Channel ice-free, 301
  finds oldsquaw's nest, 327
  finds second wife, 51
  freezes ears, 229
  freezes nose, 227
  Hall sends back for missing items, 201
  helps Bessels disinter old sledge, 300
  hunts for seals, 211, 418, 421, 423, 426, 433, 434, 600n6
  identifies old iceberg, 215
  is sick, 427
  joins Hall's expedition from Prøven, 101
  joins Hayes's expedition (with family), 52
  joins Kane's expedition, 51
  kills dogs, 426
  leaves muskoxen in snow house, 590n5
  listens to ice noises, 421
  loses last dog, 434
  marooned on small ice floe, 422
  moves ashore with family, 232
  occupies own snow house with family, 418
  paddles kayak across thin ice, 600n6
  paddles kayak to *Tigress*, 464

pitches tent on deck, 295
pulls Sonntag out of water, 127, 572n7
rescues Joseph with kayak, 428
runs ahead of dogs, 176
shares meager Thanksgiving dinner, 599n9
shoots bear, 452
shoots hooded seals, 444
shoots kittiwake, 163
skill at sketching ice conditions, 328–29
thought he heard walrus, 249
tracks missing party, 120
with Bryan and Bessels to Cape Constitution, 287–89
with Hall on last sledge trip, 197–216
with Morton to Cape Constitution, 121–23
with Tyson shoots 12 muskoxen, 293
Hendrik, Charles Polaris, *xiii*
birth of, 332
carried in mother's hood, 340
Hendrik, Josephine (Augustine), *xiii*, 134, 579n4
younger version of mother, 102
Hendrik, Merkut, *xiii*, 134
appearance of, 102
brings lemmings on board, 298
contribution of as seamstress, 101
gives birth to Charles Polaris, 332
has bad dream, 225
joins expedition with Hans, 52
pregnant state of not noticeable, 595n1
Hendrik, Sussi (Susanne, Suschen), *xiii*
in mother's hood, 134
still breast-feeding, 102
Hendrik, Tobias
dressed as monkey at Thanksgiving, 233
voracius appetite of, 102, 134
Henry, Joseph, 568n23, 568n24
Henry Kater Peninsula, 600n9
Herald, 533
Herbert Island, 474
Herrnhuter Brüdergemeinde, 573n36
Herron, John, *xiii*
develops scurvy, 292, 590n1
English, 600n2
hands Hall cup of coffee, 216, 585n22

member of ice-floe party, 596n17
Heuglin, Theodor von, 479
high tide at Polaris House, 386
highest latitude reached, 148, 214
Hilgard, Julius E., 569n29
Hill, Stephen J., 39
invites Hall and his officers to lunch, 571n35
Hinlopenstretet, *xxv*
hoary redpoll, 575n11
Hobby, Heinrich, *xiii*
acts as cook, 357
assigned to *George Robeson*, 302, 590n20
crew member of *Hopes dashed*, 471
lookout in crow's nest, 142, 347
makes dovekie soup, 414
member of party left on board ship, 596n15
returns to Newman Bay, 328
saves Little Fritz from drowning, 312
spills soup in fire, 358
spotted open polynyas, 328
sent to *Ravenscraig*, 495
to accompany Bessels on final northern trip, 403, 599n14
transfers from *Ravenscraig* to *Arctic*, 500
view of from crow's-nest, 142
Hoffmann, Heinrich, 588n22
Holsteinsborg, 67–79, 82, 522
coordinates of, 573n34
tidal range at, 573n34
Hopes dashed (boat), 470, 473, 475, 483
beset in ice, 480
salvaged, 497
Hopen, *xxvii*
Hospital for Mental Diseases, St. John's, 571n38
House of Representatives, 12, 13
Howgate, H.W., 549
Hudson Bay, 12
Hudson Strait, 43, 210
Humboldt Glacier, 121, 122, 208, 336, 364, 581n11
Hume, James, *xv*
Hydrographic Office, 569n28

I

Iberville, Pierre le M. de, 582n6
ice,
  details of, 138, 139, 144, 261
  observations on, 543
ice chisels, 144
ice floe
  filthy conditions on, 435
  land sighted from, 436
  progressive shrinkage of, 418, 438, 444, 446–47
  rate of drift of, 432, 433, 439, 441, 449
ice floe party
  cooking equipment of, 424
  desperate boat trips of, 445–46, 451, 452–53
  hang on to boat, 450
  plan to walk to land, 436
  playing cards of, 425
  provisions of, 420, 436, 451
  rescued, 464
  see a ship, 454
  snow houses of, 418, 420, 425
ice foot, 398, 404, 405
ice pressures, 144–147, 231–32, 317–18, 333, 336, 343
icebergs
  capsizing, 444
  colliding, 453
  erosive effects of, 108
  in Petermann Fiord, 279–80
  in St. John's harbour, 571n22
  rock transport by, 178
Iceland gulls, 478, 602n9
Igaliku, 169
Iglorpait, 85
Ilordlik Glacier, 171
Ilulissat, 573n18
Ingegerd, 67–68, 574n51
Inglefield, Edward A, 85, 116, 498, 575n17, 578n9
  encounters Qidtlarssuaq's group, 597n9
  soundings by, 265
Inglefield Land, 567n5
Inland Island, 202
insects, 324–25, 592n10

Intrepid, 536
Inughuit, 586n2, 596n4
Inuk, 357
  divorced by Manik, 379
Inuit
  assist shipwrecked survivors, 350
  at Admiralty Inlet, 512
  bow and arrows of, 373
  children, 377–78
  concepts of beauty, 380–83
  crowd into Polaris House, 354
  dialects of, 367
  diet of, 377
  drum, 383
  harpoon, 373–76
  lamps, 371
  lance, 373
  marriage arrangements, 378
  old artifacts of, 299
  on East Greenland, *xxvii*, 300
  possible origins of, 300–301
  pots, 73–74, 371
  related to Paleolithic man, 365
  singing, 384
  sledges, 371
  tattoos, 378, 512
  women's hair and dress of, 512
Ireland, 87
Isabel, 575n17
Isabella, 113
Issungoak, 85
Ivalu, 355, 356, 597n11
Ivigtut (Ivittuut), 528–30
  cryolite mine at, 528–29, 572n11
  later crucial importance of, 606n23
  mine output, 530
Ivnarssuk (Sharky), 400
  breaks sledge runner, 402, 599n12
ivory gull, 269, 307, 308, 478, 489, 509, 589n10, 594n19

J

Jackson, William, *xiii*
  English, 600n2
  replacement cook, 29, 570n9
  lives in cramped upper saloon, 581n13

member of ice-floe party, 596n16
jaeger, 485
   long-tailed, 594n19
   parasitic, 594n19
   pomarine, 489, 603n22
Jakobshavn, 59, 82, 89
James Bay, 575n9
Jamka, Friedrich, *xiii*
   assigned to *George Robeson*, 346, 590n18
   known as "Big Fred", 588n18
   opens gift prematurely, 237, 588n18
   member of ice floe party, 596n22
   suffers from snow blindness, 590n5
Jan Mayen, *xxv*, 87, 442, 479
Jane, 566n9
jellyfish, 138
Jennie (cat), 358
Jennie (dog), 434
Jensen, Peter, 106–108, 577n51
   as pilot, 131
Jérémie, Nicolas, 582n6
Jimmy (Itokirsuk(Ittukasuk)), 373
   accompanies Bessels on northward trip, 389, 598n9
   assistance of, 356
   life story of, 354–56
   procrastinations of, 389–90
   promises to look after depot, 471
   sent to Sorfalik for dog food, 403
Jockey Club (perfume), 573n26
Joe (Joseph, Ebierbing), *xiii*, 4
   accompanies Hall in United States, 22
   adrift on small ice floe, 421–22
   acts as interpreter, 522, 605n16,
   almost shoots Hans, 423–24
   biographical sketch of, 558–60
   builds snow house, 446, 447, 448
   cutting snow blocks, 275
   description of, 23
   experiences hunting fever, 163
   experiences mirage, 284
   experiences reaction, 465
   fails to shoot bear, 439
   finds reindeer antler, 300, 593n19
   first meets Hall, 561, 567n8
   gets lost in fog, 451
   gives Bessels account of ice-floe journey, 4
   harpoons seal, 433
   has two wives, 23
   Hall's informant about muskoxen, 195
   hears call of snowy owl, 593n19
   helps build house on ice, 595n9
   helps Tyson recover boat, 599n4
   hunting a bear, 285–87
   hunts seals from ice floe, 418, 419, 421, 423, 426, 428, 434, 436, 441, 449, 453
   is ill, 601n6
   joins *Polaris*, 22, 569n35
   kills dogs, 426
   leaves muskoxen in snow house, 590n5
   lights fire, 177
   lists good qualities of a dog, 162
   mistakes boulders for muskoxen, 177
   mistakes Hans for a bear, 423–24
   on muskox hunting trip, 180–88, 211, 581n12
   on second short trip south, 293
   on sledge trip north to Cape Lupton, 305–6
   on sledge trip south, 274–90
   on third short trip south, 299
   paddling an ice floe, 279
   prevents dogs from fighting, 96
   provides details on muskox, 188–94
   pulls Meyer out of water, 448
   recovers whaleboat, 418
   rescues Hannah from wave, 448
   sketches ice distribution, 328
   sent back to ship, 280–81
   shoots bear, 443, 452
   shoots bearded seal, 437, 438
   shoots black guillemot, 433
   shoots hooded seals, 444, 453
   shoots narwhal, 435
   sings for Bessels, 384
   spots first black guillemots, 268
   stays with Budingtons, 558, 558–60
   suffers frozen cheek, 226–27, 229
   thrown over by wave, 450
   tracks dogs, 432
   traps a fox, 428

unaffected by eating raw meat, 581n4
watches dance, 57
with family shares snow house with Tyson, 419
with Hall on his second expedition, 561–62
with family occupies own snow house, 599n5
Johanna Island, 282–83
John Brown Coast, 333
Johnson, Peter, *xiii*
  assigned to *George Robeson*, 302, 590n22
  becomes ill but recovers, 425
  leads donkey at Thanksgiving party, 233, 587n16
  member of ice-floe party, 346, 596n18
  tells pirate stories, 310
Jones Sound, 113, 116
Julianehaab, 100–103
  collides with *Polaris*, 103
Julianehåb, 71, 82, 169, 581n16, 581n17
Julius Caesar, 500
Juncus, 321
Juniata
  a screw-steamer 604n3
  is recalled, 535
  to renew search, 535
  to support *Tigress*, 521
Jupiter, 215

K

Kamchatka, 210
Kane, Elisha Kent, 10, 364
  determines longitude of Rensselaer Harbour, 599n15
  expedition of, 117–25, 567n6, 576n42, 578n12
  log of lost in fire, 578n15
  soundings by, 265
Kane Basin, 567n6, 567n7
Kangersuatsiaq, 576n39
Kara Sea, 7, 22
Karluk, 601n1
Kasorsoak, 98
Karl Ritter Bay, 332

kayak
  design of, 77
  handling of, 77
Kejser Fanz Joseph Fjord, *xxvii*
Kennedy Channel, 205, 208, 214, 580n1, 583n13
  open water in, 281, 301
Kingiktok, 105
King William Island, *xix*, 566n1, 580n3
Kirkcaldy, 496
kittiwake, 133, 163, 269, 501, 580n9, 594n19
Kleinschmidt, Samuel P., 367, 598n10
knot, 475, 594n19, 602n4
Knuth, Count Eigil, 537
Kongsfjorden, 133, 177
Koldewey, Karl, *xxiv*, *xxvi*, 582n9, 590n15
Kolyuchinskaya Guba, 566n11
Krarup-Smith, Sophus T, 84, 575n13
  arranges for storage of provisions, 576n32
Krarup-Smith, Mrs
  acts as interpreter, 575n15
  entertains Hall and Bessels, 89
  plays piano, 88–89
  sends gifts for Hall and Bessels, 96
Krüger, John W.C. (Robert), *xiii*
  assigned to *George Robeson*, 590n17
  assigned to *Ulysses S. Grant*, 302
  breaks through ice, 419
  catches lemmings, 297, 590n11
  climbs hill near Cape Brevoort, 91n13
  collects ancient wood, 313
  helps search for Hans, 423
  member of ice-floe party, 346, 596n21
  member of *Tigress*'s crew, 522
  reads tide gauge, 221
  returns to Newman Bay, 328
  saw ptarmigan, 589n13
  sent back to ship for bread, 591n15
  spots open polynyas, 328
Krusenstjerna, Captain von, 67
Kvitøya, *xxv*

L

La Recherche, 588n1
Labrador, 442
Labrador City, 572n42

Notes 631

Labrador Current, 43, 49, 570n17
Lady Franklin Bay, 129, 208, 209, 329, 592n2
ladybugs, 90
  three-banded, 575n24
Lake Alida, 407
Lake Tannick, 69
lake
  saline, 177
lake ice
  features of, 182
lamps
  Inuit, 72–73
Lancaster Sound, 114, 116, 210, 497, 498, 511, 532, 567n2, 577n5, 583n4
Lapland bunting, 534
  range of, 606n4
Lassen, Governor, 89
  receives Hall, 575n15
Leach's storm petrels, 560n19
Leidy's Camp, 584n14
lemming, 593n19, 597n13
  collared, 581n2
  burrows and runs of, 298
  kept on board, 297–98
  predated upon, 298
  tracks of, 181, 269
Leonora, 575n22
Leroux, Guillaume, 598n11
Lichtenfels, 62–65, 169, 573n36
Lively (Godhavn), 81
Lifeboat Cove, 351, 526
Lincoln Bay, 209
Lincoln, Abraham
  statue of, 540
Lincoln Hall, 567n9
Lincoln Sea, *xx*, 6, 566n7, 579n11
Lindahl, Joshua, 68
Lindquist, Gustav, *xiii*
  assigned to *George Robeson*, 301, 590n19
  goes to Newman Bay, 328
  member of ice floe party, 346, 596n19
  member of *Tigress*'s crew, 522
linnet, 83, 534
  range of, 606n3
Little Juniata, 523–26, 531

Littleton Island(s), *xxiii*, 117, 126, 134, 347, 352, 355, 386, 473, 526, 596n1
  geology of, 398
Liverpool, 536, 566n2
Loch Shin, 69, 574n40
Lockhart, Ninian
  owner of *Tigress*, 496
  presents survivors' boat to Smithsonian, 603n3
Lottin, V.C., 257, 588n1
looms, 109
Loomis, Chauncey C., *xxiii*
  concludes Hall possibly murdered, 537, 540
lotus, 602n19
Louis Napoleon Island, 116
Lübeck, 573n22, 576n45

M

magnetic observations, 251–53, 543
magnetic observatory, 223–24
  melting of, 295
Majuk, 350, 356
  funeral of, 380
  grave of, 475
  meaning of name of, 597n13
mammals
  seen at Polaris Bay, 593n19
Manik, 355
  divorced from Inuk, 379
Markham, Albert, 6, 499
  Bessel's dedication to, 1
  disparaging remarks of about Inuit, 604n14
  examines Thomas's grave with Bessels, 515
  kills a whale, 603n7
  makes boat trip with Bessels, 517–19
  on George Nares's expedition, 565n2, 566n3, 603n5
  reaches record high latitude, 566n3
  shoots reindeer, 518, 519
  thrown into water, 514
Massachusetts Department of Public Safety Laboratory, 538
Matochkin Shar, 566n10

Mauch, Joseph, *xiii*
  as surveyors' assistant, 166
  breaks through ice, 167, 596n6
  found barely conscious, 581n4
  finds *Pedicularis,* 592n8
  helps to build house on ice, 595n9
  hikes to Cape Lupton, 250
  hikes to Cape Sumner, 301
  in Budington's boat, 370
  member of party left on board ship, 596n15
  reads barometer, 353
  shoots Sabine's gulls, 327
  skins animals, 327
  travels to Lichtenfels with Bessels, 573n19
  transfers from *Ravenscraig* to *Intrepid,* 533
Maury Bay, 208
May, S.H., 523, 525
McGary Island, 121
McClintock, F. Leopold, 568n23
  encounters Qidtlarssuaq's group, 597n9, 597n10
Melville, George W.
  engineer on board *Tigress,* 605n7
  survives *Jeannette* expedition, 605n7
Melville Bay, 125, 131, 209, 491, 524, 583n5
Melville Island, 479
mercury
  frozen, 386, 432, 433
meteoric iron, 67
meteorites, 68–69, 573n32
meteorological observations, 29, 147, 223, 307–8, 544
  at Polaris House, 353
  difficulties of in blizzard, 225–27
  on board *Arctic,* 502
meteorological screen, 221–23
  location of, 166
Meyer, Frederick, *xiii*
  develops scurvy, 339
  assigned to *Ulysses S. Grant,* 302
  barely manages to return to ship, 167
  breaks through ice, 167
  brings biscuits to observatory for Bessels, 226
  leaves message in cairn at Cape Brevoort, 591n13
  can barely stand, 451
  combines meteorological and magnetic observations, 253
  Davenport threatens to imprison, *xxii*
  determines highest latitude, 579n11
  determines ice-floe's position, 427, 431, 432, 433, 439, 441, 446, 448, 449, 453
  drifts away from ice-floe, 447
  errors of in determining longitude, 600n4
  examines ice from Cape Brevoort, 311
  freezes eyelids and hands, 227, 465, 601n6
  freezes toes, 601n6
  has swollen feet and ankles, 601n6
  helps Hall to measure baseline, 156
  helps Hall to take bearings, 137
  makes deck of cards, 424
  is carried under ice, 448
  lives in cramped upper saloon, 581n13
  makes measuring scales, 420
  makes short trips to take bearings, 293
  makes trip to Newman's Bay, 328
  member of ice-floe party, 346
  observation schedule of, 223
  occupies trigonometric stations, 166
  on loan from Army, *xxii*
  records of left on ice, 596n2
  recovers health, 601n8
  refuses to be Hall's secretary, *xxii*
  reluctant to eat raw meat, 595n10
  returns to ship from Cape Brevoort, 591n21
  sees Cape Joseph Henry, 293
  shares pendulum observations, 244
  shares magnetic observations, 251
  shares snow house with Ebierbing and family, 419
  shares *Tigress*'s captain's cabin, 464
  stands in for snow-blind Bessels, 292
  threatens to leave expedition, *xxii*
  waits on board for tailor, 467
Middle Head, 85
Middle Ice, 117, 525

Notes   633

Ministry for Greenland, 537
mirages, 97–98
Mirquiti, 576n46
Molloy, Thomas N., 36, 467, 571n27, 602n8
mollusks, 171, 306, 516
Moravians
  population of in Greenland, 65
Mortillet, Louis L.G. de, 365, 597n5
Morton, William, *xiii*, 262, 474, 576n41
  finds hypothermic Mauch, 581n14
  furthest north on Kane's expedition, 121–123, 262
  Hans did not immediately recognize, 101
  helps build emergency house on ice, 595n9
  in Budington's boat, 470
  in charge of stores and provisions, 200, 247
  keeps vigil over Hall, 585n24, 586n28
  lays out and dresses Hall's corpse, 585n29
  member of council meeting, 141, 142
  member of party left on board ship, 596n15
  notices Hall has died, 585n28
  on Kane's expedition, 121–23
  reaches Cape Independence, 121, 578n17
  reports open polar sea, 205
  retreating south with Kane, 474
  sees Cape Consitution, 121
  speaks at American Geographical Society, 569n38
  suffers snow blindness, 486
  transfers to *Arctic*, 533
Morton's Bay, 34
mosquitoes, 89, 150
Mosselbukta, 588n2
moths, 90–91, 325
Müller-Wille, Ludger, *xv*
Munik, 357
Murchison Promontory, 519
Murray, Andrew D., 582n13
murres, 478, 485, 501, 511
  common, 577n52
  thick-billed, 577n52, 595n19
muskox, 593n19

absent from Baffin Island, 582n10
attacks on man, 194
behaviour of when attacked, 193
Bessels's alleged plan to hunt, 389
classification of, 189
description of, 188–189
faeces of, 212
foetus of found, 590n3
habits of, 191–92
herd size, 582n15
hunts for, 186–88, 292, 293, 301, 590n8
injures dog, 192–93
Joseph's unsuccessful hunt for, 211
predators on, 192
range of, 189–90, 581n11
smell of, 190
taste of meat of, 582n5
tracks of, 163, 177, 180, 184, 190–91
Musset, Alfred de, 273, 589n2

N

naked sea butterfly, 572n3
Nanortalik, 479
Nantucket Island, 570n16
Nanuki (Sorkak, Baleen), 357
Nares, George S., 5, 6
Nares Strait, *xx*
Narwhal, 512
narwhals, 333, 486
  shot and harpooned, 512
  shot but lost, 434–35, 489
  spouting, 435, 600n7
National Academy of Sciences, 13
Nauckhoff, Gustav, 68, 69
Navy Board Inlet, 511
Naval Minister, 141, 143
Navy Department, 3, 4, 14, 17, 467, 527, 535
  organizes search, 521
Navy Yard, 14, 521
Nettilling Lake, 582n11
needle
  Inuit, 74
Nero (dog), 226
Netilik, 526
Nestroy, J., 577n50
Neuruppin, 573n23

Newfoundland and Labrador
  agriculture of, 44, 571n40
  climate of, 43
  economy of, 44
  flora of, 42–43
  geology of, 42
  mining in, 572n42
  population of, 572n41
Newfoundland seal hunt, 455–61
  number of ships and men involved in, 455
  procedures of, 456–59, 465–66
  onshore processing of pelts from, 459–60
  sharing of profits from, 460
  ships lost during, 460
New London, *xx*
  church service at, 29–30
  expedition's visit to, 29–32
New Mexico, 574n39
New Year's
  celebrations on ice floe, 431
  celebrations on *Polaris,* 240
  temperature during, 599n1
New York, 10, 14, 15, 117, 536
  expedition departs from, 27
New York Times, xvii, xix
Newman, John P., 30, 213, 569n31, 583n10
  Chaplain to the US Senate, 570n14
  gives expedition his blessing, 576n36
  prayer of, 30–31
Newman Bay, 142, 213, 263, 292, 293, 301, 307, 311, 314, 316, 328, 583n9
Niantilik, 528
nickel, 574n39
Nile Delta, 210
Nindemann, William, *xiii*
  assigned to *George Robeson,* 302, 590n21
  breaks through ice, 419
  capsizes kayak, 78–79
  delivers rubber sheets to Bessels, 276
  fastens ice anchor on iceberg, 229
  finds fossil corals on Offley Island, 276
  member of ice-floe party, 346, 596n20
  member of *Tigress*'s crew, 522
  suffers frozen nose, 229

  survives *Jeannette* expedition, 605n6, 605n7
  travels to Lichtenfels with Bessels, 573n19
Nordenskiöld, Nils A.E., 67, 68, 69, 86, 573n32, 575n19, 588n2
  completes first transit of Northeast Passage, 566n11
Norn, 603n2
Norfolk, Virginia, 568n20
Norsemen, 7
North Capers (orcas), 516–17
North Greenland, 82
North Magnetic Pole, 518
North Pole
  bill to fit out expedition to, 12, 13
  Congress unenthusiastic about, 12
  goal of Hall's expedition, *xix, xx,* 3, 197, 199, 200, 213, 546, 568n18
  goal of Hayes's expedition, 567n7
  Koldewey's possible goal, *xxiv, xxv*
  Markham's attempt at, 6
  prayer for, 31–32
North Somerset, 519
North Star, 364, 578n18, 598n7
North Star Bay, 16, 526
North Water, 342, 497
Northumberland Island, 421, 474, 526, 572n7
  description of, 483
  ice cap and glaciers on, 484
  reached by retreating party, 478
  reached for second time, 483
Northwest Passage, 10, 111
Novaya Zemlya, *xxvii,* 479, 566n10
Nuuk, 573n18
Nuussuaq Peninsula, 85, 87, 93
Nyström, C., 68

O

observatory
  construction of, 154–55
  depot left at, 315
  drifted up during blizzard, 230
  lay-out of, 223
  remains of examined by Loomis, 537

Odell, Alvin, *xiii*, 102
　climbs cliff on Dalrymple Island, 486
　hired in place of Wilson, 570n8
　in Budington's boat, 470
　member of party left on board ship, 596n15
　suffers snow blindness, 485
　transfers from *Ravenscraig* to *Arctic*, 533
Offley Island, 275, 299
　geology of, 276
Ohio, 12
Ohlsen, Christian, 120, 473–74
Oldenburg, *xxvi*
oldsquaw, 485, 594n19
　nest of, 327
Ommanney, Erasmus, 387
　takes Erasmus York to England, 598n5
Onkel Adam, 588n2
Open polar sea, 123, 136, 205
orca (North Caper), 516–17, 603n10, 604n21
Orkneymen, 496, 603n2
Osten-Sacken, Carl-Robert von, 592n10
Otter, Frederik W. von, 573n33
　soundings taken by, 574n37
Otterndorf, *xxiv*
Ovifak, 68
Owen, Richard, 582n8
Oxyria, 322

P

Paamiut, 575n8
Packard, A.S., 593n11
Paddock, Franklin, 537, 538
Palander, Louis, 257, 588n4
Paleocrystic Sea, 6
Pancake Rock, 35
Pannik (Punny, Sylvia), *xiii*
　is bought by Hall for Hannah, 22
　sends Bessels a "letter", 281
　shares snow-house with family, Tyson and Meyer, 419
pans
　of sculps, 601n4
　theft of, 466, 601n5

Pansch, Adolf, *xxvi*, 598n9
Parry, William Edward, xxiii, 113, 279, 514, 577n5, 604n18
　remarks of on Inuit songs, 384
Parry Point, 123
Payer, Julius, *xxvi*, *xxvii*
Payer Tinde, *xxvii*
Peabody, George, 117, 578n13
Peaked Hill, 524
Peary, Robert, 601n1
Pedley, Charles, 38, 571n32
pemmican, 274
　cost of for dogs, 588n21
　ingredients of, 178–79
pendulum observations, 241–45, 387–88
Pendulum Øer, *xxvi*
Pentland Firth, 534
Periwinkle, 13, 15
　originally named *America*, 568n19
Peteravik Glacier, 116, 132
Peterhead, 116, 534
Petermann, August, 568n23
　as promoter of arctic research, xxiv–xxvii
　biographical sketch of, 562–63
Petermanns Geographische Mitteilungen, 563
Petermann Fiord, 209, 275, 293, 299, 307
　exploration of, 278
Peschel, Oscar F., 84n15
Petersen, Mr., 105
Peuerbach, 577n8
Phipps, Weldy, 537
Phoenix, 597n9
photography
　attempt at, 271
Pingel, Peter C., 581n17
plant adaptations, 323–24
plant succession, 321
playing cards, 481
Poa, 321
Poduridae, 325
Poitras, Robin, *xv*
Polar Current, 33
Polaris, xx, xxii, xxiii
　access staircase to, 196
　afloat again, 316

636　　　　　　　　　　　　　　　　　　　　　　　　　　　　　　*POLARIS*

aground, 318
as source of firewood, 362
beset, 337
Bessels's first impressions of, 14
canvas housing installed on, 166, 196
   removed, 271
cargo unloaded from, 154
changes to, 568n21
description, layout and equipment of, 15–17
driven against Providence Berg, 228–29
encounters first ice, 135
engine of moth-balled, 166
half the crew abandoned by, 343, 346
ice drift of, 340–42
last sight of, 417
leaking, 293–94, 315, 316, 335, 338–39, 345, 592n1, 595n12
listing, 240
makes final attempts at getting north, 316–17
muster-roll of, 101–2
poor performance of under sail, 33
reaches highest latitude, 214, 579n11, 580n22
rearrangement of accommodations etc. on, 163–65
run ashore, 348
temperatures in, 165–66, 238–39
threatened by an iceberg, 317
sawing a dock for, 230
suffers storm damage, 15
warped to wintering location, 587n12
wreck of disappears, 526
Polaris (star), 431
Polaris Bay, 5, 153, 316, 317, 331, 332, 341
   erratic material at, 171–72
   evidence of uplift at, 170–71
   precipitation at, 254
   sun disappears at, 586n1
   winter temperatures at, 234–35, 255
Polaris Peninsula, 301, 313, 332
Polaris House, *xxiii*
   building of, 349–50, 351
   cooking facilities at, 357–58, 362
   departure from, 473
   depot left at, 471, 602n1
   schedule at, 358
   trashed, 605n18
   visited by Commander Greer, 526–27
Polhem, 588n2
Pond's Bay, 502, 580n4
Port Bowen, 514
Port Foulke, 126, 128, 130, 134, 170, 352, 355, 398, 550, 572n7, 579n5
Potentilla, 322
Potomac River, 14, 568n20
Potter, Russell, 540
Pouillet, Claude S.M., 596n7
Pouillet actinometer, 353
prehistoric art, 381
preparations for wintering, 337
President of the Unites States, 12, 13, 16
President's Land, 328
Prince Regent Inlet, 513, 531
Prøven, 100, 101, 125, 576n40
Providence Berg, 153, 317, 580n1
   disintegrates, 318
   drifts down on ship, 231
   meat stored in cave on, 296
provisions, complete inventory of, 20–22
ptarmigan, 91, 92, 150, 180, 269, 292, 589n13, 594n19
   diet of, 269
   distribution of, 575n26
   tameness of, 92
pteropods, 50, 572n3
puffin
   Atlantic, 109
   range of in Greenland, 577n54
Pullen, William, 578n18
Punigkpa, 355
Purchas, Samuel, 577n2
purple saxifrage, 56, 92, 305, 322, 475, 501, 511

Q

Qaqortoq, 574n44
Qasigiannguit, 575n7
Québec, 604n1
Queen Maud Gulf, 566n1
Queen of the Isles, *xxiv*
Qeqertarsuatsiaat, 572n5

Qeqertarssuak, 573n29
Qidtlarssuaq, 596n9, 597n10
Quidi Vidi Pond, 38

R

Radcliff Point, 398
Radford, Harry, 598n11
Rae, James
  makes Avatok's wooden leg, 598n7
Rapahannock River, 568n20
Rattler (dog breed), 356, 597n12
Rave Rock pilot station, 32, 570n15
raven, 64, 359, 449, 474, 479, 573n25, 594n19
Ravenscraig, xxiii
  beset, 496
  meets *Arctic* again, 533
  sighted by shipwrecked party, 493
  takes shipwrecked party aboard, 496
  working through ice, 497–98
Ream, Vinnie, 540–42
  dines with Hall, 541
  gives Hall photo of statue of Lincoln, 541
Red Sea, 210
refuge hut built on ice, 337–38, 595n9
  reached by ice floe party, 419
Regiomontanus, 577n8
reindeer, 593n19
  decline in, 100
  shot, 518, 519
  tracks of, 190–191, 352
Release, 579n20, 580n20
Rensselaer Harbour, 118, 127, 134, 170, 341, 393, 567n6, 595n11, 598n2
Renwick Smallpox Hospital, 570n2
Repulse Harbour 139, 311, 580n2
Rescue, 10, 567n2, 583n4
Resolute Bay, 537
Resolution, 566n8
Reynolds, Commodore William, 549
Revolutionary War, 570n6
Rhein, 14
Ridgway, Robert, 480, 602n18
Rikers Island, 570n3
Rink, Hinrich J., 68, 71, 123, 574n38, 574n38
Ritenbenk, 9

Robeson, George, 570n10, 579n1
  chairs Board of Inquiry, 549, 550
  visits *Tigress*,605n5
Robeson Channel, 143, 205, 210, 213, 214, 301, 579n11
  remained open, 253
  rough ice in, 293
  tides in, 313
Roosevelt Island, 570n1
Rona, 534
Rosa, S., 260, 589n5
Rosenthal, Albert, *xxvii*
Ross, John, *xxiii*, 68, 364, 515
  first expedition of, 113–14
  chart of, 115, 577n4
  names Crimson Cliffs, 577n6
  sights "Croker Mountains", 577n5
  soundings by, 265
Ross's gull, 489, 603n21
Rothspohn, 63, 573n22
Rouvière, Jean-Baptiste, 598n11
rove beetle, 575n25
Royal Greenland Trading Department, 70, 94, 574n41
Royal St. John's Regatta, 571n33
rubber boots
  as fuel, 487
rubber breeches
  used for melting snow in sun, 492
Rudolph, Dr.Christian N., 103, 522, 576n38

S

Sabine Ø, *xxvi,* 582n9
Sabine's gull, 327, 594n19
Sable Island, 467, 524
Saguenay River, 575n9
Samson, 602n16
Sanderson's Hope, 112
sand martin, 479, 602n14
sanderling, 325, 479, 594n19
  eggs of, 327
sandpiper, 163
  purple, 580n10, 594n19
Sands, Benjamin F., 569n26
Sandy Hook, 536, 605n5
Saunders Island, 132, 133, 579n3

sawing ice, 315
Schönheyter
   welcomes Hall and Bessels, 56, 58
Schoonmaker, C.N. , 467
Schott, Carl A., 569n30
Schuhmacher (dog)
   as messenger, 275–76
Schumann, Emil, *xiii*
   accompanies Bessels to Lichtenfels, 573n19
   brings willow catkins aboard, 269
   crew member of *Hopes dashed*, 470
   erects initial grave marker, 592n4
   finds piece of meteoric iron, 300
   lives in cramped upper saloon, 581n13
   member of party left on board ship, 596n15
   pack-rat habits of, 247–48, 588n4
   uses small boiler, 339
   makes stoves for boat trip, 470
   transfers from *Ravenscraig* to *Arctic*, 500
scientific instruments
   inventory of, 18–20
Scoresby, William, 50, 87, 572n2, 575n20
Scoresby Bay, 208
Scoresbysund, 581n111
sculps, 601n3, 601n4
scurvy, 314, 339, 434
   first case of, 292
   on Kane's expedition, 120
sea lice, 572n3
sea spiders, 327, 593n18
Sea of Japan, 210
Sea of Okhotsk, 210
sea water
   colour of, 49–50
   specific gravity of, 543
seals, 139
   bearded, 278, 437, 438–439, 441, 593n19
   division of among ice floe drifters, 428–29
   Greenland (harp), 439, 441, 593n19, 600n12, 601n2
   hauled out on ice, 296
   hooded, 441–43, 444, 446, 453, 600n1, 600n3
   hunt for on ice, 296, 339, 423, 426, 428, 433, 436
   Newfoundland hunt for, 455–61
   ringed, 593n19
Secretary of the Navy, 13, 16
Second German North Pole Expedition, *xxv*, 189, 301, 591n1
Second Grinnell Expedition, 11, 50
Second Kamchatka Expedition, 580n7
selachians, 402, 599n13
Senate, 12, 13
Shakespeare, William, 603n6
shark
   Greenland, 77, 574n48
   methods of fishing for, 77–78
Sherman, John, 567n12
Shetlanders, 496, 603n2
Siemens, Hermann, *xiii*
   assigned to *Ulysses S. Grant*, 302, 590n16
   blown over in gale, 226, 587n9
   carries caribou meat, 604n24
   climbs hill near Cape Brevoort, 591n13
   crew member of *Hopes dashed*, 471
   finds driftwood, 313, 314
   finds hypothermic Mauch, 581n14
   member of party left on board ship, 596n15
   reads tide gauge, 221
   returns to Newman Bay, 328
   saves Anthing from drowning, 312
   sent back to ship for bread, 591n15
   signs offer of thanks to Hall, 582n16
   transfers from *Ravenscraig* to *Arctic*, 500
   with Bessels on boat trip near Bellot Strait, 517, 604n22
Signal Hill, 35, 39
Simms, Charles, 579n20
Siorapaluk, 474
Sisimiut, 573n31
sledge
   for hauling boats, 254
sledging equipment, 176
Smith Land, 11
Smith Sound, *xix*, 3, 6, 111, 112, 114, 117, 121, 123, 125, 134, 210, 364, 584n14

Smithsonian Institution, 549, 568n23, 578n17
　burns down, 578n5
snow blindness, 291–292, 397, 406, 486
snow bunting, 109, 147, 150, 269, 479, 594n19
　nest of, 511–512
snow houses
　construction of, 367–70
　interior layout of, 370
snowy owl, 292, 339, 593n19
　capturing lemmings, 298–99
　range of in Greenland, 590n4
solar radiation
　measurement of, 268
sole, 82, 575n5
Somerset House, *xxiii*, 604n20
　remains of, 515
Somerset Island, *xxiii*
Sonntag, August, 50, 579n24
　on Hayes's expedition, 572n7
　on Kane's expedition, 572n7
　death of, 127, 572n7
Sorfalik, 397
Sørkapp, *xxv*
soundings, 265, 334
　in Kennedy Channel, 137
　in Petermann Fiord, 280
South Greenland, 82
South Pole, 6, 25
South Shoal Lightship, 32
southward retreat
　begins, 473
　boats for, 470
　instruments for, 470
　provisions for, 470
spiders, 325, 593n17
　wolf, 183
Spitsbergen, *xxv*
staphylins, 90
Starick, I.L., 62, 573n20
starling
　feather of, 512
　introduction of to North America, 604n13
Staten Island, 28

St. John's, *xxi*, 456, 535
　description of, 35–37
　entrance to habour of, 34
　Mental Hospital at, 41
　noon time signal at, 39–41
St. Lawrence River, 575n9
Stefansson, Vilhjalmur, 601n1
Steller, Georg W., 156, 159, 180n7
Street, Thomas, 598n11
Stevenson, Job E., 567n10
storm petrels, 33
stove
　portable wood-burning, 175
stovepipe as heat source, 595n8
Strait of Belle Isle, *xix*, 601n2
Strømfjord, 82
Struwwelpeter, 239, 588n22
Sukkertoppen, 66, 82, 479, 522, 605n8
Sula Sgeir, 606n6
Sullorsuaq Strait, 575n16
sun
　disappears for winter, 202, 214, 219, 586n1, 596n3, 598n1
　reappears, 266–267, 386, 432, 589n8, 598n1
survey work, 166–167
Sumner, Charles, 213, 567n13
Sutherland, 574n40
Sutherland, Peter C., 116
Sutherland Island, 400
Svalbard, *xxiv, xxvii,* 6, 87, 257, 442
Svarte Huk, 98
swallow
　debate as to species of, 479
Symmes, John C., 30, 570n13

S

Tallapoosa, 468, 536
　Board of Inquiry held on, 549
　runs down schooner, 536
Tarrilikitak, 569n36
Tasiusaq, 105, 125, 523, 526, 527, 531, 577n54
Tasiusaq Hat, 486
Tay, 513, 533

tea
　poor quality of, 21
　smoked, 488
teetotal nature of expedition, 22
Temperance Society, 22, 175
tent
　Inuit, details of, 74
tern, 486, 594n19
Terror
　wreck of discovered, 566n1
Terror Bay, 566n1
Thames River, 29, 116, 570n15
Thank God Harbour, 153, 198, 537, 580n25
Thanksgiving
　celebration, 225, 232–33, 426
　dinner menu, 587n14, 599n9
thimble
　Inuit, 74
Third Cape, 250, 307, 591n5
Thomas, Chimham
　grave of, 515
Thorell, Tord, 593n17
Thorvaldsen, Bertel, 576n33
Three Sisters Bees, 133
throwing stick
　Inuit, 75
Thule culture houses, 517–18
tides, 587n4
tide gauge, 219–21, 232–33
　impossibility of installing at Polaris House, 353
tidal current, 476–77
tidal observations, 543
tidal waves, 139, 341
Tiger (dog), 332, 595n3
Tilt Cove, 572n43
Tigress, 536
　almost collides with iceberg, 605n19
　cost of, 604n1
　details of, 604n1
　experiences fire in coal bunker, 605 n.19
　leaves New York, 522
　modifications to, 604n2
　reaches Disko, 522
　reaches St. John's, 467
　reaches Tasiusaq, 605n14
　reaches Upernavik, 522

　rescues ice floe party, 464
　returns to New York, 536, 606n25
　searches for missing party, 521–22, 526–28
tobacco,
　chewing, 410
　hoarded, 488
Tom (cat), 358, 471
　disappears, 477–78
　ode to, 482
Tookoolito (Hannah,Taqulittuq), *xiii*
　accompanies Hall in United States, 22
　accomplishments of, 23
　appearance of, 23
　biographical sketch of, 558–60
　did not know own age, 22
　dress of, 57
　earlier children of, 569n36
　finds old sledge, 299
　is sick, 601n6
　makes skin pants, 201
　Pannik bought for by Hall, 22
　prepares furs and footwear, 196
　sees raven, 594n19
　shares snow-house with family, Tyson and Meyer, 419
　stays with Budingtons, 558
　swept away by wave, 448
　tans dog skins, 235
　tries to talk to Greenlanders, 54
　weeps over Hall's death, 217
topography
　around Polaris Bay, 168
Torrrington, John, 567n3
trawling, 75, 326
Trumbull, Jonathan, 570n6
turnstones, 325, 339, 474, 478, 594n19
　migrations of, 593n16
twilight, 204, 216, 219, 235, 236, 249, 260, 261, 266, 358, 386, 421, 424, 425, 427, 435, 443, 448,
Tyson, George, *xiii, xvii, xx*
　accuses Budington of trouble-making, 551
　accuses Budington of murdering Hall, 600n5

appointed assistant navigator, 570n10, 576n30
assesses expedition's achievements, 592n3
assesses muskox meat positively, 582n5
assists Hall's sledge party, 583n2
boards HMS *Resolute*, 563
biographical sketch of, 563–564
builds emergency house on ice, 595n9
commands boat *George Robeson*, 291, 302
commission of arrives with *Congress*, 576n30
critical of everything, 247
death of, 564
describes progress of Hall's illness, 585n24
describes Hall's final days, 585n26
earlier encounters with Hall, 564
gives critical assessment of canvas boat, 591n9
Hall's first choice as sailing master, 570n10
health of endangered, 423
hikes north to Cape Sumner, 301
ice pilot on *Tigress*, 522
joins expedition at New London, 29
journal of published, *xx*
keen to find winter quarters, 142
laid up with illness, 423, 599n7
last sighting of the ship by, 596n1
lays out and dresses Hal's corpse, 586n29
leader of ice-floe party, 346
maintains break-up of party was off Littleton Island, 605n5
makes boat trip north, 303–12
meets American consul at Bay Roberts, 602n8
meets Hall on his return from sledge trip, 585n211
mounts hunting trip to north, 293
persuades men not to burn boat, 432
persuades men not to head for Disko, 434
present at council meeting, 141
proposes heading north overland, 591n16
reaches Third Cape, 306
recognizes Cape Seward, 436
reports ice slackening, 332
reports interpersonal frictions, *xxi*
rescues boat, 599n4
rescues Eskimos and Meyer, 448
rescues Hans's children, 596n14
salvages materials from Polaris House, 605n18
shares Bartlett's cabin, 465
shares snow-house with Joe and family, 410
shoots bear, 433
spots surviving *Polaris* hawser, 605n17
suffers from rheumatism, 426
suffers swollen feet and ankles, 601n6
supports Budington, 247
tries to rescue endangered survivors, 416
tries to signal *Polaris*, 596n1
unable to understand German spoken by men, 600n2
warns men against bear liver, 600n10
winters in Cumberland Sound, 563, 564
writes will, 600n5

U

umiak, 84
Uellner, J.W., 62, 573n21
Ulve, Erik, 479, 602n16
Ulysses S. Grant (boat), 291, 302
  crushed by ice, 304
United States, 125, 567n7
United States Exploring Expedition, 569n40
Upernavik, 82, 98, 117, 124, 125, 130, 523, 527, 567n6
  dances held at, 605n20
  details of, 99
  reached by *Juniata* and *Tigress*, 522
Uumannaaq, 82, 577n54
Uumannaaqfjord, 78, 98

V

Vaigat, 85, 87, 93, 98, 575n16
Van Dyck, Anthony, 573n24
vascular plants at Polaris Bay, 592n8
Vega, Jurij B., 273, 589n1
Vega, 7, 566n11
Verlegenhuken, *xxv*
veronica, 90
Victor, 533
Victoria Day, 602n11
Victoria Head, 116
Vienna, 577n50
Vincennes, 569n40
Virchow, Rudolf C., 598n8
Voisey's Bay, 572n42

W

Wabush, 572n42
Walker, Captain, 536
Walker, David
    first choice as chief scientist, 568n23
walrus, 132–33, 386, 486, 487, 579n3
    hunt for, 400
Walrus, 466
Wards Island, 570n5
Washington, *xxi*, 14, 536
    Navy Yard, 549
Wellington Channel, 124
Weddell, James
    reached record southerly latitude, 566n9
Weddell Sea, 566n9
Welcker, Hermann, 597n6
Wellington Channel, 567n2, 583n4
Werner, Reinhold, *xxiv*
whales, 439
    bowhead, description of, 506–508
whale hunt
    details of, 503–10
Whale Sound, 112, 127, 480
whaleboat
    almost capsized by whale, 514
Whalefish Islands, 92
white-fronted geese, 478, 602n11
white wgtail, 534
    range of, 606n5

Wijkander, August, 257, 588n3
Wilcox Head, 523
Wilhelmøya, *xxv*
Wilkes, Charles, 569n40
Wilkes expedition, 25
Wilcox Point, 117
Winter Island, 384
wolverine, 192
Wollaston Islands, 511
Wolstenholme Island, 132, 133, 486, 579n3
Wolstenholme Sound, 112, 114, 132, 170, 364, 598n7
Women Islands, 112
wolf, 100, 593n19
    faeces of, 181, 269
    howling of heard, 269
World War II, 571n25
Wrangel, Ferdinand von, 162
Wrangel Bay, 209
Wrangel Island, *xxv*
Wyman, Robert H, 569n28

Y

Yedzo, 112
York, Erasmus, 387, 598n4

Z

zeeoliths, 90
Zorgdrager, Cornelis G., 603n8

www.ingramcontent.com/pod-product-compliance
Lightning Source LLC
Chambersburg PA
CBHW042117300426
44117CB00021B/2971